Economic Theory and its History

T0331416

This collection brings together leading economists from around the world to explore key issues in economic analysis and the history of economic thought. This book deals with important themes in economics in terms of an approach that has its roots in the works of the classical economists from Adam Smith to David Ricardo. The chapters have been inspired by the work of Neri Salvadori, who has made key contributions in various areas including the theory of production, the theory of value and distribution, the theory of economic growth, as well as the theory of renewable and exhaustible natural resources.

The main themes in this book include production, value and distribution; endogenous economic growth; renewable and exhaustible natural resources; capital and profits; oligopolistic competition; effective demand and capacity utilization; financial regulation; and themes in the history of economic analysis. Several of the contributions are closely related to the works of Neri Salvadori. This is demonstrated with respect to important contemporary topics including the sources of economic growth, the role of exhaustible resources in economic development, the reduction and disposal of waste, the redistribution of income and wealth, and the regulation of an inherently unstable financial sector.

All contributions are brand new, original and concise, written by leading exponents in their field of expertise. Together this volume represents an invaluable contribution to economic analysis and the history of economic thought. This book is suitable for those who study economic theory and its history, political economy and philosophy.

Giuseppe Freni is Professor of Economics at the University of Naples Parthenope, Italy.

Heinz D. Kurz is Professor Emeritus of Economics at the University of Graz, Austria.

Andrea Mario Lavezzi is Associate Professor of Economics at the University of Palermo, Italy.

Rodolfo Signorino is Associate Professor of Economics at the University of Palermo, Italy.

Routledge Studies in the History of Economics

Economic Theory and its History

Essays in honour of Neri Salvadori

Edited by Giuseppe Freni, Heinz D. Kurz, Andrea Mario Lavezzi and Rodolfo Signorino

Routledge
Taylor & Francis Group

LONDON AND NEW YORK

First published 2016
by Routledge

2 Park Square, Milton Park, Abingdon, Oxfordshire OX14 4RN
52 Vanderbilt Avenue, New York, NY 10017

Routledge is an imprint of the Taylor & Francis Group, an informa business

First issued in paperback 2019

British Library Cataloguing in Publication Data
A catalogue record for this book is available from the British Library

Library of Congress Cataloging in Publication Data
  Economic theory and its history: essays in honour of Neri Salvadori /
  edited by Giuseppe Freni, Heinz D. Kurz, Andrea Mario Lavezzi,
  Rodolfo Signorino.
    pages cm
  1. Economics–History. 2. Economics. I. Salvadori, Neri, honoree.
  II. Freni, Giuseppe, editor.
  HB75.E325 2016
  330.01–dc23   2015031445

ISBN: 978-1-138-18659-0 (hbk)
ISBN: 978-0-367-87633-3 (pbk)

Typeset in Times New Roman
by Sunrise Setting Ltd, Paignton, UK

Contents

Figures

Tables

Contributors

Martín Puchet Anyul, Universidad Nacional Autónoma de México, anyul@servidor.unam.mx

Enrico Bellino, Università Cattolica del Sacro Cuore di Piacenza, enrico.bellino@unicatt.it

Christian Bidard, University of Paris Ouest-Nanterre La Défense, christian.bidard@u-paris10.fr

Edwin Burmeister, Duke University and University of Virginia, eb@econ.duke.edu

Pasquale Commendatore, University of Naples Federico II, pasquale.commendatore@unina.it

Antonio D'Agata, University of Catania, adagata@unict.it

Simone D'Alessandro, University of Pisa, s.dale@ec.unipi.it

Amitava Krishna Dutt, University of Notre Dame and FLACSO-Ecuador, Amitava.K.Dutt.1@nd.edu

Silvia Faggian, University Ca' Foscari of Venice, faggian@unive.it

Luciano Fanti, University of Pisa, luciano.fanti@unipi.it

Riccardo Faucci, University of Pisa, faucci@dse.unipi.it

Duncan K. Foley, New School for Social Research, foleyd@newschool.edu

Giuseppe Freni, University of Naples Parthenope, giuseppe.freni@uniparthenope.it

Christian Gehrke, University of Graz, Christian.Gehrke@uni-graz.at

Eiji B. Hosoda, Keio University, hosoda@econ.keio.ac.jp

Bruno Jossa, University of Naples Federico II, bruiossa@unina.it

Ingrid Kubin, Vienna University of Economics and Business Administration, ingrid.kubin@wu.ac.at

Heinz D. Kurz, University of Graz, heinz.kurz@uni-graz.at

Andrea Mario Lavezzi, University of Palermo, mario.lavezzi@unipa.it

Edward Nell, New School for Social Research, ejnell2@gmail.com

Arrigo Opocher, Università di Padova, arrigo.opocher@unipd.it

Carlo Panico, University of Naples Federico II, carlo.panico@unina.it

Man-Seop Park, Korea University, manseop@korea.ac.kr

Sergio Parrinello, University of Rome, La Sapienza, sergio.parrinello@uniroma1.it

Carmelo Petraglia, University of Basilicata, carmelo.petraglia@unibas.it

Antonio Pinto, University of Naples Federico II, antpinto@unina.it

Alberto Quadrio Curzio, Università Cattolica di Milano and Accademia Nazionale dei Lincei, alberto.quadriocurzio@unicatt.it

Alessandro Roncaglia, University of Rome, La Sapienza, alessandro.roncaglia@uniroma1.it

Paul A. Samuelson, formerly of Massachusetts Institute of Technology

Stefan F. Schubert, University of Bozen-Bolzano, stefanfranz.schubert@unibz.it

Rodolfo Signorino, University of Palermo, rodolfo.signorino@unipa.it

Ian Steedman, Manchester Metropolitan University, I.Steedman@mmu.ac.uk

Marta Vazquez Suarez, Universidade de Santiago de Compostela, marta.vazquez@usc.es

Stephen J. Turnovsky, University of Washington, Seattle, sturn@u.washington.edu

Takashi Yagi, Meiji University, yagi8@meiji.ac.jp

1 Introduction

Giuseppe Freni, Heinz D. Kurz,
Andrea Mario Lavezzi and
Rodolfo Signorino

This collection of essays is a tribute to Neri Salvadori, the man and scholar, teacher and friend, whom the scientific community owes important works in the tradition of Piero Sraffa's revival of the classical economists' approach to the problems of value, income distribution, capital accumulation, technical progress, scarce natural resources, economic development and growth. The essays in this book have all been freshly written and contain original work with novel ideas in the areas mentioned.

In this introduction we first summarize briefly Neri Salvadori's academic career, his work and his intellectual and organizational activities, and then provide a short overview of the essays collected in this volume.

Academic career and work

Neri Salvadori was born on 3 February 1951 in Naples, Italy, where he studied economics at the Facoltà di Economia e Commercio of the University of Naples and graduated in 1976 with the highest marks. He received two study grants, one from the Fondazione Einaudi for the academic year 1976/77 the other from the Banca d'Italia for 1977/78, which he used to study at the University of Manchester with Ian Steedman and then at the University of Cambridge. In 1978 he became a research assistant for the chair of Financial Mathematics at the University of Naples and then a researcher at the Institute of Finance. In 1979 he joined the Faculty of Political Science of the University of Catania, Sicily, as a lecturer of economic analysis; in 1985 he was promoted to the position of associate professor. In 1987 he moved to the Istituto Navale di Napoli, where in 1990 he was appointed to the chair of Political Economy. In 1991 he joined the University of Pisa, where he teaches and researches.

Early on in his career Neri Salvadori became deeply fascinated with the writings of the classical economists from Adam Smith to David Ricardo, and with Piero Sraffa's revival of the classical approach to the theory of value and distribution. Sraffa's work has been a major source of inspiration for virtually all his research activities ever since. With regard to various problems studied, Neri Salvadori elaborated new solutions and moved the frontier of research outward. These concern, in particular, the problem of the choice of technique, the determination of long-period prices and income distribution, the role of the quantities of commodities in effectual demand in the case of joint production, fixed capital and scarce natural resources, and the problem of renewable and exhaustible resources. The upshot of his respective endeavour and intellectual achievements is his book (co-authored by Heinz D. Kurz), *Theory of Production: A Long-Period Analysis*. The book is now widely considered a *locus classicus* of the literature of classical orientation. However, Neri Salvadori also contributed novel insights to several other fields of research. He studied the problem of price formation in the short period in a Kaleckian framework. He extended the Sraffian approach to deal with the problem of economic growth and development. He thereby did not limit the analysis to one-good models, as is typically the case in much of growth economics, whether old or new, but tackled the intricate case of economies with many industries. A major focus of his work was on neo-Keynesian contributions in the tradition of Nicholas Kaldor and Joan Robinson to the theory of economic growth and functional income distribution. Several of his contributions deal with what is known as 'new' or 'endogenous' growth theory. He showed that some of the new growth models, while couched in neoclassical terms, contain an analytical structure that is 'classical' in spirit. In all these works Neri Salvadori made effective use of his remarkable mathematical skills and analytical sharpness, and demonstrated an amazing knowledge of the economics literature, both modern and ancient. In more recent times he got interested in the theory of oligopoly and has produced a number of papers with new results.

His interest and expertise in the history of economic analysis materialized in a number of essays dealing with major economists, such as Adam Smith, David Ricardo, Léon Walras, Knut Wicksell, John von Neumann, Wassily Leontief, Kenneth Arrow and Gérard Debreu, and especially Piero Sraffa. A characteristic feature of his contributions is his analytical grip on their works, which allows him to put into sharp relief similarities and differences and to elaborate on aspects these authors left undeveloped. His interest in past authors is not antiquarian; he rather wishes to know in which way economic theory has developed, and why, and what can still be learned from the masters of our discipline. Involved in editing the unpublished papers and correspondence of Piero Sraffa, Neri Salvadori has managed to solve a number of puzzles concerning the interpretation of Sraffa's analysis and has explored the latter's collaboration with his 'mathematical friends', Frank P. Ramsey, Abram S. Besicovitch and Alister Watson. In addition he has published on questions of methodology in the context under consideration.

Neri Salvadori's publication record is outstanding. He has published and edited numerous books, several hundred papers (well over a hundred of them in peer-reviewed journals), many entries in dictionaries, book reviews etc. (See the list of his publications at the end of this book.) His work has been widely appreciated in the literature, reflected in numerous citations and references to it and by translations of his works into other languages. His excellent standing in the profession is also documented by several prizes he received, including the Premio Linceo (a lifetime achievement award given by the Accademia dei Lincei, the Italian Academy of Science) in 2004, several visiting professorships in many countries, numerous invitations to give keynote lectures, talks and seminars all over the world, several participations as lecturer in international summer schools, and highly appreciated work as referee by leading economic journals and publishing houses. Neri Salvadori also organized highly successful serial annual lectures in economic growth and development published by Cambridge University Press. Since 2004 Neri Salvadori has served as general editor (together with Heinz D. Kurz) of *Metroeconomica*; in addition he is a member of several editorial boards of economic journals, including *The European Journal of the History of Economic Thought*.

Neri Salvadori has earned himself not only the respect of his peers and colleagues, but also of his students because of the care with which he looked after them and the support he gave them. An inspiring academic teacher, he attracted numerous bright young people and interested them in promising approaches and themes, irrespective of whether they were fashionable in the profession or not. He was able to instil into them his standards of rigour, meticulousness and dedication; several of them made an academic career. His social competence is reflected in many joint papers with former students of his.

The contents of this book

Chapter 2 contains 'personal reminiscences' of one of us, who has had the privilege of collaborating with Neri Salvadori over more than thirty years (and expects to continue to do so) and whose intellectual life is closely interrelated with his.

The thematic essays are subdivided in four parts that reflect well Neri Salvadori's main areas of interest and research. Part 1 is dedicated to 'economic growth and income distribution' and has four chapters. Chapter 3, by Pasquale Commendatore, Ingrid Kubin and Carmelo Petraglia, elaborates on the standard footloose capital model by Martin and Rogers and allows for two groups of capital owners (workers and capitalist rentiers). Following the insights of Pasinetti and Kaldor, the authors assume that capital ownership is more diffused at home than abroad and that the two groups exhibit different consumption patterns. On the basis of these assumptions new results on the impact of free trade on the long-run international distribution of capital and welfare are derived. Chapter 4, by Andrea Mario Lavezzi, argues that Adam Smith's theory of the division and labour and economic growth, and its development by Alfred Marshall, Allyn Young and Nicholas Kaldor, exhibits characteristics that allow one to classify it as belonging to complexity economics. This claim is supported by a historical reconstruction of Smith's growth theory against the background of complex systems analysis. This novel perspective is confronted with the traditional one, rooted, as it is, in general equilibrium economics, and a simple alternative model is proposed. Chapter 5 is by Sergio Parrinello and deals with attempts to extend Keynes's theory of effective demand from the short- to the long-run and to the theory of economic growth. A useful description of a normal state of a growing capitalist economy, the author insists, must not be confined to a pure steady growth, despite the fact that such a state can be used as an ideal configuration for some preliminary analytical purpose. The main analytical result derived is that in the presence of obsolete machines, the margins of changes in capacity utilization, driven by changes in effective demand, are wider if prices and distribution are allowed to deviate from their long-period values associated with free competition and a given conventional wage rate. Chapter 6, by Stefan Schubert and Stephen Turnovsky, proposes a model in which search unemployment and wage bargaining are introduced into an endogenous growth model to analyse the effects of a permanent and a temporary negative total factor productivity (TFP) shock on growth, unemployment and public debt. Motivated by the recent Italian experience following the global financial crisis, the model is calibrated to approximate that economy, showing that both the permanent and the temporary TFP shocks have long-lasting effects on unemployment and on growth and debt dynamics. The model describes well the Italian economy's performance in the immediate aftermath of the crisis and is particularly successful in tracking the time path of the unemployment rate.

Part 2 turns to 'resource economics' and has three chapters. Chapter 7, by Silvia Faggian and Giuseppe Freni, has a new look at the famous forestry problem. It uses the tools of the modern literature on optimal forest management to provide a continuous time 'Ricardian' model of forestry. It is assumed that the land on which timber is produced is not uniform in quality and it is shown that in response to an increase in timber demand forest cultivation is progressively intensified on the most fertile lands and/or extended to less fertile lands. At a given level of the rate of interest, a set of 'breakthrough timber prices' gives the order of fertility – the order in which the different qualities of land are taken into cultivation – while a set of 'threshold timber prices' gives the order in which timber contained in the old trees standing on the different lands is extracted. It turns out that for each land the breakthrough price is higher than the threshold price. The properties of the model are used to discuss a claim of Ricardo's that the compensations received by the owners of marginal forestlands in Norway following the rise of timber demand (and hence of timber price) in southern countries of Europe were not rents. Chapter 8, by Eiji Hosoda, explores the choice of technique problem for an economic system confronted with a problem of post-consumption waste disposal. If households are supposed to pay for the waste disposal at post-consumption stage and there is no constraint on waste generation, then waste is discharged as much as possible. In this case, without any environmental restriction, the existence of a gap between the wage–profit and consumption–growth frontiers implies that per capita consumption is not maximized. To cut an excessive amount of waste discharge, authorities in many countries have introduced an upstream policy represented by extended producer responsibility (EPR). A proper EPR policy can make the gap between the two frontiers disappear, internalizing the waste disposal cost in the price of the consumption commodity which generates waste at the post-consumption stage. Chapter 9, by Alessandro Roncaglia, looks at the oil market as a test in order to assess alternative interpretations of prices of production ('long-period method' and 'photograph'). The story of the oil sector is sketched, stressing the role of technical change on both the production and the utilization side, and the complex and changing nature of the market forms prevailing in the sector (including the influence of antitrust policies). The (marginalist) interpretation of oil as a scarce natural resource is criticized. Although oil should better be treated as a produced and reproducible commodity rather than as a non-reproducible natural resource, the Ricardo–Sraffa approach presupposes free competition, and the oil sector is far from that. The conclusion is that this kind of approach is useful for a critique of the mainstream (scarcity) approach, but is not directly applicable to the oil market.

Part 3 is devoted to 'capital theory and marginalism' and has six chapters. Chapter 10, by Christian Bidard, introduces so-called 'ghost goods' in the analysis; that is, goods that do not appear on markets, but are positively priced. Various cases of ghost goods are discussed: from Sraffa's 'beans' to intermediate goods which are specific to non-operated processes of production, from 'tractors' (intermediate goods in neo-Austrian models) to intermediate goods in two-period Austrian models. It is shown that while the price of a ghost good may generally vary within a certain interval, the price of some intermediate ghost goods in Austrian models can be calculated exactly. Chapter 11 was not written for this book, but has been included upon the recommendation of Edwin Burmeister, who knows how much the late Paul A. Samuelson appreciated Neri Salvadori's work. It can be surmised, would Samuelson still be with us and in good health, that he would have written a piece for this volume. In this unfinished handwritten Samuelson manuscript kindly transcribed by Edwin Burmeister, Samuelson sketches a non-neoclassical model in which output (corn) is producible by a finite number of alternative known techniques, each involving, along with labour and corn seed, non-reproducible land (and where possibly each category of inputs could involve heterogeneous varieties: male and female labours; more fertile and less fertile acreages; coal, iron, and durable produced machines). It is suggested that for the case of homogeneous one-quality land, homogeneous one-quality labour, and homogeneous one-quality corn seed, the corn–labour–land–capital competitive factor pricing can be reduced down to a primal and dual linear programming problem. It is stated that as the interest rate falls from one steady state to another, as soon as there are *joint* products and/or *multiple* heterogeneous capital goods, there need *not* be an induced rise in the plateau of permanently consumable output. In Chapter 12, by Edward J. Nell, it is pointed out that since the classical approach represents the total labour used by society during any period of production as a single, homogenous quantity, we are faced with a fundamental epistemological question: to what common measure are the various grades and kinds of labour reducible? In the chapter it is argued that the only possible common denominator is exchange value. But if this is correct, it requires a reconsideration of Sraffa's construction of the 'invariant measure of value' because his standard system cannot be shown to exhibit the linear inverse relation between wages and the rate of profit if the 'quantity of labour' is expressed in terms of value and not as a homogenous and given quantity that is independent of value and capable of being set equal to unity as a numéraire. Sraffa's derivation of the standard system is therefore said to fail. Chapter 13, by Arrigo Opocher, examines some preliminary aspects of long-period duality in the simple case of an individual, isolated industry. It is shown that firms earning maximum profits of zero can be characterized not by strict constant returns to scale, but by local constant returns, at the bottom of u-shaped average cost curves. If all inputs are 'primary' and the generating technology is perfectly smooth, only a lower dimensional region of the 'true' production function can ever be active, however variable primary input prices can be. If an industry's own output is an input and the rate of interest is zero, then an isoquant cannot be inferred from any number of real primary input prices even under strictly constant returns. A positive and variable rate of interest gives *more* information on the generating technology and, in the case of a Leontief unit isoquant, the generating technique can be inferred from knowledge of a sufficient number of different real primary input price–rate of interest combinations. Chapter 14, by Ian Steedman, examines corn/tractor, Wicksellian and simple input–output models of production. Varying the rate of interest to yield alternative long-period positions, the relationship between capital per unit of output and labour per unit of output are traced out in the consumer good industry. Reswitching is strictly excluded. Remarkably enough, it is found repeatedly that the consumer good isoquant need not be downward sloping and convex from above; it need not even be monotonic. This spells trouble for conventional assumptions in production theory. In Chapter 15, Takashi Yagi studies income distribution in a system with fixed capital and depreciation and introduces a new surplus approach in the theory of distribution and capital. The ratio of the rate of profit and the wage rate, called the surplus rate, is distinguished from the rate of profit for capital. The properties of the standard system introduced by Sraffa are then used to analyse the shares in distribution and the measurement of the aggregate value of capital in an actual system with fixed capital.

'Sraffian themes' are dealt with in Part 4, which has four chapters. Chapter 16, by Enrico Bellino, starts from Pasinetti's 1960 mathematical formulation of the Ricardian system, which is reformulated in such a way as to provide a mathematical formulation of the income distribution theory contained in Ricardo's early writings. This analytical formulation of Ricardo's early writings has the pedagogical function of fully appreciating the final objective that Sraffa was pursuing with his standard commodity: that of studying the relation concerning income distribution independently of prices. In simpler terms, Sraffa sought to depict the economy as a system where the division of the social product, or 'cake', does not affect the magnitude of the cake. In Chapter 17 Christian Gehrke investigates whether Sraffa's unpublished manuscripts provide some hints for interpreting his reaction to Joan Robinson's objections to the use of the concept of 'subsistence-cum-surplus wages'. It is shown that Sraffa regarded the problem emphasized by Robinson of specifying the amounts of commodities consumed for subsistence independently of the consumption out of surplus wages as nonexistent, because he conceived of subsistence requirements as notional parts of the commodities actually consumed. Chapter 18, by Carlo Panico, Antonio Pinto, Martín Puchet Anyul and Marta Vazquez Suarez, presents a Sraffian interpretation of the evolution of the US financial regulation after the Second World War, in which it is emphasized that the formation of monetary policy and legislation is affected by the conflicts over the distribution of income. This approach has been widely overlooked in the literature. The chapter argues that during the period considered, financial regulation evolved from a 'discretionary' to a 'rules-based' regime. That conversion was gradual and reflected the strengthening position of the financial industry. It is also stressed that the ability of the financial industry to affect political life has influenced the reforms proposed and adopted after the crisis. Chapter 19, by Man-Seop Park, starts from an accounting equation that is widely used in the recent neoclassical literature modelling production and growth. The models are set in continuous time and the equation refers to a productive process (or an aggregate economy) at 'time *t*' where (ultimately) both a nondurable input and a durable input are utilized. Two characteristics of the equation in particular attract our attention. The first is that the user cost of the nondurable input does not, whereas that of the durable input does, involve the rate of interest. The second is that the quantities appearing in the equation are all treated as real quantities. The present essay draws the attention to the logical difficulties besetting the first characteristic and concludes that the approach cannot be sustained as it is.

Part 5 deals with 'imperfect competition' and has three chapters. Chapter 20, by Antonio d'Agata, develops a simple model of product differentiation *à la* Hotelling with quantity-setting firms in which producers of identical goods collude because of kinks in demand. It is shown that producing homogeneous goods may be optimal because of the existence of collusion-supporting kinks in demand. The results achieved suggest also that positioning can be strategically used for generating kinks in demand and, therefore, collusion. Chapter 21, by Simone d'Alessandro and Luciano Fanti, analyses a vertically integrated industry with a monopolistic upstream firm and two downstream firms choosing their capacity for strategic reasons and then competing *à la* Bertrand in the final product market with differentiated products. It is shown that the common wisdom according to which (i) the profit of the monopolistic supplier is higher when it is price-discriminating, and (ii) consumers' surplus and social welfare are higher when it is non-price-discriminating, is always contradicted. Moreover, interpreting the monopolistic upstream firm as a centralized union, it is shown that an 'egalitarian' wage policy is preferred not only by the union but also by consumers and society as a whole. Both results hold in certain conditions even when strategic entry is taken into consideration. In Chapter 22 Rodolfo Signorino provides a close textual comparison between the 1957 second Italian edition and the 1962 first American edition of *Oligopoly and Technical Progress*, showing that Sylos Labini added to the later edition some sections concerning new firms' entry and incumbent firms' reaction, which partially contradict Modigliani's 1958 presentation of the Sylos Postulate. The theoretical differences between Sylos Labini and Modigliani with regard to the assumption of constant output are traced back to their different modelling strategies on how to tackle the issue of external firms' conjectures in determining the long-run oligopoly equilibrium price.

Part 6 deals with the 'history of economic analysis' and has five chapters. Chapter 23, by Amitava K. Dutt, examines whether there is anything useful left in Malthus's analysis of population and economic growth. Distinguishing between theoretical frameworks of analysis and specific predictions made using such frameworks, it argues that even though Malthus's predictions proved to be incorrect, his theoretical framework has much to offer, and deserves careful attention. Moreover, using this framework can be useful in addressing whether his fears are still justified. This is done by developing a simple formulation of Malthus's theory of population and economic growth and by extending it to examine a number of relevant and important issues that were neglected or not sufficiently emphasized by him, that is, technological change, the demographic transition, aggregate demand and the environment. In Chapter 24 Riccardo Faucci reconstructs the evolution of the thought of the Italian economist Federico Caffè, born in 1914, who mysteriously disappeared between 14 and 15 April 1987. Federico Caffè was among the most important post-1945 Italian economists. As a professor at the University of Rome for almost thirty years, he authored more than 150 academic publications. An outstanding teacher, he supervised the diploma theses of a huge number of students and educated many excellent scholars, including Mario Draghi, Ignazio Visco, Guido M. Rey, Ezio Tarantelli, Marcello De Cecco, and Nicola Acocella (his successor in the Rome chair). A militant intellectual, his opinions leaned strongly toward the left. The chapter reconstructs his political commitments, his post-war economic policy and economics contributions, his warm admiration of Cambridge economics and his hostility to monetarism. Chapter 25, by Duncan Foley, revisits the labour theory of value developed by classical economists and Marx. It claims that classical political economists and Marx conceptualized human labour in terms of the subjective cost of production, but regarded labour nonetheless as comparable and aggregatable across individuals. Labour in this sense is both universal across workers and fungible among different productive employments. In commodity-producing systems where labour is mobile among different employments, the rate of exploitation in the sense of the ratio of labour effort to money income will tend to be equalized across employments. This proportionality is sufficient to establish a proportionality between value added and labour effort over a commodity-producing system, and the conservation of surplus value in a capitalist commodity-producing system, despite the competition of capitals to maximize their share of the pool of surplus value. Chapter 26, by Bruno Jossa, argues that the establishment of a system of cooperative firms reversing the current capital–labour relation is tantamount to a revolution, in that it results in the introduction of a new production mode. It then asks whether the idea of a revolution enacted by peaceful and democratic means is fully compatible with Marx and Engels's writings. Although the best proxy for the system imagined by Marx is doubtless an economy in which labour-managed firms operate within a centrally planned system, the chapter argues that a system with self-managed firms would be consistent with Marx's theoretical edifice even if it should fail to adopt central planning. In Chapter 27 Alberto Quadrio Curzio analyses the works of two Italian 'institutional economists', Carlo Cattaneo (1801–1869) and Giuseppe Colombo (1836–1921), who, in the nineteenth and twentieth century, contributed significantly to building an industrialized nation. Attention is drawn to the Italian industrial development, which 150 years after national unification has not yet spread to the whole country. Cattaneo and Colombo were both influenced by the civil ethics of the *Risorgimento* and had a structural concept of political economy in which economics (in particular industrial growth with a focus on technological innovation) and finance were seen to be complementary rather than alternative. Finally, they both were conscious that overcoming the existing territorial dualism was a step on the way to national unification.

We take this opportunity to thank all contributors for their fine work and the colleagues we involved in assessing first versions of the chapters for helping to improve them. We are grateful to them and the publisher, especially Emily Kindleysides and Laura Johnson, for a smooth collaboration.

Last but not least, we thank Neri Salvadori for his generosity, kindness, support and friendship over many years.

2 Personal reminiscences of a close friend and colleague

Heinz D. Kurz

Neri and I saw each other for the first time on the occasion of a research seminar organised by Domenico Mario Nuti and Bob Rowthorn in the Faculty of Economics of the University of Cambridge in the spring of 1978. Neri was then a research student in Cambridge after he had studied under the supervision of Ian Steedman at the University of Manchester. I was a British Academy visiting scholar, coming from Kiel University, Germany, where I had recently finished my PhD thesis on Piero Sraffa's work and wished to meet the man whose work I admired. Neri and I saw each other in the seminar, but we did not get in closer contact.

We met again in 1981 at the Trieste International Summer School at the Centro di Studi Economici Avanzati. The school had freshly started the year before in Udine and was organised by Sergio Parrinello, who did a marvellous job in bringing together scholars with a critical orientation towards mainstream economics. He, Pierangelo Garegnani and Jan Kregel represented the school, but Sergio, I believe, made it all happen, raised the funds, booked the venue, etc. The school was of the utmost importance for my intellectual life, because there I made friends with a number of scholars whose work I appreciated and with whom I cooperated during the following years in a number of ways. The scholars included, amongst others, in alphabetical order: Tom Asimakopoulos, Amit Bhaduri, Krishna Bharadwaj, Christian Bidard, Paul Davidson, Pierangelo Garegnani, Geoff Harcourt, Hyman Minsky, Edward J. Nell, Sergio Parrinello, Fabio Petri, Alessandro Roncaglia, Bertram Schefold, Ian Steedman, Josef Steindl, Sidney Weintraub – and, of course, Neri. He attended the 1981 meeting as a junior fellow, but his interventions showed that he was anything but junior. The mathematician and economist Ulrich Krause, a friend and colleague of mine in Bremen, had come across a paper by Neri and had asked me contact him and invite him to Bremen. Neri and I had plenty of opportunities to talk in Trieste and got on friendly terms with one another.

In 1979 I had been appointed to a chair in the economics department of the recently founded University of Bremen and had begun to invite major representatives of the classical approach to the theory of value and distribution, including several of the aforementioned scholars. In November 1981 Neri visited us in Bremen and stayed with my wife, Gabriele, and I for two weeks. He gave a splendid lecture on the problem of the choice of technique in Sraffa and then also one in a workshop in the Mathematical Department organised by Uli. He came again to Bremen in late November–early December of the following year, and then in 1983 when there was a meeting of, among others, Uli, Sergio, Ian and us, devoted to discussing the role of 'demand' in the classical theory of value and distribution. Neri, who had arrived a few days earlier, gave a talk in the Mathematics Department. After having witnessed his great intellectual prowess and impeccable logic, Neri also insisted on coddling Gabi and me with his cooking expertise. He produced a vegetarian lasagne – a culinary delight; easily the best we ever had. Cooking this type of lasagne necessitated the use of a great many bowls, platters and pans, many more than we were aware of possessing, and it left behind a totally exhausted cook. Neri fell ill and had to stay in bed for a few days.

Whenever Neri does not feel well, he puts on a grey woollen hat. He wore it while still in bed, when two days after his performance as a speaker and cook, Sergio and Ian arrived in Bremen and visited us. Thankfully, Neri soon recovered.

The academic year 1982–1983 I spent as a visiting professor at the University of Rome, 'La Sapienza', where my friendship with Sergio and Pierangelo became closer. Neri, Uli (who was also on a sabbatical in Rome) and I were invited to a round table on joint production at the Institute of Economics. Neri, who in the meantime had joined the Faculty of Political Science at the University of Catania as a lecturer ('professore incaricato'), visited us in Rome and invited me to give lectures in Catania. I spent most enjoyable days there and saw how young Neri unofficially 'ran' the department. He was both the youngest and most authoritative person there, highly respected by colleagues, students and staff.

In early 1985 I went to the Department of Economics of the Graduate Faculty of the New School for Social Research, with which my faculty in Bremen had signed a cooperation agreement initiated by Harald Hagemann, Edward Nell and me. Neri, who at the time was an associate professor at the University of Denver (he was there in this position from September 1984 to May 1986), came over to New York and invited me to give a talk in Denver. Our cooperation gradually gained momentum and bore fruit. We planned to write our first paper in March 1985 while attending a conference in Pittsburgh. Ed Nell was supposed to have reserved rooms for us, but had forgotten about it. Eventually he managed to get us a room with two twin beds in a hotel near the conference venue. To be put up in the same room was somewhat odd and so we spent almost the entire first night discussing, which greatly propelled our collaboration and then our tiredness. The second night we slept like logs. The first joint papers materialised soon afterwards and were published in the *Journal of Post Keynesian Economics* in 1986 and in the *Journal of Political Economy* in 1987, respectively. These were comments on other people's works. The first piece we wrote during a meeting in Bremen devoted to editing the second one. We sat in my office on the first floor of our house and had a lot of fun. Roars of laughter came from the room, which prompted Gabi to question the seriousness of the subject and us.[1]

A start was made and both of us seem to have enjoyed the cooperation. A mutually fruitful cooperation typically involves a division of labour, and this works well if the persons involved are sufficiently different in some respects and sufficiently similar in others. It was a surprising but pleasing experience for me to find out how swiftly Neri and I understood what the other was saying and how quickly our points of view converged. We had some conflicts of opinion, but they always vanished rapidly. We are clearly possessed of different talents and capabilities, but these appear to be complementary to one another. We also share similar work attitudes. For fun, I variously called Neri my 'slave driver' and, being a free man, I retaliated by acting like his slave driver. This increased our productivity tremendously, measured in terms of the number of pages we published together.

We met variously at the annual Trieste summer school and published a few further papers. I do not remember when exactly Neri invited me to join him writing a big book along the classical-Sraffa-von Neumann line, but it must have been in late 1988 or early 1989, shortly before I joined the Graduate Faculty of the New School as Theodor-Heuss-Professor for the academic year 1990–1991.[2] The book was designed not only to summarise the results of the relevant literature up until then in a coherent and rigorous way; it had also the following goals: to apply the classical approach to problems that had not yet been dealt with at all, or dealt with in a way that we found wanting; to compare the classical approach with other approaches, especially with the different variants of the marginalist or neoclassical ones; and to trace the historical geneses of competing ideas, concepts and theories.

In New York Gabi and I lived in a most convenient apartment in the Zeckendorf tower, Irving Place, close to Union Square and five minutes' walk from the Department of Economics at the corner of 5th Avenue and 14th Street. At the time the Internet was not yet publicly available, so Neri and I communicated by exchanging floppy discs, which contained the latest versions of the chapters of the book on which we were working at the time. After having revised and added to what the sender had developed, the disc went back, and so on. I had bought a MacClassic, which had been released in October 1990 as the first Apple Macintosh for less than US\$1,000. I learned how to use it, and whilst working hard on our book, I gradually ruined my eyes staring at the tiny screen of the grey, small box in front of me, with the Empire State Building at a distance. Neri came to see me in New York many times. This simplified matters considerably, but I wonder whether he was attracted only by the fact that we could work together face to face. There were a number of excellent Japanese restaurants in the neighbourhood, and with the exception of breakfast, we essentially lived on sushi, sashimi, udon noodles and the like. According to Ludwig Feuerbach's dictum 'Der Mensch ist, was er ißt' – 'man is what he or she eats' – we had every reason to think that the quality of the food consumed would show in the quality of the book we were writing.

The manuscript progressed quickly. Mark Knell, then my teaching assistant at the New School, read drafts of the chapters and corrected our English. We then sent a set of chapters to good friends (see the preface to our book), asking them for criticisms and comments. Amongst them was Paul Samuelson at the MIT. We were extremely pleased to learn that he took an interest in our work and replied quickly after having received book chapters from us, sending us most useful and valuable remarks and observations. He also invited us to visit him in Boston, which we gladly did a couple of times. We had the privilege of discussing with him various matters and problems. We were impressed by his erudition that reached far beyond economics narrowly defined. Paul was interested in what we did and why we did it and shared his immense knowledge with us. It was clear to him that our orientation was different from his, but this did not prevent him from treating us very favourably. He thought highly of Piero Sraffa and David Ricardo, the sung heroes of the approach we had chosen, and he also held in high esteem important representatives of this approach, most notably Luigi Pasinetti, Bertram Schefold and Ian Steedman.[3] As he wrote in private correspondence to one of us, he regretted that in important respects we did not coalesce with his point of view, but he respected our stance.

Whilst in New York in August 1991, one of us contacted the American branch of Cambridge University Press to find out whether they would be interested in publishing our book. This brought us into contact with Scott Parris, the economics editor of the Press. The cooperation with him was excellent throughout the process and we became very good friends. He contacted referees who read early versions of some of the chapters, gave most useful comments and suggestions, and recommended publication.

In February and March 1992 we were kindly invited by the Istituto di ricerca sulla Dinamica dei Sistemi Economici (IDSE) in Milan to give six seminars on Chapters 1 to 10 and 12 of the book we were writing and received most valuable responses from a great many economists attending the seminars. In addition, we presented several of the chapters at conferences and seminars in the USA and Europe.

After five years of hard work we finally sent a second version of the entire manuscript to the Press. We did so after an ultimate round of discussions and corrections of our work in early February 1994 in the house of my aunt in Frankfurt. When we had posted the tome to Scott Parris we felt that it was time to celebrate the event by a decent sushi dinner.

The book was swiftly copyedited at the Press and when the person in charge of it informed us that the manuscript was on the way to us, we met in Neri's apartment in Pisa in late March 1994 to check the result. This was an excruciating experience that put our friendship to the test. Time and again we came across passages we felt we had already corrected on the occasion of our February meeting. Had one of us not accomplished his task, that is, had not incorporated the changes in the electronic version of the manuscript he was supposed to have done following our division of labour? We became ever angrier at each other as we proceeded from chapter to chapter, each putting blame on the other. Our mood deteriorated swiftly and could not even be cheered up by Rosa Lucia's fine cooking. It was only on the fifth day of extremely enervating revisions when we turned to Chapter 12 that it became crystal clear that we had been sent the wrong manuscript. After extensive discussions we had decided in February to change the title of the chapter to 'On limits to the long-period method' and had immediately carried out the correction in the electronic version of the work. Neither of us had blundered or failed to accomplish his task, the copyeditor (not, of course, Scott!) had wrongly edited an old version of our work. We were upset because of all the hours we had worked in vain, but we were also relieved to see that there was no reason to question each other's reliability. I called the office of the Press in New York and was put through to the copyeditor. He told me ruefully that he had two manuscripts in his possession, but had not known which was the final one. He erroneously took the wrong one for it. I asked him: 'Why did you not ask us which is the right one?' He answered disarmingly: 'I did not wish to look foolish in your eyes.' 'You succeeded', I replied. The entire work had to be done anew.

Theory of Production: A Long-Period Analysis was eventually published in early 1995. With the exception of the experience just mentioned, the way we saw our collaboration is well expressed in the preface of the book:

> Economics is known as the 'dismal science.' We cannot confirm this judgment. Despite the hardship we encountered in finishing the manuscript, our collaboration was a continuous source of pleasure and excitement. Indeed, given all the fun we had while writing [the book] we were at times inclined to think that economics is a laughing matter.
>
> (Kurz and Salvadori, 1995: xviii)

Shortly after the book had come out we received an invitation to give a PhD seminar based on it in September 1995 at the Postgraduate Division of the Faculty of Economics, Universidad Nacional Autónoma de México (UNAM), in Mexico City. Our host was Ignacio Perrottini. He and Adriana Suarez-Blanch looked after our wives and us extremely well. Apart from the overwhelming hospitality, the beauty of the country and its rich cultural heritage, we were given the opportunity to experience the Guerrero earthquake on 14 September (with a magnitude of 7.4 on the Richter scale). It happened in the morning around 8 o'clock and lasted for about one minute – a subjectively felt eternity. I wanted to get out of my bed, but could not stand upright and was thrown to the floor. Lying on my back I saw the chandelier hitting the ceiling from left to right. I was scared to death, called my wife who was in the bathroom, holding fast onto the washbasin, and Neri and Rosa Lucia who were still in bed in the second bedroom. 'We must get out of here,' I screamed. I desperately looked for the keys to unlock the door, but in my panic could not find them. Neri tried to calm me, telling me that he had experienced several earthquakes in Naples and Sicily and that the best to do is to place oneself under the door lintel and wait until the quake was over. Most casualties, he added, are because of heart attacks and not because of collapsing buildings. I was not fully convinced, seeing the walls of our apartment move in all directions at the same time, or so I felt. We were lucky, though, because after the big earthquake of 1985 the house had been made quakeproof.

In late November of that year we attended an input–output conference in New Delhi, followed by a one-week trip with our wives and Christian Lager through Rajasthan. It was a marvellous excursion. Yet in my judgment a trip to Arusha, Tansania, where we attended another input–output conference in 1999, was even more exciting. After the conference Neri, Rosa Lucia, Gabi, Christian Gehrke and I planned to climb Mount Meru, a volcano near Kilimanjaro, 4,566 m in height, displaying a stunningly beautiful landscape and flora. I was very sceptical that it was a good idea for Neri to accompany us, because I feared that his physical condition was not up to the task. He proved me to be quite wrong. While he and Rosa did not accompany us to the peak, they climbed Little Meru (3,801 m), and as Neri told me afterwards, he could easily have gone up higher. He also displayed his excellent organisational skills when arranging for the climb and the visit to the Serengeti afterwards.

The years that followed the publication of *Theory of Production* were filled with much joint work, which resulted in numerous publications. These are collected in, by now, four volumes of essays by the two of us, by one of us alone, or by one or the two of us with some other authors. The volumes, published by Routledge, are entitled *Understanding 'Classical' Economics* (1998), *Classical Economics and Modern Theory* (2003), *Interpreting Classical Economics* (2007), and *Revisiting Classical Economics* (2015a). Reviving the classical approach to economic theory is indeed the common thread that connects much of our work and covers areas from the theory of value and distribution to the theory of development, economic growth and technical change to the theory of scarce natural resources, and so on. See also the recent *Elgar Companion to David Ricardo* (2015b) that we edited. In addition, we share a strong interest in features of Keynesian theory and in the history of economic thought and published several papers on major economists and their doctrines.

There are two further areas in which Neri and I collaborated closely and smoothly for many years. First there is *Metroeconomica*, which had for a long time been successfully edited by Sergio Parrinello. In 1998 he asked me to take over and in 2004 I approached Neri inviting him to join me as general editor. He put all his organisational talent, academic connections and a great part of his remarkable capacity to work at the service of the journal. This soon showed in terms of sustained and substantial increases in the journal's social science citation index.

In 1995 Pierangelo Garegnani had invited me to join a group of scholars with a set division of labour amongst them to help him with editing a judicious selection from Piero Sraffa's unpublished papers and correspondence kept at Trinity College, Cambridge. In 1997 he asked me to become the general editor of the project on the grounds that he could not do it. After some hesitation I agreed to assume what turned out to be a Herculean task. I did not anticipate the kind of difficulties I was to encounter during the following years. I was keen to accomplish the task in good time and brought in Neri and Christian Gehrke, two meticulous and circumspect scholars, whose extraordinary talents and skills were badly needed in the project. The three of us spent several summers in Cambridge, often together, and managed to solve some intricate puzzles, which at first sight looked impenetrable. Neri's contribution was especially valuable in regard to interpreting Sraffa's work on his equations of production and the help he had received from his 'mathematical friends', Frank P. Ramsey, Abram S. Besicovitch and Alister Watson.

We published several papers on this collaboration, some of which were reprinted in the collections of essays mentioned above. The most intricate problems Sraffa faced concerned pure joint production on the one hand and fixed capital, nondepletable and exhaustible resources, which he analysed using a multiple-products framework, on the other. As is well known from Sraffa's 1960 book and the discussions it triggered, these areas are studded with hard nuts to crack and Sraffa deserves the credit for having cracked many of them.[4] Neri and I were especially keen to deal with the problem of exhaustible resources on which there are only a few remarks in Sraffa's book, but which concerned him from an early time onwards. We published a number of papers on the problem, dealing inter alia with the approaches elaborated by Sergio Parrinello, Bertram Schefold, Christian Bidard and Guido Erreygers.

When Pierangelo Garegnani died prematurely in October 2011, the publication of the edition of Sraffa's works and correspondence had already been delayed for several years for reasons that need not concern us here. A true friend, Neri offered to help me with the project and overcome the numerous remaining stumbling blocks on the way to the completion and publication of the edition. I am deeply grateful to him for this and I am optimistic that with his help the project, all the difficulties notwithstanding, will eventually materialise. With a friend like Neri, you are bound to master problems instead of problems mastering you.

The Sraffa edition will be, in all probability, the last huge enterprise in which we collaborate together with a number of other scholars, but I am sure we will not be able to resist the temptation of doing some work on other topics on the side. Having experienced Neri's friendship and having benefitted from his numerous talents, I am addicted to them. Therefore: Ad multos annos! When Aristotle insisted that one's best friend is the man who in wishing one well wishes it for one's sake it may be assumed it has been understood that there are positive externalities involved.

Notes

1 August 1985 saw also the memorable conference 'Sraffa's *Production of Commodities by Means of Commodities* after twenty-five years' in Florence, organised by Krishna Bharadwaj, Pierangelo Garegnani, John Eatwell and Bertram Schefold. The speakers were placed in alphabetical order in the lecture hall, and so I had the pleasure to sit right next to Lord Nicholas Kaldor. Kaldor had the habit of falling asleep every once in a while, and whenever he woke up in the morning session he would ask me: 'Heinz, when is lunch?' In the afternoon session he would surprisingly ask me: 'Heinz, when is dinner?'

2 The Heuss chair was donated to the New School by the German government as a tribute to its role as the University in Exile during the Nazi period. It is typically given for one academic year and circulates amongst its various departments.

3 The respect Paul had for Sraffa and some scholars working in the Sraffian tradition is well reflected by the fact that, when asked whether he would like to contribute an essay to a Festschrift in honour of Ian Steedman, Samuelson not only answered in the affirmative but asked one of us if he could be an editor and write a preface (see Vint *et al.*, 2010). Sadly, Samuelson died in 2009 and so did not see the published volume.

4 Given the importance of the areas under consideration stressed by Sraffa, it is amazing that the majority of scholars looking and commenting on Sraffa's unpublished papers sidestepped these areas, focusing attention exclusively on single production, as if this had not only been the starting point, but the core of his analysis.

References

Kurz, H. D. and Salvadori, N. (1995), *Theory of Production. A Long-Period Analysis*, Cambridge: Cambridge University Press.

Kurz, H. D. and Salvadori, N. (1998), *Understanding 'Classical' Economics*, London: Routledge.

Kurz, H. D. and Salvadori, N. (2003), *Classical Economics and Modern Theory*, London: Routledge.

Kurz, H. D. and Salvadori, N. (2007), *Interpreting Classical Economics*, London: Routledge.

Kurz, H. D. and Salvadori, N. (2015a), *Revisiting Classical Economics*, London: Routledge.

Kurz, H. D. and Salvadori, N. (2015b), *The Elgar Companion to David Ricardo*, Cheltenham and Northampton: Edward Elgar.

Vint, J., Metcalfe, S., Kurz, H. D., Salvadori, N. and Samuelson, P. A. (Eds) (2010), *Economic Theory and Economic Thought. Essays in Honour of Ian Steedman*, London: Routledge.

Part 1

Economic growth and income distribution

3 Ownership concentration, industrial agglomeration and welfare distribution

Pasquale Commendatore, Ingrid Kubin and Carmelo Petraglia

Introduction

Standard New Economic Geography (NEG) models are concerned with the effect of trade integration on the distribution of economic activity between two countries or regions within an economic integrated area (Krugman, 1991). Typically, a NEG model – in any of its alternative variants – focusses on trade costs, increasing returns of monopolistically competitive firms and factor mobility, and determines endogenously the spatial distribution of firms by the interplay of agglomeration and dispersion forces.

Agglomeration forces depend on the proximity of firms and households to the larger market, while dispersion forces depend on the competition in goods and factors markets which occurs as firms become more concentrated in one location. The nature of the two types of forces changes depending on the assumptions made on different ingredients of the model. The basic framework we deal with in this paper is the so-called footloose capital (FC) model, whose main features – as compared to the Krugman's core-periphery (CP) model – are as follows.

In Krugman's CP model, mobile workers spend their incomes locally and the spatial distribution of industrialized activities is driven by three effects. The 'market-access' effect (i.e. the tendency of imperfectly competitive firms to locate in a large market and export to small markets) and the 'cost-of-living' effect (i.e. goods are cheaper in regions with higher concentration of industrial firms) encourage agglomeration. The 'market-crowding' effect (i.e. the tendency of imperfectly competitive firms to locate in regions with fewer competitors) favours dispersion. Combining the 'market-access' effect and the 'cost-of-living' effect with migration creates the potential for cumulative causality and self-reinforcing agglomeration processes (Baldwin *et al.*, 2003). As a result, complete agglomeration in one region may be a stable equilibrium. Indeed, the standard result of the CP model is that a sufficient reduction in trade barriers will destabilize the symmetric equilibrium and will result in complete agglomeration of the industrial activity in one location.

Within the NEG, the CP model impresses with the richness of delivered results. However, due to cumulative causality, it is difficult to manipulate analytically and most results are obtained via numerical simulation.

The FC variant of the CP model, originally proposed by Martin and Rogers (1995), departs from the CP model for two assumptions: a fixed capital requirement for each variety of the differentiated good and international immobility of workers. The mobile factor in the FC model is physical or, in other versions of the FC model, knowledge capital. These assumptions cut off 'cumulative causality' and the outcome of catastrophic agglomeration, thus rendering the analysis much more tractable.

It is assumed that capital earnings are repatriated and spent where the capital owner resides. Therefore, the typical CP feature of demand-linked circular causality – production changes brought about by factor movements yield expenditure switching that in turn generates further production changes – does not occur. Furthermore, the cost-linked circular causality of the CP model – shifts in production alter prices inducing workers migration with further production shifting – is eliminated.

However, agglomeration still occurs due to the working of the 'market-access' effect. Compared to the CP model, the FC model has the advantage of obtaining closed form solutions for the spatial distribution of industry, while it does not feature the circular causality that is so much of the source of the CP model's richness and intractability (Baldwin *et al.*, 2003).

In the FC model, there exists a clear separation between workers and capitalists as workers solely supply labour and are not allowed to be shareholders of firms, while capital owners are modelled as 'pure capitalists'. This may not be an innocuous assumption as countries significantly differ in their distribution of capital ownership between workers and rentiers.

According to the well-known Pasinetti theorem (Pasinetti, 1962),[1] the workers' propensity to save has no effect on the rate of profit or on the distribution between profits and wages, while it does have an influence on the distribution of income between capitalists and workers.

Inspired by the work of Pasinetti and Kaldor, we aim to enrich the FC model by considering a world economy composed of two trading countries where the concept of classes enters in two ways.

First of all, workers' and capitalists' consumption behaviour may differ. In particular, we will assume that consumers belonging to the two classes in the home country can allocate a different share of their income to the consumption of the manufactured good.

Secondly, we allow for differences between the two countries in terms of concentration of capital ownership, explicitly referring to the case of workers owning a higher share of capital in the home country as compared to the foreign country.

Allowing for workers to own a share of capital, we depart from the standard Pasinetti framework – corresponding to a more traditional capitalism. We consider instead a framework more similar to the managerial capitalism conceived by Kaldor (1966) where ownership and control are separated and ownership is diffused.[2]

In our framework, which departs from the standard FC model, there are two types of representative agents/households: a capitalist–rentier, who controls the firm and decides capital relocation, and the other, dubbed 'worker', who supplies labour and owns part of the firm. According to our interpretation, workers own a larger share of capital in a country where ownership is more diffused; on the contrary, a smaller share corresponds to a country characterized by a more concentrated ownership.

Extending in this direction the CP model enriches the model with respect to both the long-run international equilibrium allocation of capital and welfare distribution among groups. The rest of the paper unfolds as follows. The next section presents the structure of the model by introducing the main assumptions. In the third section we characterize the short-run general equilibrium contingent on a given capital distribution between the two countries. The fourth section deals with the derivation of the long-run equilibrium by looking at the capital relocation process between the two countries. The assumption of asymmetric countries in terms of capital ownership concentration turns out to have a strong impact on the international equilibrium allocation. The impact of trade freeness on the long-run stationary equilibrium allocation of capital is studied under two alternative scenarios concerning consumption preferences of workers and rentiers. The fifth section focusses on welfare analysis. We study how the welfare of workers and rentiers in the two countries is affected by a higher degree of ownership diffusion in the home country. The final section concludes by summarizing our main results.

The model structure

The economy is composed of two countries, home and foreign (h and f); two sectors, agriculture and manufacturing (A and M); two factors of production with a given endowment, labour and capital (L and K); and two types of households, workers and capitalist-rentiers or rentiers (w and r). Rentiers own only capital, whereas workers may own both capital and labour. Capital is only used in manufacturing and it is mobile across countries; labour instead can only move across sectors.

Workers and rentiers own the same proportion of capital units and are equally distributed between the two countries. It follows that the two countries have the same labour endowment, with $L/2$ representing the number of workers in country h (and in country f). Instead, the capital ownership distribution is not necessarily equal in the two countries. Denoting by θ_h and θ_f the shares of workers' ownership in h and f respectively, two possible scenarios emerge: capital ownership is more diffused in the home country, $\theta_h > \theta_f$; or, alternatively, capital ownership is more concentrated in the home country, $\theta_h < \theta_f$.

The preferences of consumers belonging to the two groups (rentiers and workers) are represented by the two-level utility functions U^w and U^r. At the upper level the choice is between agricultural and manufactured goods according to a Cobb–Douglas specification, where the shares of income allocated to goods A and M by the two groups may differ:

$$U^w = C_M^{\mu w} C_A^{1-\mu w} \tag{3.1}$$

$$U^r = C_M^{\mu r} C_A^{1-\mu r} \tag{3.2}$$

where C_M (C_A) is consumption of the M (A) good, μ_w and μ_r are the shares of income allocated to the consumption of the manufactured varieties (the complement to unity being the shares allocated to the consumption of the homogeneous agricultural good) by workers and rentiers, respectively, where $0 < \mu_w$, $\mu_r < 1$. At the lower level, the choice is among the varieties of the manufactured good according to a CES specification. The quantity index for consumption of the manufactured varieties C_M is

$$C_M = \sum_{i=1}^{n} c_i^{\frac{\sigma-1}{\sigma}}$$

where σ is the constant elasticity of substitution between the manufactured varieties $i = 1, \ldots, n$, that, for convenience, is the same for all consumers. The lower σ, the greater the consumers' taste for variety; c_i is consumption of variety i; n is the total number of varieties produced in the two countries.

Each worker provides inelastically one unit of labour per period (thus L represents both the number of workers and labour units). The A-sector is characterized by perfect competition and constant returns: the agricultural good is produced with labour as the sole input, one unit of labour yielding one unit of product. We assume that neither country has enough labour to satisfy the total demand of the economy for the agricultural good. Thus, both countries always produce the agricultural good – the so-called non-full-specialization condition. Transportation of the agricultural product between the two countries is costless.

The M-sector is modelled as a Dixit–Stiglitz monopolistically competitive sector. Manufacturing involves increasing returns: each manufactured good requires a fixed input of 1 unit of capital to operate and has a constant marginal labour requirement β. Given the consumers' preferences for variety, a firm would always produce a variety different from the varieties produced by other firms. Thus the number of varieties is always equal to the number of firms. Furthermore, since 1 unit of capital is required for each manufacturing firm, the total number of firms/varieties, n, is always equal to the total supply of capital:

$$n = K.$$

The number of varieties in country j $(=h, f)$ is

$$n_h = \lambda n = \lambda K$$
$$n_f = (1 - \lambda)n = (1 - \lambda)K$$

where $0 \leq \lambda \leq 1$ denotes the share of physical capital used in country h.

Transport costs for manufactures take an iceberg form: if 1 unit is shipped between the two countries, $1/T$ is delivered, where $T \geq 0$. Following Baldwin *et al.* (2003), to compact the notation, we introduce parameter ϕ which is conventionally labelled 'trade freeness'. We have that $0 < \phi \leq 1$, with $\phi = 1$ $(T = 1)$ and $\phi \rightarrow 0$ $(T \rightarrow \infty)$ corresponding to the cases of no trade cost and trade cost becoming prohibitive, respectively.

Short-run general equilibrium

In this section we characterize the short-run general equilibrium (SRGE) contingent on a (given) capital distribution between the two countries, λ. In the A-sector, with the instantaneous establishment of market equilibrium and zero transport costs, the agricultural price is the same in both countries. Since competition results in zero agricultural profits, the equilibrium nominal wage of workers equates to the agricultural product price in both countries. We take this wage/agricultural price as the *numeraire*.

In the M-sector, under the assumption of identical behaviour, each firm sets the same local (mill) price p using the Dixit–Stiglitz pricing rule. Given that the wage is 1, the local price of every variety is

$$p = \beta \frac{\sigma}{\sigma - 1}. \tag{3.3}$$

The effective price paid by consumers for one unit of a variety produced in the other country is pT. Short-run general equilibrium requires that each manufacturer meets the demand for its variety.[3] For a variety produced in country j,

$$q_j = d_j \tag{3.4}$$

where q_j is the output of each manufacturer in country j and d_j is the demand for that manufacturer's variety. From equation (3.3), the short-run equilibrium profit per variety in country j is

$$\pi_j = pq_j - \beta q_j = \frac{pq_j}{\sigma} = \left(\frac{\beta}{\sigma - 1}\right) q_j. \tag{3.5}$$

This profit per variety defines the national rental per unit of capital. The shares θ_j and $(1 - \theta_j)$ are distributed to workers and rentiers, respectively ($j = h, f$).

Consumers face national manufacturing price indices given by

$$G_h = [\lambda K p^{1-\sigma} + (1 - \lambda) K p^{1-\sigma} \phi]^{\frac{1}{1-\sigma}} = [\lambda + (1 - \lambda) \phi] K^{\frac{1}{1-\sigma}} p \tag{3.6}$$

$$G_f = [\lambda K p^{1-\sigma} \phi + (1 - \lambda) K p^{1-\sigma}]^{\frac{1}{1-\sigma}} = [\lambda \phi + (1 - \lambda)] K^{\frac{1}{1-\sigma}} p. \tag{3.7}$$

The overall demand for each variety originating from both countries is

$$d_h = \left[M_h G_h^{\sigma-1} + M_f G_f^{\sigma-1} \phi \right] p^{-\sigma} \tag{3.8}$$

$$d_f = \left[M_h G_h^{\sigma-1} \phi + M_f G_f^{\sigma-1} \right] p^{-\sigma} \tag{3.9}$$

where

$$M_h = \mu_w \left(\frac{L}{2} + \theta_h \frac{\Pi}{2} \right) + \mu_r (1 - \theta_h) \frac{\Pi}{2}$$

$$M_f = \mu_w \left(\frac{L}{2} + \theta_f \frac{\Pi}{2} \right) + \mu_r \left(1 - \theta_f \right) \frac{\Pi}{2}$$

denote the expenditure on manufactured goods in country h and f, respectively; M defines the world expenditure on manufactures, with $M = M_h + M_f$, and $s_E = M_h/M$ its international split. We see below that M_j, M and s_E are independent of λ. These expressions take into account that the ownership distribution of home and foreign capital between workers and rentiers is identical in the two countries. Considering the equilibrium condition (3.4), after substituting (3.7) and (3.6) into (3.9) and (3.8) and the latter two into (3.5), short-run equilibrium profits per variety in the two countries correspond to

$$\pi_h = \left[\frac{s_E}{\lambda + (1 - \lambda)\phi} + \frac{(1 - s_E)\phi}{\lambda\phi + (1 - \lambda)} \right] \frac{M}{\sigma} \frac{1}{K} \tag{3.10}$$

$$\pi_f = \left[\frac{s_E\phi}{\lambda + (1 - \lambda)\phi} + \frac{(1 - s_E)}{\lambda\phi + (1 - \lambda)} \right] \frac{M}{\sigma} \frac{1}{K}. \tag{3.11}$$

For future reference, note that national and world profit incomes, Π_r and Π respectively, are given by[4]

$$\Pi_h = \lambda K \pi_h \tag{3.12}$$

$$\Pi_f = (1 - \lambda) K \pi_f \tag{3.13}$$

$$\Pi = \Pi_h + \Pi_f = \frac{M}{\sigma} \tag{3.14}$$

and world income by

$$Y = L + \frac{M}{\sigma}.$$

Observing that the Cobb–Douglas utilities for workers' and rentiers' (3.1) and (3.2) imply constant and different expenditure shares for manufacturing μ_w and μ_r, and recalling that θ_h and θ_f represent the share of capital owned by workers in countries h and f, respectively, the expenditure for the manufactured varieties in the two countries are

$$M_h = \mu_w \left(\frac{L}{2} + \theta_h \frac{\Pi}{2} \right) + \mu_r \left(1 - \theta_h \right) \frac{\Pi}{2} \tag{3.15}$$

$$M_f = \mu_w \left(\frac{L}{2} + \theta_f \frac{\Pi}{2} \right) + \mu_r \left(1 - \theta_f \right) \frac{\Pi}{2} \tag{3.16}$$

and world expenditures for manufactures are

$$M = \mu_w L + \left[\mu_r + (\mu_w - \mu_r) \left(\frac{\theta_h + \theta_f}{2} \right) \right] \Pi.$$

Taking into account (3.14), it follows that

$$M = \frac{\mu_w}{\sigma - \left[\mu_r + (\mu_w - \mu_r)\left(\frac{\theta_h + \theta_f}{2}\right)\right]} \sigma L.$$

Its international split is

$$s_E = \frac{1}{2} + \frac{(\mu_w - \mu_r)(\theta_h - \theta_f)}{4\sigma}$$

with $s_E \leq (> 0)$ for $(\mu_w - \mu_r)(\theta_h - \theta_f) \leq (> 0)$.

As mentioned above, it is possible to distinguish two possible scenarios:

1   capital ownership is more diffused in the home country, $\theta_h > \theta_f$;
2   capital ownership is more concentrated in the home country $\theta_h < \theta_f$;

with $\theta_h = \theta_f$ representing the limiting case of an equal degree of ownership distribution in the two countries.

From now on, we will consider only the first scenario by assuming $\theta_h > \theta_f$. The results obtained for this case apply by symmetry to the second scenario after switching h with f.[5]

There are also two subcases:

a $\mu_w > \mu_r$: that is, workers allocate a larger share of income to the manufactured good compared to rentiers. It follows that $s_E > 1/2$. Moreover, $\partial s_E / \partial \mu_w > 0$, $\partial s_E / \partial \mu_r < 0$ and $\partial s_E / \partial \theta_h > 0$.
b $\mu_w < \mu_r$: that is, workers allocate a smaller share of income to the manufactured good as compared to rentiers. It follows that $s_E < 1/2$. Moreover, $\partial s_E / \partial \mu_w > 0$, $\partial s_E / \partial \mu_r < 0$ and $\partial s_E / \partial \theta_h < 0$.

In the limiting case $\theta_h = \theta_f$ (and / or equivalently $\mu_w = \mu_r$), it follows that $s_E = 1/2$.

Crucial for the subsequent analysis is the relative profitability of capital $R(\lambda) = \pi_h / \pi_f$, given by

$$R(\lambda) = \frac{s_E [\lambda \phi + (1 - \lambda)] + (1 - s_E) \phi [\lambda + (1 - \lambda) \phi]}{s_E \phi [\lambda \phi + (1 - \lambda)] + (1 - s_E) [\lambda + (1 - \lambda) \phi]}. \tag{3.17}$$

For a constant s_E, the relative profitability of capital depends upon the allocation of capital λ via the so-called 'competition effect': a higher λ increases the competition in country h and therefore reduces relative profitability. The competition effect implies a negative slope of $R(\lambda)$, that is, $\partial R(\lambda)/\lambda < 0$. In addition, relative profitability depends upon workers and rentier consumption choices and on capital ownership distribution since s_E depends (positively) upon $(\mu_w - \mu_r)(\theta_h - \theta_f)$. Any parameter change that increases s_E, increases relative profitability, i.e.

$\partial R(\lambda)/\partial s_E > 0$. If, according to our assumption $\theta_h > \theta_f$ and μ_w is increased (reduced), the share of expenditures for manufactured goods in country h, s_E rises (diminishes) and relative profitability is increased (reduced) as well.

Capital movements and long-run equilibrium

In the FC model capital owners do not move themselves, but allocate the physical capital they own between the two countries (Martin and Rogers, 1995). In our framework – in which we do not take into consideration the existence of a separate group of managers – rentiers alter the international allocation of physical capital in response to relative profitability of real capital $R(\lambda)$. Since profit is spent in the country where rentiers live, cost-of-living does not impact on the capital allocation decision.

The dynamic relocation process resembles the replicator dynamics from evolutionary game theory (Weibull, 1997).[6]

Taking into account the constraint $0 \leq \lambda \leq 1$, the dynamic process is specified as follows:

$$Z(\lambda) = \begin{cases} 0 & \text{if } F(\lambda) < 0 \\ F(\lambda) & \text{if } 0 \leq F(\lambda) \leq 1 \\ 1 & \text{if } F(\lambda) > 1 \end{cases} \qquad (3.18)$$

where

$$F(\lambda) = \lambda + \gamma \lambda (1 - \lambda) \frac{R(\lambda) - 1}{\lambda R(\lambda) + (1 - \lambda)}.$$

According to $F(\lambda)$, capital is relocated in country $h(f)$ when relative profitability is larger (smaller) than 1, with γ representing the 'speed' with which the representative rentier alters the allocation of capital between the two countries in response to economic incentives.

$Z(\lambda)$ is a piecewise smooth one-dimensional map which determines the time evolution of the share of capital λ; we do not study here its dynamic properties, limiting our attention to its fixed point properties.

Fixed points for the dynamic system (3.18), which correspond to points of rest or long-run equilibria, are defined by $Z(\lambda) = \lambda$. Given that with perfectly free trade, i.e. $\phi = 1$, all capital allocations between the two countries are fixed points, we assume henceforth $\phi < 1$. Moreover, since we do not allow capital to move in a country with no manufacturing sector, the agglomeration of all manufacturing in one (either) country is necessarily a fixed point. That is, from equation (3.18), $Z(0) = 0$ and $Z(1) = 1$. We refer to $\lambda^{CP(0)} = 0$ and $\lambda^{CP(1)} = 1$ as the core-periphery fixed points or equilibria. Since capital migration does not occur when profits in the two countries are equal, λ^* is a fixed point if $R(\lambda^*) = 1$. Since $R(\lambda^*)$ is monotonically decreasing, there can be at most one interior fixed point λ^*. If an interior fixed point exists, then from (3.17) equality of profits implies that the long-run equilibrium share is

$$\lambda^* = \frac{1}{2} + \frac{1+\phi}{1-\phi}\left(s_E - \frac{1}{2}\right).$$

The following results apply:

- $\lambda^* \geq (<)1/2$ for $s_E \geq (<)1/2$, that is, $\lambda^* > 1/2$ when subcase a holds ($\mu_w > \mu_r$) and $\lambda^* < 1/2$ when subcase b holds ($\mu_w < \mu_r$);

- $\frac{\partial \lambda^*}{\partial s_E} = \frac{1+\phi}{1-\phi} > 0$;

- $\frac{\partial \lambda^*}{\partial \phi} = \frac{s_E - \frac{1}{2}}{2(1-\phi)^2} \geq (<)$ for $s_E \geq (<)1/2$, that is, $\frac{\partial \lambda^*}{\partial \phi} > 0$ when subcase a holds ($\mu_w > \mu_r$) and $\frac{\partial \lambda^*}{\partial \phi} < 0$ when subcase b holds ($\mu_w < \mu_r$);

- $\frac{\partial \lambda^*}{\partial \mu_w} > 0 \left(\frac{\partial \lambda^*}{\partial \mu_r} < 0\right)$ and $\frac{\partial \lambda^*}{\partial \theta_h} > 0$ when subcase a holds $\frac{\partial \lambda^*}{\partial \theta_h} < 0$ when subcase b holds; and

- $0 \leq \lambda^* \leq 1$ for $\frac{\phi}{1+\phi} \leq s_E \leq \frac{1}{1+\phi}$ or, equivalently, $\lambda^* > 0$ for $s_E < 1/2$ and $\phi < \phi_{S(0)} \equiv \frac{s_E}{1-s_E}$ (subcase a holds) and $\lambda^* < 0$ for $s_E > 1/2$ and $\phi < \phi_{S(1)} \equiv \frac{1-s_E}{s_E}$ (subcase b holds).

The meaning of these results are better understood by looking at Figure 3.1.

This figure shows the effect of increasing trade freeness ϕ on country's h capital share considering the two subcases of the first scenario. In Figure 3.1(a), that represents the subcase a $\mu_w > \mu_r$, the dashed line corresponds to the limiting case $s_E = 1/2$. The two countries have the same ownership distribution between workers and rentiers, which implies $\lambda^* = 1/2$ for $0 < \phi < 1$. That is, capital is symmetrically distributed between the two countries. By increasing the share of workers' capital in country h to θ_h' (keeping that in country f constant), the equilibrium capital

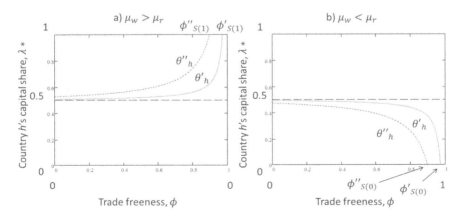

Figure 3.1 The impact of trade freeness ϕ on the long-run stationary value of the share of capital located in country h.

share λ^* rises above 0.5 (solid line). Moreover, it is increasing in ϕ within the range $0 < \phi < \phi'_{S(1)}$. At $\phi'_{S(1)}$, the so-called sustain point, the interior equilibrium exits the $(0,1)$ interval and all the manufacturing activity agglomerates in country h, as the core-periphery equilibrium $\lambda^{CP(1)} = 1$ prevails.[7] As the workers' capital ownership is further increased up to θ''_h, the equilibrium curve for λ^* shifts upwards (dashed line) and the share of capital located in country h becomes larger for all values of ϕ within the interval $0 < \phi < \phi''_{S(1)}$. Moreover, the interior equilibrium exits the $(0,1)$ interval at a smaller value of the sustain point $\phi''_{S(1)} < \phi'_{S(1)}$. That is, full agglomeration prevails at a smaller value of trade freeness. The economic intuition of the shift upwards of the λ^* curve in subcase a is the following. Since workers spend, compared to rentiers, a higher share of their income on the manufactured good, a redistribution of ownership (and therefore of capital income) in their favour determines a positive demand effect: consumption of the good produced in the M-sector rises. The interior equilibrium involves a larger share of capital located in country h. Moreover, as the share of workers' capital increases, full agglomeration occurs at a lower degree of international economic integration.

In Figure 3.1(b), representing subcase b $\mu_w < \mu_r$, the lines have the same interpretation as in Figure 3.1(a): the dashed line corresponds to the case of symmetric ownership distribution in the two countries, which implies $\lambda^* = 1/2$ for $0 < \phi < 1$. When the share of workers' capital ownership in country h is increased to θ'_h (keeping that in country f constant), the equilibrium capital share λ^* falls below 0.5 and it is decreasing with ϕ in the interval $0 < \phi < \phi'_{S(0)}$. At the sustain point $\phi'_{S(0)}$, the interior equilibrium exits the interval $0 < \phi < \phi'_{S(0)}$ and all the manufacturing activity agglomerates in country f, as the core-periphery equilibrium $\lambda^{CP(0)} = 0$ prevails.[8] As the workers' share of capital ownership is further increased up to θ''_h, the equilibrium curve for λ^* shifts downwards (dashed line) and the share of capital located in country h becomes smaller for all values of ϕ within the interval $0 < \phi < \phi''_{S(0)}$, with $\phi''_{S(0)} < \phi'_{S(0)}$. Full agglomeration now prevails at a lower value of trade freeness. The economic intuition of the shift downwards of the λ^* curve in subcase b is the following. Since workers spend, compared to rentiers, a smaller share of their income in the manufactured good, a redistribution of ownership (and therefore of capital income) in their favour determines a negative demand effect: consumption of the good produced in the M-sector shrinks. The interior equilibrium involves a smaller share of capital located in country h. Moreover, as the share of workers' ownership becomes larger, full agglomeration in country f occurs at a lower degree of international economic integration.

Welfare analysis

As seen in the previous section, once we let ownership distribution between workers and rentiers differ in the two countries, this has a strong impact on the allocation of capital between those countries, depending on the consumption preferences of the two groups. We now explore the effect of this difference on the welfare of households living in countries h and f, taking into account the origin of their incomes. We base our study on the Dixit–Stiglitz indirect utilities of workers and rentiers in the two countries evaluated at the interior equilibrium:

$$V_{hw} = \vartheta_w \frac{M_{hw}}{G_h^{\mu w}} = \vartheta_w \frac{\mu_w \left(\frac{L}{2} + \theta_h \frac{\Pi}{2}\right)}{\left([\lambda^* + (1-\lambda^*)\phi] K^{\frac{1}{1-\sigma}} \beta \frac{\sigma}{\sigma-1}\right)^{\mu w}}$$

$$V_{hr} = \vartheta_r \frac{M_{hr}}{G_h^{\mu r}} = \vartheta_r \frac{\mu_r (1-\theta_h) \frac{\Pi}{2}}{\left([\lambda^* + (1-\lambda^*)\phi] K^{\frac{1}{1-\sigma}} \beta \frac{\sigma}{\sigma-1}\right)^{\mu r}}$$

$$V_{fw} = \vartheta_w \frac{M_{fw}}{G_f^{\mu w}} = \vartheta_w \frac{\mu_w \left(\frac{L}{2} + \theta_f \frac{\Pi}{2}\right)}{\left([\lambda^*\phi + (1-\lambda^*)] K^{\frac{1}{1-\sigma}} \beta \frac{\sigma}{\sigma-1}\right)^{\mu w}}$$

$$V_{fr} = \vartheta_f \frac{M_{fr}}{G_f^{\mu r}} = \vartheta_r \frac{\mu_r (1-\theta_f) \frac{\Pi}{2}}{\left([\lambda^*\phi + (1-\lambda^*)] K^{\frac{1}{1-\sigma}} \beta \frac{\sigma}{\sigma-1}\right)^{\mu r}}$$

where $\vartheta_k = \mu_k^{\mu_k} (1-\mu_k)^{1-\mu_k}$ and $k = w, r$.

Given that households' nominal income does not depend on trade freeness, trade integration only affects real incomes via the price index. In the FC model, we have that at the interior equilibrium, $\partial G_h/\partial\phi > 0$ and $\partial G_f/\partial\phi > 0$, which implies a reduction in price indexes, and an increase of welfare for the households living in both countries as a consequence of trade integration.[9] Looking instead at the effect of a change of welfare in relative terms $\frac{V_{hw}}{V_{hr}} = \frac{\vartheta_w M_{hw}}{\vartheta_r M_{hr}} G_h^{\mu_r - \mu_w}$, it is easy to verify that $\partial(V_{hw}/V_{hr})/\partial\phi \geq (<) 0$ for $\mu_w \geq (<)\mu_r$; whereas considering an international comparison between workers and rentiers the ratios V_{hw}/V_{fw} and V_{hr}/V_{fr} evaluated at the stationary interior equilibrium are not affected by changes in ϕ, even though it can be shown that $V_{hw} \geq (<) V_{fw}$ and $V_{hr} \geq (<) V_{fr}$ for $\theta_h \geq (<) \theta_f$ and that (as long as $\theta_h \neq \theta_f$), the difference is increasing in ϕ.

The economic intuition of these results is as follows. Let us assume that workers allocate a larger share of their income to manufacturers compared to capitalists in both countries and let workers in country h own the larger share of capital: h-workers' welfare – relative to rentiers's welfare – improves with trade integration as their consumption bundle becomes cheaper. Comparing the two countries, residents in country h enjoy a higher welfare than residents in country f, since in h a larger share of income is allocated to manufacturers, a larger amount of capital units are used in production and more manufactured varieties are available locally.

Tables 3.1 and 3.2 show how θ_h impacts on the welfare of the two types of households living in the two countries under the assumption $\mu_w > \mu_r$.

There exist three channels through which the welfare of the two groups living in the two countries is affected. A higher share of capital owned by country h-workers: (i) alters the distribution of profits within the country in favour of that group ($\theta_h \Pi$ increases); (ii) determines an increase in the world level of profits Π, since it rises the overall expenditure allocated to manufactures; and (iii) as seen in

Table 3.1 Effects of an increase in h-workers' share of capital in the home country ($\mu_w > \mu_r$)

$\mu_w > \mu_r$	$\theta_h \Pi$	Π	λ^*	*Net effect*
Workers	+	+	+	+
Rentiers	−	+	+	?

Table 3.2 Effects of an increase in h-workers' share of capital in the foreign country ($\mu_w > \mu_r$)

$\mu_w > \mu_r$	$\theta_h \Pi$	Π	λ^*	*Net effect*
Workers	0	+	−	−
Rentiers	0	+	−	?

Table 3.3 Effects of an increase in h-workers' share of capital in the home country ($\mu_w < \mu_r$)

$\mu_w < \mu_r$	$\theta_h \Pi$	Π	λ^*	*Net effect*
Workers	+	−	−	?
Rentiers	−	−	−	−

the previous section, it causes a new international distribution of capital λ^* with a relocation in country h. As shown in Table 3.1, the three effects produce unambiguously welfare improvements only for workers in the home country as they all act in the same direction.

Rentiers in the home country will benefit from the increase in world profits and from the higher share of capital located in the country. However, the reduction in their capital share will sooner or later prevail on the other two (positive) effects. In the foreign country, only two effects affect workers' and rentiers' indirect utilities: a positive effect due to the rise of overall profits and a negative effect due to the shrinking of the manufacturing sector in their country. It is possible to show that the net effect for country f-workers' welfare of an increase of the capital ownership of h-workers is always negative, due to workers' larger share in the consumption of manufactures. Instead, the effect on rentiers' welfare is not univocal: following an increase in the capital ownership of h-workers – depending on parameter values – it could (i) always increase; (ii) always decrease or (iii) it could have an initial fall and then recover.

Finally, Tables 3.3 and 3.4 show how increasing θ_h alters the welfare of the two groups living in both countries under the assumption $\mu_w < \mu_r$. Now, the effects on the overall profits and on the share of capital located in country h are negative.[10] The combined effect on country h-workers is ambiguous, since – depending on parameter values – their indirect utility could monotonically

Table 3.4 Effects of an increase in h-workers' share of capital in the foreign country ($\mu_w < \mu_r$)

$\mu_w < \mu_r$	$\theta_h \Pi$	Π	λ^*	*Net effect*
Workers	0	−	+	+
Rentiers	0	−	+	+

increase, monotonically decrease or, alternatively, increase and then decrease in the relevant range. The welfare of country h-rentiers instead univocally worsens with θ_h. Concerning country f, as reported in Table 3.4, it is possible to show that the reduction in the overall profits is more than compensated by the increase in the share of capital located in this country, so that the overall effect is an increase in welfare of both country f-workers and rentiers.

Conclusions

Inspired by the work of Pasinetti and Kaldor, in this paper we have extended the standard FC model accounting for the presence of two groups of capital owners (workers and capitalist–rentiers) with different consumption preferences. We have studied the properties of the long-run stationary fixed points for increasing levels of trade freeness, assuming that workers spend a higher/lower share of income in manufactured goods. We have obtained results on the impact of trade freeness on the long-run international allocation of capital as well as on the welfare impact of higher ownership diffusion in the home country.

We have shown that the equilibrium international allocation of economic activities depends on the consumption preferences of the two groups of capital owners. In the limiting case of equal shares of workers' and capitalists' incomes devoted to the consumption of manufactured goods, results are similar to the original FC model. On the other hand, when in the home country, capital ownership is more diffused and local workers allocate a relatively higher share of income to manufactured goods, the 'home market' effect brought about by higher economic integration will be magnified as compared to the standard FC model.

In our framework, a change in the degree of capital ownership diffusion in the home country impacts on the welfare of all groups as a result of the interplay of three different effects: a change in the distribution of profits in the same country, a change in the world level of profits and a change in the international distribution of capital. We have provided a full picture of such effects under the two alternative cases concerning the consumption preferences of workers and rentiers.

Notes

1 Pasinetti started from the consideration that the previous contribution by Kaldor was flawed; see Pasinetti (1962) and Kaldor (1956). In particular, Pasinetti criticized the fact that Kaldor did not consider – in his distinction between saving out of profits and saving out of wages – that the existence of workers' savings necessarily implies that a

share of the overall capital must belong to this group or 'class'. Many years later, Fazi and Salvadori (1981) have shown that Kaldor's analysis was not incoherent by letting the rate of interest received by workers on their loans to capitalists differ from the rate of profit obtained by capitalists out of their investments. Moreover, Salvadori (1991) presents a general framework that encompasses both Pasinetti's and Kaldor's models.

2 Commendatore (1999) and Commendatore (2003) extend the Pasinetti's model in the direction suggested by Kaldor.

3 As a result of Walras' Law, equilibrium in all product markets implies equilibrium in the national labour markets.

4 For (3.14), use (3.10) and (3.11).

5 Moreover, in what follows, we dedicate our attention mostly to country h.

6 See also Fujita *et al.* (2001).

7 Looking at the stability properties of the fixed points, for γ sufficiently small, the interior fixed point λ^* is stable for $0 < \phi < \phi_{S(1)}$, and it loses stability via a transcritical bifurcation at $\phi = \phi_{S(1)}$. In correspondence of this value of the trade freeness parameter, the core-periphery equilibrium $\phi = \phi^{CP(1)}$ gains stability. The stability of $\phi^{CP(1)}$ is preserved within the interval $\phi_{S(1)} < \phi < 1$. The other core-periphery equilibrium $\phi = \phi^{CP(0)}$ is never stable for $0 < \phi < 1$.

8 Looking at the stability properties of the fixed points, for γ sufficiently small, the interior fixed point λ^* is stable for $0 < \phi < \phi_{S(0)}$ and it loses stability via a transcritical bifurcation at $\phi = \phi_{S(0)}$. In correspondence of this value of trade freeness, the core-periphery equilibrium $\phi = \phi^{CP(0)}$ gains stability. The stability of $\phi^{CP(0)}$ is preserved within the interval $\phi_{S(0)} < \phi < 1$. The other core-periphery equilibrium $\phi = \phi^{CP(1)}$ is never stable for $0 < \phi < 1$.

9 An increase in trade freeness has two effects on the price index: (1) firms relocation induced by trade integration alters the number of domestically produced varieties; (2) the price of the imported varieties decreases. In a FC model, the size of the second effect is always positive and larger in absolute value than the size of the first effect.

10 When $\mu_w = \mu_r$, an increase in θ_h only alters the home distribution of capital ownership in favour of workers. There is no effect in the foreign country.

References

Baldwin, R.E., Forslid, R., Martin, P., Ottaviano, G. and Robert-Nicoud, F. 2003. *Economic Geography and Public Policy.* Princeton University Press: Princeton, New Jersey.

Commendatore, P. 1999. Pasinetti and dual equilibria in a post Keynesian model of growth and institutional distribution. *Oxford Economic Papers*, 51(1): 223–36.

Commendatore, P. 2003. On the post Keynesian theory of growth and institutional distribution. *Review of Political Economy*, 15(2): 193–209.

Fazi, F. and Salvadori, N. 1981. The existence of a two-class economy in the Kaldor model of growth and distribution. *Kyklos*, 34(4): 582–92.

Fujita, M., Krugman, P.R. and Venables, A. 2001. *The Spatial Economy: Cities, Regions and International Trade.* The MIT Press: Cambridge, Massachusetts. p. 7.

Kaldor, N. 1956. Alternative theories of distribution. *Review of Economic Studies*, 23(2): 83–100.

Kaldor, N. 1966. Marginal productivity and the macroeconomic theories of distribution: comment on Samuelson and Modigliani. *Review of Economic Studies*, 33(4): 309–19.

Krugman, P. 1991. Increasing returns and economic geography. *Journal of Political Economy*, 99(3): 483–99.

Martin, P. and Rogers, C.A. 1995. Industrial location and public infrastructure. *Journal of International Economics*, 39(3–4): 335–51.

Pasinetti, L.L. 1962. Rate of profit and income distribution in relation to the rate of economic growth. *Review of Economic Studies*, 29(4): 267–79.

Salvadori, N. 1991. Post-Keynesian theories of distribution in the long run. In: Nell, E. and Semmler, W. (eds), *Nicholas Kaldor and Mainstream Economics: Confrontation or Convergence*? Macmillan: London.

Weibull, J.W. 1997. *Evolutionary Game Theory*. The MIT Press: Cambridge, Massachusetts.

4 Smithian growth and complexity[1]

Andrea Mario Lavezzi

Introduction

Adam Smith argued in the *Wealth of Nations* that the main force driving economic growth is the division of labour. In this paper we claim that the process of economic growth based on the division of labour, that we define *Smithian growth* (Kelly, 1997), initially described by Adam Smith, and subsequently analysed by Alfred Marshall, Allyn Young and Nicholas Kaldor, has the nature of a *complex phenomenon* (see, e.g., Arthur *et al.*, 1997).

This interpretation puts the process of growth based on division of labour in a different perspective with respect to the one developed by traditional economics (see below), in particular by the endogenous growth theory (EGT) (e.g. Romer, 1987).

The classification of Smithian growth as an instance of *complex dynamics* aims at giving fresh capacity to an 'old' growth theory to provide insights even on recent phenomena such as the polarization in the world income distribution (e.g. Quah, 1997), and the wide fluctuations experienced by many economies in recent years. From the empirical point of view, the first remark is taken into account by Hidalgo *et al.* (2007), while the second remark refers to the importance given by the current literature on output fluctuations to the network structure of the economy,[2] which we will see is a fundamental aspect in the Smithian growth process.

The paper is organized as follows. The next section describes what we mean by Smithian growth the third section describes the complexity approach; the fourth section explains the claim that Smithian growth is a complex phenomenon; the fifth section presents an example of a formalization of Smithian growth; the final section contains some concluding remarks.

What is Smithian growth?

We define Smithian growth as the process of economic growth based on division of labour, envisaged by Adam Smith in the *Wealth of Nations* (WN), and subsequently developed by Alfred Marshall, Allyn Young and Nicholas Kaldor.[3]

As is well known, economic growth according to Adam Smith is based on the division of labour, or specialization. In particular, the division of labour favours economic growth because it increases the productivity of workers who, through learning by doing, can increase their *dexterity* in a restricted set of tasks.[4] The process of specialization can take place not only among workers but also among firms, through the creation of specialized trades.

In analysing the factors acting in favour or against the division of labour, Smith assumes first of all that there exists an exogenous predisposition for social and economic interaction. That is, there exists 'a certain propensity in human nature: ... the propensity to truck, barter and exchange one thing for another' (WN I.i:1). Specifically, when an individual knows that s/he can exchange the surplus product obtained by specializing with other agents, s/he has the incentive to specialize.[5] This can occur even when individuals are originally similar, i.e. the differences 'which [appear] to distinguish men of different professions, when grown up to maturity, is not upon many occasions so much the cause, as the effect of the division of labour' (WN I.ii: 4).

This line of reasoning implies the identification of the main limit to the process of specialization; that is, the extent of the market. Specifically, the existence of a market (i.e. demand) for surplus production is the crucial condition for specialization. Moreover, this reasoning highlights the 'interactive nature' of growth based on specialization: an agent chooses to specialize if sufficient demand exists for his/her surplus product, but by specializing s/he also will obtain a surplus product that can be exchanged for other agents' surpluses. This aspect would later be elevated to a central principle by Allyn Young.

Alfred Marshall, in Book IV of the *Principles*, provides elements that contribute to the development of the Smithian growth theory. In particular, Marshall considers a fourth factor of production, i.e. organization, in addition to land, labour and capital, as organization increases the efficiency of labour. This introduces Marshall's discussion on the division of labour, which is explicitly reconducted to Adam Smith. In particular, Marshall (1910, pp. 240–241) claims that superior organisms, social and biological, are those characterized by a higher specialization of their intimately connected components. Among these, economic systems are characterized by specialization of skills, trades, knowledge and machinery, and the connections among productive units (the separate parts of the industrial organisms) are secured by, e.g., credit markets, means of transportation and information.

The dynamics characterizing such systems is defined 'organic growth' which, according to Marshall, represents a better perspective than the one offered by 'statical equilibrium' (Marshall, 1910, p. 461). In addition, in discussing the division of labour, Marshall (1910, p. 261) notes another instance of the interactive nature of the process. That is, Marshall argues that specialized labour may be substituted by machines, whose introduction generates demand for new types of skills such as those of machine operators or of workers with a high level of 'judgment'.[6]

A fundamental step in characterizing economic growth based on specialization as a complex phenomenon is taken by Young (1928). In particular, Young was able to unveil such nature of the growth process by proposing a development of the insights of Adam Smith that allowed the identification of elements, that we will see in the third section, characterize Complex Systems.

In particular, when considering that the division of labour represents a reorganization of the productive process, within or between firms, Young emphasized that other parts of the economy are affected by it: '[e]very important advance in the organisation of production ... alters the conditions of industrial activity and initiates responses elsewhere in the industrial structure which in turn have a further *unsettling* effect' (Young, 1928, p. 533).[7]

This process is endogenously fuelled by the division of labour itself: the increase in supply from a firm made possible by higher productivity due to specialization represents increase of demand for other products, i.e. it is an increase of the extent of the market, which allows further specialization, other increases of the extent of the market, etc. In Young's words: 'the division of labour depends in large part upon the division of labour' (Young, 1928, p. 533).[8]

The relevant implications are: (i) the process should be considered 'as a whole' (Young, 1928, p. 533) or, using another convincing definition, the economy should be studied in its 'togetherness'.[9] (ii) Economic growth is a disequilibrium process. Here it is worth fully quoting Young who warned not to focus on individual (or representative) firms or industries, but to look:

> [o]ut beyond, in that obscurer field from which [the firm] derives its external economies, [where] changes of another order are occurring. New products are appearing, firms are assuming new tasks, and new industries are coming into being. In short, changes in this external field are qualitative as well as quantitative. No analysis of the forces making for economic equilibrium, forces which we might say are tangential at any moment of time, will serve to illuminate this field, for movements away from equilibrium, departures from previous trends are characteristics of it. Not much is to be gained by probing into it to see how increasing returns show themselves in the costs of individual firms and in the prices at which they offer their products.
>
> (Young, 1928, p. 528)

(iii) Growth is a cumulative path dependent process as this endogenous process of change 'becomes progressive and propagates itself in a cumulative way' (Young, 1928, p. 531).

This view of specialization and growth remained peripheral until Nicholas Kaldor revived it in a more general argument against economics based on general economic equilibrium (see Kaldor, 1972, 1975, 1979, 1981, 1985).[10] First of all, Kaldor argued for the necessity of basing growth on increasing returns, after observing the stylized facts on economic growth in developed countries (see Kaldor, 1961). Since this assumption was absent from the formulations of general economic equilibrium he was criticizing, Kaldor considered this theory as incapable of constituting the base for a theory of economic growth.[11]

Consequently, an alternative starting point for the analysis of growth had to be sought in Smith and Young, who took increasing returns seriously, by considering the process of division of labour. The roots of increasing returns are to be found 'in the nature of technological processes' (Kaldor, 1972, p. 1242).

In particular, Kaldor emphasized the importance of economies deriving from specialization, defined as 'dynamic' or 'irreversible' (see Kaldor, 1966, p. 106 and Kaldor, 1972, p. 1253), and played down the importance of indivisibilities as sources of increasing returns. In the presence of economies of specialization:

> [t]he whole issue, as Young said, is whether an equilibrium of costs and advantages is a meaningful notion in the presence of increasing returns. When every change in the use of resources – every reorganisation of productive activities – creates the opportunity for a further change which would not have existed otherwise, the notion of an optimum allocation of resources – when every particular resource makes a great or greater contribution to output in its actual use as in any alternative use – becomes a meaningless and contradictory notion: the pattern of the use of resources at any one time can be no more than a link in the chain of an unending sequence and the very distinction, vital to equilibrium economics, between resource-creation and resource-allocation loses its validity.

The conclusion is that: '[t]here can be no such thing as an equilibrium state with optimum resource allocation where no further advantageous reorganization is possible, since every such reorganization may create a fresh opportunity for a further reorganization' (Kaldor, 1975, p. 355).[12]

Finally, Kaldor argued that the competitive process is more about creation and change than about allocation guided by prices. He did not accept the definition of competition as a situation where agents merely take prices as given, but on the contrary attributed to agents a higher capacity of price-making (for instance through mark-ups). Interpreting competition as the stimulus for creation and change is essential for an understanding of the process of economic growth.[13]

Summing up, we argue that the process of economic growth based on specialization, in the view advanced by Adam Smith and subsequently developed by Alfred Marshall, Allyn Young and Nicholas Kaldor, has the following characteristics: economic growth is endogenous, it is a cumulative, path-dependent process and it is a disequilibrium process. In the next section we discuss the characteristics of Complex Systems and of their dynamics, while in the following section we compare the two contexts.

What is a complex system?

In this section we describe the characteristics of 'Complex Systems', with particular reference to the developments of this concept in economics. Following Agliardi (1998, p. 6), we read: '[a] remarkably good definition of what makes a system complex is provided by Philip Anderson, the Nobel laureate physicist ... : complexity is the science of emergence; that is, it is about how large interacting ensembles exhibit collective behaviour that is very different from anything one might have expected from simply scaling up the behaviour of the individual units'. A similar definition is found in Farmer and Geanakopoulos (2009,

p. 34): '[c]omplex systems refers to the idea that systems composed of simple components interacting via simple rules can give rise to complex emergent behaviors, in which in ... the whole is greater than the sum of its parts'.

From the two definitions, it is possible to highlight the following elements: a Complex System features the interaction of a large set of simple units; the rules governing interaction are also simple and the overall result of the interaction is an *emergent phenomenon*, i.e. a phenomenon that could not have been inferred from 'zooming' in on one part of the system. Complex Systems, in addition, are inherently dynamic, as the process of *emergence* highlights a bottom-up process of motion, from the constituent parts to the aggregate level.

Arthur *et al.* (1997) proposed a specific definition of a 'complexity perspective in economics'.[14] Models elaborated in such a perspective focus on six features of real economies. (i) *Dispersed interaction* of many heterogeneous agents acting in parallel, whose actions depend upon 'the anticipated actions of a limited number of other agents and on the aggregate state these agents co-create'. (ii) *No global controller* of interactions; 'controls are provided by mechanisms of competition and coordination between agents ... Economic actions are mediated by legal institutions, assigned roles, and shifting associations'. Moreover, 'no single agent can exploit all opportunities in the economy'. (iii) *Cross-cutting hierarchical organization*: '[t]he economy has many levels of organization and interaction. Units at any given level – behaviours, actions, strategies, products – typically serve as building blocks for constructing units at the next higher level'.

Other characteristics are: (iv) *Continual adaptation behaviours*, according to which 'actions, strategies, and products are revised continually as the individual agents accumulate experience – the system constantly adapts'. (v) *Perpetual novelty*, so that '[n]iches are continually created by new markets, new technologies, new behaviours, new institutions. The very act of filling a niche may provide new niches. The result is ongoing, perpetual novelty'. (vi) *Out-of-equilibrium dynamics*: '[b]ecause new niches, new potentials, new possibilities, are continually created, the economy operates far from any optimum or global equilibrium. Improvements are always possible and indeed occur regularly'. Systems with these characteristics, such as economies, can be defined *adaptive nonlinear networks*.[15]

It can be observed that some of these characteristics provide foundations for the 'complexity' approach that differ from those of traditional economics.[16] There is first of all a different assumption on agents' behaviour: economic agents are not rational utility maximizers, able to gather all relevant information and to cope with uncertainty 'probabilistically, revis[ing] their evaluations in the light of new information via Bayesian updating' (Arthur *et al.*, 1997, p. 5).[17] Agents in the complexity approach are instead typically assumed to be boundedly rational (Farmer *et al.*, 2012, p. 307).[18] However, even if boundedness depending on limited cognitive capacities is ruled out, 'agents generally do not optimize in the standard sense ... because the very concept of an optimal course of action often cannot be defined' (Arthur *et al.*, 1997, p. 5).

A related aspect regards the interaction among agents. In the complexity approach, the interaction is *local*. That is, it does not feature either interaction among all of a large number of agents, as in general equilibrium (in which inter-action is mediated by prices), or interaction among few agents, as in game theory, where each player typically interacts with all other players.[19] In the framework of local interactions the *network structure* connecting the agents becomes, therefore, crucial. In particular, it is important for the definition of the amount of information the agents utilize for their decisions, assumed to come mostly from their *neighbourhood*, i.e. from the set of connected agents.

Finally, in the complexity approach there is no compelling need for the existence of equibria, as systems following 'complex dynamics' may not settle to a state where improvements are exhausted, because of the characteristic of 'perpetual novelty'.

Discussion

In this section, on the basis of the characteristics of Smithian growth and complex systems, we claim that the former represents an example of the dynamics envisaged by the complexity approach.

Let us consider first the aspect of interaction among agents. According to Smith, as remarked, interaction among agents is 'natural', and represents an essential precondition for specialization. In addition, for him, the decision to specialize depends on the extent of the market. Allyn Young insightfully pointed out that the extent of the market crucially depends on the decision of other agents to specialize: the decision of some agents (or firms) to specialize may induce other agents (or firms) to specialize.

Unless one assumes that each agent or firm is connected to all the other agents and firms in the economy, a natural assumption is that the interaction involved by the dynamics of specialization is local, but how much local interaction there is depends on various factors. For example, in early stages of economic development, when agents are initially unspecialized and means of transportation, communica-tion, and payment are underdeveloped, each agent can be assumed to be connected to a limited number of other agents. In more advanced stages, in which communi-cation is developed and money is a widespread means of payment, interaction may nonetheless be local, for example for firms deciding to specialize in the produc-tion of a good and, say, giving up the production of an intermediate input, whose production is taken up by another specialized firm.[20] In this case, the input–output structure defines the relevant network structure: some sectors (or firms) are 'con-nected' to many others (e.g. electricity), while others are connected to few (e.g. hybrid corn).[21]

The effect of one agents' specialization on the incentives for other agents to specialize can be defined as a network externality (Lavezzi, 2003b, p. 282), and represents a self-reinforcing mechanism.[22] This makes the dynamics of specializa-tion cumulative and path dependent. The implication for the present discussion is that, as postulated by the complexity approach, it is unrealistic to assume that agents are rational optimizers, because the paths taken by the economy can-not be defined in advance as the system is characterized by 'perpetual novelty'.

This makes the economic growth process based on specialization a disequilibrium process – another crucial characteristic of Complex Systems.

Path dependence is discussed by Hidalgo *et al.* (2007), who consider as the relevant network structure the *space of products*. In particular they define a bipartite network in which countries and products are the relevant sets of nodes, and are connected through capabilities: each good can be produced by some capabilities; a country is able to produce a good if it possesses the necessary capabilities. The empirical evidence they present shows that the development of products by a country is significantly dependent on the set of existing products, demonstrating in this way the path dependent nature of the process of specialization. Moreover, they demonstrate that countries displaying a higher level of *complexity*, i.e. those more diversified, have the highest levels of income, providing support for the theory of growth based on specialization.[23]

Another important feature advocated in the Smithian growth approach is Young's emphasis on the importance of observing the economy in its 'togetherness', without focusing on individual firms or sectors. This perspective is consistent with the idea of emergent state, i.e. of an aggregate state whose characteristics cannot be grasped by looking at one or a few components of the system.

The version of growth based on specialization proposed in the endogenous growth literature[24] incorporates the effect of increasing specialization on growth by postulating the existence of an intermediate goods sector, where monopolistic competition prevails. Each intermediate good is produced by an individual firm, and enters symmetrically the production of the final consumption good by a Dixit–Stiglitz–Ethier production function implying imperfect substitution among intermediates.[25] The implication is that the higher the number of intermediate goods produced in equilibrium, the higher the production level of the final good.

However, this representation of the process of specialization is questionable for different reasons. First of all, it fails to capture what we argued are the main features of Smithian growth.[26] In addition, as noted by Yang and Borland (1991, pp. 461–462): 'models ... which ... fix the level of specialization of an individual agent [or firm], are unable to explain why an economy evolves from autarky ... to a state in which there is a highly developed division of labour'. Finally, as empirically demonstrated by Hidalgo *et al.* (2007), it contains the unrealistic assumption that the current level of specialization is independent from the history of production of intermediate goods, i.e. the level of specialization attained in the past, as if: 'the cost of developing a regional jet aircraft is the same whether the firm or country has previously developed a transcontinental aircraft and a combustion engine or whether it produces only raw cocoa and coffee' (Hausmann and Hidalgo 2011, p. 311).[27]

Other relevant formalizations of the process of specialization and growth are provided by Kelly (1997), Becker and Murphy (1992) and Yang and Borland (1991). Kelly (1997) focuses on the dynamics of aggregate growth when specialization diffuses, i.e. when local economies become connected by trading linkages and production can be taken over by some specialized agents, assumed to be more efficient than nonspecialized agents. Kelly (1997) shows that growth displays 'threshold behaviour', i.e. it may abruptly increase when linkages have reached a critical density.[28] This model, however, assumes that specialization is exogenously given.

Becker and Murphy (1992) instead consider the role of coordination costs among specialized workers and the role of accumulation of general knowledge (as opposed to specialized knowledge) on the division of labour. In this model, individuals may choose to form teams of specialized agents on the supply side: the larger the team, the smaller the set of tasks performed by each worker. The optimal division of labour is found by equating the marginal benefit from increased specialization to the marginal cost, assuming that the larger the team, the higher the coordination costs for its members.

As a consequence of the assumptions of the model, output per task increases with team size, i.e. with the division of labour. This effect is similar to the effect on growth of a higher number of intermediate goods in the EGT models of specialization and growth. In the Becker and Murphy's framework, focused on the supply side, the aspect of 'elasticity' in Young's terms is however not featured.[29]

Finally, Yang and Borland (1991) (YB) focus on specialization of individual agents. They consider a dynamic general equilibrium model in which agents may specialize in producing a good under increasing returns due to learning by doing, and purchase other goods from other agents, incurring a transaction cost.

The evolution of the division of labour depends on the balance of gains in production from learning by doing *vis-à-vis* the transaction efficiency.[30] For low levels of a and k, autarky forever is the equilibrium; for high levels of a and k, the equilibrium is, from the outset, full specialization, where each individual is a specialized producer; for intermediate values, the economy undergoes a gradual evolution in which the full specialization is the final state (each individual produces one good and each good is traded in the market). The model may generate a phase of increasing growth rates if the number of existing goods m (i.e. the potential for specialization) is large, and the number of traded goods n_t is close to m.[31]

YB is probably the model in the equilibrium approach that more closely captures some relevant aspects of Smithian growth.[32] To secure the existence of an intertemporal Walrasian equilibrium, however, it assumes that complete future markets exist, and that all trades are carried out in the initial period, so each individual can be price taker in the infinite number of periods that follow.[33] On the one hand, these assumptions can be criticized as instances of sacrificing realism for mathematical rigour,[34] on the other hand the way in which YB consider Young's insight that the 'division of labour is limited by the division of labour' can be questioned.

In the YB model, the division of labour is measured by the number of traded goods. Assuming that the extent of the market can be measured by trade volume per head (Yang and Borland, 1991, p. 476), given that the latter magnitude positively depends on n_t, it results that the extent of the market is limited by the division of labour. This, however, does not seem to be what Young meant when he discussed the role of elasticities, i.e. the capacity for increased production due to specialization to become increased demand for other goods, which can become increases of production, etc. originating an endogenous chain reaction where the limit is set by the elasticities themselves. In the YB model, the key parameters are transaction efficiency and parameter a: when 'fine-tuned' they trigger a symmetric equilibrium process that brings the agents to specialize. In addition, this model features the essential characteristic of general equilibrium models in which agents interact globally, through a price system that operates in the initial period. The next section discusses a model of Smithian growth which follows the complexity approach.

An example

In this section we present an example of a model of Smithian growth developed following the insights of the complexity approach, from Lavezzi (2003c). In the model initially identical agents are located in a network with a simple structure (a circular lattice). They can be unspecialized and produce two goods, or they may specialize in the production of one good. They specialize in one good if the market is sufficiently large, in particular if other agents in their *neighbourhood*, i.e. the agents with whom they are connected, are specialized in the production of the other good. That is, each agent locally interacts with a fixed number of other agents. Agents must consume both goods: if unspecialized, an agent produces small quantities of both goods, if specialized s/he produces a larger quantity of a single good.

The model assumes the presence of a force acting against specialization: if there is insufficient demand in their neighbourhood, in particular if there are 'too many' agents of the same type in the neighbourhood, an agent de-specializes, and returns to producing both goods. The structure of the agents' network and the agents' 'activation' rule (see Eq. 4.1) give this artificial economy (see Axtell and Epstein, 1996) the form of a *cellular automata* (see, e.g., Wolfram, 2002).

Formally, in every period t, one agent is 'active' and has the possibility to make a transition across states: *unspecialized*, *specialized* in good 1 or *specialized* in good 2.[35] The transition rule governing the change of state is

$$x_i(t+1) = F\{x_i(t), \Psi(N_i(t))\} \tag{4.1}$$

where $x_i(t)$ is the state of agent i in period t, $F\{.\}$ is the transition function and $\Psi(N_i(t))$ is a vector indicating the demand for both goods expressed by agents in the neighbourhood N_i of agent i in period t. The size of the neighbourhood N_i is indicated by D.

Figures 4.1 and 4.2 present examples of the dynamics that can be generated by the model, given some assumptions on the relevant parameters and on their values.[36] The left panel of each figure contains a graphical representation of the evolution of the configuration of the system. Each line corresponds to a round of the simulation, i.e. to a number of periods equal to the number of

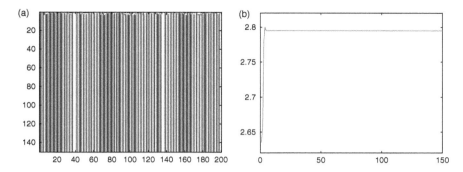

Figure 4.1 Growth dynamics: convergence to steady state. Parameters: $N = 200$, $t = 30,000$, $D = 5$. (a) Network dynamics. (b) Time series of per capita output.

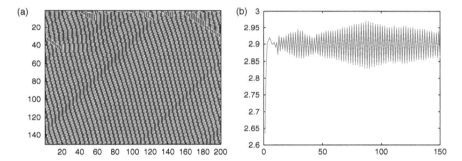

Figure 4.2 Growth dynamics: continuous fluctuations. Parameters: $N = 200$, $t = 30,000$, $D = 7$. (a) Network dynamics. (b) Time series of per capita output.

agents N where each agent is activated once.[37] When 'activated', an agent, given its state, evaluates the level of $\Psi(N_i)$ and makes a transition following the rule in Eq. (4.1). The colour white indicates 0-agents, while grey and black respectively indicate 1-agents and 2-agents. The right panel contains the time series of the simulated aggregate output.[38] The two simulations share the same (randomly generated) initial configuration, and the same parameters except for the size of the neighbourhood D.

Figure 4.1 shows a case in which the system rapidly converges to a steady state configuration in which most of the agents are specialized. Aggregate output shows fast convergence to a level of 2.79, i.e. near to the maximum level. Figure 4.2 instead represents the case of a higher level of the dimension of the neighbourhood, i.e. of parameter D. Figures 4.2(a) and 4.2(b) show that an equilibrium configuration is not reached and aggregate output displays irregular fluctuations. The aggregate output increases, as the theory suggests, reaching an average level of 2.89, but also its variability increases. The insight for this qualitative and quantitative change is the following: the increase of the size of the neighbourhood in relation to the thresholds increases the probability of transitions to specialization for each agent, but it also introduces more variability, as each agent is affected by the possible transitions of a higher number of agents.

Other possibilities are explored in Lavezzi (2003c).[39] The example presented in Figures 4.1 and 4.2 is sufficient to highlight the emergence of complex dynamics from a slight perturbation of the conditions that led to a steady state, opening the way for a rich characterization of the possible dynamical paths that such a simple economy can follow.

Concluding remarks

In this paper we have proposed a characterization of the process of growth based on the division of labour as an instance of complex dynamics. This claim was supported by the reconstruction of the theory through the contributions of Alfred Marshall, Allyn Young and Nicholas Kaldor. This representation puts Smithian growth in a very different perspective than the one developed by traditional economics. In other words, we have argued that Smithian growth has been mis-classified as an equilibrium process, as Beinhocker (2006, p. 99) argues that the economy as a whole has been misclassified as an equilibrium system by traditional economics.

Our claim can open the way to novel formalizations of the growth process, as exemplified by the model described in the previous section, which may provide new insights on the functioning of real economies, in particular on growth and fluctuations, which the equilibrium approach still treats in an unsatisfactory way, as debates following the crises of 2008 demonstrate.[40]

Notes

1 This essay is written in honour of Neri Salvadori. Neri supervised my Ph.D. dissertation and provided invaluable advice and support throughout my career. I keep in mind his lessons and intellectual rigour each time I have to advise a younger researcher.
2 See, in particular, Gabaix (2011) and Acemoglu *et al.* (2012) and, for earlier insights, Bak *et al.* (1993) and Durlauf (1993).
3 This section draws on Lavezzi (2001, 2003a,b).
4 In addition, specialization allows workers to spare the time required to switch among different tasks and, as individuals focus on a limited number of tasks, they can devise new tools and machines to facilitate their work. See Lavezzi (2003a, p. 83).
5 Surplus product is the production above subsistence level.
6 The important part of Marshall's reasoning on the implied aspects of increasing returns and competition is discussed in Lavezzi (2003a, pp. 92–93).
7 Young was not fully persuaded by the Marshallian distinction between internal and external economies, as concepts related to a static view of the economy. Young opposed the concept of economies of specialization, i.e. those that are captured by firms that reorganize their production in the specialization process. See Young (1928, p. 528).
8 Young introduced the concept of reciprocal demand among firms: 'demand for each commodity is elastic, in the special sense that a small increase in its supply will be attended by an increase in the amounts of other commodities which can be had in exchange for it. Under such conditions an increase in the supply of one commodity

is an increase in the demand for other commodities, and it must be supposed that every increase in demand will evoke an increase in supply'.

9 In the LSE lecture notes taken by Kaldor, we read: 'Seeking for equilibrium conditions under increasing returns is as good as looking for a mare's nest. Certainly the matter cannot be explained by this curve apparatus, which does not see things in their togetherness'. See Young (1999, p. 45). Buchanan and Yoon (2000, p. 45) argue that: 'the Smithean proposition that relates the division or specialization of labor to the extent of the market is best captured by the notion of *generalized increasing returns*, which implies only that the degree of specialization utilized increases with the size of the *whole nexus of economic interaction* thereby increasing the ratio of positively valued outputs to inputs' (emphasis added).

10 A notable exception is Richardson (1975), who argued for a disequilibrium interpretation of the growth model envisaged by Smith.

11 Kaldor considered increasing returns as sufficient condition to rule out equilibrium. Later developments of growth theory, see, e.g., Romer (1987, 1990), proved the possibility of existence of equilibria in presence of increasing returns under the assumption of monopolistic competition in the relevant markets, i.e. those producing innovations.

12 Smith himself noted that as the process of specialization proceeds, further subdivisions of labour that: 'might never otherwise been thought of' become possible (1976 [1776], V.i., p. 271).

13 On competition in Adam Smith, see, e.g., Richardson (1975, p. 354) and Lavezzi (2003a, p. 89).

14 The quotations that follow in the paragraph are from Arthur *et al.* (1997, pp. 3–4).

15 For a similar characterization of *complexity economics* see Beinhocker (2006, p. 97).

16 By *traditional economics* we follow Beinhocker (2006, Ch. 2) and refer to the approach based on the effort of Walras, Jevons and Pareto to provide economics with a rigorous mathematical basis, further developed by Arrow and Debreu and general equilibrium analysis, to the macroeconomic theory of Friedman and Lucas based on rational expectations. See also the definition of *equilibrium theory* of Farmer and Geanakoplos (2009, pp. 12–15).

17 See also Farmer and Geanakoplos (2009, p. 12).

18 Farmer and Geanakoplos (2009, pp. 20–21) offer a concise discussion of the critiques to the rationality hypothesis.

19 See Kirman (1999) for a discussion on interactions among agents, which includes game theory.

20 Young's discussion on reciprocal demands can be interpreted in such context. See footnote 7.

21 See, e.g., Acemoglu *et al.* (2012, p. 1980). See also Hidalgo and Hausmann (2009) for a definition and analysis of a network structure in the product space.

22 Beinhocker (2006, p. 101) notes that reinforcing mechanisms, or positive feedbacks, are at the root of disequilibrium dynamics, while negative feedbacks, i.e. effects of opposite sign elicited by changes of an element of the system, contribute to pushing the system towards a state of equilibrium. In the present discussion, this would amount to the case in which specialization of one agent creates incentives for less specialization of other agents.

23 So, does path dependency reduce the unpredictability of the development path and restore the possibility for agents to be rational optimizers, contradicting the claim by Arthur *et al.* (1997, p. 5) mentioned above? The compatibility between path dependency and the impossibility of defining an 'optimal course of action' (Arthur *et al.*, 1997, p. 5), requires that each step of specialization is a link in an unending sequence, but every possible step becomes known only when the previous step has been reached. This seems to be the interpretation of Kaldor's claims. The consequence for optimization is that these steps cannot be predicted in advance. The implication for

equilibrium in the allocative sense is that the value of a resource in alternative uses cannot be known in advance, and equilibrium as optimal resource allocation cannot be computed.

24 See Romer (1987, 1990).

25 Dixit and Stiglitz (1977) considered a utility function reflecting preference for variety in consumption, while Ethier (1982) proposed to utilize that functional form for a production function.

26 For thorough discussion of this claim see Lavezzi (2003b).

27 Let us also remark that the assumption of the symmetric role of intermediate goods on final goods production implies the possibility of inferring characteristics of the aggregate picture from the observation of a component, in contrast with the view of economic growth as an emergent phenomenon.

28 The property of the networks considered by Kelly (1997) is reminiscent of the phase transition of random graphs, when a giant component appears by merging many smaller, disconnected components of the network. See Newman (2003, p. 21).

29 Lavezzi (2003b) discusses in more details the role of supply and demand in Smithian growth.

30 In the model the relevant parameters are, respectively, the exponent of specialized labour in the production function, a, and the index k. The smaller k, the higher the transaction costs.

31 The number of traded goods, n_t, is a measure of the degree of division of labour attained: the higher the number of traded goods, the lower the number of goods produced by each individual. When it reaches the maximum given by m, it means that each individual produces only one good and buys the other goods.

32 On the relevance of the YB model, see also Buchanan and Yoon (2000, p. 45).

33 These assumptions, along with the assumption on the existence of transaction costs, limit the possibility that specialized agents become monopolists, which would be implied by the assumption of increasing returns from specialization at the individual level.

34 According to Beinhocker (2006, p. 48), trading off realism for mathematical rigour is a characteristic of the equilibrium approach introduced by Walras.

35 There exist, therefore, three types of agents: 0-agents, 1-agents, 2-agents.

36 $\Psi(N_i)$ depends on the following parameters: $d_{10} > 0$ and $d_{20} > 0$, representing the demand of good 1 and 2 coming from 0-agents; d_{21} and d_{12} respectively referring to the demand of good 2 from 1-agents and for good 1 from 2-agents; d_{11} and d_{22}, representing demand for good 1 from 1-agents and for good 2 from 2-agents. The latter parameters take on negative values as specialized agents evaluate the presence of agents of the same type in their neighbourhood as negative potential demand. To capture the role of the extent of the market on the decision to specialize, we introduce t_{01} and t_{02} which, respectively, denote the threshold levels of demand for good 1 and good 2 which may induce a 0-agent to specialize. The decision to de-specialize instead requires a demand above t_{11} and t_{22}, which respectively represent the threshold levels of demand for good 1 or good 2 in the neighbourhood of 1-agent or a 2-agent, which causes the decision to remain specialized.

37 This is the case of asynchronous activation.

38 We compute output in the following way: the production of good 1 and 2 by an unspecialized agent counts 1 (hence their total production counts 2), while production by specialized agents counts 3. Therefore, the range for per capita output is $[2; 3]$.

39 In particular, Lavezzi (2003c) found other parameter combinations, different activation rules and the diffusion process when in the initial configuration one or few agents are specialized.

40 See, among others, Farmer and Geanakoplos (2009) and Farmer *et al.* (2012) and the references therein.

References

Acemoglu, D., Carvalho, V. M., Ozdaglar, A. and Tahbaz–Salehi, A. (2012), The Network Origins of Aggregate Fluctuations, *Econometrica*, 80(5): 1977–2016.

Agliardi, E. (1998), *Positive Feedbacks Economies*, London: Macmillan.

Arthur, W. Brian, Durlauf, S. N. and Lane, D. A. (1997), Introduction: Process and Emergence in the Economy, in Arthur, W., Durlauf, S.N. and Lane, D.A. (Eds.), *The Economy as an Evolving Complex System II*, Reading, MA: Adison Wesley, pp. 1–20.

Axtell, R. and Epstein, J. M. (1996), *Growing Artificial Societies: Social Science from the Bottom Up*, Washington, DC: Brookings Inst. Press.

Bak, P., Chen, K., Scheinkman, J. and Woodford, M. (1993), Aggregate Fluctuation from Independent Sectoral Shocks: Self-Organized Criticality in a Model Production and Inventory Dynamics, *Ricerche Economiche*, 47(1): 31–64.

Becker, G. S. and Murphy, K. M. (1992), The Division of Labor, Coordination Costs, and Knowledge, *Quarterly Journal of Economics*, 107(4): 1137–1160.

Beinhocker, E. D. (2006), *The Origin of Wealth*. Boston: Harvard Business School Press.

Buchanan, J. M. and Yoon, Y. J. (2000), A Smithean Perspective on Increasing Returns, *Journal of the History of Economic Thought*, 22(01): 43–48.

Dixit, A. K. and Stiglitz, J. E. (1977), Monopolistic Competition and Optimum Product Diversity, *The American Economic Review*, 67(3): 297–308.

Durlauf, S. N. (1993), Nonergodic Economic Growth, *Review of Economic Studies*, 60(2): 349–366.

Ethier, W. J. (1982), National and International Returns to Scale in the Modern Theory of International Trade, *American Economic Review*, 72(3): 389–405.

Farmer, J. D. and Geanakoplos, J. (2009), The Virtues and Vices of Equilibrium and the Future of Financial Economics, *Complexity*, 14(3): 11–38.

Farmer, J. D., Gallegati, M., Hommes, C., Kirman, A., Ormerod, P., Cincotti, S., Sanchez, A. and Helbing, D. (2012), A Complex Systems Approach to Constructing Better Models for Managing Financial Markets and the Economy, *The European Physical Journal – Special Topics*, 214(1): 295–324.

Gabaix, X. (2011), The Granular Origins of Aggregate Fluctuations, *Econometrica*, 79(3): 733–772.

Hidalgo, C. A. and Hausmann, R. (2009), The Building Blocks of Economic Complexity, *Proceedings of the National Academy of Sciences*, 106(26): 10570–10575.

Hidalgo, C. A., Klinger, B., Barabasi, A. L. and Hausmann, R. (2007), The Product Space Conditions the Development of Nations, *Science*, 317(5837): 482–487.

Hausmann, R. and Hidalgo, C. A. (2011), The Network Structure of Economic Output, *Journal of Economic Growth*, 16(4): 309–342.

Kaldor, N. (1961), Capital Accumulation and Economic Growth, in Lutz, F. A. and Hague, P. C. (Eds.), *The Theory of Capital*, London: MacMillan, pp. 177–222.

Kaldor, N. (1966), *Causes of the Slow Growth of Economic Growth in the United Kingdom*, Cambridge: Cambridge University Press. Reprinted in Kaldor, N. (1978), *Collected Economic Essays*, Vol. V, London: Ducksworth, pp. 100–130.

Kaldor, N. (1972), The Irrelevance of Equilibrium Economics, *The Economic Journal*, 82(328): 1237–1255.

Kaldor, N. (1975), What is Wrong with Economic Theory, *Quarterly Journal of Economics*, 89(3): 347–357.

Kaldor, N. (1979), Equilibrium Theory and Growth Theory, in Baskin, M. (Ed.), *Economics and Human Welfare – Essays in Honour of Tibor Scitovsky*, New York: Academic Press, pp. 271–291.

Kaldor, N. (1981), The Role of Increasing Returns, Technical Progress and Cumulative Causation, *Économie Appliqée*, 34(6): 593–617.

Kaldor, N. (1985), *Economics Without Equilibrium*, Armonk, New York: M.E. Sharpe.

Kirman, A. (1999), Interaction and Markets, in Kirman, A. and Gallegati, M. (Eds), *Beyond the Representative Agent*, Cheltenham: Elgar.

Kelly, M. (1997), The Dynamics of Smithian Growth, *Quarterly Journal of Economics*, 112(3): 939–964.

Lavezzi, A. M. (2001). Division of Labor and Economic Growth: from Adam Smith to Paul Romer and Beyond, University of Pisa: Mimeo.

Lavezzi, A. M. (2003a), Smith, Marshall and Young on Division of Labour and Economic Growth, *European Journal of the History of Economic Thought*, 10(1): 81–108.

Lavezzi, A. M. (2003b). Division of Labour and Economic Growth: Paul Romer's contribution in an historical perspective, in N. Salvadori (Ed.), *The Theory of Economic Growth: A Classical Perspective*, Cheltenham: Elgar, pp. 272–284.

Lavezzi, A. M. (2003c), Complex Dynamics in a Simple Model of Economic Specialization, Discussion Papers 2003/2, Dipartimento di Economia e Management (DEM), University of Pisa.

Marshall, A. (1910), *Principles of Economics*, Sixth Edition. London: Macmillan.

Newman, M. E. (2003), The Structure and Function of Complex Networks, *SIAM Review*, 45(2): 167–256.

Quah, D. T. (1997), Empirics for Growth and Distribution: Stratification, Polarization, and Convergence Clubs, *Journal of Economic Growth*, 2(1): 27–59.

Richardson, G.B. (1975), Adam Smith on Competition and Increasing Returns, in Skinner, A. S. and Wilson, T. (Eds), *Essays on Adam Smith,* Oxford: Oxford University Press, pp. 350–360.

Romer, P. M. (1987), Growth Based on Increasing Returns Due to Specialization, *American Economic Review*, 77(2): 56–62.

Romer, P. M. (1990), Endogenous Technological Change, *Journal of Political Economy*, 98(5): S71–102.

Smith, A. (1976 [1776]), *An Inquiry into the Nature and Causes of the Wealth of Nations*, Campbell, R. H. and Skinner, A. S. (Eds), Oxford: Clarendon Press.

Wolfram, S. (2002), *A New Kind of Science*, Champaign: Wolfram Media Inc.

Yang, X. and Borland, J. (1991), A Microeconomic Mechanism for Economic Growth, *Journal of Political Economy*, 99(3): 460–482.

Young, A. A. (1928), Increasing Returns and Economic Progress, *The Economic Journal*, 38(152): 527–542.

Young, A. A. (1999), *Particular Expenses and Supply Curves (Nicholas Kaldor's Notes on Allyn Young's LSE Lectures, 1927–29)*, in Mehrling, P. G. and Sandilands, R. J. (Eds), *Money and Growth. Selected Papers of Allyn Abbot Young*, London: Routledge, pp. 391–398.

5 Capacity utilization, obsolete machines and effective demand

Sergio Parrinello[1]

Introduction

This paper is related to the efforts which aim to extend Keynes's theory of effective demand from the short to the long period and to the theory of economic growth.[2] Starting from a state of the economy characterized by a uniform rate of profit and an unlimited supply of labour at a fixed conventional wage, an autonomous change in demand for the social product becomes *effective* through a regime of flexible *quasi-rents*. This claim, which will be argued in the next sections, suggests that a certain flexibility in the distribution of income should be admitted to cope with the assumption of variable capacity utilization within investment-constrained growth models.

A useful description of a normal state of a growing capitalist economy should not be confined to a pure steady growth, despite the fact that such a state can be used as an ideal configuration for some preliminary analytical purpose. In particular, a normal state should include the co-existence of obsolete and non-obsolete machines. A production economy in long period equilibrium with obsolete machines has been analysed rather cursorily in Sraffa (1960, Ch. XI, Section 91) and extensively in Schefold (1989, Part II, Section B) and Kurz and Salvadori (1995, Ch. 12), in the context of the theory of joint production. The latter authors have used this case to stress some limitations of the classical method of long period equilibrium. A distinction should be made within types of obsolete machines: a machine can be said to be obsolete in a *strong sense* if it cannot be produced *and* used any more in any profitable process. In a *weak sense*, a machine is obsolete if it is not produced any more, but it can still be used in a profitable way. The profitability is relative to the existing technology and the corresponding range of possible prices and income distribution. In this paper, *obsolete* machines mean obsolete in a weak sense: machines that can be used and may receive non-negative Marshallian *quasi-rents*, but are not produced anymore. From now onwards, we shall use the word '*rent*' instead of '*quasi-rent*', since the absence of Ricardian land and pure rent from the present analysis does not require such a qualification.

Obsolete machines are ubiquitous and their number is an important component of the capital stock of any capitalist economy, in comparison with the available non-obsolete machines. We shall argue that obsolete capital goods should play a substantial role in modelling a growing economy where changes in capacity utilization depend on driving deviations of demand and income distribution from normal values. In the next section a simple model of variable capacity utilization will introduce a more complex model – the topic of the rest of the paper – in which the state of capacity is related to the existence of obsolete machines, and is consistent with a cost-minimizing choice of techniques. Only a few properties of the model will be analysed to provide some examples of possible capacity adjustments. The main analytical result of this paper conforms to common intuition. In the presence of obsolete machines, the margins of changes in capacity utilization, driven by changes in effective demand, are wider if prices and distribution are allowed to deviate from their long period values associated with free competition and a given conventional wage rate. Some related questions remain analytically unsettled and are left to speculative reasoning. Different types of changes in effective demand (a once-for-all impulse versus a persistent shift in the absolute level or in the rate of growth of demand) can have different qualitative consequences in the long period after a transition phase: a convergence either towards the initial income distribution or to a different one associated with a different conventional wage rate. Furthermore, different speeds of adjustment may characterize the prices and quantity proportions of non-obsolete machines compared with those of obsolete machines.

A simple treatment of variable capacity utilization

A simple approach to variable capacity utilization has been adopted in slightly different variants, either explicitly[3] or implicitly, in many works which aim to extend Keynes' theory of effective demand to the long period and to a growth theory.

Let us assume a one-commodity model, where a commodity is produced by means of labour and the same commodity. Suppose that only one technique is available and is subjected to constant returns to scale and to a variable degree of capacity utilization defined as follows. Let us assume that a change in capacity utilization affects the productivity of labour and capital in the same proportion, u, and define the critical ranges of capacity utilization

$u = 1$: normal capacity,
$0 < u < 1$: excess capacity,
$1 < u < u_\mathrm{m}$: capacity overutilization, where u_m is a technical maximum.

Let λ, μ denote technical coefficients: respectively the amount of labour and physical capital per unit of output when productive capacity is used at the *normal* rate $u = 1$. Define

$Y \equiv \frac{K}{\mu}$: normal output of a given stock of capital K,
uY: actual output,
$u_\mathrm{m}Y$: full capacity output.

Let us denote the nominal values

  w: wage rate,
  p: price of commodity C,
  ϱ_c: rent on capital good C.

The nominal price equation: $w\lambda + \varrho_c\mu = pu$.
The relative price equation with commodity C chosen as the *numéraire* ($p = 1$):

$$w\lambda + \varrho_c\mu = u \tag{5.1}$$

where wages are supposed to be paid *post factum*. Given a conventional real wage rate, $w = \bar{w}$, equation (5.1) with $u = 1$ determines the *normal* rent ϱ_c. Depending on the assumption about the lifetime of the capital good and its efficiency performance, combined with equation (5.1), it is possible to derive the normal rate of profit r. For simplicity assume that the capital good lasts n periods with constant efficiency.[4] Next r must be a solution to the following equation derived from the equality between the price ($p = 1$) of the currently produced commodity and the present value of a constant annuity ϱ_c paid for n periods and discounted at a constant rate of interest r:

$$\varrho_c = \frac{r(1+r)^n}{(1+r)^n - 1}$$

with the important special cases: $\varrho_c = 1 + r$ if $n = 1$ (the case of circulating capital); $\varrho_c \to r$ if $n \to \infty$ (the case of land).

  This simple notion of variable capacity utilization can be used in preliminary demand-led growth models, but it should be revised for at least two reasons.[5] Firstly, it can be argued that a single number (u) is an excessively simplified measure of the degree of capacity utilization even in a one-commodity model, considering that what is at issue in many industrial experiences (e.g. electric power supply) are *distributions* of utilization over time, falling in a certain range of normality which preserve the long term expectations, versus abnormal distributions outside that range which lead to revised expectations and investment plans. Secondly, and more importantly, variable u is used in those models as an adjustment variable between aggregate capacity savings and investments, but its 'equilibrium' value may not be consistent with a cost-minimizing choice of techniques. A change in u above or below the norm $u = 1$ may not leave unaffected the unit costs of production. If the change in aggregate demand is persistent, it should be explained why producers do not pursue the technical efficiency which is implicit in the cost-minimizing choice of techniques. This paper is focused on the second shortcoming, leaving aside the first one. It aims to offer a model of production where a variable degree of capacity utilization is admitted and can make *effective* a change in demand, but at the same time is consistent with that cost-minimizing choice.

An economy with obsolete machines under two regimes

Let us assume an economy with labour L and three commodities: a produced commodity C used as a means of production (machine of type C) and for consumption; and two types of obsolete machines M_1 and M_2. Three processes are available for the production of C, and are described by vectors of positive (output) and negative (input) *absolute* quantities:

$$\mathbf{m}_0 \equiv \begin{bmatrix} C^{(0)} \\ -L_0 \\ -C_0 \\ 0 \\ 0 \end{bmatrix} ; \quad \mathbf{m}_1 \equiv \begin{bmatrix} C^{(1)} \\ -L_1 \\ -C_1 \\ -M_1 \\ 0 \end{bmatrix} ; \quad \mathbf{m}_2 \equiv \begin{bmatrix} C^{(2)} \\ -L_2 \\ -C_2 \\ 0 \\ -M_2 \end{bmatrix} .$$

Inputs of labour and commodity C intervene in each process; instead machines of types M_1 and M_2 are used only in processes $\mathbf{m}_1$ and $\mathbf{m}_2$ respectively. Quantities M_1 and M_2 are given; the total product $C^{(0)} + C^{(1)} + C^{(2)}$ is not constrained by a limited supply of labour and is determined by a given effective demand D.

Let us denote the total quantities

D: demand for C, equal to the total product $C^{(0)} + C^{(1)} + C^{(2)}$;
$K = C_0 + C_1 + C_2$: total number of machines C in use;
$L = L_0 + L_1 + L_2$: total employment of labour;

and the *nominal* values

w: wage rate;
p: price of commodity C;
ϱ_c, ϱ_1 and ϱ_2: rents on machines C, M_1 and M_2.

For the sake of argument *we assume* that, despite the fact that both obsolete machines M_1 and M_2 by definition are not produced any more, because their *own* cost of production is too high, there is a partial ranking of cheapness among $\mathbf{m}_0$, $\mathbf{m}_1$ and $\mathbf{m}_2$ in terms of increasing costs of production of C, *net* of rents ϱ_1 and ϱ_2, such that, as the effective demand D hypothetically increases, the processes can be activated in the partial order:[6] $\mathbf{m}_1$, $\mathbf{m}_0$ first; $\mathbf{m}_2$ second. Let us start from a state of reproduction in which the level of demand D is such that, at the given wage rate, process $\mathbf{m}_2$ is not operated ($C^{(2)} = 0$) and D is allocated to method $\mathbf{m}_1$ up to the full capacity of M_1, whereas the residual quantity of D is supplied by method $\mathbf{m}_0$. This state can be interpreted as a quasi-long period equilibrium and will be called a *steady state*. Let us write the price and quantity equations corresponding to the assumptions $C^{(2)} = 0$; ϱ_c, $\varrho_1 > 0$. In conditions of free competition, the price equations in the unknowns w, ϱ_c ϱ_1 are

$$\left.\begin{aligned} wL_0 + \varrho_c C_0 &= pC^{(0)} \\ wL_1 + \varrho_c C_1 + \varrho_1 M_1 &= pC^{(1)} \end{aligned}\right\} \tag{5.2}$$

subject to the productivity constraint $0 \leq C_j/C^{(j)} < 1$, $j = 0$, 1. We assume constant returns to scale and choose commodity C as the *numéraire* ($p = 1$). The price equations in terms of technical coefficients are

$$\left.\begin{aligned} w\lambda_0 + \varrho_c c_0 &= 1 \\ w\lambda_1 + \varrho_c c_1 + \varrho_1 \mu_1 &= 1 \end{aligned}\right\} \tag{5.3}$$

where $\lambda_j = L_j/C^{(j)}$, $c_j = C_j/C^{(j)}$, $j = 0$, 1; $\mu_1 = M_1/C^{(1)}$. The quantity equations in the unknowns $C^{(0)}$, $C^{(1)}$, K, L are

$$\left.\begin{aligned} C^{(0)} + C^{(1)} &= D \\ c_0 C^{(0)} + c_1 C^{(1)} &= K \\ \lambda_0 C^{(0)} + \lambda_1 C^{(1)} &= L \\ \mu_1 C^{(1)} &= M_1. \end{aligned}\right\} \tag{5.4}$$

Let us consider two distributive regimes and closures of the model.

A surplus regime with rents

Suppose that the wage rate is fixed at a conventional level, $w = \bar{w}$, so that equations (5.3) determine the rents ϱ_c and ϱ_1 sequentially. The rate of profit follows from the formula (see the second section) of the present value of the constant annuity ϱ_c. The unknowns of systems (5.3) and (5.4) are w, ϱ_c, ϱ_1, $C^{(0)}$, $C^{(1)}$, K and L, with $w = \bar{w}$. In Figure 5.1 the D, K, L and M lines represent equations (5.4) and the point of intersection E describes a steady state on the quantity side.

A pure rent regime

By contrast, suppose that the economy has reached a full employment equilibrium represented by point E, through an adjustment process where the demand is endogenous and the assumption of unlimited supply of labour with a fixed conventional wage is replaced by that of a limited supply with a flexible wage. The amounts K, L and M_1 are *given* but not arbitrarily given; E is the common intersection point of the resource constraints and can be interpreted as a *degenerate*[7] solution to a linear programming (LP) problem in which D is the maximand, subject to K, L and M linear constraints. We know from the duality theorem of LP that if the primal problem is degenerate then the solutions to its dual problem are infinite. In our case, prices w, ϱ_c and ϱ_m, conceived as shadow-prices of the dual LP problem, would have one degree of freedom.[8] This degree apparently can be

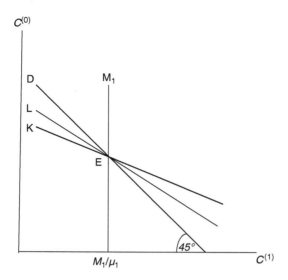

Figure 5.1 Equilibrium with more equations than variables.

filled by setting a conventional wage rate and therefore the two (surplus and pure rent) regimes seem to have been reconciled. However, this is illusory. A marginal change in the given amounts of K, L and M_1 can make only two resources binding and, as a consequence, the LP problem on the quantity side would become non-degenerate and no room would be left for a conventional wage rate in the price solution to the dual problem.

Deviations from steady states due to an autonomous change in D

Let us distinguish two alternative assumptions (**a** and **b**) on the change in D and specify the assumption (**c**) of degree of capacity utilization.

Assumption **a.** The change in D is temporary and normal, although the exact time of its occurrence may not be foreseen with certainty.

Assumption **b.** The rate of change in D is persistent.

Assumption **c.** The degree of utilization of machines can be variable according to two possibilities: a continuously variable and uniform degree of utilization of each machine or a binary degree of utilization (either active or idle) of each machine, such that a variable number of machines of each type can be operative, and the rest are kept idle. The two options may not be indifferent in terms of costs, but for simplicity we suppose that they are and therefore an idle machine *in demand* should receive the same rent paid for an active machine.

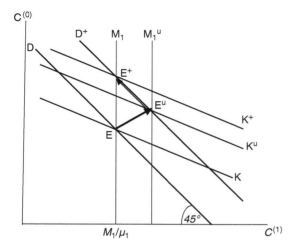

Figure 5.2 Transition between steady states driven by a 'small' increase in demand.

Let us assume that the quantity side of an initial steady state of the surplus regime is represented by point E in Figure 5.2. An autonomous increase in demand is described by a shift of the D line, say up to D^+. *How can the new demand become effective (actual) instead of remaining potential, if (i) quantities K and M are given, and (ii) only techniques m_0 and m_1 are available?*

A possible adjustment sequence is described in Figure 5.2 by points E, E^u, E^+ and two oriented connectors. For simplicity we assume, like in the second section, a single variable u which defines a *uniform* degree of capacity utilization. The revised resource constraints are

$$\left.\begin{array}{r}c_0 C^{(0)} + c_1 C^{(1)} = Ku \\ \lambda_0 C^{(0)} + \lambda_1 C^{(1)} = Lu \\ \mu_1 C^{(1)} = M_1 u \\ 0 < u < u_{\max}.\end{array}\right\} \tag{5.5}$$

At point E both types of machines, C and M_1, are used at the normal rate, $u = 1$, and this condition underlies the K and M_1 lines. Instead, the K^u and M^u lines correspond to the same number of machines used at a degree of capacity which is higher than normal, $1 < u \le u_{\max}$, and the K^+ line describes a production constraint where the number of machines of type C is fully adjusted to the higher demand and used at the normal rate, $u = 1$. Point E^u represents an intermediate equilibrium along a route towards a new steady state E^+. The normal prices and the conventional wage of the initial equilibrium E can be preserved along the path from E to E^u. A similar argument can be applied, *mutatis mutandis*, to the case of a fall in effective demand represented in Figure 5.3. The adjustment path is described by

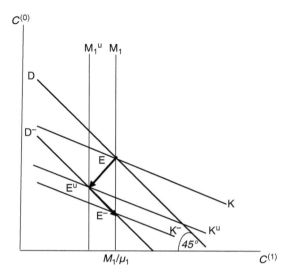

Figure 5.3 Transition between steady states driven by a 'small' fall in demand.

the succession of points E, E^u and E^-. The quantity $C^{(0)}$ may even fall to zero and $\varrho_1 = 0$, if D falls even more.

A different adjustment to a new steady state may turn out if demand D increases to such an extent that it cannot be satisfied by the given amounts of machines of type C and M_1 used at their maximum capacity $u = u_{max}$ The following case describes this possible adjustment of capacity utilization.

By assumption process $\mathbf{m}_2$, which uses obsolete machines of type M_2, is not profitable at the normal prices prevailing in E ($\varrho_2 < 0$). However, a change from the surplus regime to a rent regime can make process m_2 profitable and $C^{(2)}$ positive. Such a regime is not a 'pure' rent regime, because the corresponding equilibrium wage rate, despite the fact that it may deviate from the conventional level, does not clear the labour market and is consistent with the assumption of an unlimited labour supply. The following price equations, where λ_2, c_2 and μ_2 are the technical coefficients of process $\mathbf{m}_2$, determine the rent ϱ_c and the wage w which allow machines M_2 to be used at the margin and receive a rent equal to zero, provided that $C^{(2)} \leq M_2/\mu_2$:

$$\left.\begin{array}{r} w\lambda_0 + \varrho_c c_0 = 1 \\ w\lambda_2 + \varrho_c c_2 + \varrho_2\mu_2 = 1 \\ \text{with } \varrho_2 = 0 \text{ and } w, \varrho_c \geq 0. \end{array}\right\} \tag{5.6}$$

A positive solution to (5.6) may not exist and we shall recall this possibility in the final section.

By assumption the order of cheapness among processes $\mathbf{m}_0$, $\mathbf{m}_1$ and $\mathbf{m}_2$ is such that $C^{(1)}$ in a steady state is equal to the normal capacity output of machines M_1, that is $\bar{C}^{(1)} = M_1/\mu_1$. Suppose that $\mathbf{m}_2$ is more labour intensive and less capital intensive compared with process $\mathbf{m}_0$: $\lambda_2/c_2 > \lambda/c_0$. Therefore the wage rate will have to decrease below the conventional level, the rate of profit implicit in ϱ_c increase and part of K will be reallocated from process $\mathbf{m}_0$ to process $\mathbf{m}_2$ allowing for a positive product $C^{(2)}$, a further decline of $C^{(0)}$ and a higher employment. Figure 5.4 describes a quantity adjustment in two dimensions $(C^{(0)}, C^{(2)})$ due to a higher increase of demand. It starts from steady state E^+, where $C^{(0)} = \bar{C}^{(0)}$, $C^{(1)} = \bar{C}^{(1)}$ and $C^{(2)} = 0$, and passes through the intermediate state E^{u+}, in which part of the total amount M_2 is used, up to the new steady state E^*, where machines of type M_2 are idle again. The lines D^N, K^N and L^N are isoquants of net quantities $D^N \equiv D - \bar{C}^{(1)}$, $K^N \equiv K - c_1\bar{C}^{(1)}$ and $L^N \equiv L - \lambda_1\bar{C}^{(1)}$.

This argument suggests that a wider range of excess capacity exists in the economy with obsolete machines, if we admit the possibility of a deviation of relative prices from their normal values; in particular, a deviation of the wage rate from its conventional level. Only through a process of induced accumulation, which increases the number of non-obsolete machines C, is it possible to reach a new steady state represented by points E^+ in Figure 5.3 or E^* in Figure 5.4, and possibly recover the original income distribution associated with the conventional wage rate $\bar{w}$. The adjustment process requires that effective demand persists at the higher level D^*. This would not be the case if the *rate of growth* of the demand should rise, instead of a constant level of higher demand D^*, and become persistent. This change in the rate of growth cannot be accommodated only through a change in capacity utilization, which eventually restores the initial income distribution.[9]

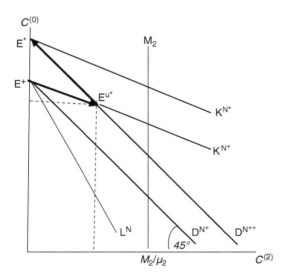

Figure 5.4 Transition between steady states driven by a 'large' increase in demand.

Normal prices corresponding to the terminal point E* may not be equal to the prices of the initial steady state E. Our argument does not imply full employment either in a steady state or along the adjustment path with a rent regime. In any case, the possibility that the change in effective demand is abnormal, to such an extent that it will remain potential instead of actual, cannot be ruled out.

A similar argument applies to the case of a 'large' fall in demand, where the *mutatis mutandis* clause includes the activation of another type of obsolete machine used at the margin with its own null rent and by a more capital intensive and less labour intensive process compared with process $\mathbf{m}_0$.

Modelling an intermediate-short period

Different fragments of modelling presented in the previous sections can be merged into a complete, albeit not general, model of capacity adjustment. The steady state model is represented by equations (5.3) and (5.4) with $D = \bar{D}$, $M_1 = \bar{M}_1$ and $M_2 = \bar{M}_2$ and the unknowns are w, ϱ_c, ϱ_1, $C^{(0)}$, $C^{(1)}$, K and L. A solution to the equations is characterized by a quantity $K = K^*$ and process $\mathbf{m}_0$ in use. The adoption of $\mathbf{m}_0$ can be interpreted as the result of a cost-minimizing choice among many available techniques which produce commodity C without using obsolete machines. It implies the achievement of *a maximum* uniform rate of profit, given the conventional wage rate, the level of demand and the amounts of obsolete machines. A short period model, confined for simplicity to a uniform normal degree of capacity utilization, where $\underline{u} = 1$ and $K = K^*$, can exemplify one among possible transition equilibrium states towards a new long period position, with a different level of effective demand D^+; $D^+ \neq D$. The formalized model:

$$\left. \begin{aligned} w\lambda_0 + \varrho_c c_0 = 1 \\ w\lambda_2 + \varrho_c c_2 + \varrho_2 \mu_2 = 1, \quad \varrho_2 = 0 \end{aligned} \right\} \tag{5.7a}$$

$$\left. \begin{aligned} w\lambda_1 + \varrho_c c_1 + \varrho_1 \mu_1 = 1 \\ \varrho_c = \frac{r(1+r)^n}{(1+r)^n - 1} \\ p_{m_1} = \sum_{t=1}^{n_1} \frac{\varrho_1}{(1+r)^t} \\ p_{m_2} = \sum_{t=1}^{n_2} \frac{\varrho_2}{(1+r)^t} \end{aligned} \right\} \tag{5.7b}$$

$$\left. \begin{aligned} C^{(0)} + C^{(1)} + C^{(2)} = D^+ \\ c_0 C^{(0)} + c_1 C^{(1)} + c_2 C^{(2)} = K^* \\ \mu_1 C^{(1)} = \bar{M}_1 \\ \lambda_0 C^{(0)} + \lambda_1 C^{(1)} + \lambda_2 C^{(2)} \equiv L \\ \mu_2 C^{(2)} \leq \bar{M}_2 \\ w, \varrho_c, \varrho_1, C^{(0)}, C^{(1)}, C^{(2)} \geq 0 \end{aligned} \right\} \tag{5.7c}$$

where p_{m_1}, p_{m_2} denote the price of machines of type M_1, M_2 and n_1, n_2 their finite lifetime under the assumption of constant efficiency. The unknowns of system (5.7a), (5.7b) and (5.7c) are w, ϱ_c, ϱ_1, r, p_{m_1}, p_{m_2}, $C^{(0)}$, $C^{(1)}$, $C^{(2)}$ and L; the givens include n, n_1, n_2, D^+, K^*, $\bar{M}_1$ and $\bar{M}_2$. Notice that a hierarchy exists in the determination of values, since w and ϱ_c can be determined before the other prices through equations (5.7a). Furthermore, the values of obsolete machines is determined *ex-post* as equal to a constant rent capitalized at the profit rate r, and therefore a uniform rate of return rules on the price of all scarce capital goods used in the economy.

A solution to equations (5.7a), (5.7b) and (5.7c) can be interpreted as an *effective deviation* from an initial normal state, driven by a downwards or upwards shift of aggregate demand. In particular, the wage rate determined by (5.7a) can be conceived as a deviation from its long period conventional level. *Effectiveness* in such a context means that the deviation can be actual and may trigger a change in the economy.

Some unsettled questions

The mechanism of variable capacity utilization exemplified so far is not heterodox, although the assumption of a finite number of techniques may lead, in the face of a change in demand D, to discrete changes in prices and distribution and to a kinked curve of labour employment L plotted against D. Other results can be derived without subverting the basis of the Keynesian theory. In particular, the Kahn–Keynes multipliers of employment and national income can be reframed in our context of flexible prices, assuming that the demand for consumption is positively related to the national income which includes rents on obsolete machines. Also, the so-called Cambridge equation[10] can be reinterpreted, assuming that savings are proportional to the sum total of profits and rents. The accumulation of capital would consist only of non-obsolete machines (commodity C in our model), since investment in obsolete machines is excluded. Still, the previous analysis suggests a reflection on some questions which have not been answered here, but cannot be avoided if the theory of the effective demand has to be applied to a theory of economic growth and cycles.

First question

In a more general model with heterogeneous capital goods, we encounter well-known 'paradoxes' of capital theory (re-switching of techniques and capital intensity reversal) and, as a consequence, a change in demand may bring about non-orthodox effects through a change in income distribution. However, even outside such cases, a problem should be noticed in the previous examples. The equations (5.6), which reappear in systems (5.7a), (5.7b), (5.7c), may not have a positive solution. In this case, processes m_0 and m_2 cannot co-exist under the condition $\varrho_2 = 0$ and a different choice of methods of production should cope with the assumed change in D and the deviation of prices from their long period values.

Second question

We have argued that a transitory change between two regimes, the surplus and a (non-pure) rent regime, can bring about a higher flexibility in capacity utilization and accommodate a change of demand in a sort of two-way avenue: from the surplus regime to the rent regime and back to the surplus regime. However, it is not said how, to use a metaphor, the shuttle can return from space (the rent regime) to the earth (the surplus regime) if, during the travel in space, the typical social connotations of the surplus regime (like a conventional wage rate on which the normal prices depend) have been abandoned. It seems plausible that the pressure of a shift of demand may temporarily overrule the surplus regime, but some trace of the institutional features of the latter has to pass to the rent regime if they should be fully recovered at the end of the adjustment process. In the simple model described in the third and fourth sections, such an institutional feature is represented by what we called a given *conventional* wage rate and by equation $w/p = \bar{w}$, where 'conventional' is used as a shorthand for the more articulated expression 'depending on institutional factors'. However, also, such an expression remains vague for an extension of the theory of effective demand from the short period to a theory of growth and fluctuations. It is not clear whether the *conventional* wage and the implicit conventions are those stressed by Keynes in his short period analysis or, instead, it reflects the conventional nature of the subsistence wage of the old classical long period theory of population. According to the first connotation, the model should be extended to the monetary side of the economy. Instead of the equation $w/p = \bar{w}$, we should assume a given *money* wage rate and a given money interest rate in order to close the system of price equations. By contrast, if we follow the classical approach, we should clarify which institutional factors can determine the *real* wage. What is at issue for the feasible two-way avenue mentioned above is whether the same conventional wage applies to the short and to the long period and whether in each case the wage is fixed at a certain level or is only subjected to a minimum floor set by $w/p \geq \bar{w}$.

Third question

We wonder how long-term expectations and investment plans are affected through the short-term changes in prices and distributional variables. The method of comparative dynamics, applied to the model with obsolete machines, allows us to determine the change in quantities between steady states; in particular, the change in K from the initial to the new amount induced by the change in demand D. Yet, the *process* of growth should be a main issue, considering also that the dynamics of the *absolute* quantities, in general, is subjected to path-dependency.[11] On this question, the composition of fixed capital in terms of obsolete and non-obsolete machines seems to be an important factor, which perhaps has not received the due attention in the recent literature dealing with effective demand and growth[12]. As a matter of fact, a normal state of an economy presents a stratification into layers of machines which embody different technologies and have been grouped in two categories – only for our analytical purpose: obsolete and non-obsolete machines. On the basis of this distinction, it is not necessary that fixed capital as a whole adjusts to a steady state in order to make it possible for the distributive variables to converge toward their normal values. The adjustment of the proportions among capital goods which belong to only one layer would suffice: the layer of the non-obsolete machines entering the sub-system of equations – first equation of system (5.2) in our simple model – which determine the rate of profit, given the conventional wage rate. This property suggests that the speed of adjustment towards those normal values is decoupled, within certain limits, from the dynamics of obsolete fixed capital. The capital composition is subjected to the interference of a multiplicity of factors, in particular to the vagaries of technical progress, and the proportions among obsolete capital goods may not possess an equilibrium configuration which can act as an attractor. This is consistent with a gravitational pull attributed to normal prices and to the quantities of non-obsolete capital associated with them.

Notes

1 Email address: Sergio.parrinello@uniroma1.it. The author would like to acknowledge the useful comments addressed by Adriano Birolo, Duncan Foley and an anonymous referee to early versions of this paper. He remains the only person responsible for possible errors and omissions. A preliminary version of this paper has been published as a working paper (Parrinello, 2014b).
2 The interested reader may consult Parrinello (2014a, available online) for a bibliography of the debate about the extensions of Keynes's theory of effective demand to the theory of growth with variable capacity utilization.
3 See Foley and Michl (1999, Ch. 11), Parrinello (2014a).
4 For a more general treatment of fixed capital and its depreciation without the restriction of constant efficiency, see Sraffa (1960, Ch. X).
5 See Parrinello (2014a).
6 It might seem strange that m_1, a process with an obsolete machine, can be cheaper or equally profitable than another process, m_0, with a non-obsolete machine. However, according to the definition of *weak* obsolescence adopted at the beginning, the source of the distinction between the two categories of capital goods is upstream of their productive efficiency. In fact, it reflects the profitability of their own production, not that of the techniques where they are used as inputs.
7 The degenerate feature of the solution derives from the fact that the number of constraints which bind the optimal solution is greater than the number of the choice variables.
8 This interpretation of a fully adjusted equilibrium in the rent regime as a degenerate problem of L.P. and its dual with infinite solutions is not new. As far as I know, beside my own early persuasion, I remember that the same property has been stressed by Harvey Grahm in his presentation at a conference held in the Nineties.
9 A similar view is advanced in (Nell, 1998: 492–493).
10 The Cambridge equation is $g = s_\pi r$, where the symbols denote: g the rate of accumulation, s_π the propensity to save out of profits and r the rate of profit.
11 The present author (see Parrinello, 2014a) has called the attention to a property of a disaggregated model of balanced growth at a geometric rate, noticed already by Solow and Samuelson (1953). This type of model in a sense is inherently unstable on the side of the *absolute* quantities of capital goods and path dependency of its steady equilibrium is

the rule; only *relative* stability (i.e. the convergence of the *proportions* among quantities and among prices) is left to demonstration.

12 See Parrinello (2014a).

References

Foley, D. and Michl, T. (1999), *Growth and Distribution*, Cambridge, Massachusetts and London, England: Harvard University Press.

Kurz, H.D. and Salvadori, N. (1995), *Theory of Production: a Long-Period Analysis*, Cambridge: Cambridge University Press.

Nell, E.J. (1998), *The General Theory of Transformational Growth: Keynes after Sraffa*, Cambridge: Cambridge University Press.

Parrinello, S. (2014a), A Search for Distinctive Features of Demand-led Growth Models, *PSL Quarterly Review*, Vol. 67, No. 270 (September), 309–342. [A slightly different version of this article was published in the *Centro Sraffa Working Papers*, No. 2, May 2014.]

Parrinello, S. (2014b), Capacity Utilization, Obsolete Machines and Effective Demand, *Centro Sraffa Working Papers*, No. 9, December 2014.

Schefold, B. (1989), *Mr Sraffa on Joint Production and Other Essays*, London: Unwin Hyman.

Solow, R. and Samuelson, P.A. (1953), Balanced Growth under Constant Returns to Scale, *Econometrica*, Vol. 21, No. 3 (July), 412–424.

Sraffa, P. (1960), *Production of Commodities by means of Commodities, Prelude to a Critique of Economic Theory*. Cambridge: Cambridge University Press.

6 Endogenous growth and unemployment

The experience of Italy following the recent financial crisis[1]

Stefan F. Schubert and
Stephen J. Turnovsky

Introduction

The global financial crisis, which began in 2007 with the bursting of the US housing bubble, rapidly infected the world economy in various ways. The output contraction in the US spilled over to other economies through a slump in exports, and the troubles that the housing bubble caused in financial markets resulted in a widespread financial crisis. This in turn led to a 'credit crunch', and the efficiency of financial intermediation suffered substantially. As a member of the European Union, Italy was not spared the adverse consequences of this crisis.

It is well documented that Italy already had severe economic problems well before 2008 and the globalization of the financial crisis. Italy's 'Achilles' heel' has been the low productivity of its economy, which had already suffered over 15 years of slow growth prior to the global financial crisis; see IMF (2010, p. 57). The Italian economy, based on many small and medium-sized enterprises, was adversely affected via three important channels: a contraction in international trade, a reduction in credit and a decline in confidence. The recession in Italy's main trading partners sharply reduced Italy's exports, financing conditions tightened, which reduced credit growth, and bankruptcies increased; see IMF (2010, p. 6). Italy found itself in the worst recession since World War II. Starting from a relatively low unemployment rate of 6.9 per cent in the third quarter of 2008, the unemployment rate increased to 8.3 per cent in the fourth quarter of 2009 and remained above 8 per cent until 2011, when another crisis, the so-called 'Euro crisis' or, more appropriately, the public debt crisis, infected Italy. However, we should point out that the government debt–GDP ratio was already well above 100 per cent before the global financial crisis emerged.[2] In August 2011, for the first time, the European Central Bank bought Italian and Spanish government bonds on the secondary market in an attempt to avoid further interest rate increases in these countries.

In this paper we shall focus on Italy's disappointing economic performance in terms of growth and unemployment in the aftermath of the global financial crisis, and shall thus abstract from the additional downturn caused by the government debt crisis. We shall also restrict our analysis to Italy's main economic problem, low productivity, and will not consider the additional channel of trade through which the Italian economy was also adversely affected. The short-run decline in Italy's output during the financial crisis can be attributed to a collapse in total factor productivity (see IMF, 2010, p. 57). Despite the fact that – compared to other economies – the Italian financial system found itself in a relatively strong position (see IMF, 2010, p. 3), which did not lead to a liquidity crunch, banks' asset quality and profitability weakened, and lending growth to the private sector was sharply curtailed (see IMF, 2010, p. 5). In these circumstances, when the financial system is unable to allocate loanable funds as productively as before the crisis and high-productivity firms go bankrupt for lack of financing, the efficiency of the production process declines and total factor productivity (TFP) falls (see IMF, 2009, Ch. 4). This view is supported by several recent studies (Estevão and Severo 2010, Haugh, Ollivaud and Turner 2009, Meza and Quintin, 2005, Cole, Ohanian and Leung 2005).[3]

An important issue to arise with respect to a TFP shock is its impact on unemployment and the government debt–GDP ratio. This paper focuses on unemployment, growth and debt dynamics in the aftermath of such a TFP shock. But in addition to unemployment and growth dynamics, we also investigate how other key economic variables such as capital, output and consumption adjust and the consequences for overall economic welfare.

To address the effects of TFP shocks, we adapt a model of endogenous growth developed by Chatterjee and Turnovsky (2012), in which the accumulation of public capital is a key source of growth. But to analyse the dynamics of unemployment, we must depart from the standard neoclassical approach employed by Chatterjee and Turnovsky, in which, having a Walrasian labour market with flexible wages, the labour market always clears and unemployment does not exist. To do this we augment and modify the standard representative agent model of a growing economy by introducing search unemployment pioneered by Mortensen and Pissarides (1994), together with wage bargaining, in a similar way into the models of Shi and Wen (1997, 1999) and Heer (2003). In these models, unemployment emerges due to the time consuming and costly matching of vacancies with agents who search for a job.[4] But in contrast to these papers, we also introduce sticky wages as suggested by Hall (2005a, 2005b). The wage resulting from Nash bargaining by workers and employers determines the target wage, to which the actual wage rate adjusts gradually. The introduction of slow wage adjustment is not only plausible, it also yields realistically slow and persistent unemployment dynamics, whereas assuming that the wage rate adjusts instantaneously to the bargained wage generates unrealistically fast unemployment adjustment; see, e.g., Heer (2003) or Schubert (2011).

The resulting macroeconomic equilibrium is described by a relatively complex high order dynamic system, for which analytical solutions are infeasible, requiring us to resort to numerical simulations. We calibrate the model so that several key economic variables closely match those of the Italian economy. In particular, the pre-shock balanced growth rate is practically zero, reflecting Italy's recent experience of low economic growth. We analyse two types of total factor productivity shocks. First, we investigate the effects of a permanent drop in TFP. Second, we consider a drop in TFP that is temporary in the sense that after the shock the level of TFP gradually reverts to an initial benchmark value. In both cases we find that the shock leads to an increase in the unemployment rate and persistent unemployment dynamics, as well as to an increase in the public debt–GDP ratio and a decline in the instantaneous growth rate of GDP.

In the case of the permanent shock, the unemployment rate increases by more than two percentage points on impact, and gradually converges to a level marginally less than its pre-shock level. The long-run debt–GDP ratio increases to 125 per cent, and the balanced growth rate falls by roughly 0.2 percentage points.[5] The shock imposes substantial welfare losses, both in the short run and in the long run. In the case of a temporary negative TFP shock, the instantaneous unemployment rate is raised by a little more than one percentage point, whereas its steady-state value is unaffected. Despite the fact that the balanced growth rate does not change for a temporary shock, the economy ends up with a higher public debt–GDP ratio. Relative to the permanent shock, the welfare losses are moderated, but still significant. Comparing these responses with Italy's unemployment and debt dynamics between the years 2008 and 2011 (before the public debt crisis fully hit Italy), we feel that the dynamics caused by a temporary TFP shock can provide a coherent explanation of a large part of Italy's experience during that period.

The remainder of the paper proceeds as follows. In the next section we set out the model and describe the sectoral structure of the economy, the labour market, and the macroeconomic equilibrium. In the third section the model is calibrated and the benchmark steady state is discussed. The economic effects of a permanent and a temporary TFP shock are analysed in the fourth section, while the fifth section concludes. Insofar as possible, formal details related to the development of the model are relegated to the Appendix, available on request from the authors.

Analytical framework

The key analytical feature of the model is to introduce search into a standard endogenous growth model, where a key source of growth is an externality composed of an amalgam of public and private capital in production, as in Chatterjee and Turnovsky (2012). Three sectors can be distinguished: households, firms, and the government, which we consider in turn.

Households

The economy is populated by N identical households. Each household, i, consists of a continuum of agents with a fixed measure. Each household member cares only about the household's utility. Thus, individual risks in consumption and leisure are completely smoothed within each household; see Shi and Wen (1997). Each household is endowed with one unit of time that can be used for supplying labour, l^s, searching for employment, s, or enjoying leisure, $L = 1 - l^s - s$. Agents who are searching are called unemployed. The labour force is defined as $l + s$, and the unemployment rate as $s/(l + s)$, where l denotes the equilibrium level of employment. Besides leisure, each household consumes a consumption good, C. For notational simplicity and without loss of generality, we drop the index i and normalize the number of households, N, to unity.

The representative household earns wage income from labour, interest income from holding capital, K, and government bonds, B, and receives the profits, Π, of the representative firm he owns. He uses his income for buying the consumption good, C, and accumulating capital and bonds, subject to his flow budget constraint:

$$\dot{K} + \dot{B} = (1 - \tau_\pi)\Pi + (1 - \tau_k)r(K + B) + (1 - \tau_w)wl^s$$
$$+ \tau_u ws - (1 + \tau_c)C - T \tag{6.1a}$$

where r is the rental rate and w the wage rate, and τ_π, τ_k, τ_w and τ_c are the tax rates levied on income received from firms (profits), interest income, labour income, and consumption. T denotes a lump-sum tax. $\tau_u ws$ are unemployment benefits, where τ_u is the rate of the unemployment subsidy as a fraction of the wage rate. As Shi and Wen (1999) note, τ_u should be interpreted as the average unemployment subsidy to all unemployed agents. Thus, τ_u can be constant over time even though in reality the subsidy to an unemployed individual typically falls with unemployment duration.

A key aspect of the model is that labour (employment) l^s changes only gradually according to

$$\dot{l}^s = \phi s - \zeta l^s \tag{6.1b}$$

where ϕ denotes the job finding rate, which the individual agent takes as given, and ζ is the exogenously given rate of job separation.[6] As Shi and Wen (1999) also observe, there are inflows into and outflows from the state of unemployment all the time, even in steady state. Since the identities of unemployed agents are constantly changing, the unemployment duration, $1/\phi$, should be interpreted as the average duration of all unemployed agents.

The representative household derives utility from consumption, C, leisure, L, and from a government provided consumption good, G_C. The unit maximizes the intertemporal iso-elastic utility function W,

$$W \equiv \int_0^\infty \frac{1}{\varepsilon}[C(1 - l^s - s)^\theta G_C^\eta]^\varepsilon e^{-\beta t} dt,$$

$$\theta \geq 0, \quad 1 > \varepsilon\theta, \quad 1 > \varepsilon(1 + \theta), \quad \eta \geq 0 \tag{6.2}$$

by choosing the rate of consumption, C, search (unemployment), s, and the rates of capital, bonds and labour accumulation, subject to the flow budget constraints (6.1a) and (6.1b), and the given initial stocks of capital, $K(0) = K_0$, bonds, $B(0) = B_0$, and labour, $l^s(0) = l_0^s$, respectively. β denotes the agent's rate of time preference, taken to be constant. The intertemporal elasticity of substitution equals $1/(1 - \varepsilon)$, and θ denotes the elasticity of leisure. The optimality conditions are given by

$$C^{\varepsilon-1}(1 - l^s - s)^{\varepsilon\theta} G_C^{\varepsilon\eta} = (1 + \tau_c)\lambda \tag{6.3a}$$

$$\theta C^{\varepsilon}(1 - l^s - s)^{\varepsilon\theta-1} G_C^{\varepsilon\eta} = \gamma\phi + \lambda\tau_u w \tag{6.3b}$$

$$\beta - \frac{\dot{\lambda}}{\lambda} = (1 - \tau_k)r \tag{6.3c}$$

$$\frac{\lambda(1 - \tau_w - \tau_u)w}{\gamma} + \frac{\dot{\gamma}}{\gamma} - \zeta = \beta + \phi \tag{6.3d}$$

together with the transversality conditions

$$\lim_{t\to\infty} \lambda K e^{-\beta t} = \lim_{t\to\infty} \lambda B e^{-\beta t} = \lim_{t\to\infty} \gamma l^s B e^{-\beta t} = 0 \tag{6.3e}$$

where λ is the marginal utility of wealth, and γ is the shadow price of employment. Condition (6.3a) equates the marginal utility of consumption to the marginal utility of wealth. Equation (6.3b) equates the marginal cost of searching (i.e. its (dis)utility) to the marginal benefit of searching, which comprises the utility value of finding a job plus the utility value of the unemployment benefits received while searching. Equation (6.3c) is the usual Euler condition, equating the rate of return on consumption to the rate of return on capital and on bonds, i.e. the interest rate. The dynamic no-arbitrage condition (6.3d) requires the rate of return on employment, comprising the 'dividend yield' of employment, $\lambda(1 - \tau_w - \tau_u)w/\gamma$, the 'capital gain' $\dot{\gamma}/\gamma$ and the loss due to job destruction ζ, to equal the 'effective' discount rate, $\beta + \phi$, which comprises the rate of time preference adjusted for the probability of finding a job, ϕ. Finally, to ensure that the agent's intertemporal budget constraint is met, the transversality conditions (6.3e) must hold.

Equations (6.3a) and (6.3b) can be solved for consumption, C, and search, s. For the latter we obtain

$$s = s(l, \lambda, \gamma, \phi, w, G_C, \tau_c, \tau_u); \quad s_l = -1, \quad s_\lambda \gtrless 0, \quad s_\gamma > 0,$$
$$s_\phi > 0, \quad s_w > 0, \quad s_{G_C} < 0, \quad s_{\tau_c} \gtrless 0, \quad s_{\tau_u} > 0 \tag{6.4}$$

where the signs are determined assuming that the intertemporal elasticity of substitution is less than one (i.e., $\varepsilon < 0$), as empirical evidence overwhelmingly suggests. The signs of s_λ and s_{τ_c} are ambiguous and depend on the level of the unemployment subsidy τ_u. If $\tau_u = 0$, then $s_\lambda < 0$, $s_{\tau_c} < 0$, and $s_w = s_{\tau_u} = 0$. The shadow price of employment, γ, is a forward-looking variable. The representative household recognizes that, in equilibrium, the job finding rate $\phi(t)$ is a function of time. By finding a job, the household's net wage increases by $(1 - \tau_w - \tau_u)w$ units of output, which provides $\lambda(1 - \tau_w - \tau_u)w$ units of utility. Solving equation (6.3d) forward and invoking the transversality condition (6.3e), we obtain

$$\gamma(t) = \int_t^\infty \lambda(z)(1 - \tau_w - \tau_u)w(z)e^{-\int_t^z (\varsigma + \beta + \phi(q))dq}dz. \tag{6.5}$$

The value of a job, expressed in terms of utility, equals the household's discounted flow of the net real wage, valued at the marginal utility of wealth. We will return to these two equations when discussing unemployment dynamics.

Firms

The economy also comprises a large number of identical firms, which for convenience we normalize to unity. Firms produce a domestic good, Y, by combining private capital, K, and labour (demand), l^d, by means of the CES production function

$$Y = A(t)[\alpha K^{-\rho} + (1-\alpha)(Xl^d)^{-\rho}]^{-1/\rho}, \quad -1 \leq \rho < \infty \tag{6.6a}$$

where $\sigma \equiv 1/(1+\rho)$ is the elasticity of substitution in production, $A(t)$ is a scale parameter summarizing total factor productivity, and α denotes the share of private capital, K, in production. The long-run level of total factor productivity equals $\bar{A}$, to which the current TFP adapts gradually in accordance with the process

$$\dot{A}(t) = \varsigma(\bar{A} - A(t)) \tag{6.6b}$$

where ς is the autoregressive adjustment speed parameter. In addition, production is influenced by an aggregate externality, X, which we take to be a geometric weighted average of the economy's aggregate stock of private capital, $\bar{K}$, and public capital (infrastructure), K_G:

$$X \equiv \bar{K}^v K_G^{1-v}, \quad 0 \leq v \leq 1. \tag{6.6c}$$

That is, 'raw' labour interacts with the composite production externality to create labour efficiency units, which in turn interact with private capital to produce output. The production function thus has constant returns to scale in both the private factors and in the accumulating factors, and accordingly can potentially sustain an equilibrium of ongoing growth. The composite externality represents a combination of the role of private capital as in Romer (1986), together with public capital as in Barro (1990), Futagami *et al.* (1993) and subsequent authors and can be justified in two ways. First, it facilitates the calibration of the aggregate economy, something that is generically problematic in the conventional one-sector AK growth model (where the term 'AK' refers to the fact that output is proportional by a factor A, to capital K). Second, the notion that the economy's infrastructure contributing to labour efficiency comprises a combination of both private and public components is itself a plausible representation of reality.

Workers separate from a job at rate, ζ. The individual firm takes the rate, ϕ, of filling a vacancy, v, as given. Hence, the firm's employment follows

$$\dot{l}^d = \phi v - \zeta l^d. \tag{6.6d}$$

The firm has to pay a cost for maintaining a number of job vacancies equal to $m\bar{Y}v$. This cost includes advertising costs (Pissarides, 1987), and can also be thought as a hiring/recruiting cost (Pissarides, 1986, Mortensen and Pissarides, 1994), and/or as the cost of a human resources division. Following Pissarides (1987), we assume that vacancy costs depend on output.[7] Vacancy costs are linearly homogeneous in average (aggregate) output, $\bar{Y}$. This assumption is necessary to support an equilibrium of ongoing growth.

The firm's operating profit (capital earnings) is given by

$$\Pi = Y - wl^d - (r+\delta)K - m\bar{Y}v \tag{6.6e}$$

where δ denotes the depreciation rate of private capital. The firm's objective is to maximize the value of the firm, i.e. the present value of profits, V,

$$V \equiv \int_0^\infty \Pi(t)e^{-\int_0^t r(z)dz}dt \tag{6.7}$$

by choosing the amount of capital K to be rented, vacancies v, and the rate of accumulating labour l^d, subject to equations (6.6) and the initial stock of labour, $l^d(0) = l_0^d$. In making its decisions, the individual firm takes the stock of aggregate private capital, $\bar{K}$, as well as average output, $\bar{Y}$, as given. Hence, from the firm's perspective the externality X is a parameter, though with all firms being identical, in equilibrium $\bar{K} = K, \bar{Y} = Y$.

Solving the firm's optimization problem gives rise to the following first order conditions:

$$\alpha A^{-\rho}\left(\frac{Y}{K}\right)^{1+\rho} = \frac{\partial Y}{\partial K} = r+\delta \tag{6.8a}$$

$$m\bar{Y} = \xi\phi \tag{6.8b}$$

$$\frac{(1-\alpha)(AX)^{-\rho}\left(\frac{Y}{l^d}\right)^{1+\rho}}{\xi} + \frac{\dot{\xi}}{\xi} - \frac{w}{\xi} - \zeta = r \tag{6.8c}$$

$$\lim_{t\to\infty} \xi l^d e^{-\int_0^t r(z)dz} = 0 \tag{6.8d}$$

where ξ denotes the shadow price of labour. Equation (6.8a) determines the amount of capital to be rented, given the interest rate r. Equation (6.8b) equates the marginal cost of vacancy to its marginal benefit. The no-arbitrage relation (6.8c) equates the rate of return on labour, comprising a 'dividend yield', a 'capital gain', and two losses due to wage payments and job destruction, to the rental rate of capital, r. Finally, the transversality condition (6.8d) must hold.

Government

The government uses its revenues to finance its current expenditures G_K on infrastructure (public capital), K_G, the provision of the consumption good, G_C, unemployment benefits, and interest on its outstanding debt, B. These expenditures are subject to the government's flow budget constraint

$$\tau_\pi \Pi + \tau_k r(K + B) + \tau_c C + \tau_w wl + T + \dot{B} = rB + G_K + G_C + \tau_u ws. \quad (6.9)$$

Public capital depreciates at rate δ_G and evolves according to

$$\dot{K}_G = G_K - \delta_G K_G. \quad (6.10)$$

Finally, since we are concerned with a growing economy, we assume that the government ties its expenditure to the size of the economy as summarized by Y, i.e.

$$G_K = g_K Y, \quad G_C = g_C Y. \quad (6.11)$$

Goods market clearing

Goods market equilibrium is obtained by combining the household's budget constraint, (6.1a), with the firm's profits (6.6e) and the government's budget constraint, (6.9). It requires that output is allocated to consumption, capital accumulation, government expenditure and financing vacancy costs, i.e.

$$Y = C + \dot{K} + \delta K + G_K + G_C + m\bar{Y}v \quad (6.12)$$

from which, using (6.11), and noting that in equilibrium $\bar{Y} = Y$, the capital accumulation equation

$$\dot{K} = (1 - g_K - g_C - mv)Y - \delta K - C \quad (6.13)$$

follows. Goods market clearance (6.12) is maintained by residual adjustments in private investment $\dot{K}$. Note that in macroeconomic equilibrium $l^s = l^d = l$, and (aggregate) output is given by

$$Y = A\left[\alpha K^{-\rho} + (1 - \alpha)\left(K^v K_G^{1-v}l\right)^{-\rho}\right]^{-1/\rho}$$

$$= AK\left[\alpha + (1 - \alpha)\left(\left(\frac{K_G}{K}\right)^{1-v}l\right)^{-\rho}\right]^{-1/\rho}. \quad (6.14)$$

Matching and wage determination

Labour markets are subject to frictions and are characterized by two-sided search. Matching vacancies with searching agents is a time consuming process. To simplify notation, v and s also denote the aggregate numbers of vacancies and unemployed agents, respectively. We assume a constant returns to scale matching technology of the Cobb-Douglas form

$$M(v, s) = \Lambda v^{\chi} s^{1-\chi}, \quad \Lambda > 0, \quad 0 < \chi < 1. \tag{6.15}$$

Thus, matches per unemployed agent can be expressed as $\phi = \Lambda(v/s)^{\chi}$, and matches per vacancy as $\phi = \Lambda(v/s)^{\chi-1}$. Hence, the rates of finding a job and of filling a vacancy are endogenously determined, whereas households and firms take them as given. Defining $x \equiv v/s$ as the vacancy-search ratio (or vacancy-unemployment ratio), which is a measure of labour market tightness, we have

$$\phi(x) = \Lambda x^{\chi}, \quad \varphi(x) = \Lambda x^{\chi-1}$$

where we see that matches per searching agent $\phi(x)$ are an increasing function in the vacancy-search ratio, whereas matches per vacancy $\phi(x)$ are a decreasing function in x.

Following Hall (2005a, b), we introduce sticky wages, and this has a profound influence on the search process and hence on unemployment dynamics. We assume that the (real) wage w is formed adaptively:

$$\dot{w} = \Omega(w_N - w) + w\frac{\dot{K}}{K}, \quad \Omega > 0 \tag{6.16}$$

where Ω is the speed of wage adjustment and thus a measure of wage stickiness and w_N is the target wage, which we define to be the wage that would result from Nash bargaining. The expression $\dot{K}/K$ reflects autonomous wage inflation. In steady state the average product of labour, Y/l, grows at the same rate as the capital stock; hence steady-state unit labour costs remain constant when wages grow along with average labour productivity.

The Nash-bargaining wage, w_N, which serves as the target wage, is determined as a weighted average of the firm's reservation wage (marginal product of labour) and the worker's reservation wage (marginal rate of substitution of leisure for consumption); see Shi and Wen (1997, 1999),

$$w_N = \pi(1-\alpha)(AX)^{-\rho}\left(\frac{Y}{l}\right)^{1+\rho} + (1-\pi)\frac{\theta C}{(1-l-s)}\frac{1+\tau_c}{1-\tau_w} \tag{6.17}$$

where $0 < \pi < 1$ measures the bargaining power of workers.[8] Any wage w that is located within the bargaining set, given by the firm's and the worker's reservation wage, is a Nash equilibrium (for details, see Hall, 2005b).

Macroeconomic equilibrium

The macroeconomic equilibrium is defined as follows (Shi and Wen, 1997, 1997; Heer, 2003).

Definition 1 The competitive search equilibrium is a collection of decision rules $\{C, s, l, \dot{K}, \dot{B}, v, K\}$ and wages $\{w\}$ such that

1   Individual variables equal (average) aggregate variables.
2   Given factor prices, profits, and matching rates, households maximize their utility (6.2) subject to (6.1).
3   Given factor prices and matching rates, firms maximize the value of the firm (6.7) subject to (6.6).
4   Wages evolve according to (6.16), and profits are given by (6.6e).
5   The rental rate r clears the capital market.
6   Capital accumulation (investment) $\dot{K}$ adjusts properly to continuously clear the domestic goods market (6.12).
7   Firms do not take into account the effect of their decisions on the aggregate capital stock and hence on the externality.
8   Agents do not take into account the effect of their decisions on the matching rates ϕ and φ. In equilibrium, $\varphi v = \phi s$.
9   The government budget constraint (6.9) is satisfied.

Since the flows of workers in and out of unemployment are equal to each other in any symmetric equilibrium, i.e. $\phi(x)s = \varphi(x)v$, equations (6.1b) and (6.6d) coincide implying that in equilibrium, $l^s = l^d \equiv l$. The derivation of the macrodynamic equilibrium is rather complicated, involving a lot of technical detail, and accordingly is relegated to the Appendix, available on request from the authors.

The benchmark economy

Given the complexity of the model, we resort to numerical simulations. We calibrate the model, using the parameter values shown in Table 6.1, which reflect a time unit of one year. The initial steady-state equilibrium of the corresponding benchmark economy is reported in Table 6.2.

Table 6.1 The benchmark economy

Preference parameters	$\beta = 0.04$, $\varepsilon = -0.5$, $\theta = 1.5$, $\eta = 0.25$
Production parameters	$\bar{A} = 1$, $\varsigma = 0.05$, $\alpha = 0.5$, $v = 0.6$, $\rho = 1/3$, $\delta = 0.05$, $\delta_G = 0.075$
Labour market parameters	$\zeta = 0.044$, $\pi = 0.5$, $\chi = 0.4$, $\Lambda = 1$, $m = 2.97$, $\Omega = 0.05$
Initial conditions	$K_0 = 1$, $B_0 = 0.37$
Expenditure parameters	$g_K = 0.05$, $g_C = 0.15$
Tax rates	$\tau_\pi = \tau_k = \tau_w = 0.308$, $\tau_c = 0.2$, $\tau_u = 0.36$

Table 6.2 Initial equilibrium of benchmark economy

UR (%)	Dur U	U	l	L	K/Y	C/Y	K_G/K	ψ (%)
6.824	1.66	1.8997	25.9372	72.1631	3.1421	0.6260	0.2112	0.0358

Notes: UR = unemployment rate in per cent of labour force $l + s$, Duration of unemployment Dur U is measured in years, Unemployment (search) U, Labour l and Leisure L are denoted in per cent of total time, and the equilibrium growth rate ψ is measured in per cent.

The model is calibrated to reflect some key features of countries in Southern Europe, in particular Italy. The rate of time preference, β, is set equal to 0.04, a standard and non-controversial value. The preference parameter ε is set equal to -0.5 and corresponds to an intertemporal elasticity of substitution $1/(1 - \varepsilon)$ of 2/3. The elasticity of leisure, θ, is the key determinant of the equilibrium labour–leisure allocation and setting $\theta = 1.5$ yields an equilibrium allocation of time of approximately 72.2 per cent to leisure, 25.9 per cent to work and around 1.9 per cent to job search, generally consistent with empirical evidence.

The elasticity of substitution in production between labour and capital, $1/(1 + \rho)$ is set equal to 0.75 (i.e. $\rho = 1/3$), reflecting recent empirical evidence.[9] The base level of total factor productivity (TFP) is normalized to $\bar{A} = 1$. We set the autoregressive parameter ς for the speed of adjustment of TFP equal to 0.05 in accordance with Ríos-Rull (1996) who chooses the AR(1) parameter 0.95 for a discrete-time process using annual data. The distributive share of capital in production is set equal to $\alpha = 0.5$, yielding a ratio of private capital to output of 3.1, which matches closely Italy's reported capital–output ratio of 3.1 in 2008 (see the AMECO database, the macroeconomic database of the European Commission's Directorate General for Economic and Financial Affairs, which can be accessed at http://ec.europa.eu/economy_finance/db_indicators/ameco/index_en.htm). The ratio of total capital $K + K_G$ to output equals 3.8. The rate of depreciation of private capital equals 0.05, a commonly assumed value, whereas the depreciation rate of public capital equals 0.075. The choice of the parameter v, determining the share of private capital in the externality, is less obvious. Following Chatterjee and Turnovsky (2012), we set $v = 0.6$. The reason for this choice is to yield a productive elasticity for public capital that falls within the range of empirical estimates reported by Bom and Ligthart (2013).

The labour market parameters are set in a way to replicate an empirically reasonable characterization of the labour market. The bargaining power of workers and firms is assumed to be equal; therefore we choose $\pi = 0.5$. The value of χ is set equal to 0.4, and the matching productivity parameter Λ is set equal to 1. Together with the vacancy cost parameter $m = 2.97$ and a job separation rate of $\zeta = 0.044$, the baseline economy is characterized by a steady-state unemployment rate $\tilde{s}/(\tilde{s} + \tilde{l})$ of 6.82 per cent and an average duration of unemployment, $1/\phi$, of roughly 1.66 years. This fits Italian data quite well. In 2008, the unemployment rate was 6.7 per cent (see AMECO database), and in 2012 the average length of job search was 21 months (see Istat, 2013). The asymptotic speed of convergence is highly sensitive to the speed of wage adjustment, and setting $\Omega = 0.05$ yields a very plausible rate of convergence of around 4.11 per cent. The initial private capital stock, K_0, is normalized to unity, and the initial stock of government debt is set to $B_0 = 0.37$ resulting in a debt–GDP ratio of 1.16, reflecting Italy's number in 2009 (see AMECO database).

The policy parameters are chosen as follows. The share of public investment in GDP, g_K, is set to 0.05, and the share of government consumption in GDP, g_C, equals 0.15, resulting in a share of government purchases in GDP of 20 per cent, approximately mirroring Italy's expenditures on government consumption and investment.[10] The tax rates on profits, capital income and labour income are set equal to the Italian average income tax plus employee social security contributions as a percentage of gross wage income (see OECD, 2013, Table 0.3).[11] The consumption tax rate equals the Italian value added tax of 20 per cent.[12] The unemployment benefit rate τ_u is set equal 0.36.[13]

The capital–output ratio equals 3.14, and the private consumption–output ratio is 0.626 and close to the year 2008 Italian value of 0.59.[14] The ratio of public to private capital equals 0.2112. Finally, the benchmark economy is characterized by a growth rate of 0.04 per cent, thus mirroring Italy's low growth rate over the period 2007–2008.

It is worth noting that the steady-state unemployment rate $\tilde{U}\tilde{R}$ is determined by[15]

$$\tilde{U}\tilde{R} = \frac{\zeta}{\phi(\tilde{x}) + \zeta}. \tag{6.18}$$

It depends only on the structural parameters job separation rate, ζ, and the matching function parameter χ, which enters the job finding rate $\phi(x) = \Lambda x^{\chi}$. As these parameters are exogenous, any change in the long-run unemployment rate must occur through a change in labour market tightness x. The higher x, the higher the job finding rate and the lower the unemployment rate.

Finally, to maintain a debt–GDP ratio of roughly 1.16, the government has to set the lump-sum tax-GDP ratio equal to -0.1125, that is, the ratio of net transfers to GDP is roughly 11.25 per cent.

Total factor productivity shock

We now turn to the effects of a negative TFP shock. Our discussion is motivated by the view expressed by the IMF that 'Italy's dismal growth performance is largely due to poor productivity' (see IMF, 2010, p. 59), and that since the beginning of the global financial crisis, Italy's productivity has dropped even further. The decline in measured TFP over 2008–2009 was about 3.5 per cent (see IMF, 2010, p. 62). According to the OECD database[16], the combined TFP drop of the years 2008 and 2009 sums up to 4.6 per cent. We therefore choose a reduction in TFP by 4.5 per cent from 1 to 0.955. We shall discuss two types of shock. In the first case we assume that the decline in TFP is both unanticipated and permanent. In the second case we assume that after its initial unanticipated drop, TFP gradually recovers over time and eventually reverts back to its original benchmark level, $\bar{A} = 1$.

A permanent TFP shock

In our scenario of a permanent TFP shock, in equation (6.6b) we set $A(0) = 0.955$ and $\bar{A} = 0.955$, so that the TPF drop is permanent and there are no dynamics in total factor productivity. Table 6.3 reports short-run and long-run effects of that shock.

Figure 6.1 illustrates the time paths of key economic variables arising from the TFP shock, where the consumption–capital ratio c, leisure L, labour l, the output–capital ratio y, and the wage–capital ratio ω are illustrated relative to their initial benchmark values. The solid lines depict the dynamics in case of a permanent shock. On impact, the TFP decline reduces output and the marginal productivities of labour and capital by the same percentage amount (4.5 per cent). This is because both labour and capital are sluggish variables and cannot change at time $t = 0$ when the shock hits the economy. Despite the fact that the marginal product of labour declines on impact, the wage rate remains constant, reflecting the fact that wage adjustment is also a sluggish process. Households, being rational, foresee the economy's evolution and know that the TFP shock is permanent. This causes a negative wealth effect, and as a consequence they reduce consumption on impact by roughly 7.9 per cent. Lower consumption in turn increases the marginal rate of substitution between consumption and leisure, and households seek to reduce their leisure time. In fact, households increase their search for jobs by roughly 2/3 percentage points. This is because households wish to work more to reduce the income losses due to the TFP shock, so as to be able to keep consumption as high as possible. More formally, the value of a job, γ, increases by more than four times, as the marginal utility of wealth increases on impact (see equation (6.5)). The higher shadow value of employment induces households to spend more of their time searching for a job (see equation (6.4)).[17] The increase in search raises the unemployment rate by roughly 2.15 percentage points on impact and the unemployment rate jumps up to 8.98 per cent.[18]

The initial reduction in consumption and the other demand components (government purchases and vacancy costs) outweigh the drop in output, leading to an initially slightly higher rate of capital accumulation, so that the growth rate of capital, ψ_K, increases on impact to roughly 0.08 per cent. On the other hand, together with the 4.5 per cent drop in the level of GDP, the instantaneous growth rate of output falls to roughly -0.075 per cent, implying that the economy will shrink. This is because as the marginal product of labour drops on impact, but the wage remains constant, firms find it less profitable to hire labour, and they cut back job openings sharply. Despite the fact that households search more for a job, they encounter fewer open positions, and employment falls during the initial stage of transition. The employment reduction outweighs the effect of the slightly increased rate of capital accumulation, and output shrinks. The growth rate of public capital falls to roughly -0.3 per cent, since, according to the policy rule $G_K = g_K Y$, the

Table 6.3 Effects of TPF shock – permanent and temporary: $A(0) = 0.955$

	$\Delta UR(0)$	$\bar{U}R_1$	$\Delta L(0)$	$\Delta s(0)$	$\Delta \tilde{L}$	$\Delta \tilde{I}$	$\Delta C(0)$	$\Delta\left(\dfrac{\tilde{C}_1}{\tilde{Y}_1}\right)$	$\dfrac{\tilde{K}_{G1}}{\tilde{K}_1}$ $\tilde{\psi}_0$	$\dfrac{\tilde{B}_1}{\tilde{Y}_1}$	$\tilde{\psi}_1$	$\Delta W(0)$	$\Delta \tilde{W}$
	(pp)	(%)	(pp)	(pp)	(pp)	(pp)	(%)	(pp)	(%)	(%)	(%)	(%)	(%)
Permanent shock	2.1594	6.787	−0.6605	0.6605	−0.0715	0.0770	−7.8970	−0.1102	0.2072 0.0358	124.95	−0.1897	−5.9669	−10.312
Temporary shock	1.0406	6.824	−0.3144	0.3144	0	0	−7.4852	0	0.2112 0.0358	121.13	0.0358	−4.8597	−6.7900

Note: The changes in the unemployment rate, leisure, labour, and unemployment (search s), and the consumption–output ratio are reported as percentage points (pp) of fraction of time. The change in initial consumption is reported in per cent. $\Delta W(0)$ is the instantaneous change in welfare and $\Delta \tilde{W}$ is the change in intertemporal welfare, all denoted in per cent.

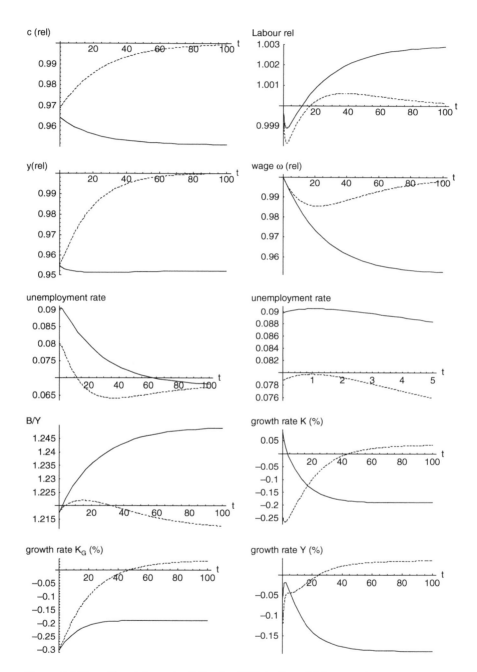

Figure 6.1 Transitional dynamics following TFP decline of 4.5 per cent.

government reduces public investment expenditures. The instantaneous welfare loss of the TFP shock amounts to 5.97 per cent.[19]

During the first phase of the transition, faster capital accumulation raises the output growth rate, as well as the growth rate of public capital. However, the output-capital ratio declines. Since the growth rate of private capital is higher than in the initial (benchmark) state, the marginal product of labour increases. This tends to increase the target wage, w_N, and this reduces the downward pressure on wages. The value of a job falls, which – viewed in isolation – reduces search. But this effect is more than compensated for by falling labour, which, viewed in isolation, increases search one to one (see equation (6.4)). Summing up all partial effects on search, search increases, and this – together with falling labour – raises the unemployment rate $s/(s+l)$ further. Intuitively, in times when the wage is still high, it would pay to have a job to take advantage of the currently still high wage rather than to find a job later, when the wage is already lower, and this provides a strong incentive to search for a job, thus contributing to the increase in the unemployment rate.

Approximately one year after the shock, the unemployment rate reaches its maximum during transition, and slightly exceeds 9 per cent. From thereon, it starts to fall gradually. The reason is simple: the value of a job falls sharply during the first year of transition, and this reduces the incentive to search. Households recognize that on average their increased search for jobs is not successful. They become discouraged and reduce their search efforts, which translates to a falling unemployment rate. After roughly two years, the growth rate of GDP, albeit still negative, reaches its maximum, and shortly after (after 2.25 years), labour employed reaches its minimum.

The growth rate of private capital falls monotonically over time, as does the wage–capital ratio. As the latter falls, thus reducing the cost of labour, firms are willing to post more jobs. More searching agents are thus matched with open positions, which increases labour over time. On the other hand, the value of a job continues to decline, and households reduce their search further. More labour and less search in turn reduce the unemployment rate over time. The growth rate of public capital remains negative and the growth rate of capital continues to fall and becomes negative after roughly four years. Slower capital accumulation (in fact, it is a decumulation) slows down GDP growth. This induces households to spend relatively less, reducing the consumption–capital ratio further. After roughly 11.5 years, labour is back at its benchmark level, increasing further thereafter.

Eventually, the economy reaches a new balanced growth path, which exhibits the following characteristics. The steady-state growth rate has fallen and is now −0.19 per cent. The consumption–output ratio is −0.11 percentage points lower, and labour is slightly higher than in the benchmark scenario (+0.077 percentage points of time). Leisure is 0.0715 percentage points lower. The new steady-state unemployment rate is marginally lower (6.787 per cent) than it was originally. The change in intertemporal welfare is substantial: the intertemporal welfare loss sums up to 10.312 per cent.

It is also of interest to discuss briefly the dynamics of the debt–GDP ratio. On impact, because of the sharp drop in GDP, the debt–GDP ratio jumps up from 116 per cent to 121.7 per cent. Thereafter, the debt–GDP ratio increases monotonically and eventually converges to 125 per cent. During the transition, the government runs a higher deficit-GDP ratio than admissible if the debt–GDP ratio is to remain constant, and this raises the debt–GDP ratio. The reason is that the time path of tax revenues became lower due to the shock, compared to the time path of expenditures. We should also stress that if the government were to keep the ratio of (net) lump-sum transfers to GDP $(-\tau = -T/Y)$ constant, the public debt would not be sustainable, and the ratio of debt to GDP would explode. It is therefore necessary to reduce the lump sum transfer–GDP ratio from -11.68 per cent to -11.25 per cent, given the tax rates, or alternatively to increase some tax rates or cut some expenditures.

A temporary TFP shock

We now investigate the second type of TFP shock. We assume again that on impact TFP drops by 4.5 per cent to $A(0) = 0.955$, *but* that the long run TFP level remains constant at $\bar{A} = 1$. TFP thus follows the monotonic dynamic, in accordance with equation (6.6b), and ultimately returns to its benchmark level. Table 6.3 contains the impact and long-run reactions of some key economic variables. The dynamics are illustrated by the dashed paths in Figure 6.1.

The impact reactions of output and the debt–GDP ratio are the same as in case of a permanent shock. The value of a job again increases, but much more moderately than for the permanent shock: it increases by 40 per cent relative to the benchmark. Households therefore increase search less than in case of the permanent shock, which – given sluggish labour – leads to an instantaneous jump of the unemployment rate by 1.04 percentage points to 7.87 per cent. The initial reaction of consumption is also moderated (-7.49 per cent). The short-run responses of the growth rates of capital and GDP contrast sharply with those obtained for a permanent reduction in TFP. As the output drop is the same as in case of a permanent shock, but the consumption response is moderated, the supply-side effect outweighs the demand reduction, and net investment becomes negative. The growth rate of capital falls to -0.3 per cent, and output growth becomes -0.17 per cent. The reason for this drop is the same as for a permanent shock.

As time passes, total factor productivity gradually increases, and this leads to a slow recovery of the economy. Eventually, the economy returns to its benchmark steady state and grows at the same rate as prior to the shock. In the long run, there is thus no growth effect, but only a level effect, as the balanced growth path is located at a lower level.

Of particular interest are the dynamics of the unemployment rate. One year after the shock it reaches its maximum of 8 per cent, it declines thereafter, and converges non-monotonically back to its benchmark level. After 15 years, it reaches its pre-shock level, but continues to decline, until after roughly 37 years it reaches

Table 6.4 Italy's unemployment rate 2008–2010

I 2008	*II* 2008	*III* 2008	*IV* 2008	*I* 2009	*II* 2009	*III* 2009	*IV* 2009	*I* 2010	*II* 2010	*III* 2010	*IV* 2010
6.5	6.9	6.9	7.3	7.5	8.0	8.3	8.5	8.5	8.3	8.4	8.2

its minimum during transition (roughly 6.4 per cent). Thereafter, it increases back to its long-run level (6.82 per cent).

The debt–GDP dynamics are non-monotonic, too. After the impact increase to 121.7 per cent, during roughly the first 15 years it increases to 122.2 per cent and falls than back to its new and higher long-run level (121.1 per cent). Again, without any change in tax rates or expenditures, the evolution of the government's budget and debt would be unsustainable. The government has to change the (net) lump-sum transfer-GDP ratio to 11.4825 per cent or to adjust other tax rates or reduce expenditures to remain intertemporally solvent.

Italy's seasonally adjusted quarterly unemployment rate over the period 2008–2010, taken from Istat, Italy's national statistics institute, is summarized in Table 6.4. It is characterized by an increase of two percentage points over the first two years, followed by a gradual decline of 0.3 percentage points during 2010. Taking into account that, of course, the TFP drop was not the only shock which hit the Italian economy during the years 2008–2009, we feel that the calibrated model gives rise to dynamics of the unemployment rate that mirror quite nicely the inverted U-shape exhibited by the data. Moreover, while both the permanent and temporary TFP shock generate unemployment dynamics of this shape, we think that the latter does a better job of tracking the Italian experience over the immediate period 2008–2010, following the global financial crisis. In 2011 the so-called Euro crisis hit Italy and resulted in a sharp increase in the unemployment rate and the debt–GDP ratio. Whereas in 2010 and 2011 the debt–GDP ratio was 119.3 per cent and 120.8 per cent, respectively, close to what our model predicts, in 2012 and 2013 the ratio soared to 127 per cent and 130.6 per cent, respectively.[20]

Conclusion

This paper has introduced search unemployment, coupled with wage bargaining, into an endogenous growth model to analyse the effects of a permanent and a temporary negative total factor productivity shock on growth, unemployment, and public debt. Motivated by the recent Italian experience as a result of the global financial crisis, we have calibrated the model to approximate that economy and found that both the permanent and the temporary TFP shock have long-lasting effects on the unemployment rate and on growth and debt dynamics. Overall, the dynamics generated by the model in response to a temporary TPF shock does a credible job in describing the Italian economy's performance in the immediate aftermath of the crisis and is particularly successful in tracking the time path of the unemployment rate.

The temporary negative TFP shock increases the unemployment rate for several years, paralyses the economy in terms of growth, and raises the public debt–GDP ratio. Despite the fact that the balanced growth rate is unchanged, the shock nonetheless has level effects, as, after transition, the economy evolves along a lower balanced growth path and a shows a higher debt–GDP ratio. Moreover, the shock requires some fiscal adjustment to maintain the government's long-run solvency. Our paper thus contributes to the explanation what happened to Italy during the years of the global financial crisis and underlines that fiscal adjustments are necessary to finance the government budget in the long run.

Notes

1 This paper was written to honor the 65th birthday of Neri Salvadori, a good friend and a fine scholar, who has made important contributions to the study of economic growth and to sponsoring research in this area. Research on this project began in January 2014 when Schubert was visiting the University of Washington. Schubert's research stay was financed by the Free University of Bozen-Bolzano. Turnovsky's research was supported in part by the Van Voorhis endowment at the University of Washington.

2 Over the period 2006–2013 the government debt–GDP ratio for Italy evolved as follows: 2006: 106.3 per cent, 2007: 103.3 per cent, 2008:106.1 per cent, 2009: 116.4 per cent, 2010: 119.3 per cent, 2011: 120.8 per cent, 2012: 127.0 per cent, 2013: 130.6 per cent, see IMF (2013), Statistical Table 4.

3 As one of the few exceptions, Petrosky-Nadeau (2010) comes to the opposite conclusion that TFP increased after the 2008 financial crisis.

4 See Pissarides (2000) for an overview.

5 At a first glance, this 'small' drop may seem negligible, but over time this accumulates to strong long-run effects.

6 Following Shi and Wen (1997, 1999) and Heer (2003), the job destruction rate is assumed to be exogenous to not further complicate the model. Moreover, as discussed in Pissarides (2000, Ch. 2), the dynamics with an endogenous job destruction rate are similar to those derived in a model where the job separation rate is exogenous.

7 See Pissarides (1987), who states that 'it is reasonable to assume that the cost of a vacancy is a constant fraction of output to avoid the implication that as output per job grows the cost of hiring labour becomes less and less important.'

8 The conventional assumption where labour is paid its marginal product corresponds to $\pi = 1$ when firms have all the bargaining power.

9 Recently, Papageorgiou (2008), using a new empirical methodology and a new data set, estimated an elasticity of substitution of roughly 0.7. Other recent studies suggesting that the Cobb–Douglas function overstates the elasticity of substitution include Antras (2004), and Klump *et al.* (2007).

10 The statistical definitions of government consumption and capital formation differ from the variables G_C and G_K.

11 Of course, the Italian tax system is much more complicated (e.g., the personal income tax is progressive with stepwise flat rates), but this number fits well on average.

12 Until the beginning of 2012 the Italian VAT was 20 per cent.

13 In 2009, the benefit was 60 per cent of the average gross earnings received over the last three months for the first six months, 50 per cent for the following two months, 40 per cent for the remaining period (for recipients aged over 50). The maximum amount of the benefit was Euro 886.31 per month, raised to Euro 1,065.26 for gross earnings exceeding Euro 1.917,48 per month. See OECD (2009).

14 See World Bank, http://data.worldbank.org/indicator/NE.CON.PETC.ZS?page=1, accessed 9 September 2014.
15 This follows from setting $\dot{l} = 0$ in equation (6.2), solving for $s = l\zeta/\phi$, inserting this in the definition of the unemployment rate $UR = s/(l + s)$, and multiplying numerator and denominator by ϕ/l.
16 See http://stats.oecd.org/Index.aspx?DataSetCode=MFP, accessed 9 January 2014.
17 The positive effect of the higher value of a job outweighs the negative effect of the increased marginal utility of wealth.
18 We should keep in mind that the unemployment rate generated by the model does not necessarily correspond with the officially reported rate, because in the model, unemployment is defined as searching for a job, whereas in official statistics several criteria have to be fulfilled to be counted as unemployed. 'An unemployed person is defined by Eurostat, according to the guidelines of the International Labour Organization, as: someone aged 15 to 74 (in Italy, Spain, the United Kingdom, Iceland, Norway: 16 to 74); without work during the reference week; available to start work within the next two weeks (or has already found a job to start within the next three months); actively having sought employment at some time during the last four weeks. The unemployment rate is the number of unemployed persons as a percentage of the labour force.' (See Eurostat, 2011, p. 679–680.)
19 The change in the welfare measure in equation (6.2) is expressed in terms of equivalent variations in the permanent flow of consumption necessary to equate the initial levels of welfare to what they would be following the shock and policies, both in the short run and in the long run.
20 The data are from IMF (2013), Statistical Table 4.

References

Antras, P. (2004). Is the US aggregate production function Cobb–Douglas? New estimates of the elasticity of substitution. *Contributions to Macroeconomics* 4(1): article 4.

Barro, R. J. (1990). Government spending in a simple model of endogenous growth. *Journal of Political Economy* 98(5): S103–S125.

Bom, P. and Ligthart, J. (2013). What have we learned from three decades of research on the productivity of public capital? *Journal of Economic Surveys* 28(5): 889–916.

Chatterjee, S. and Turnovsky, S. J. (2012). Infrastructure and inequality. *European Economic Review* 56(8): 1730–1745.

Cole, H. L., Ohanian, L. E. and Leung, R. (2005). Deflation and the international great depression: A productivity puzzle. *NBER Working Paper 11237*.

Estevão, M. and Severo, T. (2010). Financial shocks and TFP growth. *IMF Working Paper WP/10/23*.

Eurostat (2011). *Europe in Figures – Eurostat Yearbook 2011*. European Commission, Luxembourg, doi:10.2785/12017.

Futagami, K. Morita, Y. and Shibata, A. (1993). Dynamic analysis of an endogenous growth model with public capital. *Scandinavian Journal of Economics* 95(4): 607–625.

Hall, R. E. (2005a). Employment efficiency and sticky wages: Evidence from flows in the labor market. *Review of Economics and Statistics* 87(3): 397–407.

Hall, R. E. (2005b). Employment fluctuations with equilibrium wage stickiness. *American Economic Review* 95(1): 50–65.

Haugh, D., Ollivaud, P. and Turner, D. (2009). The macroeconomic consequences of banking crises in OECD countries. *OECD Economics Department Working Papers, No. 683, OECD Publishing*, doi:10.1787/226123651438.

Heer, B. (2003). Welfare costs of inflation in a dynamic economy with search unemployment. *Journal of Economic Dynamics and Control* 28(2): 255–272.

IMF (2009). *World Economic Outlook, October 2009, Sustaining the Recovery*. International Monetary Fund, Washington, DC.

IMF (2010). Italy: 2010 article IV consultation – staff report; public information notice on the executive board discussion; staff statement; statement by the executive director for Italy. *IMF Country Report No. 10/157.*

IMF (2013). *FiscalMonitor April 2013. Fiscal Adjustment in an Uncertain World.* International Monetary Fund, Washington, DC.

Istat (2013). The annual report 2013 – the state of the nation – summary. *Istituto Nazionale di Statistica*, http://www.istat.it/en/files/2013/07/Sintesi_Rapp_Annuale_inglese.pdf, accessed 25 August 2014.

Klump, R., McAdam, P. and Willman, A. (2007). Factor substitution and factor augmenting technical progress in the United States: A normalized supply-side system approach, *Review of Economics and Statistics* 89(1): 183–192.

Meza, F. and Quintin, E. (2005). Financial crises and total factor productivity. *Federal Reserve Bank of Dallas Working Paper 0105.*

Mortensen, D. T. and Pissarides, C. A. (1994). Job creation and job destruction in the theory of unemployment. *Review of Economic Studies* 61(3): 397–415.

OECD (2009). Country chapter for OECD series benefits and wages – Italy, www.oecd.org/els/social/workincentives, last accessed 30 November 2015.

OECD (2013). *Taxing Wages 2013*. OECD Publishing, http://dx.doi.org/10.1787/tax_wages-2013-en, last accessed 30 November 2015.

Papageorgiou, C. (2008). Comment on 'unwrapping some euro area growth puzzles: Factor substitution, productivity and unemployment'. *Journal of Macroeconomics* 30(2): 667–670.

Petrosky-Nadeau (2010). TFP during a credit crunch: The macroeconomics of credit and job destruction. *GSIA Working Papers 2010–E70.*

Pissarides, C. A. (1986). Unemployment and vacancies in Britain. *Economic Policy* 1(3): 499–559.

Pissarides, C. A. (1987). Search, wage bargains and cycles. *Review of Economic Studies* 54(3): 473–483.

Pissarides, C. A. (2000). *Equilibrium Unemployment Theory*. MIT Press, Cambridge, Massachusetts, second edition.

Ríos-Rull, J.-V. (1996). Life-cycle economies and aggregate fluctuations. *Review of Economic Studies* 63(3): 465–489.

Romer, P. M. (1986). Increasing returns and long-run growth. *Journal of Political Economy* 94: 1002–1037.

Schubert, S. F. (2011). The effects of total factor productivity and export shocks on a small open economy with unemployment. *Journal of Economic Dynamics and Control* 35(9): 1514–1530.

Shi, S. and Wen, Q. (1997). Labor market search and capital accumulation: Some analytical results. *Journal of Economic Dynamics and Control* 21(10): 1747–1776.

Shi, S. and Wen, Q. (1999). Labor market search and the dynamic effects of taxes and subsidies. *Journal of Monetary Economics* 43(2): 457–495.

Part 2

Resource economics

7   A Ricardian model of forestry

Silvia Faggian and Giuseppe Freni

Introduction

Ricardo's *Principles* contain just a single reference to forestry, as a whole, although in a well-known and remarkable passage in Chapter II, 'On Rent'. There, a rigorous notion of *rent* is introduced, and Adam Smith is criticized for using the term in an inconsistent way:

> Adam Smith [. . .] tells us that the demand for timber, and its consequent high price, in the more southern countries of Europe, caused a rent to be paid for forests in Norway, which could before afford no rent. Is it not however evident, that the person who paid, what he thus calls rent, paid it in consideration of the valuable commodity which was then standing on the land, and that he actually repaid himself with a profit, by the sale of the timber? If, indeed, after the timber was removed, any compensation were paid to the landlord for the use of the land, for the purpose of growing timber or any other produce, with a view to future demand, such compensation might justly be called rent, because it would be paid for the productive powers of the land; but in the case stated by Adam Smith, the compensation was paid for the liberty of removing and selling the timber, and not for the liberty of growing it.
>
> (Ricardo, 1951, p. 68)

Then Ricardo seems to contemplate two different possible effects of a higher demand for timber: the extension of forestry to new lands on a permanent basis, which could lead to the rise of the rents paid on these lands, and a temporary rise of timber production due to the extraction of timber from standing trees. In two recent insightful papers, Kurz and Salvadori (Kurz and Salvadori, 2009, 2011) emphasize the second effect, arguing that the above passage constitutes the basis of Ricardo's analysis of exhaustible resources. Then, following Marshall's advice to interpret Ricardo 'more generously than he himself interpreted Adam Smith' (Marshall, 1920, p. 813), they conclude that 'royalties are there in Ricardo's analysis, but they are not easily identifiable as such' (Kurz and Salvadori, 2009, p. 69), and that although the Hotelling rule is not yet to be found in Ricardo, it is not inconsistent with his analysis. In this paper, we set up and begin exploring a 'Ricardian' model, where abandoning, exhausting or replanting trees grown on lands of different quality are economic decisions depending on the parameters of the model. Therefore, the model we develop should accommodate both of the effects that Ricardo envisaged. Since a competitive equilibrium with sustained timber production involves a rotation period that is determined by means of the so-called 'Faustmann formula' (after Faustmann, 1849), which was probably unknown to Ricardo[1], our model is a rational reconstruction of Ricardo's scant remarks on forestry, enriched by the tools of modern theoretical literature on optimal forest management.

We recall that optimal forest management has developed since the late 1970s following Samuelson's review paper (Samuelson, 1976), and mainly focuses on the dynamics of forest rotation on a fully occupied plot of land, where new trees are immediately replanted after old trees are cut (see, e.g., Mitra and Wan, 1985, 1986; Salo and Tahvonen, 2002, 2003; Khan and Piazza, 2012; Fabbri *et al.*, 2015). Immediate replanting and continuous full occupation of the land are justified by the assumptions that cutting and replanting costs are null and that the productive life of trees is finite. Hence such a basic model is not suitable to handle spatial expansion (or contraction) of forest cultivation: a higher demand for timber simply results in a higher timber price with unchanged production.

To extend the model, we assume positive labour production costs as in Samuelson (1976) and add the Marshallian assumption that the wage rate in terms of the numeraire is given and independent of timber price. Although very specific, this assumption enables a framework in which Marshallian partial equilibrium analysis can be performed. In return, this seems to be the simplest way to shape spatial development without turning the Mitra–Wan model into an explicit multisectoral general equilibrium model.[2]

Making timber a renewable resource that cannot be exhausted, the basic Mitra–Wan model also tends to conceal the fact that optimal forest management implicitly generates dual variables governed by Hotelling-like rules. As pointed out by Salant (2013) in a recent attempt to study the equilibrium price path of timber, this fact is hardly overlooked in settings in which exhaustion is contemplated. Indeed, Salant (2013) used an extreme framework, where replanting costs are infinite, to stress the fact that if a forest is not exploited instantaneously then, at equilibrium, a Hotelling-like rule must hold as the extractor has to be indifferent whether to harvest trees immediately or later. The same kind of phenomena re-emerge in our Ricardian model whenever cutting is cost minimizing but replanting is not viable at the equilibrium prices. However, it will turn out that Hotelling-like rules are relevant in general in equilibrium forest management: indeed, it is competitive arbitrage inducing Hotelling-like asset-market-clearing conditions for aging assets such as trees.

In what follows, we concentrate on long-run equilibria, making only cursory reference to the more challenging problem of the structure of transitional dynamics, as a proper analytical treatment of our model with non-zero production costs, even if limited to the stationary states, can hardly be carried out without a deep study of the dual price system. Therefore, the extension of the basic model has, as a (methodological) side effect, the shift of focus from the quantity side to the price side of the system. According to Salant (2013), this shift is long overdue in literature both for the study of the equilibrium price system – still largely unknown – and as a first step towards the analysis of models in which externalities or other distortions are present.[3]

In building our Ricardian model, we borrow the continuous-time production structure of Fabbri *et al.* (2015), instead of using the original discrete-time Mitra–Wan formulation. The continuous-time model is mathematically more challenging than the discrete-time counterpart for two reasons: (a) the evolution of state variables is governed by a partial differential equation, as they represent a continuum of (vintage) capital goods: trees of different ages; (b) since cost minimization and competitive arbitrage imply that cutting trees is profitable only at a finite set of ages, distributed controls concentrating on single points need be allowed. Hence, in order for the model to be endowed with meaningful price-supported stationary states, intensity levels of the production processes need to be chosen in a very large space (a space of measures). However, once the technical difficulties are overcome (see Fabbri *et al.*, 2015), the clear distinction between stock and flow variables, which is lacking in discrete time (see Foley, 1975), turns into an advantage in the interpretation of the price system: the theory of long-run production prices and the role of the Hotelling rule become transparent.

The paper is organized as follows. The continuous-time Ricardian forestry model is introduced in the next section. In the third section, modified golden rules of the system are studied. The long-run timber supply curve is built in the fourth section, where also some comparative static analysis is presented. The fifth section concludes.

A Ricardian model of forestry

A number N of lands, with $N \geq 1$, are available for forest cultivation with the purpose of extracting a single final good: timber. The lands have sizes given by the coordinates of the positive vector $[h_1, h_2, \ldots, h_N]$, and $x_i(t, s)$ represents the part of land i, $i \in I \equiv \{1, 2, \ldots, N\}$, covered at time t by trees of a certain age s, with $t \geq 0, s \geq 0$. At any time t and for any land i, trees of any age s can be harvested and new saplings can be produced and planted on the land. Let $c_i(t, s)$ be the intensity of cut at time t of trees of age s on land i, and $y_i(t)$ the corresponding rate of production of new saplings. Given an N-tuple of initial distributions $x_i(0, s), i \in I$, the evolution of the system is described by the following set of transport equations and boundary conditions:

$$\begin{cases} \dfrac{\partial x_i}{\partial t}(t, s) = -\dfrac{\partial x_i}{\partial s}(t, s) - c_i(t, s) & t > 0, \ \ s > 0, \ \ i \in I \\[2mm] x_i(t, 0) = y_i(t) & t \geq 0, \ \ i \in I \end{cases} \tag{7.1}$$

where the variation of density $\frac{\partial x_i}{\partial t}(t, s)$ is due to aging of trees $-\frac{\partial x_i}{\partial s}(t, s)$, and to harvesting $-c_i(t, s)$. Note that the boundary conditions require that the numbers of saplings of age zero planted at time t on the different lands equal the amounts produced $y_i(t)$. In addition, we require the strategy couples $(c_i(t, s), y_i(t))$ to be non-negative, that is

$$c_i(t, s) \geq 0 \quad \text{and} \quad y_i(t) \geq 0 \quad \forall t \geq 0, \quad s \geq 0, \quad i \in I, \tag{7.2}$$

and the trajectories to satisfy the following pure state constraints:

$$\int_0^{+\infty} x_i(t, s)ds \leq h_i \quad \text{and} \quad x_i(t, s) \geq 0 \quad \forall t \geq 0, \quad s \geq 0, \quad i \in I \tag{7.3}$$

that is, the occupied portion of the land i equals at most the land extension, and the trees density is non-negative for all time, ages and lands. Consider now the timber extraction technology. Let $f_i(s)$ be the rate of timber production ensuing from a unitary harvesting ($f_i(s)$ is the *productivity* of a tree of age s on land i) and let $l_i(s)$, $l_i(s) > 0$ be the corresponding unitary cutting cost. Summing up the amounts $f_i(s)c_i(t, s)ds$ of timber extracted from trees of ages s on lands i at time t, we obtain the total timber $q(t)$ harvested at time t

$$q(t) \equiv \sum_{i=1}^N q_i(t) \equiv \sum_{i=1}^N \int_0^\infty c_i(t, s) f_i(s)ds. \tag{7.4}$$

Similarly, total harvesting costs at time t are given by

$$\sum_{i=1}^N \int_0^\infty c_i(t, s)l_i(s)ds. \tag{7.5}$$

Note that costs and productivities are assumed independent from the harvesting rates only for the sake of simplicity. Two additional less innocuous assumptions are the following:

(HC1) $l_i(s) \equiv \bar{l}_i$ (unit cutting costs are age-independent);

(HC2) f_i concave, $f_i \geq 0$, $f_i(0) = 0$, and there exists $\bar{s}_i > 0$ such that $f_i(s) = f_i(\bar{s}_i) = f_i^a > 0$ for each $s \geq \bar{s}_i > 0$, and $f_i(s) < f_i^a$ for $s \in (0, \bar{s}_i)$ (in particular, trees not younger than $\bar{s}_i$ are equally productive).

Note that this implies that $f_i(s)$ is strictly increasing in $[0, \bar{s}_i)$. For the sake of simplicity, we also assume that each f_i is strictly concave in $[0, \bar{s}_i]$ and differentiable in $(0, +\infty)$, see Figure 7.1.[4]

One of the main implications of (HC1) and (HC2) is that, in each land i, trees not younger than $\bar{s}_i$ can be aggregated into a single state variable $a_i(t)$ whose evolution is given by the ordinary differential equation

$$\dot{a}_i(t) = x_i(t, \bar{s}_i) - c_i^a(t), \quad i \in I, \quad t > 0 \tag{7.6}$$

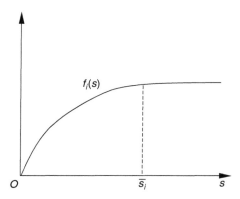

Figure 7.1 Productivity function.

where

$$a_i(t) = \int_{\bar{s}_i}^{+\infty} x_i(t, s)ds \quad \text{and} \quad c_i^a(t) = \int_{\bar{s}_i}^{+\infty} c_i(t, s)ds. \tag{7.7}$$

Clearly, if $x_i(t, \bar{s}_i) = 0$ for $t \geq 0$ then the wood in old trees on a given land i can be interpreted as the stock of an exhaustible resource in a specific deposit. To complete the description of the technology, we assume linear saplings production costs and write b_i, $b_i > 0$ for the average (and marginal) cost in producing a sapling suitable to be planted on land i. We further assume that planting costs are null *sensu stricto*. Total planting costs at time t are then

$$\sum_{i=1}^{N} y_i(t)b_i. \tag{7.8}$$

Moreover we assume the demand of timber at price $p_q(t)$, is given by the demand function $D(p_q(t))$, which is taken to be continuous and non-increasing for all $p_q(t) > 0$,[5] and that the interest rate r, $r > 0$ is exogenously given and constant.[6] Since there are constant returns to scale and production is studied under competitive conditions, without loss of generality we may consider a single producer owning all means of production specific of the timber sector who, taking the price path of timber as given, maximizes the discounted value of cash flows generated by selling the good and buying the non-specific factors of production. Using equation (7.7) both in the objective and in equations (7.1)–(7.5), we thus get the following control problem:

$$\text{Max} \int_0^{+\infty} e^{-rt} \left\{ p_q(t)q(t) - \sum_{i=1}^{N} \left[y_i(t)b_i + \bar{l}_i \left(\int_0^{\bar{s}_i} c_i(t, s)ds + c_i^a(t) \right) \right] \right\} dt \tag{7.9}$$

$$
\begin{cases}
\dfrac{\partial x_i}{\partial t}(t, s) + \dfrac{\partial x_i}{\partial s}(t, s) = -c_i(t, s) & i \in I, \quad s \in [0, \bar{s}_i], \\[2mm]
\dot{a}_i(t) = x_i(t, \bar{s}_i) - c_i^a(t) & i \in I, \\[2mm]
x_i(t, 0) = y_i(t) & i \in I, \\[2mm]
\displaystyle\int_0^{\bar{s}_i} x_i(t, s)ds + a_i(t) \leq h_i & i \in I, \\[2mm]
c_i(t, s) \geq 0 & i \in I, \quad s \in [0, \bar{s}_i], \\[2mm]
x_i(t, s) \geq 0 & i \in I, \quad s \in [0, \bar{s}_i], \\[2mm]
c_i^a(t) \geq 0 & i \in I, \\[2mm]
a_i(t) \geq 0 & i \in I, \\[2mm]
y_i(t, s) \geq 0 & i \in I, \\[2mm]
q(t) = \displaystyle\sum_{i=1}^{N}\left(\int_0^{\bar{s}_i} c_i(t, s) f_i(s)ds + c_i^a(t) f_i^a\right),
\end{cases}
\tag{7.10}
$$

where the initial conditions $x_i(0, s)$, $s \in [0, \bar{s}_i]$, and $a_i(0)$ for all $i \in I$, and the function $p_q(t)$ are given exogenously. We then define a competitive equilibrium as a price path $p_q(t)$ and a solution of the above control problem such that

$$
q(t) = D(p_q(t)). \tag{7.11}
$$

In the next sections, the focus will be the stationary solutions of problem (7.9)–(7.10) associated with any given stationary timber price path $p_q(t) = p_q^* \geq 0$. We will then use this analysis to characterize the *long-run timber supply curve* and hence to study the stationary competitive equilibria of the model. Various general remarks are here due. First, note that, except for the properties of the productivity function, the basic Mitra–Wan model in continuous-time in Fabbri et al. (2015) is recovered for $b_i = 0$, $l_i(s) = 0$, and for $N = 1$.[7,8] However, adding different lands in a single final good model (as the one in Fabbri et al., 2015) would not change much the structure of the stationary states. Since candidates for stationary equilibria are the strategy-trajectory components of the modified golden rules and, as for the Ramsey–Cass–Koopmans aggregate model, generically only a unique strategy-trajectory couple can belong to a modified golden rule of the model, the quantity of timber produced in a stationary equilibrium turns out to be independent from the demand of timber (see Mitra and Wan, 1985, Fabbri et al., 2015).[9] In this respect, what makes the extended model a two-final goods system is the introduction of the alternative numeraire good, while the two final goods sectors are interdependent because there are positive production costs on all lands.

Second, an infinite dimensional version of the second welfare theorem would be needed to link the solutions of problem (7.9)–(7.10) to competitive equilibria. However, a suitable maximum principle for our problem is technically challenging and at the moment the literature has not yet developed it, although a version of the second welfare theorem restricted to the stationary solutions has been provided by Fabbri *et al.* (2015) in continuous-time. In fact, we will show that a similar result holds for the extended model discussed here. Moreover, since the dual variables supporting a stationary solution of (7.9)–(7.10) are themselves stationary, they can be straightforwardly interpreted as the long-run production prices that would prevail at the rate of interest r.

Finally, a few preliminary observations on the types of steady states that can solve system (7.10):

(a) A stationary distribution $x_{i*}(, s)$ solving the state equation (7.1) is a non-increasing function of s, when replanting trees either on a part or on the whole land i^*. An example is provided next.

Example 7.1 Suppose $h_{i*} = 2$, $\bar{s}_{i*} = 3$, $c_{i*}(, s) = \frac{1}{2}$ for $s \in [0, 2)$ and $c_{i*}(, s) = 0$ for $s \in [2, 3]$, $a_{i*} = \frac{1}{2}$ (of course, $c_{i*}^a = 0$), and $x_{i*}(, 0) = y_{i*} = 1$. Since also $\int_0^{\bar{s}_{i*}} c_{i*}(, s) ds = 1$, that means that the above data are consistent with a stationary $x_{i*}(, s)$. Then integration of the state equation (7.1) gives the explicit form of the stationary distribution: $x_{i*}(, s) = \max(0; 1 - \frac{1}{2}s)$. Because in this steady state we have $\int_0^{\bar{s}_{i*}} x_{i*}(, s) ds = 1$; half of the land is continuously occupied by an 'uneven' cultivated forest. Of what is left, half is abandoned forest land, where old trees stand (i. e. $a_{i*} = \frac{1}{2}$), and half is bare land. □

(b) If a steady state $x_{i*}(, s)$ is optimal, with a positive aggregate steady state a_{i*}, then necessarily $x_{i*}(, s) = 0$ (for instance, the steady state in the previous example cannot be optimal). A formal proof of this result is given in the next section. Indeed, if it is optimal to incur cutting and replanting costs to sustain a stationary forest on part of a land, then it cannot be optimal leaving unextracted timber for which only cutting costs are due. Of course, if the timber extraction costs on land i^* are very high in comparison to timber price, then abandoned forest land is to be expected. Under these circumstances, the steady-state value of the aggregate state variable a_{i*} will belong to the interval $[0, h_{i*}]$, while what is left, $h_{i*} - a_{i*}$, will be bare land. But if timber extraction is optimal on land i^*, then $a_{i*} = 0$, and in this case, depending on the demand for timber and on replanting costs, $x_{i*}(, s)$ will be either positive or zero.

However, even if we had set $a_{i*} = 0$ in the stationary state of the above example, the resulting stationary state could not have been optimal for a subtle reason: since cutting activities are spread across a whole interval of ages, $x_{i*}(, s)$ is a strictly decreasing function for $s \in [0, 2]$. On the contrary, it turns out that optimal stationary cutting controls, if positive, are concentrated on a single age. This is the theme of the next section.

Modified golden rules

In this section we concentrate on the modified golden rules of the system. Given a stationary price of timber p_q^*, we formally define a modified golden rule as an N-tuples of couples $[(\bar{c}_i(, s), \bar{c}_i^a, \bar{y}_i, \bar{x}_i(, s), \bar{a}_i), (\bar{p}_i(, s), \bar{p}_i^a, \bar{p}_i^y, \bar{R}_i)]$, $\forall i \in I$, where $(\bar{c}_i(,s), \bar{c}_i^a, \bar{y}_i, \bar{x}_i(,s), \bar{a}_i)$, $s \in [0, \bar{s}_i]$, $\forall i \in I$ is a stationary N-tuples of strategy-trajectory couples that solve the state equations and satisfy the constraints in (7.10), and where the stationary N-tuples of prices for the different vintages of trees $(\bar{p}_i(,s), \bar{p}_i^a)$, $s \in [0, \bar{s}_i]$, $\forall i \in I$, the stationary N-tuples of sapling prices $\bar{p}_i^y$, $\forall i \in I$, and the stationary N-tuples of rent rates $\bar{R}_i$, $\forall i \in I$ are such that, at the given prices: (A) profits are maximized, (B) the markets for lands' services clear, (C) the asset-market-clearing conditions that hold under competitive arbitrage are satisfied. The focus is on modified golden rules because it turns out that their strategy-trajectory components are optimal solutions of problem (7.9)–(7.10) and, conversely, that any optimal stationary solution of problem (7.9)–(7.10) can be endowed with a stationary supporting price function.[10]

Consider now the implications of the above conditions (A), (B) and (C). First, observe that profit maximization and constant returns to scale imply null maximum profits both in cutting trees and in saplings production. Hence, the following inequalities must hold for all $i \in I$:

$$f_i(s)p_q^* \le \bar{p}_i(,s) + \bar{l}_i, \quad \bar{c}_i(,s)f_i(s)p_q^* = \bar{c}_i(,s)(\bar{p}_i(,s) + \bar{l}_i), \quad s \in [0, \bar{s}_i] \tag{7.12}$$

$$f_i^a p_q^* \le \bar{p}_i^a + \bar{l}_i, \quad \bar{c}_i^a f_i^a p_q^* = \bar{c}_i^a (\bar{p}_i^a + \bar{l}_i), \quad \bar{c}_i^a \ge 0, \tag{7.13}$$

$$\bar{p}_i^y \le b_i, \quad \bar{y}_i \bar{p}_i^y = \bar{y}_i b_i, \quad \bar{y}_i \ge 0, \tag{7.14}$$

$$\bar{c}_i(,s) \ge 0, \quad s \in [0, \bar{s}_i]; \tag{7.15}$$

where, in particular, the meaning of conditions (7.12) (7.13) and (7.15) is that no cutting process generates extra profits and that only processes with zero losses can be activated, whereas conditions (7.13) and (7.14) imply that sapling production can occur only if costs are covered.

Second, since lands are supplied inelastically, requirement (B) is satisfied if and only if the following conditions hold for all $i \in I$:

$$\int_0^{\bar{s}_i} \bar{x}_i(,s)ds + \bar{a}_i \le h_i \tag{7.16}$$

$$\bar{R}_i \left[\int_0^{\bar{s}_i} \bar{x}_i(,s)ds + \bar{a}_i \right] = \bar{R}_i h_i \tag{7.17}$$

$$\bar{R}_i \ge 0. \tag{7.18}$$

Finally, we note that standing trees are exhaustible resources, so the asset-market-clearing conditions must be instances of the Hotelling rule, even if, different from the standard case, two specific facts affect the precise structure of the price equations: (1) a rent rate is due to hold a tree of any age *in situ*, (2) young trees are subject to aging. Fact (1) implies that for each i the price of mature trees evolves according to

$$\dot{p}_i^a(t) \le rp_i^a(t) + R_i(t), \quad a_i(t)\dot{p}_i^a(t) = a_i(t)[rp_i^a(t) + R_i(t)]. \tag{7.19}$$

Hence, for the price of old trees on land i to be stationary at least one of the following systems must hold:[11]

$$0 = r\bar{p}_i^a + \bar{R}_i, \quad \bar{a}_i \geq 0, \tag{7.20}$$

or

$$0 \leq r\bar{p}_i^a + \bar{R}_i, \quad \bar{a}_i = 0. \tag{7.21}$$

On the other hand, fact (2) implies that if prices of young trees on different lands are stationary, then the Hotelling rule holds *across* ages.[12] Hence, for all $i \in I$ we have the following conditions:

$$\frac{d\bar{p}_i}{ds}(,s) \leq r\bar{p}_i(,s) + \bar{R}_i \quad s \in [0, \bar{s}_i] \tag{7.22}$$

$$\bar{x}_i(,s)\frac{d\bar{p}_i}{ds}(,s) = \bar{x}_i(,s)[r\bar{p}_i(,s) + \bar{R}_i] \quad s \in [0, \bar{s}_i] \tag{7.23}$$

$$\bar{x}_i(,s) \geq 0 \quad s \in [0, \bar{s}_i]. \tag{7.24}$$

Competitive arbitrage has a further implication: the price of a tree cannot jump up at junction points (otherwise there would be a rush to buy the asset just before it appreciates), while jumps down can occur only if no agent holds the asset (otherwise there would be a rush to sell the depreciating tree). This implies

$$\bar{p}_i(,0) \leq \bar{p}_i^y, \quad \bar{x}_i(,0)\bar{p}_i(,0) = \bar{x}_i(,0)\bar{p}_i^y, \tag{7.25}$$

and

$$\bar{p}_i(,\bar{s}) \geq \bar{p}_i^a, \quad \bar{x}_i(,\bar{s})\bar{p}_i(,\bar{s}) = \bar{x}_i(,\bar{s})\bar{p}_i^a, \tag{7.26}$$

for all $i \in I$. We now identify the modified golden rules of our Ricardian model. Since the system comprising the stationary versions of (7.10) and of the supporting price conditions (7.12)–(7.26) can be split into N independent systems, each referring to a single land, we state the results for a generic land i. We start from what was anticipated in the second section.

Proposition 7.2 *Assume* $(\bar{x}_i(,s), \bar{a}_i)$ *belong to a modified golden rule. Then:*

(i) $f_i^a p_q^* > \bar{l}_i \Longrightarrow \bar{a}_i = 0.$
(ii) $f_i^a p_q^* \leq \bar{l}_i \Longrightarrow \bar{x}_i(,s) = 0 \quad \forall s \in [0, \bar{s}_i].$

Moreover, if $f_i^a p_q^* \leq \bar{l}_i$, *then the strategy-trajectory couple* $\bar{c}_i(,s) = 0 \quad \forall s \in [0, \bar{s}_i]$, $\bar{c}_i^a = \bar{y}_i = 0$, $\bar{x}_i(,s) = 0 \quad \forall s \in [0, \bar{s}_i]$, $\bar{a}_i \in [0, h_i]$, *and the price system* $\bar{p}_i(,s) = 0 \quad \forall s \in [0, \bar{s}_i]$, $\bar{p}_i^y = \bar{p}_i^a = \bar{R}_i = 0$ *constitute a modified golden rule.*

Proof. For (i), note that $f_i^a p_q^* > \bar{l}_i$ and inequality (7.13) imply $\bar{p}_i^a > 0$, so (7.20) cannot hold and (7.21) holds instead. To prove (ii), assume by contradiction that $f_i^a p_q^* \leq \bar{l}_i$ and there exists an age s such that $\bar{x}_i(, s) > 0$. Since there is planting, i.e. $\bar{y}_i > 0$, then (7.14), and (7.25) imply $\bar{p}_i(, 0) = b_i$. Moreover, since stationary paths are non-increasing, there exists a maximum age $\hat{s}$ of standing trees on $[0, \bar{s}_i]$, more precisely, $\hat{s} \equiv \sup\{s \in [0, \bar{s}_i] : \bar{x}_i(, s) > 0\}$. Then (7.22) holds with equality up to age $\hat{s}$, implying

$$\bar{p}_i(, s) = b_i e^{rs} + \frac{\bar{R}_i}{r}(e^{rs} - 1) \quad s \in [0, \hat{s}] \tag{7.27}$$

so that $\bar{p}_i(, s) > 0$ for all $s \in [0, \hat{s}]$. Now, the productivity function is increasing from zero to maturity age, so that

$$f_i(s) p_q^* \leq f_i^a p_q^* < \bar{p}_i(, s) + \bar{l}_i \quad \forall s \in [0, \bar{s}_i].$$

From (7.12) one derives that no standing tree can be cut, implying $\dot{a}_i(t) > 0$, and hence a contradiction. Direct substitution of the candidate modified golden rule into inequalities (7.12)–(7.18), (7.20) and (7.26), with $\frac{\partial x_i}{\partial t}(t, s) = 0$ and $\dot{a}_i(t) = 0$ into system (7.10), gives the last claim. $\qquad\square$

Remark 7.3 Interpreting p_q^* as the choke-off price at which timber demand is nil, Proposition 7.2(i) is the standard result in theory of exhaustible resources that exhaustion of a deposit is optimal if the choke-off price is higher than the extraction cost. $\qquad\square$

It remains to be determined if forest cultivation takes place in the modified golden rules when $f_i^a p_q^* > \bar{l}_i$, and to find which technique is chosen if this occurs. If it does, proceeding as in the proof of Proposition 7.2(ii), one derives $\bar{p}_i(, s)$ given by (7.27). That, substituted into the no-extra profits condition (7.12) and rearranging terms, provides

$$\frac{f_i(s) p_q^* - b_i e^{rs} - \bar{l}_i}{e^{rs} - 1} \leq \frac{\bar{R}_i}{r} \quad s \in [0, \bar{s}_i). \tag{7.28}$$

Note also that, using (7.13) and (7.26), this last condition can be extended to the closed interval $[0, \bar{s}_i]$. So in the end, if forest cultivation takes place in a modified golden rule, (7.28) needs to be verified everywhere, and it has to hold with equality for at least an age $\hat{s}$ in the interval $[0, \bar{s}_i]$. Of course, whenever timber price is too low, a negative rent would be required to verify this condition, implying that forest cultivation is not profitable at that price.

This line of argument leads to the basic problem of the choice of technique, that is, finding the ages at which the land value $\bar{R}_i/r$ attains a minimum in the set of values that satisfy (7.28) or, equivalently, the ages that solve the Faustmann problem of maximizing 'the present discounted value of all net cash receipts [. . .]

calculated over the *infinite chain* of cycles of planting on the given acre of land from now until Kingdom Come' (Samuelson, 1976, p. 122), namely

$$V_i^F(s) = \sum_{n=1}^{\infty} e^{-rns} [f_i(s)p_q^* - b_i e^{rs} - \bar{l}_i] = \frac{f_i(s)p_q^* - b_i e^{rs} - \bar{l}_i}{e^{rs} - 1}. \tag{7.29}$$

This requirement, emerging in different forms in all forest management problems where replanting is possible, is also used here to characterize modified golden rules for timber prices greater than $\bar{l}_i / f_i^a$.

To begin with, since $V_i^F(s)$ is continuous in the interval $s \in [\lambda, \bar{s}_i]$ for all $0 < \lambda \le \bar{s}_i$ and $V_i^F(s) \to -\infty$ for $s \to 0_+$, the Faustmann problem has a solution for each $p_q^* \ge 0$. Moreover, the maximum value as a function of the timber price $M_i^F(p_q^*)$ is negative for low values of the price p_q^*, increasing with p_q^*, and eventually positive when p_q^* is sufficiently high. Therefore, we can define the 'break-through' price $\hat{p}_{qi}^*$ as the minimum timber price for which the maximum of the Faustmann function is non-negative.

Now note that $\hat{p}_{qi}^*$ is strictly greater than $\bar{l}_i / f_i^a$: for timber price levels that are only slightly higher than $\bar{l}_i / f_i^a$, even if cutting costs can be covered by waiting for new planted trees to reach maturity, forest cultivation still results in losses due to strictly positive planting costs. Hence, for all $p_q^* \in (\bar{l}_i / f_i^a, \hat{p}_{qi}^*)$,

$$\max_{s \in [0, \bar{s}_i]} [f_i(s)p_q^* - b_i e^{rs} - \bar{l}_i] < 0,$$

and it is easy to see that there exists $m_i(p_q^*)$, with $0 < m_i(p_q^*) < b_i$, such that

$$\max_{s \in [0, \bar{s}_i]} [f_i(s)p_q^* - m_i(p_q^*)e^{rs} - \bar{l}_i] = 0.$$

With this fact established, we are ready to characterize modified golden rules for $p_q^* \in (\bar{l}_i / f_i^a, \hat{p}_{qi}^*)$.

Proposition 7.4 *Assume* $p_q^* \in (\frac{\bar{l}_i}{f_i^a}, \hat{p}_{qi}^*)$ *and that* $(\bar{x}_i(, s), \bar{a}_i)$ *belongs to a modified golden rule. Then:*

(i) $\bar{x}_i(, s) = 0$, $\forall s \in [0, \bar{s}_i]$, *and* $\bar{R}_i = 0$.
(ii) *The strategy-trajectory couple* $\bar{c}_i(, s) = 0$, *for all* $s \in [0, \bar{s}_i]$, $\bar{c}_i^a = \bar{y}_i = 0$, $\bar{x}_i(, s) = 0$ *for all* $s \in [0, \bar{s}_i]$, $\bar{a}_i = 0$, *and the price system* $\bar{p}_i(, s) = m_i(p_q^*)e^{rs}$, *for all* $s \in [0, \bar{s}_i]$, $\bar{p}_i^y = m_i(p_q^*)$, $\bar{p}_i^a = m_i(p_q^*)e^{r\bar{s}_i}$, $\bar{R}_i = 0$ *constitute a modified golden rule.*

Proof. To prove (i), one may replicate the argument used to establish Proposition 7.3(ii). Assume by contradiction $\bar{x}_i(, s) > 0$ at an age s in $[0, \bar{s}_i]$, then both planting and cutting at some age have to occur. Hence there exists $\check{s} \in [0, \bar{s}_i]$ such that (7.28) holds as an equality at $s = \check{s}$. Since by assumption $V_i^F(\check{s}) < 0$, this contradicts the non-negativity of the rent rate. Hence $\bar{x}_i(,s) = 0$, for all $s \in [0, \bar{s}_i]$. Moreover, since $p_q^* > \bar{l}_i$ implies $\bar{a}_i = 0$, it is immediate from (7.16) and (7.17) that $\bar{R}_i = 0$.

To prove (ii), note that the strategy–trajectory couple in the candidate modified golden rule is a stationary solution of system (7.10) and that inequalities (7.12)–(7.18) and (7.21) are verified by the candidate price system. Finally, note that for our candidate modified golden rule inequalities (7.22), (7.25) and (7.26) hold as equalities. □

The next two propositions show that forest cultivation becomes profitable for $p_q^* \geq \hat{p}_{qi}^*$ and describe modified golden rules when $p_q^* = \hat{p}_{qi}^*$ and when $p_q^* > \hat{p}_{qi}^*$, respectively. But first, consider the Faustmann problem for $p_q^* \geq \hat{p}_{qi}^*$. A key fact is that the maximizer $s_i^F(p_q^*)$ is unique.[13] This is quite apparent from Figure 7.2, where we drew the graph of the function

$$g_i(s) := \frac{M_i^F(p_q^*)(e^{rs} - 1) + b_i e^{rs} + \bar{l}_i}{p_q^*} \tag{7.30}$$

along with the graph of the productivity function $f_i(s)$. Since $M_i^F(p_q^*) \geq 0$, $g_i(s)$ is a strictly convex increasing function, and this, together with the concavity of $f_i(s)$, implies uniqueness of the age that maximizes the Faustmann function (7.29). The implication of this fact is, as we will show, that forest cultivation in modified golden rules is characterized by a uniform density function on the cultivated land, with cutting concentrated at the Faustmann age. Formally, we will consider the uniform density functions given by

$$x_{\theta_i}^{U_i}(,s) := \frac{\theta_i h_i}{s_i^F(p_q^*)} \chi_{[0, s_i^F(p_q^*)]}(s), \tag{7.31}$$

where $\theta_i \in [0, 1]$ is the share of land i that is cultivated, in which all ages in the range $[0, s_i^F(p_q^*)]$ are uniformly distributed and equal to $\frac{\theta_i h_i}{s_i^F(p_q^*)}$, while those in the range $[s_i^F(p_q^*), \bar{s}_i]$ are null, and the cutting intensity vectors given by

$$c_{\theta_i}^{D_i}(,s) \equiv \frac{\theta_i h_i}{s_i^F(p_q^*)} \delta_{s_i^F(p_q^*)}, \tag{7.32}$$

where $\delta_{s_i^F(p_q^*)}$ is the Dirac delta at point $s_i^F(p_q^*)$, that is, the action undertaken by $c_{\theta_i}^{D_i}(,s)$ is cutting exactly the trees reaching age $s_i^F(p_q^*)$. Note that if $\theta_i > 0$, then $c_{\theta_i}^{D_i}(,s)$ is not a function of s but a positive measure.

Proposition 7.5 *Assume $p_q^* = \hat{p}_{qi}^*$. Then:*

(i) $\bar{R}_i = 0$ *for any modified golden rule. In addition, a strategy-trajectory couple belongs to a modified golden rule only if it has the following*

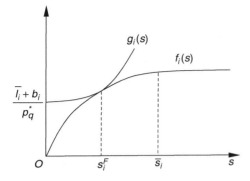

Figure 7.2 Uniqueness of $s_i^F(p_q^*)$.

form: $\bar{c}_i^a = \bar{a}_i = 0$, $\bar{x}_i(\,,s) = x_{\theta_i}^{U_i}(\,,s)$, $\bar{c}_i(\,,s) = c_{\theta_i}^{D_i}(\,,s)$ and $\bar{y}_i = \frac{\theta_i h_i}{s_i^F(\hat{p}_{qi}^*)}$, for any choice of $\theta_i \in [0, 1]$. Moreover, if $\theta_i > 0$, then $\bar{p}_i^y = b_i$, $\bar{p}_i(\,,s) = b_i e^{rs}$ for all $s \in [0, s_i^F(\hat{p}_{qi}^*)]$.

(ii)   The strategy-trajectory couple $\bar{x}_i(\,,s) = x_{\theta_i}^{U_i}(\,,s)$, $\bar{c}_i(\,,s) = c_{\theta_i}^{D_i}(\,,s)$ and $\bar{y}_i = \frac{\theta_i h_i}{s_i^F(p_q^*)}$, any $\theta_i \in [0, 1]$, $\bar{c}_i^a = \bar{a}_i = 0$, and the price system $\bar{p}_i(\,,s) = b_i e^{rs}$ for all $s \in [0, \bar{s}_i]$, $\bar{p}_i^y = b_i$, $\bar{p}_i^a = b_i e^{r\bar{s}_i}$, $\bar{R}_i = 0$ constitute a modified golden rule.

Proof. To prove (i), consider any modified golden rule. It is immediate from $\hat{p}_{qi}^* > \bar{l}_i$ that $\bar{c}_i^a = 0$ and $\bar{a}_i = 0$ hold. Then, if no planting occurs, $\bar{R}_i = 0$, as in Proposition 7.3. On the other hand, if $\bar{x}_i(\,,s) > 0$ for at least an age s in $[0, \bar{s}_i]$, then there exists $\check{s} \in [0, \bar{s}_i]$ such that (7.28) holds as an equality at $s = \check{s}$ and, since $V_i^F(s) < 0$ for all $s \in [0, \bar{s}_i] \setminus \{s_i^F(\hat{p}_{qi}^*)\}$ while $V_i^F(s_i^F(\hat{p}_{qi}^*)) = 0$, this implies that $\check{s} = s_i^F(\hat{p}_{qi}^*)$ and $\bar{R}_i = 0$. When $\theta_i > 0$, $\bar{p}_i^y = b_i$ follows from (7.14), and $\bar{p}_i(\,,s) = b_i e^{rs}$, for all $s \in [0, s_i^F(\hat{p}_{qi}^*)]$ from the fact that on this set of ages (7.22) holds as an equality. Finally, (ii) is verified by direct substitution. $\square$

The following proposition shows that the multiplicity of modified golden rules arising for $p_q^* = \hat{p}_{qi}^*$ disappears for higher levels of timber price.

Proposition 7.6 *Assume $p_q^* > \hat{p}_{qi}^*$. Then:*

(i)   *For any modified golden rule,* $\bar{R}_i = r M_i^F(p_q^*)$, $\bar{x}_i(\,,s) = x_1^{U_i}(\,,s)$, $\bar{c}_i(\,,s) = c_1^{D_i}(\,,s)$, $\bar{y}_i = \frac{h_i}{s_i^F(p_q^*)}$, $\bar{p}_i^y = b_i$, *and* $\bar{p}_i(\,,s) = b_i e^{rs} + M_i^F(p_q^*)(e^{rs} - 1)$ *for all* $s \in [0, s_i^F(p_q^*)]$.

(ii)   *The strategy-trajectory couple* $\bar{x}_i(\,,s) = x_1^{U_i}(\,,s)$, $\bar{c}_i(\,,s) = c_1^{D_i}(\,,s)$, $\bar{y}_i = \frac{h_i}{s_i^F(p_q^*)}$, $\bar{c}_i^a = \bar{a}_i = 0$, *and the price system* $p_i(\,,s) = b_i e^{rs} + M_i^F(p_q^*)(e^{rs} - 1)$

for all $s \in [0, \bar{s}_i]$, $\bar{p}_i^y = b_i$, $\bar{p}_i^a = b_i e^{r\bar{s}_i} + M_i^F(p_q^*)(e^{r\bar{s}} - 1)$, $\bar{R}_i = r M_i^F(p_q^*)$ constitute a modified golden rule.

Proof. After noting that $\bar{R}_i < r M_i^F(p_q^*)$ is inconsistent with the no extra profits condition (7.12) and that forest cultivation results in losses whenever $\bar{R}_i > r M_i^F(p_q^*)$, we can proceed as in the proof of Proposition 7.4, taking into account that $\bar{R}_i > 0$ implies that (7.16) holds with equality. □

Having characterized modified golden rules for the different values of the timber price, we have also implicitly derived the 'long-run timber supply correspondence', defined by equation (7.4) when cutting intensity levels belong to modified golden rules. We can now turn our attention to the properties of the long-run timber supply curve and to the analysis of the competitive stationary equilibrium of our forestry model.

Long-run supply curves and comparative statics effects of an increase in timber demand

As ordinary supply functions (or correspondences) are the sum of individual firms' supply functions, our aggregate timber supply correspondence is simply the horizontal summation of the single lands' supply correspondences. Thus our first task is the construction of land i timber supply:

- For $0 \leq p_q^* < \hat{p}_{qi}^*$, timber supply on land i is constant at zero. Indeed Proposition 7.2(i) implies $\bar{c}_i^a f_i^a = 0$ for all $p_q^* \geq 0$, and (ii) of the same proposition and Proposition 7.3(i) implies $\int_0^{\bar{s}_i} \bar{c}_i(, s) f_i(s) ds = 0$.
- However, when $p_q^* > \bar{l}_i / f_i^a$, something economically relevant happens under the surface of the constant supply function. Since now it is worth extracting the timber they contain, the price of old trees is no longer zero. Old trees have become a valuable resource, destined to be exhausted.
- When $p_q^* = \hat{p}_{qi}^*$, the supply curve has a flat. This follows from Proposition 7.4(i) and the definition of the Dirac delta, that is $\delta_{s_i^F(\hat{p}_{qi}^*)} f_i(s) = f_i(s_i^F(\hat{p}_{qi}^*))$, so that

$$\int_0^{\bar{s}_i} c_{\theta_i}^{D_i}(, s) f_i(s) ds = \theta_i \frac{h_i f_i(s_i^F(\hat{p}_{qi}^*))}{s_i^F(\hat{p}_{qi}^*)}, \quad \text{for any } \theta_i \in [0, 1].$$

The amount of timber supplied is any quantity in the interval $[0, h_i f_i(s_i^F(\hat{p}_{qi}^*))/ s_i^F(\hat{p}_{qi}^*)]$.
- Finally, for $p_q^* > \hat{p}_{qi}^*$ we can use Proposition 7.5(i) to get

$$\int_0^{\bar{s}_i} c_1^{D_i}(, s) f_i(s) ds = \frac{h_i f_i(s_i^F(p_q^*))}{s_i^F(p_q^*)},$$

and hence to establish that the supply correspondence is univalued. In addition, the supply function is increasing at all $p_q^* > \hat{p}_{qi}^*$. To prove that, we show that the Faustmann critical age $s_i^F(p_q^*)$ is decreasing at any price greater than $\hat{p}_{qi}^*$.

Proposition 7.7 *Assume* $p_q^* \geq \hat{p}_{qi}^*$. *Then* $s_i^F(p_q^*)$ *is a continuous decreasing function. As a consequence, land i supply function* $h_i f_i(s_i^F(p_q^*))/s_i^F(p_q^*)$ *is continuous and increasing for all* $p_q^* > \hat{p}_{qi}^*$.

Proof. Let p_q^* be any price that satisfies the hypothesis $p_q^* \geq \hat{p}_{qi}^*$ and let $\Delta p_q^* > 0$. Recall the definition of $g_i(s)$ in (7.30), and define

$$k_i(s) := \frac{M_i^F(p_q^* + \Delta p_q^*)(e^{rs} - 1) + b_i e^{rs} + \bar{l}_i}{p_q^* + \Delta p_q^*}, \quad \alpha := \frac{(p_q^* + \Delta p_q^*)(M_i^F(p_q^*) + b_i)}{p_q^*(M_i^F(p_q^* + \Delta p_q^*) + b_i)}.$$

Note that the following hold: $g_i(0) > k_i(0)$, and $g_i'(s) = \alpha k_i'(s)$. Now, since $\alpha \geq 1$ would lead to the contradiction $k_i(s_i^F(p_q^*)) < g_i(s_i^F(p_q^*)) = f_i(s_i^F(p_q^*))$, $\alpha < 1$. Hence, at $s_i^F(p_q^* + \Delta p_q^*)$ the following hold true: $k_i'(s_i^F(p_q^* + \Delta p_q^*)) = f_i'(s_i^F(p_q^* + \Delta p_q^*)) > g_i'(s_i^F(p_q^* + \Delta p_q^*))$. Since we have $f_i'(s_i^F(p_q^*)) = g_i'(s_i^F(p_q^*))$ and since $f_i(s) - g_i(s)$ is a strictly concave function, the last inequality implies $s_i^F(p_q^* + \Delta p_q^*) < s_i^F(p_q^*)$. Finally, uniqueness of the maximizer of the Faustmann function implies that $s_i^F(p_q^* + \Delta p_q^*) \to s_i^F(p_q^*)$ for $\Delta p_q^* \to 0$, and hence the continuity of the function $s_i^F(p_q^*)$. The last fact is a direct consequence of (HC2), since $h_i f_i(s)/s$ is decreasing in s. $\square$

This completes the construction of the supply correspondence on land i for all $p_q^* \geq 0$. We have depicted a typical supply curve in Figure 7.3.

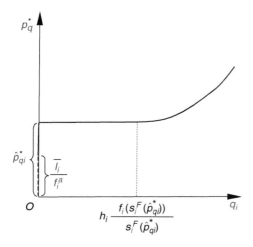

Figure 7.3 Supply curve.

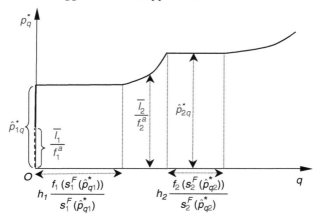

Figure 7.4 Aggregate supply.

Now we can construct the aggregate timber supply correspondence that, as already noted, is simply the horizontal sum of the N individual correspondences. If, to avoid singular cases, we assume $\hat{p}^*_{qi} \neq \hat{p}^*_{qj}$ and $(\bar{l}_i / f^a_i) \neq (\bar{l}_j / f^a_j)$, for all $i, j \in I, i \neq j$, then the aggregate supply curve contains exactly N flats in correspondence of the break-through prices $\hat{p}^*_{qi}$ and N threshold prices $\bar{l}_i / f^a_i$ that trigger extraction of the timber contained in old trees.

The construction of the curve is illustrated in Figure 7.4 for the case $N = 2$. Note that through this process lands are ranked both in terms of their threshold prices $\bar{l}_i / f^a_i$ and in terms of their break-through prices $\hat{p}^*_{qi}$. The order in terms of break-through prices, which is called the *order of fertility* (see Kurz and Salvadori, 1995, p. 287), is one of the building blocks of the Ricardian theory of extensive rent, and gives the order in which the lands are taken into cultivation when the demand for timber increases. Timber production begins when the price of timber equals the minimum $\hat{p}^*_{qi}$, that is the break-through price of the most fertile land ($\hat{p}^*_{q1}$ in the example in Figure 7.4). Since at this price any share of the most fertile land can be cultivated, the supply curve has a flat. Before passing to the second most fertile land (that in the example in Figure 7.4 occurs when the price $\hat{p}^*_{q2}$ is reached), forest cultivation on the first land is intensified (recall that the Faustmann age of the cost minimizing technique is a decreasing function of the price of timber), with the effect that timber supply increases and a *Faustmann intensive rent* is paid on the most fertile land (see Sraffa, 1925 p. 334 ff., for a similar construction).

When the break-through price of the second most fertile land is reached ($\hat{p}^*_{q2}$ in Figure 7.4), there is a second flat on the supply curve. If not fully cultivated, the second most fertile land is now the *Ricardian marginal land* on which no rent is paid, so that the rent paid on the most fertile land is now the usual *Ricardian extensive rent* that eliminates the extra profits that the use of the cost-minimizing technique on the most fertile land would otherwise generate. For higher levels of the timber price, cultivation is intensified on both the first two most fertile lands until the break-through price of the third most fertile land is reached, where there is a new flat in the supply curve. And so on.

On the other hand, and quite naturally, the order in terms of threshold prices, which we call the *order of extraction*,[14] does not affect the shape of the long-run aggregate supply correspondence, although it determines the structure of the state variable in the modified golden rules that are behind the supply curve. We will say that there is an *order of the lands* if each land occupies the same position in the two orders described above. An order of lands will be called *strong* if, in addition, $\hat{p}_{qi}^* < \bar{l}_j / f_j^a$ for each land j that follows land i in the order of lands (for example, that depicted in Figure 7.4 is a strong order of lands).

Once the properties of the supply correspondence have been established, the comparative static effects of an increased demand for timber are fairly obvious: if at the initial equilibrium the marginal land exists, then a higher demand could simply lead to an increase of the timber produced on that marginal land, without any increase in timber price and in rents of the intra-marginal lands. If on the contrary the lands in use are fully occupied, then a rise in the price of timber and in the rents of the fully occupied lands necessarily occurs. As suggested by Ricardo, in both cases a sufficiently high demand for timber causes a 'rent to be paid for forests [. . .], which could before afford no rent', as future demand cannot be met without fully cultivating some of previously unoccupied or partially cultivated lands.

The other part of Ricardo's argument – that not all of what 'is annually paid by a farmer to his landlord' can be considered rent, and that a higher demand for timber could simply raise those components of the compensation paid by the farmer that are not rent – has the clearest counterpart in our model when there is a strong order of lands. Figure 7.5 illustrates the point. Let the initial demand curve be the one labelled A in the figure. Then, since in equilibrium the timber price is lower

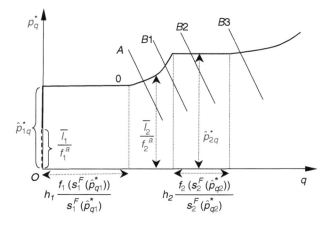

Figure 7.5 Effects of an increasing timber price.

than $\bar{l}_2/f_2^a$, all trees standing on land 2 have no value. If an increase in demand shifts the curve to $B3$, then both the prices of standing trees and the rent on land 2 become positive, but if instead the increase is such that the demand curve is either $B1$ or $B2$, then no rent will be paid on land 2, although in both cases the owners of land 2 will receive compensation whenever they sell the now valuable assets standing on their land.

Concluding remarks

We have provided a rational basis for Ricardo's tenet that the compensations received by the owners of marginal forestlands in Norway following the raise of timber demand (and hence of timber price) in more southern countries of Europe were not rents. To do that, relying on the insights in Kurz and Salvadori (2009, 2011) and on the continuous-time forest management theory developed in Fabbri *et al.* (2015), we have built a 'Ricardian' forestry model whose comparative statics properties, we think, well mimics Ricardo's claims.

Beyond its use as an interpretive tool, our model improves that contained in Fabbri *et al.* (2015) by introducing, although in a simplified way, a second sector in the continuous-time Mitra–Wan forestry framework. Starting from this basis, it should be no hard task to develop alternative two-sector models with, for example, a second agricultural sector or an energy sector that uses both fossil fuels and renewable energy technologies. With these modifications, the model can be adapted to the analysis of important contemporary economic issues as, for example, the following ones (e.g. Piazza and Roy, 2015). Is it truly inevitable that forestry or trees conservation will be adversely affected by rising food demand or the introduction of policies encouraging the use of biofuels?

Notes

1 However, a recent study has shown that the formula was already known in England at the end of seventeenth century and that its discovery is linked to the institutional developments that changed the English financial markets after the 1690s; see Viitala (2013).
2 Using a Sraffian terminology, we are treating timber as a non-basic commodity.
3 Stokey and Lucas (1989) advocated the direct study of the equilibrium price system, to supplement what they called 'the indirect approach'.
4 Besides Ricardian extensive rents, an intensive rent arises in the model because a higher timber price leads to a shorter rotation period, with higher timber production and higher rent, on fully occupied lands. We call this type of intensive rent the *Faustmann rent*.
5 Note that a perfectly elastic timber demand curve would not satisfy the requirements in the text, as it would be multivalued. We avoid this 'linear' case because it complicates the comparative statistics. It should be noted that, in the continuous-time version of the basic Mitra–Wan model, the closed form of the dynamics of competitive equilibrium is known only as the linear case (see Fabbri *et al.*, 2015).
6 Although the case $r = 0$ is important in forestry literature (price-supported steady states of the original undiscounted Mitra–Wan model fulfil the foresters' goal of *maximum sustained yield*), its analysis would require the introduction of specific optimality criteria. However, on a first inspection, it seems some of the results in Fabbri *et al.* (2015) may extend to the model discussed in this paper.

7 In Fabbri *et al.* (2015), $f(s)$ is not required to be concave, has support contained in $(0, \bar{s})$, with $0 < \bar{s} < \infty$, meaning that trees older than $\bar{s}$ are considered unproductive and that some time after planting is needed before a tree becomes productive. Moreover, since cutting/replanting costs are null, Fabbri *et al.* (2015) assume consistently that the aggregate variables $a(t)$ and $c_a(t)$ are zero at any time.

8 Fabbri *et al.* (2015) consider an optimal growth model with the Ramsey-like objective $\int_0^{+\infty} e^{-\rho t} u\left(q^D(t)\right) dt$, where $\rho \geq 0$ is the rate of discount and $u(q^D(t))$ is the instantaneous utility function. To compare the two models, it is sufficient to re-interpret the rate of interest as the rate of discount and the demand function $q^D(t) = D(p_q(t))$ as the inverse of the function $p_q = u'(q^D(t))$.

9 Following the terminology of optimal growth theory, we call any stationary strategy–trajectory couple satisfying (7.10) and supported by a stationary price path a modified golden rule. A formal definition is given in the third section.

10 The proofs of these results, which are not given here, can be obtained by adapting Theorem 4.5 in Fabbri *et al.* (2015).

11 In principle, negative prices are possible in this model. For example, suppose that on land i the cost of removal of the trees is very high, so that $f_i^a p_q^* - \bar{l}_i < 0$, and $a_i(0) = h_i$. In this case, a stationary state in which $\bar{a}_i = h_i$ can be sustained by negative prices of mature trees and positive rent rates that satisfy $f_i^a p_q^* - \bar{l}_i \leq \bar{p}_i^a$ and $0 = r \bar{p}_i^a + \bar{R}_i$. Note that in this kind of equilibria, even if the rent rate is positive, what is 'annually paid by a farmer to his landlord' equals zero because a positive rent exactly compensates for the interests the landlord pays on the value of the 'bad' standing on his land. However, this case is not particularly relevant as, besides a stationary solution with negative price of the old trees, there also exists the more natural non-negative solution $\bar{R}_i = 0$, $\bar{p}_i^a = 0$. Assumptions (HC1)–(HC2), implying that the rent on land i can be positive only if $f_i^a p_q^* - \bar{l}_i > 0$, preclude a more interesting case of a negative price for mature trees that would occur when a high removal cost would prevent cultivation of the part of the land that is covered with old trees, even if the land were in short supply for forest cultivation.

12 A simple argument that explains the statement in the text runs as follows. Buying at time t a tree of age s on land i, holding it *in situ* till time $t + \Delta t$, and then selling it, generates a net revenue at time $t + \Delta t$ of $p_i(t + \Delta t, s + \Delta t) - p_i(t, s) - \bar{R}_i \Delta t$. Under competitive arbitrage, this sum equates the foregone interest on the sum used to buy the asset, $r p_i(t, s) \Delta t$. Hence:

$$\frac{[p_i(t + \Delta t, s + \Delta t) - p_i(t, s + \Delta t)] + [p_i(t, s + \Delta t) - p_i(t, s)]}{\Delta t} = r p_i(t, s) + \bar{R}_i.$$

With stationary prices, letting $\Delta t \to 0_+$ one gets the Hotelling-like condition in the text.

13 Uniqueness can be proved for all $p_q^* \geq 0$; however, it is irrelevant when $p_q^* < \hat{p}_{qi}^*$.

14 Although our analysis is static, we abuse the term *order of extraction* to underline the fact that if planting costs were infinite and all standing trees were old, then our model would be reduced to a standard exhaustible resource model with multiple deposits. Provided the demand choke-off price is greater that the maximum of the $\bar{l}_i / f_i^a$, $i \in I$, the order in term of threshold prices in this model would correspond to the order of extraction of the N deposits of timber (see Herfindahl, 1967).

References

Fabbri, G., Faggian, S. and Freni, G. 2015. On the Mitra–Wan forest management problem in continuous time. *Journal of Economic Theory*, **157**, 1001–1040.

Faustmann, M. 1849. Berechnung des Wertes welchen Waldboden sowie noch nicht haubare Holzbestände für die Waldwirtschaft besitzen. *Allgemeine Forst-und Jagd-Zeitung*, **15**, 441–455.

Foley, D. K. 1975. On two specifications of asset equilibrium in macroeconomic models. *Journal of Political Economy*, **83**(2), 303–324.

Herfindahl, O. C. 1967. Depletion and economic theory. In Gaffney, Mason (ed.), *Extractive Resources and Taxation*. Madison, WI: University of Wisconsin Press, pp. 63–90.

Khan, M. A. and Piazza, A. 2012. On the Mitra–Wan forestry model: a unified analysis. *Journal of Economic Theory*, **147**(1), 230–260.

Kurz, H. D. and Salvadori, N. 1995. *Theory of Production. A Long-Period Analysis*. Cambridge: Cambridge University Press.

Kurz, H. D. and Salvadori, N. 2009. Ricardo on exhaustible resources, and the Hotelling Rule. In Aiko, Ikeo, and Kurz, Heinz D. (eds), *The History of Economic Theory: Festschrift in Honour of Takashi Negishi*. London: Macmillan, pp. 68–79.

Kurz, H. D. and Salvadori, N. 2011. Exhaustible resources: rents, profits, royalties and prices. In Caspari, Victor (ed.), *The Evolution of Economic Theory: Essays in Honour of Bertram Schefold*. London: Routledge, pp. 39–52.

Marshall, A. 1920 [1890]. *Principles of Economics*. 8th edn. London: Macmillan.

Mitra, T. and Wan, H. Y. 1985. Some theoretical results on the economics of forestry. *The Review of Economic Studies*, **52**(2), 263–282.

Mitra, T. and Wan, H. Y. 1986. On the Faustmann solution to the forest management problem. *Journal of Economic Theory*, **40**(2), 229–249.

Piazza, A. and Roy, S. 2015. Deforestation and optimal management. *Journal of Economic Dynamics and Control*, **53**, 15–27.

Ricardo, D. 1951 [1817]. *On the Principles of Political Economy and Taxation*. In *The Works and Correspondence of David Ricardo*, edited by Piero Sraffa with the collaboration of Maurice H. Dobb, Vol. I. Cambridge: Cambridge University Press.

Salant, S. W. 2013. The equilibrium price path of timber in the absence of replanting: does hotelling rule the forests too? *Resource and Energy Economics*, **35**(4), 572–581.

Salo, S. and Tahvonen, O. 2002. On equilibrium cycles and normal forests in optimal harvesting of tree vintages. *Journal of Environmental Economics and Management*, **44**(1), 1–22.

Salo, S. and Tahvonen, O. 2003. On the economics of forest vintages. *Journal of Economic Dynamics and Control*, **27**(8), 1411–1435.

Samuelson, P. A. 1976. Economics of forestry in an evolving society. *Economic Inquiry*, **14**, 466–492. (Reprinted in 1995, *Journal of Forest Economics*, **1**(1), 115–150).

Sraffa, P. 1925. Sulle relazioni fra costo e quantitá prodotta. *Annali di Economia*, **2**, 277–328. English translation by John Eatwell and Alessandro Roncaglia in Luigi L. Pasinetti (ed.), Italian Economic Papers. Bologna: Il Mulino and Oxford: Oxford University Press, 1998, pp. 323–363 and in Heinz D. Kurz and Neri Salvadori (eds), 2003. *The Legacy of Piero Sraffa*. Cheltenham, UK: Edward Elgar, Vol. 1, pp. 3–43.

Stokey, N. L. and Lucas, R. E. Jr. 1989. *Recursive Methods in Economic Dynamics*. Cambridge, MA: Harvard University Press.

Viitala, E.-J. 2013. The discovery of the Faustmann Formula in natural resource economics. *History of Political Economy*, **45**(3), 523–548.

8 Choice of technique made by an upstream policy for waste reduction

Eiji B. Hosoda[1]

Introduction

The cost-minimization principle is a core concept for analysing a capitalist economy.[2] Without the principle, important problems such as re-switching of techniques, capital reversing and so on could not have been properly formalized nor solved. Then, it is quite natural to apply the principle to environmental problems, since solving environmental problems requires a choice of technique different from the one adopted in a competitive market, and since the cost-minimization principle coupled with an upstream policy is expected to guide a capitalist economy to a more environmentally friendly equilibrium. This paper addresses the problem, focussing upon a household waste problem.

Recently, many countries have adopted upstream policies such as extended producers responsibility (EPR), which are expected to guide producers to the choice of technique for reduction of waste discharged at a post-consumption stage. In particular, EPR is considered to be a very powerful policy tool for waste reduction. The purpose of this paper is to formalize the policy and analyse how effective it is, showing that EPR is successful in making households' decisions on green consumption compatible with producers' cost-minimizing decisions.

This paper is a direct extension of Hosoda (2010), which deals with a zero-one type of choice of technique made by EPR. He shows that households' preference for non-waste generating goods is harmonized with producers' cost-minimizing behaviour by means of EPR, although it is not the case without the policy: if EPR is not introduced, the cost-minimization principle may possibly lead producers to choose a technique for waste-generating goods, which is not chosen by consumers.

In this paper, instead of a zero-one type of choice of technique, a multiple type of choice of technique is dealt with. The latter type of choice of technique has quite a different nature from the former, particularly when infinitely many production processes are considered for waste reduction. Indeed, this is the case for producers who face reduction of the amount of the container or package of consumption goods. There could be infinitely many choices of reduction and, accordingly, infinitely many input-output combinations might be possible for the producers' option.

Choice of technique by the cost-minimization principle is adopted for solving environmental problems in a Sraffian framework. Typical examples are Gehrke and Lager (1995), Lager (1999) and Hosoda (2012, 2014). The first two papers demonstrate that taxation on environmentally unfriendly substances may possibly give a perverse effect to an economy: the technique which uses those substances may be chosen by virtue of the taxation, since it is a cost-minimizing technique.

The last two papers, on the other hand, deal with problems which are caused by degradation of recycled materials. Based upon the cost-minimization principle, they show that recycling is sometimes preferred to waste disposal even if waste is negatively priced so that it is bads: negative price of waste does not necessarily mean that recycling of waste is economically disadvantageous compared with waste disposal. Furthermore, correct sorting is shown by Hosoda (2014) to be an important factor for the grade of recycled resources.

Upstream policies for effective waste reduction are also analysed in detail by mainstream economists like Calcott and Walls (2000), Dinan (1993), Eichner and Pethig (2001), Fullerton and Kinnaman (1995), Fullerton and Wu (1998), Walls and Palmer (2001) and so on. It is worth pointing out that those seminal papers appeared when EPR was about to be adopted in developed countries. The practical importance of EPR was theoretically endorsed by those papers in a timely manner.

The structure of this paper is as follows. The next section displays the fundamental structure of the model and the basic assumptions. In the third section, some fundamental mathematical deductions and main propositions are demonstrated. Choice of technique corresponding to a point of the wage–profit frontier plays a crucial role in the analysis. Clearly, this is nothing but the cost-minimization principle. In the final section, concluding remarks are made.

The basic model and assumptions

The structure of the model

Let me assume that there are two production sectors and one disposal sector: The first production sector produces a commodity which is used only as circulating capital by every sector. The second production sector produces a commodity which is used as a consumption commodity as well as circulating capital. The second commodity is also assumed to be input into every sector. The third sector is a disposal sector, which treats waste generated by consumption of the second commodity by households. It is assumed that θ units of waste are generated by consumption of a unit of the consumption commodity. Let me call θ a *waste generation rate*.

Producers of the consumption commodity are supposed to have controllability of the waste generation rate θ: they can choose a production process which generates more waste at the post-consumption stage or one which generates less waste. This choice may be a zero-one type or a multiple type, depending upon the technological assumption. It may be conceivable that a consumption commodity is presented with or without a package or a container. This is the first type of choice.

Although this type of choice may be possible and should not be excluded from consideration, it is not so easy to find good examples to match this case. It is more possible for producers to control the amount of packages or containers in various gradations. Sometimes, infinitely many changes in the amount could be possible. The weight of containers or volume of packages may possibly be changed in this way.

If the first type of choice is assumed, then the choice is expressed as $\theta \in \{0, 1\}$, whose case is analysed by Hosoda (2010). The second type of choice is expressed as $\theta \in \{1, 2, \ldots, n\}$. The third type is expressed as $\theta \in \{1, 2, \ldots\} \equiv \mathbb{N}$. In an extreme case, a choice expressed by $\theta \in [0, 1]$ is possible. I adopt the last type of choice in the following, since it is so general that it includes other cases, as a special case.

Obviously, inputs of circulating capital and labour in the second sector depend upon a waste generation rate θ: if producers are required to reduce waste generation at a post-consumption stage, they have to choose a production process which satisfies the requirement. Thus, choice of the waste generation rate means nothing but choice of a production process for producers of the consumption commodity. Then the input–output structure is expressed as follows:

$$
A(\theta) = \begin{pmatrix} a_{11} & a_{12}(\theta) & a_{13} \\ a_{21} & a_{22}(\theta) & a_{23} \\ 0 & 0 & 1 \end{pmatrix} \rightarrow \begin{pmatrix} 1 & 0 & 0 \\ 0 & 1 & 0 \\ 0 & 0 & 0 \end{pmatrix}
$$

$$
L(\theta) = (l_1, \quad l_2(\theta), \quad l_3)
$$

where A is a production coefficient matrix, including waste input expressed by unity in the third (disposal) process (i.e. $a_{33} = 1$), and $a_{ij} > 0$ ($i = 1, 2$ and $j = 1, 2, 3$). $L(\theta)$ is a labour input vector, which is positive. The third process produces neither a commodity nor a dis-commodity, so that the component in the lower-right corner is zero.

Since $\theta \in [0, 1]$ is assumed, the second column of $A(\theta)$ as well as the second component of $L(\theta)$ implies that there are infinitely many production processes in the second sector. Consequently, I deal with the problem of infinitely many choices of techniques.

On the other hand, a consumption vector is expressed as

$$
C \equiv c \begin{pmatrix} 0 \\ 1 \\ \theta \end{pmatrix},
$$

where c denotes per capita consumption level. Hence, the above vector shows that c units of consumption commodity are consumed, while θc units of waste are generated from the consumption activity.

Assumptions

As for the saving behaviours of producers and households, let me adopt the simplest assumption, following the preceding researches such as Hosoda (2010, 2012, 2014): households do not save and producers do not consume. Therefore, the profit rate (r) equals the growth rate (g). It does not seem that generalization of the assumption harms the essential argument of this paper.

The household income, therefore, consists of only wages. They are assumed to pay for waste disposal as well as the consumption commodity *unless* any policy for waste reduction is adopted by the government. If an upstream policy for waste reduction is adopted, the burden of payment for waste disposal is transferred from households to producers of the consumption commodity, as shown later.

The following is a conventional assumption which guarantees the feasibility of reproduction of an economy. Defining $A^{(-)}(\theta)$ as

$$\begin{pmatrix} a_{11} & a_{12}(\theta) \\ a_{21} & a_{22}(\theta) \end{pmatrix},$$

let me make the following assumption.

Assumption 8.1 $A^{(-)}(\theta)$ *satisfies the Hawkins–Simon condition for all* $\theta \in [0, 1]$.

Thanks to this assumption, an economy can afford to reproduce itself in an expanding way. That is,

$\exists g > 0$ such that $[I - (1 + g)A^{(-)}(\theta)]$ is invertible and $[I - (1 + g)A^{(-)}(\theta)]^{-1}$ has positive components, i.e. $[I - (1 + g)A^{(-)}(\theta)]^{-1} \gg 0$.[3]

Let us denote $\bar{g}$ as $\bar{g} \equiv 1/\lambda^* - 1$, where λ^* denotes the Perron–Frobenius eigenvalue of A. Clearly, $\bar{g}$ is nothing but the maximum growth rate. Denoting $\bar{g} \equiv \bar{r}$, I may express $\bar{r}$ as the maximum profit rate.

Next, I would like to define the relationship between inputs in the second sector and the waste generation rate θ. I simply assume that there is a trade-off between economic and environmental considerations:[4] larger θ implies that producers of the consumption commodity do not have to pay more attention to waste generation, so that inputs for environmental consideration become smaller. In other words, larger waste generation means cheaper production costs. On the other hand, smaller θ implies that they have to pay more attention to waste reduction, so that inputs must become larger to cut waste at the post-consumption stage. In other words, smaller waste generation means larger production costs.

Hence, let me adopt the following assumption.

Assumption 8.2 $\dfrac{da_{i2}(\theta)}{d\theta} \le 0$ $(i = 1, 2)$ *and* $\dfrac{dl_2(\theta)}{d\theta} \le 0$ *hold, where a strict inequality holds at least in one inequality.*

Since θ can take any value between 0 and 1, there are infinitely many choices of techniques. Yet, insofar as a long-run competitive equilibrium is considered, the conventional principle, that is, the cost-minimization principle, can be applied to this type of technique. Therefore, we have the following:

Principle *The cost-minimization principle is applicable to choice of techniques here. Thus, given a profit rate, the technique which maximizes a wage rate is chosen.*

Fundamental equations

A case in which households have to pay for waste disposal treatment

First, let me give a formal description of an economy in which households are supposed to pay for waste disposal treatment. I assume that household waste is treated by the private sector in a competitive market. It might be argued that household waste is treated by the public sector in many countries, so that the assumption would be too strong. Waste treatment by the public sector can, however, be accommodated by the present model without difficulty (see Hosoda, 2010). Thus, I adopt the simple assumption.

The price and quantity systems are expressed as follows:

$$\begin{cases} (1+r)(p_1 a_{11} + p_2 a_{21}) + w l_1 = p_1 \\ (1+r)\{p_1 a_{12}(\theta) + p_2 a_{22}(\theta)\} + w l_2(\theta) = p_2 \\ (1+r)(p_1 a_{13} + p_2 a_{23} + p_3) + w l_3 = 0 \\ p_2 = 1 \end{cases} \tag{8.1}$$

and

$$\begin{cases} (1+g)\{a_{11}x_1 + a_{12}(\theta)x_2 + a_{13}x_3\} = x_1 \\ (1+g)\{a_{21}x_1 + p_2 a_{22}(\theta)x_2 + a_{23}x_3\} + c = x_2 \\ (1+g)x_3 = \theta c \\ l_1 x_1 + l_2(\theta)x_2 + l_3 x_3 = 1. \end{cases} \tag{8.2}$$

The first and second equations of (8.1) are straightforward, showing the cost-price balance for producing the first and second commodities. The third one is slightly different from those equations. It shows the cost-price balance of a disposal process. By inputting a unit of waste as well as the other inputs, the process produces valueless output whose price is zero. Thus, nothing appears on the right-hand side of the third equation of (8.1). Obviously, p_3 denotes the price of waste, which is negative.

It is possible to express the cost-price balance of the third sector in terms of waste disposal service, instead of physical input of waste or bads.[5] I use the present expression for the third process, which is slightly different from Hosoda (2010). Yet, whichever expression I may adopt, the formal procedure of the following argument should be the same, with minor modification.

The fourth equation is nothing but the normalization of prices: the second commodity is adopted as *numeraire*.

Let me look at the quantity side expressed by (8.2). The first and second equations express a supply-demand balance of the first and second commodities in a long run. The third equation shows that the waste generated by consumption is treated by the waste disposal process, and so implies a supply-demand balance of waste. It must be noted that waste is supposed to be generated at the time of consumption, so that it is inputted to the third process with a time lag. That is why x_3 is multiplied by the growth factor $(1 + g)$. The fourth equation implies the normalization of quantity variables.

From the assumption on saving behaviours, the following budget constraint must hold:

$$w = c - p_3\theta c = (1 - \theta p_3)c,$$

where p_2 before c is abbreviated, since $p_2 = 1$. The meaning is clear: the wage income is spent for consumption and waste disposal. The above equation implies that the real price of the consumption commodity is $(1 - \theta p_3)$, instead of unity.

Let me make an important remark on the possibility of illegal dumping by households. As one can find in daily life, households often throw away waste such as used containers and packages, litter, or even end-of-life products into the environment, even if they are not required to pay for disposal of such waste. They have, *a fortiori*, an incentive to dump waste illegally if they are required to pay for waste disposal.

Yet, I ignore the possibility of illegal dumping of waste by households for a while, since it does not change the general thrust of the paper. I will take up the issue in the section on illegal dumping of waste.

The wage–profit and consumption–growth frontiers

The wage–profit frontier

It would be quite natural to start from an analysis of the price system (8.1). It must be noted that the third process (the disposal process) does not affect the price formation of the first and second processes. Let me define a vector $p^{(-)}$ as $p^{(-)} \equiv (p_1, p_2)$.

Since I adopt the second commodity as *numeraire*, the following equation is obtained:

$$1 = p^{(-)} \begin{pmatrix} 0 \\ 1 \end{pmatrix} = wL^{(-)}(\theta)\left[I - (1+r)A^{(-)}(\theta)\right]^{-1} \begin{pmatrix} 0 \\ 1 \end{pmatrix},$$

where

$$L^{(-)}(\theta) \equiv (l_1, l_2(\theta)).$$

From the above equation, we know the following holds:

$$w = \frac{\{1 - (1+r)a_{11}\}\{1 - (1+r)a_{22}(\theta)\} - (1+r)^2 a_{21}a_{12}(\theta)}{(1+r)l_1 a_{12}(\theta) + l_2(\theta)\{1 - (1+r)a_{11}\}}. \tag{8.3}$$

Thus, the wage rate is expressed as a function of r and parameter θ, i.e. $w = w(r; \theta)$. Obviously, (8.3) shows a *wage–profit curve* for a given θ.

A *wage–profit frontier* is obtained as the envelope of the wage–profit curves when parameter θ is supposed to be chosen according to the cost-minimization principle. Clearly, if there is no constraint on waste generation, $\theta = 1$ is chosen due to Assumption 8.2 and the cost minimization principle. Such choice of technique does not, however, necessarily imply maximization of per capita consumption, since waste generation and its disposal are not taken into account in the deduction of the frontier.

If a constraint on waste generation, whatever it may be, is reflected on the side of the price equation, cost-minimizing θ may not be unity. This is the key point of this paper, and I will demonstrate how an upstream policy induces environmentally friendly production which matches economic efficiency: an upstream policy which makes the costs of waste disposal properly reflected in a consumption-commodity production process fulfills the maximization of per capita consumption, so that household benefits are well-harmonized with the cost-minimizing behaviour of producers.

The consumption–growth frontier

Now, let me turn to the quantity side. Substituting the third equation of (8.2) into the first and second equations, we can reduce the first to the third equations of the quantity system to the following equation system:

$$\begin{cases} (1+g)\{a_{11}x_1 + a_{12}(\theta)x_2\} + a_{13}\theta c = x_1 \\ (1+g)\{a_{21}x_1 + p_2 a_{22}(\theta)x_2\} + a_{23}\theta c + c = x_2. \end{cases} \tag{8.4}$$

It is convenient to express the above in a matrix form as follows:

$$(1+g)A^{(-)}(\theta)x^{(-)} + cQ = x^{(-)}, \tag{8.5}$$

where

$$Q \equiv \begin{pmatrix} a_{13}\theta \\ a_{23}\theta + 1 \end{pmatrix} \quad \text{and} \quad x^{(-)} \equiv \begin{pmatrix} x_1 \\ x_2 \end{pmatrix}.$$

Clearly, c denotes per capita consumption when Q is taken as a unit of a consumption vector.

From (8.5), we have

$$x^{(-)} = c[I - (1+g)A^{(-)}(\theta)]^{-1}Q, \tag{8.6}$$

which implies

$$x^{(-)} = c\frac{\begin{pmatrix} 1 - (1+g)a_{22}(\theta) & (1+g)a_{12}(\theta) \\ (1+g)a_{21} & 1 - (1+g)a_{11} \end{pmatrix}}{\det\,[I - (1+g)A^{(-)}(\theta)]}Q \gg 0,$$

due to Assumption 8.1.

Notice $L(\theta)x = 1$ is equivalent to

$$L^{(-)}(\theta)x^{(-)} = 1 - \frac{1}{1+g}l_3\theta c. \tag{8.7}$$

Coupling (8.6) with (8.7), we have

$$1 = \left\{ \frac{1}{1+g}l_3\theta + L^{(-)}(\theta)\left[I - (1+g)A^{(-)}(\theta)\right]^{-1}Q \right\}c. \tag{8.8}$$

Per capita consumption c is a function of g and a parameter θ, so that it may be expressed as $c = c(g; \theta)$. More explicitly, the above equation can be expressed as follows:

$$c = \frac{(1+g)\left[\{1 - (1+g)a_{11}\}\{1 - (1+g)a_{22}(\theta)\} - (1+g)^2 a_{21}a_{12}(\theta)\right]}{(1+g)\left[l_1 a_{12}(\theta) + l_2(\theta)\{1 - (1+g)a_{11}\}\right] + \gamma(g; \theta)}, \tag{8.9}$$

where

$$\begin{aligned}\gamma(g; \theta) \equiv \theta\big[&(1+g)l_1\left(a_{13}\{1 - (1+g)a_{22}(\theta)\} + a_{12}a_{23}\right) \\ &+ (1+g)l_2(\theta)\left((1+g)a_{13}a_{21} + a_{23}\{1 - (1+g)a_{11}\}\right) \\ &+ l_3\left(\{1 - (1+g)a_{11}\}\{1 - (1+g)a_{22}(\theta)\} - (1+g)^2 a_{21}a_{12}(\theta)\right)\big].\end{aligned}$$

Notice $\gamma(g; \theta) \gg 0$ due to the Hawkins–Simon condition. Thus, per capita consumption is positive.

Equation (8.9) shows a *consumption–growth curve* for a given θ. As θ changes, the shape of the curve expressed by (8.9) also changes. Then, we can deduce the relationship between per capita consumption and a growth rate which maximizes per capita consumption for each growth rate. This is nothing but a *consumption–growth frontier*.

A gap between two frontiers

Let us compare the wage–profit and consumption–growth frontiers. Looking at (8.3) and (8.9), at once we notice that the functional relationship between w and r is different from that between c and g, since $\gamma(g; \theta)$ appears in the denominator of (8.9) but the corresponding term $\gamma(r; \theta)$ does not appear in the denominator of (8.3). Hence, we have $w(r; \theta) > c(g; \theta)$ for any $r(= g)$. This implies that there is a gap between the wage–profit and consumption–growth curves. Moreover, the wage–profit frontier is obtained from (8.3) by setting $\theta = 1$, while the consumption–growth frontier is obtained from (8.9) by maximization of c. Obviously, the wage–profit frontier is located above the consumption–growth frontier.

Since choice of technique is made by the cost-minimization principle, parameter θ is chosen according to maximization of the wage rate, instead of maximization of per capita consumption, so that $\theta = 1$ is chosen. Thus, insofar as there is no constraint on production of a consumption commodity which generates waste at the post-consumption stage, maximization of the wage rate is incompatible with that of per capita consumption in a long-run competitive equilibrium: The competitive power in a market economy cannot be harmonized with household benefits.

I can deduce a stronger result as follows. Define $D(g; \theta)$ and $\Phi(g; \theta)$ as

$$D(g; \theta) \equiv \det\left[I - (1+g)A^{(-)}(\theta)\right]$$

and

$$\Phi(g; \theta) \equiv L^{(-)}(\theta)\begin{pmatrix} 1-(1+g)a_{22}(\theta) & (1+g)a_{12}(\theta) \\ (1+g)a_{21} & 1-(1+g)a_{11} \end{pmatrix} Q.$$

Then, (8.8) is expressed as

$$1 = c\left[\frac{1}{1+g}l_3\theta + \frac{\Phi(g; \theta)}{D(g; \theta)}\right],$$

where $\Phi(g; \theta) > 0$ and $D(g; \theta) > 0$.

Differentiating (8.8) with respect to θ, we have

$$0 = \frac{\partial c}{\partial \theta}\left[\frac{1}{1+g}l_3\theta + \frac{\Phi(g; \theta)}{D(g; \theta)}\right] + c\left[\frac{1}{1+g}l_3 + \frac{\frac{\partial \Phi}{\partial \theta}D(g; \theta) - \frac{\partial D}{\partial \theta}\Phi(g; \theta)}{[D(g; \theta)]^2}\right].$$

$$(8.10)$$

Here, we have

$$\frac{\partial D(g; \theta)}{\partial \theta} = -(1+g)\{1-(1+g)a_{11}\}a'_{22}(\theta) - (1+g)^2 a_{21}a'_{12}(\theta) > 0,$$

and

$$\frac{\partial \Phi(g; \theta)}{\partial \theta} = l_1\left[a_{13}\{1-(1+g)a_{22}(\theta)\} + (1+g)a_{12}(\theta)a_{23}\right]$$
$$+ \theta l_1\left[-(1+g)a_{13}a'_{22}(\theta) + (1+g)a'_{12}(\theta)a_{23}\right]$$
$$+ l_2(\theta)\left[(1+g)a_{13}a_{21} + a_{23}\{1-(1+g)a_{11}\}\right]$$
$$+ \theta l'_2(\theta)\left[(1+g)a_{13}a_{21} + a_{23}\{1-(1+g)a_{11}\}\right]$$
$$+ (1+g)l_1a'_{12}(\theta) + l'_2(\theta)\{1-(1+g)a_{11}\}.$$

Defining $||f(\theta)|| \equiv \max_{\theta \in [0,1]} f(\theta)$, I can show the following result.

Lemma 8.1 *Suppose that l_3 is sufficiently large or $||a'_{12}(\theta)||$, $||a'_{22}(\theta)||$ and $||l'_2(\theta)||$ are sufficiently small so that $\frac{1}{1+g}l_3 + \frac{\frac{\partial \Phi}{\partial \theta}D(g;\theta)-\frac{\partial D}{\partial \theta}\Phi(g;\theta)}{[D(g;\theta)]^2} > 0$ holds. Then, we have $\partial c/\partial \theta < 0$.*

Proof. It is clear from (8.10). □

Let me show another lemma.

Lemma 8.2 *Suppose that $r = g$ and $\partial c/\partial \theta < 0$ hold. Then, for $\theta_1 < \theta_2$, we have*

$$c(\theta_2) < c(\theta_1) < w(\theta_1) < w(\theta_2).$$

Proof. The first inequality is clear from the hypothesis, and so is the last from $\frac{\partial w}{\partial \theta} > 0$ which is guaranteed by Assumption 8.2. From $\gamma(g;\theta) > 0$, it is confirmed that the middle inequality holds. □

From the above lemmata, we can deduce the following important proposition.

Proposition 8.1 *Suppose that l_3 is sufficiently large or $||a'_{12}(\theta)||$, $||a'_{22}(\theta)||$ and $||l'_2(\theta)||$ are sufficiently small so that $\frac{1}{1+g}l_3 + \frac{\frac{\partial \Phi}{\partial \theta}D(g;\theta)-\frac{\partial D}{\partial \theta}\Phi(g;\theta)}{[D(g;\theta)]^2} > 0$ holds. Then, the wage rate is maximized whereas per capita consumption is minimized in a long-run competitive equilibrium.*

Proof. Clear from the above lemmata. □

The result has a clear message: If the waste disposal sector is very labour intensive or the cost structure of the consumption commodity process is not affected very much as θ changes, there is a trade-off between households' and producers' benefits. In other words, households' benefits are ignored in a long-run equilibrium where there is no constraint on waste generation and the costs of waste disposal are not reflected in the production process of a consumption commodity.

Let me explain why. Notice that a waste generation rate θ affects per capita consumption c through two separate courses. If θ increases, the input coefficients of the second sector decrease, meaning that the productivity of the consumption sector increases. This contributes to an increase in per capita consumption.

On the other hand, an increase in the waste generation rate means more resources should be withdrawn from other production sectors and allocated to the waste disposal process, so that more waste can be properly treated. This works adversely for per capita consumption.

When $a_{i2}(\theta)$ and $l_2(\theta)$ are insensitive to θ, the former effect is relatively small compared to the latter effect. In addition to this, if l_3 is sufficiently large, the second effect is also large. Thus, per capita consumption decreases as the waste generation rate increases.

Illegal dumping of waste

In this subsection, I pick up the issue of illegal dumping of waste. Although this issue is not the main part of the present paper, it has some connection with an upstream policy for waste reduction which is soon formulated. Hence, I would like to briefly describe a model in which the possibility of illegal dumping of waste is accommodated. Here, too, I adopt the assumption that $r = g$ holds.

Households have an incentive to avoid paying part of waste disposal and dumping it illegally. I assume that only part of the waste goes to legal waste treatment, while the rest of it goes to illegal dumping: the proportion of waste which goes to legal waste treatment is denoted as $\alpha \in (0, 1)$. The rate α possibly depends upon the price of waste p_3, so that $\alpha = \alpha(p_3)$. I do not assume how α is related to p_3, although $d\alpha/dp_3 < 0$ is a natural assumption.

Then, $\alpha(p_3)\theta c$ goes to legal waste treatment, while $\{1 - \alpha(p_3)\}\theta c$ goes to illegal dumping. It is assumed that illegally dumped waste is cleaned up by the authority, and the clean-up service is more costly than the ordinary waste treatment service. I also assume that the clean-up costs are covered by income tax.

Denoting the input coefficient vector of the clean-up process as (a_{14}, a_{24}, l_4), I assume the following holds:

$$(a_{13}, a_{23}, l_3) < (a_{14}, a_{24}, l_4).$$

Now, I can express the new price and quantity systems as follows:

$$\begin{cases} (1+r)(p_1a_{11} + p_2a_{21}) + wl_1 = p_1 \\ (1+r)\{p_1a_{12}(\theta) + p_2a_{22}(\theta)\} + wl_2(\theta) = p_2 \\ (1+r)(p_1a_{13} + p_2a_{23} + p_3) + wl_3 = 0 \\ (1+r)(p_1a_{14} + p_2a_{24} + p_4) + wl_4 = 0 \\ p_2 = 1, \end{cases} \tag{8.11}$$

and

$$\begin{cases} (1+g)\{a_{11}x_1 + a_{12}(\theta)x_2 + a_{13}x_3 + a_{14}x_4\} = x_1 \\ (1+g)\{a_{21}x_1 + p_2a_{22}(\theta)x_2 + a_{23}x_3 + a_{24}x_4\} + c = x_2 \\ (1+g)x_3 = \alpha(p_3)\theta c \\ (1+g)x_4 = \{1 - \alpha(p_3)\}\theta c \\ l_1x_1 + l_2(\theta)x_2 + l_3x_3 + l_4x_4 = 1. \end{cases} \tag{8.12}$$

By the assumption that the clean-up costs of illegally dumped waste are covered by income tax, we have the following budget constraints:

$$\begin{cases} (1-\tau)w = c - \alpha(p_3)\theta cp_3 \\ \tau w = \{1 - \alpha(p_3)\}\theta cp_4, \end{cases}$$

where τ is the income tax rate.

It is easy to show that the above systems are consistent and solved. Suppose $g(=r)$ is given. For an arbitrarily given θ, all the prices and the wage rate are determined by (8.11), and so is $\alpha(p_3)$. Substituting this $\alpha(p_3)$ to the third equation of (8.12), the quantity system (8.12) is solved, and the solution is meaningful. The income tax rate τ is determined so that the budget constraints are satisfied.

Now, let us deduce the wage–profit and consumption–growth curves. The former curve is the same as the one obtained before, namely (8.3). The latter curve is deduced as follows. From the third and fourth equations of (8.12), we have

$$x_4 = \frac{1 - \alpha(p_3)}{\alpha(p_3)} x_3.$$

Substituting this to (8.12) and calculating as we have done before, we arrive at the following:

$$\begin{cases} (1+g)A^{(-)}(\theta)x^{(-)} + c\tilde{C}^{(-)} = x^{(-)} \\ L^{(-)}(\theta)x^{(-)} = 1 - \dfrac{1}{1+g}\tilde{l}_3(p_3)\theta c, \end{cases}$$

where

$$\tilde{C} \equiv \begin{pmatrix} \tilde{a}_{13}\theta \\ \tilde{a}_{23}\theta + 1 \end{pmatrix},$$

$\tilde{a}_{i3} \equiv \alpha(p_3)a_{i3} + \{1 - \alpha(p_3)\}a_{i4}$ $(i = 1, 2)$ and $\tilde{l}_3(p_3) \equiv \alpha(p_3)l_3 + \{1 - \alpha(p_3)\}l_4$.

From these, we finally obtain

$$c_{IL} = \frac{(1+g)\left[\{1 - (1+g)a_{11}\}\{1 - (1+g)a_{22}(\theta)\} - (1+g)^2 a_{21}a_{12}(\theta)\right]}{(1+g)\left[l_1 a_{12}(\theta) + l_2(\theta)\{1 - (1+g)a_{11}\}\right] + \tilde{\gamma}(g; \theta, p_3)},$$

$$(8.13)$$

where

$$\begin{aligned} \tilde{\gamma}(g; \theta, p_3) \equiv \theta\big[& (1+g)l_1\,(\tilde{a}_{13}\{1 - (1+g)a_{22}(\theta)\} + a_{12}a_{23}) \\ & + (1+g)l_2(\theta)\,((1+g)\tilde{a}_{13}a_{21} + \tilde{a}_{23}\{1 - (1+g)a_{11}\}) \\ & + \tilde{l}_3\,(\{1 - (1+g)a_{11}\}\{1 - (1+g)a_{22}(\theta)\} - (1+g)^2 a_{21}a_{12}(\theta))\big]. \end{aligned}$$

Since $(a_{13}, a_{23}, l_3) < (\tilde{a}_{13}, \tilde{a}_{23}, \tilde{l}_3)$ holds by construction, we have $\gamma(g; \theta) < \tilde{\gamma}(g; \theta, p_3)$. Therefore, $c(g; \theta) > c_{IL}(g; \theta, p_3)$ holds.

The conclusion is clear: if there is a possibility of households throwing away part of the waste to avoid waste disposal payment, per capita consumption becomes lower than that in the circumstance where there is no illegal dumping of waste.

An upstream policy

In this section, I try to extend the basic model so that I can analyse how introduction of an upstream policy such as EPR attains the maximization of per capita consumption while waste reduction is taken into account. Although there are many types of EPR in a real economy, I would like to adopt the simplest one in this paper: Producers of consumption commodities which generate waste at the post-consumption stage are supposed to pay the charge for waste treatment.

The extended model in which EPR is built-in

Let me show the price and quantity systems in which EPR is built-in. They are expressed as follows respectively:

$$\begin{cases} (1+r)(p_1 a_{11} + p_2 a_{21}) + w l_1 = p_1 \\ (1+r)\{p_1 a_{12}(\theta) + p_2 a_{22}(\theta) - \delta p_3\} + w l_2(\theta) = p_2 \\ (1+r)(p_1 a_{13} + p_2 a_{23} + p_3) + w l_2 = 0 \\ p_2 = 1, \end{cases} \tag{8.14}$$

and

$$\begin{cases} (1+g)\{a_{11}x_1 + a_{12}(\theta)x_2 + a_{13}x_3\} = x_1 \\ (1+g)\{a_{21}x_1 + a_{22}(\theta)x_2 + a_{23}x_3\} + c = x_2 \\ (1+g)x_3 = \theta c \\ l_1 x_1 + l_2(\theta)x_2 + l_3 x_3 = 1, \end{cases} \tag{8.15}$$

where δ is assumed to be a policy variable determined by the authority. How δ is determined is a very important issue, which affects choice of technique. I will discuss this matter soon.

There seems to be only a slight difference in the new systems expressed by (8.14) and (8.15) from the original ones expressed by (8.1) and (8.2), by the term $-\delta p_3$ which appears as the third term in the curly brackets in the second equation of (8.14). Yet, this brings about a big difference to the whole economy, as demonstrated later.

In the price system (8.14), the term $-\delta p_3$ expresses the waste treatment charge which the producers of the consumption commodity have to pay due to the requirement of EPR. Since this payment must cover the total amount of costs on waste treatment by the waste disposal process, the following must hold:

$$p_3 \delta x_2 = p_3 x_3 = p_3 \theta c \frac{1}{1+g}. \tag{8.16}$$

A few remarks follow. Firstly, the authority must calculate the ratio $\delta \equiv x_3/x_2$ precisely for a given θ, while producers of a consumption commodity should deduce the value of δ correctly. I assume that the authority is wise enough to calculate δ, although I take into account the situation in which producers may not be able to deduce δ correctly if the rule of how to determine δ is too complicated. I will demonstrate a simple rule which leads the producers to the correct calculation of δ.

Secondly, assuming that households do not save their income and producers do not consume as I have assumed so far, it is easily demonstrated that the rate of profit equals the growth rate, i.e. $r = g$, from (8.14), (8.15) and (8.16).

Thirdly, the cost-minimization principle is still valid in the new equation systems: if a policy variable δ is determined by the authority for a given θ, the technique which maximizes the wage rate is supposed to be chosen, given the rate of profit. This is quite a natural supposition, since the same cost-minimizing pressure as in the original systems still exists in the new systems.

Finally, the price system is no longer independent of the quantity system, so that the price equations cannot be solved without the help of the quantity equations. Obviously, the quantity system is also dependent upon the price system, since the former depends upon parameter θ, which is determined by the cost-minimization principle.

In order to solve the new equation systems, by utilizing (8.16), let me transform (8.14) and (8.15) into the following:

$$\begin{cases} (1+r)(p_1a_{11} + p_2a_{21})wl_1 = p_1 \\ (1+r)\left\{p_1a_{12}^{\dagger}(\theta, \delta) + p_2a_{22}^{\dagger}(\theta, \delta)\right\} + wl_2^{\dagger}(\theta, \delta) = p_2 \end{cases}$$

and

$$\begin{cases} (1+g)\left\{a_{11}x_1 + a_{12}^{\dagger}(\theta, \delta)x_2\right\} = x_1 \\ (1+g)\left\{a_{21}x_1 + a_{22}^{\dagger}(\theta, \delta)x_2\right\} + c = x_2 \\ l_1x_1 + l_2^{\dagger}(\theta, \delta)x_2 = 1, \end{cases}$$

where $a_{12}^{\dagger}(\theta, \delta) \equiv a_{12}(\theta) + \delta a_{13}$, $a_{22}^{\dagger}(\theta, \delta) \equiv a_{22}(\theta) + \delta a_{23}$ and $l_2^{\dagger}(\theta, \delta) \equiv l_2(\theta) + \delta l_3$. Defining $A^{\dagger}(\theta, \delta)$ and $l^{\dagger}(\theta, \delta)$ as

$$A^{\dagger}(\theta, \delta) \equiv \begin{pmatrix} a_{11} & a_{12}^{\dagger}(\theta, \delta) \\ a_{21} & a_{22}^{\dagger}(\theta, \delta) \end{pmatrix} \quad \text{and} \quad L^{\dagger}(\theta, \delta) \equiv \left(l_1, l_2^{\dagger}(\theta, \delta)\right),$$

I can transform the above equations into the following matrix equations:

$$(1+r)p^{(-)}A^{\dagger}(\theta, \delta) + wL^{\dagger}(\theta, \delta) = p^{(-)} \tag{8.17}$$

$$(1+g)A^{\dagger}(\theta, \delta)x^{(-)} + \begin{pmatrix} 0 \\ c \end{pmatrix} = x^{(-)} \tag{8.18}$$

$$L^{\dagger}(\theta, \delta)x^{(-)} = 1. \tag{8.19}$$

Notice that (8.18) is equivalent to (8.5), so that maximization of c in (8.18) is the same as that in (8.5).

EPR formulae

In this subsection, I explore how EPR leads the economy to harmonization of households' benefits with the competitive power of markets *if a formula to determine a policy variable δ is properly presented by the authority and understood by producers*. First, let me explain how the wage–profit and consumption–growth frontiers are modified when an EPR policy is implemented.

The wage–profit and consumption–growth frontiers in the new systems

For an EPR policy to be implemented correctly, a parameter θ and a policy variable δ must be properly correlated, and not independent: Otherwise, (8.16) would not hold, so that the quantity system would be inconsistent. There must be a formula to determine a policy variable δ, depending upon a parameter θ. I can deduce the relationship between θ and δ easily from (8.18) and (8.19):

$$\delta = \frac{x_3}{x_2} = \frac{\{1 - (1+g)a_{11}\}\{1 - (1+g)a_{22}(\theta)\} - (1+g)^2 a_{21}a_{12}(\theta)}{(1+g)^2 a_{21}a_{13} + \{1 - (1+g)a_{11}\}(1+g)\left(a_{23} + \frac{1}{\theta}\right)}.$$

Thus, once θ is given, a policy variable δ is determined. Let me denote this relationship as $\delta = \phi(\theta)$. Obviously, $\phi'(\theta) > 0$ holds.

Based upon this formula, I can deduce the wage–profit and consumption–growth curves. Actually, from (8.17), the following is obtained:

$$w = \frac{\det\left[I - (1+r)A^{+}(\theta, \delta)\right]}{(1+r)l_1 a_{12}(\theta, \delta) + l_2^{+}(\theta, \delta)\{1 - (1+r)a_{11}\}}. \tag{8.20}$$

On the other hand, from (8.18) and (8.19), the following is obtained:

$$c = \frac{\det\left[I - (1+g)A^{+}(\theta, \delta)\right]}{(1+g)l_1 a_{12}(\theta, \delta) + l_2^{+}(\theta, \delta)\{1 - (1+g)a_{11}\}}. \tag{8.21}$$

Clearly, (8.20) and (8.21) have the same functional form, and thus, the wage–profit and consumption–growth curves have exactly the same shape. Moreover, the two functions above have the same form even if θ and δ change. Therefore, I can deduce the following proposition.

Proposition 8.2 *The wage–profit frontier and the consumption–growth frontier have the same functional form in the systems represented by (8.14) and (8.15).*

Consequently, the discrepancy between households' and producers' benefits found in the original model disappears in the present model.

Two formulae of EPR

In the above, I have shown that a formula $\delta = \phi(\theta)$ implements an EPR policy. If the formula is shown to economic actors by an authority, a competitive power, as I have supposed in the original systems, is also at work in the systems where an EPR policy is implemented, and thus, the cost-minimization principle operates in the following systems:

$$
\begin{cases}
(1+r)(p_1 a_{11} + p_2 a_{21}) + w l_1 = p_1 \\
(1+r)\{p_1 a_{12}(\theta) + p_2 a_{22}(\theta) - \phi(\theta) p_3\} + w l_2(\theta) = p_2 \\
(1+r)(p_1 a_{13} + p_2 a_{23} + p_3) + w l_2 = 0 \\
p_2 = 1,
\end{cases}
\tag{8.22}
$$

and (8.15). Therefore, given the rate of profit, the technique which maximizes the wage rate is chosen.

Provided that only the production and labour coefficients represented by $a_{12}(\theta)$, $a_{22}(\theta)$ and $l_2(\theta)$ in the second equation above were taken into account, clearly a larger θ should be preferred, so that $\theta = 1$ would be chosen. Yet, an EPR coefficient $\phi(\theta)$ counteracts that effect, since $\phi(\theta)$ is an increasing function. Consequently, a θ which is smaller than unity may possibly be chosen in a long-run competitive economy. Anyhow, since the wage rate is determined once θ is given, and since this relationship $\theta \in [0, 1] \mapsto w \in [0, w_{max}]$ is continuous in an ordinary sense, there exist some θ^* (and so δ^*) which maximize the wage rate.

It must be remembered that the wage–profit frontier coincides with the consumption–growth frontier by means of an EPR policy (Proposition 8.2). Coupling this result with the above, we know that per capita consumption is maximized by the cost-minimization principle.

Proposition 8.3 *Suppose the EPR policy formula $\delta = \phi(\theta)$ is demonstrated by the authority and fully comprehended by producers, then per capita consumption is maximized while waste is properly disposed of on the responsibility of producers of a consumption-commodity.*

I would like to note that this proposition refers to compatibility of economic and environmental factors. The economic factor is clearly the maximization of per capita consumption, while the environmental factor is disposal of waste. Waste generation at the post-consumption stage is fully taken into account by producers of the relevant commodity, and the waste disposal charge is paid by them. Thus, waste reduction is also considered by them at the ante-consumption stage. Obviously, this is the implication of EPR.

I would like to make an important remark. For the above proposition to hold, the formula $\delta = \phi(\theta)$ must be understood precisely by the producers of the second commodity. Otherwise, a θ^* which maximizes per capita consumption is not chosen. Suppose that the producers do not understand how δ changes as θ changes, and misunderstand δ as a fixed parameter. Then, a larger θ is preferred for any given δ, so that $\theta = 1$ is finally chosen by the competitive power, even though δ is changed as θ changes.

Although the formula $\delta = \phi(\theta)$ is theoretically possible and understood by producers of a consumption-commodity, it looks very complicated and is actually impractical. I would like to show that there is a much simpler formula.

Setting $\theta = 1$ in (8.17), we have

$$(1 + r) p^{(-)} A^\dagger(1, \delta) + w L^\dagger(1, \delta) = p^{(-)}.$$

Then, we can regard w as a continuous and decreasing function of δ. Hence, there exists $\hat{\delta}$ such that corresponding $\hat{w}$ is smaller than $w^* \equiv w_{\max}$, namely $\hat{w} < w^*$.

Now, let me make the following formula:

$$\delta = \psi(\theta) \equiv \begin{cases} \phi(\theta^*) & \text{for } \theta \in [0, \theta^*] \\ \hat{\delta} & \text{for } \theta \in (\theta^*, 1], \end{cases}$$

where θ^* corresponds to w^*. By construction,

$$w < w^* \text{ for all } \theta \in [0, \theta^*) \text{ and for all } \theta \in (\theta^*, 1], \text{ and } w = w^* \text{ for } \theta = \theta^*.$$

Then, the cost-minimizing technique based upon the formula $\delta = \psi(\theta)$ is the one which corresponds to $\theta = \theta^*$. This formula is much simpler than $\delta = \phi(\theta)$, and easily understood by producers. Since the same pair (θ^*, δ^*) as under the formula $\delta = \phi(\theta)$ is chosen under the formula $\delta = \psi(\theta)$, the same equilibrium price and quantity vectors are obtained in the long-run equilibrium. Thus, we have the following result:

Proposition 8.4 *Under the formula $\delta = \psi(\theta)$, the same equilibrium price and quantity vectors as under the formula $\delta = \phi(\theta)$ are obtained in (8.14) and (8.15).*

EPR and price changes

It is clear that the introduction of an EPR policy affects price formation. Let me explore how the price system is modified in the EPR environment, comparing the new prices with the ones in the original model in which an EPR policy is not introduced.

In order to make the comparison clear, let me give superscripts I and II respectively to the variables which correspond to economies in non-EPR and EPR policy environments. Furthermore, as a reference point, let me consider a case in which a waste generation coefficient is somehow restricted to θ^* by the authority but households are supposed to pay the waste treatment charge.

Now, I can show the following proposition.

Proposition 8.5 *Adopting the price of a consumption commodity as numeraire, we have (i) $w^{II}(\theta^*) \leq w^I(\theta^*) \leq w^I(1)$, and (ii) $p_2^{II}(\theta^*) \leq p_2^I(\theta^*) - \theta p_3^I(\theta^*)$*

$\leq p_2^I(1) - \theta p_3^I(1)$, *where a strict inequality holds when* $0 < \delta^*$ *holds in the former inequality and when* $\theta^* < 1$ *holds in the latter inequality for both (i) and (ii).*

In the proposition, the price of the consumption commodity is unity, i.e. $p_2^{II}(\theta^*) = p_2^I(\theta^*) = p_2^I(1) = 1$ by definition.

Proof. See Appendix 8.A. □

The price $p_2^{II}(\theta^*)$ includes the waste disposal charge following the upstream policy EPR, which is represented by $\delta = \phi(\theta)$ or $\delta = \psi(\theta)$, so that the waste disposal charge is internalized in $p_2^{II}(\theta^*)$. This is not larger than (actually smaller than in most cases) the price of the consumption commodity $p_2^I(\theta^*)$ plus the waste disposal charge $\theta^* p_3^I(\theta^*)$, which means the total payment on consumption when the waste generation coefficient θ^* is imposed on producers by the authority on one hand, while households are supposed to pay for waste disposal on the other. Furthermore, this total payment is not larger than (actually smaller than in most cases) the total payment on consumption when there is no restriction on waste generation and households are supposed to pay for it. This shows how an EPR policy affects the price formation and waste charge payment.

It is interesting to see what happens to changes of the price formation after the EPR implementation, when labour is adopted as *numeraire*, instead of the consumption commodity. Adopting the notation $p^i(\theta) \equiv (p_1^i(\theta), p_2^i(\theta), p_3^i(\theta))$ ($i = I, II$), I can demonstrate the following proposition.

Proposition 8.6

(i) $\dfrac{p^I(1)}{w^I(1)} \leq \dfrac{p^I(\theta^*)}{w^I(\theta^*)} \leq \dfrac{p^{II}(\theta^*)}{w^{II}(\theta^*)}$ *holds, where the first inequality holds strictly when* $\theta^* < 1$, *while the second inequality holds strictly when* $0 < \delta^*$.

(ii) $\dfrac{p_2^{II}(\theta^*)}{w^{II}(\theta^*)} = \dfrac{p_2^I(\theta^*)}{w^I(\theta^*)} - \theta^* \dfrac{p_3^I(\theta^*)}{w^I(\theta^*)} \leq \dfrac{p_2^I(1)}{w^I(1)} - \dfrac{p_3^I(1)}{w^I(1)}$ *holds, where a strict inequality holds when* $\theta^* < 1$.

Proof. See Appendix 8.B. □

The first half of this proposition tells us that prices measured in terms of labour are the highest when an EPR policy is implemented, and the lowest when there is no restriction on waste generation and households are supposed to pay for waste disposal at the post-consumption stage. The prices are between two extremes when the same restriction on waste generation as under EPR is implemented by the authority but households are supposed to pay the waste disposal charge.

The second half of the proposition tells us the following: if prices are measured in terms of labour, the price of the consumption commodity in which the waste disposal charge is internalized by EPR equals the price of the consumption commodity plus the waste disposal charge when the charge is paid by households at the post-consumption stage but the same waste generation coefficient as under EPR is imposed on producers by the authority. Yet, it is not larger than (actually smaller in most cases) the price of the consumption commodity plus the waste disposal charge when the charge is paid by households at the post-consumption stage and there is no restriction of waste generation (i.e. $\theta = 1$).

Proposition 8.6 is contrasted with the second part of Proposition 8.5, which demonstrates that, if prices and a wage rate are measured by the consumption commodity, the price of the consumption commodity in which the waste disposal charge is internalized by EPR is not larger than (actually smaller in most cases) the price of the consumption commodity plus the waste disposal charge when the charge is paid by households at the post-consumption stage but the same waste generation rate as under EPR is imposed on producers by the authority. It must, however, be noted that per capita consumption is the same in both cases since the same waste generation rate θ^* is supposed to be given.

Concluding remarks

By means of a variation of a Sraffa model, I have explored how an EPR policy which places the responsibility for waste disposal on producers waste generation affects per capita consumption as well as the price formation. The idea of choice of technique by the cost-minimization principle is fully utilized. The main results are as follows.

Firstly, if households are supposed to pay for the waste disposal at post-consumption stage and there is no constraint on waste generation, waste is discharged as much as possible, while per capita consumption is not maximized. This means that such an economy is wasteful not only in an environmental sense, but in an economic sense. The defect is due to the fact that there is a gap between the wage–profit and consumption–growth frontiers.

Secondly, a proper EPR policy rectifies this defect, internalizing the waste disposal cost in the price of the consumption commodity which generates waste at the post-consumption stage. The gap between the two frontiers disappears, thanks to EPR, so that households' and producers' benefits are well matched in a long-run competitive economy.

Finally, it may be worth noting that the same result is obtained without an EPR policy on some specific conditions. Even if households are supposed to pay the waste disposal charge after consumption, per capita consumption is maximized, provided that the authority can impose the same waste generation rate as under EPR directly on producers *and* there is no illegal dumping of waste by households. In addition, if labour is adopted as *numeraire*, the price of the consumption-commodity which internalizes the waste disposal cost under EPR is the same as the price of the consumption-commodity plus the waste disposal charge at the post-consumption stage without EPR. Thus, there is no difference between the two policies, insofar as the aforementioned conditions are met.

It would, however, be unrealistic to assume that there is no illegal dumping by dischargers of waste when they are required to pay for waste disposal. If there is illegal dumping of waste, households' benefits may be unimproved in a competitive economy, even if the authority is so wise that it can impose the same waste generation rate as under EPR on producers. Internalization of waste treatment costs by an upstream policy in the relevant production activity is effective in eliminating illegal dumping of waste, and an EPR policy which harmonizes households' and producers' benefits may be one of the most powerful policy tools for waste reduction.

Appendix 8.A

Proof of (i) of Proposition 8.5.

$$\left(p_1^I(1), p_2^I(1)\right) = w^I(1)L^{(-)}(1)\left[I - (1+r)A^{(-)}(1)\right]^{-1}$$
$$\left(p_1^I(\theta^*), p_2^I(\theta^*)\right) = w^I(\theta^*)L^{(-)}(\theta^*)\left[I - (1+r)A^{(-)}(\theta^*)\right]^{-1} \text{ and}$$
$$\left(p_1^{II}(\theta^*), p_2^{II}(\theta^*)\right) = w^{II}(\theta^*)L^{\dagger}(\theta^*)\left[I - (1+r)A^{\dagger}(\theta^*)\right]^{-1}$$

must hold, where $\delta^* = \phi(\theta^*)$. Then, we have

$$1 = w^I(1)L^{(-)}(1)\left[I - (1+r)A^{(-)}(1)\right]^{-1}\begin{pmatrix} 0 \\ 1 \end{pmatrix}$$

$$= w^I(\theta^*)L^{(-)}(\theta^*)\left[I - (1+r)A^{(-)}(\theta^*)\right]^{-1}\begin{pmatrix} 0 \\ 1 \end{pmatrix}$$

$$= w^{II}(\theta^*)L^{\dagger}(\theta^*)\left[I - (1+r)A^{\dagger}(\theta^*)\right]^{-1}\begin{pmatrix} 0 \\ 1 \end{pmatrix}.$$

Since

$$L^{(-)}(1)\left[I - (1+r)A^{(-)}(1)\right]^{-1} \leq L^{(-)}(\theta^*)\left[I - (1+r)A^{(-)}(\theta^*)\right]^{-1}$$
$$\leq L^{\dagger}(\theta^*)\left[I - (1+r)A^{\dagger}(\theta^*)\right]^{-1} \qquad (8.A.1)$$

hold, we have $w^{II}(\theta^*) \leq w^I(\theta^*) \leq w^I(1)$. If $0 < \delta^*$ holds, then $\ll$ holds in the first vector inequality above, so that $w^{II}(\theta^*) < w^I(\theta^*)$ holds. If $\theta^* < 1$ holds, then $\ll$ holds in the second vector inequality above, so that $w^I(\theta^*) < w^I(1)$ holds. $\qquad\square$

Proof of (ii) of Proposition 8.5. Notice $w^{II}(\theta^*) = p_2^{II}(\theta^*)c^{II}(\theta^*)$, $w^I(\theta^*) = \{p_2^I(\theta^*) - \theta^* p_3^I(\theta^*)\}c^I(\theta^*)$ and $w^I(1) = \{p_2^I(1) - p_3^I(1)\}c^I(1)$ hold, where the second commodity is *numeraire*, i.e., $p_2^I(\theta^*) = p_2^I(1) = p_2^{II}(\theta^*) = 1$.
    Since $c^I(\theta^*) = c^{II}(\theta^*) \geq c^I(1)$ and $w^{II}(\theta^*) \leq w^I(\theta^*) \leq w^I(1)$ hold, we have

$$p_2^{II}(\theta^*) \leq p_2^I(\theta^*) - \theta^* p_3^I(\theta^*) \leq p_2^I(1) - p_3^I(1),$$

where strict inequalities hold when $0 < \delta^* = \phi(\theta^*)$ and $\theta^* < 1$ hold, since we have $a_{i2}(\theta) < a_{i2}^{\dagger}(\theta)$ ($i = 1, 2$) and $l_2(\theta) < l_2^{\dagger}(\theta)$ ($i = 1, 2$) in the case of $0 < \delta^*$, and $c^{II}(\theta^*) > c^I(1)$ as well as $w^I(\theta^*) < w^I(1)$ in the case of $\theta^* < 1$. $\qquad\square$

Appendix 8.B

Proof of (i) of Proposition 8.6. This is clear from (8.A.1).   □

Proof of (ii) of Proposition 8.6. Notice

$$w^I(1) = \{p_2^I(1) - p_3^I(1)\}c^I(1), \; w^I(\theta^*) = \{p_2^I(\theta^*) - \theta^* p_3^I(\theta^*)\}c^I(\theta^*) \quad \text{and}$$
$$w^{II}(\theta^*) = p_2^{II}(\theta^*)c^{II}(\theta^*)$$

holds. Hence, we have

$$1 = \left(\frac{p_2^I(1)}{w^I(1)} - \frac{p_3^I(1)}{w^I(1)}\right)c^I(1) = \left(\frac{p_2^I(\theta^*)}{w^I(\theta^*)} - \theta^* \frac{p_3^I(\theta^*)}{w^I(\theta^*)}\right)c^I(\theta^*) = \frac{p_2^{II}(\theta^*)}{w^{II}(\theta^*)}c^{II}(\theta^*),$$

where $c^I(1) \leq c^I(\theta^*) = c^{II}(\theta^*)$ and a strict inequality holds when $\theta^* < 1$ holds. Therefore, the result follows.   □

Notes

1 The author is grateful to Professor Ken-ichi Akao for his comments. This research was supported by the Environment Research and Technology Development Fund (K123002) of the Ministry of the Environment, Japan.
2 See Kurz and Salvadori (1995) for detailed discussion on the principle.
3 For $x = (x_1, x_2, \ldots, x_n)$, $x \gg 0$ means that $x_i > 0$ for all i, and $x \geq 0$ means that $x_i \geq 0$ for all i. Finally, $x > 0$ means that $x \geq 0$ and $x \neq 0$. The same notation is applicable to matrix inequalities.
4 It must be noted that a so-called material balance is not considered in this paper.
5 In this case, the cost-price balance is expressed by $(1+r)(p_1 a_{13} + p_2 a_{23}) + w l_3 = P_3$. Then, $P_3 \equiv -(1+r)p_3 (> 0)$ is the price of waste disposal service. This expression is adopted in Hosoda (2010).

References

Calcott, K. and M. Walls (2000) 'Can Downstream Waste Disposal Policies Encourage Upstream "Design for Environment"?', *American Economic Review*, Vol. 90, pp. 233–237.

Dinan, T.M. (1993) 'Economic Efficiency Effects of Alternative Policies for Reducing Waste Disposal', *Journal of Environmental Economics and Policy Studies*, Vol. 25, pp. 242–256.

Eichner, T. and R. Pethig (2001) 'Product Design and Efficient Management of Recycling and Waste Treatment', *Journal of Environmental Economics and Policy Studies*, Vol. 41, pp. 109–134.

Fullerton, D. and T. Kinnaman (1995) 'Garbage, Recycling, and Illicit Burning or Dumping', *Journal of Environmental Economics and Policy Studies*, Vol. 29, pp. 78–91.

Fullerton, D. and W. Wu (1998) 'Policies for Green Design', *Journal of Environmental Economics and Policy Studies*, Vol. 36, No. 2, pp. 131–148.

Gehrke, C. and C. Lager (1995) ' Environmental Taxes, Relative Prices and Choice of Technique in a Linear Model of Production', *Metroeconomica*, Vol. 46, No. 2, pp. 127–145.

Hosoda, E. (2010) 'Malfunction of a Market in a Transaction of Waste – A Reason for the Necessity of an Upstream Policy in Waste Management', contained in J. Vint, J.S. Metcalfe, H.D. Kurz, N. Salvadori and P.A. Samuelson (eds), *Economic Theory and Economic Thought – Essays in Honour of Ian Steedman*, London: Routledge, pp. 234–253.

Hosoda, E. (2012) 'Recycling of Waste and Downgrading of Secondary Resources in a Classical Type of Production Model', *Journal of Economic Structures*, Vol. 1, No. 7, DOI: 10.1186/2193-2409-1-7.

Hosoda, E. (2014) 'An Analysis of Sorting and Recycling of Household Waste: A Neo-Ricardian Approach', *Metroeconomica*, Vol. 65, No. 1, pp. 58–94, DOI: 10.1111/meca.12029.

Kurz, D.H. and N. Salvadori (1995) *Theory of Production – A Long-Period Analysis*, Cambridge: Cambridge University Press.

Lager, C. (1999) 'Perverse Results of a Greening of the Tax System', contained in J.R. Teixeira and F.G. Carneiro (eds) *Economic Dynamics and Economic Policy*, Brasilia: DF-Brazil, pp. 147–160.

Walls, M. and K. Palmer (2001) 'Upstream Pollution, Downstream Waste Disposal, and the Design of Comprehensive Environmental Policies', *Journal of Environmental Economics and Policy Studies*, Vol. 41, pp. 94–108.

9 How should prices of production be interpreted?

The case of oil

Alessandro Roncaglia[1]

Introduction

The issue of the interpretation of prices of production has long been an object of debate, ever since the publication of Sraffa's *Production of Commodities by Means of Commodities* in 1960. My own interpretation (in short, prices of production photographing the economy at a given moment in time, see Roncaglia, 1975, 2009) in some respects differs from the one (the so-called long-period method) adopted by Neri Salvadori and Heinz Kurz, following Garegnani (see Garegnani, 1990; Kurz and Salvadori, 1995).[2]

I shall not repeat my interpretation here, nor illustrate theirs – apart from recalling two points which will be relevant to the following pages. First, the long-period method requires a factual assumption, namely that the givens in the analysis of prices of production change slowly, relative to the adjustment of (actual) market prices to prices of production. The photograph interpretation, instead, considers Sraffa's analysis of the relationship between prices and income distribution as capturing some basic relations holding in the economy at a point in time, with no assumption about how the economy changes over time. Second, in a world where technical change is ubiquitous, and showing a rate and characteristics which differ from one sector to another (and, as a consequence, in a world in which uncertainty about the future path of the economy also reigns), there is a need for a great deal of caution in the use of some tools of price of production theory – such as analysis of rent for non-reproducible resources – when considering real-world economic issues.

The aim of this paper is to illustrate this point by analysing the characteristics of the oil market. Here, not only technical change and uncertainty but also market forms other than competition play an important role. As a consequence, the analytical tools developed in the context of the Sraffian framework for non-reproducible natural resources[3] cannot be utilized, and prices of production remain in the background. Since oil is a basic commodity for the world economy, the facts of its price of production have an important part to play in our interpretation of the system of prices of production in general.

The next section provides a historical overview of the oil sector, stressing the role of technical change on both the production and the utilization side, and the complex and changing nature of the market forms prevailing in the sector (including the influence of anti-trust policies). The third section considers the issue of oil resources and reserves, showing the role of uncertainty and the fact that, contrary to widespread opinion, oil should better be treated as a produced and reproducible commodity rather than as a non-reproducible natural resource. The final section concludes, coming back full circle to the references to interpretation of Sraffian prices of production made in this section.

An overview of the oil sector history and characteristics

Oil is a complex sector, with a sequence of technologically diverse productive stages: exploration, production, transport, refining, distribution of a number of distinct products, such as lubricants, gasoil and gasoline. Oil fields also vary in location, technological characteristics and the quality of oil (density, sulphur content, etc.). International political relations are important, with strong interdependence between exporting and importing countries and global environmental implications which call for multilateral coordination of policies, while the various countries show marked juridical differentiation concerning property and control of oilfields, environmental regulations, taxation and so on.

One characteristic common to all stages of activity in the oil sector and persistent through time is the high ratio of fixed to variable costs.[4] Under freely competitive conditions this element is a source of instability, since every firm has an interest in expanding production up to the limit of full utilization of productive capacity due to decreasing unit costs (and has a strong inducement to do so when confronted with falling prices); in the history of the oil sector, it has been a source of market power concentration, since the larger firms enjoy a cost advantage over the smaller firms and entrance is constrained by the relatively large minimum size of plants compared to the size of the market (suffice it to consider, for instance, the scale of a refinery or a pipeline).

Thus, in the last decades of the nineteenth century, Rockefeller's Standard Oil Trust grew to a near-monopoly position in the United States through the advantage acquired in the transport of crude oil by railway between the oilfields and the refineries in the Pennsylvania area. The size of the market for oil products was limited at the time, the main use of oil being for oil lamps. Intervention by the US Supreme Court was necessary, in 1911, to break the Standard Oil Trust down into 34 separate corporate entities, among which the Standard Oil of New Jersey (later Exxon) and the Standard Oil of New York (later Mobil), recently merged into Exxon–Mobil.[5]

The period immediately following the First World War was characterized by competitive outbursts and price instability. New companies appeared, such as Texaco with the discovery of the Texas oil fields; outside of the United States, Shell and BP grew in size and market power. In 1927–28 a price war broke out between Exxon and Shell, initially in the Indian market but later with worldwide impact: a disastrous price fall followed.

As was later discovered by a US Senate commission of inquiry (Federal Trade Commission Staff Report, 1952; see also Blair, 1976), the so-called oil majors reacted to this situation by entering into two separate agreements, both in 1928. The first agreement ensured joint control over the most abundant and least costly sources of crude, the Middle East oilfields: the oil majors agreed to joint exploitation of oil reserves within an area drawn with a red pencil on a Middle East map (hence the name 'Red Line Agreement'). The second ('As Is') agreement ensured coordination in the supply of oil products in major consuming countries, through regular country-by-country meetings between representatives of the companies.[6]

Traditionally, the US anti-trust authorities are keen on pressing for competition within the country but ready to disregard collusion in foreign parts involving US-based companies. However, even within the United States, when confronted with the huge Texas discoveries and the fall in demand following upon the 1929 crisis, the authorities were induced to intervene, legislating elements of control on the supply side: a ban on oil imports (reinforced in 1959, and lasting up to 1973) and a 'prorationing' mechanism, namely oil well stoppage in rotation enforced by a public body, the Texas Railroad Commission.

Oil demand rose sharply in the aftermath of the Second World War, but the market structure remained more or less unaltered, with the Seven Sisters (five US majors plus Shell and BP) and later the French company Elf and (after the death of Mattei) the Italian ENI continuing their joint exploitation of Middle East oil and their dominance of the international oil market. The prices of crude oil and oil products remained relatively stable, while production and demand grew *pari passu*. In 1950 the Seven Sisters plus Elf controlled 99.4 per cent of the crude oil produced outside the United States.

However, the growth in the size of the market and the growing production of countries outside the Red Line (such as the Soviet Union, Egypt and Libya on whose crude oil ENI relied for its original development outside of the system of control of the majors) brought about a slow but continuous decrease of this share: in 1957, the Seven Sisters and Elf controlled 92 per cent of crude oil production outside the US; in 1970 the share was down to 68.4 per cent.[7] The oil majors were vertically integrated companies, active in all stages – from exploration and production of crude oil to transport, refining and distribution of oil products – with a relatively balanced internal structure and with long-term agreements between oil-short companies such as Mobil and oil-long companies such as Exxon.[8] Thus, crude oil prices were mainly internal prices, set with a mind to tax minimization. The 'official' prices set by the oil companies – the so-called posted prices – were in fact maximum prices: 'only fools and affiliated pay posted prices', was a widespread opinion among market insiders, while inter-company deals took place at (well-kept secret) discounts.

This market structure underwent a massive upheaval in the early 1970s, around the period of the first oil crisis. Occasioned by the Arab–Israeli war, but also by the sudden abolition of the ban on imports on the part of the US,[9] the 1973 crisis led not only to a multi-fold price increase (with heavy imbalances on current accounts for importing countries, inflation and a worldwide economic crisis) but also to recognition of a shift of power from importing countries and oil companies to oil exporting countries, especially in the Arab peninsula; this element was reinforced by the second oil crisis, in 1979–80, sparked off by the Iranian revolution.

Since 1973 OPEC, the petroleum exporting countries' organization, took the lead in price-setting, taking care to adjust crude oil supply to demand, namely accommodating increases in crude production in non-OPEC countries through decreases in its own share, thanks mainly to Saudi Arabia, who willy-nilly acquired the role of swing producer (namely, the producer who adapts its own supply so as to balance overall world supply with overall world demand (or more precisely, given geographical constraints to international oil trade, overall supply of OPEC oil with overall demand for it).

Producing countries also acquired control of their oil fields, in most cases through national oil companies such as Aramco, with long-term agreements with the oil majors for technical assistance in the production and sale of crude oil.

Competitive pressure from non-OPEC oil exporting countries slowly accumulated; finally, when in August 1985 Saudi Arabia saw its production reduced to 2.2 million barrels per day (from a customary level of around 10 million barrels at the beginning of the 1970s and a production capacity around 12 million barrels), it decided to abandon its role as swing producer, abruptly and indeed dramatically increasing its production, thereby bringing about an equally dramatic price fall.

After a brief period in which Saudi Arabia set prices for its crude oil on the basis of the prices obtained by refined oil products (thus ensuring that refineries buying Saudi crude were able to fetch their margin of earnings whatever happened to the prices of their refined products), there was a general move to a 'formula pricing' system based on 'marker' prices, the main marker being Brent, a North Sea crude. According to this system, oil sales are indexed to the prices realized on a 'competitive' market – the 'dated Brent' market – where single cargoes are bought and sold so that the rhetoric of the oil sector can maintain that equilibrium prices are continuously determined by the opposite forces of supply and demand.

Markets such as that for 'dated Brent' are relatively thin, and slimming over time; buyers and sellers deal over the counter, with no obligation to reveal the price of their deals (and, when they choose to do so, there is no penalty for false declarations). Thus, the prices are 'assessed' by price reporting agencies, an activity dominated by two companies: Platt and Argus (who see themselves as news agencies, and as such exempt from the surveillance of the financial sector authorities).

Over time, a gigantic system of futures and options grew on the shoulders of the 'physical' price of Brent. The idea that the physical price could be considered independent of such financial markets, a necessary precondition for it to be utilized as the basis for the settlement of the financial contracts, was becoming increasingly awkward to sustain.[10] After a while there was a shift on the part of the price reporting agencies towards assessing oil prices on the basis of the futures market itself, the implicit assumption being, of course, that as predicated by the theory of efficient financial markets (Fama, 1970), the prices determined in such markets reflect the 'fundamentals' of supply and demand (or better the financial agents' evaluations of such fundamentals). Finally, Saudi Arabia and other exporting countries shifted to direct use of futures prices as the 'marker' to which their contracts are indexed.

After the 2007–08 financial crisis, the theory of efficient financial markets appears to have fallen somewhat out of fashion (and deservedly so), with a widespread return to Keynes's theory of the beauty contest, according to which prices in organized financial markets such as the stock exchange are determined not by 'fundamentals' but by a complex game of expectations on the other operators' expectations, with a relevant role assigned to 'conventions' on how the market works – the conventions holding good for a stretch of time and then abruptly breaking down.[11]

It is by no means easy to get a clear idea of the convention now ruling in the financial market for oil futures; operators appear to look mainly to data on US inventories (one of the few reliable data series in the oil sector) and the political news regarding the exporting countries. This would be a logical thing to do if the scarcity of oil were an immanent characteristic driving the day-by-day behaviour of 'physical' oil markets; however, as we shall seek to demonstrate in the following section, the situation appears to be quite different.

The assumed scarcity of oil

Why should oil prices be driven by day-by-day changes in supply and demand, rather than by cost of production?

Two aspects must be considered in this context: first, the flexibility of supply in the short run to meet unexpected changes in demand; second, the influence exerted by the ultimate scarcity of oil on current prices.

With regard to the first aspect, as a matter of fact we can see that over time production and demand grew *pari passu*, as shown by Figure 9.1. This is due to the existence of margins of unutilized capacity in the main oil exporting countries and, in the not-very-short period, to some flexibility in the timetable of investment plans already under way in existing giant oilfields.

The small differences between production and consumption are met by inventory changes. Commonly it is commercial inventories which adapt; such inventories are held by producers, by refineries or along the transport chain, at the mouth or end of pipelines (as in the case of the huge reserves at Cushing, Oklahoma) or in oil cargoes (quite simply, speeding them up or slowing them down). Major consuming countries also hold strategic reserves, recourse to which is limited to extraordinary events; a common target size for these is about 90 days' consumption.[12]

As a rule, for produced–reproducible commodities, especially under oligopolistic market conditions, the vagaries of current demand do not influence prices, which are determined, rather, by production costs (computed for a normal degree of utilization of plants) plus a margin of profits which depends on the market power of firms. (Without expanding on the issue here, illustrated at length elsewhere, we may recall here that the international oil market can be characterized as a 'trilateral oligopoly', with the international companies together with the

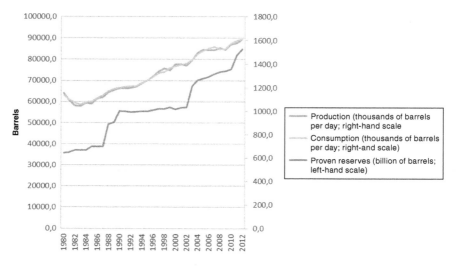

Figure 9.1 Production, consumption and reserves.

Source: U.S. Energy Information Administration (EIA).

exporting and importing countries constituting the three sides of the game and a differentiated power structure within each group.)[13]

The idea that crude oil prices could quite simply be determined by costs of production, were it not for the oligopolistic conditions characterizing the market, is commonly rejected by mainstream economists through reference to the ultimate scarcity of oil. Under these conditions, the Hotelling theorem (Hotelling, 1931) indicates that the price of the scarce exhaustible resource must grow over time at a rate equal to the rate of interest, eventually reaching, as the resource is fully exhausted, a level high enough to bring about its full substitution by other means of production and a change in the structure of consumption.

A classical counterpart to this theory is represented by simplistic direct recourse to the analytical tools of the Ricardian theory of rent.[14] In both cases there is the need to assume a given amount ultimately available of the resource, known ex ante, and a known technological path. In both cases, too, the most meticulous theorists indicate that when ultimate exhaustion is far off in time and the exhaustion path lies in a penumbra of uncertainty, then the ultimate exhaustion does not influence current prices. In fact, technical progress can in the meantime render the resource overabundant, due to better use of it and, especially, to substitution by a superior resource, as happened in the case of coal (largely substituted by oil) and as is happening in the case of oil (increasingly substituted by natural gas).

In order to show that this is the case, we must consider how distant the ultimate exhaustion of oil may be. Here, obviously, one has to take into consideration the available data on oil reserves.

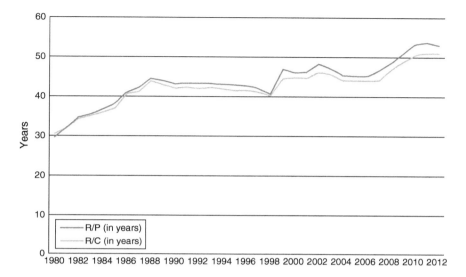

Figure 9.2 Proven reserves (R) as years of production (P) and consumption (C) – (BP).

Source: BP, Statistical Review of World Energy, 2013.

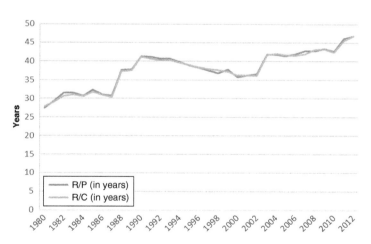

Figure 9.3 Proven reserves (R) as years of production (P) and consumption (C) – (US EIA).

Source: US Energy Information Administration.

Figures 9.2 and 9.3 show proven reserves (to be defined below) expressed in years of current production, according to two different sources: BP (Figure 9.2) and the US Energy Information Administration (Figure 9.3). Both figures show an increase over time in proven reserves, from about thirty to a bit more or less than fifty years. It is thus clear that proven reserves vary over time, and may register significant growth. It is also clear that there are discrepancies between the two sets of data. What lessons can we infer from these facts?

First, the differences between the two series point to the limited reliability of data on the oil sector,[15] as energy economists are well aware, which should suggest a great deal of caution when interpreting the data, especially when drawing inferences from econometric exercises concerning the oil sector. There is an impact, too, in terms of the uncertainty which surrounds decision-making in the energy field.

Second, the significant growth over time of proven reserves, not only in absolute terms but also as a ratio to current production (which also tends to increase over time), shows that proven reserves can be 'produced'. This depends on the very definition of proven reserves: reserves whose location, size and characteristics (quality of crude, depth and pressure of the field) are already known, and which on the basis of such data are confidently held to be economically recoverable with known technology at prevailing price–cost ratios.[16] Thus, reserves can be 'produced' not only by exploratory activity but also, and especially, by technical progress reducing extraction costs and increasing the rate of recovery of oil in the field. The growth of this rate from about 10–15 per cent for Middle East oilfields in the 1960s to about 40 per cent and more in difficult oilfields such as the North Sea ones, through secondary and tertiary recovery techniques, meant a gigantic increase in proven reserves, more than sufficient to compensate for the gradual exhaustion of currently exploited oilfields.[17] In recent years, the so-called unconventional oil (heavy oil, tar sands and shale oil) also entered the scene, more or less doubling the amount of economically recoverable oil with current techniques.[18]

In fact, the proven reserves can be likened to a shelf inventory of means of production, which can be increased when needed.[19] In order to evaluate the ultimate scarcity of oil we should rather look to ultimate reserves (namely the total quantity of oil available on earth); but the estimates for these are most uncertain, with wild differences from one source to another, and even such estimates have a tendency to grow over time as a consequence of technical progress (as happened, for instance, when unconventional oil – shale oil, tar sands etc. – came to be included in the definition). Overall, we can certainly reject the doomsday prophecies envisaging an imminent exhaustion of oil;[20] we can also consider the ultimate exhaustion of oil to be so far off in the future as not to justify the thesis that it has an impact on current prices.

When we consider the distribution by quality of the reserves and the ratio between current production and reserves at the level of individual fields, another aspect becomes clear. Low-cost Middle East reserves, huge as they are, are relatively under-utilized in comparison to the higher-cost reserves in OECD countries; the current exploitation of unconventional oil reserves (with production costs higher than conventional oil, but in most cases lower, indeed much lower, than the currently prevailing oil prices) is accompanied by under-utilization of the conventional reserves.[21]

The implication of these facts is also clear. It is not the high cost of producing oil in the 'marginal' oil field[22] that determines the price of crude oil; rather, the converse is true: it is the current price of oil which allows for the exploitation of 'inferior' (relatively higher cost) reserves. In other words, the Ricardian theory of rent cannot be applied to the oil sector.[23] Also, it is clear that the oil sector cannot be considered as characterized by free competition exerting a downward pressure on prices to the point of expelling higher-cost oil from the market.

In conclusion, there can be no getting away from the fact that technology is important in determining the price of oil, as for every commodity that is produced; to this we should add the crucial role of market forms, and hence the strategies adopted by the main actors on the scene: the major companies, the major exporting countries (and their organization, OPEC) and the major consuming countries.

Conclusions: some implications for the interpretation of production prices

The thesis that the price of crude oil is mainly determined by technology (cost of production) and the prevailing market forms (and the strategies of the main actors) may be proposed as plausible, in the light of the previous pages, but certainly not fully demonstrated. The purpose of this paper is rather to bring some elements of concrete reality to bear on the debate on interpretation of the scope of production price analysis.

First of all, we can see from the above that the traditional marginalist tools applied to account for the prices of exhaustible natural resources, such as the Hotelling theorem, cannot be of much help, since crude oil, while being by definition an exhaustible natural resource, cannot be considered economically scarce, and the moment of its ultimate exhaustion is wrapped in the future mists of time.

Second, recourse to the tools of a Ricardian–Sraffian type can be considered. Uncertainty about the future is here irrelevant, since these tools are constructed for analysis 'at a point in time' – a sort of photograph of the technical relations prevailing 'now' (see Roncaglia, 2009). Here, the problem is of a different nature: the Ricardian theory of rent (and its Sraffian developments for the case of exhaustible natural resources) presupposes free competition, and the oil sector is far from that.

Sylos Labini (1984, pp. 141–3) suggests considering market forms departing from free competition in a Sraffian setting by recourse to sectorial multiplicative coefficients for the rate of profits. This leaves open the issue as to what determines such coefficients, and the even bigger issue as to what influence the market forms exert on the strategies of the main agents and the path of development of the sector itself. Given the importance of the oil sector in the world economy, this is no small issue.

The account given above of events in the oil sector suggests that political events (including anti-trust policies) and technical progress play a decisive role in determining the evolution of the market structure, which in turn determines production costs and profit margins. This implies that the issue is better tackled with a dynamic–historical type of analysis, rather than trying to determine an equilibrium (or better, in our context, a 'long-period position').[24]

Thus, we might draw the conclusion that in the case of oil the Sraffian–Keynesian approach provides help for a critique of the mainstream (scarcity) approach but not an easy direct solution along the lines of the Ricardian theory of rent as perfected by Sraffa in Chapter XI of his 1960 book. However, the general conceptual framework of the Sraffian–Keynesian analysis may provide a useful background.[25]

What the example of the oil sector discussed in the preceding sections suggests is that the reconstruction of a classical Keynesian approach for application to real-world issues should not proceed along the lines of a general all-encompassing model for the entire economy, but along the path of separate pieces of analysis tailored to the specific problem at hand, where the unifying element is provided by the conceptual compatibility with the general features of the classical Keynesian (reproducibility) approach.

Notes

1 Department of statistical sciences, Sapienza University of Rome. In this paper I utilize material drawn from my writings on the subject of oil markets (Roncaglia, 1983, 1991, 2015). In particular, for more details on the history of the oil sector, see Roncaglia (1983); and for a more detailed treatment of the current situation, see Roncaglia (2015).
2 My discussions with Neri Salvadori on the interpretation of Sraffa's work date back to the early 1970s, when I had just graduated and Neri was still an undergraduate student. Disagreements are possible even within a basic common classical framework, and they represent the salt of an ongoing debate which is all the more fruitful if it is accompanied, as in our case, by decades-long friendship and mutual respect – indeed, this is a case where I believe that a 'long-period position' in academic and human relations can be recognized.
3 For a thorough analysis of these tools, see Kurz and Salvadori (1995), Chapter 10; Chapter 12 points to the 'limits to the long-period method', with Section 4 (pp. 357 ff.) specifically devoted to the case of exhaustible resources, for which fossil fuels and oil are cited as typical examples. Indeed, what Kurz and Salvadori say concerning these limits on pp. 357–60 (in particular the reference to treating the 'deposits', in my case oil reserves, 'as if they were a machine', p. 360) corresponds to the situation I shall try to illustrate in the following pages.
4 Originally pointed out by Frankel (1946), this element is the foundation stone for Sylos Labini's (1956) theory of concentrated oligopoly.
5 In the following decades, a web of relations (interlocking shareholdings and interlocking directorates involving oil corporations and banks) favoured the implicit coordination of long-term strategies of the major international oil companies. See Roncaglia (1983), pp. 47–79.
6 The Report of the Federal Trade Commission documents, for instance, over fifty meetings per year in Sweden, deciding on, for instance, the set of apparently independent bid prices for the supply of gasoil for Stockholm public transport.
7 ENI, 1981, Table 133b.
8 Oil-short companies are those with refining subsidiaries requiring more crude oil as input than the crude lifted by production subsidiaries. For oil-long companies the opposite situation holds: their internal production of crude oil is greater than the amount of crude required as input in their refineries.
9 On the importance of the second element, commonly overlooked, see Roncaglia (1983), pp. 99–100.

10 The system is very complex. There is in fact a chain of different contracts: from 'dated Brent' to 'Brent forward' connected by a contract called CFD, contract for differences, then to Brent futures, connected to Brent forward by a contract called 'exchange for physicals'; for detailed illustration of the system, see Fattouh (2011).

11 See Keynes (1936), pp. 150–63. On the limits of risk evaluation in finance, see Roncaglia (2012).

12 To evaluate the security allowed by such reserves, let us consider an example. When Iraq invaded Kuwait and Kuwaiti production suddenly disappeared from the market, assuming that in a Western country such as Italy or the United States Kuwaiti imports represented 10 per cent of national consumption of oil (a fair approximation to the real data, here adopted for the sake of simple computation), such imports can be fully substituted by drawing on strategic reserves for 900 days – a time span more than sufficient to expand oil production elsewhere in the world. Let us remark in passing that joint management of such reserves on the part of the major consuming countries could do wonders in stabilizing oil prices; even a strong assertion to this effect – strong enough to be credible – could change the conventions ruling in the oil futures market and obtain the desired result. Unfortunately such a possibility has never been seriously considered, notwithstanding the negative impact on the real economy of the current marked variability in oil prices. (For a proposal of a stabilization mechanism for oil prices, see Roncaglia (1991); buffer stocks for the stabilization of raw material prices are a traditional Keynesian proposal: see Sabbatini (1989), for an account of this proposal).

13 This interpretation of the oil market is developed in Roncaglia (1983). See also Roncaglia (2015), for a re-proposal of this interpretation in the present context, in opposition to the view of a succession of stages in the oil sector (first domination on the side of multinational oil companies, then the OPEC era, and subsequently the era characterized by 'competitive' price determination in spot and financial markets assumedly driven by supply and demand fundamentals).

14 As far as I know, no economist ever tried to explain oil prices with direct recourse to the Ricardian theory of rent. A variant of the Ricardian rent theory based on the 'marginal barrel' in a supposedly increasing long-run Marshallian supply curve was proposed by Adelman (1972, 1995); for critical comment, see Roncaglia (1983), pp. 31–4. The media occasionally explain oil price increases referring to increases in extraction costs due to the shift to more technologically difficult oilfields occasioned by growth in demand and exhaustion of old oilfields; however, this cannot be considered as a general rule, since it assumes away technical progress.

15 Oil companies have an embedded interest in optimistic evaluations of their own proven reserves, since such data commonly affect the price of their shares in the stock exchange; official evaluations tend to be more conservative.

16 There are in fact a number of different definitions of proven reserves. A partition in nine categories of resources/reserves has recently acquired some ground; see IEA (2013), pp. 29–35. Among the institutions pressing for clear definitions, to be consistently adopted over time, there is the US Stock Exchange Commission, given the importance of the data on reserves supplied by oil companies for the evaluation of their share prices in the stock exchange.

17 On the technologies presently in use (thus, for an illustration of secondary and tertiary recovery techniques) and on technological perspectives, see IEA (2013).

18 Often the data on proven reserves of unconventional oil are provided separately from the data on proven reserves of conventional oil. See e.g. IEA (2013).

19 Part of the growth of proven reserves expressed as a ratio to current production in recent years is due to the slowing down of the world economy, hence of oil consumption relatively to forecasts on the basis of which the oil companies took exploration and development decisions before the crisis; another part may be due to the strategy of vertical re-integration (namely, a re-balancing of proprietary reserves and own crude

oil production relatively to own refining and distribution activities) followed by major multinational oil companies after the nationalization in the 1970s of the reserves they held in Middle East countries, and indeed to the growth of political uncertainty in major oil exporting countries.

20 The best known of these prophecies in the last few decades was that of the Club of Rome Report (Meadows *et al.*, 1972), which not only foresaw the imminent exhaustion of oil (in about eighteen years: more than forty years ago!) but also depicted the outcome in apocalyptic terms (on the cover of the Report): 'a world where industrial production has sunk to zero. Where population has suffered a catastrophic decline. [...] Where civilization is a distant memory.' As has happened time and again in the past, such Malthusian prophecies are politically motivated, which incidentally helps to explain the attention they repeatedly meet with (see Roncaglia, 2005, pp. 158–64 and pp. 286–7 for the examples of Malthus, 1798 and Jevons, 1865, concerning respectively agricultural production and coal).

21 In the Middle East, where most low-cost oilfields are located, there is both a by no means insignificant margin of underutilization of productive capacity and, especially, under-investment in development of proven reserves. The data available are far from reliable, and it is difficult to distinguish between 'structural' constraints (political unrest, in the first place) and deliberate decisions not to exploit proven reserves fully. However, it is common opinion that there is ample availability of low-cost oil, in the Middle East as well as in Africa and elsewhere. There are also many estimates, and few certainties, regarding costs in the different oilfields. But even the relatively pessimistic cost estimates of the IEA (2013, pp. 227–30: the IEA explicitly takes the high cost situation to be transitory, associated with an increase in input prices due to the large-scale investments in shale oil in the US) point to a level of costs far lower than current prices even for relatively high-cost production. We can find much lower estimates in the literature, e.g. Golombek *et al.* (2014), p. 37, suggesting less than ten dollars per barrel for OPEC oil and less than fourteen dollars per barrel for non-OPEC oil (in 1996 dollars).

22 Determining the marginal oilfield is a difficult exercise. For example, costs in a given oilfield may be higher, indeed much higher, than had been foreseen when planning investment, due to incidents and more generally unforeseen circumstances: in such cases, as in that of the Kashagan field in Kazakhstan, the project may be kept alive since past investment expenditures can be considered sunk costs. However, such (ex post) mistaken decisions should not be considered in the determination of a well-behaved supply curve.

23 There is a parallel here to the point Carey (1837–40) made about the non-applicability of the Ricardian theory of rent to Northern America.

24 An analogous approach was suggested in Roncaglia (2010), for the analysis of income distribution.

25 See Roncaglia (2009), pp. 151–4; and Roncaglia and Tonveronachi (2014).

References

Adelman M. (1972), *The World Petroleum Market*, Baltimore: Johns Hopkins University Press.

Adelman M. (1995), *The Genie out of the Bottle. World Oil since 1970*, Cambridge, Mass.: MIT Press.

Blair J. M. (1976), *The Control of Oil*, New York: Pantheon Books.

Carey H. C. (1837–40), *Principles of Political Economy*, 3 vols., Philadelphia: Carey, Lea and Blanchard.

ENI (1981), *Energy and Hydrocarbons*, Rome: ENI.

Fama E. (1970), 'Efficient capital markets: a review of theory and empirical work', *Journal of Finance*, vol. 25 n. 2, pp. 383–417.

Fattouh B. (2011), 'An anatomy of the crude oil pricing system', *Working Paper* WPM.40, January, Oxford: Oxford Institute for Energy Studies.

Federal Trade Commission, Staff Report (1952), *The International Petroleum Cartel*, Washington: US Government Printing Office.

Frankel P. H. (1946), *Essentials of Petroleum*, 2nd edn., London: Frank Cass, 1969.

Garegnani P. (1990), 'Sraffa: Classical versus marginalist analysis', in Bharadwaj and Schefold (eds.), *Essays on Piero Sraffa. Critical Perspectives on the Revival of Classical Theory*, London: Routledge, pp. 112–41.

Golombek R., Irarrazabal A. and Ma L. (2014), 'OPEC's market power: An empirical dominant firm model for the oil market', *Working Paper* n. 3, Norges Bank Research.

Hotelling H. (1931), 'The economics of exhaustible resources', *Journal of Political Economy*, vol. 39, Apr., pp. 137–75.

Jevons W. S. (1865), *The Coal Question*, London: Macmillan.

Keynes J. M. (1936), *The General Theory of Employment, Interest and Money*, London: Macmillan.

Kurz H. and Salvadori N. (1995), *Theory of Production. A Long Period Analysis*, Cambridge: Cambridge University Press.

IEA (2013), *Resources to Reserves 2013*, Paris: IEA.

Malthus T. R. (1798), *An Essay on the Principle of Population as it Affects the Future Improvement of Society*. London; 2nd edn., 1803; critical edn., edited by P. James, Cambridge: Cambridge University Press, 1989.

Meadows D. H., Meadows, D. L., Randers, J. and Behrens III, W. W. (1972), *The Limits to Growth*, New York: New American Library.

Roncaglia A. (1975), *Sraffa e La Teoria dei Prezzi*, Roma–Bari: Laterza; English translation. *Sraffa and the Theory of Prices*, Chichester: Wiley 1977.

Roncaglia A. (1983), *L'Economia del Petrolio*, Roma–Bari: Laterza; English translation, *The International Oil Market*, London: Macmillan,1985.

Roncaglia A. (1991), 'La Stabilizzazione del Prezzo del Petrolio: Alcuni Commenti', *Economia delle Fonti di Energia*, vol. 34 n. 44, pp. 71–8.

Roncaglia A. (2005), *The Wealth of Ideas*, Cambridge: Cambridge University Press.

Roncaglia A. (2009), *Piero Sraffa*, Basingstoke: Palgrave Macmillan.

Roncaglia A. (2010), 'Prezzi e distribuzione del reddito: una nota', *Studi Economici*, vol. 65 n. 100, pp. 261–73.

Roncaglia A. (2012), 'Keynesian uncertainty and the shaky foundations of statistical risk assessment models', *PSL Quarterly Review*, vol. 65 n. 263, pp. 437–54.

Roncaglia A. (2015), 'Oil and its markets', *PSL Quarterly Review*, vol. 68 n. 273, pp. 151–75.

Roncaglia A. and Tonveronachi M. (2014), 'Post–Keynesian, post-Sraffian economics: an outline', in Papadimitriou D. B. (ed.), *Contributions to Economic Theory, Policy, Development and Finance. Essays in Honor of Jan A. Kregel*, Basingstoke: Palgrave Macmillan, pp. 40–64.

Sabbatini R. (1989), 'Il Progetto di Keynes di Stabilizzazione dei Prezzi delle Materie Prime', *Quaderni di Storia dell'Economia Politica*, vol. 7 n. 1, pp. 55–73.

Sraffa P. (1960), *Production of Commodities by Means of Commodities*, Cambridge: Cambridge University Press.

Sylos Labini P. (1956), *Oligopolio e Progresso Tecnico*, Milano: Giuffrè; fourth edn. Torino: Einaudi 1967; English translation, *Oligopoly and Technical Progress*, Cambridge, Mass.: Harvard University Press 1962; 2nd edn., 1969.

Sylos Labini P. (1984), *The Forces of Economic Growth and Decline*, Cambridge, Mass.: MIT Press.

Part 3

Capital theory and marginalism

10 The dropbox and the ghosts

Christian Bidard[1]

Production[2] cannot take place out of nothing. Some scholars have attempted to find the origin of such a rare agreement among economists. According to Monseigneur Vittrant, the famous historian, the grounds of that no-Cockaigne land axiom are found in the Bible: production from scratch did occur during the week of Creation, but the experience has not been repeated and, after the Original Sin, men must work to produce and live. Sociologists argue that, though production out of nothing would be beneficial to people, it would endanger the economists themselves and condemn the profession to the same fate as dinosaurs: markets and prices would disappear. Physicists claim that the axiom has a material basis, the conservation of mass. That explanation is the least satisfactory of all: if economists did pay attention to physical laws, why is the free disposal axiom, which is the reverse of the no-Cockaigne land axiom, so universally accepted?

We start from a reinterpretation of the free disposal axiom which makes it compatible with the law of conservation of mass: instead of setting the physical disappearance of the freely disposed goods, it assumes their storage in a gigantic dropbox. These goods, however, are zero-priced. We suggest pursuing the exploration until the discovery of another type of goods, the ghost goods, which do not appear on markets but play a role in their working and are positively priced. The Austrian model and others widely used in the study of production, for instance in the theory of truncation, presume their existence, which however remains so far from sight that it is generally ignored. Let us be fair with ghosts. The best way to rehabilitate them in all their dignity is to calculate their prices and to point at their role in a central problem of capital theory.

The free disposal axiom

Walras (1874) defined equilibrium as a state in which demand equals supply on all markets. He argued that such a state could be reached by choosing the price vector adequately, the equilibrium prices being the result of a tâtonnement process. The argument is not totally convincing (some scholars are not convinced at all), and its final form was found by Arrow and Debreu (1954) eighty years after the publication of the *Éléments*. It only concerns existence and leaves apart both the tâtonnement and the study of stability, on which further researches have led to inconclusive results. Moreover, Arrow and Debreu modified the initial notion of equilibrium: it is a state in which every market is either balanced or in excess supply but, in the second case, the price of the corresponding good must be zero. That adaptation, introduced by Zeuthen (1933), soon proved to be fruitful and led to the replacement of Walras's equalities by inequalities with complementarity relationships. Von Neumann (1937) already made use of that formalisation, and the modern basic tool to prove the existence of a general equilibrium, viz. the Gale–Nikaido–Debreu lemma, is adapted to it.

Let us look at Sraffian economics. The notion of 'given requirements for use' is usually interpreted as meaning that the demand basket and the rate of accumulation are given. This is not in line with Sraffa's own conception, if only because Sraffa (1960) stressed that no hypothesis on returns is set, but the interpretation of long-term prices as those sustaining a steady growth path allows us to solve some puzzles that Sraffa's analysis left unanswered. For single-product systems, the net product can be adjusted exactly to the requirements for use and there is no need for the free disposal axiom, not even for an explicit reference to the requirements. But consider a multiple-product system in which every available process produces more iron than corn (when measured in adequate units), while the final demand vector has more corn than iron. (Sraffa's note 2 in Chapter VII does not take that possibility into account.) Both markets cannot be balanced simultaneously and it becomes necessary to enlarge the notion of a long-run equilibrium: an excess supply is admitted, provided that the corresponding good is zero priced. This amounts to admitting the free disposal axiom. Kurz (1986) and Kurz and Salvadori (1995) attribute the first application of the rule to Adam Smith (1776), although in a still rudimentary form. The axiom also discards the presence of negative prices (the free disposal of the corresponding goods would yield extra profits) and is the answer retained today to Sraffa's remark in Section 70 (Chapter IX):

> [A]lthough in actual fact all prices were positive, a change in the wage might create a situation the logic of which required some of the prices to turn negative: and this being unacceptable, those among the methods of production that gave rise to such a result would be discarded to make room for others which in the new situation were consistent with positive prices.

The free disposal axiom avoids any reference to 'book-keeping' (Sraffa, 1960, Appendix B, p. 91) but sets a more general question to Sraffa's two-step methodology: Sraffa first studied a productive system in isolation, with as many methods as commodities, then proceeded to comparisons between systems and introduced the choice of methods. The phenomenon at stake requires taking into account the coexistence of methods of production, including the free disposal methods, from the very beginning.

Free disposal is conceived as a method which, on the input side, shows an amount of some commodity and, on the output side, nothing. Steedman (1987) objected that the axiom violates the law of conservation of mass. A way to solve that jigsaw is to consider that free disposal does not consist of the destruction of the excess supply but in its storage at no cost in a dropbox located near the market. When considered as an economic activity, the storage of a zero-priced good yields zero penny out of zero penny and is compatible with competition for any rate of profit. After total or partial disposal of some goods, supply is adjusted exactly to demand. That is, the free disposal axiom allows the economists to reduce a definition of equilibrium which distinguishes two cases to only one. Thanks to the introduction of the dropbox, the law of conservation of mass is no longer violated. The story is a bit convoluted but acceptable by both economists and physicists.

Competition and the dropbox

What about entrepreneurs? The notion of competition retained, at least in a post-Walrasian tradition inherited from the invention of the auctioneer, is that the entrepreneur has an exhaustive knowledge of goods, methods and prices. His favourite reading is the Great Catalogue which assigns a price to each commodity and describes how goods are produced and transformed. As soon as he discovers an opportunity to combine inputs in a profitable way, he asks for these items and produces the good. Coordination by prices implies that, if an entrepreneur finds a profitable combination, the corresponding inputs must be available on the market in the required quantities. It is also assumed that each entrepreneur is potentially specialised in a one-period production process: a seven-year production process is deemed to be the work of seven successive entrepreneurs, with no coordination between them other than the one ensured by prices; each year, the intermediate product is sold by an entrepreneur and bought by another. The prices of intermediate goods sustain the ruling rate of profit year after year, not only over the whole seven-year period.

That conception explains why some positively-priced commodities may not appear on the markets. Let us give a few examples of that possibility, starting from a case considered by Walras himself (1874, 7th lesson of the *Éléments*, § 64). Consider an exchange economy with two agents and a pure consumption good owned by agent 1. Suppose that agent 1 does not want to supply it below a minimum price p_1 and that agent 2 does not want to buy it above a maximum level p_2, with $p_2 < p_1$. Curiously, Walras concluded that 'there is no solution': he had in mind that the demand curve does not cross the supply curve. But the demand curve $d = d(p)$ must be extended on its right (for $p > p_2$) by the horizontal line, and the supply curve $s = s(p)$ on its left (for $p < p_1$) by the same line, so that any price between p_1 and p_2 is an equilibrium price, with, however, a zero demand and a zero supply. (In modern parlance, the corresponding equilibrium is inessential.) Such a good is positively priced but not exchanged on the market: it is a ghost good. Ghost goods have a price and an address in the list of commodities, but no agent cares for them.

Let us consider capital goods. In Appendix B of *Production of Commodities* (1960), Sraffa referred to a self-reproducing non-basic commodity ('beans') such that 'for every 100 units sown no more than 110 units are reaped', while the ruling rate of profit in the economy exceeds 10 per cent. Sraffa suggested a way to allow for the effective production of beans by distinguishing a book price and a market price, or the price of beans as inputs from that as an output. In our view this is an unsuccessful attempt to deny the ghostness of beans: for any positive price, farmers decide not to produce beans because they are too costly.

A third example deals with pure capital goods, which are not consumed. Imagine that some consumption good can be produced by two ways, which both take two periods. The first process requires seven units of labour in the first year and one unit of labour in the second year, while the second requires five units in the first year and five units in the second year. The choice of the operated method depends on distribution: the first process is cost-minimising for low rates of profit (high wages) and the second for high rates (low wages). For simplicity, assume that the rate of profit is zero and let labour be chosen as numeraire, so that comparisons can be made directly in terms of labour contents. Then the first process is operated and the price of the final good amounts to eight. Production with the first method involves an intermediate good A, which is sold by the first-year entrepreneur to the second-year entrepreneur. The value of that intermediate good amounts to seven. The alternative process, which is not operated, also admits an intermediate good B. Good B is typically a ghost good, i.e. a good with an address in the dropbox and a price, but which does not appear on the market. The equilibrium price of good B must be such that no entrepreneur wants either to produce or to use it. The first condition is met when the price of B is low enough: since the production cost of B is five, its price must be smaller than five. The second condition concerns the second-year producer: it is written in the Great Catalogue that one unit of B and five units of labour can be used to produce one unit of final good. The view of competition held by economic theory is that it cannot be objected to that producer who wants to use good B as an input that this good is not available on the market: the scarcity constraint must be incorporated in the price vector itself. That condition is met when the price of B is so high that its use would imply over-costs. Since the price of the final good is eight and that of five units of labour is five, over-costs occur when the price of B is greater than three. On the whole, good B is not on the market but is positively priced, its price lying somewhere (anywhere) between three and five. The prices of ghost commodities are a part of the whole price system and their knowledge is essential to the working of the market. As a general rule, intermediate goods which are specific to a non-operated process are ghost goods.

Truncation and ghost goods

The previous example refers to an Austrian model. Neo-Austrian models, with a flow of dated quantities of labour giving rise to a flow of dated final goods, are slightly more complex. When decomposed year after year and written down as multisector models, neo-Austrian models are of the fixed-capital type (of a very specific type: no basic good and no maximum rate of profit). It is in that framework that the theory of truncation was first elaborated at the end of the fifties before being extended to general multisector fixed-capital models by Sraffian scholars.

Let us continue our exploration with a neo-Austrian process: a nine-year flow of labour inputs, with one unit of labour every year, produces one unit of corn after four years and another unit after nine years. The truncation theory is based on the remark that it is more efficient (and, first, more profitable!) to stop that process after four years and start another four-year investment: one unit of corn is then obtained every four years, while the original process leads to an alternation of four and five years. The truncation theory is more elaborated than suggested here, as the lifetime of a process may depend on distribution, but the example suffices for our purpose. Let us call tractors the intermediate goods of different ages, from zero to seven (since the new tractor produced by the first yearly process is deemed to have age zero, whereas no tractor is produced by the ninth yearly process, the oldest variety of tractor in a nine-year neo-Austrian model is indeed seven years old), and assume again that the rate of profit is zero. At equilibrium, the shortened (truncated) four-year process is operated, the price of the final good is four, and the three-year-old tractor produced jointly with the crop is disposed of freely: it is zero priced and thrown away in the dropbox. (The truncation hypothesis is but a special form of the free disposal hypothesis.) Tractors of ages four to seven, which do not appear on the market, are on the list printed in the Great Catalogue and a price is attributed to each variety. What is the price of the tractor aged seven? It is written in the Great Catalogue that combining that good with one unit of labour allows an entrepreneur to get one quarter of corn. With a price of labour equal to one and that of the final good to four, the entrepreneur would ask for that machine if its price p_7 was either zero or small: competition presumes that p_7 is greater than three, otherwise that variety of tractor would be demanded and not produced.

What can be said of the other non-produced and non-used tractors at equilibrium? A generalisation of the above reasoning leads to inequality $p(t) + 1 \geq p(t + 1)$ for the non-produced varieties of tractor: that condition ensures that it is not profitable to ask for a tractor of age t ($t \geq 3$) and one unit of labour to produce a tractor of age $t + 1$. On the whole, the equilibrium prices are: $w = 1$ for labour, $q = 4$ for corn, $p_0 = 1$, $p_1 = 2$, $p_2 = 3$ for the effectively produced tractors, $p_3 = 0$ (the 3-year-old tractor is disposed of freely), then $p_4 \leq 1$ (otherwise the production of a tractor of age 4 by means of a 3-year-old tractor and labour would be profitable) and $p_4 + 1 \geq p_5$, $p_5 + 1 \geq p_6$, $p_6 + 1 \geq p_7$, $p_7 \geq 3$. The price conditions relative to the ghost tractors are written more synthetically as

$$4 \geq p_4 + 3 \geq p_5 + 2 \geq p_6 + 1 \geq p_7 \geq 3. \tag{10.1}$$

Then the price of a ghost tractor is sufficiently low to discourage its production and, at the same time, sufficiently high to discourage the production of the next type of tractor. A truncation theory which would only refer to the prices of the produced machines would be incomplete, as those of the non-produced varieties should also be mentioned: the important point is that, even if the truncated variety is zero priced (this being the signal for truncation), the other non-produced varieties are positively priced: they are ghost goods.

A two-period model

Infinitely many prices satisfy the conditions (10.1): it is a quite general phenomenon that the price of a ghost good may vary within a certain interval, whereas that of a produced commodity is determined (without excluding the possibility of multiple equilibria). But formula (10.1) also shows that the range of variations of prices p_4 to p_7 is rather small. We now identify a case in which the value of a ghost can be calculated exactly.

Let us return to two-period Austrian models of the flow-input point-output type, already mentioned in the second section. However specific those models are, their study is instructive and provides many hints on a general ghost theory. In the decomposition of the overall process as a sequence of two one-period methods, the first yearly method produces a tractor by means of labour l_1 alone, while the next produces one quarter of corn by means of that tractor and the amount l_0 of labour. Truncation is excluded. Consider a family $(l_1(u), l_0(u))$ of such two-period processes:

$$l_1(u)L \rightarrow 1M(u)$$

$$1M(u) + l_0(u)L \rightarrow 1 \text{ quarter corn}$$

where tractor $M(u)$ is the intermediate good produced by the first yearly method and used up in the second. Inefficient processes are costly and can be ignored: if a method requires more labour than another at date -1, it requires less labour at date 0. There is no restriction in assuming that $l_1(u)$ is increasing with u (this is but a reordering of the processes), and then $l_0(u)$ is decreasing with u. When the rate of interest r increases, present labour is substituted for past labour and the index $u = u(r)$ of the operated method decreases. The intermediate tractor $M(u)$ is specific to process u and cannot be used in another process. We may think of $M(u)$ as a tractor of quality u: tractors of higher quality require more labour to be produced but are more efficient. There is a continuum of processes and, at rate r, each variety u of tractor has its own price which we denote as $p(u \mid r)$ (conditional price of variety u when the rate of interest is r).

Where are the ghost goods? At equilibrium at rate r, the cost-minimising method denoted t is operated and only the quality t of tractor is produced and used. All other varieties are ghosts: ghosts are much more numerous than visible beings. (One of the main puzzles of contemporary physics concerns the 'missing mass' in universe, made of a mysterious 'dark matter'. As the missing mass represents 90 per cent of total mass, it has been suggested that the universe might be filled with ghosts: 'There are more guests at table than the hosts invited.') Let labour be chosen as numeraire. As the operated method is cost-minimising, t is the solution to $\min (1 + r)l_1(u) + l_0(u)$ and the price q of corn is

$$q = \min(1 + r)l_1(u) + l_0(u) = (1 + r)l_1(t) + l_0(t).$$

The price $p(t \mid r)$ of the quality t of tractors is such that

$$l_1(t) = p(t \mid r)$$
$$(1+r)p(t \mid r) + l_0(t) = q.$$

The principle governing the pricing of the ghost tractor of any other variety u is that its price $p(u \mid r)$ is too low to sustain its effective production, and simultaneously too high to sustain its use: both inequalities

$$l_1(u) \geq p(u \mid r) \tag{10.2}$$
$$(1+r)p(u \mid r) + l_0(u) \geq q \tag{10.3}$$

hold. They define an upper and a lower bound for the price of the tractor of quality u, and the price can take any value in that interval. In the case of a continuum of methods, with u varying, the two curves defining the bounds of $p(u \mid r)$ are tangent at point t. As a consequence, the price of the variety $t + du$ close to the produced variety t can be determined up to the first order. The calculation is as follows. First, inequality (10.2) for $u = t + du$ implies

$$l_1' du + (du)\varepsilon_0 \geq p'(t \mid r)du.$$

(All derivatives are with respect to t for a given rate of profit.) Similarly, inequality (10.3) with equality for $u = t$ implies

$$(1+r)p'(t \mid r)du + l_0' du + (du)\varepsilon_1 \geq 0.$$

One gets from the last two inequalities that

$$(1+r)^{-1}l_0' + \varepsilon_1 \leq p'(t \mid r) \leq l_1' + \varepsilon_0.$$

As equality $(1+r)l_1' + l_0' = 0$ holds by the cost-minimisation property of the selected method, there follows

$$p'(t \mid r) = -(1+r)l_0' = l_1'. \tag{10.4}$$

The price of the variety $t + du$ of tractors is $p(t \mid r) + p'(t \mid r)du$, where $p'(t \mid r)$ is defined by (10.4).

Numerical application. Consider the Austrian family defined by $l_1(u) = u^2$, $l_0(u) = 2u^{-1}$ where u is a positive parameter. The operated method t at rate r is the solution to $\min(1+r)u^2 + 2u^{-1}$; hence $t(r) = (1+r)^{-1/3}$. The price in terms of wage of the operated variety t is $p(t) = p(t \mid r) = l_1(t) = (1+r)^{-2/3}$. Since $p'(t \mid r) = l_1'(t)$, the price of the ghost variety $t + du$ is $p(t) + 2tdu$.

When the rate of profit changes, so does the price of the operated variety of tractor, for two reasons: first, the price of any commodity is sensitive to distribution (price effect); and, second, the operated tractor itself is changing (quality effect). The overall effect is measured by the magnitude $p'(t \mid r)$ given by formula (10.4). Since the operated variety of tractors is produced by $l_1(t)$ units of labour and labour is the numeraire, the price effect is nil. The quality effect measures the change in $l_1(t)$ implied by a change in r and amounts to $l_1't'(r)\mathrm{d}r$. The equality of the quality effect and the overall effect can be stated as in the following proposition.

Proposition 10.1 *In a two-period Austrian model and with labour as numeraire, the price of the ghost tractor $M(t + \mathrm{d}u)$ coincides with its price when, after a change in the rate of profit, that tractor is operated.*

Let us use the above numerical example to illustrate that statement. It has already been shown that the price at rate r of the ghost tractor $M(t + \mathrm{d}u)$ is $p(t) + 2t\mathrm{d}u$. Consider alternatively the price of that tractor when it is operated. As $t(r) = (1+r)^{-1/3}$, the variety $t + \mathrm{d}u$ is operated when the rate of interest moves by $\mathrm{d}r$ such that $t + \mathrm{d}u = (1 + r + \mathrm{d}r)^{-1/3}$; hence $\mathrm{d}r = -3(1+r)^{4/3}\mathrm{d}u$. Since, for a given rate of profit, the price of the operated tractor is known (it is equal to $l_1(t)$, with $t = t(r)$), it is easy to check that the price of the operated tractor at rate $r - 3(1+r)^{4/3}\mathrm{d}u$ is indeed $p(t) + 2t\mathrm{d}u$.

Proposition 10.1 states that two measures coincide locally: the first concerns the price of a ghost tractor for a given rate of profit, the second the price of an effectively operated tractor. It is that coincidence which, in our opinion, constitutes the microeconomic foundation of the specific properties of the two-period Austrian model. Note that the second magnitude is observable by a 'man from the moon' (when the rate of profit changes) whereas the first is non observable.[3]

General Austrian models

We now consider a general Austrian model with $T + 1$ periods, where the quantities $(l_T, \ldots, l_0)$ of labour are successively invested to produce one quarter of corn at date 0. These quantities depend on a parameter u. Here, we pay attention to the last stage of the process, i.e. to the consumption good industry. The rate of interest r being given, the capital invested in the consumption good industry is a tractor M. Again, our aim is to determine the prices of that tractor and of its neighbouring varieties. From a backward point of view, the price of the operated variety of tractor is equal to the present value of the successive labour investments required for its construction. From a forward point of view, it is equal to the present value of the crop it produces, once labour l_0 is paid. The non-operated varieties of tractors satisfy similar conditions written as inequalities instead of equalities: these inequalities express that there is no incentive to produce these varieties or to use them. Leaving calculations to the reader, it can be shown that, with labour as numeraire, formula

$$p'(t \mid r) = -(1+r)l_0' \tag{10.5}$$

still holds. (The hypothesis that we consider the value of the last tractor is essential for the simplicity of the result.)

The numeraire

Another important hypothesis used in the above calculations is that labour is chosen as numeraire. Consider for instance Proposition 10.1: does it resist a change of numeraire? For instance, does it still hold with corn (the final good) as numeraire? Following that change, all nominal prices are multiplied by w/q. Proposition 10.1 compares two measures. In the first, w/q is a constant because the rate of profit is given. In the second, the rate of profit changes and the ratio w/q admits a first order variation. It is therefore expected that Proposition 10.1 does not survive a change of numeraire. This does not mean that it is useless: equality (10.5) with labour as numeraire can be rewritten as

$$(p/w)' = -(1+r)l_0'$$

and, since that equality has become independent of the numeraire, one can derive from it other equalities for any specific numeraire.

Let corn be the new numeraire ($q = 1$). From equality $p/q = (p/w)(w/q)$, one concludes that the price of the variety $t + du$ of tractors close to the operated variety is $p(t + du) = p(t) + p'(t)du$ with

$$p'(t) = (p/w)'w + (p/w)w' = -w(1+r)l_0' + (p/w)w'.$$

The last term on the right-hand side makes the difference with formula (10.5). The unexpected phenomenon is that this term vanishes: with corn as numeraire, equality $w' = 0$ holds by the wage-maximisation property and, therefore, the change of numeraire from labour to the final good does not matter here:

$$p'(t) = -w(1+r)l_0'. \tag{10.6}$$

Experience has told us that lucky phenomena of that type have contributed to play down the role of the dimensional equation in economics: testing whether a formula relative to value resists a change of numeraire or can be adapted to such a change remains an essential experiment.

Ghost goods and capital theory

An important problem of capital theory concerns the marginal productivity of capital. Marginal productivity deals with the production per head and is equal to the ratio between an infinitesimal change in the value of the product (the effect of the change) and an infinitesimal change in the value of capital (the cause of the change). We consider an Austrian model and proceed to an estimate of that magnitude in the consumption-good industry. Since capital in that industry is made of a tractor, a change in capital means that we are substituting a tractor of type

$t + dt$ for a tractor of type t: that is why ghost goods play a role in the calculation. The change in the value of capital per head takes two effects into account: a quantity effect, because the number of tractors per head depends on the operated method; and a quality effect, because the quality of the tractor changes with the method.

In the above formalisation, the generic production process in the consumption good industry was written as $1M(t) + l_0(t)L \to 1$ C. We may rewrite it in terms of production per worker:

$$\mu M(t) + 1L \to q \text{ C}$$

where $\mu = l_0^{-1}$ is the number of machines per worker and $q = l_0^{-1}$ the product per head. For any infinitesimal variation in the method t and therefore in l_0, we have

$$d\mu = dq = d(l_0^{-1}) = -l_0^{-2}dl_0. \tag{10.7}$$

These quantity effects measure the change in the number of tractors per worker and the change in the product per head. To estimate the quantity effects in value terms, one takes into account the price of the tractor and that of corn. Here, we choose corn as numeraire.

The quality effect per tractor stems from the change in quality from $M(t)$ to $M(t + dt)$, as reflected in the change of its price from $p(t)$ to $p(t + dt)$. The overall quality effect per worker is equal to the quality effect per tractor times the number of tractors per head. The sum of the quantity and quality effects gives the change dk in the value of capital per head:

$$dk = d(p(t)\mu) = p(t)d\mu + \mu dp(t).$$

Since one tractor of quality t and l_0 units of labour produce one unit of corn, we have $p(t) = (1 - wl_0)(1 + r)^{-1}$. The variation $d\mu$ in the number of tractors is given by formula (10.7), that $dp(t) = p(t)'dt$ in the value of the tractor by formula (10.6). On the whole,

$$dk = (1 - wl_0)(1 + r)^{-1}(-l_0^{-2}dl_0) - l_0^{-1}w(1 + r)^{-1}l_0'dt.$$

The terms involving w disappear and one gets

$$dk = (1 + r)^{-1}(-l_0^{-2}dl_0) = (1 + r)^{-1}dq$$

or

$$dq/dk = 1 + r. \tag{10.8}$$

These calculations can be extended and, by following the same steps as above, it can be shown that the marginal equality (10.8) holds at all stages of the production process. It therefore also holds at the global level, when the economy is considered as a whole.

Proposition 10.2 *There is some way to measure capital such that the gross marginal productivity of capital is equal to the factor of profit.*

Wicksell (1923) studied an elegant variant of a neo-Austrian model in which the quality of a fixed capital good (an axe) is measured by the time spent in its production, which is positively correlated with its lifetime. He concluded that there is divergence between the marginal productivity of capital and the rate of interest. Garegnani (1970) studied a more complex model and concluded more radically that 'no definition of "capital" allows us to say that its marginal productivity is equal to the rate of interest': this does not seem to be the case, if Proposition 10.2 holds. In the absence of mistakes in the calculations, the divergences between the conclusions suggest that there would be different ways to measure the marginal productivity of capital: the question at stake is therefore the very notion of marginal productivity of capital, well before any discussion about its equality, or not, with the rate of interest. Two types of arguments are worth considering for clarifying the distinction between the two approaches:

- The first mixes technical and conceptual considerations. As marginal productivity is conceived as a real magnitude (even if it is estimated in value terms), the robustness of calculations with regard to a change of numeraire is a significant test for the consistency of the concept. In models with a unique final good, labour and corn are two sensible numeraires, and the magnitude dq/dk should be defined in order to be insensitive to that choice. Wicksell, Garegnani and the present paper proceed to an estimate of dq/dk with the final good as numeraire. In all these calculations, it would be worth considering if the alleged 'marginal productivity' changes with the numeraire. This can be done along the lines sketched in the previous section, and the exercise is left to the reader.
- The second remark is of a methodological order: should an economic theory of long-term prices be based on observable magnitudes only? This was apparently Sraffa's own position, if we understand it correctly (see the reference to Kurz and Salvadori, 2007). The present paper leaves no part to psychological considerations but is invaded by ghosts, which are virtual beings: they are not observed on the stage but play their role behind it, from which they direct the show.

Conclusion

Economists often dispute the respective places of objective and subjective elements in their constructions. Their divergences cannot hide a deeper agreement on the objective: they claim to be scientists. With regard to any academic criterion of that type, there is no doubt that Neri Salvadori made numerous significant contributions to economic theory and that his works on long-period positions will also remain a reference for a long time. The only slight reservation we introduce concerns the economists' work in general: even if economics is no longer identified as a gloomy science, it has not become very popular and fails to raise the same enthusiasm as, say, soccer or pop music. We suggest that this state may be explained by a certain lack of dream in the economists' approach. For instance, why are the Classicals so much praised by Neri (and others) for their analytical works when one can hardly find a single reference to their contemporary Charles Fourier, whose unleashed imagination was never failing and who inspired attempts for a better organisation of society? Where is the new Utopia, five centuries after Thomas More? Where is lyricism in economics when a rare attempt in that direction, the Fable of the Bees, is ignored by all anthologies of poetry? As a first step, we plea for the recognition of the existence of supernatural beings who inspired visionary innovators such as the great American poet Henry W. Longfellow:

> Through the open doors
> The harmless phantoms on their errands glide,
> With feet that make no sound upon the floors.
> We meet them at the door-way, on the stair,
> Along the passages they come and go,
> Impalpable impressions on the air,
> A sense of something moving to and fro.
> There are more guests at table than the hosts
> Invited; the illuminated hall
> Is thronged with quiet, inoffensive ghosts,
> As silent as the pictures on the wall.

Notes

1 EconomiX, University Paris-Ouest, Department of economics, Nanterre (France).
2 With acknowledgements to Heinz D. Kurz, Antoine Rebeyrol and Ian Steedman for comments, with the usual caveat concerning the opinions expressed in the present paper.
3 For the reference to the 'Man from the moon' in Sraffa's papers and its methodological implications, see Kurz and Salvadori's (2007) analysis.

References

Arrow, K. J. and Debreu, G. (1954), Existence of an equilibrium for a competitive economy, *Econometrica*, 22, 255–90.
Garegnani, P. (1970), Heterogeneous capital, the production function and the theory of distribution, *Review of Economic Studies*, 37, 407–36.
Kurz, H. D. (1986), Classical and early neoclassical economists on joint production, *Metroeconomica*, 38, 1–37.
Kurz, H. D. and Salvadori, N. (1995), *Theory of Production. A Long-Period Analysis*, Cambridge University Press: Cambridge.
Kurz, H. D. and Salvadori, N. (2007), 'Man from the moon'. On Sraffa's objectivism, in H. D. Kurz, N. Salvadori (with C. Gerhke, G. Freni and F. Gozzi) (eds.) *Interpreting Classical Economics. Studies in Long-Period Analysis*. Routledge: New York, pp. 120–9.

Neumann, J. von (1937), über ein ökonomisches Gleichungssystem und eine Verallgemeinerung des Brouwerschen Fixpunktsatzes, in K. Menger (ed.) *Ergebnisse eines mathematischen Kolloquiums*, 8, 73–83 (Leipzig, Franz Deuticke); transl. A model of general equilibrium, *Review of Economic Studies*, 1945–6, 13, 1–9.

Smith, A. (1776 [1976]), *An Inquiry into the Nature and Causes of the Wealth of Nations*, first edition 1776, Vol. II of *The Glasgow Edition of the Works and Correspondence of Adam Smith*, edited by R.H. Campbell, A.S. Skinner and W.B. Todd, Oxford University Press: Oxford.

Sraffa, P. (1960), *Production of Commodities by Means of Commodities*, Cambridge University Press: Cambridge.

Steedman, I. (1987), Free goods, in J. Eatwell, M. Milgate and P. Newman (eds.) *New Palgrave Dictionary of Economics*, 1st edition, vol. 2, pp. 419–21.

Walras, L. (1874 [1988]), *Éléments d'Economie Politique Pure ou Théorie de La Richesse sociale* (Paris, Guillaumin); reprint in Auguste and Léon Walras, *Oeuvres Economiques Complètes*, vol. VIII (Paris, Economica), 1988.

Wicksell, K. (1923 [1934]), Dr. Akerman's Realkapital und Kapitalzins, *Ekonomisk Tidskrift*, 1923, 5–6, 145–80; reprint in Wicksell (1934), A mathematical analysis of Dr. Akerman's problem, *Lectures on Political Economy*, vol. I, London, Georges Routledge and Sons, pp. 274–99.

Zeuthen, F. (1933), Das Prinzip der Knappheit, technische Kombination und ökonomische Qualität, *Zeitschrift für Nationalökonomie*, 4, 1–24.

11 Sraffa–Samuelson marginalism in the multi-primary-factor case

A fourth exploration

Transcription of unfinished handwritten Paul A. Samuelson manuscript by Edwin Burmeister[1]

In his 100-page classic, Piero Sraffa did include a brief 4-page chapter on land. However, its paragraphs dealt with some definitional formalities and never did for land the extended analysis provided for labor working with one or more produced inputs. In order to specify a labor–land–capital model of the simplest Ricardian type, which can then be subjected to an unbiased comparison with the post-Clark neoclassicism that Sraffa did not like, I plan here to spell out a non-neoclassical model in which output such as corn is producible by a finite number of alternative known techniques that each involve, along with labor and say corn seed, non-reproducible land (and where possibly each category of inputs could involve heterogeneous varieties: male and female labors; more fertile and less fertile acreages; coal, iron, and durable produced machines).

Abstractly, inputs $(x_1, x_2, \leftrightharpoons, x_n)$, $n > 2$, are needed to produce an output, Q. However, in contrast to Clark–Douglas–Solow neoclassicism, I do not postulate a smoothly differentiable neoclassical function such as any of the following:

$$
\begin{aligned}
Q &= f(x_1, \leftrightharpoons, x_n) \\
&= x_1^{k_1} \cdots x_n^{k_n}, \quad k_j > 0, \quad \sum_{j=1}^{n} k_j = 1, \quad \text{or} \\
&= \left(\sum_{j=1}^{n} c_j x_j^{\gamma} \right)^{\frac{1}{\gamma}}, \quad 1 \geq \gamma \neq 0, \quad \gamma \geq 0.
\end{aligned}
\tag{11.1}
$$

Leontief–Sraffa analysis can be done for first-degree-homogeneous, smoothly concave functions. However, the present purpose is to prepare the way for Sraffa and Leontief and von Neumann's reliance on solely a finite number of discrete alternative techniques, M in number over the present state of technological knowledge is posited.

To keep the complicated exposition from being unnecessarily difficult, in the present installment I play down the intertemporal phasing of technology. That can come in a later installment. And also, for later treatment, is any concentration on how the produced input(s) currently used were themselves the output(s) of earlier periods. Thus, the crucial novelties of Sraffa–Robinson capital theory are reserved for leisurely later microscopic examination.

For the case of three factors– $n = 3$, corresponding say to homogeneous one-quality land, A, homogeneous one-quality labor, L, and homogeneous one-quality corn seed, K, in place of the neoclassical equation(s) (11.1), here we postulate

$$Q = \min \left(\frac{A}{a_A}, \frac{L}{a_L}, \frac{K}{a_K} \right), \qquad (a_A \, a_L \, a_K) > 0 \qquad (11.2a)$$

and where $(a_A \, a_L \, a_K)$ take on at first only $M = 3$ alternative vector numbers corresponding to different known techniques: namely α, β, and γ

(α : 4 acres of land & 3/4 of labor & 1/4 of corn seed)

    will produce each 1 of corn (11.2b)

(β : 1 acre of land & 3 of labor & 1 of corn seed)

    will produce each 1 of corn (11.2c)

(γ : 2 acres of land & 1 of labor & 1 of corn seed)

    will produce each 1 of corn (11.2d)

Stipulate along with (11.2)'s menu of techniques knowable to all competitors, that society has <u>exogenously</u> fixed input endowments

$A = 40$ acres, $L = 30$, $K = 30$.

Sraffa (1960) never poses and grapples with the following question.

Under Darwinian selfish competition between and among society's numerous independent owners of land, labor, and corn seed, what has to be the resulting distribution of income—of Q—between landowners' corn-rent rate, (2) laborers' corn wage-rate, and (3) capital owners' (gross!) rent rate? Understand that these factor returns—R_A for land rent, W for wage, and R_K for corn seed—are payable at the end of any short unit period of production; therefore we can ignore any endogenous interest rate that would "discount" the factor owners' returns. When market clearing supply and demand determines equilibrium $\left(R_A^*, \ W^*, \ R_K^* \right)$, absolute and relative income shares are determined for the $(A \ L \ K) = (4 \ 30 \ 30)$ fixed factor endowments:

$$R_A^* 40 + W^* 30 + R_K^* 30 = Q^*$$

$$= \text{gross corn output}$$

Remark 11.1 When K is a produced input like corn seed, which is totally used up in one period's use (which is the case for Sraffa's 1960 Part I), we avoid all joint-production complications. In this case $R_K - 1$ is the "own corn rate of interest."

However, if K were a "durable machine" that in each use depreciates by say 10%, then $R_K - 0.1$ would be the own rate of interest in any stationary state. The reader and I have no need in the present exposition to concern ourselves with profit or interest rates so long as we do keep in focus K's gross rental rate R_K^*.

For convenient mathematical notations, we can employ the following:

$$(A \ L \ K) \equiv (x_1 \ x_2 \ x_3) = \mathbf{x}; \quad \text{corn output} = Q$$

$$(R_A \ W \ R_K) \equiv (y_1 \ y_2 \ y_3) = \mathbf{y}$$

$$\left(a_A^\alpha \ a_L^\alpha \ a_K^\alpha; \ a_A^\beta \ a_L^\beta \ a_K^\beta; \ a_A^\gamma \ a_L^\gamma \ a_K^\gamma\right) \equiv \mathbf{a} = \begin{pmatrix} a_{11} & a_{12} & a_{13} \\ a_{21} & a_{22} & a_{23} \\ a_{31} & a_{32} & a_{33} \end{pmatrix},$$

$$(A \ L \ K \ \cdots) \equiv (E_1 \ E_2 \ \cdots \ E_n) = \mathbf{E}, \quad n \geq 1.$$

Instead of $n = 3$ and $M = 3$, $\mathbf{a}$ can be any $M \times n$ matrix, while $\mathbf{x}$, $\mathbf{y}$, and $\mathbf{E}$ can be any n vectors.

If we ignore antiquarian gabble about labor theory of value and other metaphysical paradigms, the corn–labor–land–capital competitive factor pricing can be reduced down to a Primal and Dual linear programming problem involving the specified $\mathbf{a}$ matrix and the endowment vector $\mathbf{E}$, the different "Sraffa–Samuelson marginalism" that bases itself on the post-1960 technological model—of Leontief (1941), von Neumann (1935, 1945), and Sraffa—and which posits empirically a finite number of alternative *discrete* input–output techniques. By the late 19th century writers like Walras (1874, 188), von Wieser (18), and Fred Taylor (1920) had already in a casual way chanced upon the analysis of alternative discrete technologies; indeed the frequent use of numerical examples in the pre- and post-Smith classical literature did advert to the same methodology—as for example in Ricardo's cloth & wine trade 'twixt England and Portugal.

Robinson in her later decades became increasingly fond of the verb "bamboozle" when writing on capital theory! Sraffa, after effectively debunking one's ability to define unambiguously when capital was "more roundabout," "more deepened," more qualitatively productive, announced his 1960 intention to publish a future critique of modern economic theory. But both he and Robinson went to their graves leaving undone the task of comprehensively weighing the pros and cons of conventional time-phased produced-inputs interest and profit theory. Before going to my grave, I assay here to explicate objectively what reswitching and all that implies for the pretensions of Clarkian smooth technologies and the pretensions of Sraffa–Samuelson discrete technique marginalisms.

For readers on the run, I will merely state at this point that solely two classical and neoclassical tenets are shown to be in need of careful justification: in the absence of technical innovations, as the interest rate falls from one steady state to another, as soon as there are <u>joint</u> products and/or <u>multiple</u> heterogeneous capital goods, there need <u>not</u> be an induced rise in the plateau of permanently consumable output. None of the other of my numerically stated points listed above turn out to be negated. Furthermore, qualitatively, all that gets ruled out in either the Clark paradigm or in the non-Clark Sraffa–Samuelson paradigm, must also get ruled out in both of these non-identical paradigms.

Court Verdicts on Smooth Clarkian Neoclassicism

I concentrate on simplest essentials. Corn is the sole consumer good, C or $C\,(t+1)$. It is produced by 4 inputs (and with <u>no</u> joint products):

(input land, input labor, capital good 1, capital good 2) $\equiv \left[A(t)\ L(t)\ {}^{1}K(t)\,{}^{2}K(t) \right]$.

No aggregate of Kapital will enter into my present pages.

In Clark–Ramsey–Solow fashion, or as well in von Thünen (1850) fashion, society's production functions are defined to be smooth and concave and subject to all the West–Malthus–Ricardo–Knight laws of return.

$$C\,(t+1) + {}^{1}K\,(t+1) = A\,(t)^{0.2}\,L\,(t)^{0.4}\,{}^{1}K\,(t)^{0.4} + \frac{5}{6}\,{}^{2}K\,(t)$$

$$\quad\quad {}^{2}K\,(t+1) =$$

Edwin Burmeister note: This is the end of the handwritten manuscript; the remainder of the final page is blank.

Note

1 Research Professor of Economics Emeritus, Duke University, and Commonwealth Professor of Economics Emeritus, University of Virginia. The Estate of Paul A. Samuelson has kindly granted Edwin Burmeister permission to publish this transcription of Samuelson's handwritten, unfinished and unpublished manuscript that is housed in the Duke University Rubinstein Rare Book & Manuscript Library. The manuscript evidently was a first draft, and the attempt here is to transcribe it verbatim. The research assistance of John D. Singleton both in helping to uncover this manuscript and in proofreading my first transcription of it is gratefully acknowledged

12 The quantity of labour, the wage rate and the standard system[1]

Edward Nell

The Classical approach represents the total labour used by society during any period of production as a single, homogenous quantity. Upon this quantity a uniform wage is paid – uniform within an industry, across all industries and the same rate for all grades of labour. This requires explaining; the measure of that quantity, denoted by L, in terms by which a sum can be taken, and a rate figured. Just as 'capital', denoted by K, does not consist of a single homogeneous article measurable in units particular to it, so too does 'labour' consist of various grades and qualities of differing skills and aptitudes. While the Cambridge Capital Controversy made the problem of quantifying capital famous, economic theory has not seriously confronted the corresponding problem with L. The non-homogeneity of labour has been obscured by the common time dimension of the labour input. Yet the fact that the work of a surgeon and a ditch digger can both be expressed in hours is, by itself, meaningless.[2] So we are faced with a fundamental epistemological question: to what common measure are the various grades and kinds of labour reducible?

I shall argue, *only to the common denominator of exchange value*. But if this is correct, it requires a reconsideration of Sraffa's construction of the 'invariant measure of value' because his Standard System cannot be shown to exhibit the linear inverse relation between wages and the rate of profit if the 'quantity of labour' is expressed in terms of value and not as a homogenous and given quantity that is independent of value and capable of being set equal to unity as a *numeraire*. Sraffa's derivation of the Standard System, therefore, fails.

Overview of problems in Sraffa's construction

The approach to the concept of labour in his construction is open to quite serious objections.[3] The difficulty involves aggregating different types of labour within and across types, and levels of skills. Specifically, three objections must be raised: (i) labour is not a quantity measurable independently of value; (ii) the wage rate is not a fraction of the actual net product or the standard net product; and (iii) the subsistence of workers and managers must be included in the measure of capital (think of business practices – a line of credit for 'working capital').

The difficulties here can be removed by measuring labour as the sum of the values of the various subsistence goods required by the various grades (i.e. types) of labour, and including this sum as part of capital. The net wage is then paid *as a proportional return on the value of labour*. This solution to the quantification of labour, however, upsets the analysis that Sraffa has provided. This is most evident in the rate of return equation

$$r = R(1 - w)$$

where R is the maximal profit rate obtainable in the Standard System and w is the wage rate. K, capital, is not independent of prices, so cannot be uniquely defined, and the same is true for L. Furthermore, the actual–Standard relationship will not be simple and linear. The implication is that w is not the 'true' wage let alone one that can be nominally set to unity. Nor is it legitimate to define the wage as a fraction of the Standard System.

This means that if labour is expressed in terms of value and if the necessaries of subsistence are included in capital, so that wage can be expressed as a proportional increment of the basic subsistence wage, then Sraffa's construction breaks down. This will now be shown in detail.

Examination of the specific issues

Sraffa initially represents labour by the goods that support it, but he soon rejects that (Sraffa, 1960, p. 10) and introduces labour as a homogenous, unchanging factor within the economic system:

> The quantity of labour employed in each industry has now to be represented explicitly taking the place of the corresponding quantities of subsistence. We suppose labour to be uniform in quality or what amounts to the same thing, we assume any differences in quality to have been previously reduced to equivalent differences in quantity so that each unit of labour receives the same wage.

There are insurmountable difficulties in defining '*the quantity of labour*' as being formed by '*equivalent labour*' which '*corresponds to quantities of subsistence*' earning '*the same wage*'. As noted, these difficulties can be resolved by aggregating labour in terms of the value of the goods and services that support labour, or go into producing it – but then important steps in Sraffa's project are rendered invalid. And each of the above phrases can be seen to be flawed in similar ways.

Yet Sraffa is not alone in trying to reduce differences in quality of labour to ones of quantity. In spite of the all-too-obvious variety, virtually all schools of economic thought treat the total labour of society as a homogeneous magnitude, measured by the total number of workers, multiplied by the average workweek, with the differences in skills and intensity and level of work somehow 'reduced' to simple common average labour. (In Marxian theory, this could be considered the practical equivalent of expressing the many various kinds of labour as different quantities of 'abstract' labour.) The reason surely lies in the idea of 'factors of production' – land, labour and capital (Marshall added 'organization') – that are *given* at any particular time and are combined to produce output. This idea is common to Classical and Neo-Classical thinking. The Classics and Marx need it for the labour theory of value, Neoclassicals need it for marginal productivity theory, and it appears to be generally considered necessary for the study of distribution (e.g. Piketty, 2013). The Classicals see each factor as giving rise to characteristic long-run problems, population and the iron law of wages for Labour, rising rent for Land, and the falling rate of profit for Capital. In each case the analysis of the problem rested on treating the factor as measurable in its own units. For neo-Classicals, the basic economic question is an optimizing problem, to find the best, or least-cost, combinations of factors, each given in its own units, to produce output. Factors in turn will be valued by their productive contributions, i.e. their 'scarcity' values. 'Homogeneous' labour does not seem to be a mere simplification, which might be dispensed with in more advanced work.

The quantity of labour

Lumberjacks in Maine do not need swimsuits, water-ski instructors in Florida do not need snowshoes. Different lines of work often call for very different levels and kinds of training or education and also often either require or characteristically lead to very different patterns of consumption, even to different lifestyles. And, of course, the various kinds of work are paid very differently, and while wage and salary differentials are usually stable in the short and medium term, they do shift over time, and they sometimes change very suddenly and sharply.

At one time most labour might have seemed quite similar, an output of effort fuelled by food and drink, protected by clothing and shelter. Moreover, if there were, in practice, a workable and generally accepted method of expressing skilled labour in terms of simple or abstract labour, then this expedient assumption of homogeneity could be accepted – even if there were nagging difficulties. For example, skilled labour would be ordinary labour that had undergone training by specialists, themselves trained by further specialists. But what goes into training these specialists? How are different kinds of work to be compared? Yet in conditions of simple technologies, surely skilled observers could make sound judgements. But these would be special circumstances.

For whatever may have been the case in the past, the work done in different fields today is not similar, and different work requires different equipment; the training for skilled work is highly varied, and usually requires many non-labour inputs; while both the training for and performance of managerial and professional work call for non-labour inputs completely different from those needed in manual work These problems can be managed in a set of equations, which will generate 'reduction coefficients'; but these coefficients are in fact *relative valuations*. The 'reduction' amounts to adding up different kinds of labour in terms of its value. There is no other general method by which to carry out a 'reduction' So 'homogeneous labour' is not a mere simplifying assumption; it is a misrepresentation of workers' activities across time, location and skills.

'Equivalent labour'

Applying the same argument to the meaning of 'equivalent labour' in Sraffa's phrase 'differences in quality [. . .] reduced to equivalent differences in quantity', how can this 'equivalence' be established? How does the qualitative difference between water-ski instruction and brain surgery become a quantitative difference? Is it a matter of the length of the education/training period? Compare neurosurgeons and priests. Or is it personal qualities – brain surgeons must be precise, meticulous. So must the anthropologists who restore dinosaur skeletons, the art restorers who work on damaged Old Masters. . . . In terms of what unit could we measure these different kinds of work?

As noted, we could answer this by measuring labour in terms of its *value*. Labour can be measured directly no more than can capital. Like capital, labour consists of heterogeneous items; different jobs require different skills, aptitudes and knowledge and many jobs require specialized training.[4] But even granted that the quantity of labour must be measured in value, the matter is still not settled, for the question arises whether the measure should be established according to labour's (marginal) *productivity* or to its *cost of production*. The wage paid can be thought to reflect the workers' contribution to productivity, the concern of employers, or it can be interpreted as covering their cost of living and supplying labour, the concern of households. In equilibrium, of course, these measures should coincide. But then what is the measure out of equilibrium? If labour is valued by productivity (as is ubiquitous today), the issue is further complicated by the distinction between 'labour' and the 'job'. Any worker, whatever their background and training, on a production line will have a certain 'productivity' – determined by the speed of the line. If the worker moves to another line, he or she will have a different productivity, associated with that line. Productivity is tied directly to output, which of course depends on many things other than the labour input. In spite of many efforts there is no generally accepted way to measure the quantity of labour by the value it contributes to output, because that value cannot be separated from the contributions of other inputs.

Labour is not productive in the abstract; it can only produce when on the *job*, and its productivity there depends on techniques, materials, energy and the organization of work. Jobs cannot be aggregated, except by the outputs attributable to them, and outputs have to be aggregated in value. Labour considered apart from its *jobs* can be divided into grades and skill levels. But each quality of labour does have a cost largely separable from what it does. The cost of sustaining, training and replacing workers is the cost of labour regardless of what they do with their skills, or with the time during which they are supported. This cost depends on the values of the goods required as 'inputs' to maintain and train labour. But if labour value is posited on the cost of supporting and producing labour as Marx and Sraffa both suggest in places, then we are back to the problem that the composition of 'subsistence' in different sectors and for different grades will be different. The indeterminacy of the 'quantity of labour' stems from the fact that the proposed measure of labour itself is its basic consumption cost. And the cost of such subsistence must be reckoned in terms of commodities' *exchange values*. But if the quantity of labour is expressed as a sum of exchange-value, then that quantity cannot be set equal to unity arbitrarily, since this sum of exchange value, like any other value sum, will vary as the distribution of the net product changes. The exception, of course, would be the case of the invariant measure of value. The important implication here is that labour, like capital, is a factor of production that is itself *produced by 'means of production', including labour*. The amount of labour is not given exogenously; it is an outcome of the working of the system.[5]

Sraffa's assumption of a fixed quantity of labour might still be defended if the value of labour changed *pari passu* in every industry. It could be argued that this would be the case if there were only one grade of labour in the system. Such an assumption, while restrictive and unrealistic, might be defensible for some purposes. But even if there were only one grade of labour, Sraffa's system could be made to work *only if workers in every industry had the same basic consumption pattern*. This would of course imply proportional shifts in labour values across industries for any change in the value of the bundle of subsistence commodities.[6]

However, since a major point of the Sraffian approach is to avoid restrictive and unrealistic assumptions about the technical characteristics of industry, it is unreasonable to assume that labour grades and subsistence are all the same, or that different employments make the same kinds of demands on the worker. If the ratio of labour to capital differs between industries it is reasonable to suppose that the nature of the work will be very different; work may be indoor or outdoor, relatively safe or relatively dangerous; it may involve working in cooperation with other people, or it may be relatively independent; it may be active or repetitive or varied and interesting, and it may be clean or messy, hot and hard, or cool and light. These distinctions are clearly related to the patterns of consumption of workers, since their diets, medical care and clothing will vary with most of the above. But if different jobs require different consumption patterns by their workers, then the value of labour in different industries will necessarily change in different ways when prices change.

In short, Sraffa's treatment of labour as a quantity measurable without reference to prices may be as unfortunate as the attempt to measure the quantity of capital without reference to prices. Even if there were only one grade of labour, it would be necessary to express it in terms of value in order to know how much labour the net product commanded; nor would assuming a single grade be sufficient to entail that every industry had the same subsistence pattern. But in a system which assumes that different industries have different ratios of capital to labour there must be both many grades of labour and many lines of employment, with the result that the 'quantity of labour' must be expressed in value and cannot be taken as an arbitrary constant.

Remember that Adam Smith saw the division of labour and specialization of function as the foundation for increases in productivity. Division of labour means that workers will come to be doing not only different activities, but *different kinds* of activities (e.g. cutting and shaping materials – blue collar – versus keeping records of what has been done – white collar – and these differences in turn lead to differences in consumption and lifestyle. Division of labour will bring about changes in the *class composition* of the society. The different social classes, in turn, will educate and prepare their children differently, aiming them for different roles and careers. The resulting 'social products' cannot be aggregated in their own units: it is surely difficult to argue that a typical upper class child is some multiple of a representative lower class child.

Reducing heterogeneous labour to a single magnitude

There have been many attempts to solve the problem of expressing heterogeneous labour as a homogeneous magnitude, without appealing to valuations.[7] The simplest has been to reckon that more complex or more advanced labour is just a multiple of ordinary labour, in proportion to the time required for education and training for the more advanced form. Units of various kinds of labour and other inputs ('reduced' to dated labour... which poses problems) combine to produce a certain kind of skill as output – as in an education or training program. A matrix of these programs can be written and *provided we can measure all the inputs in simple labour*, without recourse to exchange-values, we can express the outputs as multiples of such labour.

But this approach assumes that degree of skill is the only problem in regard to heterogeneity. It does not deal with how to aggregate two different types, or grades, of simple labour! Again, labour differs qualitatively when workers both perform wholly different tasks using different talents, and consume different vectors of basic wage goods. In short this proposed solution begins by taking for granted that we already have a *general* measure of 'simple' labour.

A natural extension would be to treat each kind of labour as a separate output, produced by other kinds of labour and commodities; then the system could be solved for the relative prices of the different labours, along with other prices.[8] But, of course, such a solution would require that the various wages and the rate of profit be known in order to solve the system. This would certainly enable us to price and aggregate the different kinds of labour – in terms of exchange-value!

Instead of trying to aggregate by the time required for education and training, a second approach, based on Adam Smith and endorsed by Keynes, and actually adopted by Sraffa, aggregates by treating relative wages as weights, assuming them to be stable. These wage differentials presumably reflect differentials in consumption patterns, and/or differentials in productivity. Keynes (1936, pp. 41–2), for example, writes:

> ... in so far-as different grades and kinds of labour and salaried assistance enjoy a more or less fixed relative remuneration, the quantity of employment

can be sufficiently defined for our purpose by taking an hour's employment of ordinary labour as our unit and weighting an hour's employment of special labour in proportion to its remuneration; i.e. an hour of special labour remunerated at double ordinary rates will count as two units. . . . This assumption of homogeneity in the supply of labour is not upset by the obvious fact of great differences in the specialised skill of individual workers and in their suitability for different occupations. For, if the remuneration of the workers is proportional to their efficiency, the differences are dealt with by our having regarded individuals as contributing to the supply of labour in proportion to their remuneration.

But this calls for a *prior* theory to explain the wage differentials. If they depend on relative efficiencies then we require an account of 'efficiency' which is independent of prices and productivity since these concepts cannot be determined without appeal to labour quantities. How is the ratio of one kind of output to one kind of labour to be compared to the ratio of *another* kind of output to *another* kind of labour? If the differentials depend on differences in the cost of living, it means already knowing the values of the consumption goods. Moreover, this approach assumes that two workers who are paid the same wage per hour do the same amount of labour, even though they may do completely different tasks, calling for different skills, and they may consume different bundles of goods.

The relative remuneration of different grades of labour is either based on stable market relationships, reflecting well-considered choices or not. If not, it is plainly not a sound basis for aggregation, perhaps being accidental or reflecting conventional prejudices. But a stable and well-grounded relationship must be based on the differential costs of supporting labour or on the different labour type's productivity in the output, or some combination of both. Such differences, however, must be expressed in value terms, since the relevant comparisons cannot be made in purely quantitative terms.[9]

This creates an insurmountable problem. If the real consumption supporting labour is given as different consumption bundles in different industries,[10] then as prices change with changes in distribution, the value ratio of these bundles will change. Likewise if real output consists of different bundles in different industries, the comparisons will have to be made in value terms. Hence as distribution changes, the differentials would apparently change, even though real consumption relativities and real production coefficients were constant. Differences in pay cannot be the basis for aggregating labour of different grades and qualities.[11]

On the other hand, in every capitalist economy, some labour supported by a defined set of goods spends its time teaching and training potential labour. The outcomes of the various education and trainings programs will be the various skill grades of labour. We have, in other words, labour that has been trained to be teachers and trainers applied to potential workers, supported by basic subsistence, in programs such that they graduate with qualifications: labour producing labour. A set of equations could (and should) be written for this – call it the 'education sector'. Such equations should make it possible to 'reduce' skilled labour to basic subsistence. This procedure can be carried out both for training of skilled blue collar workers and for various kinds of white collar and managerial work. The equations will be different. In each case skilled labour can be valued in relation to basic labour, and to other skilled labour – but the ratios will normally change as prices change. Moreover, the value of basic labour in relation to capital goods may also change. Useful expressions of 'higher order' labour in terms of basic labour can be obtained – but they are not independent of prices and distribution.

This conclusion is not far from that of Kurz and Salvadori, who ask 'whether it is possible to aggregate different concrete labours via relative wages', noting that this requires that relative wages be unaffected by changes in the general rate of profit and in the techniques used. In general, they answer, this will not be the case. 'With a rise in the general rate of profit not only the values of physical capital will generally be affected, but the values of human capitals also' (Kurz and Salvadori, 1995, pp 333–4). However, they propose to carry on, using particular labours measured in own units. The argument here is that labour should be aggregated in units of exchange-value, analogously to capital.

The 'true wage' from labour's perspective

Going back to the quote from Sraffa: what does 'taking the place of ... subsistence' mean here? The 'corresponding quantities of subsistence' will change in value as the distribution changes so that the value required to support a given level of employment will vary. Hence a given fraction of the net product will sustain more or less labour depending on the prices of subsistence goods, which vary as the distribution changes.

Explaining capitalism requires examining socio-economic *classes*, where the different classes will have different consumption and saving patterns. The higher classes will normally invest more in education and training. The different grades of labour may be considered different 'social products', the different results of bringing up children according to the norms of class structure. Classes may also have different patterns of remuneration as well as consumption – think of daily or weekly wages vs. monthly salaries, bonuses, stock options, etc. With heterogeneous labour we may have different social *sub*-classes, as well, further complicating the picture. Some of these compete against each other; and their prosperity is likely to be affected differently by different types of investment. Indeed, the investment in social capital varies through cultures, classes and over the normal lifecycle; but these expenditures are critical aspects of social life and, as such, should be considered part of the normal 'subsistence' for the various grades of labour (especially as they accord with social class). As Bourdieu reminds (*Distinction*, 1984; Chapter 7, p. 375) us:

> One man's extravagance is another man's prime necessity – and not only because the marginal value of those two million francs varies with the number of millions possessed. *Many of the expenditures that are called conspicuous are in no way a squandering* and, as well as being obligatory elements in

a certain style of life, they are very often – like engagement parties – an excellent investment in social capital. [emphasis added].

Thus, 'subsistence' is not defined once and for all in social terms – it evolves and vacillates with society and one's position in it.[12] But at any given time it will be defined, and argued over, in popular culture.

From the point of view of labour the important issue is the ratio of payments for labour to the cost of 'subsistence', as defined above. From the employer's point of view, the relevant ratio would be that of payments to labour to the value of net output. If both households and employers are satisfied by the payments we may call this ratio the 'true wage' and it is what the market will tend to equalize across different lines of employment. This wage rate is analogous to the rate of profit – being a bonus rate on a basic wage covering the cost of living, *it is a rate of return on the value of labour*. If workers in one sector are receiving 10 per cent over their cost of living, and in another sector, 20 per cent, workers will tend to migrate from the first to the second, *ceteris paribus*.

But neither Sraffa nor Sraffians have thought in terms of this ratio. Quite the contrary: Sraffa treats the wage first as a fraction of the net product, then as a fraction of the standard net product – the employer's perspective.[13] Neither fits into the normal bargaining framework of labour. Worse, neither is related to labour's major concern – the cost of living. It is not clear how to translate the wage as a fraction of net product into the wage as a proportional return to labour because the quantity on which this proportional return will be received must be the value of labour, which changes as the distribution changes and prices vary. Such changes also make it difficult to speak of labour in different industries receiving the same wage, especially when the labour is supported by different bundles of subsistence goods, since it is necessary to separate out the 'true' net wage bill from the total wage bill. How are we to determine the relative shares of the net product? Moreover, it should be clear that when the fraction of the net product going to labour increases, the 'true' net wage should also increase. But how are we to show this? It might increase non-proportionally or at a variable rate; intuitively, it surely would not fall, but this should be demonstrated.

Institutionally, the wage rate, far from being a fraction of the net product, is a proportional payment to man-hours in which different grades of labour receive different rates of pay corresponding to their different costs of support, education and training. Moreover, the 'net product' in the traditional sense requires that it should be net of the subsistence wage. This quantity must therefore also be defined for each sector and each grade of labour, in spite of all of the socio-economic difficulties discussed above. Thus we have a simple relation

Payment to labour = net wage + basic subsistence

$$= (\text{Wage rate} \times \text{subsistence}) + \text{subsistence} = (1 + w)q'$$

where the normal net wage rate is w and S is the matrix of subsistence wage goods that must be paid to each grade of labour. The vectors q' and p are relative quantities and relative prices. The net wage is then the surplus each grade of labour in each sector receives over and above *its* subsistence level.

The wage share – let alone the standard wage share – is not a concern either of labourers or of employers. The issue for labourers is the ratio of pay to the cost of living; for employers, pay in relation to productivity and product price is the central focus. (Employers must at least cover the cost of living in the long run.) Competition among workers will imply that they will move to the employers paying the most in relation to cost of living, driving down such pay, while competition among employers implies that those paying the least in relation to normal productivity and price will earn the highest profit. To keep pace, others will have to cut their wage offers. However, those who pay the least will tend to get the poorest workers, those who pay the most, the best. Those swamped with workers will be able to cut wage offers, those facing shortages of labour will be obliged to raise them. Hence there will be a tendency for competition to force a convergence to a common wage rate between employees and employers. For workers this central wage rate is defined in terms of the ratio of money payments to cost of living. For employers the wage rate concerns the ratio of money outlays to the excess of productivity over the funds required needed to meet fixed costs for firms.

So 'the wage' should be thought of as a net wage, net of the cost of living, thus analogous to the profit on capital, so that the wage *rate*, like the profit rate, will be a proportional return to the amount of value already productively employed This approach to the net wage considers it a 'bonus' paid out of the economy's net product, in contrast to the subsistence wage, which is advanced out of capital during the period of production.[14] Capital, then, would consist of two parts: (1) the technical goods for production, represented by a matrix T and; (2) goods that make up the (socially defined) basic or 'subsistence' wages of workers and salaried managers, represented by S.

To put it another way, Sraffa treats the payments to labour very differently from the return to industry. Industries must replace their means of production out of their sales proceeds, and their return is calculated as the value ratio of their net proceeds to cost of production. By contrast only the gross earnings of labour appear in his construction, and the way labour is supported (or produced!) is not shown explicitly.

There is no reason to suppose that the true wage would vary directly with 'the payment to labour', since the values of the wage-goods will depend on the ratio of labour to capital in the industries which produce them. Even if all labour were supported by the same wage-goods consumed in the same proportions, so that differences in quality could be reduced to differences in quantity, the prices of subsistence goods could, for example, fall by less than a decrease in the payment to labour, or even rise. Only if the industries producing wage goods employed the 'balancing proportions' of labour and capital, and if their suppliers and suppliers' suppliers, etc. did likewise, could the prices of wage goods remain constant as the wage-payment varied.

Only if the prices of wage-goods remain constant, or change in such a way that the effects exactly cancel one another, will the true wage vary proportionally with the payment to labour. But that would mean supposing, in effect, that the subsistence of labour had the same composition as the standard commodity. This would imply either that only labour was used, which confines the story to Ricardo's shrimps and broken stones, or that all industries have the same ratio of labour to capital.

A crucial difficulty when the wage is not a fraction of net product

Sraffa defines the wage as a fraction of the net product, and this has an important implication. Basic macro-accounting definitions mean the sum of the payments to labour and to capital can be expressed in the familiar macroeconomic notation as

$$Y = wL + rK$$

where both rates are given in *net of cost* terms But since Sraffa takes the wage a fraction of net product, his national income equation must be written as[15]

$$Y = wY + rK$$

as is shown by the fact that the latter equation, *but not the former*, can be put in the form

$$r = (Y/K)(1 - w)$$

This raises a critical question for Sraffa's construction. In the normal case

$$r = (Y/K) - w(L/K)$$

and there is no reason to suppose that $Y = L$ is ever the case, let alone for all distributions!

Yet what Sraffa has done is to set both Y and L equal to unity, as a matter of choosing *numeraires*. At the very least this needs justification: in Sraffa's system the equation $Y = L$ does not match up dimensionally, since Y and L are measured in different units. The unit of Y is exchange-value while L is a measure of physical quantities, specifically labour time. What does it mean to say that one unit of exchange value equals one unit of labour? Is this a postulate or a condition of reproduction, or a kind of equilibrium? Why is the relationship between r and w such that $Y = L$ is implied?

When the rate of profit varies prices will rise or fall depending on the ratio of labour to means of production (Sraffa, 1960, Chapter 3); there will be a 'watershed' or critical ratio according to which, for example, the funds saved from the fall in the rate of profit are just sufficient to pay the rise in wages, without the need for a price change. If the goods used as means of production for this industry also had this critical ratio, their prices would not need to change either. If this ratio were 'recurrent' at every stage in production, then no prices would change. Sraffa then argues (in his Section 22) that this implies that the net output of such an industry cannot change relative to the value of its aggregate means of production, thus shifting from considering the 'hybrid' ratio of labour to means of production, to the ratio of net product to means of production. And this latter ratio can be 'recurrent', for when the wage is zero the ratio of net product to means of production is the same in every industry, and equal to the maximum rate of profit. And when total labour is set equal to unity, as a choice of numeraire, the two ratios coincide. Or do they?

Recall the dispute between Schefold and Flaschel, mentioned earlier: Flaschel argues that the 'watershed proportion', or balancing proportion, is a ratio of the exchange value of means of production to labour (in time units), and so cannot be equated to the Standard Ratio, which is a pure number. This is essentially the above dimensional problem. Schefold argues, in effect, that when both Y and L are set equal to unity (in standard proportions), as a matter of choosing *numeraires*, labour units are equated to exchange-value units and the watershed proportion also becomes a pure number. But can the arbitrary choice of numeraire trump the difference in dimensions? Surely a justification is needed for equating a unit of exchange value to a unit of labour?

Moreover, it seems that Sraffa's wage–profit equation depends on the fact that the derivation does not actually involve either the quantity of labour or the real wage. There is no term of the form: 'wage rate × quantity of labour'; instead the wage is given as a fraction, between 0 and 1, of the Standard Net Product (Sraffa, 1960, Sections 29 and 30). Suppose, instead of the wage, the fraction were interpreted as the government's take. The equation would then be a linear profit–tax tradeoff. The derivation does not give us a true wage–profit curve.

This is all problematic to say the least. The larger point concerns the quantity of labour, which cannot be a given. Instead it is argued here that quantities of labour, like quantities of capital, must be expressed in units of value (preferably units of *invariant value*, but that is a further issue). The wage must be a rate on the cost of living, showing the percentage over that basic cost that labour is earning, as its share in the surplus. However, then the construction of the Standard System will not work.

The standard system with subsistence capital

If the system is modified to meet these difficulties by introducing 'subsistence capital' (subsistence wages that are advanced from capital) and a net wage, a new set of problems arises. To introduce subsistence capital means exhibiting the amount of labour employed by an industry by showing the corresponding subsistence goods (which constitute the 'cost of living'), whose prices will alter as the distribution changes, rising or falling according to the conditions of production in their respective industries. The net wage then appears as a proportional return on the value of the subsistence capital. That is, when subsistence goods are included as a part of capital, then the wage paid over and above those subsistence goods is defined as a premium wage. It follows that the Sraffian wage–profit equation cannot be derived in the usual way.[16]

The matrix equation for a single product circulating system is

$$(1+r)Cp + wSp = Pp \quad \text{or}$$
$$(1+r)C - Pp + wSp = 0.$$

Here r is the rate of profit, w the net wage rate, p prices, P the matrix of outputs, and S of subsistence. C is capital, consisting not only of the technical goods needed as inputs, but also including the inputs needed for the subsistence of workers and managers, who receive a basic wage advanced from capital. C may therefore be regarded as partitioned into T, the matrix of technical inputs, and S, the subsistence matrix.

Now let us apply the q matrix to the equation

$$q'[[(1+r)C - P]p + wSp] = 0$$

and then add

$$rq'Cp - q'Pp + q'Cp + wq'Sp = 0 \quad \text{or}$$
$$rq'Cp = q'(P - C)p - wq'Sp$$

which implies

$$r = [q'(P - C)p - wq'Sp]/q'Cp.$$

The q' system is so defined that $q'(P - C)/q'C$ will be a ratio of quantities, independent of prices, since every good will appear in the same proportions in both numerator and denominator.[17] S, however, is part of C, which equals (T/S); consequently if $q'(P - C)$ and $q'C$ have the same composition, i.e. are different quantities of the same composite commodity, then clearly $q'S$ will be a different composite commodity from $q'C$, of which it is a partition (C will normally possess elements not in S). Price changes will therefore affect S differently than they affect C. The value ratio of $q'Sp$ to $q'Cp$, or, as it might be called, the internal composition of capital, will therefore change as the distribution changes.

This implies that the simple linear and inverse relation between the wage rate and the rate of profit cannot be derived in a Standard System in which the 'subsistence capital' is shown,[18] except in the special case – 'shrimps and broken stones' – where there is no technical capital, i.e. where $q'S = q'C$. This means, among other things, that in such a 'Standard System' the relation between the wage and the rate of profits would not be independent of prices.[19]

Labour as a produced means of production

Sraffa actually suggests the idea of 'subsistence capital' and net wages. He does not adopt it, perhaps because he intended his system to be the basis for a critique of the dominant ideas, so wanted it to be similar in basic assumptions. But he also wanted to lay the basis for a better approach, and the assumption of exogenously given labour, measurable in its own units, is not an adequate foundation for studying advanced capitalism.

When it comes to determining the total quantity of labour in the economy, all the ways of aggregating heterogeneous labour can be useful. Marx was surely correct that 'different labours are set equal by the market', if this means not just the market, but the economy as a whole. Reduction equations can be helpful. Labour is aggregated in terms of prices, which in turn are based not only on the market but also on norms and normal behaviour, including traditional wage differentials, as Keynes suggested. The relationships between different grades of labour are established in the process of reproduction. Labour is supported by consumer goods, and the amount of such goods depends on the amount of *time* the work will take and further, these labour times and *the timing of work* are also coordinated across industries. Both of these – the support of labour and the coordination of production times – are needed to determine the quantity of labour. There is also a coordination problem in the long run: education, schooling and training have to produce appropriate labour force replacements at the appropriate time. For example, graduations stemming from education/training programs have to be coordinated with retirements and deaths.

But this means that the 'quantity of labour' depends on prices and therefore *cannot enter as a given* into the basic equations that determine prices. Rather, labour is a *constructed* magnitude, which is determined as part of the integrated whole. Moreover, this approach means that 'the quantity of labour' does not constrain the economy. Instead we replace 'labour' with the bundles of goods that support labour for the appropriate lengths of time.

Clearly there is a similarity to the case of capital – capital cannot be aggregated, except by adding up the elements of capital in terms of exchange value, and the capital controversy shows that there is no reason to suppose that such an aggregate of prices times quantities will vary inversely as the rate of profit changes. A similar case can be made for the aggregate of labour, also an expression of prices of consumer basics times the quantities needed to support basic labour for the time needed in production. There is no reason to suppose that this aggregate will move inversely to the wage rate. If consumer goods industries were relatively labour intensive and remained so as the wage rose, then consumer goods prices would rise relatively to other goods as the wage rises. So as the wage rose the aggregate 'quantity of labour' would increase. Conversely, if consumer goods industries were capital intensive, and remained so as the wage rose, the quantity of labour would decrease as the wage rose. In general, however, it is not possible to identify an industry or group of industries as being 'capital-intensive' or 'labour-intensive', except for a *given* level of the wage rate, as these ratios will change as prices change.

We then take a crucial step: we determine the productivity of labour in general, for the economy as a whole, *as a purely quantitative ratio* denoted by ω (Nell, 1998, Chapter 7). The numerator of this ratio consists of the net output of the system, adjusted so that it is made up of the consumer goods that support labour, in the proper ratio to each other, while the denominator is the aggregate quantities of basic consumer goods supporting labour, in the same proper ratio to each other. That is, the consumer goods making up the net product must be in the same proportions as the basket of basic subsistence goods. This is analogous to Sraffa's standard commodity where the net product of the system as a whole (of basics) stands in the same proportions as the set of goods making up the aggregate means of production.

The effects of speeding up or slowing down production

As a thought experiment the analysis can begin with an economy that produces just enough to support its labour and replace the goods used up each period. Each kind of labour in each industry will be represented by the bundle of goods required to support and train that labour for the time necessary for it to perform the work. The amount of work that needs to be done in each case depends on the engineering and the design of the technology; these will determine not only the activities to be performed, but also the *speed* with which they are completed. This determines the time for which labour will have to be supported – i.e., how many days of consumer goods. Moreover the timing of the work in each industry will be coordinated with the industries that supply it, and with its customers. Supplies will be needed when production is to start, and delivery should take place when production is finished – carrying inventory is costly. Such coordination will ensure that the economy as a whole will start and finish its productive cycle in a regular and efficient manner – something that an industrial economy has to arrange, but which was imposed on pre-industrial economies by the seasons and the weather. (This temporal coordination of different kinds of work, coordinating the inputs and outputs of different sectors, may provide a basis for the idea of 'abstract labour' – any particular labour depends for its success on its interaction with all other basic labour.)

The amount of steel needed for a certain level of automobile output is *constant*, it does not matter when or how fast the output in question is produced. But the amount of sandwiches and beer needed to process the steel is *variable;* it depends on how long it takes, one week or two, to produce the output.

So there are two different kinds of coefficients in our approach, a difference that may correspond to Marx's distinction between 'constant' and 'variable' capital. Constant capital coefficients are those which show the inputs required per unit of output, regardless of the time required for production. So much wood per table is needed, whether it takes a day or a week to make the table. Variable capital coefficients are those which apply to inputs that vary with respect to output, according to the speed of production. If workers work faster, then fewer units of subsistence goods will be required per unit of output, since workers will need to be supported for less time. A surplus can thus be created by *speeding up throughput*, so that more work is done in the time during which labour is supported by its consumption. A speed-up will typically involve a re-organized division of labour, and more careful and more efficient movements in carrying out work. Quantitatively, such a speed-up reduces the amount of consumer goods needed to support unit production, thus reducing unit costs in relation to revenues. Qualitatively, a speed-up will change the way work is carried out, and may change the skills needed.

Now we come to the crucial step: defining labour productivity in purely quantitative terms. Starting from a 'no-surplus' economy (Nell, 1998, Chapters 5 and 7) consider a uniform speed-up in the turnover of the 'technical' capital – in the simplest case, the result will be the exact reproduction of the technical capital, together with the basic subsistence goods, *and a surplus of the composite subsistence good*, the size of which depends on the speed-up.[20] The net output, a vector of subsistence goods in the correct proportions, will stand in the ratio ω to the subsistence capital, that is, to the vector of basic consumer goods needed to support and train labour.

(This could be seen another way, by starting from an existing surplus, which implies a high speed of turnover, that is, workers are working fast. This surplus can be reduced and, eventually eliminated by *slowing down* the speed of production (and changing relative sector sizes). For example, consider the system that is reached, starting from a productive economy, by a uniform slowdown of production, proceeding until the surplus disappears.)

Let us start from an economy with no surplus, and further examine the productive system reached by a uniform speed-up.[21] In the no-surplus economy we can see the relationships between the different categories of labour very easily. This device will be useful, because in the productive economy resulting from a uniform speed-up, the surplus will consist of *the same goods in the same proportions as the aggregate support for labour* – and the prices will also be the same, taking account of ω (Nell, 1998). The result of a speed-up is an increase in the purely quantitative ratio between the bundle of goods making up the surplus and the bundle that supports labour, whatever the varieties of labour. This ratio is ω, which we can now see will be the maximum wage rate, when the whole surplus goes to labour. But in the case of a uniform speed-up or slowdown, it will appear as a purely quantitative ratio. The measure of labour, then, is the volume of goods that support labour, in the right proportions, as this appears in the no-surplus economy; the measure of this labour's productivity is the uniform slowdown that would eliminate the surplus (Nell, 1998, Chapter 7).[22] This measure, of course, corresponds to the 'rate of exploitation' in Marx, and equals the maximum possible wage rate. Thus it can be combined with R to form a wage–profit equation.

Further analysis could explore the wage–profit–price system, and could examine the symmetrical consumption–growth–relative size relationships. We could demonstrate that the 'Golden Rule' – rate of profit equals rate of growth – can be drawn upon to reconstruct something like Sraffa's project: it can be shown that the system exhibits 'conservation of value'. This makes it possible to define an 'invariable' measure of value, different from the standard commodity, and moreover, one that fits together with a (revised and reinterpreted) quantity equation (Nell, 2004, 2010, 2011). The measure of value is incorporated in money. But all this is beyond the scope of this paper,[23] which has been concerned to argue that labour is as heterogeneous as capital, and like capital, must be aggregated in value terms – with the result that Sraffa's construction fails.

Notes

1 Appropriately for a commentary on Sraffa, these ideas have been a long time in the making, and were discussed with Sraffa himself on one occasion. Several important passages have been taken almost verbatim from my 1965 Oxford thesis; others are close to Nell (1998), Chapter 7. This paper is a first step towards pulling it all together; a follow-up paper is available on request. Many thanks to all those I have discussed these issues with over the years.

2 If all labour inputs are measureable by a reduction to scalar multiples in the time dimension (i.e. how many hours of John's work equals an hour's worth of Jane's work) then all output can be measured in units of labour time. John is a ski-instructor at Aspen, Jane a water-ski instructor in Miami. Even if the 'output' of successful pupils can be measured and compared – we can say how much water-skiing equals a unit of snow-skiing – it is still the case that John needs ski jackets and Jane bathing suits. Their basic living costs differ. To say nothing of another issue in reducing different kinds of labour to a common measure: how do we account for ingenuity, creativity, collaboration and problem-solving? How do they figure in labour's value? If labour is valued by its productivity they must be accounted for.

3 Cf. Peter Flaschel's criticisms, Chapters 11 and 12 in Flaschel (2010). He argues that the linear wage–profit tradeoff merely 'hides' the non-linearities, transferring them to the expression for the national income. He also argues that Sraffa's derivation of the 'invariant measure' is defective, because the 'recurrent watershed proportion' (also known as the 'balancing proportion') cannot be legitimately identified with the Standard Ratio. Schefold (1997) disputes this, arguing that Sraffa is entitled to choose his numeraire, and that by setting the standard net product equal to unity he equalizes the two ratios. Below we will show that there is a dimensional problem here. However, the problems go deeper. Sraffa treats labour as measured in units of time (adjusted for skills), so *independent of value;* thus the amount of labour can be summed up and set equal to unity. But it is argued here that labour cannot be treated as independent of exchange value; labour must be measured in the consumer goods that support it, so must be a sum of exchange value. Hence the 'amount of labour' will vary with changes in distribution, and Sraffa's procedure is invalid.

4 The Dictionary of Occupational Titles, in 1965, listed more than 44,000 distinct jobs in the modern United States, together with a description of the different skills and training needed for each. As the economy shifted from an industrial system to services and information, listings increased so rapidly and the nature of jobs changed so much that the US Department of Labour stopped updating the DOT in 1999 and instead produced a new kind of listing, the O*NET, Occupational Information Network, an online system that describes occupations in terms of the skills and characteristics required of workers, rather than the tasks to be performed. It began with about 1,300 different categories.

5 The 'amount of labour' is sometimes confused with *the number of workers* or *level of employment,* but it is different from both, even if hours are given. Hours of one *kind of work* are not the same as hours of another; hours of one *grade of labour* or level of skill are not the same as hours of another. The number of workers comes from the long-run interaction of family dynamics – and migration – with technology and job creation; hours come from the results of social and economic bargaining. The level of employment is a macroeconomic issue. The amount of total employment offered by the system – working at normal capacity – depends on the jobs offered by the capital structure, and will vary with aggregate demand. The ratio of employment to available workers is a measure of utilization. (Labour is not normally a constraint.) But the contention here is that the 'amount of labour' depends first on the number of jobs offered in the various industries, and the training required, and then on the pattern of basic consumption in those industries and finally on the prices of the basic wage goods, since

total basic consumption will be aggregated in value terms. The amount of labour will then be aggregated in terms of value (long-run normal prices). Like capital it is a cost of production.

6 In early capitalism consumption patterns of the working class in different sectors might well have been similar. Smith, Ricardo and Marx seem to have assumed this. Moreover, even where these patterns differed in *particular* goods, the *broad categories* Food, Clothing, Fuel, Shelter, Transport and Entertainment might have stood in the same proportions in the support bundle for labour in the different sectors. If teachers and trainers also shared this common consumption pattern there would be some justification for assuming that all grades of labour could be expressed in a common measure. This would make it possible to formulate the Labour Theory of Value. However, even in early capitalism the professional classes, creative workers, soldiers and priests had sharply divergent consumption patterns, not to mention the huge difference between agricultural and industrial workers. Approximations may be possible from time to time, but 'Reduction to Simple Labour', without relying on values, is not generally feasible, and the Labour Theory must always be suspect.

7 Homogeneous labour could be rejected, and, instead, a number of different kinds of labour could be accepted. At first this looks promising, and some writers have been led to the interesting and perhaps important problem of the potential conflicts in distribution between different groups of workers (Bowles and Gintis, 1977). But within these categories it would still be necessary to aggregate the working time of various workers who do not do exactly the same thing in the same way, or consume exactly the same goods, yet their working times must be aggregated. The difficulty here is similar to that for capital.

8 This is the approach taken in Nell (1998), Chapter 7.

9 In quantitative terms a differential could only be calculated in terms of the *support* labour requires, or in terms of the *output* that labour produces – or perhaps in some combination of the two. To establish the differential, the support and/or the output would have to be compared, presumably per unit time. But the bundle of goods that supports a day of one kind of work may be quite different from the bundle that supports a day of another type, and the productivity of one kind of work will be expressed in a different bundle of goods from that of another.

10 'Production costs' might be extended to cover different subsistence inputs to different grades of labour. Special inputs to labour could be treated as supplied directly by employers (rather than purchased out of wages); so these inputs-into-the-input might, therefore, be considered part of the means of production. This might work for the uniforms of security guards and police, and protective goggles of welders, but it cannot account for the across-the-board differences in the normal consumption patterns of lumberjacks and water-ski instructors, fishermen and cowboys, let alone janitors and attorneys, doctors and bus drivers, not to mention differing 'cost of living' bundles based on culture and custom.

11 Another interpretation contends that different labours are 'set equal by the market'. One kind of labour can be taken as the standard; it will then be equated through exchange to various amounts of other kinds of labour. It is possible to determine a set of 'reduction coefficients' which express the various kinds of labour in terms of an abstract standard (Ulrich Krause, *Value and Abstract Labour* 1981), but to do this, it is necessary to settle the question of exploitation: are all forms of labour exploited to the same degree? If so, can we assume that the market establishes a uniform rate of exploitation in terms of abstract labour, that is, actual labour multiplied by the reduction coefficients? There seems to be no reason whatever to suppose that the market would do this.

12 'Having millions does not in itself make one able to live like a millionaire; and parvenus generally take a long time to learn that what they see as culpable prodigality is, in their new condition, expenditure of basic necessity' (Bourdieu, 1984, p. 374).

13 Sraffa defines the wage as the wage per unit of labour, 'which like prices will be expressed in terms of the chosen standard' (Sraffa, 1960, p. 11). He then provisionally sets 'the national income of a system in a self-replacing state' equal to unity, thereby expressing prices and wages in terms of this sum. The whole of the wage is taken as variable, ranging from 0 to 1 though he notes that this 'relegat[es] the necessaries of consumption to the limbo of non-basic products' (p. 10). He suggests that 'it would be [more] appropriate ..., [...] to separate the two component parts of the wage and regard only the 'surplus' part as variable; whereas the goods necessary for the subsistence of the workers would continue to appear, with the fuel, etc., among the means of production' (pp. 9–10). Thus he notes the difference between basic and net wages, but he considers the former to be on a footing with means of production. (Later we will see that the subsistence of workers and the means of production differ in regard to time in a most important respect – a difference that underlies the ability to produce a surplus.) Finally he expresses the wage as a fraction of the Standard Net Product.

14 The net wage need not, of course, be paid at the end of the period, provided that whatever funds finance its payment are suitably replenished at that point.

15 Sraffa (1960), 'We shall also hereafter assume that the wage is paid post factum as a share of the annual product ...', p. 10. 'We proceed to give the wage (w) successive values ranging from 1 to 0; these now represent fractions of the national income ...', p. 12. See footnote 3 commenting on Flaschel and Schefold.

16 In Nell (1998), Chapter 7 the relation of subsistence capital to the net product is examined. It is shown that we can define a purely quantitative ratio of net product to subsistence capital by putting the net product in the same proportions as subsistence capital; the result is an analogy for labour to the maximum rate of profit on capital.

17 When there is fixed capital building ahead of demand implies excess capacity; and for Marx's reasons there will normally be a 'reserve army of labour'. So it should be easy to adjust the relative size of industries and sectors. What limits the size of the economy is the existing structure of fixed capital and the amount of arable land.

18 It might be thought that the condition that $q'Sp = 1$ could be added, in place of the equation determining the units in which to express prices. But this equation is misleading, for we have just seen that the value of $q'Sp$ is *not* invariant, as distribution changes, so cannot be set equal to unity. On the contrary, unlike Sraffa's standard commodity, it changes with the changes in the distribution of the surplus.

19 To be useful, the Standard System must bear a definite and ascertainable relationship to the actual system, which means in the present context that it must be possible to express the actual system's wage rate as a fraction of the Standard national income. This can be done, but the relationship is not simple and linear. When the actual wage is paid as a proportional return to the value of labour we have w_a, the actual system's wage, and w_s as that of the Standard System, so that the relationship of the actual and the Standard System will be given by the transformation

$$w_a W = w_s q' (P - C)p, \quad \text{where } W = q'Sp.$$

This will normally have a solution for w_s, given a feasible w_a. When the distribution changes, $W = q'Sp$ will also change; but the changes will not be proportional to the changes in net product. So the relationship will be non-linear.

20 If the new production speed is twice the old, the total output of consumer goods (in the correct proportions) will be twice the old, and the net output will be equal to the subsistence capital, so that $\omega = 1$.

21 'Wasting time' is costly, so competitive pressures will tend to ensure that slowdowns and speed-ups will be, if not uniform, then *coordinated* (Nell, 1998, pp. 309–11). When they are non-uniform, coordination will require differences in speed of production to be offset by differences in relative sizes and in the carrying of inventory. A non-uniform

speed-up (slowdown) can be paired with an equivalent uniform speed-up (slowdown) by re-allocating labour, changing relative sizes to offset the differences in production speeds; the two systems will have the same prices and the same productivity of labour, but the uniform system will show this in purely quantitative terms. Cf. Nell (1998), pp. 338–9.

22 Treating labour as an endogenously produced commodity immediately presents the challenge of defining the scale of the system. In most economic models, Sraffa's included, the size of the labour force sets the scale of the system. In early capitalism, the availability of land and agricultural technology – the land/labour ratio – set the size of the agricultural sector, and the surplus of that sector limited the size of the urban sector and urban industry. Later the capacity of industry sets a limit to the level of employment and output. Here the scale of the economic system, implicitly or explicitly reflects past investment and development.

23 A follow-up paper is available on request, and will be published separately.

Bibliography

Bowles, S and Gintis, H. 1977. 'The Marxian theory of value and heterogeneous labour: a critique and reformulation' *Cambridge Journal of Economics*, 1, 173–192.

Bourdieu, P. 1984. *Distinction: A Social Critique of the Judgement of Taste, translated by Richard Nice*. Cambridge, MA: Harvard University Press.

Flaschel, P. 2010. *Topics in Classical Micro- and Macroeconomics: Elements of a Critique of Neoricardian Theory*. Berlin, Heidelberg: Springer-Verlag.

Keynes, J. M. 1936. *The General Theory of Employment, Interest and Money*. London: Macmillan.

Krause, U. 1981. *Value and Abstract Labour*. New York: Verso.

Kurz, H and Salvadori, N. 1993. 'The "Standard Commodity" and Sraffa's Search for an "Invariable Measure of Value" ', in Baranzini, M and Harcourt, G., eds., *The Dynamics of the Wealth of Nations – Essays in Honour of Luigi Pasinetti*. London: Macmillan and New York: St Martin's Press.

Kurz, H and Salvadori, N. 1995. *Theory of Production: A Long-Period Analysis*. Cambridge: Cambridge University Press.

Marx, K 1965. *Capital Vols, I, II, III*. New York: Modern Library.

Nell, E. J. 1982. 'Understanding the Marxian Notion of Exploitation: The "Number One Issue"', in Feiwel, G. W. ed., *Samuelson and Neo-Classical Economics*, Boston: Kluwer-Nijoff. Reprinted in Nell, 1992, *Transformational Growth and Effective Demand*. New York: New York University Press.

Nell, E. J. 1998. *The General Theory of Transformational Growth*. Cambridge: Cambridge University Press.

Nell, E. J. 2004. 'Monetizing the Classical Equations', *Cambridge Journal of Economics*, 28(2), 173–203.

Nell, E. J. 2010. 'The Quantity Equation and the Classical Theory of Production and Distribution', in Ciccone, R, Gehrke, C, and Mongiovi, G, eds., *Sraffa and Modern Economics, Vol. II*. London and New York: Routledge, pp. 186–204.

Nell, E. J. 2011. 'On the Circulation of Real and Fiat Money in Fix-Price and Flex-Price Economies', in Birolo, A, Foley, D, Kurz, H, Schefold, B and Steedman, I, eds., *Production, Distribution and Trade: Alternative Perspectives, Essays in Honour of Sergio Parrinello* London and New York: Routledge, pp. 254–85.

Piketty, T. 2013. *Capital in the Twenty-First Century*. Cambridge, MA and London: The Belknap Press of Harvard University Press.

Schefold, B. 1989. *Mr Sraffa on Joint Production and Other Essays.* London: Unwin Hyman.

Schefold, B. 1997. *Normal Prices, Technical Change and Accumulation.* New York: St Martin's Press.

Smith, A. 1776. *The Wealth of Nations.*

Sraffa, P. 1960. *Production of Commodities By Means of Commodities.* Cambridge: Cambridge University Press.

13 Duality theory and full industry equilibrium

A diagrammatic analysis[1]

Arrigo Opocher

My tribute to Neri Salvadori's scholarship concerns some aspects of the duality between a technology and the long-period prices generated by it. This broad topic has been investigated by Neri in at least two pioneering works: one written jointly with Ian Steedman (Salvadori and Steedman, 1985), the other with Christian Bidard (Birdard and Salvadori, 1995). The former has shown that a Sraffa system can be formulated on the basis of a vector of given unit cost functions, rather than from an explicit description of technology; the latter has shown that a sufficient number of possible price vectors contain all the information on their common generating technique (assuming there is only one). I have myself examined the Bidard–Salvadori duality principle in the case of any number of techniques (Opocher, 2002).

This chapter takes so to speak, a step *backward* by examining some preliminary aspects of long-period duality in the simple case of an individual, isolated industry. The crucial point is that this industry makes *net* profits of zero. This is a simple case of what Steedman and I call a *Full Industry Equilibrium* (FIE). (See Steedman, 1998; Opocher and Steedman, 2015.)

We begin with an industry characterized by u-shaped average cost curves and two primary inputs, land and labour. Then we turn to strict constant returns to scale and introduce a third input, consisting of the industry's own output. In both cases it is found that, in FIE, the degrees of freedom on the production function/isoquant are sharply reduced and the 'true' production function/isoquant may *not* be implicit in the knowledge of long-period prices. Even fixed coefficients may not be determined on the basis of any number of long-period prices, differently from the case discussed by Bidard and Salvadori.

Duality at the bottom of u-shaped average cost curves

Let $C(w, r, Q)$ be a twice differentiable cost function of the (identical) firms forming our industry where (w, r) denote, respectively, the wage and rent rates and Q denotes the firm output. $C()$ is homogeneous of degree one in w, r and, at any given input prices, is a reverse s-shaped function of Q. (Hence the *average* cost curve is always u-shaped.)

By competition, each firm gravitates towards a zero-profit equilibrium at the bottom of its average cost curve. (A good discussion of this case is in Silberberg, 1974.) Denoting by p the output price, an FIE is therefore characterized by

$$\frac{\partial C\,(w,\,r,\,Q)}{\partial Q} = \frac{C\,(w,\,r,\,Q)}{Q} \tag{13.1}$$

$$C\,(w,\,r,\,Q) = pQ. \tag{13.2}$$

Needless to say, $C\,(w,\,r,\,Q)$ contains all the relevant information concerning the generating production function, say $Q\,(L,\,T)$, however complicated the duality relations between the two functions might be. But we are concerned here with a different (and perhaps simpler) problem which is specific to long-period positions. We want to extract all possible technological information from knowledge not of the entire cost function, but of prices $(w,\,r,\,p)$ and total cost satisfying (13.1) and (13.2).

It is convenient to distinguish between two cases, according to whether $C\,(w,\,r;\,Q)$ is homothetic or not.

The homothetic case

In the first case $C\,(w,\,r,\,Q)$ can be written as $g\,(Q)\,\gamma\,(w,\,r)$ (see Shephard, 1970, p. 93). Equations (13.1) and (13.2) become, therefore

$$\frac{dg}{dQ} = \frac{g}{Q} \tag{13.1'}$$

$$g\,(Q)\,\gamma\,(w,\,r) = pQ. \tag{13.2'}$$

We see from (13.1') that only *one* critical output is consistent with FIE. Therefore only *one isoquant* and not the entire production function, is relevant. Denoting by Q^* the unique critical output which solves (13.1'), substituting Q^* in (13.2'), and by the homogeneity properties of cost functions, we obtain

$$\frac{g\,(Q^*)}{Q^*}\,\gamma\left(\frac{w}{p},\,\frac{r}{p}\right) = 1. \tag{13.2''}$$

(13.2'') defines a real wage–real rent frontier (in terms of the industrial output). It will be convenient to express w/p and r/p on the frontier as parametric functions of the r/w ratio, z. Shephard's Lemma tells us that $\partial C/\partial w = L$ and $\partial C/\partial r = T$. We have, therefore, by the implicit function theorem and the zero-profit condition

$$\frac{T}{L} = -\frac{dw}{dr}\,(z) \tag{13.3}$$

$$\frac{w}{p}\,(z)\,L + \frac{r}{p}\,(z)\,T = Q^*. \tag{13.4}$$

If the real wage–real rent frontier has no kinks (i.e. the cost function is everywhere twice differentiable) then (13.3) and (13.4) determine T and L as parametric functions of z: in principle we can therefore map each point of the frontier into a corresponding point of the Q^* isoquant.

In practice, of course, one may not know the entire frontier, but only some $(w/p, r/p)$ combinations on the frontier, such as, for instance, $(w^A/p^A, r^A/p^A)$, $(w^B/p^B, r^B/p^B)$. The (L, T) combinations that could have generated these two given pairs of real input prices can be inferred from the inequalities

$$w^A L + r^A T \geq p^A Q^*$$
$$w^B L + r^B T \geq p^B Q^*$$

with at least one strict equation. Geometrically, the estimated isoquant is the outer envelope of the two isocost lines. In relation to Bidard and Salvadori (1995), it is of interest to note that, if the true isoquant is L-shaped (and the frontier is a straight line), then we can determine the (L, T) combination at the corner by simply imposing a strict equation in *both* inequalities This is largely standard duality theory, of course, except for the fact that only one isoquant and not the entire production function is relevant.

The non-homothetic case

But now assume that the cost function is *not* homothetic. For given (w, r, p) satisfying (13.1) and (13.2) we still have a critical long-run output, but a small change in the rent/wage ratio determines an output change (its direction depending on the specific cost function). There can be no input substitution on an isoquant: a change in input proportions implies *ipso facto* also a change in the output level. Specifically, we can derive from (13.1) the long-run output as a function of (w, r), homogeneous of degree zero, which can be reduced to $Q(z)$. We can also extract from (13.2) a real wage–real rent frontier along which the long-run output is variable.

What information on the generating production function can be inferred from real input prices in this case? Let us first notice that the absolute slope of the frontier is still equal to relative input use, as can be seen by differentiating (13.2) while taking (13.1) into account. Hence (13.3) still holds. By contrast, (13.4) becomes

$$\frac{w}{p}(z)L + \frac{r}{p}(z)T = Q(z). \tag{13.4$'$}$$

At a given z, (13.1), (13.2), (13.3) and (13.4$'$) uniquely determine the relevant (L, T, Q) combination (that is, the relevant point of the production function); a change in z determines now a change in all three quantities: geometrically, we have a *curve* on the three-dimensional production function: the rest of the production surface is irrelevant in FIE.

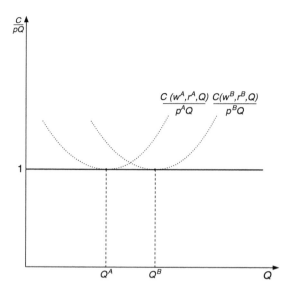

Figure 13.1 Two alternative FIE outputs.

As before, let us also consider the case in which only *some* values of input and output prices and of total cost are known, say $(w^A, r^A, p^A; C^A)$ and $(w^B, r^B, p^B; C^B)$ which are assumed to satisfy (13.1) and (13.2). With no loss of generality let $w^A/p^A > w^B/p^B$, $r^A/p^A < r^B/p^B$ and $Q^A < Q^B$.

By definition, $C^A/p^A = Q^A$ and $C^B/p^B = Q^B$; moreover, we know that

$$C\left(w^A, r^A, Q\right) \geq p^A Q \quad \text{and} \quad C\left(w^B, r^B, Q\right) \geq p^B Q \qquad (13.5)$$

with equality, in turn, (only) when $Q = Q^A$ and when $Q = Q^B$. A geometric representation is given in Figure 13.1 (which reproduces Figure 2.2 of Opocher and Steedman, 2015, p. 29). Now we can associate to each point of equilibrium an isocost defined, respectively, by

$$\left(w^A/p^A\right) L + \left(r^A/p^A\right) T = Q^A \qquad (13.6)$$
$$\left(w^B/p^B\right) L + \left(r^B/p^B\right) T = Q^B. \qquad (13.7)$$

By (13.5), the (L, T) combinations that could have generated prices and total cost 'A' must also satisfy

$$\left(w^B/p^B\right) L + \left(r^B/p^B\right) T > Q^A. \qquad (13.8)$$

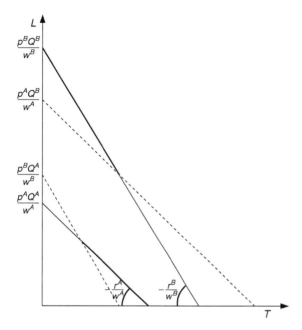

Figure 13.2 The isoquant map implicit in two FIE price vectors.

Conversely, the (L, T) combinations that could have generated prices and total cost 'B' must also satisfy

$$\left(w^A/p^A\right) L + \left(r^A/p^A\right) T > Q^B. \qquad (13.9)$$

The estimated isoquants are drawn as bold lines in Figure 13.2, where the dotted lines represent the *hypothetical* isocost lines defined by (13.8) and (13.9) as equations. The interested reader can easily verify that the two points where the dotted lines cross the solid lines have the same land/labour ratio, equal to $(p^B w^A - p^A w^B)/(p^A r^B - p^B r^A)$.

We may, of course, be more interested in the possible combinations of inputs *per unit of output*, (l, t), than in absolute inputs. Assuming two pairs of real input prices to be known, (13.6) to (13.9) reduce to

$$\left(w^A/p^A\right) l + \left(r^A/p^A\right) t \geq 1$$
$$\left(w^B/p^B\right) l + \left(r^B/p^B\right) t \geq 1$$

with at least one strict equality. It should be stressed, however, that this outer envelope of isocost lines generally does *not* approximate any 'unit isoquant', because a specific output is associated to each pair of real input prices.

Duality theory and produced inputs

Now let us assume that the industry uses as input its own output. This introduces some significant variations in the description of technology which is implicit in the real input prices. In the interest of simplicity it is convenient to assume strictly constant returns thus concentrating on input use per unit of output.

Let us first assume that the rate of interest is identically zero (as before) and let $c\,(w,\ r,\ p)$ be the *unit* cost function. In FIE we have

$$c\,(w,\ r,\ p) = p, \quad \text{or}$$

$$c\left(\frac{w}{p},\ \frac{r}{p},\ 1\right) = 1. \tag{13.10}$$

It is clear from (13.10) that, even though we have three inputs, the FIE 'real input price frontier' is in fact a curve, not a surface. On this curve, drawn as *ab* in Figure 13.3, the relative price of the commodity input is identically equal to one, while the real rent and real wage rates are inversely related and range from zero to their respective maximum values; the vertical projection of the *ab* line on the $w/p - r/p$ plane is the real wage–real rent frontier (drawn as $\omega\rho$). What information on the generating unit isoquant can we infer from knowledge of the *ab* line or, perhaps, of some points on it? Let $(w^A,\ r^A,\ p^A), (w^B,\ r^B,\ p^B), (w^D,\ r^D,\ p^D)$ be three distinct price vectors satisfying (13.10) and let a denote the use of the 'own commodity' per unit of output.

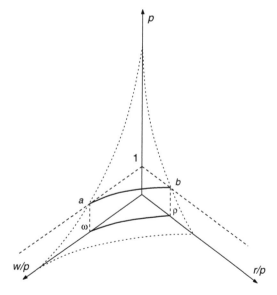

Figure 13.3 The FIE real input price frontier *ab* and the real wage–real rent frontier $\omega\rho$.

By cost minimization and the equality between minimum unit cost and price, the set of (l, t, a) combinations that could have generated those price vectors must satisfy

$$\frac{w^A}{p^A}l + \frac{r^A}{p^A}t + a \geq 1 \tag{13.11}$$

$$\frac{w^B}{p^B}l + \frac{r^B}{p^B}t + a \geq 1 \tag{13.12}$$

$$\frac{w^D}{p^D}l + \frac{r^D}{p^D}t + a \geq 1 \tag{13.13}$$

with at least one strict equality. The unit isoquant that can be derived from knowledge of the three price vectors is therefore the outer envelope of the three isocost planes, drawn with bold lines in Figure 13.4. It is worth noting that by setting $a = 0$ we obtain a two-dimensional broken isoquant on the (l, t) plane which shows the alternative *vertically integrated* labour and land requirements implied by the three price vectors. Needless to say, if we know the entire $\omega\rho$ line, then we obtain a

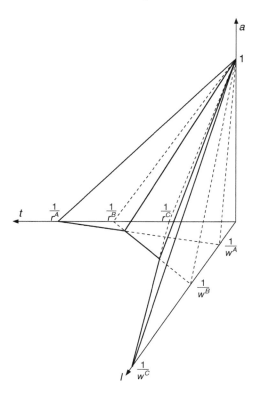

Figure 13.4 The unit isoquant implicit in three price vectors.

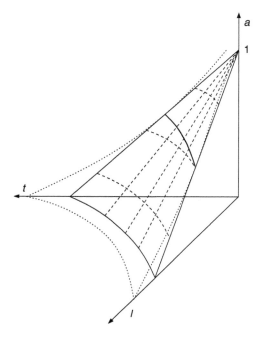

Figure 13.5 The unit isoquant implicit in the FIE frontier and the 'true' isoquant.

smooth curve on the (l, t) plane: joining each point with the $a = 1$ point on the 'a' axis we obtain the whole set of implied *direct* coefficients, as in Figure 13.5.

It should be stressed that the 'implied' unit isoquant is generally different from the 'true' unit isoquant (drawn with dotted lines). What we can say generally is that the 'true' isoquant cannot lie 'below' the 'implied' isoquant. If it is a conventional smooth isoquant (as in Figure 13.5), then the 'true' and the 'implied' isoquants are tangent on a curve: just as the FIE real input price frontier is a curve in three-dimensional space, so the input coefficients which are relevant in FIE, too, form a curve in three-dimensional space. All other input coefficients on the 'true' unit isoquant are completely irrelevant. By contrast, if the 'true' unit isoquant is of the 'Leontief' kind, the ab and $\omega\rho$ lines are in fact *straight lines* and there can be only two linearly independent price vectors: only the two isocost planes with, respectively, $((w/p)^{\text{max}}, (r/p)^{\text{min}})$ and $((w/p)^{\text{min}}, (r/p)^{\text{max}})$ contribute to form the envelope. The common intersection of the various isocost planes, which is found by setting (13.11)–(13.3) as strict equations, does *not* determine the generating technique, but only a relationship between l, t and a. Specifically

$$l = \frac{r^B - r^A}{w^A r^B - w^B r^A} (1 - a) = \frac{r^D - r^B}{w^B r^D - w^D r^B} (1 - a)$$

$$t = \frac{w^A - w^B}{w^A r^B - w^B r^A} (1 - a) = \frac{w^B - w^D}{w^B r^D - w^D r^B} (1 - a).$$

Setting $a = 0$ we obtain the unique *vertically integrated* land and labour coefficients, but the three direct input coefficients *cannot* be inferred from the knowledge of price vectors alone.

This result might seem to be at odds with the Bidard and Salvadori finding that a sufficient number of long-period prices fully determine their generating technique, but in fact it is not. Bidard and Salvadori analysed the dual properties of price systems in an economy characterized by *one* primary input and a positive and variable rate of interest and in that case, there *are* indeed as many linearly independent prices as needed to determine the generating technique.

In order to make our analysis more comparable with that of Bidard and Salvadori, let us now introduce a positive and variable rate of interest (i). Equation (13.10) becomes

$$c\left(\frac{w}{p}, \frac{r}{p}, (1+i)\right) = 1 \tag{13.14}$$

which determines a three-dimensional real wage–real rent–rate of interest frontier defined for $(w/p) \geq 0$, $(r/p) \geq 0$, $(1+i) \geq 1$, as in Figure 13.6. Differently from the previous case, the real rental of the commodity input is now *variable*, ranging from 1 to $(1/\hat{a})$, where $\hat{a}$ is the use of the commodity input per unit of output when $w = 0 = r$. The FIE real wage–real rent–interest rate frontier is a surface of the kind marked by the bold lines in Figure 13.6: more exactly it is *a portion* of a wider surface, the latter being defined for $(1+i) \geq 0$. There is now 'much more' input price variability than in the previous cases and more information can be obtained on the generating unit isoquant. Assuming a Leontief isoquant, the

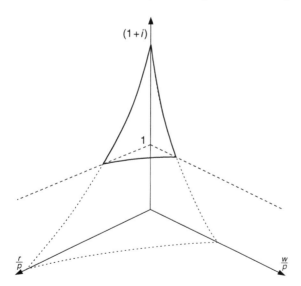

Figure 13.6 The real wage–real rent rate of interest frontier.

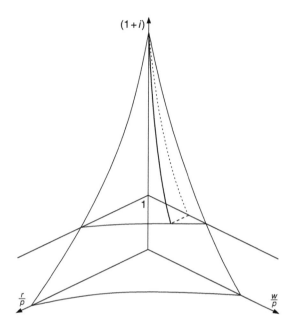

Figure 13.7 The FIE real rate–real rent–interest rate frontier (bold line).

surface in Figure 13.6 becomes a plane and any three linearly independent real input rentals would suffice to determine uniquely the generating technique, as in Bidard and Salvadori. But also in the other polar case of infinitely many techniques (implicit in the figure), the knowledge of the entire FIE frontier would determine 'much' of the 'true' isoquant, as the interested reader can easily see on the basis of standard duality-theory arguments.

A final case can be briefly considered. Let the two primary input prices in (13.10) be the wages of two different kinds of labour and let their ratio, $r/w \equiv z$, be *fixed*. If we interpret the homogeneous-labour assumption of much Sraffian literature in a metaphorical sense, then this case in which different kinds of labour have constant wage ratios becomes important.

Similarly to Figure 13.3, the FIE frontier in Figure 13.7 is again a curve in three-dimensional space. With such a limited variability, the knowledge of long-period real input rentals cannot contain much information on the generating unit isoquant. Assume that there are infinitely many techniques (as in the figure) and that n points of the frontier are known. Once again, we can associate to each point an isocost plane and determine the implied isoquant as their outer envelope, defined by

$$l + zt + \frac{\left(1 + i^J\right) p^J}{w^J} \geq \frac{p^J}{w^J}, \quad J = 1, 2, \ldots, n$$

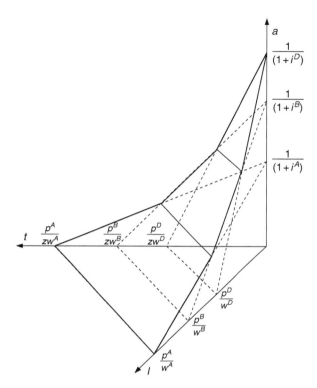

Figure 13.8 The unit isoquant implicit in three price vectors.

with at least one strict equation. Figure 13.8 provides an illustration for the case with $n = 3$. If just one technique is known, the FIE frontier will be a *straight* line in three-dimensional space because r/w is fixed: any three real input rentals are in fact linearly *dependent* and knowledge of them *cannot* possibly determine the generating technique.

Concluding remarks

Twenty years ago Bidard and Salvadori reached an important duality result on a system of production characterized by n industries, one (constant returns) technique, homogeneous labour and a variable rate of interest on circulating capital. Yet some more can still be said on the duality properties of long-period real input prices, even in the much simpler case with only one industry.

First, firms earning maximum profits of zero can be characterized not by strict constant returns to scale, but by local constant returns, at the bottom of u-shaped average cost curves. Even if all inputs are 'primary' and the generating technology is perfectly smooth, the sole assumption of zero net profits introduces some significant differences with respect to standard duality theory: only a lower dimensional region of the 'true' production function can ever be active, however variable primary input prices can be.

A produced input introduces further unconventional aspects even under strictly constant returns. With two primary inputs, a zero rate of interest and a three-dimensional smooth unit isoquant, only a *curve* on the generating isoquant can ever be active and the knowledge of all real primary input prices consistent with zero net profits can only approximate it. Not even a Leontief isoquant can be inferred from any number of real primary input prices (in contrast to the Bidard–Salvadori case). A positive and variable rate of interest gives *more* information on the generating technology and, in the case of a Leontief unit isoquant, we can indeed infer the generating technique from knowledge of a sufficient number of different real primary input price–rate of interest combinations.

Note

1 This chapter is part of wider joint work with Ian Steedman. It has not developed into a joint chapter to stress my personal affection to Neri.

References

Bidard, C. and Salvadori, N. (1995), 'Duality Between Prices and Techniques', *European Journal of Political Economy*, **11**: 379–389.

Opocher A. (2002), 'Duality Theory and Long-Period Price Systems', *Metroeconomica*, **53**(4): 416–433.

Opocher A. and Steedman I. (2015), *Full Industry Equilibrium. A Theory of the Industrial Long Run*, Cambridge: Cambridge University Press.

Salvadori, N. and Steedman, I. (1985), 'Cost Functions and Produced Means of Production: Duality and Capital Theory', *Contributions to Political Economy*, **4**: 79–90.

Shephard R.W. (1970), *Theory of Cost and Production Functions*, Princeton, NJ: Princeton University Press.

Silberberg E. (1974), 'The Theory of the Firm in Long-Run Equilibrium', *American Economic Review*, **64**(4): 734–741.

Steedman I. (1998), 'Produced Input Use per Unit of Output', *Economics Letters*, **59**: 85–95.

14 The 'capital–labour isoquant' in the consumer good industry[1]

Ian Steedman

It is a great pleasure to offer this essay in honour of Neri Salvadori, once my brilliant student and then a friend, colleague and sometime co-author and co-editor. Needless to say, he has made enormous contributions to the literature on capital theory and this paper seeks to take up certain familiar themes in the capital theory literature but to push them in a relatively unusual direction. More specifically, the focus of most of the capital theory discussions was on the economy as a whole, asking whether the aggregate capital–labour ratio fell as the interest rate increased, whether that rate was equal to 'dy/dk', whether upward sloping 'input demand curves' would cause problems for uniqueness and/or stability, etc. Yet it was always implicit in those discussions that certain familiar economic relationships did or did not hold good at the level of specific industries. Here we shall focus on the 'capital–labour isoquant' in the consumer good industry that is implied by various models of production of the Hicks–Samuelson–Spaventa 'corn-tractor(s)' kind. (Appendix 14.A, however, considers the same question in the context of two other models of production.) We begin by considering a famous example from the capital theory literature and then move on to present some new examples, in which we emphasize the irrelevance, for our present concern, of reswitching.

A famous example

Of all the many examples presented during the discussions on capital theory, one of the most celebrated is certainly that given in the Appendix to Garegnani (1970). While he was concerned with various properties of the economy as a whole, the data provided in his Tables 1 and 2 make it easy to derive both the labour per unit of output and the capital per unit of output in the consumer good industry, at various rates of interest. The 'capital–labour isoquant' can then be plotted; see Figure 14.1, in which the arrows show the direction of movement as the rate of interest rises. As that rate, r, increases from zero, the capital–output ratio, K, first decreases, while the labour–output ratio, β, increases and, indeed, the K/β isoquant looks quite conventional for small enough r. With further increases in r, however, the K/β relationship becomes thoroughly unconventional and almost forms a perfect loop; it does not quite do so because, while β takes exactly the same value at both the minimum and the maximum values of r, K is slightly lower at the latter than at the former value.

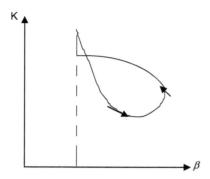

Figure 14.1 The 'capital–labour isoquant' in which the arrows show the direction of movement as the rate of interest rises.

That β, in this example, is exactly the same when the interest rate is zero and when the wage rate is zero, reflects the fact that Garegnani's example is replete with reswitching techniques. It is also an example defined by rather complex functions – so much so that Kurz and Salvadori (1999) devoted an entire 12-page paper to simplifying it! It would be quite wrong, however, to deduce that an unconventional K/β relationship in the consumer good industry presupposes either reswitching or complexity of the underlying technical possibilities. In what follows, we shall use only very simple functional relationships and will completely exclude the reswitching of techniques.

Three simple cases

Consider the familiar 'corn-tractor(s)' model of production in which, for a given technique, a specific kind of machine can be used by labour to produce either machines of the same kind or the consumer good. Machines are fully used up in one period of production and there are constant returns to scale. In the Hicksian notation, the production of one machine requires inputs of 'a' machines and 'b' units of labour, while that of one unit of the consumer good requires 'α' machines 'β' units of labour. As is well known, the variables α and b only appear in the form of the product αb, so we simplify our notation by defining $\gamma \equiv \alpha b$. (Note that, dimensionally, γ is, like β, an amount of labour per unit of consumer good.) The wage rate in terms of the consumer good, w, is given by

$$\frac{1}{w} = \beta + \frac{(1+r)\gamma}{1 - (1+r)a}$$

and thus the first order condition for the maximization of w, given r, is

$$d\beta + \left[\frac{(1+r)}{1 - (1+r)a} \right] d\gamma + \left[\frac{(1+r)}{1 - (1+r)a} \right]^2 \gamma \, da = 0.$$

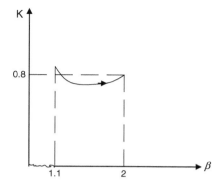

Figure 14.2 The qualitative nature of the K/β relation.

The three simple cases of this section are obtained by taking, first, '*a*' to be constant, then β to be constant and, finally, γ to be constant.

Constant a

In this case, $(d\gamma/d\beta) < 0 < (d^2\gamma/d\beta^2)$ must be assumed and, as r increases, β will always rise and γ fall. (Thus there is no reswitching.) If the constant value of a is a_0 $(0 < a_0 < 1)$ then the capital–output ratio in the consumer good industry is

$$K = \frac{\gamma}{\beta + (\gamma - a_0\beta)(1+r)}.$$

When the wage is zero, and $a_0(1+r) = 1$, we naturally have $K = a_0$. But $K = a_0$ *also* holds if $\gamma = a_0\beta$. So if – as r rises, γ falls and β rises – it happens that $\gamma = a_0\beta$ for some value of r then we know at once that, while $\beta(r)$ is monotonic, $K(r)$ is not. Hence the K/β relationship is *non-monotonic*.

A numerical example of this possibility is provided by $a_0 = 0.8$ and

$$9\gamma = 13 - 4\beta + \beta^2.$$

As r increases from 0 to 25 per cent, β rises from 1.1 to 2.0 and γ falls from 1.01 to 1.00. Hence (γ/β) falls from above 0.99 down to 0.50, being equal to $a_0 = 0.8$ when r is just above 5 per cent and β is just above 1.315. The qualitative nature of the K/β relation is as shown in Figure 14.2. The $\gamma(\beta)$ function defining the technical possibilities is very simple and there is no reswitching – but the 'capital–labour isoquant' in the consumer good sector is far from conventional in nature.

Constant β

With β constant, at $\beta = \beta_0$ say, there is no possibility of a conventional K/β relationship, of course; the only question is how K varies with r. (Certainly '*a*' always falls and γ rises, as r increases.) If, for example, $\beta_0 = 10$ and $\gamma = 2a^{-1}$ then

$$K = \frac{4(1+r)}{(9+8r+4r^2)}.$$

As r increases from zero to 11.8 per cent, K increases slightly (from $4/9$ to $1/\sqrt{5}$) and thereafter decreases towards zero as r increases without limit. Thus the 'iso-quant' is a segment of the vertical line above $\beta = \beta_0$, with K first rising with r and then falling to zero. Again, there are infinitely many techniques, the definition of the alternatives – $a\gamma = 2$ – is very simple and there is no reswitching.

Constant γ

The first order condition can now be written as, say,

$$d\beta + \gamma_0 \left[\frac{(1+r)}{1-(1+r)a} \right]^2 da = 0$$

and we must have $(d\beta/da) < 0 < (d^2\beta/da^2)$. As r rises from zero, 'a' always falls and β rises.

Suppose now that

$$\beta = \beta_0 - 2\lambda^2 \sqrt{a - a_0}.$$

The value of 'a' is given by

$$\lfloor \lambda a + \sqrt{\gamma_0}(a - a_0)^{1/4} \rfloor (1 + r) = \lambda$$

and it can then be calculated that $K = a_0$ not only when $a_0(1 + r) = 1$ but also when

$$\sqrt{\gamma_0}\,\lambda(a - a_0)^{3/4} + 2\lambda^2 a_0(a - a_0)^{1/2} = (a_0\beta_0 - \gamma_0). \tag{14.1}$$

It can be shown that there are numerical values of $(a_0, \beta_0/\gamma_0, \lambda^2/\gamma_0)$ such that the solution of (14.1) is both greater than a_0 and less than the value of 'a' at $r = 0$. Hence the K/β 'isoquant' is non-monotonic in the presence of a simple, continuous $\beta(a)$ relation and the absence of reswitching.

Since unconventional K/β isoquants can arise even when any one of (a, β, γ) is constant, they can of course also arise when more general $[\beta(a), \gamma(a)]$ relationships are supposed. Rather than elaborate this point, however, we now turn to consider a particular restriction on these relationships.

Restricted $\beta(a)$ and $\gamma(a)$ relations

In the above-mentioned example due to Garegnani, every one of the infinitely many techniques has the special property that the maximum wage it can generate (at $r = 0$) is exactly equal to the maximum rate of interest it can generate (at $w = 0$). This means that, in our notation,

$$\gamma = a - \beta + a\beta$$

for *every* technique and hence that the $\beta(a)$ and $\gamma(a)$ functions could not be chosen independently. Here, too, we shall stipulate that the wage–interest rate frontiers for the different techniques all have a common property. In our case, however, that common property is that *every* individual technique $w(r)$ frontier passes through a common point $(\bar{r}, \bar{w})$, where $-1 < \bar{r} < 0$. More specifically, in order to save on notation, we shall stipulate that every $w(r)$ frontier passes through the point $(-\frac{1}{2}, 2)$. (The reader is of course welcome to generalize the argument.) It follows at once that there will be no reswitching as r increases from zero and that, as it does so, *both* 'a' and β will decrease. (An inverse relation between β and r is, of course, an unconventional one.) Consequently, γ will increase as r rises.

As already noted, $\beta(a)$ and $\gamma(a)$ are here not independent functions and every $w(r)$ frontier passes through $(-\frac{1}{2}, 2)$ if and only if

$$2\gamma(a) = (2 - a)[1 - 2\beta(a)]. \tag{14.2}$$

(Clearly, $2\beta < 1$ is always required.)

When our three coefficients are restricted by (14.2), the first-order condition for the maximization of w, given r, is

$$[1 - (1 + r)a]\,d\beta = (1 + r)(\frac{1}{2} - \beta)da$$

and the second-order condition is $\left(d^2\beta/da^2\right) < 0$. Suppose then that $\beta = 0.1 + \frac{4}{3}\sqrt{2/5}\sqrt{a - 0.8}$.

It follows that

$$20a = 41 - 20(1 + r)^{-1} - \sqrt{369 - 360(1 + r)^{-1}}.$$

As r rises from zero to its maximum value of 25 per cent, 'a' falls from 0.9 to 0.8, 30β falls from 11 to 3 and 30γ rises from 4.4 to 14.4. It follows that $K = 0.8$ not only when $r = 25\%$ but also when $r = 0$, so that the K/β isoquant is non-monotonic. (When $9r = 1$, K is a little over 0.858 and 30β a little greater than 6.) Once again, then, simple $\beta(a)$ and $\gamma(a)$ functions, giving rise to no reswitching, are found to generate an entirely unconventional 'capital–labour isoquant' in the consumer good industry.

(While the restriction that the various techniques must all generate $w(r)$ curves passing through a common $(\bar{r}, \bar{w})$ point has here been used only for the particular purpose of examining K/β relationships, the reader might perhaps find other uses for this kind of argument. An analogous remark may also be made concerning the argument of the following section.)

A straight line $w(r)$ frontier

Let t be a continuous variable $(1 \leq t \leq 1.25)$ defining infinitely many (a, β, γ) techniques by

$$25a = 20 + (5 - 4t)^2$$
$$25\beta = 5 + 4t^2$$
$$25\gamma = 4(1 - t + 4/5t^2)^2.$$

Note that as t increases, 'a' falls but β and γ both rise. Note too that $5(a\beta - \gamma) = 1$ for *all* values of t.

On choosing t to maximize w for given r, one finds that $t = (1 + r)$ satisfies both the first- and second-order conditions. It then follows that the economy's $w(r)$ frontier is

$$w = 1 - 4r,$$

a straight line! There are infinitely many techniques, each with a $w(r)$ frontier that is convex from below, and the outer envelope of these individual frontiers is a straight line.

(It follows, of course, that if k is the capital–labour ratio for the whole (stationary) economy then $(k + \frac{dw}{dr}) < 0$ always holds $(r > 0)$. If y is the output–labour ratio for the (stationary) economy then the capital–output ratio (k/y) is equal to 4 at both $r = 0$ and $r = 25\%$ and is less than 4 for all intermediate values. There is thus capital-reversing (with no reswitching). It can be shown that

$$\left(\frac{dy}{dk}\right) = \left(\frac{2r}{1-r}\right).$$

Not only is this greater than r $(r > 0)$, it is much greater for large r; when $r = 1/4$, $(\frac{dy}{dk}) = \frac{2}{3}$, for example.)

Returning now to our main concern, the consumer good industry, it can be shown that

$$K = 4\beta - 2\sqrt{\beta - 0.2}$$

for $36 \leq 100\beta \leq 45$. As r increases from zero to 25 per cent, 100β rises from 36 to 45 and $25K$ *increases* from 16 to 20. Thus our K/β relationship is monotonically increasing (with $d^2K/d\beta^2 > 0$ in fact). Even for small values of r, there is no chance that the K/β isoquant could be misinterpreted as being of the conventional form.

Concluding remarks

The above discussion should suffice to show that simple models of production involving infinitely many alternative techniques and no reswitching can give rise to 'capital–labour isoquants' in the consumer good sector that are utterly unlike those so often presented in the textbooks (and, indeed, even in more advanced literature). There really is no excuse for blithely assuming that $(dK/d\beta) < 0 < (d^2K/d\beta^2)$! Our discussion might also encourage those working in the Sraffian tradition to devote more attention to *individual industries* and to the economic relationships that characterize them.

Appendix 14.A

Here, we first show how the 'capital–labour isoquant' in the consumer good industry can be examined in the three-period Wicksellian model, *subject to the restriction* that every individual $w(r)$ frontier passes through $(r, w) = (-\frac{1}{2}, 2)$. In a familiar notation, the $w(r)$ frontier is given by

$$w[l_0 + (1+r)l_1 + (1+r)^2 l_2] = 1$$

and it satisfies our restriction if and only if

$$2l_0 + l_1 + \left(\frac{1}{2}\right)l_2 = 1.$$

The maximization of w, given r, requires that

$$2\left(\frac{dl_0}{dl_2}\right) = (1+r) \quad \text{and} \quad \left(\frac{d^2l_0}{dl_2^2}\right) < 0.$$

Hence, as r rises, l_0 and l_2 both fall and l_1 increases. Now consider the case $3l_0 = \sqrt{l_2}$, for which

$$3l_0(1+r) = 1 = 3l_2(1+r)^2$$
$$6l_1(1+r)^2 = 1 + 8r + 6r^2.$$

Denote the capital–output ratio in the consumer good industry by k_0; it is readily calculated that

$$k_0 = \frac{(3+10r+6r^2)}{(1+r)(5+10r+6r^2)}.$$

At $r = 0$, $k_0 = (3/5)$. But it also takes this value when

$$6r = -3 + \sqrt{19} \quad \text{or} \quad r \approx 22.65\%,$$

and thus $(3 + \sqrt{19})l_0 = 2$.

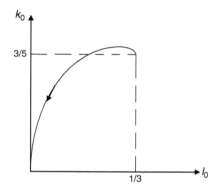

Figure 14.A.1 The k_0/l_0 relation.

The k_0/l_0 relation is as shown in Figure 14.A.1, where the arrow indicates the direction of movement as r rises. Even the simplest of production models, with no reswitching, can generate an utterly unconventional 'capital–labour isoquant' in the consumer good industry.

Any Wicksellian model of production suffers from the defect that the productive process begins with the use of unassisted labour. To remedy this, suppose now that l_1 units of labour work with 'a' units of the consumer good to produce one unit of some intermediate good, which is then worked on by l_0 units of labour to produce one unit of the consumer good. (Note that this Nuti model of production is a simple 2×2 input–output system with an imprimitive matrix.) The corresponding wage/interest rate frontier is

$$w = \frac{1 - a(1+r)^2}{l_0 + l_1(1+r)}.$$

If the available alternatives are defined by 'a' $= l_0$ and $l_0 l_1 = 1$, w is maximized, for given r, when

$$l_0^2 + 2(1+r)^3 l_0 - (1+r) = 0$$

or

$$l_0 = -(1+r)^3 + \sqrt{(1+r)^6 + (1+r)}$$

(l_0 is zero when $(1+r) = 0$ and tends to zero as r increases without limit; it reaches its maximum value when $24(1+r)^5 = 1$ and is thus decreasing in r for all relevant r).

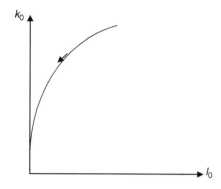

Figure 14.A.2 The k_0/l_0 isoquant is always *upward*-sloping.

The economy-level wage/interest rate frontier is given by $2(1+r)w = l_0$ and it follows that

$$k_0 = \frac{1 - 2(1+r)^5 + 2(1+r)^2\sqrt{(1+r)^6 + (1+r)}}{2(1+r)}.$$

Like l_0, k_0 always falls, as r rises, and tends to zero as r increases without limit. Hence the k_0/l_0 isoquant is always *upward*-sloping. See Figure 14.A.2.

Yet again, a very simple model, involving no reswitching, can generate an entirely unconventional 'capital–labour isoquant' in the consumer good industry.

Note

1 I thank Uli Krause (Bremen) for encouraging discussion about the derivation of the straight-line $w(r)$ frontier and Christian Bidard (Paris), Heinz Kurz (Graz), Arrigo Opocher (Padua) and Sergio Parrinello (Rome) for more general encouragement.

References

Garegnani, P. (1970) Heterogeneous capital, the production function and the theory of distribution. *Review of Economic Studies* 37, 407–36.

Kurz, H.D. and Salvadori, N. (1999) Reswitching: simplifying a famous example. In: Fase, M.M.G., Kanning, W. and Walker, D.A. (eds), *Economics, Welfare Policy and the History of Economic Thought*, Cheltenham, Edward Elgar, pp. 169–80.

15 Distribution and capital

Takashi Yagi[1]

Introduction

A surplus – shares other than wages – is defined as a social product minus necessary consumption (Garegnani, 1987, p. 561). We extend this view to examine distribution in a system with fixed capital and depreciation and introduce a new surplus approach in the theory of distribution and capital. If we consider a system without scarcity of land, the profits are equivalent to a surplus. Ricardo considered the wage for labourers as capital, and the rate of profit is defined as the ratio of profit to wage as capital. Marx defined the rate of profit as the ratio of the surplus value to the sum of variable and constant capital. Böhm-Bawerk treated capital through his theory of the average period of production, where the rate of profit is the ratio of profit to wage as capital. When fixed capital enters the distribution discussion, we face difficulties in constructing a consistent theory to define the rate of profit and measure the aggregate value of capital. Garegnani (1960) included both the Marxian theory of value and distribution and the theory of the average period of production of Böhm-Bawerk as theories of the Ricardian tradition. Garegnani (1960) suggested that the Ricardian theory might provide a consistent explanation for the problem of measuring the value of capital. In this study, we denote the rate of profit to the wage as r_w and call it the surplus rate to distinguish it from the rate of profit for capital, which has an ordinary meaning. The rate of profit for capital of ordinary meaning is expressed as r_K. Sraffa (1960) introduced the standard system, which is a useful framework for the analysis of distribution. In the Sraffa system, if the share of wages in standard income is denoted as ω_v, the share of profits in standard income becomes equal to $r_w\omega_v$ and then we have $\omega_v + r_w\omega_v = 1$. This property is very interesting because using the standard system and the notion of the surplus rate allows an examination of the distribution in one number line as a one-dimension theory of distribution. We apply this property of the Sraffa system to an actual system with fixed capital and depreciation to analyse the shares in distribution and the measurement of the aggregate value of capital.

In our model, the exogenous variables are the matrices of the output and the produced means of production (circulating capital); the vector of the labour input; the vectors of depreciation, fixed capital and commodity prices, which are measured in terms of money; and the scalars of the money wage rate and total profit.

The important unknowns of our model are the surplus rate r_w, the wage share, the real wage and the rate of profit r_K. Furthermore, it is important to examine the notion of capital that corresponds to the surplus rate and the real value of capital that corresponds to the rate of profit.

The next section explains the properties of the Sraffa system. The third section explains our model to measure real values, which combines Sraffa's standard system and the system with fixed capital and depreciation. We then explain the surplus rate and the shares in distribution, define the real wage and provide our formulation of the average period of production. Finally, we examine the relationship between the rate of profit r_K and the real value of capital of ordinary meaning.

The Sraffa system

This section explains a simple system of *Part I* of Sraffa (1960) (Kurz and Salvadori, 1995, Garegnani, 1987, Pasinetti, 1977, Schefold, 1989, Yagi, 2007, 2012). The number of commodities is n. Two quantity systems exist in the Sraffa system: the actual system and the standard system. We denote the actual output vector as **x**, the actual net product vector as **y** and the vector of the actual produced means of production (circulating capital) as $\mathbf{z}_Y$. These vectors are assumed to be positive. The relationship between these vectors becomes $\mathbf{x} = \mathbf{y} + \mathbf{z}_Y$. On the other hand, we denote the output vector of the standard system as **q**, the standard net product as **s** and the vector of the produced means of production of the standard system as $\mathbf{z}_S$. Then, we have $\mathbf{q} = \mathbf{s} + \mathbf{z}_S$. The labour input coefficient vector is expressed as $\mathbf{l}_A$. The total labour of the standard system is expressed as

$$L_S = \mathbf{q}\mathbf{l}_A. \tag{15.1}$$

We refer to L_S as standard labour. The output vector **q** should be normalised by the actual labour amount to connect the standard system to the actual system.

The vectors of the standard system are defined by using the eigenvector and the maximum eigenvalue of the transposed input coefficient matrix. We denote the transposed input coefficient matrix as **A** and its maximum eigenvalue as λ. We assume that **A** is a semi-positive and an indecomposable matrix. The vector **q** becomes positive. The maximum physical surplus rate is given as

$$R = 1/\lambda - 1. \tag{15.2}$$

The standard system of Sraffa (1960) is given as

$$\mathbf{q} = (1 + R)\mathbf{q}\mathbf{A} \tag{15.3}$$

$$\mathbf{s} = R\mathbf{q}\mathbf{A} = \mathbf{q}[\mathbf{I} - \mathbf{A}] \tag{15.4}$$

$$\mathbf{z}_S = \mathbf{q}\mathbf{A}. \tag{15.5}$$

Next, we turn to the price system. The rate of profit is assumed to be uniform throughout the economic system. The wage is paid at the end of the production period and is assumed to be uniform throughout the economic system. We denote the column vector of the commodity prices as $\mathbf{p}_A$, the rate of profit as r_K and the uniform post factum wage rate as w_A. The maximum rate of profit is expressed as R, which is equal to the maximum physical surplus rate. The rate of profit takes real numbers ranging from 0 to the maximum rate of profit R ($0 \leq r_K < R$). We introduce a notion of the value of labour and denote it as v_L. Then the total value of standard labour becomes equal to $v_L \mathbf{ql}_A$, which is larger than $w_A \mathbf{ql}_A$ when the rate of profit is positive, and is equal to $w_A \mathbf{ql}_A$ when the rate of profit is equal to zero. Then, for all r_K ($0 \leq r_K < R$), we have the following production equation of the standard net product and the price system (Yagi, 2012, pp. 253–255)

$$\mathbf{sp}_A = v_L \mathbf{ql}_A \tag{15.6}$$

$$\mathbf{p}_A = (1 + r_K)\mathbf{Ap}_A + w_A \mathbf{l}_A. \tag{15.7}$$

Equation (15.6) represents the virtual production equation of the standard net product, which is produced by means of unassisted standard labour. In the system of (15.6), (15.7), $(n + 1)$ independent equations and $(n + 3)$ unknowns ($\mathbf{p}_A$, v_L, w_A, r_K) exist. If the rate of profit or the wage rate is exogenously given, the price system becomes determinate. In the system of (15.6), (15.7), we have the following equivalent conditions[2]

$$v_L = 1 \tag{15.8}$$

$$\Leftrightarrow r_K = R(1 - w_A). \tag{15.9}$$

Under the condition of $v_L = 1$, the price vector $\mathbf{p}_v$, which is measured in terms of quantities of labour, is expressed as

$$\mathbf{p}_v = \mathbf{p}_A/v_L = (1 - r_K/R)[\mathbf{I} - (1 + r_K)\mathbf{A}]^{-1}\mathbf{l}_A. \tag{15.10}$$

This equation represents one interpretation of the reduction equation of Sraffa (1960) (Yagi, 2007). The prices in this equation are subject to the changes in the rate of profit and in the technological condition of production. Under the condition of $v_L = 1$, the standard income measured in terms of labour becomes equal to the standard labour. Therefore, we obtain

$$\mathbf{sp}_v/\mathbf{ql}_A = 1. \tag{15.11}$$

This equation indicates that the value of one unit of the standard net product produced with one unit of unassisted standard labour becomes equal to unity. The ratio between the produced means of production and the standard income becomes equal to the inverse of the maximum rate of profit and is represented as

$$\mathbf{z}_s\mathbf{p}_v/\mathbf{sp}_v = 1/R. \tag{15.12}$$

The profit share π_v of the standard system is given as

$$\pi_v = \frac{r_K \mathbf{Z}_S \mathbf{p}_v}{\mathbf{sp}_v} = \frac{r_K}{R}. \tag{15.13}$$

Because we have $w_A \mathbf{ql}_A / v_L \mathbf{sp}_v = w_A \mathbf{ql}_A / v_L \mathbf{ql}_A$ from (15.6), the wage share of the standard system is expressed as

$$\omega_v = w_A / v_L. \tag{15.14}$$

This value is equal to the wage rate under the condition of $v_L = 1$. The ratio of the profit share to the wage share can be represented as

$$r_w = \frac{1 - \omega_v}{\omega_v}. \tag{15.15}$$

In this equation, r_w indicates profit to wage as capital, and it is called the surplus rate. Because profit share is given as r_K / R, the surplus rate is expressed as

$$r_w = \frac{r_K \mathbf{Z}_S \mathbf{p}_v}{\omega_v \mathbf{ql}_A} = \frac{r_K}{\omega_v R}. \tag{15.16}$$

From (15.13) and (15.16), we obtain $r_w \omega_v = \pi_v$ and then, under the condition of $v_L = 1$, from (15.15), we have

$$1 = \omega_v + \pi_v = \omega_v + r_w \omega_v. \tag{15.17}$$

Using the notion of the surplus rate and the properties of the standard system, we obtained the one-dimension theory of distribution.

A new surplus approach

A system to evaluate real values

We proceed to the system with fixed capital and depreciation. We assume that no scarcity of land, no joint production, no exports and no imports exist. The number of commodities is n. We denote the diagonal matrix of the output as $\mathbf{X}$, the matrix of the produced means of production as $\mathbf{Z}$, the column vector of the labour amount as $\mathbf{L}_A$ and the column vector of depreciation measured in terms of money as $\mathbf{D}_M$. The column vector of the nominal values of fixed capital at the end of the previous production period is expressed as $\mathbf{K}_M$, which is assumed to be exogenously given. The uniform rate of money wage is expressed as w_M. The vector of money prices of commodities of the system with fixed capital and depreciation is expressed as $\mathbf{p}_M$. The total profit measured in terms of money is expressed as Π. We assume that the $\mathbf{X}$ and $\mathbf{Z}$ matrices are semi-positive, the vectors of $\mathbf{L}_A$, $\mathbf{D}_M$, $\mathbf{K}_M$ and $\mathbf{p}_M$ are positive and the scalars of w_M and Π are positive. The net product will be used as both consumer goods and investment goods. Therefore, no special production process exists for fixed capital, and durable goods are treated in the same manner as in the case of input–output tables. A set of exogenously given data is [$\mathbf{X}$, $\mathbf{Z}$, $\mathbf{L}_A$, $\mathbf{D}_M$, $\mathbf{K}_M$, $\mathbf{p}_M$, w_M, Π]. The rate of profit is expressed as r_K, which is assumed to be uniform throughout the economic system. Then, we have the following system:

$$\mathbf{X}\mathbf{p}_M = (1+r_K)\mathbf{Z}\mathbf{p}_M + w_M\mathbf{L}_A + r_K\mathbf{K}_M + \mathbf{D}_M. \tag{15.18}$$

The only variable of this equation is the rate of profit. If we divide $\mathbf{K}_M$ and $\mathbf{D}_M$ by the money wage rate w_M, we obtain the following vectors:

$$\mathbf{K}_w = \mathbf{K}_M/w_M, \quad \mathbf{D}_w = \mathbf{D}_M/w_M. \tag{15.19}$$

The components of these vectors are measured in terms of wage unit or labour commanded. We multiply the matrix $\mathbf{Z}$ and the vectors $\mathbf{L}_A$, $\mathbf{K}_w$ and $\mathbf{D}_w$ by the inverse matrix of $\mathbf{X}$ from the left-hand side. Then, we define the following coefficient matrix and the coefficient vectors:

$$\mathbf{A} = \mathbf{X}^{-1}\mathbf{Z}, \quad \mathbf{l}_A = \mathbf{X}^{-1}\mathbf{L}_A, \quad \mathbf{k}_w = \mathbf{X}^{-1}\mathbf{K}_w, \quad \mathbf{d}_w = \mathbf{X}^{-1}\mathbf{D}_w \tag{15.20}$$

For simplicity, the matrix $\mathbf{A}$ is assumed to be an indecomposable and a semi-positive matrix. If we denote the output vector as $\mathbf{x}$, the total labour becomes equal to

$$L_A = \mathbf{x}\mathbf{l}_A. \tag{15.21}$$

With the notation of (15.20), the price system (15.18) can be rewritten as

$$\mathbf{p}_M = (1+r_K)\mathbf{A}\mathbf{p}_M + w_M\mathbf{l}_A + r_K w_M\mathbf{k}_w + w_M\mathbf{d}_w. \tag{15.22}$$

We divide this price vector into two parts. The first and second terms of the right member, i.e. $\{(1+r_K)\mathbf{A}\mathbf{p}_M + w_M\mathbf{l}_A\}$, have the same formulation as that of the simple Sraffa system. The remainder of the right member corresponds to the gross profit for fixed capital. Combining the Sraffa system with these price equations, we analyse the distribution of the system with fixed capital and depreciation.

Now we consider how to normalise the output vector of the standard system to connect the standard system with the previously described actual system. The depreciation term ($w_M\mathbf{x}\mathbf{d}_w$) must be paid from the annual output at the end of the production period. We consider the following ratio to connect the standard labour of (15.1) with the labour amount of the actual system:

$$\varphi = \frac{w_M\mathbf{x}\mathbf{l}_A + \Pi}{w_M\mathbf{x}\mathbf{l}_A + w_M\mathbf{x}\mathbf{d}_w + \Pi}. \tag{15.23}$$

The numerator of the right member is the total amount of direct wage and profit. The denominator of the right member is the total amount of direct wage, depreciation and profit. Using the ratio of (15.23), the actual total labour is divided into two parts as

$$\mathbf{xl}_A = \varphi\mathbf{xl}_A + (1 - \varphi)\mathbf{xl}_A. \tag{15.24}$$

The term $(1 - \varphi)\mathbf{xl}_A$ corresponds to the labour amount for depreciation.[3] The term $\varphi\mathbf{xl}_A$ corresponds to the standard labour needed to produce the standard net product. We normalise the standard labour by $\varphi\mathbf{xl}_A$ as

$$L_S = \mathbf{ql}_A = \varphi\mathbf{xl}_A. \tag{15.25}$$

Equation (15.25) represents the definition of standard labour. Using this assumption, the standard system of Sraffa can be combined with the actual system. For simplicity, let us denote the ratio of $\mathbf{qd}_w$ to $\mathbf{ql}_A$ as

$$\delta = \mathbf{qd}_w/\mathbf{ql}_A. \tag{15.26}$$

Then, from (15.22), we obtain[4]

$$\left(1 - \frac{r_K}{R}\right)\mathbf{sp}_M = w_M\mathbf{ql}_A(1 + \delta)\left\{1 + \frac{r_K\mathbf{qk}_w}{\mathbf{ql}_A(1 + \delta)}\right\}. \tag{15.27}$$

Equation (15.27) determines the rate of profit r_K. However, we consider the larger equation system of (15.6), (15.7), (15.8), (15.14), (15.15) and (15.27) to determine the real values. This enlarged system has $(n + 5)$ equations and $(n + 5)$ unknowns $(\mathbf{p}_A, v_L, w_A, \omega_v, r_w, r_K)$. Equation (15.27) makes the Sraffa system of the second section determinate.

The surplus rate and distribution

We use the system of (15.6), (15.7), (15.8), (15.14), (15.15) and (15.27) to explain the surplus rate r_w and the shares in distribution.

The general price level measured in terms of money is given as

$$P_M = \frac{\mathbf{sp}_M}{\mathbf{sp}_v} = \frac{\mathbf{sp}_M}{\mathbf{ql}_A} \cdot \frac{\mathbf{ql}_A}{\mathbf{sp}_v} = \frac{\mathbf{sp}_M}{\mathbf{ql}_A}. \tag{15.28}$$

This equation indicates that the definition of the general price level is given as the ratio between the nominal value and the real value of the standard income, or as the ratio between the nominal value of the standard income and the standard labour. The general price level of (15.28) is obtained from the exogenously given data. The actual wage share ω_A is defined as

$$\omega_A = \frac{w_M\mathbf{ql}_A(1 + \delta)}{\mathbf{sp}_M} = \frac{w_M(1 + \delta)}{P_M}. \tag{15.29}$$

The actual wage share of (15.29) is also obtained from the exogenously given data. From (15.16) and (15.29) and $\omega_v = 1 - r_K/R$, equation (15.27) is rewritten as

$$\omega_v = \omega_A \left\{ 1 + r_w \times \frac{\omega_v}{\omega_A} \times \frac{\omega_A \mathbf{Rqk}_w}{\mathbf{ql}_A(1+\delta)} \right\}. \tag{15.30}$$

Let us use the following notation:

$$\kappa_Z = \frac{\mathbf{Rqk}_w}{\mathbf{ql}_A(1+\delta)} = \frac{\mathbf{qk}_w}{\mathbf{z}_s \mathbf{p}_v(1+\delta)}. \tag{15.31}$$

Then, from (15.30), we obtain

$$\frac{\omega_v}{\omega_A} = \frac{1}{1 - r_w \omega_A \kappa_Z}. \tag{15.32}$$

Therefore, from (15.15) and (15.32), the surplus rate becomes

$$r_w = \frac{1 - \omega_A}{\omega_A + \omega_A \kappa_Z}. \tag{15.33}$$

We can use equation (15.33) in place of (15.27) to close the enlarged equation system of (15.6), (15.7), (15.8), (15.14) and (15.15). Moreover, under the condition of $v_L = 1$, we have

$$1 = \omega_A + r_w \omega_A + r_w \omega_A \kappa_Z. \tag{15.34}$$

This equation indicates that the total of the wage share and the profit share becomes equal to unity, and the profit share is divided into two components: the share of profit for the produced means of production ($r_w \omega_A$) and the share of profit for fixed capital ($r_w \omega_A \kappa_Z$).

The Ricardian theory of distribution and capital

Equations (15.17) and (15.34) explain the shares in distribution on a number line, enabling us to obtain the one-dimension theory of distribution. For equation (15.17), we consider the profit share as $r_w \omega_v = \pi_v$. In contrast, for equation (15.34), the profit share becomes equal to $r_w \omega_A + r_w \omega_A \kappa_Z$, which includes the share of profit for fixed capital. For us to change the standard for distribution from that of equation (15.34) to a new one is easy because distribution is considered in one number line. Representing ω_v / ω_A as P_v and multiplying both members of equation (15.34) by ω_v / ω_A, we obtain

$$P_v = \omega_v / \omega_A = \omega_v + r_w \omega_v + r_w \omega_v \kappa_Z. \tag{15.35}$$

The left member indicates the price of the standard net product measured in terms of the standard labour. Because in equation (15.35) we have $\omega_v + r_w \omega_v = 1$, the variable ω_v has the meaning of the real wage measured in terms of the standard net product or standard labour as is seen in equation (15.17).

Because we changed the notion of the rate of profit from r_K to the surplus rate r_w, we changed the notion of capital from the produced means of production $\mathbf{z}_S\mathbf{p}_v$ to wage as capital. Now we turn to the term $\omega_v\kappa_Z$. The nominal value of fixed capital of each sector is exogenously given and the vector of fixed capital measured in terms of the wage unit is represented as $\mathbf{k}_w$. We denote the vector of fixed capital measured in terms of the standard net product as $\mathbf{k}_R$. This is expressed as

$$\mathbf{k}_R = w_M\mathbf{k}_w/P_M. \tag{15.36}$$

Using this notation, we define the ratio of the real value of fixed capital to standard labour $\mathbf{ql}_A$ as

$$\kappa_L = \frac{\omega_A\mathbf{qk}_w}{\mathbf{ql}_A(1+\delta)} = \frac{w_M\mathbf{qk}_w}{\mathbf{sp}_vP_M} = \frac{\mathbf{qk}_R}{\mathbf{ql}_A}. \tag{15.37}$$

Then, we define the following value,

$$T = R\kappa_L P_v = \omega_v\kappa_Z = \frac{\mathbf{qk}_R P_v}{\mathbf{z}_S\mathbf{p}_v}. \tag{15.38}$$

The numerator $\mathbf{qk}_R P_v$ is the real value of fixed capital measured in terms of standard labour. The denominator $\mathbf{z}_S\mathbf{p}_v$ indicates the real value of the produced means of production measured in terms of labour. Therefore, T is considered as the multiplier for standard labour. Standard labour $(\mathbf{ql}_A)$ produces the total output of the standard system, which is divided into the standard net product $\mathbf{s}$ and the produced means of production $\mathbf{z}_S$. Using equation (15.38), the real value of fixed capital is considered as T units of standard labour. The term T is considered as the average period of production in our model (Garegnani, 1960). From (15.35) and (15.38), we obtain the following equation[5]

$$P_v = 1 + r_w T. \tag{15.39}$$

Equation (15.39) is interpreted as the theory of average period of production (Garegnani, 1990, pp. 24–25). From (15.39), we obtain

$$r_w = \frac{P_v - 1}{T}. \tag{15.40}$$

Equation (15.40) indicates that the surplus rate is given by the surplus value divided by T. Additionally, from (15.33), (15.35) and (15.38), we obtain

$$r_w = \frac{1 - \omega_A}{\omega_A + T/P_v}. \tag{15.41}$$

The numerator is the surplus value, or the value of $(\mathbf{sp}_v/\mathbf{ql}_A - \omega_A)$, and the denominator is the total value of capital. Equation (15.41) is also quite interesting because it is similar to the definition of the rate of profit of Marx.[6]

The rate of profit and the real value of capital

Now, we consider the relationship between the rate of profit and the real value of fixed capital. From (15.9), (15.14), (15.16), (15.35), (15.38) and (15.41), the rate of profit is given as

$$r_K = \frac{P_v - \omega_v}{1/R + \kappa_L/\omega_A} = \frac{1 - \omega_A}{1/R + \kappa_L}. \tag{15.42}$$

Therefore, the real value of total capital (K_R) measured in terms of the standard net product is obtained as

$$K_R = \frac{1}{R} + \kappa_L = \frac{1 - \omega_A}{r_K}. \tag{15.43}$$

In equation (15.43), both $1/R$ and κ_L are obtained from exogenously given data. The right member indicates the discounted value of capital, which yields the annual return of $(1 - \omega_A)$ in perpetuity. Therefore, the right member indicates that the real value of capital should be kept constant in perpetuity. In addition, under the given wage share, the rate of profit should be consistent with the real value of capital K_R. Equation (15.43) indicates that our model's capital is considered as everlasting capital whose value is kept constant under the given conditions, including the given wage share ω_A. However, it should be stressed that our model enabled us to define the real value of capital by using the given nominal data. Equation (15.43) can be considered as the condition that our definition of the real value of fixed capital should satisfy. Sraffa (1960) treated fixed capital as a joint product. The discounted value of a machine and the amount of depreciation varies if the rate of profit changes (Sraffa, 1960, Schefold, 1989). In contrast, we have taken up an economy-wide amount of fixed capital, which should be considered as a composite of capital goods (Garegnani, 1960, Chapter 5).

Conclusion

Difficulties exist in the theory of distribution and the measurement of aggregate capital (Garegnani, 1960, Harcourt, 1972). We have explained our method for measuring the shares in distribution and the real value of capital. We have assumed that the nominal value of fixed capital at the end of the previous production period and the nominal value of depreciation are exogenously given. Though our model has restrictive constraints and conditions, the exogenously given conditions are acceptable. With a set of exogenously given data measured in terms of money, we have explained the surplus rate and the shares in distribution. We have developed the Ricardian theory of value and distribution as the one-dimension theory of distribution, and have given a formulation of the average period of production in our model. Moreover, we have given the definition of real value of fixed capital which is consistent with the rate of profit. Our new approach is considered as a theory to measure real values in distribution and capital.

Notes

1 The author would like to thank Professors Heinz Kurz, Christian Lager, Fabio Petri and Bertram Schefold for their helpful comments. The author is grateful for the financial support of the Grant-in-Aid for Scientific Research (*KAKEN*) of JSPS (Research Project: 22243019).
2 If we multiply equation (15.7) by $\mathbf{q}$ from the left-hand side, we obtain

$$\mathbf{q}[\mathbf{I} - \mathbf{A}]\mathbf{p}_A = (r_K/R)R\mathbf{q}\mathbf{A}\mathbf{p}_A + w_A\mathbf{q}\mathbf{l}_A.$$

We rewrite this equation as

$$(1 - r_K/R)\mathbf{s}\mathbf{p}_A = w_A\mathbf{x}\mathbf{l}_A.$$

From this, we obtain the equivalent conditions of (15.8) and (15.9).
3 Pasinetti (1981) calls the labour required to replace worn-out productive capacity indirect labour (see Pasinetti, 1981, p. 132).
4 The price system (15.22) can be rewritten as

$$(\mathbf{I} - \mathbf{A})\,\mathbf{p}_M - (r_K/R)R\mathbf{A}\mathbf{p}_M = w_M\mathbf{l}_A + r_Kw_M\mathbf{k}_w + w_M\mathbf{d}_w.$$

Multiplying both members of this equation by the eigenvector $\mathbf{q}$ from the left-hand side, we obtain equation (15.27).
5 Equation (15.39) can be rewritten as $P = v_L + r_w v_L T$, where the value of labour is the variable for labour in place of the wage rate.
6 Garegnani (1960) indicated the similarity between the Marxian theory and the theory of the average period of production.

References

Garegnani, P. (1960). *Il Capitale nelle Teorie della Distributione*, Giuffrè: Milano.
Garegnani, P. (1987). Surplus approach to value and distribution, *The New Palgrave Dictionary of Economics*, Eatwell, J., Milgate, M., and Newman, P. (eds.) London: Macmillan, pp. 560–574.
Garegnani, P. (1990). Quantity of capital, *The New Palgrave: Capital Theory*, Eatwell, J., Milgate, M., and Newman, P. (eds.) London: Macmillan, pp. 1–78.
Harcourt, G. C. (1972). *Some Cambridge Controversies in the Theory of Capital*, Cambridge: Cambridge University Press.
Kurz, H.D. and Salvadori, N. (1995). *Theory of Production; A Long-Period Analysis*, Cambridge: Cambridge University Press.
Pasinetti, L. L. (1977). *Lectures on the Theory of Production*, New York: Columbia University Press.
Pasinetti, L. L. (1981). *Structural Change and Economic Growth*, Cambridge: Cambridge University Press.

Schefold, B. (1989). *Mr Sraffa on Joint Production and Other Essays*, London: Unwin Hyman.

Sraffa, P. (1960). *Production of Commodities by Means of Commodities*, Cambridge: Cambridge University Press.

Yagi, T. (2007). *New Productivity Indexes and Capital Theory*, The Report of Research Project 17530137, Category (C) of the Grant-in-Aid for Scientific Research, Japan Society for the Promotion of Science (JSPS), pp. 1–186.

Yagi, T. (2012). Structural Change and Invariable Standards, Arena, R. and Porta, P. L. (eds.) *Structural Dynamics and Economic Growth*, Cambridge: Cambridge University Press, pp. 241–263.

Part 4

Sraffian themes

16 Pasinetti's Ricardo after Sraffa

A reformulation based on Ricardo's 'early writings'

Enrico Bellino

Introduction

In the literature on Ricardo's political economy we find two milestones, which were published over the span of ten years, more than one century after the publication of Ricardo's works: Sraffa's (1951) 'Introduction' to *The Works and Correspondence of David Ricardo* and Pasinetti's (1960) 'Mathematical Formulation of the Ricardian System'.

Before the publication by Sraffa of Ricardo's edition, the main focus of economists had been on the material contained in the *Principles* (Ricardo 1817). Sraffa provided a new perspective: in his 'Introduction' we find a sort of reha-bilitation of the approach followed by Ricardo in his *Essay on the Influence of a low Price of Corn on the Profits of Stock* (Ricardo 1815) and in some of his other early writings. These works deal with what is considered by Ricardo 'the principal problem in Political Economy', that is, 'the laws which regulate [income] distribu-tion' (Ricardo 1817, p. 5). In extreme synthesis rent is explained as a differential gain related to the fertility of the various plots of land, wages are determined by the subsistence level and profits absorb what remains of the social product, i.e. the surplus of the system. To provide a rigorous determination of the profits of the system (and of the rate of profit) on the basis of this 'residual' procedure, Ricardo follows two different paths. In the *Principles*, he evaluates all the aggregates rele-vant in the calculation of profits at their labour values, while in the 'early writings' he adopts the simplifying assumption that 'in agriculture the same commodity, namely corn, forms both the capital (conceived as composed of the subsistence necessary for workers) and the product'; in this way profits can be calculated before knowing the price system (Sraffa 1951, p. xxxi). Sraffa's rehabilitation of Ricardo's earlier analytical framework stands on the findings of an investigation that Sraffa had been carrying out since the late Thirties and that would appear only in 1960 in *Production of Commodities by Means of Commodities*. Sraffa writes: 'It should perhaps be stated that it was only when the Standard system and the distinction between basics and non-basics had emerged in the course of the present investigation that the above interpretation of Ricardo's theory suggested itself as a natural consequence' Sraffa (1960 Appendix D). Yet, some method-ological aspects of Ricardo's theories and of Sraffa's interpretations were clarified only later, after quite a long period of settling down of the logic of Sraffa's (1960) framework.

Pasinetti's mathematical formulation of the Ricardian system was written in the academic year 1957–58, hence after the publication of Sraffa's 'Introduction' but before *Production of Commodities*. It is thus not surprising that some aspects of Sraffa's interpretation of Ricardo, and in particular his rehabilitation of his early writings, had not been fully appreciated by Pasinetti:

> [f]ragments of an early version of the Ricardian theory of value can be traced in Ricardo's early writings and in some letters (see the evidence given by Mr. Sraffa, Works, p. XXXI). It seems that Ricardo tried at the beginning to measure the relevant variables of his system in terms of a main agricultural commodity, namely corn, claiming that this commodity has the property of being both the capital and the product and, therefore, makes it possible to determine the ratio of profit to capital in physical terms without any question of evaluation. This position was, however, very vulnerable and will not be considered in this paper, as Ricardo abandoned it long before writing the Principles.
>
> (Pasinetti, 1960, p. 78, fn. 2)

Actually Pasinetti's article was written before it was possible to appreciate how Sraffa's Standard system could provide the way to make Ricardo's 'vulnerable' position general.

I read Pasinetti's formulation of the Ricardian system in 1985 when I was a student. Some years later, I started my research in the field of classical-Keynesian political economy, and on numerous occasions I was able to be increasingly involved in this research field and in particular in study issues like the 'corn-ratio' theory of profit, the Standard commodity, etc. Since the beginning of the Nineties, I have always included the Ricardian model in my lectures. But probably I have slightly changed the way of presenting the original Pasinetti model each year so that, when in 2010 Heinz Kurz and Neri asked me to write the entry 'Pasinetti on Ricardo' for the *Companion to David Ricardo*, I perceived that what I had been teaching for all these years had slowly shifted from Pasinetti's original formulation. Pasinetti's model is in fact very flexible, and with very few changes it is possible to obtain a reformulation that includes the main features of the theoretical framework of Ricardo's early writings. Recent works of mine (Bellino, 2014, 2015a and 2015b) describe three changes to the model aimed at making it more coherent with Sraffa's interpretation of Ricardo and in general with the logical framework of surplus theories. The present essay puts together the necessary parts to provide an organic presentation of a model which formalizes a Ricardian system of Ricardo's early writings.

The analytical formulation

Consider an economic system where there are three social classes: landlords, capitalists and workers. Capitalists organize the production of commodities employing workers (against payment of a wage) and the land put at their disposal by landlords (against payment of a rent). The *residuum* from the net product after deducing rents and wages constitutes profits which goes to capitalists. Ricardo distinguishes two groups of commodities: 'necessaries', that is, the commodities that must be produced to make the working of the entire system possible, like wage goods, and 'luxuries'. We will group these broad categories of commodities in two goods: 'corn' and 'gold', respectively. For the sake of simplicity, the production processes of corn and gold do not employ capital goods. Yet, as production takes time (one 'year') workers' subsistence is *advanced* by capitalists during the whole production period. Advanced wages constitute thus the only form of capital of our economy. Technology is described by two functions expressing the link between the input and output levels:

$$Q_c = f(N_c), \tag{16.1}$$

where Q_c is the output of corn and N_c is the number of workers employed in the production of corn. Function $f : \Re^+ \mapsto \Re^+$ satisfies the following assumptions:

$$f'(N_c) > 0, \tag{16.1a}$$
$$f''(N_c) < 0, \tag{16.1b}$$
$$f'(0) \geq \bar{x}, \tag{16.1c}$$

where $\bar{x}$ is the quantity of corn which constitutes the subsistence of a worker.

Assumptions (16.1a) and (16.1b) entail that as the number of workers increases, the increase of the output of corn is less than proportional: as lands have different degrees of fertility, capitalists organize corn production at first on the most fertile plots of land, but, as population and production increase, they must expand production to less and less fertile plots of land.[1]

Assumptions (16.1a) and (16.1b) can be interpreted in *extensive* terms, i.e. the increase of output of corn is obtained by a *simultaneous* increase of land, labour and capital: the additional output is obtained by additional lands, cultivated by additional workers, requiring additional advances of wages, i.e. of capital.[2] In this sense, function (16.1) is not *stricto sensu* a 'production function', at least not in the neoclassical sense, as it does *not* allow for the possibility of varying one input at a time;[3] the same can be said for the following function, describing the technology of gold:

$$Q_g = \alpha N_g, \tag{16.2}$$

where Q_g is the output of gold, N_g is the number of workers employed in the production of gold and α is the quantity of gold produced by one worker. *Constant returns* characterizes this production, assimilable to manufacturing, where there is no reason to think that inputs have different degrees of fertility.

The production period is the same for both processes (one 'year'); the social product, constituted by the output of corn and of gold is distributed to landlords, to workers and to capitalists in the form of rents, wages, and profits, respectively. How these shares are determined is described below.

Rents. They arise just in the corn industry: the different degree of fertility of the various plots of rents determines the rent on each plot of land as the difference between the corn produced on that plot and the corn produced on the last cultivated plot of land where rent is zero; total rents (R) are thus the sum of these differences:[4]

$$R = f(N_c) - N_c f'(N_c).$$ (16.3)

Wages. The unit wage (x) is regulated by a Malthusian principle at the subsistence level, $\bar{x}$:

$$x = \bar{x}.$$ (16.4)

Total wages (W) are given by:

$$W = x(N_c + N_g).$$ (16.5)

As advanced wages are the only component of capital of our system, K, we have

$$K = W.$$ (16.6)

Profits. Profits are the *residuum* for capitalists once rents and wages are deduced from output. The analytical way to determine profits differs between the industries due to the specific characteristics of each industry. In the corn industry the calculation is simpler because

> in agriculture the same commodity, namely corn, forms both the capital (conceived as composed of the subsistence necessary for workers) and the product; so that the determination of profit by the difference between total product and capital advanced, and also the determination of the ratio of this profit to the capital, is done directly between quantities of corn without any question of valuation.
>
> (Sraffa, 1951, p. xxxi)

We have, in fact,

$$P_c = Q_c - R - x N_c,$$ (16.7)

where P_c is the amount of profit of the corn industry expressed in terms of corn. The rate of profit is given by $\pi_c = P_c/\bar{x}N_c$ which, thanks to (16.7), (16.1) and (16.3) reduces to

$$\pi_c = \frac{f'(N_c) - \bar{x}}{\bar{x}}.$$ (16.7′)

The calculation of profits is more complicated in the gold industry because the residuum must be calculated by comparing the *value* of two different commodities:

$$P_g = p_g Q_g - p_c x N_g,$$ (16.8)

where p_c and p_g are the prices of corn and of gold, respectively, and P_g is the amount of profit of the gold industry expressed in value terms. It is thus necessary to provide a theory to determine the prices of corn and gold. Following Sraffa (1951),

> if there is to be a uniform rate of profit in all trades it is the exchangeable values of the products of other trades relatively to their own capitals (i.e. relatively to corn) that must be adjusted so as to yield the same rate of profit as has been established in the growing of corn; since in the latter no value changes can alter the ratio of product to capital, both consisting of the same commodity.
>
> (Sraffa, 1951, p. xxxi)

We thus write

$$\pi_g \equiv \frac{p_g Q_g - p_c x N_g}{p_c x N_g} = \frac{f'(N_c) - \bar{x}}{\bar{x}} \equiv \pi_c.$$ (16.9)

Rearranging (16.9) we obtain

$$\frac{p_c}{p_g} = \frac{1/f'(N_c)}{1/\alpha}.$$ (16.9')

The relative price of corn in terms of gold thus identified aligns the rate of profit of the gold industry to the rate of profit of the corn industry. Incidentally, we can observe that the relative price (16.9') expresses a *labour theory of value*, with $1/f(N_c)$ being the quantity of labour necessary to produce one unit of corn on the marginal land and $1/a$ being the quantity of labour necessary to produce one unit of gold. Observe that in this formulation of Ricardo's early writings the labour theory of value expressed by equation (16.9') is just a *result* of our assumptions, not a hypothesis. In particular, it is the consequence of the assumption that capital is constituted by advanced wages only. Thus, in this model no result is based on the validity of such a theory of value.[5]

Having identified a relative price, we need to fix a *numéraire*: as in Pasinetti's formulation, the unit of value is the quantity of gold produced by one worker (α), that is

$$p_g \alpha = 1;$$ (16.10)

in this way, the price of each commodity coincides with its embodied labour,

$$p_g = 1/\alpha \quad \text{and} \quad p_c = 1/f'(N_c). \tag{16.9''}$$

We have thus 10 equations, (16.1)–(16.10), in 12 unknowns, Q_c, N_c, R, x, W, K, P_c, Q_g, N_g, P_g, p_c and p_g. We need two further equations.

Till now, we have specified the determinants of rents, wages and profits (the theory of income distribution), the determinants of prices (the theory of value), but the level of all these unknowns still depends on another unknown, the level of employment in the corn industry, N_c, which has not yet been determined.

Different closures of the model could be considered at this point. It is known that classical economists considered output levels as given in the stage of analysis concerning the determination of relative prices and of income distribution.[6] As suggested in Bellino and Nerozzi (2014, Section 3) we can adopt this solution by adding the following two equations:

$$Q_c = \bar{Q}_c \tag{16.11}$$

and

$$Q_g = \bar{Q}_g. \tag{16.12}$$

Other ways to close the system are obviously available. For example, Pasinetti proposed to close the model by introducing a theory of demand: he assumed that, with the exception of a negligible *minimum*, all rents are spent on luxuries, i.e. on gold, while wages and profits are entirely spent on corn (for subsistence and for capital accumulation).[7] It has been noted (see for example Costa, 1977) that this closure has the disadvantage of breaking the *causal* logical structure of the Ricardian income distribution theory and transforms the model into a fully interdependent one; on this see Bellino and Nerozzi (2014). Alternatively, we could follow a third way and close the model by fixing from outside the amount of capital and the output level of one industry. The other level would thus be univocally determined by the model. This solution introduces a certain degree of arbitrariness about which output level to fix from the outside. However, it has the quality of explicitly taking into account the level of the available capital stock, which constitutes the binding constraint of the accumulation process for classical economists.

Solution of the model

In this way, equation (16.11) together with (16.1) determines the number of workers employed in the corn industry, $f^{-1}(\bar{Q}_c) := N_c^*$. All the other unknowns can be easily determined as indicated in Table 16.1.

Economic characteristics of the solution

The rate of profit *of the whole system* depends simply on the technical conditions of the corn industry and on the subsistence level of the wage rate. In this case,

Table 16.1 Solution of the model: summary

	Equilibrium value of the variables	Equations used
1)	$x^* = \bar{x}$	(16.4)
2)	$Q_c^* = \bar{Q}_c$	(16.11)
3)	$Q_g^* = \bar{Q}_g$	(16.12)
4)	$N_c^* = f^{-1}(\bar{Q}_c)$	(16.11) and (16.1)
5)	$R^* = f(N_c^*) - N_c^* f'(N_c^*)$	(16.3)
6)	$P_c^* = N_c^*[f'(N_c^*) - \bar{x}]$	(16.7), (16.3) and (16.1)
	$\rightarrow \pi^* = \dfrac{f'(N_c^*) - \bar{x}}{\bar{x}}$	(16.9)
7)	$p_g^* = 1/\alpha$	(16.10)
8)	$p_c^* = 1/f(N_c^*)$	(16.9'')
9)	$N_g^* = \bar{Q}_0/\alpha$	(16.12) and (16.2)
10)	$P_g^* = N_g^*[1 - \bar{x}/f'(N_c^*)]$	(16.2), (16.4), (16.9'') and (16.12)
11)	$W^* = \bar{x}(N_c^* + N_g^*)$	(16.5)
12)	$K^* = W^*$	(16.6)

it is formally correct to state that 'it is the profits of the farmer that regulate the profits of all other trades' stated by Ricardo in his 'early writings'. This asymmetry between the industry of necessaries and that of luxuries will be fully developed subsequently in the distinction between basics and non-basics in Sraffa's (1960) framework.

Moreover, Table 16.1 shows us that the rate of profit may be calculated *before* the price system has been determined! It is thus formally correct to maintain that the rate of profit is *independent* of prices. It is, in fact, a ratio between *physical* quantities of corn (this determination of profits is often referred as the 'corn-ratio' theory of profit).

These results rest on the crucial assumption that there exists one industry where the same commodity is both the output and the (unique) input.

This independence of the rate of profit of prices has several theoretical and practical implications.

1   For Ricardo it was relevant to argue in favour of the imports of corn, that would have had the effect of reducing the price of corn *without reducing* the rate of profit. This is because corn is, at the same time, produce and means of production. A reduction of its price would thus equally affect revenues and costs, leaving the rate of profit unchanged. Moreover, the reduction of the internal cultivation of corn would result in an *increase* of the rate of profit (to the detriment of rents) as the cultivation would thus be organized over a restricted and more fertile set of plots of land.

2   It emphasizes the *real* nature of profits. They originate in the sphere of production as a *surplus*. Profits from the value sphere (for example by speculation) can be obtained only transitorily.

3   It describes Ricardo's conception of competition. In other words, a process
     that tends to *equalize* the rates of profit of the various industries through the
     movements of capital in search of the highest rate of profit, and *not* a process
     that *lowers profits* (eventually to zero), as described by Adam Smith[8] and
     subsequently encoded in the neoclassical notion of 'perfect competition'.

Last, if we allow that the wage rate is not fixed at the subsistence level and can
be changed, expression (16.7′) gives us a *decreasing* relation between the wage
rate and the rate of profit (see Figure 16.1):

$$\pi = \frac{f'(N_c^*) - x}{x}.$$ (16.13)

The drawing of (16.13) requires the knowledge of the employment level of the
corn industry, N_c^*. We need to know the marginal land, whose product can be
divided between workers and capitalists (the excess produced on all other more
fertile plots goes to landlords as rents). In other terms, we need to know the technique we can adopt to produce corn. As in Sraffa's (1960) framework, we must
consider the output of the basic industry as given. Despite the existence of a single
capital good, the ensuing relation is not linear due to the assumption that wage is
paid *ex-ante*. Contrary to the case considered by Sraffa, our system does not have
a maximum rate of profit. Since capital is constituted by advanced wages only, the
rate of profit tends to infinite when the wage rate tends to zero. We are in the case
of an 'ultimate' commodity (i.e. corn) 'produced by pure labour without means of
production except land, and which therefore [is] incompatible with a fixed limit to
the rise in the rate of profits' (Sraffa 1960, Appendix D, § 3).

Accumulation of capital

A further sphere where Pasinetti's formulation of the Ricardian system has been
fruitfully applied is the study of the process of accumulation of capital. We will go

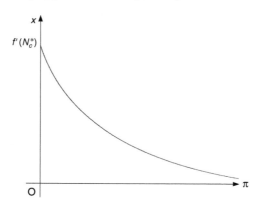

Figure 16.1 The relation between the wage rate and the rate of profit.

through this application here in order to discover some peculiarities of Ricardian methodology.

According to Ricardo, the main consequence of capital accumulation (i.e. the increase of the capital stock due to savings out of profits) is an inexorable fall in the rate of profit which tends to exhaust the accumulation process and leads the system to the stationary state. The fundamental cause for the fall in profits is to be found, according to Ricardo, in decreasing returns to scale in the production of wage goods, due to the necessity to extend the margin of cultivation on less and less fertile plots of land as the system grows. The ensuing increase of rents, together with a constant wage rate, will result in a profit squeezing.[9] This can be easily deduced by a graphical representation of the solution of the model described in the previous sections. Given the quantity produced by industries, $\bar{Q}_c$ and $\bar{Q}_g$, technology functions (16.1) and (16.2) identify the employment levels necessary to produce those quantities, N_c^* and N_g^*, which are represented on the horizontal axes of Figure 16.2. Consider the left-hand side of Figure 16.2. From the graph of the curve $f'(N_c)$ we can represent the total production of corn as the area $ON_c^* F^*C$.

Rents are represented by area R^*, the sum of the differences between the corn obtained from each plot of land and the corn obtained from the least productive cultivated plot. Total wages paid in the corn industry are represented by area $W_c^* = \bar{x}N_c^*$, where $\bar{x}$ is the natural wage. Profits of the corn industry are represented by area P_c^*, i.e. the *residuum*. The rate of profits is the ratio between area P_c^* and area W_c^* or, equivalently, between segments S^*F^* and $N_c^*S^*$, that is,

$$\frac{P_c^*}{W_c^*} = \frac{S^*F^*}{N_c^*S^*} = \frac{f'(N_c^*) - \bar{x}}{\bar{x}}.$$

The right-hand diagram refers to the gold industry. Magnitudes are represented in terms of gold (in symmetry with the left-hand diagram, where magnitudes appear in terms of corn). The unit wage ($\bar{x}$) expressed in terms of gold is $p_c\bar{x}/p_g = \alpha\bar{x}/f'(N_c^*) = w_g$. Total wages and profits of the gold industry, both

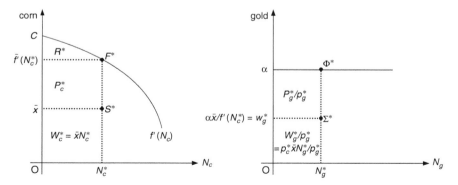

Figure 16.2 Graphical representation of the solution.

in terms of gold, are given by areas: $ON_g^*\Sigma^*w_g^*$ and $w_g^*\Sigma^*\Phi^*\alpha$, respectively. It is easy to verify that the ratio between segments $w_g^*\alpha$ and Ow_g^* yields a rate of profits equal to the rate of profits of the corn industry; in fact,

$$\frac{w_g^*\alpha}{Ow_g^*} = \frac{\alpha - \alpha\bar{x}/f'(N_c^*)}{\alpha\bar{x}/f'(N_c^*)} = \frac{f'(N_c^*) - \bar{x}}{\bar{x}}.$$

The willingness of capitalists to enlarge their capital stock brings them to save and invest in additional means of production both in the industry of the wage-good and in the industry of the luxury good. The actual division of this investment between the two industries depends on the way in which final demand evolves during the process of accumulation of capital. However, for our purposes, it is not necessary to go into this determination because *any* pattern of evolution of quantities arising in consequence of the accumulation of capital will always entail an *increase* in the quantity of corn produced, since corn is the means of production of each of the commodities produced in the system. Hence, the presence of positive profits in the solution described by Figure 16.2 engenders a movement along the arrows as indicated in the diagrams represented in Figure 16.3.

The increase of production of corn requires an increase in the number of workers employed in the corresponding industry, from N_{1c}^* to N_{2c}^* to N_{3c}^*, etc. New and less fertile plots of lands are thus being cultivated. Consequently, the amount of corn obtained on the marginal land, $f(N_c)$, decreases. By a simple inspection of expression (16.9'), an immediate consequence of this increased difficulty in producing corn is an increase of the relative price of corn in terms of gold. Moreover, while the wage rate remains fixed at $\bar{x}$, total wages increase from $ON_{1c}^*S_1\bar{x}$ to $ON_{2c}^*S_2\bar{x}$, to $ON_{3c}^*S_3\bar{x}$, etc. Rents unambiguously increase. Initially, the effect on profits is ambiguous: total profits increase for the extension of cultivation, but the profits obtained on each plot of land decrease as they are affected by the increase of rents. From a certain level of N_c onwards, the second effect prevails and total profits of the corn industry decrease.[10]

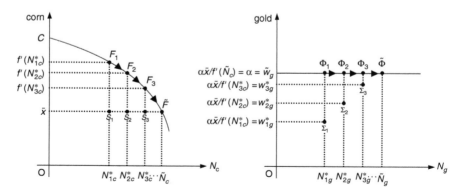

Figure 16.3 Graphical representation of the capital accumulation.

If the production of gold increases then N_g increases and total wages increase, while profits decrease from a certain point onward. In fact, the profits of the gold industry (in terms of gold) are $P_g/p_g = \alpha N_g[1 - \bar{x}f'(N_c)]$. On the basis that any increase of employment in the gold industry requires a corresponding increase of employment in the corn industry (to produce the wage-good for the additional workers of the gold industry), we can assume that $dN_c/dN_g > 0$. Hence

$$\frac{d(P_g/p_g)}{dN_g} = \alpha\left[1 - \frac{\bar{x}}{f'(N_c)}\right] + \alpha\bar{x}N_g\frac{f''(N_c)}{\left[f'(N_c)\right]^2}\frac{dN_c}{dN_g}.$$

The first addendum is positive and decreasing as long as $N_c < \bar{N}_c$, where $\bar{N}_c$ is the stationary state employment level for the corn industry, while the second addendum is always negative. When N_c approaches $\bar{N}_c$, the first addendum of the derivative tends to zero, and thus real profits in the gold industry decrease.

Moreover, the rate of profits for the whole system, given by the ratios $S_t F_t/N^*_{ct} S_t = \Sigma_t \Phi_t/N^*_{tg} \Sigma_t$, with $t = 1, 2, \ldots$, always decreases.

In conclusion, the main consequence of the accumulation of capital is that the rate of profits decreases and tends to zero while profits decrease and tend to zero from a certain point on. Here both the incentive to accumulate and the source from which to draw additional capital are exhausted. The economy has reached its stationary state. It is in the condition to indefinitely replicate the same productive cycle without expanding or contracting. More realistically, according to Ricardo, the stationary state will be reached before profits completely disappear, i.e. when the rate of profits has reached that minimum level which no longer induces capitalists to invest.

The above analysis makes it clear that the cause of the decrease in profits during the process of accumulation of capital is rooted in the decreasing returns to scale of lands. In the corn industry profits are eroded in favour of rents (this emerges clearly from the left-hand diagram of Figure 16.3). But, as corn is the wage-good, this phenomenon extends to the rest of the economy through a higher wage rate expressed in terms of the other commodity(ies). The wage rate remains constant in physical terms at the given level $\bar{x}$, but its value in terms of gold, $(p_c/p_g)\bar{x} = \alpha\bar{x}/f'(N_c)$, increases as new workers are employed on new (and less fertile) plots of land. The right-hand diagram of 16.3 depicts this effect very clearly. This reasoning faithfully replicates the description of the effects of accumulation of capital described by Ricardo (1817, pp. 120–1).

In the above analysis, we have considered the wage rate fixed at the subsistence level ($\bar{x}$) during the whole process of capital accumulation. This is clearly a shortcut, because according to the Malthusian principle, $\bar{x}$ is that level of the wage rate which keeps the population size *constant*. This is contrary to the need of increasing employment according to the accumulation requirements.[11] However, as showed by Kurz and Salvadori (2006, pp. 110–1), the conclusions reached above would not be significantly affected if a non-constant path were assumed for the wage rate. Consequently, the accumulation process could be described by the same formal apparatus described before, with the only proviso to re-interpret the given level of the wage rate $\bar{x}$ as the 'normal' wage rate prevailing during the accumulation process. This 'normal' level is affected by a set of forces—which evidently includes the speed of accumulation—whose intensity and direction are not so general and univocal as to describe it by a formal one-to-one function of the other endogenous variables of the model. Hence $\bar{x}$ is to be considered as a given value, fixed at a level *higher* than the subsistence level.[12]

Concluding remarks

Pasinetti's mathematical formulation of the Ricardian system is remarkably flexible. It was conceived to provide a formal presentation of the theoretical framework of Ricardo's *Principles*, but we have used it here to outline the logic of Ricardo's distribution and value theory of his early writings.[13] The latter has the great advantage that it can be generalized to the M-commodity case as indicated by Sraffa (1960): the supposition that in an industry the same commodity is the output and the unique input is replaced by the adoption of a suitable *numéraire*, the Standard commodity, which allows us to penetrate the intricacies of the interdependence between value and distribution with the same ease as in the case of the corn-economy.

The analytical formulation of Ricardo's early writings presented in these pages has the pedagogical function of fully appreciating the final objective that Sraffa was pursuing with his Standard commodity: that of studying the relation concerning income distribution independently of prices. In simpler terms, Sraffa aimed to depict the economy as a system where the decisions regarding the amplitude of one of the 'slices' of national income does *not* affect the magnitude of the entire 'cake'.

Notes

1 An interpretation of capitalists' behaviour in terms of game theory is provided by Salvadori (2004).
2 Pasinetti (1977, § 3.1, fn. 8) also allows for an *intensive* interpretation of the equation, although in a Ricardian framework the change of input proportions does not play the same rôle played in the marginal approach.
3 This point deeply discriminates the approach followed here from other mathematical formulations of the Ricardian system like, for example, the one proposed by Samuelson (1959a)–(1959b).
4 For an historical excursus on the origin of this theory of rent see Pasinetti (2015).
5 On the contrary, this will be the true (restrictive) assumption on which the entire analysis of the *Principles* is grounded and that Ricardo will never be able to remove.
6 See the reconstruction of the logical structure of classical surplus theories proposed by Garegnani (1984) or the first paragraph of the Preface in Sraffa (1960).
7 For details see Pasinetti (1960, p. 84).
8 Smith writes: 'The increase of stock, which raises wages, tends to lower profit. When the stocks of many rich merchants are turned into the same trade, their mutual competition naturally tends to lower its profit; and when there is a like increase of stock in all the different trades carried on in the same society, the same competition must produce the same effect in them all' (Smith 1776, Vol. I, book I, ch. ix, p. 105).

9 On this point Ricardo is resolute in disproving the view expressed by Adam Smith that this fall in profits is the result of competition engendered by capital accumulation. This position is in fact incompatible with Ricardo's theory of profits seen in the previous section.

10 Consider, in fact, the expression of profits of the corn industry, $P_c = Q_c - R - \bar{x}N_c = N_c[f'(N_c) - \bar{x}]$ and its derivative with respect to the number of workers employed in the corn industry, $dP_c/dN_c = [f'(N_c) - \bar{x}] + N_c f'(N_c)$. The first addendum is positive and decreasing with respect to N_c, while the second addendum is negative.

11 There have been some attempts to overcome this objection by introducing an alternative determination of the real wage rate during the accumulation process. All these attempts have ended up with considering the wage rate as a variable determined by the interplay of a labour demand curve with a labour supply curve. This approach has been presented as a 'new view' in Ricardian economy (the term was coined by Hicks and Hollander, 1977: see also Casarosa, 1982 and Samuelson, 1978). This approach is clearly extraneous to Sraffa's interpretation of Ricardo. It has correctly been argued that the 'acceptance of the New view would dissolve the perception of Ricardo as a "surplus theorist" in any meaningful sense' (Peach 1988, p. 111).

12 For further details see Bellino (2015a).

13 This shows us that the economic system considered in the *Principles* cannot be more general than the one considered by Ricardo in his early writings.

References

Bellino, E. (2014): "Necessary prices and necessary income distribution in classical political economy – A bridge with the notions of 'just' prices and 'just' wage," *Rivista internazionale di scienze sociali*, CXXII(2), 177–92, Vita e Pensiezo, Milano.

—— (2015a): "Accumulation of capital," in *Elgar Companion to David Ricardo*, ed. by H. D. Kurz, and N. Salvadori, pp. 1–13. Edward Elgar, Cheltenham, UK.

—— (2015b): "Pasinetti, Luigi Lodovico, on Ricardo," in *Elgar Companion to David Ricardo*, ed. by H. D. Kurz, and N. Salvadori, pp. 396–404. Edward Elgar, Cheltenham, UK.

Bellino, E., and S. Nerozzi (2014): "Causality and interdependence in Pasinetti's works and in the modern classical approach," Centro Sraffa Working Paper No. 10.

Casarosa, C. (1982): "The New View of the Ricardian Theory of Distribution and Economic Growth," in *Advances in Economic Theory*, ed. by M. Baranzini, pp. 227–42. Basil Blackwell, Oxford.

Costa, G. (1977): "Ricardo, Keynes, la causalità e la legge di Say – Alcune osservazioni e considerazioni sui 'Saggi' del professor Luigi L. Pasinetti," *Studi economici*, 2, 3–56, Franco Angeli, Milano.

Garegnani, P. (1984): "Value and Distribution in the Classical Economists and in Marx," *Oxford Economic Papers*, 36(2), 291–325.

Hicks, J., and S. Hollander (1977): "Mr. Ricardo and the Moderns," *Quarterly Journal of Economics*, XCI(3), 351–69.

Kurz, H. D., and N. Salvadori (2006): "Endogenous Growth in a Stylised 'Classical' Model," in *Economic Development and Social Change – Historical Roots and Modern Perspectives*, ed. by G. Stathakis and G. Vaggi, pp. 106–124. Routledge, Abington and New York.

Pasinetti, L. L. (1960): "A Mathematical Formulation of the Ricardian System," *The Review of Economic Studies*, XXVII(2), 78–98.

—— (1977): *Lectures in the Theory of Production*. Macmillan, London.

—— (2015): "On the Origin of the Theory of Rent in Economics," in *Resources, Production and Structural Dynamics*, ed. by M. Baranzini, C. Rotondi, and R. Scazzieri, pp. 35–52. Cambridge University Press, Cambridge.

Peach, T. (1988): "David Ricardo: a Review of Some Interpretative Issues," in *Classical Political Economy – A Survey of Recent Literature*, ed. by W. O. Thweatt, pp. 103–31. Kluwer Academic Publishers, Boston.

Ricardo, D. (1815): *An Essay on The Influence of a Low Price of Corn on the Profits of Stock*. John Murray, London, edition used: *The Works and the Correspondences of David Ricardo*, ed. by Piero Sraffa, with the collaboration of Maurice H. Dobb, Cambridge University Press, Cambridge, 1951–73, Vol. IV, pp. 1–41.

—— (1817): *On the Principles of Political Economy and Taxation*. John Murray, London, edition used: *The Works and the Correspondences of David Ricardo*, ed. by Piero Sraffa, with the collaboration of Maurice H. Dobb, Cambridge University Press, Cambridge, 1951–73, Vol. I.

Salvadori, N. (2004): "Is Ricardian Extensive Rent a Nash Equilibrium," in *Money Credit and the Role of the State: Essays in honour of Augusto Graziani*, ed. by R. Arena, and N. Salvadori, pp. 347–58. Ashgate, Aldershot.

Samuelson, P. A. (1959a): "A Modern Treatment of the Ricardian Economy: I. The Pricing of Goods and of Labor and Land Services," *The Quarterly Journal of Economics*, 73(1), 1–35.

—— (1959b): "A Modern Treatment of the Ricardian Economy: II. Capital and Interest Aspects of the Pricing Process," *The Quarterly Journal of Economics*, 73(2), 217–231.

—— (1978): "The Canonical Classical Model of Political Economy," *Journal of Economic Literature*, 16(4), 1415–34.

Smith, A. (1776): *An Inquiry into the Nature and Causes of the Wealth of Nations*. W. Strahan, T. Cadell, London, 1st edn., 2 vol.; edition used edited by R. H. Campbell, A. S. Skinner, W. B. Todd, Vol. II of *The Glasgow Edition of the Works and Correspondence of Adam Smith*, Clarendon Press, Oxford, 1976.

Sraffa, P. (1951): "Introduction," in *The Works and Correspondence of David Ricardo*, ed. by Piero Sraffa with the collaboration of Maurice H. Dobb, Vol. I, xiii–lxii.

—— (1960): *Production of Commodities by Means of Commodities – Prelude to a Critique of Economic Theory*. Cambridge University Press, Cambridge.

17 Subsistence-cum-surplus wages versus gross wages

A note

Christian Gehrke[1]

Introduction

In Piero Sraffa's unpublished papers, which are deposited in the Wren Library at Trinity College, Cambridge, is a typescript version of Joan Robinson's 1961 review article of *Production of Commodities by Means of Commodities*, entitled 'Prelude to a Critique of Economic Theory'.[2] Sraffa kept this typescript together with the following note, which he dated 27 August 1960: 'This will appear in Oxford Economic Papers January number. I hope it provides an opportunity for whatever <u>dementi</u> you want to make. J{oan}' (D3/12/111: 343). Sraffa refrained from making any *dementi* in print, but he annotated three passages in Robinson's manuscript, amongst them also the following one (Sraffa's annotations in the margin of the typescript are given in curly brackets):[3]

> Instead of the real wage being fixed by physical necessity, the workers receive a share of the surplus. The author toys with the idea of separating the wage into a part which is necessary and the rest. {!?} Happily, he rejects it. {no!} It would be very hard to imagine that, when the workers had a surplus to spend on beef, their physical need for wheat was unchanged. {?} Wage goods thus cease to be necessary for production in technically fixed proportions. {?}
> (D3/12/111: 346–7)

Sraffa's annotations clearly indicate disagreement with Robinson's statements, or at any rate doubts about her interpretation. This is somewhat surprising in view of the fact that this particular passage from Robinson's review article has met with the approval of serious Sraffa scholars; in fact it was quoted approvingly by authors like Peter Newman (1962: 68) and Heinz D. Kurz and Neri Salvadori (1995: 423, n 42). It would therefore seem interesting to investigate whether the documents in Sraffa's unpublished papers can provide some hints for interpreting these annotations.

Robinson's statements in the passage quoted above refer, of course, to Section 8 of *Production of Commodities*, which concerns the transition from subsistence wages to wages as a share in the surplus. In order to interpret Sraffa's annotations it is useful to start from this section and to first identify those elements which are in conflict with Robinson's comments. In the opening paragraph of Section 8 Sraffa notes, after observing that wages, 'besides the ever-present element of subsistence, ... may include a share of the surplus product', that

> it would be appropriate, when we come to consider the division of the surplus between capitalists and workers, to separate the two component parts of the wage and regard only the 'surplus' part as variable; whereas the goods necessary for the subsistence of the workers would continue to appear, with the fuel, etc., among the means of production.
>
> (Sraffa, 1960: 9)

Sraffa thus considered the conceptualization in terms of a separation of the wage into two component parts (designated in the following as the concept of 'subsistence-cum-surplus wages') as 'more appropriate' than, and thus as preferable to, the concept of 'gross wages', which he adopted. The only reason he gives for using the 'gross wage' concept is that of 'following the usual practice' and of not 'tampering with the traditional wage concept' (1960: 9): It is an argument based solely on expositional expedience, while conceptual or theoretical problems play no role in motivating this decision. And in the final paragraph of Section 8 Sraffa indeed emphasized that the discussion which follows 'can easily be adapted' to the alternative conceptualization in terms of 'subsistence-cum-surplus wages', thus suggesting that *no* theoretical difficulties would be involved if the latter were in fact adopted.

Apparently, then, Sraffa regarded the subsistence-cum-surplus wage conception not only as preferable to the concept of gross wages, on theoretical grounds, but he also did not believe that one would be prevented from adopting it because of theoretical problems, including the objection raised by Joan Robinson. In her view, adopting this concept would cause a serious problem, because the workers' subsistence requirements cannot possibly be treated as given quantities of commodities any more when the workers also obtain a share of the surplus, because the consumption out of their surplus share must inevitably be bound up with changes in their requirements for subsistence. In other words: the workers' subsistence consumption and their surplus consumption cannot be conceived of as independent of one another.

Why, then, did Sraffa annotate Robinson's statements with a question mark in the margin? Did he accept Robinson's criticism, signalling with his question mark that he did not have a proper answer to it, or did he consider her argument as ill-founded? In order to answer these questions, I will first take a closer look, in the next section of this note, at Sraffa's successive drafts of the relevant passage in *Production of Commodities*, which have been preserved in his unpublished papers. In the third section, the reader is then referred to some correspondence between Robinson and Sraffa, which shows that their disagreements with regard to the treatment of wages can also be related to a particular interpretation of the 'Keynes-Classics distinction' which had earlier been suggested by Robinson, and which

Sraffa had considered as 'totally misleading' (JVR/vii/431/35). The final section contains some concluding remarks.

Sraffa's drafts of the relevant passage

The first version of the passage that was later to become Section 8 of *Production of Commodities* was written on 12 and 14 March 1955, when Sraffa during an extended stay on the isle of Majorca composed a first draft of the bulk of his book manuscript (the so-called 'Majorca draft').[4] The draft version of the passage reads:

12.3.55

Hitherto we have regarded wages as being composed of the necessary subsistence for the workers & thereby being on the same footing as the fuel for the engines or the fodder for the working animals. Wages however partake of a double nature & while always containing the element of subsistence they may, *in certain social conditions*, secure also a share of the surplus product. *And it is indeed the stress & strain arising from this possibility that has given economic theory its shape.* {. . .}[5]

14.3.55

We shall designate the wage per unit of labour as w; this is a price to be determined like other prices in terms of the commodity which is chosen as a (standard). The unit of labour being the annual social labour, w will at the same time represent the fraction of the national income that goes to wages (it will be the 'proportionate wage' of Ricardo).[6]

The double nature of wages, as means of production and as share in the surplus, gives rise to the question whether the whole of the wages should be included in w; or only the 'surplus' part of them, while the subsistence part is left in its previous shape as raw materials. There is much to be said for either method. The latter separation is in many ways more reasonable, for it represents by a constant the quantity that is unchangeable and by a variable the quantity that can be more or less according to circumstances. It is the view of the classical economists, who did not regard wages as part of the net income of society, but as being advanced out of capital, although they admitted that in some cases they might succeed in getting a part of the surplus.[(1)] It has also the advantage of including the necessary wage in the year's advances which must be multiplied by the factor $1 + r$, while leaving outside the part which must come out of the product at the end of year. *Much as there is to recommend it in theory, this method would give rise to some difficulty in practical application*, if such had ever to be attempted; for the segregation of the commodities composing the two parts of the wages, whilst no doubt feasible in the early stages of society, would meet in modern conditions with 'insurmountable obstacles'

(The attempt to overcome them by a division of the 'value' of the wage would create more troubles than it overcomes).

The other method has much less logic to recommend it; but it has the decisive advantage of being in conformity with current usage, in that it treats the wage as a single unit, and it includes the whole of it as part of the national income: and it is the distribution of this (rather than that of the less inclusive 'Net National Revenue' of A. Smith) which we shall have to discuss. {...}

[1] Note on Ricardo & (if possible) A. Smith[7]

(D3/12/52: 7–8; emphasis added)

On the back of this page Sraffa added:

The question of what is included and what not in wages becomes of great importance when we consider that w & r are determined exclusively by basic commodities: so that if an improvement takes place in the production of basics R is affected, but if in not basics, not. Clearly, 'essential subsistence' wages must be included in basics for this purpose. {...}

(D3/12/52: 8, verso)

To this passage Sraffa made an addition on 15 March 1955, apparently upon re-reading what he had written on the day before:

15.3.55

P.S. Reason is entirely on the side of A. Smith & we adopt the other solution only to conform to the customary sense of 'wages' & 'Nat. Income'; but in some cases, with notice given, it will be necessary to depart from it. – As to the practical difficulty of separating 'necessary' subsistence commodities in wages, it is no greater than the existing one of deciding whether 'working clothes' are part of wages – & how to sort out shares if in quality they are better than strictly necessary.

(D3/12/52: 8 (verso); emphases added)

In Sraffa's view, then, the division of the wage into the two components of subsistence and share in the surplus involved a 'practical difficulty', not a theoretical one. Two days later, after having composed drafts of several other sections of his projected book, Sraffa returned once more to this page of his manuscript, making a further addition:

still later, 17.3.55

Most of the following discussion is independent of which of the two definitions of w is adopted, as it is natural this being mainly *a question of statistical application*. But whenever one or the other is specifically involved warning is given.

As regards the *statistical difficulties* of dividing wages [one part in commodities] in this way, they are undoubted: but they are not different in kind from the existing difficulty of deciding whether working clothes or transport to work (in own car?) are or are not part of the wage. The dividing line would be drawn at a different place, but need not be much more blurred.

(D3/12/52: 8, verso; emphasis added)

Five days later Sraffa returned to this problem again, and added:

after still later, 22.3.55

Take care that with, or without, necessaries means two distinct systems, with different algebraic properties. We show that 'basic' commodities have a role greater than luxuries; and surely, according as we include wheat etc. among basics, or not, must have a far reaching influence on the mathematical properties of the system.

(D3/12/52: 8, verso)

Although Sraffa continued to work on his manuscript after his return to Cambridge, he only returned to the issue of gross wages versus subsistence-cum-surplus wages in August 1955, when he made two important decisions. First, he decided for good to make use only of the concept of gross wages.[8] Second, he also decided that because of this decision the distinction between basics and non-basics must be introduced 'at the earliest possible moment, i.e. after the first surplus equations (with wages fixed in kind).[9] And then', he reminded himself, 'discuss the matter on the pros & cons of net or gross wage (this being the main 'con': while the main 'pro' is non-distinguishability of gum-boots etc.)' (D3/12/50: 15).[10] In a manuscript of 4 September 1955 Sraffa then sketched out a first draft of the required discussion of the 'pros & cons' of gross wages versus subsistence-cum-surplus wages:

Gross-wages or surplus-wages

My own inclination would be to take surplus wages. True there would be considerable difficulties of demarcation in distinguishing the two sorts {ªpartsª} of wages, all the greater in so far as we do it *in actual commodities*, which would confront us with the impossible task {ªinsoluble problemª} of *splitting single commodities into basic qualities & surplus qualities* {ªideal partsª} ... {later insertion in the margin: ?} These difficulties however are equally present when the line has to be drawn between articles of workers' consumption and means of production. {later insertion in the margin: a wrinkled line} {...}

whenever a commodity which in one way is part of necessaries {ᵃsubsistenceᵃ}, being consumed in a better quality than is strictly necessary, becomes to that extent part of surplus confronts us with the insoluble problem of *splitting it into* these *two notional parts*

(D3/12/50: 10; emphases added)[11]

This document is interesting, in spite of its unfinished and fragmentary character, because in it Sraffa first set out his idea of 'splitting up' single commodities into two 'notional' or 'ideal' parts. At the same time, the (undated) later annotations seem to indicate doubts about the feasibility of this approach. However, there were good reasons for pursuing further the subsistence-cum-surplus conceptualization of wages, because the adoption of the alternative conceptualization in terms of gross wages had serious implications for Sraffa's newly introduced concept of 'basic' and 'non-basic' commodities:

w, wage or surplus

It would be legitimate to ask, whether the classing of a commodity as basic or non basic is purely arbitrary; and how can the different effect they are alleged to have depend on such a decision & in that case how could any importance be attached to the distinction. The answer is that wage-goods, or necessaries, expelled by the door, re-enter by the window; & their influence on p & r now appears exerted through the fact that in reality, w cannot fall below the level where those goods can be bought by wage earners.

Awkward decision: For it will give the impression that the whole thing is tautological, play with words.

(D3/12/50: 11; emphasis added)[12]

Sraffa, although he was by no means 'happily' rejecting the subsistence-cum-surplus wage conception, did not waver in his decision to adopt the gross wage concept, which 'avoids the need of distinguishing the two parts', as he explained in the following document, where he also reiterated his view that this division must be done in terms of splitting-up 'actual commodities used':

Strictly speaking, we ought to split up the wage and only regard as variable the 'surplus' part. This method, which would be conformable with the standpoint of the classical economists (what we have described as the surplus product coincides with the 'Net Revenue' of Adam Smith and Ricardo) has some advantages. Nevertheless we follow the current practice of taking as 'dividend' the national income, a conception which includes the whole of the wage & thus avoids the need of distinguishing the two parts: this distinction, if relatively clear conceptually, would meet considerable difficulties since necessaries would have to be defined in terms of actual commodities used. (3,000 calories may be agreed as 'necessary', but how to separate them as a commodity from the 'surplus' flavours which pervade them?)

(D3/12/50: 21)[13]

In a further re-draft of this passage (D3/12/71: 9–10), which was carried out in March 1956 (and which the Sraffa catalogue describes as the 'copy used by typist for Sections 1–32' of *Production of Commodities*), Sraffa then adopted the wording which, except for some stylistic changes (see D3/12/72), corresponds to the final text.

Summing up, the following conclusions can be drawn. First, Sraffa reached the decision to adopt the concept of gross wages very reluctantly and only after having carefully contemplated the advantages and drawbacks of the two alternative concepts. Second, for Sraffa the conceptualization in terms of subsistence-cum-surplus wages involved *splitting up the commodities actually produced and consumed into two notional (or ideal) parts.* This division of individual commodities into notional parts he regarded as '*conceptually clear*', but to meet with 'insurmountable obstacles' in '*practical*' or '*statistical* application'. Third, the wording that Sraffa finally adopted in Section 8 is less clear with regard to this division of the wage, *in terms of notional parts of actual commodities*, than his earlier drafts. Fourth, Sraffa dismissed the idea of attempting to overcome the 'statistical difficulties' mentioned by using the device of a 'value concept of wages'.

Before we discuss the implications of these findings for interpreting Sraffa's annotations in Robinson's review article it seems useful to note that the formalization of subsistence-cum-surplus wages proposed by Roncaglia (1978: 86) does not conform to Sraffa's ideas, and at any rate provides no solution to the 'insurmountable obstacles' in practical applications foreseen by him. Roncaglia suggested that the alternative wage conceptualization in terms of subsistence-cum-surplus wages could be easily introduced into Sraffa's price system by introducing the notion of a minimum wage rate (the 'subsistence wage') which is determined as the production price of the commodity 'labour-power', p_l, from the following system of equations,

$$\boldsymbol{A}\boldsymbol{p}\,(1+r)+\boldsymbol{l}\,(p_l+w)=\boldsymbol{p}$$
$$\boldsymbol{a}_l\boldsymbol{p}\,(1+r)+l_l\,(p_l+w)=p_l$$

where $A \in R^{n \times n}$ is a square semi-positive input matrix, $\boldsymbol{l} \in R^n$ is a semi-positive vector of labour inputs, and $\boldsymbol{a}_l \in R^n$ is a semi-positive vector of subsistence requirements. In this formulation it is simply taken for granted that the subsistence requirements can somehow be specified in commodity terms, and the problem of the interdependence between subsistence requirements and surplus consumption noted by Robinson is simply not addressed at all.

Let us return, then, to the annotated passage in the typescript of Robinson's review article. The interpretation suggested by the draft versions of Section 8 reproduced above is that Sraffa viewed Robinson's objection to the concept of subsistence-cum-surplus wages as misplaced, because to him it was always clear that the subsistence requirements must be specified, not in terms of *hypothetical* consumption goods baskets which could only just satisfy the workers' physical needs, but in terms of notional parts of the commodities *actually* produced and consumed in the economic system under consideration. Accordingly, the problem of an incompatibility between given subsistence requirements (in terms of, say, given amounts of 'wheat') and consumption out of surplus wages (in terms of amounts of 'beef') could not possibly arise at all, and therefore could play no role in connection with the 'awkward decision' of choosing between the two alternative conceptualizations of wages.

At this point it seems useful to discuss briefly the interpretation of the subsistence-cum-surplus wage concept proposed by Newman, who regarded Robinson's objection to this concept as well-taken. He suggested that the concept could be rationalized only by presupposing the existence of two separate groups of labourers:

> Sraffa argues that when there is surplus in the system, it is only reasonable to expect that labor will share in it. He wistfully lingers over the possibility of dividing the wage into an 'inter-industry' and a 'surplus' part, but rejects it in order to conform to common usage. Such a division would seem reasonable if there were two non-competing groups of laborers – say slaves and freemen – but is (as Mrs. *Robinson* remarks p. 54) very artificial otherwise.
>
> (Newman, 1962: 68)

From an analytical point of view, Newman's interpretative suggestion can indeed be said to provide a solution to the interdependence problem noted by Robinson, because it separates the subsistence requirements (of the 'slaves') from the demand for wage goods that comes out of the surplus wages (of the 'freemen'), thus breaking the interdependence between the workers' subsistence consumption and their surplus consumption. However, Newman failed to perceive that Robinson's problem does not arise at all if one starts from the *given quantities of commodities actually produced* and defines the subsistence requirements in terms of notional parts of the latter: Sraffa sought the solution to the problem not by breaking the interdependence but rather by fully acknowledging it.

Some further discussion of Newman's interpretative suggestion may be instructive in order to clarify the meaning of Sraffa's notion of 'necessities for subsistence'. Newman's suggestion is clearly related to his view that the economic system contemplated by Sraffa up to Section 7 of his book refers to a 'slave economy' (Newman, 1962: 66–68). Now Sraffa, in an early draft of Appendix D, also related the concept of subsistence wages to slave economies when he wrote: 'The treatment of wages as part of the r.{aw} m.{aterial} of prod.{uction} came natural to writers to whom slavery was not too remote a conception. Thus, Sir W.{illiam} Petty says ... & Cantillon ...' (D3/12/98: 8).[14] However, Sraffa's reference to Petty and Cantillon in this document, as well as to Smith and Ricardo in the documents quoted above, make it perfectly clear that the concept was not meant to refer to slave economies only, but also to the Classical economists' notion of subsistence wages of 'doubly-free wage labourers' in capitalistic systems. For Sraffa, the notion of 'necessaries of consumption' or 'necessaries for subsistence' was meant to comprise the quantities of commodities which have to be used up by 'those who work' (1960: 3), that is, the quantities of commodities which are 'technically' necessary for production, independently of the particular institutional arrangements and social organization of the economic system under consideration (see, on this, also Arena, 2014).[15]

Further interpretative hints from the Sraffa–Robinson correspondence: the 'money-value of labour' versus the 'labour-value of money'

In Sraffa's papers is some correspondence with Robinson which provides further interpretative hints for the explanation of Sraffa's reaction to her statements on gross wages versus subsistence-cum-surplus wages. Some of this correspondence is from the spring and summer of 1960, that is, from the period immediately preceding Sraffa's annotations in Robinson's typescript in August 1960. However, there is also an exchange of letters from March 1951, in which their later disagreements with regard to the treatment of wages are already foreshadowed.

Robinson's reaction to Sraffa's 'Introduction' to Ricardo's Principles

As is well known, Sraffa was very secretive about his own work and most reluctant to discuss it with others – and in particular with Robinson. He only gave her an advance copy of his 'Introduction' to vol. 1 of the Ricardo edition shortly before it was published, on the occasion of a meeting on 24 March 1951 in the late afternoon, as an entry in his diary shows: '5 Joan (dato bozza Intr. I)' (E 23). Interestingly, Sraffa left Cambridge very early in the morning on the following day, 25 March, in order to spend the Easter vacation in Italy. Preserved in his papers is a letter from Robinson, dated 26 March 1951 (which Sraffa only received in Rome on 28 March, as he noted in his diary). It reads:

> My dear Piero – I cannot wait for your return to tell you how much I am delighted with your Introduction. {. . .}
>
> I am struck by the thought that the real 'Keynesian revolution' was to substitute the money-value of labour (the wage rate) for the labour-value of money. The point is that money has not got a labour cost. It is a social convention, like an alphabet. Each affair has a certain cost of upkeep (gold-mines – school teachers) but nothing corresponding to a labour cost per bushel. {. . .}
>
> Much looking forward to chewing this over when you return.
>
> (D3/11/83: 45)

The impression one gets from the available documents is that Sraffa had deliberately chosen the timing of making his Introduction available and his absence from Cambridge so as to avoid having to 'chew this over' with Robinson in private conversation. His reply to her letter, dated 31 March 1951 and sent from Rome, has been preserved in the Robinson Papers:

> My dear Joan,
>
> Many thanks for your letter. {...} Your contrast between the labour value of money & the money value of labour looks very neat but I think is totally misleading, as the word 'value' has entirely different senses in the two cases (indeed, if it hadn't, the two phrases would be identical). {...}
>
> (JVR/vii/431/35–6)

The term 'labour-value of money' in Robinson's letter refers, of course, to Ricardo's application of the labour theory of value to the determination of the value of gold (or money), whereas the term 'money-value of labour' refers to the *money* wage rate. Contrasting these two terms is misleading, because the money wage rate is not a proper value concept[16] – it could be contrasted more appropriately with the *real* wage rate, as a bundle of consumption goods.

Robinson's comments and queries on Production of Commodities

As is well known, Sraffa also refrained from discussing his constructive work on *Production of Commodities* with Joan Robinson, and there is no indication that she was shown any draft versions of the book (or even of parts of it). However, as an entry in Sraffa's diary shows, Robinson was given an advance copy of the book on 12 May 1960.[17] She began to study it carefully immediately upon receipt and in the course of the following week sent Sraffa a set of notes and queries, on 14, 15, 18 and 19 May, on 'points that I am puzzled about' (D3/12/111: 324). The following two notes are related to Sraffa's treatment of wages. On 15 May Robinson asked:

> What is the status of the assumption that there is at least one basic commodity?
>
> When there is one staple food, corn, it enters into all commodities via labour. If there are several staples, e.g. wheat and potatoes, no one is necessarily a basic. Moreover in the book no commodity is treated as basic merely by virtue of being a wage good. (*This is the great point that emancipates Ricardo's system and makes it applicable to the modern world.*)
>
> (D3/12/11: 325–6; emphasis added)

On 18 May Sraffa received another query from Joan Robinson, again relating to his treatment of wages:

> Is this right?
>
> J{oan}.
>
> Wages and the Standard of life
>
> A higher wage is associated with lower consumption per head by workers when the proportion of labour is sufficiently higher in the production of wage goods than in the Standard commodity.
>
> Adam Smith type of economies of scale are ruled out by the assumptions. All the same the composition of the basic part of national income may affect relative prices. To separate out this question compare two economies alike in every respect except that in one capitalists and workers consume the same composite commodity and in the other sharply different ones.
>
> Starting the two economies in identical positions, alter the wage rate equally in both. In one the composition of output remains unchanged and particular changes in relative prices occur, as analysed in the book. In the other economy the changes in prices will be different.
>
> Is this, in your view (a) true but uninteresting, or (b) untrue?
>
> (D3/12/111: 328–9)

There is no record of Sraffa's answers to these queries, and in fact he seems not to have discussed any of her comments on his book with Joan Robinson until some two weeks later, as his diary entry for 29 May 1960 shows: '2–7:30 Joan walk Hardwick e discusso, ahimè, il mio lavoro {and discussing, unfortunately,[18] my work}!' (E32); in addition, Sraffa also noted in his diary that later that evening they had 'champagne in hall' (E32). Although their friendship remained intact, these discussions must have been painful not only for Sraffa, but also for Robinson, as her reaction in the first paragraph of the following note, which she sent to Sraffa on 31 May 1960, shows. Interestingly, the second paragraph of this note again concerns the treatment of wages and basically repeats the point about the 'Keynes-Classics' distinction she had already made some ten years earlier in her first reaction to Sraffa's 'Introduction'. However, instead of contrasting Keynes's 'money-value of labour' with Ricardo's 'labour-value of money', she was now applying the contrast between *money* wages and *real* wages to herself and Sraffa:

> Dear Piero,
>
> I have always been baffled because, while your ideas are just what I want (apart from a few pts {points} that are above my head) you do not like mine.

I think I now see where the difference lies. I should say that a rate of profit is essentially a capitalist phenomenon, and capitalism requires wages to be agreed in some form or other of money (maybe purely material) so that the real wage emerges from the prices (the rate of profit being given from outside the system of prices).

Thus the device of putting wage goods into the non-basic category, subject to the condition that the real wage cannot fall below a certain level (which can be given a rather vague sense in this context) is to my mind absolutely essential, while you regard it merely as convenient for exposition.

(D3/12/111: 337–8)

There is, again, no record of Sraffa's reaction to this note. Presumably, his response was given only verbally in private conversation, if at all. What is important for us is to notice that this letter, together with the 1951 letter on Sraffa's 'Introduction' and Robinson's notes and queries of mid-May 1960, can also help in interpreting Sraffa's annotations in her review essay. The two letters show that Robinson attached great significance to the fact that in capitalistic systems wage bargaining takes place over *money wages*, so that the real wage only emerges *ex post*. She associated this insight specifically with Keynes, and saw it to be in sharp contrast with the classical economists' treatment of wages in terms of *given* subsistence requirements, i.e. of *given real wages*. In her view – and this is reflected also in the passage of her review essay annotated by Sraffa – it was 'absolutely essential', in order to 'emancipate Ricardo's system and make it applicable to the modern world', to put 'wage goods into the non-basic category'.

Sraffa was not of this opinion. In his understanding the classical economists, most notably Smith and Ricardo, had not confined wages to strict necessities, but had already allowed for a share of the workers in the distribution of the surplus. They also knew, of course, that the wage bargaining process concerns the determination of money wages, and although this fact was perhaps not emphasized as much by them as it was later by Marx, it certainly cannot be considered as a fundamental characteristic of Keynes's economic theory, which sets it apart from the classical approach. More importantly, Sraffa insisted on the fact that subsistence requirements are essentially basic, because he regarded the means of production *and* the means of subsistence as 'technical necessities' which are 'objectively' required in order to produce the given quantities of commodities, independently of the institutional arrangements and social organization prevailing in the economic system under consideration.

Also, in Sraffa's understanding the treatment of wages in terms of subsistence-cum-surplus wages would not undermine his research strategy of analysing the effects of changes in distribution on relative prices on the assumption of 'given quantities'. This research strategy can be linked to Ricardo's method, in Chapter I of the *Principles*, of analysing the impact of distributional changes on relative prices for given quantities of commodities produced and for given methods of production. In fact, the method of 'given quantities' adopted by Sraffa is reminiscent of the procedure adopted by Ricardo in Section VII of the chapter 'On Value' of his *Principles*, where Ricardo contemplated the case of a change in the proportional distribution of income when, due to some improvements in the methods of production, the absolute quantities of commodities produced have been doubled:

Of every hundred hats, coats, and quarters of corn produced, if

The labourers had before 25
The landlords 25
And the capitalists 50
100

And if, after the commodities were double the quantity, of every 100

The labourers had only 22
The landlords 22
And the capitalists 56
100

In that case I should say, that wages and rent had fallen and profits risen; though, in consequence of the abundance of commodities, the quantity paid to the labourer and landlord would have increased in the proportion of 25 to 44.

(1951: 50)

In this passage Ricardo proposed to analyse changes in the proportional distribution of income by holding the overall composition of consumption constant: a change in the shares going to each of the three classes is supposed to leave the composition of the 'gross produce' unchanged.

Conclusion

Joan Robinson's objection to the use of the concept of subsistence-cum-surplus wages, according to which the subsistence requirements cannot be taken as given quantities of commodities any more when the workers participate in the sharing out of the surplus, has widely been regarded as well-taken (and this view was shared also by the present writer). The implication is that one is forced to adopt the concept of gross wages, because of the *theoretical* problems associated with the alternative wage conceptualization. As the present paper has shown, Sraffa did not consider Robinson's objection pertinent, because to him it was clear that the subsistence requirements must be specified in terms of notional parts of the commodities actually produced and consumed in the economic system under consideration. The adoption of the subsistence-cum-surplus wage concept therefore would not have undermined his research strategy of analysing the impact of distributional changes on relative prices for given methods of production and given quantities of commodities produced.

Notes

1 I would like to thank the staff in the Wren Library at Trinity College for most helpful assistance in the preparation of this paper and Tony Aspromourgos and Heinz D. Kurz for critical comments on a previous draft.

2 See, for the typescript version, the document D3/12/111: 344–355 in the Sraffa papers and, for the published version, Robinson (1961).

3 In addition, Sraffa also annotated the following statement, which however is not contained in the final version, with a wrinkled line in the margin: 'Sraffa has removed the assumption of a technically determined physical real wage' (D3/12/111: 351). The third passage he annotated recurs in the published version, unchanged:

> Can the equalisation of the rate of profit throughout the economy mean anything except the equalisation of expected {last word underlined} profits on new investment in various lines? If the rate of profit has changed during the life-time of machines in existence this year, there is no equality between expected and realised profits in any one line – why should there be equality between realised {last word underlined} profits in different lines? {wrinkled line in the margin and an arrow from the word 'realised' in the last sentence to the word 'expected' in the first sentence}.
>
> (D3/12/111: 351)

In this case the interpretation of Sraffa's annotations is obvious: he considered Robinson's argument inconsistent, because it involved a switch from '*expected* profits on new investment' to '*realised* profits'.

4 This is the first draft of what was to become the final version, but Sraffa had of course worked on the problem of the treatment of wages much earlier. The distinction between gross wages and subsistence-cum-surplus wages had in fact been extensively discussed by him already in manuscripts written in 1923–1924; for a summary account of these documents see Levrero (2015).

5 The material omitted here was later used in the composition of Sections 10 and 13 of *Production of Commodities*.

6 The explicit reference to Ricardo's notion of 'proportional' or 'proportionate' wages is not to be found in the final version of *Production of Commodities*, where the concept is introduced in Sections 10, 12 and 13.

7 Here the reference – left unspecified by Sraffa – could be to Ricardo (1951: 348, note) and to Smith (1976, I.viii.15–16).

8 In fact, Sraffa had effectively made this decision already much earlier, namely when he began to elaborate his third equations' in 1929 (see Kurz and Salvadori, 2010: 206), and when he finally decided to treat wages as entirely paid out of the net product in late 1943 (see Kurz, 2007 [2006]: 146). What he decided in August 1955 was thus not to adopt the gross wage concept (this had long since been decided), but merely not to pursue further the statement in document D3/12/8 (verso), quoted above, that 'in some cases, with notice given, it will be necessary to depart' from the concept of gross wages.

9 For the introduction of the basics/non-basics distinction at this point, see document (D3/12/71: 9).

10 The word 'this' in 'this being the main con' obviously refers to the fact that adopting the notion of gross wages implies that wage goods are relegated to the category of non-basics. The main argument in favour of gross wages is that 'gum-boots', i.e. working clothes, cannot easily be classified as necessary means of production, in particular if their quality is better than strictly necessary.

11 All the documents in folder D3/12/50 were kept by Sraffa in an envelope inscribed 'Rubbish. (Transferred to clean copy) 1955 drafts etc.' (D3/12/50: 1). The 'clean copy'

referred to (see D3/12/71) contains the material which was to form pages 1–23 in the final version of the book; it was written in March 1956 and then given to a typist.

12 For a variant of this passage, see D3/12/50: 12.

13 A variant of this passage is in document D3/12/50: 20.

14 For a variant of this formulation, see also the document D3/12/98: 15.

15 This independence of institutional arrangements and social organisation is also evident in the wording that Sraffa adopted in Section 1, where commodities are assumed to be 'used, *in part as sustenance for those who work*, and for the rest as means of production' (Sraffa, 1960: 3; emphasis added). What this wording was meant to convey is that it does not matter whether 'those who work' are slaves, working animals, kibbutzniks, or 'freemen' – what matters are only the amounts of commodities which are objectively necessary, and thus must necessarily be used up, in order to produce the given quantities of commodities.

16 See Marx's critical disquisitions on the notion 'value of labour' in Chapter 19 of vol. I of *Capital* (1954).

17 See Sraffa's diary entry for 12 May 1960: 'To Joan, advance copy of my book' (E 32). The official publication dates of *Production of Commodities* were 27 May 1960 for the English edition and 6 June 1960 for the Italian edition. (In a letter to John Hicks Sraffa noted that 'Austin Robinson read the MS as a Syndic of the Press' prior to publication (D3/12/111: 269). However, there is no indication that he made the book manuscript available to his wife.)

18 The word 'unfortunately' does not fully convey the meaning of the Italian exclamation 'ahimè', which refers to something that is painful to oneself. (I am grateful to Nerio Naldi for pointing this out to me.)

References

Arena, R. (2014), The Role of Technical and Social Factors in the Distinction between Necessities and Surplus: Classical Economics after Sraffa, Contribution to the Conference 'What Have We Learnt on Classical Economy since Sraffa?', 16 and 17 October 2014, University of Paris Ouest Nanterre La Défense.

Kurz, H. D. (2007 [2006]), The Agents of Production are the Commodities Themselves. On the Classical Theory of Production, Distribution, and Value, in H. D. Kurz and N. Salvadori, *Interpreting Classical Economics. Studies in Long-period Analysis*, London: Routledge, pp. 131–158.

Kurz, H. D. and Salvadori, N. (1995), *Theory of Production. A Long-Period Analysis*, Cambridge: Cambridge University Press.

Kurz, H. D. and Salvadori, N. (2010), Sraffa and the Labour Theory of Value: A Few Observations, in J. Vint, J. S. Metcalfe, H. D. Kurz, N. Salvadori and P. A. Samuelson (eds), *Economic Theory and Economic Thought. Essays in Honour of Ian Steedman*, London: Routledge, pp. 189–215.

Levrero, E. S. (2015), Sraffa on Taxable Income and its Fiscal Policy Implications, Paper presented at the 19th Annual Conference of the *European Society for the History of Economic Thought*, 'Great Controversies in Economics', at Roma Tre University, Rome, 14–16 May 2015.

Marx, K. (1954), *Capital*, Vol. I, Moscow: Progress Publishers.

Newman, P. (1962), Production of Commodities by Means of Commodities, *Schweizerische Zeitschrift für Volkswirtschaft und Statistik*, **98**: 58–75.

Ricardo, D. (1951), *On the Principles of Political Economy and Taxation*, Vol. I of *The Works and Correspondence of David Ricardo*, edited by Piero Sraffa with the collaboration of Maurice H. Dobb, Cambridge: Cambridge University Press.

Robinson, J. (1961), Prelude to a Critique of Economic Theory, *Oxford Economic Papers*, **13**: 53–58.

Roncaglia, A. (1978), *Sraffa and the Theory of Prices*, New York: John Wiley and Sons.

Smith, A. (1976), *An Inquiry into the Nature and Causes of the Wealth of Nations*, Vol. I, *The Glasgow Edition of the Works and Correspondence of Adam Smith*, edited by R. H. Campbell, A. S. Skinner and W. B. Todd, Oxford: Oxford University Press.

Sraffa, P. (1951), Introduction, in *The Works and Correspondence of David Ricardo*, edited by P. Sraffa with the collaboration of M. H. Dobb, Vol. I, Cambridge: Cambridge University Press, pp. xii–lxii.

Sraffa, P. (1960), *Production of Commodities by Means of Commodities*, Cambridge: Cambridge University Press.

18 A Sraffian approach to financial regulation

Carlo Panico, Antonio Pinto,
Martín Puchet Anyul and
Marta Vazquez Suarez[1]

Introduction

The study of the classical tradition has been at the centre of Neri Salvadori's writings. To acknowledge his authority, we present in what follows an interpretation of the evolution of financial regulation after the Second World War, which is in line with the work of Piero Sraffa and of the classical tradition.

Several studies on the causes of the recent crisis focus on the changes that occurred in financial regulation. To evaluate the role of these changes and the content of the reforms introduced after the crisis, this paper identifies the main features of two regimes, adopted in the USA before and after the 1970s, to organize this aspect of monetary policy.

The literature examines financial regulation by focusing on the measures that can prevent the managers of financial firms, 'acting in their own interests, deviate from what a social planner would have them do' (Hanson *et al.*, 2010: 1–2). It concentrates on the identification of the appropriate mix between the use of instruments that generate disciplined behaviour through 'market mechanisms' and through 'supervisory discretion based on the competent evaluations of independent regulators'. Before the crisis the search for the 'right incentives' focused on 'micro-prudential regulation', i.e. on preventing the costly failure of individual financial firms. After the crisis many observers underlined that the search for incentives has to be applied to 'macro-prudential regulation' too. The latter seeks to limit the extent to which adverse developments hitting one financial firm can lead to problems for other firms (see Hanson *et al.*, 2010; Goodhart, 2010a: 179; Kashyap *et al.*, 2011).

Other authors (Barth *et al.*, 2009; Caprio, 2009; Levine, 2010; Barth *et al.*, 2011; Admati and Hellwig, 2013), however, point out that this standpoint fails to identify a major cause of the recent crisis, i.e. the malfunction of the governance of regulation.

> The collapse of the global financial system reflects a systemic failure of the governance of financial regulation – the system associated with designing, enacting, implementing and reforming financial policies. ... In contrast to common narrative, my analyses ... indicate that ... failures in the governance

of financial regulation helped cause the global financial crisis. ... This
conclusion ... has material implications for reforming financial regulation.

(Levine, 2010: 1)

Levine (2010) and Barth *et al.* (2011) provide several examples that illustrate
how the financial authorities and their political overseers did not act in the interest of the public. By using evidence from official documents and archives, these
authors argue that the authorities introduced policies that destabilized the financial
system. What is more, they preserved them when, before the crisis, they learned
that these policies were distorting the flows of credit towards questionable ends
and went so far as to provide Congress with false information in order to keep
them in place. These authors conclude that an assessment of the causes of the
crisis must inquire why policymakers made these choices and that it is necessary
to strengthen the independence of the authorities from the pressures of the financial industry in order to correct the governance of regulation, improve the reforms
proposed and adopted, and reduce the probability of future crises.

Admati and Hellwig (2013) do not present evidence from official documents.
Yet, they also argue that it is necessary to strengthen the independence of the
authorities from the pressures of the financial industry. For them (see Admati and
Hellwig, 2013: 204), the influence of the banking industry over politicians and
regulators favoured, after the 1970s, the change towards a new regime of financial
regulation, which failed to set and enforce proper rules to prevent the reckless
behaviour of bankers.

Banks operating under Basel II ... found many creative ways to have very
high leverage and to evade the requirements by shifting risks to others or
hiding them behind flawed risk models or misleading credit ratings.

(Admati and Hellwig, 2013: 96)

These authors suggest that the ties between the banking industry, the political
world and the financial authorities still affect decisions in this area. Basel III has
tried to deal with some abuses in this area, but several weaknesses remain since
these agreements too are

the result of an intense lobbying campaign mounted by bankers against any
major change in regulation. This campaign has continued since. By now even
the full implementation of Basel III is in doubt.

(Admati and Hellwig, 2013: 96)

For Levine, Barth, Caprio, Admati, Hellwig and others, it is necessary to
strengthen the independence of the authorities and of supervisors, making them
more capable to resist the pressures of the banking industry in order to focus on
the public interest.

We can have a financial system that works much better for the economy than
the current system without sacrificing anything. But achieving this requires

that politicians and regulators focus on the public interest and carry out the necessary steps.

(Admati and Hellwig, 2013: 228)

The analyses of these authors show that it can be misleading to examine the evolution of financial regulation without considering the power relations affecting legislation and their effects on income distribution. Nonetheless, the mainstream literature tends to disregard these issues, which are instead at the centre of the stage in some critical works.

For Palma (2009: 832), the study of the events leading to the crisis makes theoretical sense if it considers the political settlements and distributional changes in which these financial phenomena occurred. Other authors (see Panico *et al.*, 2012; Panico *et al.*, 2013) took a similar standpoint moving from Sraffa's work and from his approach to monetary problems. They show that the expansion of the financial sector affects the level of production and can generate changes in the income shares that can be unfavourable to workers.

By moving again from Sraffa's approach to monetary problems, we argue in what follows that, before the crisis, financial regulation evolved from a 'discretionary' to a 'rules-based' regime, i.e. from a regime based on the discretionary powers of the authorities over the managers of financial firms to one based on the respect of capital coefficients. Much literature assumes that this change was introduced to pursue the public interest. We argue instead that it also reflects the attempts of the financial sector to improve its income share and that it was favoured by the pressures of this sector, which benefited from the expansion of its activities allowed by the new forms of regulation. The conversion to the new regime was gradual and reflected the strengthening position of the financial industry in the economy and in society. It was attended by scarce attention of the dominant literature to the questions raised by Levine and his colleagues. This scarce attention also influenced the reforms proposed and adopted after the crisis, in spite of the formal acknowledgement by official documents of the need to reinforce the supervisory powers of the authorities over the managers of financial firms.

The paper is organized thus: the next section describes Sraffa's approach to money and banking. The third section describes how the literature classifies the instruments of regulation. The fourth, fifth and sixth sections describe the changes that occurred in financial regulation before the crisis. The seventh section deals with some of the reforms proposed after the crisis. The final section concludes.

Sraffa's approach to money and banking

Sraffa conceived income distribution as a historical and conventional phenomenon. For him, the technical conditions of production and the availability of resources affect the *relation* between distributive variables but do not fix their *levels*, which depend on how the conflicting relations among different groups and institutions are solved over a certain period of time. To identify the rules and the institutions that can best suit the financial needs of a country, Sraffa did not refer to an optimal or efficient configuration of the markets, but evaluated the most convenient configuration on the basis of the historical evolution of the economy and of the country. In his work the provision of credit was crucial for economic development and the banking sector was seen as an industry, which sells to the other industries services that are necessary for productive activity and, as any other industry, tries to, and often can, affect policy decisions in its favour.

Sraffa held this position since his earlier contributions in the 1920s, even if at that time he was not aware of its theoretical implications. His 1922 articles on the Italian banking crisis, the 1923–1927 writings on the economic policy of the fascist government and his Lecture notes on 'Continental banking', presented in Cambridge during the academic years 1928–1929, 1929–1930 and 1930–1931, focus on the formation of monetary interventions and on the benefits they offer to different entities and groups. In these analyses the evolution of financial markets and monetary policy are the results of the complex historical re-composition of the relations among groups (workers, owners and managers of industrial, financial and other firms) and economic and political institutions.

His writings show a detailed knowledge of the working of the banking system and of the exchange markets (see Sraffa Papers, D3/12/68,2; D3/12/78,6 and 13; D3/12/111). They argue that monetary events, like inflation and deflation, and monetary policies and legislation, are part of the processes that emerge when the claims of the different social groups over the distributive shares are incompatible. Monetary events, policies and legislation influence social conflicts and contribute to the determination of what is considered the *normal* or *equilibrium* level of distributive variables.

At the same time, Sraffa argued that the formation of monetary policies and legislation is affected by the attempts of the most powerful pressure groups to shape the distributive rules according to their material interests. In his 1922 essay on the Italian banking crisis Sraffa (1922: 191–197) pointed out in which cases the Italian Government acted to protect powerful pressure groups at the expenses of society as a whole. He argued for a general tendency towards the formation of large and diversified financial groups able to influence the exertion of power, to control relevant sections of the economy, of the media and of the political world and to disguise the aims of their initiatives from the majority of the population to such an extent as to represent a danger for democracy.

> The general tendency seems to be towards the ... formation of large 'groups' of companies of the most varied kinds concentrated around one or more banks, mutually related by the exchange of shares and by the appointments of Directors common to them. Within these 'groups' the various interests are all equally subject to the interests of a few individuals who control the whole group ... Very little is known ... about these groups ... What the public knows and feels ... is the enormous financial and political power which they have and the frequent use they make of it to influence both the foreign and home policy of the government in favour of their own interests. Each group keeps several press organs which support its policy, and some of the

accusations made against certain Ministries of being actuated by the interests not of a class, but of private concerns, and of favouring one financial group against another, have no doubt a basis of truth.

(Sraffa, 1922: 196)

In subsequent writings he further analysed the questions of liquidity, solvability and exertion of power, relating them to the technical operation of the financial system, and touched on issues that are still relevant in monetary debates. He said that the ability of the banking industry to affect the exertion of power can be a major problem for the working of the financial system and hinted at the necessity that legal provisions make financial authorities as independent as possible from political and economic pressures.[2]

Sraffa's approach to monetary problems leads to an analysis of financial regulation with a different perspective from that proposed by mainstream literature. It avoids the reference to an optimal configuration of the markets and escapes considering only the incentives that can best complement the operation of the markets, when these are not perfectly competitive. It moves instead from the historical evolution of the economy and of its institutions and takes into account rules and incentives that can make the working of financial markets compatible with the political agreements reached by the Government and other sectors of society over distributive rules, social welfare and development.

The laws on regulation introduce rules and controls over the exercise of powers in the formation and execution of financial contracts and are shaped by the agreements among the different sectors of the economy and the monetary and fiscal authorities over their material interests and their expectations on social and economic development. According to this approach, then, the forms assumed by financial regulation depend on the ability of the different sectors or groups to impose the distributive rules that are most convenient to them, rather than on the need to complement the imperfect operation of the markets.

Sraffa's approach is close to some institutional and evolutionary approaches but does not coincide with all of them. Already in the 1940s, Medina Echavarría, a Spanish sociologist who lived exiled in Mexico, noticed that classical economic theories, to which Sraffa's approach is related, differ from those of Commons and Veblen. Classical theories recognize the relevance of individual behaviour and assume that it depends on the legal and social frameworks in the sense that it is subject to the conventions that historically emerge from social interaction. In these theories the formation of rules, legislation and institutions is an integral part of the analysis. It is the result of the conflicting relations among the different sectors and reflects their ability to enact rules and agreements over distribution and the future of society, which are functional to their material interests.[3] For Medina Echavarría, Commons and Veblen assume instead that the legal and institutional framework emerges from a process of social selection, which favours the ability of individuals and organizations to adapt to the environment in which they operate.[4] Playing down the distributive implications of the legal framework, this approach overlooks that conventions and institutions reflect the relative power of the different sectors and that their maintenance (or rejection) depends on the value judgements prevailing in the society, i.e. on the common evaluations of the rules and agreements enacted over a certain historical period, rather than on their adequacy to favour social selection.

Sraffa paid attention to the role of value judgements in economic theorizing and, in order to limit their influence, examined how other sciences were dealing with them. He read the contributions embracing 'an objectivist philosophy' (Whitehead, 1926: 124) adopted in different sciences by Hertz, Helmholtz, Poincaré, Picard, Simiand, Labriola, Heisenberg, Dirac, Bridgman, Whyte, etc. According to this approach, scientific research must move from observable magnitudes and must look for 'efficient causes', which relate present events to existing material elements or facts of the past, instead of 'final causes', which relate present events to perceptions or foresight of future acts (see Kurz and Salvadori, 2005). The material basis of the objectivist approach prevents the formation of theories rooted in subjective and elusive factors that favour the intrusion of ideological elements.

When dealing with distributive problems, however, the use of what Sraffa called 'an entirely objective point of view' raised a question that, as Davis (2012) points out, he considered in a 1931 unpublished manuscript (Sraffa, D3/12/7: 161). Dealing with production and distribution, he noticed that since any effect must have an efficient cause, there must be correspondence between the material inputs of production (the causes) and the objects produced (the effects), according to the rule 'production can transform objects, but not create them'. How then can any surplus come about from the production process and be distributed to the different social groups? Sraffa's solution of this conundrum was to consider that the economic field is 'in communication with the world'. It is an open system within which 'outside causes' operate. In the case of the production process the outside causes are the historical elements that affect the *level* of distributive variables. They allow the identification of the surplus within the social product.

This solution allowed Sraffa to reconcile history with the materialism of the objectivist philosophy. To overtake the limits of this approach he elaborated new conceptions and anticipated a philosophical position, known as 'supervenience physicalism', developed by Davidson and Dennett in the 1970s and 1980s (Davidson, 1970; Dennett, 1987). This view, today widely held, is 'central to understanding the nature and role of modern science' (Davis, 2012: 15) and can provide a solid scientific basis on which to examine the evolution of financial regulation.

A classification of the instruments of regulation

To develop Sraffa's approach we analysed, in a recent paper (see Panico *et al.*, 2013), the evolution of financial regulation in the USA since the 1930s. We traced how regulation moved from a regime based on the discretional powers of the authorities over the managers of financial firms to a regime based on fixed capital coefficients by describing how administrative decisions and legislation affected

Table 18.1 A classification of the tools of regulation

Structural regulation	Prudential regulation	Management and resolution of the crises
Group 1	**Group 2**	**Group 4**
1. controls of entry 2. limits on economies of scale 3. limits on economies of scope and diversification 4. limits on pricing (interest ceilings)	5. capital requirements 6. disclosure requirements 7. bank examination (auditing, stress tests, etc.) **Group 3**	9. liabilities insurance 10. financial infrastructures
	8. supervision, which can be based on the discretionary power of the authorities or on controls on the application of fixed rules	

its organization. Our analysis extended a classification of the tools of regulation proposed by Mishkin (2001) and used by White (2009) to identify three periods in the evolution of financial regulation in the USA:

- the New Deal or Bretton Woods era (from the 1930s to 1970)
- the Post New Deal era (from 1971 to 1990, era that we call 'transition period')
- the Contemporary era (from 1991 to the recent financial crisis).

The instruments of financial regulation are grouped in the three categories (see Table 18.1): structural regulation, prudent regulation and management and resolution of financial firms' crisis. Structural regulation designs the financial sector in order to discipline its working. Prudential regulation aims at identifying and controlling the risk exposure of individual firms and of the whole system. The management and resolution of crises aim at reducing the costs and the damage of a distress when it occurs.

Group 1 contains tools of structural regulation ('*control of entry*', '*limits on economies of scale*', '*limits on economies of scope and diversification*', '*limits on pricing*', e.g. interest ceilings) that can be used to control the degree of competition among financial firms.

Group 2 contains some tools of prudential regulation ('*capital requirements*', '*disclosure requirements*', '*bank examination*', e.g. auditing, stress tests, etc.) that strengthen market discipline. They enhance the ability of depositors and other operators to evaluate the risk exposure of financial firms, thus reducing the degree of asymmetry in the distribution of information between sellers and buyers of financial services.

In recent years the literature has paid great attention to the instruments of *Group 2*. Disclosure requirements have been diversified and re-named as 'conduct-of-business'. They have become the subject of a large set of legislation (see de Haan *et al.*, 2009: 312–317) and now include:

- *transparency* in the provision of information to customers and shareholders
- *quality and objectivity in the provision of advice*, which is considered to be different from the provision of information
- *duty of care* towards customers, which aims at enhancing responsible behaviour by requiring financial institutions to adhere to a reasonable standard of care while dealing with their customers.

In some countries 'conduct-of-business' has been separated from the other instruments and entrusted to a different body of regulators (see de Haan *et al.*, 2009: 317–321).

Group 3 contains instruments of prudential regulation aiming at reducing the probability of systemic distress by allowing the authorities to assess beforehand the management's exposure to risk. In Mishkin's classification it is listed as 'supervision'. It may be 'discretionary' or 'rules-based' and may be enforced by the imposition of penalties. To make the enforcement effective, legislation may endow the authorities with different degrees of power over the management of financial firms. In some countries it may even allow the authorities to dismiss and replace the managers of private enterprises. The content of legislation on these matters plays a relevant role in defining the relations of power between the different actors of regulation.

Mishkin's classification of the tools that can be used for the management and resolution of financial crises (*Group 4*) only includes 'liabilities insurance', which aims at reducing the probability of bank runs by protecting depositors from the loss of their assets. Since the crisis, the literature has paid great attention to new 'financial infrastructures'. The literature has proposed the introduction of central counterparties of financial networks, the establishment of a temporary bridge bank and of firm-specific 'recovery and resolution plans', including measures like the 'accumulation of bank-financed orderly liquidation funds' and the 'prior completion of firms' 'living will' or 'funeral plans', considered able to limit contagions (see Goodhart, 2010b: 12–13).

For most literature, a major issue of financial regulation is to identify the appropriate mix between *Groups 2* and *3*, i.e. between market discipline and supervisory discretion based on the competent evaluations of independent regulators.

Regulation during the New Deal or Bretton Woods era

During the New Deal or Bretton Woods era, governments and societies showed limited faith in market discipline. Legislation imposed an approach to regulation that aimed at reinforcing the position of the authorities by fortifying their discretionary powers over the managers of financial firms and by avoiding the fact that the financial sector grew more than other sectors. To achieve these results, an important use was made of the instruments listed in *Groups 1, 3 and 4*.[5] Those listed in *Group 2* had limited relevance in those years. Capital and liquidity ratios were used as guidelines. They were not compulsory and never replaced the evaluations of the competent supervisor, whose discretion had the final word in the identification of the managers' behaviour towards risk exposure.

The strategy followed by this regulatory regime was consistent with that generally pursued by State intervention at the time. It tended to integrate different interests and to secure a consensual participation of as many sectors as possible in the benefits generated by the growth of the economy. The instruments of *Group 1* (limitations on entries, scale, scope and pricing) secured the profits and the consensual participation of the banking industry in the national programmes. The regulatory regime thus carried out a complex strategy, which took into account the relevance of the power relations between the authorities and financial firms and the fact that the stability and the growth potentials of the economy can be damaged if the size of the financial sector supersedes that of the other sectors. An increasing weight of the financial sector in the economy and in the society may bring about a situation in which speculation dominates over enterprise and may lead to policies that favour the interests of this sector at the expense of those of the others. It affects income distribution and may consequently exacerbate social conflicts over the distributive shares (see Panico *et al.*, 2012).

It is widely acknowledged (see Eichengreen and Bordo, 2003; White, 2009: 18; Goodhart, 2010b: 3) that the discretionary approach brought about positive results. The management of financial firms was adequately controlled and bank crises disappeared. The few banks that failed were very small and most of them had been involved in frauds that regulators unearthed. Yet, the dominant interpretations of these events underplay the role played by this approach. White (2009: 25–26 and 31) attributes the positive results of that period to the high and stable growth of the economies, rather than to the merits of the discretionary approach. He also refers to the weak state of the financial industry after the crisis of 1929 to argue that it led the banks to assume a conservative attitude and to become more interested in raising reserves and holding safe assets than in stimulating innovative investments. Goodhart (2010b: 3–4) too attributes the positive results of that period to the conservative attitude of the managers of financial firms, rather than to the merits of the discretionary approach. For him, the dearth of bank failures of those years

> was *not* due to any exertion of effort by central banks to maintain systemic stability; instead the controlled, constrained financial system was just a safe, but dull, place.
>
> (Goodhart, 2010b: 4)

Goodhart and White overlook that there can be interdependence between high and stable growth and the controlled situation in which the financial system operates. What is more, during the Bretton Woods era, i.e. when the financial system was a 'dull place', the economies steadily grew at higher rates than during the subsequent years, unemployment was low, income inequality shrank, education, life expectancy, health conditions and security improved (see Panico *et al.*, 2013). The 'dull place' was not as inefficient as Goodhart suggests, nor did it prevent the societies from enjoying positive results.

What is more, de Haan *et al.*, 2009, a widely used textbook, conceals the positive results achieved by the discretionary approach to regulation and induces the reader to believe that only the rules-based approach is relevant today. It states (2009: 299–330) that, as financial institutions became increasingly complex, regulation moved away from methods of direct control to methods dominated by fixed rules. This claim muddles up causes and effects. The financial system became increasingly complex as a result (not a cause) of the replacement of the discretionary approach (see Bordo, 2008; Eichengreen, 2008; White, 2009). Finally, de Haan *et al.* (2009) fail to remind the reader that the basic question of financial regulation is: 'Should supervision focus on re-enforcing market discipline or should it rely on regulators discretion and their independent evaluation?' (White, 2009: 15). It thus gives a one-sided account of the matter, preventing students from properly valuing the evolution of financial regulation and its central notions.

Regulation during the transition period

The process of revision of the dominant regime started during the subsequent years. It was gradual, complex and was characterized by an on-going erosion of the powers of the authorities. The process was stimulated by the need to give financial firms, constrained by the limits on competition prevailing before 1970, the chance to adjust to the new situation generated by the abandonment of the Bretton Woods agreements and by the oil shocks. The conversion from fixed to flexible exchange rates transferred the related risks from the public to the private sector. Moreover, the slowdown of the economy and the surge of inflation raised the nominal interest rates. It changed the cost of financial services, affected the preferences of the operators, put at risk the solvency of financial firms, and forced them to innovate in order to expand their turnover. The subsequent decision of the authorities to start the 'monetarist experiment' of 1979–1982, setting rigid controls on the money supply, further accelerated financial innovation and weakened the balance sheets of financial firms. It increased the number of bank crises, as in the case of the Saving and Loans (S&Ls), and made it necessary to bail out many of them.

The process of revision of the regulation regime was led by a political climate more favourable to the financial industry. A first sign of this change was the reduction of resources assigned to the regulatory authorities during the Nixon and Reagan administrations (*Group 3*).[6] Another sign was the relaxation of some administrative controls established in the New Deal era (*Group 1*).[7]

At the beginning of this period the Congress did not pass laws that overtly changed the main features of the discretionary approach. Legislation focusing on specific aspects was approved at a later stage. In the 1980s Congress abolished some barriers to competition. The Depository Institutions Deregulation and Monetary Control of 1980 eliminated the ceilings on interest rates and the Garn-St Germain Act of 1982 allowed the S&Ls, at the time under distress, to deal with activities previously prohibited, like consumer loans, commercial real estate and business loans.

Supervision underwent a contradictory process that testifies to the complex formation of legislation and to the need to take into account the interests of the different pressure groups to interpret the evolution of financial regulation. On the one hand, the Financial Institutions Regulatory and Interest Rate Control Act of 1978 and the Federal Institutions Reform, Recovery and Enforcement Act of 1989 strengthened the powers of regulators in order to compel compliance. On the other hand, the emergence of a political climate more favourable to the financial industry led to measures that eroded the powers of the authorities over the management of firms. The reductions in the resources attributed to them, particularly heavy under the Reagan administration, changed supervision in quantity and quality. Surprise inspections, which are the most effective, lost relevance. The authorities had to limit the scope of their reviews and to enhance a regular dialogue with banks' managers and board members. The overall result of these changes was a reduction of the ability of the authorities to effectively control a sector that was starting to grow in size and complexity (see White, 2009: 31 and 36).

The tools of *Group 2* underwent important changes too. The Financial Institutions Regulatory and Interest Rate Control Act of 1978 obliged banks to disclose more information and introduced a Uniform Interagency Bank Rating System, named CAMEL, to harmonize the criteria of the different regulatory agencies. In 1981 and 1983, in the face of the difficulties of the banks' balance sheets caused by the monetarist experiment and the Latin American debt crisis, the Federal Reserve and the Office of the Comptroller of the Currency (OCC) made compulsory the compliance of capital ratios, previously used by supervisors as first indicators of risk exposure. The resistance of the financial industry, which complained about the advantages that this measure gave to foreign banks, led to the Basel I agreements of 1988, which phased in until 1993 a set of compulsory ratios (see Bank of International Settlements, 1999; Ashcraft, 2001: 8–11).

During the transition period, the financial system, unlike the 'dull place' of the previous years, became increasingly adept at assuming risks. At the same time, the turnover and the assets of financial firms grew at higher rates than GDP, unemployment rose and inequality returned to worsen after five decades of constant improvement (see Panico *et al.*, 2013). These results make it difficult to argue that the change of the financial system during those years improved its ability to provide resources for the productive sectors and to promote the achievement of desirable social objectives.

Finally, the number of bank crises increased. Some of them occurred in the 1970s, as a result of the unstable economic environment. In the 1980s the distresses further increased as a consequence of the monetarist experiment. The crisis of the S&Ls was the most relevant case. The monetarist experiment made the whole sector insolvent, raising the percentage of unprofitable insured S&Ls from

7 per cent in 1979 to 85 per cent by 1981 (see White, 2009: 32). White (2009: 33) attributes the crisis of the S&Ls to the authorities' misuse of their discretionary powers. He claims that the S&Ls gambled, after the introduction of the Garn-St Germain Act in 1982, because they knew that the authorities would have exercised forbearance towards them. This interpretation, however, underplays the negative impact of the monetarist experiment and the costs that the economic system would have paid if these institutions had not been rescued and contagion would have spread to other firms.

Regulation during the contemporary era

In the 1990s legislation further accomplished the process of reforms and liberalization. It formalized the conversion to a rules-based approach to regulation, the abolition of the limits on competition, the emergence of universal banking and the upsurge of the OTC derivatives operations. The financial markets enjoyed an 'explosive' expansion, which was accompanied by rising distress of financial firms and decelerating growth of the economy (see Panico *et al.*, 2013). The latter was eventually disrupted by the recession produced by the financial crisis.

Some important laws approved during those years were:

- the Federal Deposit Insurance Corporation Improvement Act of 1991, which abolished what remained of the discretionary approach to regulation
- the Riegle–Neal Interstate Banking and Branching Efficiency Act of 1994, which definitely eliminated all barriers to nation-wide branching
- the Gramm–Leach–Bliley Financial Services Modernization Act of 1999, which permitted universal banking within the structure of a financial holding company
- the Commodities Futures Modernization Act of 2000, which exempted OTC derivatives market from Government oversight.

Another important measure was the 1996 Federal Reserve's decision to allow banks to use Credit Default Swaps (CDS) to reduce capital reserves (see Levine, 2010: 5).

The Federal Deposit Insurance Corporation Improvement Act of 1991 formalized the change from a discretionary to a rules-based approach to supervision by introducing the 'prompt corrective actions' with the intention to hold back the possibility that the authorities' forbearance could lead to wide financial distresses. Banks were classified according to five categories of risk exposure, defined by financial ratios calculated by dividing the value of risk-weighted assets by that of capital. The thresholds of risk exposure were automatically calculated and when banks crossed them, mandatory actions, which increased monitoring and restrictions, inevitably applied.

To evaluate their risk exposure, the 1991 Act asked financial firms to provide regulators with more information than before. This obligation and the obstacle set to forbearance gave the impression that firms were more strictly constrained.

Yet, the removal of discretionary powers from the authorities enhanced the ability of firms to evade controls.

> By ruling out discretion, banks were able to develop new complex financial instruments that are not subject to statutory standards and allow them to assume more risk with existing capital. The most notorious of these were of course, the mortgage-backed securities that were held off-balance sheet in Structured Investment Vehicles (SIVs) that skirted the rules-based control system that was sufficiently rigid that it was difficult to quickly adjust to innovations. Banks were able to increase their risk and hence their return, while regulators appeared to be faithfully executing their mandates.
>
> (White, 2009: 36)

The limited availability of resources made it difficult for the authorities to analyse the large amount of information coming from the banks and to monitor the quality of these new instruments. It forced the authorities to rely on the advice of the Ratings Agencies. Yet, the intervention of these entities raised conflicts of interest, due to their position of advisors of controllers and customers of the controlled firms, and drove the system further away from a suitable solution of the problems of regulation.

Dealing with the origin of the recent financial crisis, White (2009: 36) claims that 'the genesis of the most recent collapse has part of its root' in the shift to the rules-based regime. It generated a financial industry that grew in scale, scope and complexity and further weakened the ability of the authorities, already limited by the availability of resources, to control financial firms and the rise of systemic risk:

> The fast changing character of the financial system increased the challenge to federal bank supervisors, who had a relatively rigid rules-based statutory supervisory regime, who faced an increasingly complex and evolving banking system, adept at increasing risk.
>
> (White, 2009: 37)

The introduction in the 1990s of rules-based forms of regulation has been presented as a consequence of the problems caused by the discretionary forbearance of the authorities during the banks' crisis of the 1980s. The role attributed to the 'prompt corrective actions' in the Federal Deposit Insurance Corporation Improvement Act corroborates this view (see White, 2009: 34; de Haan *et al.*, 2009: 306, Box 10.2). There are elements, however, suggesting that other factors, like the lobbying activities of the financial industry, played a role in the formation of this legislation. Some evidence provided by the US Senate (see www. opencongress.org) testifies to the pressures put by lobbying activities on the formation of monetary legislation. This information, orderly re-organized by the Centre for Responsive Policy (see www.opensecrets.org), shows that the financial industry has the highest quota of the total expenditure in 'campaign contributions' (on average, 19.4 per cent during the period 1990–2010) and in 'lobbying activities' (on average, 14.7 per cent during the period 1998–2009) of all the sectors of the economy. These pressures still play a relevant role in the formation of the reforms and legislation introduced after the recent financial crisis, with the aim of reducing the risk of future distresses (see Schinasi and Truman, 2010; Admati and Hellwig, 2013; Panico *et al.*, 2013).

The evolution of financial regulation after the crisis

Sraffa's approach can also be used to evaluate how the reactions to the recent financial crisis have affected the evolution of financial regulation. We shall refer to the Interim Report, written by the Financial Stability Board (FSB) for the G20 in June 2010, the package of reforms named Basel III (July–September 2010), the Dodd–Frank Wall Street Reform and Consumer Protection Act signed by the US President in July 2010, and the institution of the European Systemic Risk Board (ESRB) and of the European System of Financial Supervision (ESFS) in December 2010 and January 2011.

The Interim Report and the reforms move from the standpoint that before the crisis regulation did not work effectively because the balance between market discipline and official supervisory oversight was wrong. As Schinasi and Truman (2010: 9) say, regulation 'was tilted heavily toward ex ante market discipline, which proved to be elusive until it was too late . . . It also relied too little on official oversight'.

The need to make supervision (*Group 3*) more effective is not considered contentious. Yet, this issue is seen as likely to meet opposition from the financial industry (see Cornford, 2010: 3 and Schinasi and Truman, 2010: 18–19). Moreover, the Report and the reforms devote limited space to it, focusing instead on fortifying capital requirements (*Group 2*) and on arrangements reducing the probability of contagion among troubled firms, and improving the resolution of the crisis with limited taxpayer losses (*Group 4*).

The Interim Report sets the structure that the laws on regulation of individual countries have to follow. It proposes a policy framework that introduces novelties to structural and prudential regulation and on the management and resolution of crisis.

On structural regulation the Report envisages measures for regulating the degree of competitiveness and inter-connectedness of the financial system. The aim is to control the size, the complexity and the organisational structure of Systematically Important Financial Institutions (SIFIs). The Report (2010: 5) considers it necessary to introduce for these institutions the following measures:

- reducing intra-group connectivity through intra-group exposure limits
- structural separations of financial activities within the legal and organizational structure of a group, including requirements relating to separate incorporation and stand-alone capacity of operations that are systemically important in a financial system
- simplifying structures in a manner that aligns them more closely with the applicable regulatory and resolution frameworks.

As Cornford points out, these measures are strongly resisted by the banking industry. Moreover, they are like to enhance competition among jurisdictions:

> Changes designed to simplify the structure of financial conglomerates (which SIFIs are) or to limit the range of activities in which they can engage are likely to be strongly resisted by the banks. In London suggestions that reform might include such measures have produced rumblings from this quarter about possible moves to other jurisdictions. Such threats underline the importance of coordinated action on measures for the structural reform of large, complex financial institutions on the part of FSB member countries.
>
> (Cornford, 2010: 6)

Measures consistent with this policy framework have been included in the Dodd–Frank Act. They are referred to as the 'Volcker Rule' and the 'Lincoln Provision' and are envisaged to limit the organizational structure and the operations of SIFIs:

> The Volcker Rule prohibits banks from proprietary trading (i.e. trading for one's own account in securities or derivatives) and from investing in or sponsoring a hedge or private equity fund. Exceptions to the prohibition on proprietary trading can be authorised subject to supplementary capital requirements and quantitative limits. The Lincoln Provision, also referred to as the 'spin out' or 'push out' provision, limits the ability of banks to act as OTC derivatives dealers. The limit takes the form of a prohibition of Federal assistance (in the form of access to Federal Reserve lending facilities and reliance on deposit insurance from the Federal Deposit Insurance Corporation).
>
> (Cornford, 2010: 2)

Always on structural regulation, the Report considered it necessary to introduce supplementary prudential requirements for SIFIs. The Dodd–Frank Act establishes the Financial Stability Oversight Council, which evaluates the existence of systemic risks and authorizes the Federal Reserve to introduce supplementary requirements for SIFIs, if necessary. The European System of Financial Supervision and of the European Systemic Risk Board, which have to assess the existence of systemic risks and supervise the SIFIs in the European Union, responds to similar purposes (see Deutsche Bundesbank, 2012).

Although significant for the lack of similar measures in previous legislation, these measures appear of limited significance when compared with the complex design of structural regulation existing during the New Deal and the Bretton Woods eras.

On prudential regulation the largest space of the Interim Report and of the reforms here considered is devoted to market discipline (*Group 2*) and in particular to the rise of capital, liquidity and leverage ratios. This subject is under the responsibility of the Basel Committee on Banking Supervision that in December 2009 sent out a proposal on an upward revision of these requirements. The Group of Governors and Heads of Supervision of the Basel Committee on Banking Supervision met again in July 2010 to review the proposal and in September 2010 agreed upon a set of measures that raised the minimum capital, liquidity and leverage requirements and scheduled their phasing in for all member countries. The agreement represents a progress with respect to the previous situation, but the size and timing of the increased requirements are considered inadequate to reduce the probability of future crises (see Schinasi and Truman, 2010: 11). For Admati and Hellwig (2013), the capital requirements set by Basel III are artificially low. They argue (2013: 179) that history shows that when the owners of the banks were fully responsible for their debt, capital requirements reached higher levels than 20 or 30 per cent.

Compared with what the Group of Governors and Heads of Supervision of the Basel Committee on Banking Supervision had initially envisaged in December 2009, the final agreement provides several concessions for the banking industry:

> Unfortunately, compared to the revisions to Basel II put forward in the December 2009 proposal, the agreement reached in July 2010 provided many concessions favourable to the banking industry, including a less demanding definition of Tier 1 capital, less stringent liquidity requirements, and a lower leverage limit (only 3 per cent) phased in over a longer period ending in 2017.
>
> (Schinasi and Truman, 2010: 10)

These concessions are interpreted as a sign of the ability of the banking industry to resist the introduction of measures that increase its costs. They show that the Basel Committee failed to obtain the consensus of this group on its original proposals and was bound to recede towards an agreement, which is a source of preoccupation for the evolution of regulation and for the future stability of the financial system:

> That a consensus could not be reached is disappointing: excessive leverage and poor liquidity-risk management by the major global banks played an important role in creating the conditions for the global crisis. They also contributed importantly to the virulent market dynamics that prevailed throughout 2008-09. This mixed record to date by the regulators and supervisors is not reassuring for the prospects to agree on the difficult reform trade-offs and decisions that are yet to be taken and implemented on both sides of the Atlantic, including those pertaining to SIFIs, over-the-counter derivatives markets, and resolution mechanisms for cross-border banking problems.
>
> (Schinasi and Truman, 2010: 11)

Admati and Hellwig (2013) underline that, before the crisis, low capital requirements, the introduction of securitization and of the Structured Investment Vehicles, and the use of Credit Default Swaps (CDSs) increased inter-connection among financial firms and allowed them to evade regulation by using off-balance accounting.[8] These elements have favoured the shift of financial activity towards a kind of business that differs from traditional intermediation and has greatly contributed to increase the systemic risk (see Admati and Hellwig, 2013: 70). For them (2013: 222), until these conditions remain unchanged, it is necessary to introduce higher requirements than those foreseen by Basel III.

On the other component of prudential regulation (supervision, *Group 3*), the Report considers it necessary to reinforce the powers and the resources of the authorities:

> We will call for a strengthening of the mandate, powers and resources of supervisory authorities where appropriate and recommend a range of actions to render supervisory tools and practices more effective.
>
> (FSB, 2010: 6)

Yet, the recommendations of the Report vaguely refer to measures that can strengthen the discretionary powers of supervisory authorities over the management of financial firms. The measures proposed by the Report can be summarized by the following four items:

1 production of knowledge on corporate governance, on the working of the financial system, and on measures and quantitative models to evaluate the risk exposure of financial firms (*Group 2*)
2 improvement of collection and treatment of data and information (*Group 2*)
3 improvement of coordination among supervisory authorities at home and abroad
4 'an appropriate number of sufficiently skilled supervisors overseeing systemic firms' (FSB, 2010: 6) (*Group 3*)

As can be noticed, only item 4 refers to measures that directly affect the discretionary powers of the supervisory authorities over the management of financial firms. For this reason, the call of the Report on the role that this instrument has to play in the overall organization of financial regulation can be seen as void of practical consequences.

On the management and resolution of crises, the Report proposes the introduction of financial infrastructures in the form of systemically important payment systems, securities settlements systems and central counterparties (CCPs). The aim is to 'make derivatives standardised and increase the share of the market that is clearable' (FSB, 2010: 6). The proposal is important because it shows that the authorities now see the derivatives markets as an extension of the international inter-bank markets and consider that the most useful action in this respect is to try to ensure its orderly working.

These actions can represent a step forward in the attempt to introduce some forms of discipline and control over the derivatives markets. The organization of central counterparties (CCPs) can guarantee

- an increased transparency through the records of transactions and the definition of standard contracts
- a reduction in the likelihood of a contagion due to the failure of a single counterparty owing to the sharing of costs of the failure among clearing members and the use of this infrastructure as a clearing house for exchanges whose degree of liquidity can be supported by coordinated interventions of the monetary authorities.

Finally on the resolution of crises, the Report proposes the use of systemic levies 'to build up a resolution fund and hence facilitate resolution when such firms fail' (FSB, 2010: 5). The levies can be seen as insurance for future problems, as an incentive to reduce the size of financial firms and specific operations, and as a means to pay back the cost of recapitalization. For some experts (see Schinasi and Truman, 2010: 11–12); however, these measures are not likely to be introduced for the resistance of the banking industry.[9]

Conclusions

Sraffa's approach to monetary problems allows one to consider financial regulation as a set of norms influencing the terms at which credit is provided and the conventions over the distribution of income. This perspective highlights the need to refer to the financial system as an industry, recognizing its role in the material provision of services necessary to production and its ability to make pressures on the authorities in order to obtain measures that favour the rise of its turnover and earnings.

This approach leads one to argue that the change from a discretionary to a rules-based regime of regulation, as occurred after 1970, reflects both technical considerations on how to solve the problems of liquidity and solvency of financial firms and the pressures of the financial industry to obtain legislation promoting its interests. The conversion to the new regime was gradual and reflected the strengthening position of the financial industry in the economy and in the society. It permitted the growth of this industry by enhancing the introduction of new instruments that are not subject to statutory standards and that allow financial firms to assume more risk with the existing capital. The genesis of the financial crisis, as White (2009) says, has its root in this shift to the rules-based regime.

The analysis of the recent financial crisis along the Sraffian perspective underlines the need to defend the independence of the authorities that decide and implement the rules of financial regulation. Moreover, it suggests that the emphasis on market discipline and the neglect of the supervisory powers of the authorities, which can be found in the reforms proposed and adopted after the crisis, is due to the ability of the financial industry to affect national legislation and international agreements.

These points are sometimes acknowledged in the literature, but are not elaborated in a systematic way. We can find that Levine and others have elucidated that the malfunction of the governance of regulation must be seen as a major cause of the crisis. For these authors, the economic literature has rightly developed the analysis of the monetary authorities' independence of political entities. Yet, it has overlooked the need to maintain the monetary authorities independent of the pressures of the economic groups.

The literature also confirms that financial regulation must identify an appropriate balance between market discipline and official supervisory oversight. This position is acknowledged by the official documents presented by the authorities after the crisis. Yet, as Admati, Hellwig, Schinasi and Truman point out, owing to the ability of the banking industry to resist the introduction of measures that affect their revenues, recent reforms have focused on market discipline, disregarding the need to reinforce the supervisory powers of the authorities over the management of financial firms. Strengthening the powers of the authorities to avoid the financial industry growing at higher rates than the rest of the economy is crucial to reduce the probability of future crises. The introduction of discretionary powers administered by independent authorities can enhance the efficient provision of the financial services required by production and avoid disruptive and socially undesired changes in the conventions affecting the distribution of income.

Notes

1 The paper draws from the results of the research project 'Rethinking Finance for Stability and Growth' (FP7 PEOPLE 2012 – IRSES, ReFiSt, Reference number: PIRSES-GA-2012-319014). We thank the European Commission for financial support.
2 For an analysis of Sraffa's writings on money and banking see Panico (1988; 2001).
3 According to Medina Echavarría, 'the validity and reliability of the set of principles and laws of the classical doctrine … depend on the fact that it translates in an abstract (theoretical) form a consistent organization of social reality' (2009 [1943]: 85; our translation).
4 For Medina Echevarria, the treatment of the role of institutions presented by this approach 'is in the majority of cases rough and theoretically unrefined. It may hold good as sociological doctrine, but one can easily understand why traditional economists find it hard to be persuaded by this approach. They argue that, like the historical school, this literature fails to propose a satisfactory economic theory. They are right, because it tends to loosely elaborate economic theory either as sociological empiricism or as a sociological interpretation of history' (2009 [1943]: 79–80; our translation).
5 The Banking Act of 1933 introduced liabilities insurance through the Federal Deposit Insurance Corporation (*Group 4*) and extended the authorities' discretionary powers in the supervision of financial firms (*Group 3*). The Act also separated commercial and investment banking (*Group 1*), assuming that combining these two businesses led to conflicts of interest and increasing risk, and confirmed Regulation Q, which imposed limits on deposit interest rates (*Group 1*). The Banking Act of 1935 endowed the federal authorities with large discretionary powers over the decisions granting bank charters (*Group 1*), the Bank Merger Act of 1960 entrusted similar powers to the authorities over mergers and acquisitions (*Group 1*), the Bank Holding Acts of 1956 and 1970 limited

banks' attempts to expand their business into activities like investment advice, insurance and data processing (*Group 1*), and the Financial Institutions Supervisory Act of 1966 strengthened the supervisory powers of the authorities (*Group 3*).

6 As White (2009: 36) notices,

> although bank supervisory agencies were independently funded, they came under increased pressure from several administrations, most notably Nixon and Reagan administrations that sought reductions in regulation. In 1969 the OCC was placed under an employment ceiling, leaving the Comptroller to complain that he had an inadequate staff to conduct examinations. Pressure became more intense under the Reagan administration that sought to reduce the size and scope of the federal government in the early 1980s, just as bank failures were beginning to rise. The OCC saw a decline in its expenditures and its workforce shrank. From 3,282 employees, of whom 2,282 were examiners in 1979, the OCC shrank to 2,702 employees and 1,835 examiners by 1982. Staff at the OCC turnover reached 15 per cent in 1984. The decline in supervision was particularly acute in Texas where the median exam interval in 1986 was 700 days for banks that subsequently failed or needed assistance.

7 In the 1970s the authorities weakened the requirements for obtaining bank charters and made rejections infrequent. The Federal Reserve relaxed its anti-branching rules and several States reached agreements on reciprocal privileges to their banks, weakening the barriers to geographical competition. Moreover, during the Reagan administration, the Department of Justice eased opposition to horizontal mergers. These administrative measures allowed the banks to increase their size.

8 According to these authors, attention should be also paid to the accounting procedures, because the ways derivative contracts were treated in the different accounting regimes, i.e. the Generally Accepted Accounting Principles (GAAP) in the US and the International Financial Reporting Standards (IFRS) in the European Union, generated in the balance sheets of financial institutions differences that 'have dramatic effects on how one sees the loss absorption capacity of the bank's equity' (Admati and Hellwig, 2013: 85).

9 The US Congress, for instance, discussed the need to introduce these measures and brought them in draft legislation even. None the less, the final version of the Dodd–Frank Act does not foresee any such levy.

References

Admati A. and Hellwig M., 2013, *The Bankers' New Clothes: What's Wrong with Banking and What to Do about It*, Princeton NJ: Princeton University Press.

Ashcraft A.B., 2001, Do tougher bank capital requirements matters? New evidence from the Eighties, chapter II of *Essays in Banking and Monetary Policy*, MIT Doctoral Thesis, pp. 167–178, downloadable at http://dspace.mit.edu/handle/1721.1/8657, last accessed 28 November 2015.

Bank of International Settlements, 1999, Capital requirements and bank behaviour: the impact of the Basel accord, Report of the working group led by Patricia Jackson, *Basel Committee on Banking Supervision, Working Papers*, No. 1, April.

Barth J.R., Caprio G. Jr. and Levine R., 2011, *Guardians of Finance: Making Them Work for Us*, Cambridge MA: MIT Press.

Barth J.R., Li T., Li W., Phumiwasana T. and Yago G., 2009, *The Rise and Fall of the US Mortgage and Credit Markets: A Comprehensive Analysis of the Market Meltdown*, New York: John Wiley and Sons.

Bordo M.D., 2008, A historical perspective on the crisis of 2007–2008, *National Bureau of Economic Research, Working Paper Series*, No. 14569, December.

Caprio G. Jr., 2009, Financial regulation in a changing world: lesson from the recent crisis, *Institute for International Integration Studies, IIS Discussion Paper*, No. 308, November, downloadable at, http://www.tcd.ie/iiis/documents/discussion/pdfs/iiisdp308.pdf, last accessed 28 November 2015.

Cornford A., 2010, Structural reform of systemically important financial institutions: the FSB's response to too big to fail, downloadable at http://www.networkideas.org/featart/dec2010/Andrew_Conford.pdf, last accessed 28 November 2015.

Davidson D., 1970, Mental elements, in *Essays on Actions and Events*, Oxford: Oxford University Press, 207–223.

Davis J., 2012, The change in Sraffa's philosophical thinking, *Cambridge Journal of Economics*, 36(6), November, 1341–1356.

De Haan J., Oosterloo S. and Schoenmaker D., 2009, *European Financial Markets and Institutions*, Cambridge: Cambridge University Press.

Dennett D., 1987, *The Intentional Stance*, Cambridge MA: MIT Press.

Deutsche Bundesbank, 2012, The European Systemic Risk Board: from institutional foundation to credible macroprudential oversight, *Monthly Bulletin*, April, 29–39.

Eichengreen B., 2008, *Origins and responses to the crisis*, October, downloadable at http://eml.berkeley.edu/~webfac/eichengreen/e183_sp07/origins_responses.pdf, last accessed 28 November 2015.

Eichengreen B. and Bordo M., 2003, Crisis now and then. What lessons from the last era of financial globalisation?, in Mizen P., ed., *Monetary History, Exchange Rates and Financial Markets: Essays in Honour of Charles Goodhart*, vol. 2, Cheltenham: Edward Elgar Publishing, 52–91.

Financial Stability Board (FSB), 2010, *Report to the G-20 Finance Ministers and Central Bank Governors, Guidance to Assess the Systemic Importance of Financial Institutions, Markets and Instruments: Initial Consideration – Background Paper*. Document prepared in October 2009 by: Staff of the International Monetary Fund and the Bank of International Settlements, and the Secretariat of the Financial Stability Board.

Goodhart C.A.E., 2010a, How should we regulate bank capital and financial products? What role for 'living wills'?, in *The Future of Finance. The LSE Report*, Chapter 5, London: The London School of Economics and Political Science, 165–186.

Goodhart C.A.E., 2010b, The changing role of central banks, *Bank of International Settlements, Working Papers*, No. 326.

Hanson S.G., Kashyap A. and Stein J.C., 2010, A macroeconomic approach to financial regulation, *The University of Chicago Booth School of Business, Working Paper*, 10–29.

Kashyap A.K., Berner R. and Goodhart C.A.E., 2011, The macroprudential toolkit, Initiative on Global Markets, *The University of Chicago, Booth School of Business, Working Paper*, No. 60, January.

Kurz H.D. and Salvadori N., 2005, Representing the production and circulation of commodities: on Sraffa's objectivism, *Review of Political Economy*, 17(3), 414–441.

Levine R., 2010, The governance of financial regulation: reform lessons from the recent crisis, *Bank of International Settlements, Working Papers*, No. 329.

Medina Echavarría J., 2009, *Responsabilidad de La inteligencia. Estudios sobre nuestro tiempo*, Pensar en español y FCE. (1st ed. 1943).

Mishkin F.S., 2001, Prudential supervision: why is it important and what are the issues? In Mishkin F.S. (ed.), *Prudential Supervision. What Works and What Doesn't*, National Bureau of Economic Research Working Paper Series, No. 7926, 1–36.

Palma J.G., 2009, The revenge of the market on the rentiers: why neo-liberal reports of the end of history turned out to be premature, *Cambridge Journal of Economics, Special Issue on the Global Financial Crisis*, 33(4), July, 829–866.

Panico C., 1988, Sraffa on money and banking, *Cambridge Journal of Economics*, 12(1), March, 7–28.

Panico C., 2001, Monetary analysis in Sraffa's writings, in Cozzi T. and Marchionatti R. (eds.), *Piero Sraffa's Political Economy: a Centenary Estimate*, London: Routledge, 285–310.

Panico C., Pinto A. and Puchet Anyul M., 2012, Income distribution and the size of the financial sector: a Sraffian analysis, *Cambridge Journal of Economics*, 36(6), November, 1455–1477, doi:10.1093/cje/ber022.

Panico C., Pinto A., Puchet Anyul M. and Vazquez Suarez M., 2013, The evolution of financial regulation before and after the crisis, *Economica*, 15(1), June, 9–40.

Schinasi G.J. and Truman E.M., 2010, Reform of the global financial architecture, *Peterson Institute for International Economics, Working Paper Series*, 10–14, downloadable at http://www.iie.com/publications/wp/wp10-14.pdf, last accessed 28 November 2015.

Sraffa P., 1922, The bank crisis in Italy, *Economic Journal*, XXXII (126), June, 178–197.

White E.N., 2009, Lessons from the history of bank examination and supervision in the United States, 1863–2008, in Gigliobianco A. and Toniolo G. (eds.), *Financial Market Regulation in the Wake of Financial Crises: The Historical Experience*, Workshops and Conferences, November, Roma: Bank of Italy, 15–44.

Whitehead A.N., 1926, *Science and the Modern World. Lowell Lectures 1925*, Cambridge: Cambridge University Press.

19 On the instantaneous life of a nondurable input

A reflection in the light of Zeno and Cantor

Man-Seop Park

This chapter is both 'light' and 'heavy'. It 'teases' an established practice in (mainstream) economics by means of Zeno's paradox. To 'verify' the practice for its own sake, however, and subsequently to draw attention to some logical problems arising from the practice, it calls for Cantor's theory of transfinite numbers. The 'heavy' atmosphere set by the latter is, perhaps, a cover for the 'light' atmosphere I intend for the essay. Or, perhaps, the other way round. To some, it may look as if 'a terrific steam-hammer' is being built up 'in order to crack a nut' (Sraffa, 1932, p. 45; however, this time, it is assured that the nut is cracked). Alternatively, one may take the essay to be on the verge of 'satire' (but, then, satire always carries threads of truth).

'Light and heavy' – this expression also befits, at least partially, Neri Salvadori: light always with witty banter; heavy so often with, well, heavy mathematics. This essay is offered in Neri's honour on the occasion of his sixty-fifth birthday.

Introduction: the 'Hicksian argument'

The following type of accounting equation is in wide use in the recent neoclassical literature modelling production/growth economies; the models are set in continuous time and the equation refers to a productive process (or an aggregate economy) at 'time t' where (ultimately) *both* a nondurable input and a durable input are utilised:

$$Y = wL + p_n K_n + r p_d K_d, \tag{19.1}$$

where Y = output, L = labour, K_n = nondurable input, K_d = (ever-lasting) durable input, w = wage rate, r = rate of interest, p_n = supply price of the nondurable input, and p_d = supply price of the durable input. The models I have in mind as of particular interest are horizontal innovation and vertical innovation models (however, one may find more examples in a wider range of the literature).[1]

Two characteristics of equation (19.1) in particular attract our attention. The first is that the user cost of the nondurable input does not, whereas that of the durable input does, involve the rate of interest. The second is that the quantities appearing in the equation (Y, L, K_n and K_d) are *all* treated as real (positive and finite) quantities.[2]

The present essay will take the second characteristic for granted as the literature in question always does, concentrating our scrutiny on the first characteristic. This is because we wish to observe logical difficulties facing the established practice at their maximum (the negative conclusion we shall draw relies partly on the second characteristic), and also because, even if we 'correct' this characteristic (hence considering the quantities in question to be not real but 'infinitesimal'), we shall end up with the same negative conclusion as the present essay reaches.[3]

For those authors who p use equation (19.1), the first characteristic is the natural result of the setting of *instantaneous production* where a round of production is completed *each instant* and the corresponding value accounting, represented by an equation such as (19.1), is to be established *each instant* (put in short, the unit period of production is an instant). Thus, regarding a nondurable input, one observes Acemoglu (2009, p. 435) stating (in the context of horizontal innovation models) that '[s]ince machines depreciate [fully] after use [at time t], $p^x(v, t)$ [the price of a machine of variety v at time t] can also be interpreted as a rental price or the user cost of this machine', with time t obtained by 'making the time unit as small as possible, that is, by going to continuous time' (p. 47).

We shall call this position the 'Hicksian argument'. In the setting of discrete time, says Hicks (1973) referring to 'weeks', 'interest on the net input of the week (since it was paid for on the Monday) is included in the capital at the end of the week'. He then goes on arguing that '[i]f we had worked with continuous time, this interest would have disappeared'; '[b]y shrinking the week, we can cause it to disappear' (p. 30). He also considers the case in which a productive process is 'truncated' in the first 'week' of operation so that the economically meaningful part of the process is represented, in his neo-Austrian framework, by a singleton of net output; in this case, 'input produces output instantaneously' (p. 21) and the discounted capital value of net output is outright equal to the net output itself – the net output is 'undiscounted, because it comes in immediately' (p. 20).

The Hicksian argument, though in wide use, has seldom been given a rigorous treatment. Rather, it seems, the justification of the argument is based upon a naïve strand of reasoning: the (continuous) discounting factor, $e^{-r\tau}$, approaches unity as τ approaches 'the time unit as small as possible' (Acemoglu, 2009, p. 47) – that is, the net output is 'undiscounted, because it comes in immediately' (Hicks, 1973, p. 20).[4] As will be made clear in later pages, this reasoning commits the error of extending the procedure valid for 'real-period production' (where the unit period of production is a positive real period of time) unconditionally to instantaneous production.

The subtlety of the issue is witnessed by Katzner's (1988) doomed fate in a rare example of an attempt to derive the user cost of an instantaneous nondurable input in a rigorous way. He starts with the following familiar condition for deriving the user cost of an input in the setting of continuous discounting:

$$\lim_{\zeta \to \tau} \int_0^\zeta e^{-rv} \pi \, dv = p, \qquad (19.2)$$

where π is a flow of net revenue arising from one unit of the durable input, p the supply price per unit of the input, and r the average level of the ('weekly') rate of interest over the period concerned. Equation (19.2) expresses the arbitrage condition for the production of the input, which is the equality between the present value of net revenues ensuing from the input (the left-hand side) and its supply-price value (the right-hand side). The equation gives us

$$\pi r^{-1}(1 - e^{-r\tau}) = p. \tag{19.3}$$

The user cost of an everlasting input is for the case of $\tau = \infty$, and Katzner gets the familiar and correct result: $\pi = rp$. He then states that, in instantaneous production, 'it would be necessary to set [the life of an input] $= 0$ for nondurable[s]' (p. 386, fn. 9). The conclusion he arrives at is that 'their rental values would always be infinite' (p. 387, fn. 11). With the duration of operation of an input approaches an instant (that is, $\tau \to 0$), equation (19.3) becomes

$$\pi r^{-1}\left[\lim_{\tau \to 0}(1 - e^{-r\tau})\right] = p. \tag{19.4}$$

For p and r to be positive finite real numbers (as they should be in a no-nonsense economy), one must have $\pi \to \infty$. This is a mathematically correct, but surely economically embarrassing, result. One needs another way to 'verify' the Hicksian argument.

The first objective of the present essay is, thus, to provide a rigorous way of verifying the Hicksian argument. The main objective is, however, to argue that reasoning in the way of the Hicksian argument on the one hand, applied to an instantaneous nondurable input, cannot stand side by side with reasoning in the way of condition (19.2) on the other, applied to a durable input (whether everlasting or of a finite lifetime), *though each logically valid on its own*. One will be in a dilemma in the economics of instantaneous production. The implication is that the accounting relationship of type (19.1) should be revised if an escape from the dilemma is to be secured.

A clarification of the concept of an 'instant' of time is in order before we enter the main arguments. An instant can be understood in various (equivalent) ways: (*i*) as an ever-shrinking interval of time, that is, interval $[t, t_0]$ with $t \to t_0$, hence its length being $dv \equiv \lim_{t \to t_0}(t - t_0)$; (*ii*) as a point on the real line, that is, a degenerative real interval $[t_0, t_0]$; or (*iii*) as an 'infinitesimal' interval of time in the sense given in 'nonstandard analysis' (Robinson, 1996), where an 'infinitesimal' is defined as a magnitude that is not zero but smaller than any positive real number. Expressed in different ways, an instant in any understanding is of (Lebesgue) *measure zero*. The present essay will use the second understanding (and here lie some elements of 'satire' I wish to convey). It will have to be remarked, however, that one and the same negative conclusion will be reached in whatever understanding of an instant, though the routes to the conclusion may be different.[5]

The oxymoron of instantaneous production: Zeno's paradox

Economic – indeed, any physical – events, measured in terms of separately complete units, take place either simultaneously or one 'next' to another over time. Take the example of horizontal innovation (or vertical innovation) models. The economy begins, at 'time zero', with given stocks of the final good, intermediate goods and designs. Production takes place simultaneously in each of the three sectors to produce designs, the final good and intermediate goods respectively. Thanks to this production the economy is endowed with the new stocks of the inputs to be used for the 'next' round of production. Too obvious though it may sound, the 'next' round cannot take place at the same time as the 'previous' round. If it did, this would mean that *everything* happened at the same time. The very thesis of horizontal innovation and vertical innovation models is that the increasing variety or improving quality of intermediate goods through innovations is the source of continual economic growth. If everything happened at a single instant, no one would be allowed to talk about either 'increasing variety', or 'improving quality', or, indeed, 'innovations'. The models in question, if to be meaningful, should be based upon a *sequence* of production.

This requirement of sequentiality comes to sharper relief if the horizontal innovation or vertical innovation process of production is construed in an alternative (but equivalent) way. The final good is produced by means of intermediate goods; these latter goods having been produced by means of a design, this design in turn having been produced by means of the foregone final good, this good in turn having been produced by means of intermediate goods, and so on *ad infinitum*. For horizontal or vertical innovations to be possible, there must be a sequence of 'production-events', which requires these events to take place one 'next' to another along the time line. Indeed, this should be the case for *any* economic models where commodities are produced by means of *produced* commodities.

Thus, if the models in question are *both* to take equation (19.1) for granted (which relies on instantaneous production) *and* to be meaningful (as horizontal/vertical innovation models), production must take place *both* instantly *and* sequentially along the time line. But this is where Smaug the dragon has been lying, ready to raise its head and open its fiery mouth.

'Sequential instantaneity' is the antithesis of the very property of the real numbers (on the basis of which the structure of time is construed). Any positive interval on the real line is a continuum, a linearly ordered set of more than one element that is *densely ordered*: with the linear ordering $<$, for every real number x and y such that $x < y$, there is always another real number w such that $x < w < y$. One cannot locate an element lying 'immediately next' to a given element of the set. One cannot identify *the* instant coming 'immediately next' to the present instant.[6] To wit, a *sequence* of production taking place *instant by instant* is inconceivable. The instantaneous period of production cannot accommodate 'production of commodities by means of commodities' (Sraffa, 1960) – the essential characteristic of horizontal innovations or vertical innovations.

Production can never proceed beyond a given instant. Zeno of Elea has resurrected, triumphantly.[7]

The instantaneous life of a nondurable input: production in 'no' time

There are two ways to understand the upper limit of integration ζ in equation (19.2): in usual cases, they are equivalent to each other so that, usually, no particular attention is paid to their distinction, but their distinction will prove critical in the cases of our current concern.

One way is to understand it as denoting the physical time-duration (τ) between the beginning (t_0) and the end ($\bar{t}$) of the lifetime of the input concerned, both t_0 and $\bar{t}$ standing for time coordinates in the Newtonian absolute space-time. That is, ζ is understood as the Lebesgue measure of time interval $[t_0, \bar{t}]$:

$$\zeta = \tau := \bar{t} - t_0. \tag{19.5}$$

We have seen, however, that this way of understanding ζ (call it the τ-way) ends up at a *cul-de-sac* in regard to an input that is used up at an instant. For the input should then be subject to the manner of discounting that leads to the doomed attempt by Katzner (1986) mentioned in the previous section.

Another way of understanding ζ in equation (19.2) is that it stands for the number of 'periods of production' (T) that the input concerned goes through during its lifetime: call this the T-way. The unit period of production is the minimum length of time over which a round of production is completed so that a batch of identifiable output is produced *and* a corresponding flow of revenue is generated (even if recorded purely for accounting purposes). The T-way thus conforms to the concept of revenue as a *flow* which is generated over a certain period of time: π in formula (19.2) is the magnitude of the flow of net revenue generated over each period of production. In usual cases of this understanding, T will be obtained as

$$\zeta = T := \frac{\bar{t} - t_0}{u}, \tag{19.6}$$

where u is the physical duration of the unit period of production. For an everlasting durable input one will have $T = \infty$ because $\bar{t} - t_0 = \infty$ with u being finite.

It is obvious, however, that equation (19.6), at its face value, does not work if not on the assumption that $u > 0$. If $u > 0$, indeed, the two ways of understanding the upper limit of integration in formula (19.2) are equivalent. This is because the unit period of production is the *effective* normalisation unit of time in a model at hand, so that one can always set $u = 1$.[8] When $u > 0$, a nondurable is an input with $\tau = T = 1$ and a durable with $\tau = T = 1, 2, \ldots, \infty$, whether one understands the upper limit of integration in formula (19.2) in the τ-way or the T-way. *This* is, indeed, the established definition of a nondurable and a durable input.

The state of affairs in the setting of instantaneous production is, however, where $u = 0$ and, at the same time, $\bar{t} - t_0 = 0$. The physical lifetime of an input that is defined as used up at an instant must be, *by definition*, an instant. Also, the unit period of production for a productive process that utilises an instantaneous nondurable must be an instant, because a batch of somehow identifiable output is, *by definition*, produced when the instantaneous nondurable is used up; otherwise, the meaning of the nondurable is left in the air. This must be applicable whether or not a durable input is utilised along with the nondurable; a durable is simply an input that is involved with a multiple number of periods of production. The period of time during which a nondurable is used up to generate revenue is what defines the length of the unit period of production.

With regard to instantaneous production, thus, equation (19.6) would be dividing zero by zero. One is then in a dilemma: the τ-way cannot verify the Hicksian argument and the T-way, in the way of equation (19.6) at face value, cannot help calculate the number of periods of production for an instantaneous nondurable. However, one can provide, *in the T-way*, a rigorous counting of the number of production periods of an instantaneous nondurable and, based thereupon, a rigorous explanation of its user cost appearing in equation (19.1).

The number of production periods that a nondurable input goes through during its lifetime must be, by definition, *unity*: a nondurable is an input that is 'used *only once* in some productive process' (Silberberg and Suen, 2001, p. 387, emphasis added). To obtain that number in a rigorous manner, we propose to turn to set theory (ZFC): construe the number of periods of production covered by the lifetime of an input as the *cardinality* $|S|$ of the partition set S of that period, each partition cell having the length of the unit period of production. Keeping in mind that the unit period of production for a productive process with an instantaneous nondurable is an instant, define S as follows:[9]

$$S := \{\mathcal{I}_i = [t_i, t_i] \subseteq S\}$$
$$\text{such that } \forall i, j \in \mathbb{R}_+ \ (i \neq j), \mathcal{I}_i \cap \mathcal{I}_j = \varnothing \text{ and } \cup_i \mathcal{I}_i = [t_0, \bar{t}]. \tag{19.7}$$

$\mathcal{I}_i$, representing the unit period of production, is a degenerate interval, that is, a point on the real line, and S is in fact the set of the real numbers in interval $[t_0, \bar{t}]$, each real number constituting a partition cell for the partition set S.

For an input whose life lasts for a single instant (t_0), S is the singleton consisting of that single instant, and its cardinality is *unity*:[10]

$$S = \{\mathcal{I}_0\}; \text{ therefore, } |S| = 1. \tag{19.8}$$

This is a logical explanation of the *single* occurrence of production and revenue-generation – and its accompanying *single* event of discounting (which will actually turn out to have no effect) – which takes place in a period of *zero* length when the normalisation unit of time is also a period of *zero* length.

This alone, however, does not complete the story of discounting where the unit period of production is an instant. The instantaneous period of production means that all the *flow* variables in the model are to be measured, rather oxymoronically, in reference to an instant. The flow of revenue and the rate of interest are no exceptions. One should be talking of the 'instant-wise flow' of revenue and the 'instant-wise rate' of interest: the former is the measure of revenue ensuing at an instant, and the latter is the rate of interest that is defined in reference to an instant.[11] Now, recall that the continuous discount factor in (19.2),

$$e^{-rv} := \lim_{H \to \infty} \left(1 + \frac{r}{H}\right)^{-Hv},$$ (19.9)

is defined on the basis of the procedure by which the normalisation unit of time, *to which r refers*, is divided into H smaller intervals, with H approaching infinity: r is shrunk in proportion with the duration of time to which it is applied each round, and v stands for the total duration of time to which (or the total number of rounds in which) r is applied. The continuous discount factor requires for its definition that the normalisation unit of time, to which the rate of interest refers, should be a *positive* interval – an interval which is subsequently to be divided into an infinite number of smaller (infinitesimal) intervals. But the fact is that we are now in the 'instantaneous' world where all 'flow' variables, including the flow of revenue and the rate of interest, are measured in reference to an instant – and an instant, understood as a 'point of time', is, by definition, *indivisible*. The continuous discount factor loses its ground with the instantaneous period of production.[12]

The indivisibility of the unit period of production, thus, suggests that one should use the ('*instant-wise*') *discrete* discount factor and obtain the present value of revenues as the sum of a sequence of discrete terms of discounted revenues, not as an integral of continuous flows of discounted revenues.[13] The number of terms in the series of discounted revenues is the number of production periods that an input goes through during its lifetime, and it is calculated as the cardinality of S. Thus, the general formula for obtaining the user cost would be[14]

$$\sum_{s=1}^{|S|} \pi(1+\rho)^{-s} = p,$$ (19.10)

where $\rho := rdv$ is the 'instant-wise' rate of interest (see endnote 11). Note that, as the rate of interest to prevail at the instant has been shrunk to ρ, π is the 'instant-wise flow' of revenue obtained by appropriately time-scaling the unit-period flow of revenue.[15]

The case of an (instantaneous) nondurable input is where $|S| = 1$; therefore, one has

$$\sum_{s=1}^{1} \pi(1+\rho)^{-s} = p; \text{ that is, } \pi = (1+\rho)p.$$ (19.11)

The right-hand side of the second equation expands as $p + \rho p = p + (rdv)p$. Since $dv := \lim_{t \to t_0}(t - t_0)$, the second term of the right-hand side 'disappears' in the limit so that one gets $\pi = p$. The Hicksian argument has been verified: '[i]f we had worked with continuous time, ... interest would have disappeared'; '[b]y shrinking the week, we can cause it to disappear' (Hicks, 1973, p. 30). Equation (19.11) is, we propose, a logically consistent interpretation of the Hicksian argument.

Logic, verifying an instantaneous nondurable, however, does not let pass without a toll. The toll falls on the other member of the production partnership – a *durable* input.

The 'eternal' life of *any* durable input: counting the uncountably infinite

If a nondurable is an input that is exhausted at an instant, a durable is any input that lasts for longer than an instant – that is, any input that stays in production for a *positive* interval of time, no matter how short[16]

If one is to have $\cup_i \mathcal{I}_i = [t_0, \bar{t}]$, $\bar{t} > t_0$, with $\mathcal{I}_i = [t_i, t_i]$ as in (19.7), it must be the case that

$$|S| = \aleph_1. \tag{19.12}$$

Georg Cantor tells us that the cardinality of *any* positive interval on the real line is $\aleph_1$ (aleph-one). Then, for *any* durable input, whether of finite or infinite duration in calendar time, one would have, if applying formula (19.10),

$$\sum_{s=1}^{\aleph_1} \pi (1 + \rho)^{-s} = p \tag{19.13}$$

(*assuming* for the moment that the notation of the left-hand side has a meaning).

It would be foolhardy, however, should one jump straightforward into the calculation of the left-hand side of equation (19.13) in the manner of calculating a series in the ordinary sense. The left-hand side is expressed as the sum of a sequence of discrete terms. A sequence of discrete terms, in its ordinary notion, is indexed by the *natural numbers*: there is a one-to-one correspondence between its 'ith' term and a natural number i. A sequence involves listing its terms, and this listing amounts, in the ordinary notion of a sequence, to *counting* the terms following the sequence of the natural numbers. If a sequence is *infinite* (in the ordinary sense of ∞), the number of its terms is the same as the number of all the natural numbers, $\aleph_0$ (aleph-null). By contrast, the 'number of terms' in the left-hand side of equation (19.13) is $\aleph_1$, which is 'larger' than $\aleph_0$.[17] The left-hand side proposes to sum *more* than the *infinite* (∞) number of terms that the usual infinite series refers to: the size of a positive real interval as a set of real numbers is *transfinite*.

Looking at the opposite side of the same coin, if we tried to calculate the left-hand side of equation (19.13) in the same way as for an ordinary infinite series, we would be leaving *uncounted* some terms that are supposed to be included in the left-hand side. Indeed, Cantor tells us, the left-hand side has infinitely more uncounted terms than counted ones. The left-hand side refers to a sequence indexed by the real numbers in a positive interval – a 'net' (or a 'Moore–Smith sequence') on a positive real interval. Now, the sum of a sequence indexed by an uncountable set converges only if at most countably many terms in the sequence are nonzero (Bonar and Khoury, 2006, p. 94).

We earlier noted (and have been taking for granted) the second characteristic of equation (19.1): all the quantities in the equation are of (positive and finite) real magnitudes. We are now invoking it because it has a critical implication for our present discussion: the instant-wise flows of revenue, π's in equation (19.13), are of real magnitudes larger than zero.[18] It follows that the left-hand side of equation (19.13) has *uncountably many* nonzero (real) terms. Then, the conclusion we must arrive at is that the left-hand side fails to converge – this, *despite the fact that the flows of revenue are discounted geometrically*.[19] A logically consistent formula for an instantaneous nondurable, equation (19.13) squarely fails, in the setting of the instantaneous period of production, as a formula for obtaining the present value for a durable input.[20]

Result (19.12) allows us to see another, more fundamental, difficulty. The cardinality of a set measures the 'size' of the set. In the case of a finite set, the cardinality of the set coincides with the number of its elements. The two may be different to each other in the case of an infinite set. The cardinality of the set of the natural numbers, $\aleph_0$, corresponds uniquely to infinity (∞) when ∞ is applied to an infinite sequence. Meanwhile, $\aleph_1$ is the cardinality of *any* positive real interval. A nondurable input being defined in reference to an instant, *any* input that lasts for a positive real period, is classified as a durable. Durable inputs are not all the same, however, as they may have different physical lifetimes: one lasting for a second, another for a day, a third for a millennium. Now, with the instantaneous period of production, the number of periods of production in which these different durables are in operation is *uncountable*: $\aleph_1$, though representing the size of any positive real interval, does not 'count' the number of elements in it. To wit, using the T-way for a durable in instantaneous production is tantamount to *counting the uncountable*. One is, again, situated in a dilemma: the T-way succeeds in counting the number of production rounds that an instantaneous nondurable goes through over its lifetime but fails to do so for any durable input.[21]

The reader will be amused to note the contrast with the dilemma we have fallen into with the τ-way: one succeeds in calculating the user cost of a durable, on the basis of its lifetime being of a positive measure, but fails to do so for a nondurable since the latter's lifetime should be of measure zero. Indeed, the real dilemma one is confronted with is a bigger one: the τ-way cannot verify the Hicksian argument whilst it leads to a correct user cost of a durable; the T-way cannot be followed for calculating the user cost of a durable whilst it provides a logically consistent explanation of the Hicksian argument. In the economics of instantaneous production, one is standing perilously on thin ice, which is soon to give way due to the imbalance of weight of the two horns of dilemma.

It seems the tension arising from this dilemma that has made Katzner (1988), whose (economically) absurd result was mentioned before, resort to some nonsensical 'solution'. He may have been conscious of the result, for he stashes his 'proof' of an infinite user cost of a nondurable in footnotes. In the main text, he refers to the 'conventions' that '[the life of a nondurable input] is expressed in terms of numbers of instants (that is, numbers of infinitesimal lengths of time) and assumed to be unity' whilst 'lives of durable inputs are scaled as numbers of periods of finite length such as years and months', so that '[the life of a durable input] can be any positive real number' (p. 386). From this he infers that 'the limit of [the life of a durable input] as [it] declines is zero – not the life of a nondurable input' (p. 386).

This 'solution' is even more bizarre. Katzner is blind to the close relationship, and the necessary distinction, between the physical lifetime of an input and the number of production rounds it goes through during its lifetime. His solution is applying the τ-way to one of the two types of inputs and the T-way to the other, even though they are used side by side in productive processes. Thereby an absurd conclusion is forced upon him that some durable inputs would have a shorter lifetime (less than unity, declining to zero) than a nondurable input (always unity). His confusion in this matter is revealed also in his understanding of an instant of time: 'the concept of "instants of time" hereafter is characterised specifically as an arbitrarily small time interval. The alternative possibility of thinking of an instant as the limit of a sequence of smaller and smaller intervals . . . no longer is allowed' (p. 380). These two alternatives must be equivalent, in the sense that both must be of measure zero.

Conclusion: the more-than-instantaneous life of a nondurable input

Zeno of Elea and Cantor of Saint Petersburg – both would have a say in the economics of instantaneous production. Cantor would wonder how the economist could count the uncountable and also, by doing so, obtain a finite value. Zeno would be amazed with the story of the economist who caught up with the tortoise by making, he claimed, a sequence of instantaneous motions. Homer the economist has nodded in the economics of instantaneous production.

Homer the economist should awake and replace the instantaneous period of production with that of a *positive* period of production ('real-period production'). He will then revise the accounting relationship (19.1) into

$$Y = wL + (1+r)p_nK_n + rp_dK_d, \tag{19.14}$$

with r, K_n, Y and L all defined in reference to a common positive interval of time.[22] This is a revision that is required, not by the realism of an economic model, but by the minimal logical consistency that a theoretical model should satisfy.

One important implication of this revision is for the measure of 'capital' in multi-sector models where production of different commodities is sequentially connected. For, in these models, it will now be the case that 'interest on the net input of the week (since it was paid for on the Monday) is included in the capital at the end of the week' (Hicks, 1973, p. 30). In horizontal innovation or vertical innovation models (the object of particular attention in the present essay), if a nondurable input is used in any of the first two stages of production (the R&D and the intermediate-good sectors), the interest on the input – which now has its legitimate existence – should be taken into account (and compounded) in the measure of capital in the final stage of production (the final good sector). It is a fact, however, that Romer's (1990) 'accounting measure of capital', Barro and Sala-i-Martin's (2004, Ch. 6) measure of the 'assets' of the economy, and Jones's (2005) measure of 'financial assets' are some measures of 'capital' where the effect of (compounding) interest has been completely eliminated. Whatever convenient role they may play in their models, none of them is a correct measure of the totality of the means of production used in the economy, in the sense of the measure in reference to which the rate of interest on the means of production is calculated in a logically (and economically) consistent way. Then, yet to come are further implications for which the revision in the measure of 'capital' will have some important conclusions of these models, and which may prove seriously troublesome.

Notes

1 Gancia and Zilibotti (2005) and Aghion and Hewitt (2005) are excellent surveys of horizontal innovation and vertical innovation models, respectively. My particular attention to these models is due to an essential feature they share: production of commodities by means of commodities, or sequentially connected production. For it is this feature that is particularly vulnerable to various difficulties associated with an instantaneous nondurable input, to be identified in the following pages.
2 Of course, the price variables (w, p_n and p_d) must be positive, finite and real if the economy is to be no-nonsensical.
3 Park (2015) shows that, in the setting of instantaneous production, some of the quantities must not be real but 'infinitesimal' (in the sense of 'nonstandard analysis'; see Robinson, 1996) whilst the others must be real. He then proves that, *due to that very fact*, instantaneous production is logically impossible in the 'no-nonsense capitalist economy', the no-nonsensicality being defined in terms of the no-nonsensicality of the key economic variables (the finite positivity of the rate of interest, the unit supply price and the unit user cost) and the establishment, at each instant, of value accounting relations regarding production.
4 Or, an equally naïve way of reasoning may run as follows. The user cost of an input that depreciates at the rate of δ is $(\delta + r)p$. If an input does not depreciate at all, then $\delta = 0$; therefore, the user cost of the input is rp. If, by contrast, an input depreciates fully in a negligible interval of time, then $\delta = 1$ and the rate of interest applicable to the case also becomes negligible – that is, zero in the limit; therefore, the user cost of the input is simply p.
5 The aforementioned paper of Park (2015) adopts the third understanding and, using some concepts of nonstandard analysis, proves the 'impossibility of capitalist instantaneous production'.
6 There will always be another instant 'after' the present instant, but this 'after' can be by a second, by a nanosecond, by a yoctosecond, by 100 attoseconds (the shortest time interval ever measured physically), or by any arbitrarily small duration. It is no wonder that the ultimate measurement unit of time in (current) theoretical physics, a Plank time has a positive length. The Big Bang marked Time Zero; then, it took one Plank time (about 5.39124×10^{-44} seconds) for the first-ever 'next' event after the Big Bang – the separation of gravitation from the other fundamental forces (electromagnetism, the weak

interaction and the strong interaction) – to take place. In anticipation of our discussion in later pages, we say that when one mentions 'a sequence of production', one is restricting the meaning of a 'sequence' to an ordinary sequence indexed by the natural numbers (a countable set), excluding a (Moore–Smith) sequence indexed by the real numbers (an uncountable set).

7 Directly relevant to the current case is the paradox of 'dichotomy': In a race with a tortoise, Achilles must first run half of the initial distance between them; however, before he can complete this half, he must run half of that half; before he can complete the quarter, he must run half of the quarter, and so on; there is no first member in this regression; therefore, Achilles cannot even get started (see, *e.g.*, Salmon, 2001). The less well-known paradox of 'plurality' (which is in fact more fundamental than all the other well-known of Zeno's paradoxes) has the direct relevance to our argument in the section dealing with a durable input: 'the units in a collection can have no size at all: else they would have parts and be not units but collections of units. ... [O]n the contrary, there cannot be anything that has no size at all; for there cannot be a thing which if it were added or subtracted from something else would not affect the size of that thing' (Owen, 2001, p. 140; see also Salmon, 2001).

8 This must be the case because each period of production is associated, by definition, with a *new* measurement of a flow of revenue. In order to be consistent in the matter of measurement, then, all the other *flow* variables in the economy – including the rate of interest, whose numerator is a flow of interest accruing during a certain period of time – are to be measurement-synchronised with the flow of revenue.

9 The reader can easily construct S for the case of a positive unit period of production.

10 The same result can be obtained in terms of the first understanding of an afore-mentioned instant: an instant as an ever-shrinking interval, hence the duration of an instant being $dv := \lim_{t \to t_0} (t - t_0)$. Then one has $T = \frac{dv}{dv} = \frac{\lim_{t \to t_0} (t - t_0)}{\lim_{t \to t_0} (t - t_0)} = 1$, by L'Hôpital's rule.

11 The 'instant-wise rate of interest' is to be distinguished from what the literature calls the 'instantaneous rate of interest'. The latter refers to the rate, $r(t)$, that prevails at instant t but which is defined in reference to the (positive) unit period of time (a 'week'). The 'instant-wise rate of interest', to be denoted $\rho(t)$, is defined, in contrast, in reference to an instant. The two rates have the following relationship: $\rho(t) = r(t)dt$ or $r(t) = \int_t^{t+1} r(v)dv$ on the condition that $r(v)$ is *constant* in interval $[t, t+1]$. As Hayek (1941, pp. 175–6) puts it, the instantaneous rate of interest 'assumes concrete meaning only if we express it in terms of the increase in the original quantity which it would have caused if it had continued to operate for a definite period, say one year'.

12 In nonstandard analysis, where an instant is conceived as having an infinitesimal length, an instant is itself a continuum, capable of further infinite division. The smaller parts after the infinite division are of second-order infinitesimal lengths; these parts can be further divisible infinitely into infinitesimals of third order, etc. In this case, one may use the continuous discounting factor, with the rate of interest of an appropriate order of magnitude.

13 Thus there is an irony here: whilst the use of a positive time interval as the unit period of production (thus, measuring flows in discrete terms) allows continuous discounting, the use of an instant as the unit period of production (which points to the measurement of flows in continuous terms) would lead to '(instant-wise) discrete discounting'.

14 This formula is similar to that of discrete discounting where the unit period of production is positive and net revenue is realised at the *end* of the period. Note, however, that the instantaneous period of production annuls the distinction between the beginning and the end of a period.

15 We are here insinuating the question of the order of magnitude of the quantities appearing in equation (19.1); however, we do not probe further.

16 Logically there may be inputs that last for more than one instant but for less than any real period of time. We ignore this type of input.

17 The expressions such as the 'number of terms' and 'larger' are not really exact; see the discussion of the 'more fundamental difficulty' below.

18 In equation (19.1), $rp_d K_d$ is the total user cost of the durable, that is, $rp_d K_d = \pi x$ where x is the number of physical units of the durable put in operation each instant (with π appropriately time-scaled) and K_d is the magnitude of service generated each instant by those units of the durable. Since x cannot but be a positive natural number, a positive and finite real value of $rp_d K_d$ implies a positive and finite real value of π. (Indeed, an implicit assumption in the established practice is that $K_d = x$. Park (2015) shows that this should not be the case.)

19 The reader will note that this criticism of divergence refers to a *logical* difficulty in deriving the user cost of a durable. It is another matter to point out that, if quantities in an instant are positive real, they will become infinite as soon as the economy enters a real period of time – though this is surely unrealistic; such a criticism touches upon the matter of realism, not the matter of logic.

20 If π's, appropriately time-scaled, are nonzero but of 'infinitesimal' magnitudes in the sense of nonstandard analysis (thus, smaller than any positive real number), then the LHS *does* converge to a nonzero real number. Indeed, it must be the case that π's are infinitesimal in the case of a durable. This means that the second characteristic of equation (19.1) in the established practice is a logically invalid supposition. These points are discussed in detail in Park (2015).

21 Let us consider the matter in terms of the limit (the first understanding of an instant). For *any* $\bar{i} > t_0$, one obtains uniformly $T = \frac{\bar{i}-t_0}{dv} = \infty$. In a similar way as considered in the main text (with the second understanding of an instant), the T-way cannot tell us how to distinguish between different durables which have different lifetimes. Indeed, the first understanding gets the exposure of the problem to be sharper. Suppose the flow of revenue generated in each instant is the same across durable inputs of different lifetimes; then, since these inputs generate revenue over different durations of time, it *must* be the case that the value of the flows of revenue, whether discounted or not, is different across them. But this *cannot* be the case when we count the number of production periods in terms of ∞. Different lifetimes of the durables (which are the *physical* criterion by which to distinguish between them) are of no relevance at all in identifying the number of production periods they go through during their lifetimes and, therefore, in identifying the total amount (discounted or not) of revenues they respectively give rise to (which are the *economic* criterion by which to distinguish between them): an input that lasts for a nanosecond and another that lasts for a millennium would, even if it is supposed that the amount of revenues generated each instant is the same for both inputs, generate the same amount of revenues, whether undiscounted or discounted, during their lifetimes. Moreover, if one simply applies the infinite (∞) number of production periods to formula (19.10), one gets $\sum_{s=1}^{\infty} \pi (1 + \rho)^{-s} = \rho^{-1}\pi = p$, from which is derived $\pi = \rho p$. Since $\rho = rdv$, this means that the user cost of a durable, of any lifetime, is uniformly *zero*! – the counterpart of the *infinite* user cost of a nondurable which one obtains when one considers the matter in the τ-way.

22 The user cost of a nondurable in equation (19.14), $(1 + r)p_n$, is in accordance with discrete discounting; if one applies continuous discounting, it will be $(1 - e^{-r})^{-1}rp_n$. The use cost of an everlasting durable is, of course, rp_d whether in discrete or continuous discounting.

References

Acemoglu, D. (2009) *Introduction to Modern Economic Growth*, Princeton, NJ and Oxford: Princeton University Press.

Aghion, P. and Hewitt, P. (2005) 'Growth with Quality-Improving Innovations: An Integrated Framework', in P. Aghion and S. Durlauf (eds) *Handbook of Economic Growth*, Amsterdam: North Holland, pp. 67–110.

Barro, R. and Sala-i-Martin, X. (2004) *Economic Growth*, 2nd edition, Cambridge, MA and London: The MIT Press.

Bonar, D. D. and Khoury, Jr., M. (2006) *Real Infinite Series*, Washington, DC: Mathematical Association of America.

Gancia, G. and Zilibotti, F. (2005) 'Horizontal Innovation in the Theory of Growth and Development', in P. Aghion and S. Durlauf (eds) *Handbook of Economic Growth*, Amsterdam: North Holland, pp. 111–170.

Hayek, F. A. (1941) *The Pure Theory of Capital*, London: Routledge & Kegan Paul.

Hicks, J. (1973) *Capital and Time. A Neo-Austrian Theory*, Oxford: Oxford University Press.

Jones, C. (2005) 'Growth and Ideas', in P. Aghion and S. Durlauf (eds) *Handbook of Economic Growth*, Amsterdam: North Holland, pp. 1063–1111.

Katzner, D. W. (1988) *Walrasian Microeconomics: An Introduction to the Economic Theory of Market Behavior*, Reading, MA: Addison-Wesley Publishing Company.

Owen, G. E. L. (2001) 'Zeno and the Mathematician', in W. C. Salmon (ed.) *Zeno's Paradox*, Indianapolis/Cambridge: Hackett Publishing Company, Inc, pp. 139–163.

Park, M.-S. (2015) 'The Impossibility of Capitalist Instantaneous Production' *Metroeconomica*, 66(1): 28–50.

Robinson, A. (1996) *Non-standard Analysis*, revised edition, Princeton, NJ: Princeton University Press.

Romer, P. M. (1990) 'Endogenous Technological Change', *Journal of Political Economy*, 98(5): S71–S102.

Salmon, W. C. (2001) 'Introduction', in W. C. Salmon (ed.) *Zeno's Paradox*, Indianapolis/Cambridge: Hackett Publishing Company, Inc, pp. 5–44.

Silberberg, E. and Suen, W. (2001) *The Structure of Economics. A Mathematical Analysis*, third edition, New York, NY: McGraw-Hill Companies, Inc.

Sraffa, P. (1932) 'Dr. Hayek on Money and Capital', *Economic Journal*, 42(165): 42–53.

Sraffa, P. (1960) *Production of Commodities by Means of Commodities*, Cambridge: Cambridge University Press.

Part 5

Imperfect competition

20 Product differentiation, kinked demand and collusion

Antonio D'Agata

Introduction

This paper attempts a rehabilitation of the kinked demand approach (Hall and Hitch, 1939; Sweezy, 1939) in explaining collusion among producers of homogeneous goods. The kinked demand approach is one of the most known and still used approaches to deal with collusion (Maskin and Tirole, 1988; Sen, 2004; Currarini and Marini, 2011; Garrod, 2012), although it has been strongly criticized because of its behavioural assumption of asymmetric reaction of competitors to price changes (Stigler, 1947; Primeaux and Bomball, 1974; Bhaskar *et al.*, 1991). However, this assumption is not necessary for having a kink: actually, Salop (1979) shows that kinked demand curves can exist in Hotelling models of product differentiation with Nash-like firms. However, neither Salop nor successive scholars have investigated the implications of this result for collusion.

In this paper we provide a simple Hotelling model of product differentiation in which collusion among Nash-like quantity-setting firms[1] producing identical goods is possible because of kinks in demand. In this kind of model, homogeneity of products is a quite restrictive condition in the light of the Principle of Maximum Differentiation which has amended Hotelling's Principle of Minimum Product Differentiation (see d'Aspremont *et al.*, 1979). Nevertheless, we show that in our model production of homogeneous products by collusive firms can occur in equilibrium just because of the opportunity of collusion generated by the kinks. So, our results can also be used to rehabilitate Hotelling's Principle of Minimum Product Differentiation as well.[2] Finally, our result can be useful in explaining empirical results showing collusion in differentiated product markets where firms produce very similar or identical products (Breshanan, 1987; Lambson and Richardson, 1992; Parker and Röller, 1997) and the strategic use of product line length (see Draganska and Jain (2003) and references therein).

The paper is organized as follows. The next section shows how and under which conditions kinked demand can support collusive equilibria in quantity-setting Cournotian oligopolies. The third section shows that in a linear differentiated product model three different kinds of kinked demand can emerge and it analyses the implications of this result for the sustainability of collusive market configurations. As previously said, homogeneity of products is problematic in

product differentiation models; thus the fourth section provides an example showing that in equilibrium firms find it profitable to choose the same product thanks
to the existence of collusive-supporting kinks in demand curves. The fifth section
provides some final remarks.

Kinked demand and collusion with Nash-like firms

In this section we shall analyse the role of kinks in Cournotian oligopolies. Before
getting into technical details, let us provide an intuitive argument of our main
result. In a Cournot oligopoly with n firms the monopoly equilibrium is not stable
because the quantity effect is greater than each firm's share of the price effect
(D'Agata, 2010). The former is inversely related to the (absolute value of the)
slope of the demand curve, so the monopolistic configuration could be a collusive
equilibrium for the n-oligopoly if at this configuration the demand curve has a
'big enough' kink. We show also that the greater the number of oligopolists, the
greater the kink has to be in order to support collusion.

More formally, consider the market of an homogeneous product x with linear demand function $p = A - bq$, with $A, b > 0$. Production is carried out at
zero cost and firms are quantity-setting and follow the Cournot–Nash conjecture. Denote by $p^{(1)}$ and $q^{(1)}$ the monopolistic price/quantity configuration and for
$n = 2, 3, 4, \ldots$, a n-*firm Cournot symmetric equilibrium* (simply n-*equilibrium*) is
a price/quantity couple $(p^{(n)}, q^{(n)})$ such that $p^{(n)} = A - bq^{(n)}$ and $q^{(n)}/n$ is the profit
maximizing level of production for each firm, given the aggregate production level
$(n-1)q^{(n)}/n$ of all other firms. In general, for $n = 1, 2, \ldots$,

$$q^{(n)} = \frac{n}{(n+1)} \cdot \frac{A}{b}, \ p^{(n)} = \frac{A}{(n+1)}. \tag{20.1}$$

Collusive firms in an n-firm oligopoly seek to ensure the lowest possible pro-
duction level in interval $[q^{(1)}, q^{(n)}]$. Set $C_x(n) = \{(p, q) | p = A - bq, q^{(1)} \le q \le q^{(n)}\}$
is the *collusive interval* for the n-firm oligopoly in market x with demand func-
tion $p = A - bq$. Let (p^*, q^*) be a market configuration in $C_x(n)$, where set
$C_x(n; p^*, q^*) = \{(p, q) | (p, q) \in C_x(n), q^* \le q \le q^{(n)}\}$ is the *competitive portion*
of $C_x(n)$ with respect to market configuration (p^*, q^*). The next result follows
immediately from (20.1).

Fact 20.1 *Market configuration* $(p^*, q^*) \in C_x(n)$ *is an n-equilibrium for a market
with demand function* $p = A^{(q^*,n)} - b^{(q^*,n)}q$, *where* $A^{(q^*,n)} = (n+1)(A - bq^*)$ *and*
$b^{(q^*,n)} = \frac{n(A - bq^*)}{q^*}$.

As a consequence of Fact 20.1, we have the following.

Fact 20.2 *If* (p^*, q^*), $(p^{**}, q^{**}) \in C_x(n)$ *with* $q^* \le q^{**}$, *then* $b^{(q^*,n)} \ge b^{(q^{**},n)} \ge b$,
where the last inequality holds as an equality only if $q^{**} = q^{(n)}$.

The following result, whose proof is provided in Appendix 20.A, highlights the role of kinks in supporting collusive behaviour in homogeneous markets with Nash-like firms.

Fact 20.3 *If $(p^*, q^*) \in C_x(n)$, then (p^*, q^*) is an n-equilibrium for any market with kinked demand function:*

$$p = \begin{cases} A - bq & \text{for } 0 \leq q \leq q^* \\ A' - b'q & \text{for } q \geq q^* \end{cases} \tag{20.2}$$

with $A' \geq A^{(q^*,n)}$, $b' \geq b^{(q^*,n)}$ and $A' - A = (b' - b)q^*$, where $A^{(q^*,n)}$ and $b^{(q^*,n)}$ are defined in Fact 20.1.

Following Salop (1979, p. 143) we call the monopoly region of the demand curve that region in the interval $[0, q^*]$ in function (20.2) and the competitive region that region in the interval $\left[q^*, \frac{A'}{b'}\right]$.[3]

Example 20.1 Figure 20.1 illustrates Fact 20.2 for two price/quantity configurations in $C_x(2)$:

(a)   the monopolistic configuration $p^{(1)} = \frac{A}{2}$ and $q^{(1)} = \frac{A}{2b}$ (point b) is supported as a duopolistic equilibrium by the market demand curve Abd defined by the function

$$p = \begin{cases} A - bq & \text{for } 0 \leq q \leq q^{(1)} \\ \dfrac{3}{2}A - 2bq & \text{for } q \geq q^{(1)}; \end{cases} \tag{20.3}$$

(b)   configuration $\hat{p} = \frac{2}{5}A$ and $\hat{q} = \frac{3}{5} \cdot \frac{A}{b}$ (point e) is supported as duopolistic equilibrium by the market demand curve Aef defined by the function

$$p = \begin{cases} A - bq & \text{for } 0 \leq q \leq \hat{q} \\ \dfrac{6}{5}A - \dfrac{4}{3}bq & \text{for } q \geq \hat{q}. \end{cases} \tag{20.4}$$

Fact 20.3 ensures that these configurations are supported as duopolistic equilibria also for demand curves with steeper competitive regions.

The next result is an immediate consequence of Facts 20.2 and 20.3.

Fact 20.4 *Let $(p^*, q^*) \in C_x(n)$ be an n-equilibrium for the market with a given demand function defined by (20.2). Then $(p^{**}, q^{**}) \in C_x(n, p^*, q^*)$ is an n-equilibrium for the market with demand function*

$$p = \begin{cases} A - bq & \text{for } 0 \leq q \leq q^{**} \\ A'' - b'q & \text{for } q \geq q^{**} \end{cases}$$

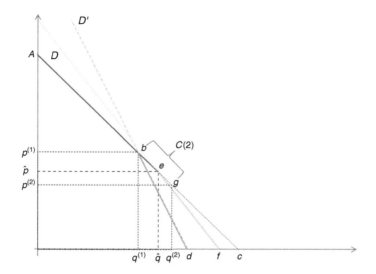

Figure 20.1 Demand curves supporting collusive market configurations.

where $A'' = A + (b' - b)q^{**}$ *and* b' *is the slope of the demand function given by* *(20.2)*.

Referring to Figure 20.1, Fact 20.4 means that, for example, since demand curve *Abd* supports $(p^{(1)}, q^{(1)})$ as a duopolistic equilibrium, any kinked demand curve obtained by curves D and D' when intersecting along segment *bg* will also support a duopolistic equilibrium at the kink. Intuitively, Facts 20.3 and 20.4 set lower bounds to the value of the slope of the demand curve in the competitive region ensuring collusion at the kink.

Facts 20.2 and 20.3 can be reinterpreted as follows. Consider, for example, a duopoly facing an initial demand function $p = A - bq$. The monopolistic configuration $(p^{(1)}, q^{(1)})$ is not a stable collusive equilibrium for the Cournotian duopoly, but it can become so if at this configuration an 'appropriate' kink, as defined by (20.3) and illustrated by curve *Abd* in Figure 20.1, is somewhat generated. Similar argument for configuration $(\hat{p}, \hat{q})$ with reference to kinked demand (20.4) and illustrated by curve *Aed*. Now the issue is how to generate kinks. As said in the first section, Salop (1979) shows that kinks can be generated endogenously by casting the Cournotian model within an address model of product differentiation. Given the endogenous nature of these kinks, it is not clear whether they meet the lower bound requirements set out by Facts 20.3 and 20.4. The next section shows that in a differentiated product model *à la* Hotelling, three kinds of kinks can be generated on the demand curve market of any given product due to the existence of either boundaries or goods which are positioned 'close enough' to the original one in the product space. Then we determine the kind of collusion, in terms of

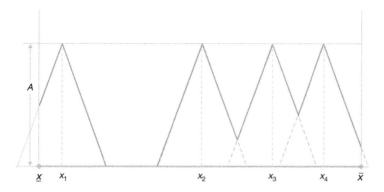

Figure 20.2 Types of markets.

number of oligopolists and market configuration, which can be supported by the three kinds of kinks.

Product differentiation, kinked demand and collusion

Consider the linear version of Salop's 1979 model, with consumers uniformly distributed along the segment $L = [\underline{x}, \bar{x}]$, each buying only one unit of good. Set L also defines the product space, so each point in L also describes a product. Consumer $c \in L$ has a reservation price for product $x \in L$ equal to $R(c, x) = \max[0, A - 2b|c - x|]$.[4] Consumer c buys product x at price p_x only if $R(c, x) - p_x \geq 0$. If p_{x_1} and p_{x_2} are the prices of products x_1 and x_2 in L, respectively, then consumer c buys product x_1 if $R(c, x_1) - p_{x_1} \geq R(c, x_2) - p_{x_2}$.

Our aim is to provide a complete list of kinked demand curves and, consequently, of potentially collusive market configurations which are generated by the existence of differentiated products or boundaries 'close enough' to the relevant product. Five possible cases can occur:[5] (a) monopoly; (b) market with unilateral boundary constraint; (c) market with unilateral competition; (d) market with bilateral competition; (e) market with unilateral competition and boundary constraint.[6]

Figure 20.2 illustrates cases (b)–(e), case (a) being obvious. Market of product x_1 exhibits a boundary constraint, market of product $x_2(x_3)$ shows unilateral (bilateral) competition, finally, market of product x_4 exhibits unilateral competition with boundary constraint. We show that in these markets demand curves show different kinks in terms of the slopes of the competitive regions. Then, on the basis of the results in the previous section, we show the implications of these possibilities for collusion. Since all claims are obtained by routine calculations and follow as direct implications of Facts 20.1–20.4, the proofs of statements are omitted.

(a)   *Monopoly.* The inverse demand function of the monopolistic product x is: $p = A - bq$, so demand has no kinks.

(b)   *Market with boundary constraint.* Product x_1's inverse demand curve is

$$p_1 = \begin{cases} A - bq_1 & \text{for } 0 \le q_1 \le 2H_1 \\ A + 2bH_1 - 2bq_1 & \text{for } q_1 \ge 2H_1, \end{cases} \tag{20.5}$$

where H_1 is the distance of product x_1 from the constraining boundary.

(c)   *Market with unilateral competition.* Product x_2's inverse demand curve is

$$p_2 = \begin{cases} A - bq_2 & \text{for } 0 \le q_2 \le \bar{q}_2 \\ \dfrac{2b(x_3 - x_2) + 2A + p_3}{3} - \dfrac{4b}{3}q_2 & \text{for } q_2 \ge \bar{q}_2 \end{cases} \tag{20.6}$$

where $\bar{q}_2 = 2(x_3 - x_2 - \frac{A-p_3}{2b})$ is the demand level at which the market of x_2 overlaps the market of product x_3 (see Salop, 1979, Figure 4).

(d)   *Market with bilateral competition.* Under symmetry of markets x_2 and x_4 with respect to market x_3 (that is: $x_4 - x_3 - \frac{A-p_4}{2b} = x_4 - x_3 - \frac{A-p_2}{2b}$),[7] the inverse demand curve of x_3 is

$$p_3 = \begin{cases} A - bq_3 & \text{for } 0 \le q_3 \le \bar{q}_3 \\ \dfrac{2b(x_4 - x_2) + (p_4 + p_2)}{2} - 2bq_3 & \text{for } q_3 \ge \bar{q}_3 \end{cases} \tag{20.7}$$

where $\bar{q}_3 = 2(x_4 - x_2 - \frac{A-p_2}{2b}) = 2(x_3 - x_2 - \frac{A-p_2}{2b})$ is the demand level at which the market of product 3 overlaps products x_2 and x_4 markets.

(e)   *Market with unilateral competition and boundary constraint.* Under symmetry of markets x_3 and x_4 with respect to market x_3 and to the boundary (that is: $H_4 = x_4 - x_3 - \frac{A-p_3}{2b}$, where H_4 is the distance of product x_4 from the constraining boundary),[8] the inverse demand of x_4 is

$$p_4 = \begin{cases} A - bq_4 & \text{for } 0 \le q_4 \le \bar{q}_4 \\ 2b(2H_4 + x_4 - x_3) + p_3 - 4bq_4 & \text{for } q_4 \ge \bar{q}_4 \end{cases} \tag{20.8}$$

where $\bar{q}_4 = 2H_4 (= 2(x_4 - x_3 - \frac{A-p_3}{2b}))$ is the demand level at which the market of product 4 overlaps the product 3 market or intersects the boundary.

Once noticed that, from Fact 20.1, $b^{(q^{(1)},n)} = nb$, by Facts 20.1, 20.3 and 20.4 and from (20.1), (20.5)–(20.8), the following proposition can be made.

Proposition 20.1 *The following assertions hold true:*

(1)   *in markets with monopolistic products (product x), only the n-equilibrium configuration $(p^{(n)}, q^{(n)})$ defined by (20.1) can be supported as an n-equilibrium;*

(2) in markets with boundary constraint, or with bilateral competition (products x_1 and x_3), any configuration in set $C_{x_i}(n, \frac{2}{n+2}A, \frac{n}{n+2}\frac{A}{b})(i = 1, 3)$ can be supported as an n-equilibrium;

(3) in markets with unilateral competition (product x_2), any configuration in set $C_{x_2}(n, \frac{4A}{3n+4}, \frac{3nA}{(3n+4)b})$ can be supported as an n-equilibrium;

(4) in markets with unilateral competition and boundary constraints (product x_4), any configuration in set $C_{x_4}(n, \frac{4A}{n+4}, \frac{nA}{(n+4)b})$ can be supported as an n-equilibrium.

To be more specific, in the monopolistic market x, only the duopolistic configuration $p_1^{(2)} = \frac{A}{3}$, $q_1^{(2)} = \frac{2}{3} \cdot \frac{A}{b}$ can be supported as a 2-equilibrium. In markets with boundary constraints or with bilateral competition any price/quantity configuration in set $C_{x_i}(2, p^{(1)}, q^{(1)})$, $i = 1, 3$, can be supported as a duopolistic equilibrium. In markets with unilateral competition any price/quantity configuration $(p^*, q^*) \in C_{x_2}(2, \hat{p}, \hat{q})$ can be supported as a duopolistic equilibrium, where $\hat{p} = \frac{2}{5}A$ and $\hat{q} = \frac{3}{5} \cdot \frac{A}{b}$ as introduced in Example (b). Finally, in markets with unilateral competition and boundary constraints any price/quantity configuration in set $C_{x_4}(n, p^{(1)}, q^{(1)})$ can be supported as an n-Cournot equilibrium, with $n \leq 4$.

The minimum product differentiation principle revisited

We show that the results in the previous section imply that oligopolists may choose the same product even in one-shot games, unlike Jehiel (1992) and Friedman and Thisse (1993), and in a standard model of product differentiation, unlike De Palma *et al.* (1985). Consider the model in the previous section and suppose that there are four firms, a, b, c and d, and three products, $x_1, x_2, x_3 \in [\underline{x}, \bar{x}]$. Firms a (firm d) produces good x_1 (good x_3), while firms b and c produce the same good x_2. Suppose also that $L = \frac{3A}{b}$, $x_1 = \underline{x} + \frac{A}{2b}$, $x_2 = \underline{x} + \frac{3A}{2b}$, $x_3 = \underline{x} + \frac{5A}{2b}$ and $p_1 = p_2 = p_4 = \frac{A}{2}$. The first four equalities ensure that in the product space there is room exactly for three monopolists who face a kink at the monopolistic price. By fact (20.2) in the proposition, firms b and c collude and split equally the market of good x_2, so their profits are equal to $\frac{A^2}{8b}$. Suppose now that either firm b or firm c changes its product to $x' \neq x_2$. Then if $x' \in [\underline{x} + \frac{A}{2b}, \underline{x} + \frac{5A}{2b}]$, the optimal price is still equal to the monopolistic one and the relevant firm's profits are equal to $\frac{A^2}{8b}$, otherwise profits are lower. So, given the location and price choice of rivals, producing good x_2 is an optimal product choice for both collusive firms b and c.

Conclusions

The third section deals only with market configurations which can *potentially* be supported by collusion. The fourth section shows that *actual* market configurations depend upon the specific position of the kink in the competitive portions of the collusive sets $C_{x_i}(n)$, if any. This, in turn, depends upon the existence of boundaries or products 'close enough' in the product space (see (20.5)–(20.8)). If we consider multiproduct firms, the analysis suggests that firms actually can strategically choose the location of their products in such a way to support collusive equilibria, possibly the monopolistic one. This extension could be of some interest also in the analysis of multiproduct firms (see, for example, Brander and Eaton, 1984).

Appendix 20.A

Lemma 20.A.1 *Consider a market with demand function*

$$
p = \begin{cases} A - bq & \text{for } 0 \le q \le q^* \\ A' - b'q & \text{for } q \ge q^* \end{cases}
$$

where $A - A' = (b - b')q^*$ and $q^* \ge 0$. Then (p^*, q^*) is an n-Cournot equilibrium if $\frac{n}{(n+1)} \cdot \frac{A'}{b'} \le q^* \le \frac{n}{(n+1)} \cdot \frac{A}{b}$.

Proof. The assertion follows from the fact that inequalities $\frac{n}{(n+1)} \cdot \frac{A'}{b'} \le q^* \le \frac{n}{(n+1)} \cdot \frac{A}{b}$ imply that $\frac{\partial \pi_i(q_i)}{\partial q_i} = A - (n+1)bq_i \ge 0$ and $\frac{\partial \pi_j'(q_i)}{\partial q_i} = A' - (n+1)b'q_i \le 0$, with $q_i = q^*/n$, $\pi(q_i) = (A - b(n+1)q_i)q_i$ and $\pi'(q_i) = (A' - b'(n+1)q_i)q_i$. $\square$

Proof of Fact 3. Let $(p^*, q^*) \in C_x(n)$; then $q^{(1)} \le q^* \le q^{(n)} = \frac{n}{n+1} \cdot \frac{A}{b}$. By the fact that $q^* = \frac{n}{(n+1)} \cdot \frac{A(q^*,n)}{b(q^*,n)}$ it follows that $\frac{n}{(n+1)} \cdot \frac{A(q^*,n)}{b(q^*,n)} = q^* \le \frac{n}{n+1} \cdot \frac{A}{b}$. By the lemma, the claim is valid for $A' = A^{(q^*,n)}$ and $b' = b^{(q^*,n)}$. For $A' \ge A^{(q^*,n)}$ and $b' \ge b^{(q^*,n)}$ with $A' - A = (b' - b)q^*$ the inequalities $\frac{n}{(n+1)} \cdot \frac{A'}{b'} \le q^* \le \frac{n}{n+1} \cdot \frac{A}{b}$ a fortiori have to be satisfied, because $\frac{A'}{b'} = \frac{A - bq^*}{b'} + q^*$, so $\frac{A'}{b'}$ is decreasing with respect to b'. $\square$

Notes

1 For a survey of models of product differentiation with quantity-setting firms, see Biscaia and Mota (2012).
2 For alternative approaches used to rehabilitate Hotelling's Principle of Minimum Product Differentiation, see, for example, De Palma *et al.* (1985), Jehiel (1992) and Friedman and Thisse (1993).
3 We do not consider the supercompetitive region: see Salop (1979, p. 143).
4 Parameters in $R(c, x)$ are chosen in order to allow a direct comparison with the results in the previous section.
5 A sixth case, that is markets with bilateral boundary constraints, is not considered as it is empirically implausible and analytically obvious once case (b) below is taken into account.
6 In Salop's circular city model only cases (a), (c) and (d) can occur.
7 Without symmetry, market of product x_3 overlaps markets x_2 and x_4 at different prices, so the demand curve exhibits two kinks. The kink associated to the low level of production is the one in case (c), while the kink associated to the highest production level is the one given by (20.7). By contrast, symmetry ensures that market of product x_3 overlaps markets x_2 and x_4 at the same price, so the demand curve exhibits only the kink defined by (20.7). From the point of view of kink types and opportunities of collusion, symmetry does not yield any loss of information.

8 The reason for assuming symmetry is, *mutatis mutandis*, similar to the one provided for the previous case (d) (see Note 7). Without symmetry, in this case the kink associated at the low level of production may be either of type (b) or of type (c).

References

Bhaskar V., Machine, S. and Reid, G. (1991), Testing a model of the kinked demand curve, *Journal of Industrial Economics*, 39(3), March, 241–254.

Biscaia, R. and Mota, I. (2012), Models of spatial competition: a critical review, *Papers in Regional Science*, 92(4), November, 851–871.

Brander, J. A. and Eaton, J. (1984), Product line rivalry, *American Economic Review*, 74(3), June, 323–334.

Breshanan, T. F. (1987), Competition and collusion in the American automobile industry: the 1955 price war, *Journal of Industrial Economics*, 35(4), June, 457–482.

Currarini, S. and Marini, M. (2011), Kinked norms of behaviour and cooperation, *Economics Letters*, 110(3), March, 223–225.

D'Agata, A. (2010), Geometry of Cournot-Nash equilibrium with applications to commons and anticommons, *Journal of Economic Education*, 41(2), April–June, 169–176.

d'Aspremont, C., Gabszewicz, J. J. and Thisse, J. F. (1979), On Hotelling's 'Stability in competition', *Econometrica*, 47 (5), September, 1145–1150.

De Palma, A., Ginsburgh, V. Papageorgiou, Y. Y. and Thisse, J. F. (1985), The Principle of Minimum Differentiation holds under sufficient heterogeneity, *Econometrica*, 53(4), July, 767–781.

Draganska, M. and Jain, D. (2003), Product line length as a competitive tool, *Journal of Economics and Management Strategy*, 14(1), February, 1–28.

Friedman, J. W. and Thisse, J. F. (1993), Partial collusion fosters minimum product differentiation, *RAND Journal of Economics*, 24(4), Winter, 631–645.

Garrod, L. (2012), Collusive price rigidity under price-matching punishment, *International Journal of Industrial Organization*, 30(5), September, 471–482.

Hall, R. and Hitch, C. (1939), Price theory and business behaviour, *Oxford Economic Papers*, 2, May, 12–45.

Jehiel, P. (1992), Product differentiation and price collusion, *International Journal of Industrial Organization*, 10(4), December, 633–641.

Lambson, V. E. and Richardson, J. D. (1992), Empirical evidence for collusion in the U.S. auto market, *NBER Working Papers*, N. 4111.

Maskin, E. and Tirole, J. (1988) A theory of dynamic oligopoly II: price competition, kinked demand curves and Edgeworth cycles, *Econometrica*, 56(3), May, 571–599.

Parker P. M. and Röller, L. H. (1997), Collusive conduct in duopolies: multimarket contact and cross-over ownership in the mobile telephone industry, *RAND Journal of Economics*, 28(2), Summer, 304–322.

Primeaux, W. J. and Bomball, M. R. (1974) A reexamination of the kinky oligopoly demand curve, *Journal of Political Economy*, 82(4), July, 851–862.

Salop, S. C. (1979), Monopolitic competition with outside goods, *Bell Journal of Economics*, 10(1), Spring, 141–156.

Sen, D. (2004), The kinked demand curve revisited, *Economics Letters*, 84(1), July, 99–105.

Stigler, G. (1947), Kinky oligopoly demand and rigid prices, *Journal of Political Economy*, 55(5), October, 432–449.

Sweezy, P. M. (1939), Demand under conditions of oligopoly, *Journal of Political Economy*, 47(4), August, 568–573.

21 Unionised oligopoly, capacity choice and strategic entry under Bertrand competition

Simone D'Alessandro and
Luciano Fanti

Introduction

The analysis of the existence of an equilibrium in the Bertrand model with homogeneous product is a very long lasting issue. The standard result, known as the Bertrand 'paradox' – i.e. the duopoly (and oligopoly) equilibrium with linear cost-symmetric firms is the perfect competition equilibrium and with linear cost-asymmetric firms is the monopoly[1] – has been deeply investigated by an extensive literature. A particular case is given by the homogenous good capacity-constrained Bertrand–Edgeworth model, where the firms may serve less than the demand they are facing. However, these latter models often are lacking – for the interesting cases – equilibrium in pure strategies and thus mixed-strategy equilibria have to be considered (e.g. Vives, 1999). Unfortunately, such mixed-strategy equilibria are difficult to handle in closed forms and under sufficiently general assumptions:[2] a complete characterisation of the mixed strategy equilibrium is lacking even in the case of identical (and constant) unit cost and concave demand, unless firms have equal capacities.

A relevant contribution in this direction has been provided by De Francesco and Salvadori (2010) who allow for differences in size among the firms and characterise, especially for the triopoly case, the mixed strategy equilibria showing that (1) the supports of the equilibrium distributions no longer need to coincide or be connected for all the firms; (2) the equilibrium no longer needs to be unique, especially when the capacity of the largest firm is high enough. Although the analysis of the homogenous good capacity-constrained Bertrand–Edgeworth model is still worthwhile, especially along the lines introduced by De Francesco and Salvadori (2010), we take another well-known way to avoid the Bertrand 'paradox' as well as to consider investments on capacity, that is the differentiated goods Bertrand duopoly model (Dixit, 1979; Singh and Vives, 1984) with strategic capacity costs (Dixit, 1980; Vives, 1986a; Fanti and Meccheri, 2013).

Under this framework we investigate some issues which have not been so far, to the best of our knowledge, explored. The first one regards the choice of a discriminated versus uniform price by a monopolistic supplier in a vertical duopoly, showing that the traditional result (see Appendix 21.A) that the monopolistic supplier can discriminate input prices instead of fixing a uniform price in the presence of asymmetric downstream firms (while, conversely, downstream firms would prefer uniform input prices) is always reversed when the downstream firms may choose capacities. Moreover, since consumers' and society's welfare is always larger under uniform input price, then our result is favourable for consumers and society as a whole. Finally, when goods are sufficiently complementary, i.e. $\gamma < -0.717$, the choice of uniform input prices is even Pareto-superior because it is preferred not only by upstream firms, consumers and society as a whole, but also by the downstream firms.

The second issue is related to strategic entry. More precisely, we investigate whether the results above are robust in a context where a firm is already in the market and there is an entry threat by a second firm. Strategic entry is an old issue in oligopoly theory, since the seminal contributions by Bain (1956), Sylos Labini (1957), Modigliani (1958) and, more recently, Dixit (1980). Our aim is to determine the effect of the behaviour of a centralised union on entry when wages are uniform or discriminated between firms. Few contributions investigate strategic entry in a unionised oligopoly. Ishiguro and Shirai (1998), Majumdar and Saha (1998), Pal and Saha (2006, 2008) and Mukherjee and Wang (2013) consider this issue with a certain degree of asymmetry in the cost structure between incumbent(s) and entrant. To the best of our knowledge, our study is the first attempt to clarify the role of union wage determination when firms choose the capacity and compete on prices in a differentiated oligopoly. We find, as expected, that uniform input price behaviour increases wages and strengthens entry deterrence. Nevertheless, upstream monopoly profit is higher, not only when fixed costs are low and entry is accommodated – confirming the result of the duopoly in a framework *à la* Stackelberg – but also when entry is deterred and fixed costs are relatively high. The same holds for consumer's surplus and social welfare.

An interesting by-product of these results is the interpretation of the monopolistic supplier of an input as a trade union supplying labour input.[3] In such a case, our results indicate that an 'equalitarian' behaviour by unions is (1) a 'maximising' behaviour rather than an 'ideological' or customary behaviour, and (2) a 'social welfare' preferred behaviour. Both the results hold, under some circumstances, even when strategic entry is taken into consideration. Therefore this finding is interesting in regard to the recent political debate about the effects of unions on employment and economy as a whole. In fact, the mainstream point of view attacks the centralised wage setting because of its rigidities which are supposed to be detrimental for overall economic performance and more decentralised and, hence, more flexible structures as a recipe for enhancing employment as well as overall economic prosperity are often invoked by policy-makers and scholars (e.g. OECD, 1996; Nickell, 1997; Siebert, 1997). In particular, the recommendation by the OECD Jobs Study (OECD, 1996) to make wage more flexible by eliminating the obstacles for allowing a 'discrimination' of wages according to the specific local conditions seems to mirror emblematically the request that industry union abandons an 'equal pay for equal work' policy for a 'discriminating' wage policy. Therefore, under this policy pressure, tendencies to switch from centralised wage systems towards intermediate union structures, introducing, although still in a frame of wage-setter industry-wide unions, more flexibility through adjustments to local conditions at the firm-level, are widespread at the moment. For instance, Haucup and Wey (2004, C150) note that

> for example, in Germany collective wage agreements between industry unions and employer associations have started to contain so-called 'opening clauses' according to which firms are allowed to pay wages below the collectively agreed rate under certain conditions. Trends towards less centralised wage setting in other countries, such as Denmark, Sweden or New Zealand, have led to more decentralised wage setting at the firm-level and, thereby, substantially reduced unions' monopoly power.

We also note that very recently the so-called Job's Act legislation by the Italian Government is an example of this tendency.

Therefore our findings contribute to this debate, showing two unconventional results: (1) also admitting that the social welfare effects of centralised unions are an open issue, or even are harmful as mainstream point of view believes, the 'equalitarian' wage policy of the central union is not at all an 'ideological' or 'ethical' principle but a fully rational policy maximising the utility of workers. To put the matter differently, the request to abandon the 'equal pay for equal work' principle is equivalent to the request that the union has to be 'irrational' instead of (as for instance many policy-makers say) 'less conservative'; (2) more importantly, an 'equalitarian' central union is social-welfare preferred. The latter result seems to fully reverse the common wisdom on which most current policy acts and recommendations are grounded.

The model

We develop a model of a duopoly in which firms acquire inputs from single suppliers. In particular, we consider a differentiated product market duopoly (following Dixit, 1979 and Singh and Vives, 1984).

Preferences of the representative consumer are given by

$$U(q_i, q_j) = a(q_i + q_j) - \frac{(q_i^2 + 2\gamma q_i q_j + q_j^2)}{2} \tag{21.1}$$

where q_i, q_j denote outputs by firm i and j, respectively, $a > 0$, and $\gamma \in (-1, 1)$ denotes the extent of product differentiation. If $\gamma = 0$, then goods of variety 1 and 2 are independent (i.e. each firm behaves as if it were monopolist in its specific market); if $\gamma = 1$, then goods 1 and 2 are perfect substitutes (i.e. homogeneous goods with the Bertrand 'paradox'); $0 < \gamma < 1$ describes the case of imperfect substitutability between goods. The degree of substitutability increases, or equivalently, the extent of product differentiation decreases as the parameter γ raises; a negative value of γ instead implies that goods 1 and 2 are complements, while $\gamma = -1$ reflects the case of perfect complementarity.

The derived product market demand is linear and, for firm i, for example, is given by

$$p_i(q_i, q_j) = a - \gamma q_j - q_i. \tag{21.2}$$

Both firms have identical cost functions: firm i faces a cost given by both the cost of labour and the cost of excess capacity $C_i(q_i, x_i)$, where q_i and x_i are the production quantity and capacity of firm i, respectively.

Moreover, we assume that both firms produce according to a standard production function with constant returns to scale

$$q_i = L_i \tag{21.3}$$

where L_i represents the level of input used by firm i (that is, as usual, a one-to-one input–output relationship).

Following an established literature (i.e. Vives, 1986b; Horiba and Tsutsui, 2000; Nishimori and Ogawa, 2004; Ogawa, 2006; Barcena-Ruiz and Garzon, 2007, 2012; Tomaru *et al.*, 2009; Barcena-Ruiz and Garzon, 2007; Fanti and Meccheri, 2013; and many others) we assume that the cost function takes the form

$$C_i(q_i, x_i) = w_i\, q_i + z(q_i - x_i)^2 \tag{21.4}$$

where w_i is the input price, and the parameter z determines the steepness of the average cost's U-shape, which, taking into account equation (21.2), may be rewritten as

$$C_i(q_i, x_i) = w_i\, L_i + z(q_i - x_i)^2. \tag{21.5}$$

Under this cost function,[4] it is easy to see that the long-run average cost is minimised when quantity equals production capacity, and both excess capacity and under-capacity are 'inefficient'.[5] We remark that this cost structure implies that the cost of having excess or under capacity is symmetric, although other non-symmetric cost structures could be assumed. However, for the sake of tractability, the symmetric cost function (21.5) is adopted here.

This paper considers the case in which there is a single supplier for both firms in an environment of a price-setting supplier. The supplier's objective is to maximise its own profit with respect to w_i:

$$\max_{w.r.t.\, w_i} \pi^U = \sum_{i=1}^{2} (w_i - c)\, L_i. \tag{21.6}$$

Equation (21.6) states that the upstream monopolist may fix different prices to different downstream firms for the same input (i.e. price discrimination), for a given constant input production cost, c. Alternatively, the upstream monopolist may fix a uniform input price according to the following:

$$\max_{w.r.t.\ w} \pi^U = \sum_{i=1}^{2} (w - c)\, L_i. \tag{21.7}$$

Profits of firm i are defined as

$$\pi_i = p_i q_i - w_i\, L_i - (q_i - x_i)^2. \tag{21.8}$$

We consider the following three-stage game. In the first stage, each firm chooses its production capacity (generally incurring costs of over or under-capacity). In the second stage a monopolistic upstream firm chooses input prices knowing both firms' capacity choices. In the third stage, each firm chooses its price knowing both firms' capacity choices and both input prices.

As usual, to look for a subgame perfect equilibrium, we solve the game backwards and examine first the last stage of the game. From (21.1) and its counterpart for firm j, we can write product demand facing firm i as

$$q_i(p_i, p_j) = \frac{a(1-\gamma) - p_i + \gamma p_j}{1 - \gamma^2}. \tag{21.9}$$

Under Bertrand profit of a firm, i is defined as

$$\pi_i = (p_i - w_i) \frac{a\,(1-\gamma) - p_i + \gamma p_j}{1 - \gamma^2} - \left(\frac{a\,(1-\gamma) - p_i + \gamma p_j}{1 - \gamma^2} - x_i \right)^2. \tag{21.10}$$

From the maximisation of (21.7) and the solution of the system of first-order conditions of the product game between downstream firms, we obtain price and quantity as functions of input prices and capacity choices:

$$p_i(w_i, w_j, x_i, x_j) =$$
$$\frac{a(\gamma^4 + \gamma^3 - 7\gamma^2 - 3\gamma + 12) + 4x_i(\gamma^2 - 2) + 2\gamma x_j(\gamma^2 - 3) - (2\gamma^2 w_i + \gamma^3 w_j - 4w_i - 3\gamma w_j)}{16 - 9\gamma^2 + \gamma^4} \tag{21.11}$$

$$q_i(w_i, w_j, x_i, x_j)$$
$$= -\frac{a(\gamma^2 + \gamma - 4) + 2x_i(\gamma^2 - 4) + 2\gamma x_j - (\gamma^2 w_i + \gamma w_j - 4w_i)}{16 - 9\gamma^2 + \gamma^4}. \tag{21.12}$$

Now in relation to the second stage we consider two alternative cases: (1) the single supplier applies the input prices discrimination;[6] (2) the single supplier applies a uniform input price.

Input prices discrimination

The upstream monopolist maximises its objective function with respect to input prices, taking the firms' output decisions into account. Substituting (21.12) in (21.6) and maximising with respect to w_i, we get:

$$w_i(w_j, x_i, x_j) = \frac{(a+c)(\gamma^2 + \gamma - 4) + 2x_i(\gamma^2 - 4) + 2\gamma x_j - 2\gamma w_j}{2(\gamma^2 - 4)}. \quad (21.13)$$

Solving the system composed by (21.13) and its counterpart for j, we obtain the subgame perfect equilibrium prices for given capacity choices, x_i and x_j:

$$w_i(x_i) = \frac{2x_i + a + c}{2}. \quad (21.14)$$

By substituting (21.14) in (21.12), we get output as a function of capacity choices only, $q_i(x_i, x_j)$, and subsequently, substituting both $w_i(x_i)$ – equation (21.14) – and $q_i(x_i, x_j)$ in the profit function – equation (21.6) – leads to profits as functions of capacity choices, $\pi_i(x_i, x_j)$.[7]

At the first stage, each firm i simultaneously chooses x_i, knowing the profits of each possible third- and second-stage games as a function of x_i and x_j. In particular, maximising profit function and solving with respect to x_i leads to the following reaction function for the firm i:

$$x_i(x_j) = \frac{\left[(a-c)(-\gamma^2 + 4 - \gamma) - 2\gamma x_j\right](-6\gamma^2 + 8 + \gamma^4)}{2(-17\gamma^6 + \gamma^8 + 103\gamma^4 - 256\gamma^2 + 224)} \quad (21.15)$$

and, in symmetric equilibrium $(x_i = x_j = x)$, we get

$$x = \frac{(a-c)(6\gamma^2 - 8 - \gamma^4)}{2(\gamma^6 - \gamma^5 - 12\gamma^4 + 9\gamma^3 + 46\gamma^2 - 16\gamma - 56)}. \quad (21.16)$$

Thus, the symmetric equilibrium output $(q_i = q_j = q)$, is derived by substituting equation (21.16) in $q_i(x_i, x_j)$:

$$q = \frac{(a-c)(\gamma^2 + \gamma - 4)(-\gamma^2 + \gamma + 4)}{2(\gamma^6 - \gamma^5 - 12\gamma^4 + 9\gamma^3 + 46\gamma^2 - 16\gamma - 56)}. \quad (21.17)$$

Therefore the equilibrium outcomes as regards input price, upstream (U) firm's profit and downstream (D) firms' profits are the following:

$$w_i = w_j = w =$$
$$\frac{a(\gamma^6 - \gamma^5 - 13\gamma^4 + 9\gamma^3 + 52\gamma^2 - 16\gamma - 64) + c(\gamma^6 - \gamma^5 - 11\gamma^4 + 9\gamma^3 + 40\gamma^2 - 16\gamma - 58)}{2(\gamma^6 - \gamma^5 - 12\gamma^4 + 9\gamma^3 + 46\gamma^2 - 16\gamma - 56)}$$

$$(21.18)$$

$$\pi^U = \frac{(a-c)^2(\gamma^6 - \gamma^5 - 13\gamma^4 + 9\gamma^3 + 52\gamma^2 - 16\gamma - 64)(\gamma^2 + \gamma - 4)(-\gamma^2 + \gamma + 4)}{2(\gamma^6 - \gamma^5 - 12\gamma^4 + 9\gamma^3 + 46\gamma^2 - 16\gamma - 56)^2}$$

(21.19)

$$\pi^D = \frac{(a-c)^2(-137\gamma^6 + 19\gamma^8 + 462\gamma^4 - \gamma^{10} - 736\gamma^2 - 736\gamma^2 + 448)}{4(\gamma^6 - \gamma^5 - 12\gamma^4 + 9\gamma^3 + 46\gamma^2 - 16\gamma - 56)^2}.$$

(21.20)

Uniform input price

In this case the upstream monopolist maximises its objective functions with respect to a uniform input price, taking the firms' output decisions into account. Substituting (21.2) in (21.7) and maximising with respect to w, after standard calculations we get the subgame perfect equilibrium uniform input price, for given capacity choices, x_i and x_j:

$$w(x_i, x_j) = \frac{x_i + x_j + a + c}{2}.$$

(21.21)

At the first stage, each firm i simultaneously chooses x_i, leading to the following reaction function for the firm i,

$$x_i(x_j) = \frac{(12 - 3\gamma^2 + \gamma)(2 - \gamma^2)[(4 - \gamma - \gamma^2)(a-c) - (4 + 3\gamma - \gamma^2)x_j]}{4\gamma^8 - 63\gamma^6 - 6\gamma^5 + 363\gamma^4 + 36\gamma^3 - 866\gamma^2 - 48\gamma + 736}$$

(21.22)

and subsequently the equilibrium outcomes as regards capacity, output, input price, the upstream (U) firm's profit and the downstream (D) firms' profits are the following:

$$x_E = \frac{(a-c)(3\gamma^4 - \gamma^3 - 18\gamma^2 + 2\gamma + 24)}{2(2\gamma^6 - 2\gamma^5 - 23\gamma^4 + 17\gamma^3 + 86\gamma^2 - 30\gamma - 104)}$$

(21.23)

$$q_E = \frac{(a-c)(\gamma^2 + \gamma - 4)(-\gamma^2 + \gamma + 4)}{2(2\gamma^6 - 2\gamma^5 - 23\gamma^4 + 17\gamma^3 + 86\gamma^2 - 30\gamma - 104)}$$

(21.24)

$$w_i = w_j = w_E =$$

$$\frac{a(\gamma^6 - \gamma^5 - 13\gamma^4 + 9\gamma^3 + 52\gamma^2 - 16\gamma - 64) + c(\gamma^6 - \gamma^5 - 10\gamma^4 + 8\gamma^3 + 34\gamma^2 - 14\gamma - 40)}{(2\gamma^6 - 2\gamma^5 - 23\gamma^4 + 17\gamma^3 + 86\gamma^2 - 30\gamma - 104)}$$

(21.25)

$$\pi_E^U = \frac{2(a-c)^2(\gamma^2 + \gamma - 4)(-\gamma^2 + \gamma + 4)(\gamma^6 - \gamma^5 - 13\gamma^4 + 9\gamma^3 + 52\gamma^2 - 16\gamma - 64)}{(2\gamma^6 - 2\gamma^5 - 23\gamma^4 + 17\gamma^3 + 86\gamma^2 - 30\gamma - 104)^2}$$

(21.26)

$$\pi_E^D = -\frac{(a-c)^2(4\gamma^{10} - 71\gamma^8 - 6\gamma^7 + 489\gamma^6 + 48\gamma^5 - 1592\gamma^4 - 120\gamma^3 + 2460\gamma^2 + 96\gamma - 1472)}{4(2\gamma^6 - 2\gamma^5 - 23\gamma^4 + 17\gamma^3 + 86\gamma^2 - 30\gamma - 104)^2}$$

(21.27)

where the subscript E refers to the uniform input price case.

Armed with the equilibrium outcomes above, we are in a position to compare the effects under the two different price behaviours of the monopolistic supplier. Then the following lemmas and results can be stated.

Lemma 21.1 *Input price and output are higher under uniform input price (than under discriminated input prices). This follows simply by observing that $w_E > w$, $q_E > q$. As known by previous literature, when downstream firms compete on prices, an under-capacity choice emerges. In the present case we may ascertain whether the level of under-capacity is larger when the single supplier is price discriminating or not.*

Lemma 21.2 *The under-capacity levels are lower under uniform input price (than under discriminated input prices). This follows simply by observing that $(x_E - q_E) > (x - q)$.*

Proposition 21.1 *The upstream monopolist always prefers to fix a uniform input price. This straightforwardly follows by observing that $\pi_E^U > \pi^U$.*

Proposition 21.2 *For the downstream duopolists, it is more profitable when the supplier fixes discriminated input prices (a uniform input price) if $\gamma > -0.717$ ($\gamma < -0.717$).*

Lemma 21.3 *Consumer's surplus and social welfare as a whole are always higher under a uniform price input. This follows simply by observing that output is a sufficient measure for the above mentioned welfares and that $q_E > q$.*

Proposition 21.3 *Given the above lemmas and propositions, the choice of a uniform input price is Pareto-superior (with respect to the choice of discriminated input prices) when $\gamma < -0.717$.*

Proposition 21.4 *The upstream firm's profit in both cases of input price determination may be reduced when the product substitutability in the product market is sufficiently high by a higher product differentiation.*

Proof. $\frac{\partial \pi_E^U}{\partial \gamma} \gtrless 0$ if and only if $\gamma \gtrless 0.630$; $\frac{\partial \pi^U}{\partial \gamma} \gtrless 0$ if and only if $\gamma \gtrless 0.635$.   □

Strategic entry

In this section, we investigate the issue of strategic entry by assuming that only one downstream firm is already in the market, the incumbent, and that a second firm, the entrant, has to decide whether to enter the market. Hence, we add a new stage in the timing of the game: in the first stage, the incumbent, firm 1, chooses the level of its capacity, $x_1 > 0$. In the second stage the entrant, firm 2, chooses the level of its capacity, $x_2 \geq 0$; $x_2 = 0$ implies that firm 2 chooses to stay out of the market. In the third stage the monopolistic upstream firm chooses input prices knowing both firms' capacity choices. In the fourth stage, the two firms compete on prices if firm 2 actually enters the market; otherwise the incumbent sets the price.

We maintain the same assumptions of the previous section with respect to the product market demand, and on the profits of the upstream monopolist, that is, equations (21.2), (21.6) and (21.7). Differently from the previous section, in the case of entry, both the downstream firms face a positive fixed cost, $F > 0$. Hence, the cost function takes the form

$$C_i(q_i, x_i) = w_i q_i + (q_i - x_i)^2 + F. \tag{21.28}$$

Thus, profits of downstream firms are given by

$$\pi_i = p_i q_i - w_i q_i - (q_i - x_i)^2 - F. \tag{21.29}$$

The analysis follows by working backwards from the fourth to the first stage. Note that the product market game (the fourth stage) and the input price game (the third stage) are identical to the third and the second stage in the previous section. Thus, equations (21.11) and (21.12) hold, and the level of input price(s) chosen by the upstream monopolist is given by equation (21.14) under input prices discrimination, and by equation (21.21) under uniform input price. First, we characterise the equilibrium under input price discrimination and then the one under uniform input price.

Input prices discrimination

Second stage

At the second stage, firm 2 chooses the level of its capacity x_2. In taking this decision it considers as given x_1, and the input and output prices that will be determined in the third and in the fourth stage, respectively, as a reaction to x_1 and x_2. Firm 2 may also stay out of the market: it enters the market if and only if the profit it can get in the fourth stage is positive.

In the case of entrance, the reaction function for firm 2 is given by equation (21.15). Note that

$$x_2(x_1) \geq 0 \quad \text{if and only if } x_1 \leq \bar{x}_1, \quad \text{where } \bar{x}_1 \equiv \frac{\left(4 - \gamma^2 - \gamma\right)(a - c)}{2\gamma}.$$

By substituting equations (21.12), (21.14) and (21.15) in equation (21.29) we get the profit of firm 2 along with its reaction function to the incumbent's capacity. It is easy to verify that such a profit depends only on x_1. Let us define this function $\pi_2(x_1)$.[8] As expected, if products are complementary, i.e. $\gamma \in (-1, 0)$, this function is always increasing in x_1. Instead, when products are substitutes, i.e. $\gamma \in (0, 1)$, $\frac{\partial \pi_2(x_1)}{\partial x_1} \leq 0$ if $0 \leq x_1 \leq \frac{\left(4 - \gamma^2 - \gamma\right)(a - c)}{2\gamma} = \bar{x}_1$, that is, entrant's profit is a decreasing function of x_1 for any $x_2 \geq 0$.

We further assume that the cost function of firm 2 is such that if $x_1 = 0$, $\pi_2(0) > 0$. This means that

$$F < \bar{F} \equiv \frac{(2 - \gamma^2)(-\gamma^2 + 4 - \gamma)^2 (a - c)^2}{4(224 - 17\gamma^6 + \gamma^8 + 103\gamma^4 - 256\gamma^2)}. \tag{21.30}$$

Firm 2 enters the market if and only if $\pi_2(x_1) > 0$. Thus, given equation (21.30), in the case of complementary products it is impossible to deter the entry of firm 2. For this reason, we limit our analysis to $\gamma \in (0, 1)$. By solving inequality $\pi_2(x_1) > 0$ for x_1, we find a critical level of incumbent capacity, that is

$$Y \equiv \frac{\left(4 - \gamma^2 - \gamma\right)\left(2 - \gamma^2\right)(a - c) - \sqrt{F(2 - \gamma^2)\left(224 - 17\gamma^6 + \gamma^8 - 256\gamma^2 + 103\gamma^4\right)}}{2\left(2 - \gamma^2\right)\gamma}. \tag{21.31}$$

Hence, the reaction function of firm 2 is

$$x_2 = \begin{cases} \dfrac{\left[(a - c)\left(-\gamma^2 + 4 - \gamma\right) - 2\gamma x_1\right]\left(-6\gamma^2 + 8 + \gamma^4\right)}{2\left(-17\gamma^6 + \gamma^8 + 103\gamma^4 - 256\gamma^2 + 224\right)} & \text{if } 0 < x_1 < Y \\[4mm] 0 & \text{if } Y \leq x_1. \end{cases} \tag{21.32}$$

First stage

At the first stage, firm 1 chooses the level of capacity taking into account the best response of firm 2 in the second stage given by equation (21.32). Note that if we assume that the strategic set of the incumbent is $x_1 \in [0, a]$, then if $Y > a$, the entrance of firm 2 cannot be deterred. Let us call F^{ID} the value of F such that for any

$$F < F^{ID} \equiv \frac{(2 - \gamma^2)[(a - c)\gamma^2 + (3a - c)\gamma - 4(a - c)]}{4(224 - 17\gamma^6 + \gamma^8 + 103\gamma^4 - 256\gamma^2)}$$

it is impossible to deter the entry. From equations (21.11), (21.12), (21.14), (21.15) and (21.29) we obtain the function of incumbent profit. Firm 1 maximises its profit through the standard procedure, and we obtain

$$x_1^{ID} = \frac{\left(4 - \gamma^2\right)\left(2 - \gamma^2\right)\left(14 + \gamma^4 - 8\gamma^2\right)(a - c) A\left(\gamma\right)}{2D\left(\gamma\right)} \tag{21.33}$$

where ID stands for 'impossible to deter' the entry of firm 2,

$$A(\gamma) = (56 - \gamma^6 - \gamma^5 + 12\gamma^4 + 9\gamma^3 - 46\gamma^2 - 16\gamma),$$

and

$$D(\gamma) = \left(43904 - 101248\gamma^2 + 99608\gamma^4 - 3730\gamma^{10} + 18073\gamma^8 + 469\gamma^{12}\right.$$
$$\left. - 33\gamma^{14} - 54460\gamma^6 + \gamma^{16}\right).$$

When $F \geq F^{\mathrm{ID}}$, there is a level of incumbent capacity $Y \leq a$ such that firm 2 does not enter the market. Thus, the incumbent profit is given by two segments of parabolas:

(i)   If $0 < x_1 < Y$ firms 2 enters the market and we define $\pi_1^D(x_1)$ the incumbent profit, where the superscript D stands for the duopoly case.[9]

(ii) If, instead, $Y \leq x_1$ firm 2 stays out of the market and the incumbent obtains the following profit

$$\pi_1^M(x_1) = \frac{4x_1(a-c) - 28x_1^2 + 2(a-c)^2}{32} - F. \tag{21.34}$$

By maximising this two-profit function and solving with respect to x_1, we obtain the optimal level of capacity when entry is accommodated and blockaded, respectively.

In the case of blockaded entry, by maximising equation (21.34) we get

$$x_1^{\mathrm{BE}} = \frac{(a-c)}{14}. \tag{21.35}$$

Firm 1 can choose this capacity and obtain the profit of monopoly if and only if $x_1^{\mathrm{BE}} \geq Y$, that is

$$F \geq F^{\mathrm{BE}} \equiv \frac{(2-\gamma^2)(7\gamma^2 + 8\gamma - 28)^2(a-c)^2}{196(224 - 17\gamma^6 + \gamma^8 - 256\gamma^2 + 103\gamma^4)}. \tag{21.36}$$

In this case, $w_1^{\mathrm{BE}} = \frac{4a+3c}{7}$, $p_1^{\mathrm{BE}} = \frac{(1-d)[6a-c-(a-c)\gamma]}{7}$, $q_1^{\mathrm{BE}} = \frac{a-c}{7}$.

In the case of accommodated entry, the optimal level of capacity is x_1^{AE}, which is the same expression of x_1^{ID}, see equation (21.33).[10] Given x_1^{AE}, from equations (21.34) and (21.15), we get the equilibrium values for the capacity of firm 2, that is

$$x_2^{\mathrm{AE}} = \frac{\left(4-\gamma^2\right)\left(2-\gamma^2\right)(a-c)\,C(\gamma)}{2D(\gamma)} \tag{21.37}$$

where $C(\gamma) = 784 - 224\gamma - 1100\gamma^2 + 256\gamma^3 + 598\gamma^4 - 103\gamma^5 - 157\gamma^6 + 17\gamma^7 + 20\gamma^8 - \gamma^9 - \gamma^{10}$.

From (21.34), (21.37), (21.11) and (21.14), we obtain the prices of inputs and of the final output. At equilibrium, the level of entrant capacity is lower than incumbent capacity for any $\gamma \in (0, 1)$, and the two levels of capacity are equal when $\gamma = 0$. This difference in the capacity choice brings about a higher input price, a lower output price, a higher output level and a higher profit for the incumbent (w.r.t. the entrant), i.e. $w_1^{AE} \geq w_2^{AE}$, $p_1^{AE} \leq p_2^{AE}$, $q_1^{AE} \geq q_2^{AE}$ and $\pi_1^{AE} \geq \pi_2^{AE}$, respectively. This result is coherent with the standard Stackelberg oligopoly model.[11]

When $F^{ID} < F < F^{BE}$, firm 1 chooses to accommodate or deter the entry of firm 2. In order to deter the entry, the incumbent has to choose a level of capacity equal to Y. It chooses to deter the entry of firm 2 if the profit of deterrence, i.e. equation (21.35) calculated in $x_1 = Y$, is higher than the maximum profit of accommodated entry. Let us define $\hat{x}_1$, the level of capacity x_1, such that the incumbent is indifferent between deterring or accommodating the entry of firm 2. If $\hat{x}_1 \geq Y (\hat{x}_1 < Y)$, firm 1 chooses to deter (to accommodate) the entry of firm 2. There is a value of the fixed cost, $\hat{F}$, such that for any $F \in [F^{ID}, \hat{F}]$ the entry is accommodated, while for any $F \in [\hat{F}, F^{BE}]$ the entry is deterred.[12] Figure 21.1 shows a numerical representation of the functions F^{ID}, $\hat{F}$ and F^{BE} in the plane $\{\gamma, F\}$ and identifies the region where it is impossible to deter the entry (ID), where entry is accommodated (AE), deterred (DE) and blockaded (BE). Note that as long as γ tends to zero, the three values of F converge to the same value.

When entry is deterred, $x_1^{DE} = Y$ and $x_2^{DE} = 0$. From (21.31), (21.11), (21.12) and (21.14) we obtain the input and output prices and the quantity produced at equilibrium: $w_1^{DE} = \frac{a+c}{2} + Y$, $p_1^{DE} = \frac{7a+c-2Y}{8}$, and $q_1^{DE} = \frac{a-c+2Y}{8}$.

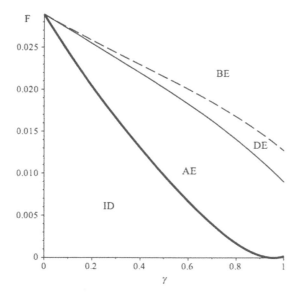

Figure 21.1 The functions F^{ID}, $\hat{F}$ and F^{ID} in the plane $\{\gamma, F\}$. The solid curve is F^{ID}, the dashed $\hat{F}$ and the dotted F^{BE}. In region ID, it is impossible to deter the entry, in region AE entry is accommodated, in region DE, entry is deterred, in region BE, entry is blockaded. Value of parameters: $a = 1$ and $c = 0.1$.

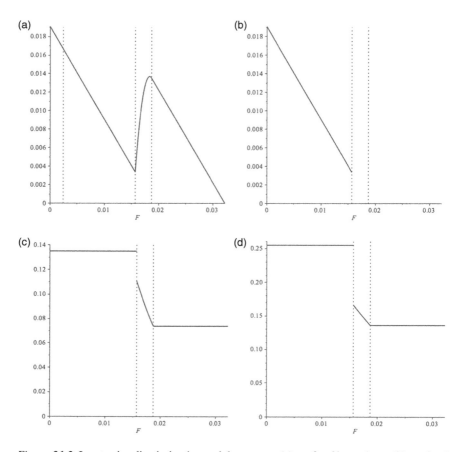

Figure 21.2 Input price discrimination and deterrence. (a) profit of incumbent. (b) profit of entrant. (c) profit of upstream monopoly. (d) total quantity produced. Values of parameters: $a = 1$, $c = 0.05$, $\gamma = 0.8$.

Figure 21.2 shows a numerical illustration of the results when fixed cost varies: for the profit of the incumbent (21.2a) and the entrant (21.2b), for the utility of upstream monopolist (21.2c), for the total quantity produced – i.e. the consumer's surplus (21.2d). Figure 21.2a is consistent with the Dixit model: under entry deterrence, the profit of firm 1 can increase as fixed cost increases. When $F < \hat{F}$ total output and prices (of inputs and output) do not depend on F. Entry deterrence brings about a social cost that emerges with the discontinuous reduction in total output and in the utility of the upstream monopolist.

Uniform input price

Under the assumption of uniform input price, the entry of firm 2 directly increases the wage of incumbent, see equation (21.21). Hence, there is a strong incentive to deter the entry of firm 2. Indeed, even when $\gamma = 0$, the profit of incumbent depends on the entry of firm 2, while, in the case of input price discrimination, the entry of firm 2 does not have any effect on incumbent profit.[13]

We solve the game through backward induction limiting our analysis to the case of substitute products $\gamma \in (0, 1)$. Given the results of the previous section, we analyse only the first two stages.

Second stage

The reaction function of firm 2 is given by equation (21.22). By substituting equations (21.11), (21.12), (21.21) and (21.22) in equation (21.29), we get the profit of firm 2 along with its reaction function to the incumbent's capacity. This profit function has a U-shaped form: $\frac{\partial \pi_2^E (x_1^E)}{\partial x_1^E} \leq 0 (> 0)$ if $0 \leq x_1^E \leq \frac{(4-\gamma^2-\gamma)(a-c)}{(1+\gamma)(4-\gamma)}$ $(x_1^E > \frac{(4-\gamma^2-\gamma)(a-c)}{(1+\gamma)(4-\gamma)})$, where the superscript E stands for the uniform input price case (equal). As before we assume that $\pi_2^E (0) > 0$, that is

$$F < \bar{F}^E = \frac{(2-\gamma^2)(4-\gamma-\gamma^2)^2(a-c)^2}{4\gamma^8 - 63\gamma^6 - 6\gamma^5 + 363\gamma^4 + 36\gamma^3 - 866\gamma^2 - 48\gamma + 736}.$$

(21.38)

Firm 2 enters the market if and only if $\pi_2^E (x_1^E) > 0$. By solving this inequality for x_1^E, we found a critical level of incumbent capacity, that is

$$Y^E \equiv \frac{(4-\gamma^2-\gamma)(2-\gamma^2)(a-c) - \sqrt{F(2-\gamma^2)(4\gamma^8 - 63\gamma^6 - 6\gamma^5 + 363\gamma^4 + 36\gamma^3 - 866\gamma^2 - 48\gamma + 736)}}{(2-\gamma^2)(1+\gamma)(4-\gamma)}.$$

(21.39)

Hence the reaction function of firm 2 is

$$x_2 = \begin{cases} \dfrac{(12 - 3\gamma^2 + \gamma)(2-\gamma^2)\left[(4-\gamma-\gamma^2)(a-c) - (4+3\gamma-\gamma^2)x_1^E\right]}{4\gamma^8 - 63\gamma^6 - 6\gamma^5 + 363\gamma^4 + 36\gamma^3 - 866\gamma^2 - 48\gamma + 736} \\ \qquad \text{if } 0 < x_1^E < Y^E \\ 0 \quad \text{if } Y^E \leq x_1^E \end{cases}.$$

(21.40)

First stage

In the first stage, the incumbent chooses the level of its capacity taking in to account the reaction of firm 2, given by equation (21.40). From equation (21.38) we found that the maximum value Y^E is always lower than a; thus, if $F > 0$, the incumbent may always choose a level of capacity to deter the entry of firm 2.

Hence, as before, incumbent profit is given by two segments of parabola, $\pi_1^{DE}(x_1^E)$ if $x_1^E < Y^E$, and $\pi_1^{ME}(x_1^E) = \frac{4x_1(a-c)-28x_1^2+2(a-c)^2}{32} - F$ if $Y^E \leq x_1^E$. When firm 2 does not enter the market, the incumbent profit function is the same in both the cases, the input price discrimination and the uniform input price; see equation (21.35). In the case of accommodated entry, from equations (21.11), (21.12), (21.21), (21.22) and (21.29), the optimal level of capacity is

$$x_1^{AE,E} = \frac{4(12-3\gamma^2+\gamma)(2-\gamma^2)(3-\gamma^2)(a-c)A^{E(\gamma)}}{D^E(\gamma)} \tag{21.41}$$

where $A^E(\gamma) = -(\gamma^6+\gamma^5-10\gamma^4-10\gamma^3+34\gamma^2+18\gamma-40)$ and

$$D^E(\gamma) = -\begin{pmatrix} 953284\gamma^4 - 554948\gamma^6 - 914176\gamma^2 + 375805 - 147696\gamma^5 - 98304\gamma + 189120\gamma^3 + 16\gamma^{16} \\ -468\gamma^{14} + 1524\gamma^{11} - 72\gamma^{13} + 197137\gamma^8 + 59808\gamma^7 + 6013\gamma^{12} - 13236\gamma^9 - 43874\gamma^{10} \end{pmatrix}.$$

Similarly to the discriminated input prices case, $x_1^{AE,E}$ is always lower than Y^E. Thus, from equations (21.41) and (21.22), we get the equilibrium values for the capacity of firm 2, and from (21.41), (21.22) and (21.11), the input and output prices. Even under uniform input price, firm 2 chooses a level of capacity lower than the incumbent for any $\gamma \in (0, 1)$. This difference in the levels of capacity implies that, at equilibrium, $p_1^{AE,E} \leq p_2^{AE,E}$, with $q_1^{AE,E} \geq q_2^{AE,E}$. Hence, when entry is accommodated, incumbent profit is higher than entrant profit.

In the case of blockaded entry, we obtain the same equilibrium as in the case of discriminated input prices. However, the level of fixed cost, $F^{BE,E}$, such that $x_1^{BE,E} \geq Y^E$, is different. More precisely, $x_1^E = Y1^E$ if and only if

$$F \geq F_{BE,E} \equiv \frac{(2-\gamma^2)(13\gamma^2+17\gamma-52)^2(a-c)^2}{196(4\gamma^8-63\gamma^6-6\gamma^5+363\gamma^3+36\gamma^3-866\gamma^2-48\gamma+736)}. \tag{21.42}$$

When $0 < F < F^{BE,E}$, firm 1 chooses to accommodate (or to deter) the entry of firm 2 if the profit function (21.32) in $x_1^E = Y^E$ takes a value lower (higher) than the maximum level of profit when entry is accommodated. There is a value of fixed cost, $\hat{F}^E$, such that for any $F \in (0, \hat{F}^E)$ the entry is accommodated, while for any $F \in [\hat{F}^E, F^{BE,E}]$ the entry is deterred.

When entry is deterred, $x_1^{DE,E} = Y^E$. From (21.39), (21.11), (21.12) and (21.21) we obtain the input and output prices and the quantity produced at equilibrium $w^{DE,E} = \frac{a+c}{2} + Y^E$, $p_1^{DE,E} = \frac{7a+c-2Y^E}{8}$, and $q_1^{DE,E} = \frac{a-c+2Y^E}{8}$.

Deterrence, under-capacity and welfare

The results of the game when the upstream monopolist sets a uniform or a discriminated input price allow us to discuss three important issues, the implications of the two different pricing behaviour on: (i) deterrence, (ii) under-(over-)capacity and (iii) welfare. Particularly relevant is the interpretation of the upstream monopolist as a trade union that may set wages according to a centralised or a decentralised rule.

First, as expected, when the upstream monopolist sets a uniform input price, the incentive of the incumbent to deter the entry of competitors increases. In the language of our model, this means that the level of fixed cost that makes deterrence optimal for the incumbent is lower in the centralised than in the decentralised regime, i.e. $\hat{F}^E < \hat{F}$. This result is difficult to prove analytically, given the high degree of complexity of the two expressions. However, numerical simulations confirm the expected result. Furthermore, it holds that $F^{\mathrm{BE},E} > F^{\mathrm{BE}}$ for any $\gamma \in (0, 1)$. Thus, the monopoly outcome is easier under the discriminated input price than under the uniform input price regime. Hence, in order to compare the results in the discriminated input price (DIP) and in the uniform input price (UIP), we must consider five regions, i.e. intervals in the value of the fixed cost:

(i) $0 < F < \hat{F}^E$, entry is accommodated under both the regimes;
(ii) $\hat{F}^E \leq F < \hat{F}$, entry is accommodated under DIP and deterred under UIP;
(iii) $\hat{F} \leq F < F^{\mathrm{BE}}$, entry is deterred under both the regimes;
(iv) $F^{\mathrm{BE}} \leq F < F^{\mathrm{BE},E}$, entry is blockaded under DIP and deterred under UIP;
(v) $F \geq F^{\mathrm{BE},E}$, entry is blockaded under both the regimes.

Thus, the following results hold.

Lemma 21.4 *In region (i), $w^{AE,E} > w_1^{AE} \geq w_2^{AE}$, and $q_1^{AE,E} + q_2^{AE,E} \geq q_1^{AE} + q_2^{AE}$; in (ii) $w^{DE,E} > w_1^{AE} \geq w_2^{AE}$ and $q_1^{AE} + q_2^{AE} \geq q_1^{DE,E}$; in (iii) there is a level of fixed cost, $\tilde{F} \in (\hat{F}, F^{BE})$, such that for $\hat{F} \leq F \leq \tilde{F}$, $w_1^{DE} \geq w^{DE,E}$ and $q_1^{DE} \geq q_1^{DE,E}$, while for $\tilde{F} < F < F^{BE}$, $w_1^{DE} < w^{DE,E}$ and $q_1^{DE} < q_1^{DE,E}$; in (iv) $w_1^{BE} < w^{DE,E}$ and $q_1^{BE} < q_1^{DE,E}$; in (v) $w_1^{BE} = w^{BE,E}$ and $q_1^{BE} = q_1^{BE,E}$.*

Lemma 21.5

(i)   *When entry is accommodated, the result of under-capacity presented in Lemma 21.2 is confirmed for the firms. The downstream firms choose a level of capacity lower than the quantity produced at equilibrium in both the input price regimes. It holds that $(x_1^{AE,E} - q_1^{AE,E}) > (x_1^{AE} - q_1^{AE}) > (x_2^{AE,E} - q_2^{AE,E}) > (x_2^{AE} - q_2^{AE})$.*

(ii) *When entry is deterred, $(x_1^{DE,E} - q_1^{DE,E}) > (x_1^{DE} - q_1^{DE})$. In this case, there is a degree of substitutability between the two products, $\tilde{\gamma} \in (0, 1)$, such that for any $\gamma > \tilde{\gamma} (\gamma < \tilde{\gamma})$ the incumbent faces over-capacity (under-capacity) at equilibrium. In other words, if the two products are relatively homogeneous, the incumbent finds it convenient to face over-capacity costs by deterring the entry of competitors.*

(iii) *When entry is blockaded, the same degree of under-capacity emerges under the two input price regimes.*

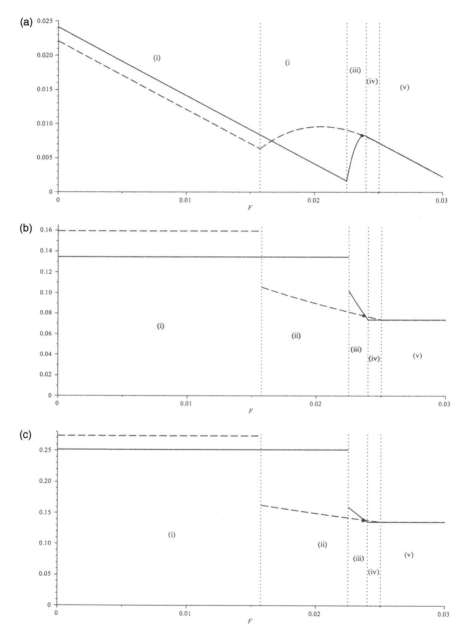

Figure 21.3 Uniform input price (dashed) versus input price discrimination (solid).
(a) utility of upstream monopoly, (b) incumbent profit, (c) total product,
(d) social welfare. Value of parameters: $a = 1$, $c = 0.05$, $\gamma = 0.8$.

Lemma 21.6 *In both the regimes, the profit of the incumbent is a continuous function of F. It is decreasing when entry is accommodated, first increasing and then decreasing when entry is deterred, and is decreasing when entry is blockaded. The level of profits in region (i) is higher under DIP than under UIP, while in region (v) it is the same under the two regimes. In region (ii) there is a value of fixed cost $\widehat{\widehat{F}} \in \left(\hat{F}^E, \hat{F} \right)$, such that for $\hat{F}^E < F < \widehat{\widehat{F}}$ the profit of the incumbent is higher under DIP than under UIP, while for $\widehat{\widehat{F}} \leq F \leq \hat{F}$ the reverse holds. In region (iii) for $\hat{F} \leq F < \tilde{F}$ the profit of the incumbent is higher under UIP than under DIP, while for $\tilde{F} \leq F < F^{BE}$ the reverse holds.*

Proposition 21.5 *The upstream monopolist prefers to fix a uniform input price in (i), (iii) if $\tilde{F} < F < F^{BE}$ and (iv); while it prefers to fix discriminated input prices in (ii) and (iii) if $\hat{F} \leq F \leq \tilde{F}$. It is indifferent between DIP and UIP if $F \geq F^{BE,E}$.*

Proposition 21.6 *The entrant prefers a DIP regime when entry is accommodated, in regions (i) and (ii).[14] The incumbent prefers DIP regime in regions (i), (ii) if $\hat{F} < F < \widehat{\widehat{F}}$, (iii) if $\tilde{F} \leq F < F^{BE}$ and (iv), UIP regime in regions (ii) if $\widehat{\widehat{F}} \leq F \leq \hat{F}$ and (iii) if $\hat{F} \leq F \leq \tilde{F}$, and it is indifferent between the two regimes in region (v).*

Proposition 21.7 *Consumer's surplus and social welfare as a whole are higher under UIP than in DIP in regions (i), (iii) if $\tilde{F} < F < F^{BE}$ and (iv), lower in regions (ii) and (iii) if $\hat{F} \leq F \leq \tilde{F}$. Finally, in region (v) consumer's surplus and social welfare are the same.*

Figure 21.3 shows a numerical illustration of the three propositions: (a) the utility of upstream monopolist, (b) the incumbent profits, (c) the total product, (d) social welfare. The results of Propositions 21.5 and 21.7 are relevant for at least two reasons. First, when entry is accommodated in both the regimes, i.e. in region (i), the analysis confirms all the results of the second section generalised in a framework *à la* Stackelberg. More surprisingly, second, even when only the incumbent stays in the market, if $\tilde{F} < F < F^{BE,E}$, i.e. in part of region (iii) and in region (iv), the uniform price behaviour maximises union utility and social welfare.

Concluding remarks

This paper deals with a context of a vertical industry with a monopolistic upstream firm and two downstream firms choosing, for strategic reasons, their capacity and then competing on price (*à la* Bertrand) between them in the final product market with differentiated products. In such a context, the effects of alternative price policies by a monopolistic input supplier (i.e. fixing either a uniform or a discriminated price) are investigated under a given exogenous market structure as well as under strategic entry. In the latter case also, the effects of the alternative input price behaviours on the entry are studied. As regards the former case, we show that the common wisdom according to which (1) the profit of the monopolistic supplier is higher when it is price-discriminating; (2) consumer's surplus and social welfare are higher when it is non-price-discriminating, is always reversed. Moreover, interpreting the monopolistic upstream firm as a centralised union, we show that the 'equalitarian' wage policy (which is, by definition, less flexible than a wage-discriminating policy) is preferred not only by the union but also by the consumers and society as a whole, arguing that the current tendency towards more flexibility in the union's behaviour might be harmful. Both the results hold, under some circumstances, even when strategic entry is taken into consideration. Indeed, as regards the entry issue, we show that, as expected, uniform input price behaviour increases input prices (wages) and strengthens the deterrence. Nevertheless, upstream monopoly profit is higher under uniform input price behaviour, not only when fixed costs are low and entry is accommodated – confirming the result of the duopoly – but also when entry is deterred and fixed costs are relatively high. Moreover, consumers and society as a whole also prefer the uniform input price behaviour whenever it is preferred by the upstream monopoly.

Appendix 21.A

Standard calculations along the lines of the main text holding exogenous asymmetric values x_i, x_j, lead to the following:[15]

$$(\pi^U - \pi_E^U) = \frac{(x_i - x_j)^2}{2(4 - \gamma)} > 0 \quad \text{and} \quad (\pi^U - \pi_E^U) = \frac{(x_i - x_j)^2}{2(4 - \gamma - \gamma^2)} > 0.$$

This clearly illustrates the traditional wisdom that the upstream profit is higher when the monopolistic supplier 'discriminates' input prices than when fixing a uniform input price.

Notes

1 Note that under convex costs Dastidar (1995) has shown that the Bertrand 'paradox' may no longer hold.
2 For mixed-strategy equilibrium solutions under quite restrictive assumptions such as linear demand or identical firms see, among others, Beckmann (1965), Levitan and Shubik (1972), Vives (1986a) and Cheviakov and Hartwick (2005). Under less restrictive assumptions, non-closed form solutions limited to the duopolistic setting are found by Kreps and Scheinkman (1983), Davidson and Deneckere (1986), Osborne and Pitchik (1986) and Allen and Hellwig (1993).
3 This interpretation and subsequent comments draws from Fanti (2014).
4 For simplicity in the rest of the paper we assume $z = 1$. However, to the extent that this parameter is a measure of the flexibility of technology, it is also a measure of the importance of the long-run capacity decision relative to the short-run quantity decision. As argued by Horuba and Testui (2000, 210):

> If z is small, then the short-run average cost curve tends to be flat and the choice of x is not relevant to the choice of q. On the other hand, if z is large, the short-run average cost curve tends to be steeply sloped so that it can be quite costly to produce

q that is different from x, whence the long-run capacity decision becomes closely tied to the short-run quantity decision.

The investigation of the role of z in the present model is left for further research.

5 As noted by Lu-Poddar (2005, 367): 'This cost function clearly shows the advantage of well-coordinated capacity-quantity choice. Excess capacity or under capacity would result in inefficiency. Under this U-shaped cost function, the long-run average cost is actually minimised when quantity equals production capacity, i.e. $q_i = x_i$.'

6 In broad terms, one can say that price discrimination exists when two 'similar' products which have the same marginal cost to produce are sold by a firm at different prices by a dominant firm which 'exploits' buyers by means of price discrimination, with the result that final consumer and societal welfare are reduced.

7 The formulas of the output $q_i(x_i, x_j)$ and profit $\pi_i(x_i, x_j)$ functions are not reported here for economy of space, given their rather unmanageable form.

8 For the sake of clearness, we avoid writing this long equation in the text. The formal derivation of this and other expressions are available on request.

9 Even in this case, for the sake of clearness we avoid writing explicitly the functional form, see footnote 8.

10 Note that since $x_1^{AE} < x_1^{BE}$ and $x_1^{BE} < Y$, $x_1^{AE} < Y$. Otherwise entry is blockaded.

11 Note that the capacity level, x, in the previous section is such that $x_2^{AE} < x < x_1^{AE}$.

12 The expression for $\hat{F}$ as a function of the other parameters is very complicated and does not give much insight.

13 In principle, firm 1 may find it convenient to deter the entrance of firm 2 even in the case of complementary products. More precisely, in this case, there is a value of complementarity $\hat{\gamma} \in (-1, 0)$, such that for any $\gamma < \hat{\gamma}(\gamma < \hat{\gamma})$ the maximum profit in the case of entry is higher (lower) than the maximum profit in the case of monopoly. However, we find that as long as products are complementary, the level of fixed cost that implies entry deterrence is higher than the level of fixed cost that makes null the profit of incumbent. Hence, in what follows, we analyse only the case of substitute products.

14 If $F > \hat{F}$ firm 2 stays out of the market, and it is indifferent between the two regimes.

15 The results are omitted here for economy of space and of course are available on request.

References

Allen, B. and M. Hellwig (1993), Bertrand–Edgeworth Duopoly with Proportional Demand, *International Economic Review*, 34(1), 39–60.

Barcena-Ruiz, J. C. and M. B. Garzon (2007), Capacity Choice in a Mixed Duopoly under Price Competition, *Economics Bulletin*, 12(26), 1–7.

Barcena-Ruiz, J. C. and M. B. Garzon (2012), Endogenous Timing in a Mixed Duopoly with Capacity Choice, *The Manchester School*, 78(2), March, pp. 93–109.

Beckmann, M. (1965), Bertrand–Edgeworth Duopoly Revisited, in *Operations Research*, *Verfahren*, Vol. III, ed. by R. Henn, Hain: Meisenheim, pp. 55–68.

Bain, Joe S. (1956), *Barriers to New Competition: Their Character and Consequences in Manufacturing Industries*. Cambridge, Massachusetts: Harvard University Press.

Cheviakov, A. and J. Hartwick (2005), Beckmann's Bertrand–Edgeworth Duopoly Example Revisited, *International Game Theory Review*, 7(4), 1–12.

Dastidar, G. S. (1995), On the Existence of Pure Strategy Bertrand Equilibrium, *Economic Theory*, 5(1), 9–32.

Davidson, C. and R. Deneckere (1986), Long-run Competition in Capacity, Short-run Competition in Price and the Cournot Model, *Rand Journal of Economics*, 17, 404–415.

De Francesco, M. and N. Salvadori (2010), Bertrand–Edgeworth Games under Oligopoly with a Complete Characterization for the Triopoly, Munich Personal RePEc Archive, MPRA Paper No. 24087.

Dixit, A. (1979), A model of duopoly suggesting the theory of entry barriers, *Bell Journal of Economics*, 10, 20–32.

Dixit, A. (1980), The Role of Investment in Entry Deterrence, *Economic Journal*, 90(357), 95–106.

Fanti, L. (2014), Equalitarian Union and Social Welfare in Duopolies with Capacity Choice, Discussion Paper n. 193, Department of Economics and Management, University of Pisa.

Fanti, L. and N. Meccheri (2013), Capacity Choice, Duopoly and Union Structures, Discussion Paper n. 176, Department of Economics and Management, Pisa.

Haucup, J. and C. Wey (2004), Unionisation Structures and Innovation Incentives, *The Economic Journal*, 114(494), C149–C165.

Horiba, Y. and S. Tsutsui (2000), International Duopoly, Tariff Policies and the Case of Free Trade, *Japanese Economic Review*, 51(2), 207–220.

Kreps, D. M. and J. A. Scheinkman (1983), Quantity Precommitment and Bertrand Competition Yield Cournot Outcomes, *Bell Journal of Economics*, 14(2), 326–337.

Ishiguro, S. and Y. Shirai (1998), Entry Deterrence in a Unionized Oligopoly, *Japanese Economic Review*, 49(2), 210–221.

Levitan, R. and M. Shubik (1972), Price Duopoly and Capacity Constraints, *International Economic Review*, 13(1), 111–122.

Lu, Y. and S. Poddar (2005), Mixed Oligopoly and the Choice of Capacity, *Research in Economics*, 59(4), 365–374.

Majumdar, S. and B. C. Saha (1998), Job Security, Wage Bargaining and Duopoly Outcomes, *The Journal of International Trade & Economic Development*, 7(4), 389–403.

Modigliani, F. (1958), New Developments on the Oligopoly Front, *Journal of Political Economy*, 66(3), 215–232.

Mukherjee, A. and L. F. S. Wang (2013), Labour Union, Entry and Consumer Welfare, *Economic Letters*, 120(3), 603–605.

Nickell, S. (1997), Unemployment and Labour Market Rigidities: Europe versus North America, *Journal of Economic Perspectives*, 11(3), 55–74.

Nishimori, A. and H. Ogawa (2004), Do Firms always Choose Excess Capacity? *Economics Bulletin*, 12(2), 1–7.

OECD (1996), *The OECD Jobs Study: Implementing the Strategy*, Paris: OECD.

Ogawa, H. (2006), Capacity Choice in the Mixed Duopoly with Product Differentiation, *Economics Bulletin*, 12(8), 1–6.

Osborne, M. J. and C. Pitchik (1986), Price Competition in a Capacity-Constrained Duopoly, *Journal of Economic Theory*, 38(2), 238–260.

Pal, R. and B. C. Saha (2006), Wage Commitment, Signalling, and Entry Deterrence or Accommodation, *Labour*, 20(4), 625–650.

Pal, R. and B. C. Saha (2008), Union-Oligopoly Bargaining and Entry Deterrence: a Reassessment of Limit Pricing, *Journal of Economics*, 95(2), 121–147.

Siebert, H. (1997), Labour Market Rigidities: at the Root of Unemployment in Europe, *Journal of Economic Perspectives*, 11(3), 37–54.

Singh, N. and X. Vives (1984), Price and quantity competition in a differentiated duopoly, *RAND Journal of Economics*, 15, 546–554.

Sylos Labini, P. (1957), *Oligopolio e Progresso Tecnico*. Second and revised edition, first edition 1956, Milano: Giuffrè.

Tomaru, Y., Y. Nakamura and M. Saito (2009), Capacity Choice in a Mixed Duopoly with Managerial Delegation, *Economics Bulletin*, 29(3), 1904–1924.

Vives, X. (1986a), Rationing Rules and Bertrand–Edgeworth Equilibria in Large Markets, *Economics Letters*, 21(2), 113–116.

Vives, X. (1986b), Commitment Flexibility and Market Outcomes, *International Journal of Industrial Organization*, 4(2), 217–229.

Vives, X. (1999), *Oligopoly Pricing: Old Ideas and New Tools*. Cambridge, Massachusetts: MIT Press.

22 The Sylos Postulate reconsidered

Rodolfo Signorino

Introduction

Within the great stream of the imperfect/monopolistic competition revolution of the early 1930s much was written concerning the role of excess capacity and potential entry in less-than-perfectly competitive markets. (Harrod, 1934, 1952; Kaldor, 1935, 1938; Bain, 1949, 1950, 1954a, b; Clark, 1940; Osborne 1964 and Pyatt 1971 provide early critical assessments of this literature.) The bone of contention was the pricing policy chosen by oligopolistic firms facing the threat of external firms' entry.[1] One of the analytical outcomes of the above literature was the static limit-pricing model with symmetric information, also referred to as the Bain–Sylos Labini–Modigliani model. That model now belongs to the history of oligopoly *cum* entry theory: Gilbert, in his 1989 review article on the role of potential competition within industrial organization theory, refers to it as the 'classic limit pricing model'. According to Gilbert, a basic assumption in the model concerned (when scale economies are included in the picture) is that 'entrants expect that established firms will not accommodate entry by reducing their output' (Gilbert 1989: 108). In a footnote, Gilbert adds:

> A particular example of the non-accommodation assumption is the 'Sylos Postulate' that established firms will maintain their pre-entry outputs, named after the work of Sylos Labini (1962, originally published in Italian in 1958). *Game theorists will recognize this assumption as Nash-Cournot behavior on the part of entrants, with the incumbent acting as a Stackelberg leader.*
>
> (Gilbert 1989: 108 fn 1, emphasis added;
> in the same vein see Osborne 1973)

Irrespective of their intrinsic worth, Gilbert's and Osborne's game-theoretical appraisals of Sylos Labini's oligopoly theory end up describing a piece of past economics as little more than an imperfect anticipation of contemporary economics. In short, they fall squarely within the boundaries of so-called Whig historiography (see Blaug 1997, 1999, 2002 and Klaes, 2003). Almost inevitably, Whig reconstructions of past economics tend to minimise the theoretical and methodological originality, if any, of past economics. As argued by Roncaglia (2006),

Arena (2007) and Rancan (2012), Sylos Labini's oligopoly theory has not escaped such a gloomy fate: the villain of this story is Modigliani (1958) who deeply influenced what subsequently became the received interpretation of Sylos Labini (1962).

Rancan (2012) has extensively investigated the analytical and methodological differences between Modigliani's and Sylos Labini's approaches to oligopoly theory. Relying on fresh evidence provided by their private correspondence in the Modigliani Papers preserved at Duke University, Rancan (2012) points out that the differences between Sylos Labini's 1957 Italian book and Modigliani's 1958 *JPE* review were not exclusively analytical but also and significantly methodological:

> Modigliani's review examined only Sylos' microeconomic static analysis, notably the role of firms' expectations and the Sylos postulate for determining long-run equilibrium price and output. In doing so, Modigliani departed from Sylos' objective approach to the oligopoly problem as an alternative to subjective analysis based on reaction functions.
>
> (Rancan 2012: 4–5; see also Rancan 2014: 272)

Moreover, Rancan (2012) argues that Modigliani's methodological stance may be traced back to his early acquaintance with game theory and his deep involvement in research projects sponsored by the University of Illinois and Carnegie Tech on decision making under uncertainty (on this aspect of Modigliani's thought, see Rancan 2013).[2]

While I agree with the gist of Rancan's interpretation, I have just a minor point of departure. Rancan (2012: 11 and 17), following Roncaglia (2006), claims that Sylos Labini considered constant output as an established fact of the modern industrial system and, on this basis, he adopted it in his model. By contrast, in my view, Sylos Labini agreed with Modigliani that external firms do make conjectures on what he calls the 'long-period demand curve for the industry', that is, post-entry market demand conditions. Accordingly, I claim that the point at stake between Sylos Labini and Modigliani was the modelling strategy scholars ought to follow in order to formalise such conjectures. Granted that external firms' conjectures are part of the subject observed, it is the observer who has to choose the assumptions best fitted to capture what may be considered the basic features of the subject under investigation. However, freedom to choose does not mean arbitrariness. What I call 'modelling strategy' is just the set of rules that observers, more or less consciously, impose on themselves, on the basis of their *a priori* beliefs, research goals etc., in order make methodologically consistent analytical choices. Obviously, different observers will probably choose different assumptions because of their different *a priori* beliefs, research goals etc. From this perspective, Sylos Labini's assumption of constant output should be defended not so much on the grounds of its (alleged) empirical soundness; but rather as the assumption which he thought was the one which best fitted the methodological requirements of his objectivistic approach to oligopoly theorising.[3]

To support my interpretation, in this Chapter I propose a textual comparison between the 1957 second Italian edition (that reviewed by Modigliani in 1958) and the 1962 first American edition of Sylos Labini's book. In the later edition of his book, Sylos Labini added some fresh sections concerning the issue of new firms' entry and incumbents' reaction that partly contradict Modigliani's 1958 discussion of the Sylos Postulate. I also show that, unlike Modigliani, Sylos Labini sided with those economists such as Bain, Kaldor and Sweezy who, in the aftermath of the imperfect/monopolistic competition revolution of the early 1930s, (i) questioned the ability of an analytical approach based on subjectivist magnitudes to cope with the value problem in oligopoly theory and (ii) were willing to explore different theoretical routes. Unfortunately, the oligopoly literature which stemmed from Modigliani (1958) and his Sylos Postulate totally lost sight of Sylos Labini's objectivistic bias and modelling strategy, with the unfortunate outcome that theoretical subversion has been traded for analytical refinement.

The chapter is structured as follows. The next section compares Modigliani's 1958 presentation of the Sylos Postulate with the text of Sylos Labini (1957 and 1962) and sketches Sylos Labini's assessment of Modigliani (1958) over the years. The third section focuses on Sylos Labini's analytical discontent towards the then blossoming literature on 'conjecturizing' oligopoly models and his preference for a sharply different modelling strategy to cope with demand issues in oligopoly theory. The issue is further analysed in the fourth section, which explores the methodological constraints on the analysis of external firms' entry implied by Sylos Labini's objectivism. The final section concludes.

Showing the evidence: Modigliani (1958) and Sylos Labini (1957 and 1962) on the Sylos Postulate

As is well known, Modigliani (1958) is a comparative review of Joe Bain's *Barriers to New Competition* (1956) and Paolo Sylos Labini's *Oligopolio e Progresso Tecnico* (1957). Modigliani introduced the Sylos Postulate in the following way:

> [Bain and Sylos Labini have] proceeded to explore systematically the implications of the following well-defined assumption: that potential entrants behave as though they expected existing firms to adopt the policy most unfavorable to them, namely, the policy of maintaining output while reducing the price (or accepting reductions) to the extent required to enforce such an output policy.
>
> (Modigliani 1958: 217)

According to Modigliani,

> the significance of Sylos' postulate lies in the fact that it enables us to find a *definite solution to the problem of long-run equilibrium price and output under homogeneous oligopoly*, or at least a definite upper limit to the price,

to be denoted by *Po* [the limit price] and a corresponding lower limit to aggregate output, say, *Xo* [the limit quantity].

(Modigliani 1958: 217, emphasis added)

Modigliani's remark is worth stressing since the issue of the (in)determinacy of equilibrium, together with the problem of formalising the conjectures of an oligopolistic firm about its rivals' reactions, was the *crux* of classical oligopoly models, before the advent of game theory (see Chamberlin 1929: 87–91).[4] In fact, to exploit scale economies a potential entrant should expect to be able to sell a significant fraction of their pre-entry output. This fact implies that the basic magnitude relevant to a potential entrant in order to calculate the expected entry profitability, i.e. post-entry equilibrium market price, may well sharply differ from the pre-entry equilibrium market price. Expected post-entry equilibrium market price depends on the quantities actually produced by the entrant *and* the incumbents after entry and thus on the anticipated incumbents' reaction to actual entry. Therefore, an assumption concerning the issue of potential entrant's conjectures on incumbents' likely reactions is crucial in order to determine long-run oligopoly equilibrium in the presence of scale economies.

Yet, quite surprisingly, Modigliani failed to provide his readers with an exact bibliographic quote from the two books under review. With regard to Sylos Labini, he just pointed out that the Sylos Postulate 'underlies, more or less explicitly, most of his analysis' (Modigliani 1958: 217). The language barrier prevented English-speaking readers checking the text of Sylos Labini's 1957 book by themselves until the appearance of *Oligopoly and Technical Progress* in 1962. However, the 1962 book is not a mere English translation of its Italian precursor. As concerns the assumptions about external firms' entry into a concentrated oligopoly (characterised by the interaction of different scale and cost functions firms producing a homogeneous commodity) the text of the 1957 Italian book reviewed by Modigliani markedly differs from that of the 1962 book: as noted by Rancan (2012: 17), in the former, unlike the latter, there is no explicit evidence of any Sylos Postulate. Indeed, in *Oligopolio e Progresso Tecnico* Sylos Labini went no further than the following cryptic sentence:

> Non vi sono ostacoli all'entrata di nuove imprese se non quelli impliciti nelle ipotesi e assunzioni fatte. (Sylos Labini 1957: 47) There are no obstacles to the entry of new firms except as implied by the previous assumptions.
>
> (My translation)

From this perspective, Arena (2007: 38) is on firm ground when he speaks of 'Modigliani et l'invention du "Postulat de Sylos Labini"'.[5] By contrast, five years later in *Oligopoly and Technical Progress* Sylos Labini wrote:

> There are no obstacles to the entry of new firms except as implied by the previous assumptions. If new firms enter the market, the existing ones continue to produce as much as before. They do so not only to discourage the entry of

new firms, whose additional output in these circumstances depresses the price and so makes the whole market less profitable, but also because by lowering their output the existing firms would raise their total average cost (since on our assumptions total average cost is decreasing up to the limit of plant capacity). For the sake of simplicity, we have ruled out any reduction of output by existing firms as a result of the entry of new firms; if existing firms decide to produce less than maximum output, they do so not under pressure from new entry, but on the basis of independent economic calculations.

(Sylos Labini 1962: 43)[6]

Appended to this passage is a footnote where Sylos Labini explicitly referred to Modigliani (1958: 230). The passage in question is worth citing in full:

as long as we are dealing with homogeneous oligopoly, it is hard to find a well-defined sensible alternative [to the Sylos Postulate]. Certainly, the diametrically opposite assumption that existing firms will adopt a policy of maintaining price, by contracting their output, would generally be a rather foolish one for the entrant to make. It implies that established firms will graciously allow the entrant to carve out for himself whatever slice of the market he pleases, while suffering losses on two accounts: (1) by losing sales and (2) by incurring a higher average cost, at least in the short run and possibly even in the long run, if their original plant was of no more than optimal size.

(Modigliani (1958): 230)

We may only speculate on the reasons that pushed Sylos Labini to clarify his own thinking on this specific issue in the 1962 edition of his book. A plausible guess is that he was not fully satisfied with Modigliani's 'invention' of the Sylos Postulate, at least as concerns the way Modigliani defended it in the first part of his 1958 article, that is, as an arbitrary conjecture on the part of a potential entrant about the likely incumbents' reaction in the event of actual entry. In my view, it is no mere coincidence that when Sylos Labini tackled the entry issue once again in the 1962 book he approvingly quoted the final part of Modigliani's 1958 article where Modigliani emphasised the technological and cost-based rationale of the alleged postulate.

Before concluding this section, a word of caution is needed. Although it is fair to say that Sylos Labini never explicitly rejected Modigliani's 1958 interpretation of his book, he appeared to have some reservations on it. In the Preface to *Oligopoly and Technical Progress* Sylos Labini pointed out that

[c]onsidering the scientific value of Modigliani's analysis and the original approach to certain specific problems and their solution, his [1958] paper is to be regarded as more than a critical review of the book; *it is a new and significant contribution to the theoretical problem of oligopoly.*

(Sylos Labini 1962: vii, emphasis added)

Moreover, he informed his readers that he had chosen to revise Parts II and III of his book substantially (devoted to macroeconomic issues) while leaving Part I basically unaltered (devoted to equilibrium analysis in oligopoly). He explained the decision not to take Bain (1956) and Modigliani (1958) into consideration in the revised edition of his book in the following way:

> It seemed to me that if I were to recast my whole analysis, this would not only involve a *radical revision of the logic structure of my book*, but, just because of the kinship between my analysis and the two others mentioned, might also impair the homogeneous texture of my argument.
>
> (Sylos Labini 1962: viii, emphasis added)

Sylos Labini's reservations appear explicitly in his personal correspondence of the mid-1950s with Modigliani. After a reading of the 1956 provisional Italian edition of Sylos Labini's book, Modigliani anticipated much of the content of his future 1958 *JPE* paper in the course of a long letter, dated 14 September 1956 (quoted in Rancan 2012: 10 ff and now published as Modigliani [1956] 2014).[7] Sylos Labini annotated Modigliani's letter with several notes of open disagreement. In particular, commenting upon the passage where Modigliani discussed entry conditions and introduced the hypothesis of constant output, Sylos Labini wrote:

> This is not my hypothesis, the interpretation of this point is not correct.
>
> (Quoted in Rancan 2012: 14, Rancan's translation;
> see also Modigliani [1956] 2014: 291 fn 12)

Some fifty years later, Sylos Labini had the opportunity to reconsider the question of Modigliani's interpretation of his 1957 book. In his 2005 personal recollections on Modigliani, Sylos Labini claimed that

> [a]s was to be expected, [Modigliani] had some reservations about certain points of my analysis in his review. I, too, had some reservations about his interpretation of my model, the main one being that he found in it an essentially static approach with promising leads for dynamic analysis, while I set out to present a dynamic analysis from beginning to end.
>
> (Sylos Labini 2005: 42)

In particular, as concerns the Sylos Postulate, Sylos Labini stressed that

> It is in any case not the rigid assumption one might expect when the term 'postulate' is brought in: my point is that the assumption applies in certain market conditions – I begin with a market situation 'criée au hasard', considering a certain economic space and a given 'empirical elasticity' of demand – but not in others. Nevertheless, the fact remains that the existing firms do not necessarily adjust production when other firms attempt entry. *Between myself*

and Franco there are no logical contrasts, but different assumptions, and thus different lines of analysis.

(Sylos Labini 2005: 43, emphasis added)

Taking Sylos Labini's words at face value, one is led to conclude that an unfortunate consequence of Modigliani's 1958 algebra and graphs has been to obscure the theoretical divide between Sylos Labini's and Modigliani's analysis of the same questions: which is the best modelling strategy to follow in order to analyse market demand and incumbents' likely reactions to external firms' entry within oligopoly theory. I tackle these two issues in the next two sections, respectively.

Market demand in oligopoly theory: Sylos Labini... *et al.*

Sylos Labini manifested a critical attitude towards the ever-growing role played by subjectivist magnitudes within the oligopoly literature as early as the 1957 Italian edition of his book. His strictures targeted not only oligopoly models such as those *à la* Cournot and *à la* Edgeworth which, in his view, were based on 'ipotesi astratte, che hanno essenzialmente carattere psicologico' (Sylos Labini 1957: 24) – 'abstract hypotheses of an essentially psychological nature' (Sylos Labini 1962: 19). With regard to oligopoly models based on 'reaction curves' and 'conjectural variations' *à la* Bowley (1924), Sylos Labini claimed that

> [l]a produzione di ipotesi e soluzioni siffatte ha raggiunto proporzioni allarmanti [...] La verità è che, sulla via delle "variazioni congetturali" (*Io credo ch'ei credette ch'io credesse*), non ci si ferma mai. Le soluzioni possono essere aumentate all'infinito ed il proporre siffatte ipotesi e soluzioni può divenire una sorta di mestiere.
>
> (Sylos Labini 1957: 24–25)[8]

Endless model proliferation is not the only drawback Sylos Labini envisaged in the conjectural variation approach. In his view, the major drawback was the risk of falling into circular reasoning in price determination and thus filling oligopoly literature with 'empty economic boxes'. For Sylos Labini, the only way out of such a deadlock was an oligopoly analysis based on objective magnitudes:

> dobbiamo tendere a individuare elementi obiettivi che, nella realtà, possano servire di base alla determinazione del prezzo. Altrimenti, rischiamo di rimanere nel mondo fantastico delle "curve di reazione" e delle "variazioni congetturali" — un mondo dove tutto è possibile e nulla è necessario. E rischiamo di proporre spiegazioni che, se pure formalmente valide, possono essere di scarso o di nessun aiuto allo studioso che si accinga all'analisi concreta di industrie particolari, perpetuando lo iato, tuttora gravissimo, fra schemi teorici dell'oligopolio e realtà industriale moderna; spiegazioni che si aggirano in circoli viziosi e che offrono il fianco all'arguta frecciata di R. A. Gordon: 'Rifugiarsi in interpretazioni soggettive delle funzioni del costo e del ricavo non è certo una soluzione. Teorie fondate su tali interpretazioni non dicono

altro che questo: che gli uomini d'affari fanno quel che fanno perché lo fanno'.

(Sylos Labini 1957: 38)[9]

At this juncture, a possible source of misunderstanding must be clarified: when Sylos Labini spoke of 'objective elements as may, in real situations, serve as a basis for price determination' he was referring to (i) technology *and* (ii) market demand conditions.[10] Indeed, market demand conditions determine what Sylos Labini called 'the structure of an industry':

> Per "struttura" dell'industria intendiamo: 1) *l'estensione assoluta del mercato*, ossia il volume delle vendite ad un certo prezzo; 2) la capacità di assorbimento del mercato, ossia *l'elasticità della domanda* rispetto a variazioni di prezzo; 3) *la distribuzione del volume delle vendite* fra un numero determinato di *imprese di tipi diversi*.
>
> (Sylos Labini 1957: 40, Sylos Labini's emphasis)[11]

The role of this structural element is to guide scholars in their assessment of whether a given market price *crié par hasard à la* Walras is or is not an equilibrium price (Sylos Labini, 1957: 40). Therefore, Sylos Labini's objectivism does not imply that scholars should develop an oligopoly model where market demand conditions simply play no role in equilibrium price determination. Rather, it should be considered as a binding constraint on scholars' modelling strategy concerning the analysis of market demand. For Sylos Labini, the introduction of conjectures on (actual and potential) rivals' behaviour into the demand curves of oligopolistic firms involves a serious analytical drawback, namely the development of a theoretical object whose empirical foundations are at best shaky. For Sylos Labini the market demand curve based *only* on the tastes of consumers is a theoretical object that has a solid empirical foundation (see Sylos Labini 1957: 35 and 1962: 31). This is the reason why Sylos Labini preferred to concentrate his oligopoly analysis on the homogeneous commodity case:

> Dobbiamo distinguere fra domanda ed elasticità della domanda per l'industria e domanda ed elasticità della domanda per la singola impresa oligopolistica. (Se si fa astrazione dalla differenziazione dei prodotti, non sussiste una curva di domanda per la singola impresa, distinta dalla curva di domanda per l'industria). Solo la domanda per l'industria si può dire che rifletta i gusti e quindi le possibili reazioni dei consumatori. L'altra curva di domanda riflette invece, commistamente, le reazioni dei consumatori e quelle dei rivali dell'impresa considerata (rivali già operanti e rivali potenziali). È una curva di domanda spuria, una curva "immaginata", come l'hanno chiamata Kaldor e Sweezy.
>
> (Sylos Labini 1957: 37–38)[12]

With regard to the analytical discontent towards 'imagined' demand curves based on oligopolistic firms' conjectures about (actual and potential) rivals' reactions, Sylos Labini was definitely not a lone rider. Besides the two economists, Nicholas Kaldor and Paul Sweezy, explicitly mentioned by him, other scholars whose works exerted a deep influence on his thought were treading a similar path. I refer to Hall and Hitch (1939) and Bain (1942). The former wrote:

> The 'current doctrine' of the equilibrium of the firm, which runs in terms of marginal cost and marginal revenue, is held to apply in its simpler form only to ... pure competition, pure monopoly, and monopolistic competition. It breaks down in the [case of] oligopoly and monopolistic competition with oligopoly; these, as special cases, are relegated to footnotes or left to mathematicians, because the *demand curve for the product of the individual firm, and therefore marginal revenue, is indeterminate where the price and output policies of the firms are interdependent.*
>
> (Hall and Hitch (1939: 17, emphasis added)

Bain's criticism was even more destructive and assumes an explicit methodological perspective. In his view, Joan Robinson's oligopoly price theory was devoid of empirical content and amounted to nothing more than *ex post* rationalization of market equilibrium. According to Bain, the theory in question was based on two theoretical price determinants, i.e., the demand curve and the cost curves: unlike the latter, the former was not even conceivably ascertainable independently of the prices it is supposed to determine.[13] The relevant passage is worth citing in full:

> The theoretical demand curve is always an *ex ante* demand curve which exists in the expectations of a producer. An *ex post* demand curve, no matter how adequate the statistical technique which prepared it, is not the same thing, nor does it bear any specific or necessarily close relationship to it. Not only have those demand curves which exist in the minds of producers not been ascertained, but it is very questionable whether they are practically susceptible of ascertainment. Insofar as this is true, a price theory stemming from 'given' demand curves is devoid of empirical content, on the ground that the curves are practically non-ascertainable. *The same difficulty is reinforced in any case where conceptually the demand curve for the individual seller is contingent as regards its shape and position upon reactions of rival sellers which are likely to be induced by movements along it – i.e., in every case of oligopoly. Here the demand curve is doubly a matter of the subjective of the seller – as regards not only his expectations concerning the demand for the product, but also his expectations regarding the probable reactions of his rivals.* The demand schedule for the individual oligopolist is hardly susceptible of practical ascertainment. It is such a highly tenuous concept that one might question its explicit existence in the mind of the producer and therefore whether it is even conceivably ascertainable.
>
> (Bain 1942: 563–564, emphasis added)

Needless to add, Bain's criticism is part and parcel of the then blossoming Harvard approach to Industrial Organization theory that eventually led to the Structure–Conduct–Performance paradigm: three years before Bain, Mason (1939: 62, 64 and 70) had already raised the empirical applicability issue of Joan Robinson's 'box of tools'.

Objectivism and external firms' entry within Sylos Labini's oligopoly theory

The argument proposed in the previous sections invites a few obvious questions. Since Sylos Labini's objectivist bias was already evident in *Oligopolio e Progresso Tecnico*, how could Modigliani turn a blind eye to it by 'inventing' his Sylos Postulate? Should Modigliani be sentenced for malicious misinterpretation of his Italian friend's oligopoly analysis? My answer to these questions is that Modigliani actually turned a blind eye to the methodological underpinnings of Sylos Labini's oligopoly model; yet he should be granted extenuation since the text of the 1957 Italian book, reviewed by him, unlike the 1962 American edition, is far from crystal clear as regards the relationship between objective foundations of oligopoly theory and the issue of new firms' entry. Obviously, it may be argued that Modigliani's review worked as a kind of catalyst which pushed Sylos Labini to make up his mind on this specific aspect of his model. Moreover, it should not be forgotten that Modigliani's aim in 1958 was to 'channel' a book written in Italian by a not-yet-famous economist to an English-speaking audience. Be that as it may, the fact is that Sylos Labini seized the occasion of the new American edition of his book to clarify his thinking.

Right at the end of Chapter I, 'Aspetti generali del problema teorico', ['General aspects of the theoretical problem'], of *Oligopolio e Progresso Tecnico* (1957) Sylos Labini wrote:

> Bain [Sylos Labini refers to Bain 1949] parla esplicitamente di un "livello critico" del prezzo, che nessun oligopolista vorrà superare per non far invadere il mercato da nuovi produttori. Ma, non diversamente da Harrod [Sylos Labini refers to Harrod 1952], esprime osservazioni generiche sulle forze che contribuiscono a determinare questo livello critico.
>
> (Sylos Labini 1957: 36)

> Bain explicitly speaks of a 'critical level' of price, which no oligopolistic firm would like to exceed in order to prevent market invasion by new producers. But, just like Harrod, he makes generic observations on the forces which contribute to bring about such a critical level.
>
> (My translation)

By contrast, in the same place of *Oligopoly and Technical Progress* (1962) the above passage was deleted and replaced by the following one:

> Bain, who has contributed the most significant writing on the problem of oligopoly [Sylos Labini refers to Bain 1949, 1954a and b and 1956], rightly emphasizes the importance of studying the conditions of entry. Indeed,

as long as we assume a fixed and unalterable number of firms, we are led either to place disproportionate stress on the demand curve and on demand elasticity or to go back to the psychological-reaction curves. It would seem a more fruitful approach to an adequate explanation of the equilibrium price, and thus of the level of the markup q, to drop that assumption. Our analysis of price determination, like Bain's, will concentrate on the conditions of entry.

(Sylos Labini 1962: 31–32, emphasis added)

This newly added passage clarifies that, for Sylos Labini, the issue of external firms' entry plays a basic role in the process of clearing oligopoly value theory off subjectivist magnitudes. In Chapter II, 'La determinazione del prezzo', ['Price determination'], of *Oligopolio e Progresso Tecnico* (1957), Sylos Labini did not provide a general analysis of the pricing policy followed by the price leaders, i.e. incumbent large-plant firms, and preferred to discuss a few numerical examples. Yet his numerical examples were built to show that there is no *a priori* reason why the price fixed by large-plant firms should be an equilibrium price, given technology and market demand conditions, once the issue of potential external firms' entry is included in the analysis: external firms enter the market whenever they find it profitable, given the price fixed by incumbent large-plant firms, and their entry provokes an increase of production and a fall of market price.

Sylos Labini's numerical examples take as given (i) technological discontinuities, which determine the number of incumbent firms of various dimensions, and (ii) market demand conditions, which determine the absolute extension of the market, its price-elasticity (which Sylos Labini assumed equal to unity) and the distribution of sales among the incumbent firms of various dimensions. These two *objective* magnitudes determine the boundaries of large-plant firms' market power and the relative convenience of alternative pricing policies, ranging from an aggressive policy to a more accommodating 'live and let live'. Indeed, to analyse large-plant firms' pricing decisions Sylos Labini distinguished between an entry-preventing price, 'prezzo di esclusione', and an elimination price, 'prezzo di eliminazione': see Sylos Labini (1957: 44–45 and 1962: 40) and claimed that, unlike what happens in competitive markets, oligopolistic firms, when they fix their price, 'worry much more about the reactions of existing or potential rivals than about those of consumers' (Sylos Labini 1962: 51; see also Sylos Labini 1957: 55).[14] His numerical examples allowed him to conclude that the general tendency for the equilibrium price is that '[t]he price tends to settle at a level immediately above the entry-preventing price of the least efficient firms which it is to the advantage of the largest and most efficient firms to let live' (Sylos Labini 1962: 50; see also Sylos Labini 1957: 54). Though Sylos Labini was silent on this issue, it may be inferred from his discussion of the numerical examples that such a general price tendency is common knowledge among incumbent firms and the external ones and thus constitutes the objective basis on which external firms calculate their entry profitability.

Granted my interpretation, it may be argued that Sylos Labini was aware that external firms do make conjectures on what he calls the 'long-period demand curve for the industry', that is, post-entry market demand conditions:

> Anybody proposing to enter the market must reckon not only with the present size of demand, but must also make some estimate of the market's capacity to absorb an additional quantity of goods – either (a) at lower prices if the market is stationary, (b) at the ruling price if the market tends to expand, or (c) at lower prices if the market tends to expand but the entrant want to speed up its expansion.
>
> (Sylos Labini 1962: 34. See also Sylos Labini 1957: 38)

Accordingly, the crux of the matter between Modigliani and Sylos Labini is the choice of the modelling strategy in order to formalise such conjectures. An objectivistic approach to oligopoly theory requires that when, modelling external firms' conjectures, scholars should look at the same objective elements which they identify as those determining incumbents' pricing policy. From this perspective, ruling out 'any reduction of output by existing firms as a result of the entry of new firms' may be defended as the assumption that Sylos Labini considered as that consistent with an objectivistic approach to oligopoly theory.

Final remarks

The Sylos Postulate is one of the main analytical pillars on which Modigliani built his 1958 interpretation of Sylos Labini's *Oligopolio e Progresso Tecnico* (1957). Taking my lead from a few contributions which have critically assessed such a postulate and clarified the methodological foundations of Sylos Labini's oligopoly pricing model, in this chapter I proposed a textual comparison between the 1957 second Italian edition (that reviewed by Modigliani in 1958) and the 1962 first American edition of Sylos Labini's book. The aim of such an exercise was twofold. The first aim was to emphasise that, in the later edition of his book, Sylos Labini added some fresh sections concerning the issue of new firms' entry and incumbents' reaction that partly contradicted Modigliani's presentation of the Sylos Postulate. The second was to show that, unlike Modigliani, Sylos Labini sided with those economists such as Bain, Kaldor and Sweezy who, in the aftermath of the imperfect/monopolistic competition revolution, (i) questioned the ability of an analytic approach based on subjectivist magnitudes to cope with the value problem in oligopoly theory and (ii) were willing to explore different theoretical routes.

Though Modigliani's 1958 neglect of the methodological underpinnings of Sylos Labini's contribution may be partly justified, the fact remains that it paved the way for a Whiggish assessment of Sylos Labini's contribution that does less than full justice to its originality. Sylos Labini's analysis of large firms' pricing policy was far from fully satisfactory since it was based on restrictive assumptions (such as unit price-demand elasticity) and was developed by means of simple numerical examples. Subsequent oligopoly theorists did not miss the opportunity to report such drawbacks (see Osborne 1964: 397 fn 8). Yet these critical commentators went so far as to throw out the baby (an objectivistic approach to oligopoly theory) with the bathwater (the shortcomings of Sylos Labini's numerical examples).

Notes

1 To the best of my knowledge, the issue was first raised by Roy Harrod in his review of Edward Chamberlin's *The Theory of Monopolistic Competition* (Chamberlin, 1933):

> It is pertinent to inquire why the oligopolistic competitors, whose special attribute is that they trace out to the last stage the effect of their policy on the existing competitors, give no thought to the possibility of attracting new competitors and spoiling their position in that way. Why are they so long-sighted with regard to their existing rivals' reactions, and yet in blinkers with regard to the possibility of new competitors?
>
> (Harrod 1933: 665).

2 According to Sent (2002), in the mid-1950s to the early-1960s, Franco Modigliani, Charles Holt, Herbert Simon and John Muth constituted at Carnegie a four-man team deeply involved into the project of developing and applying innovative mathematical techniques to decision making under uncertainty and forecasting: Grunberg and Modigliani (1954) is probably the best-known outgrowth of Modigliani's thought on these issues in the mid-1950s. On this aspect of Modigliani's work at Carnegie, see Hartley (2004).

3 Granted my interpretation, it may be argued that Sylos Labini's approach was somewhat similar to that followed by Piero Sraffa in his 1925–1926 articles and 1960 book as concerns the analysis of demand conditions. As shown by Neri Salvadori, 'Sraffa was not of the opinion that demand does not matter but, on the contrary, that demand based on preferences (utility) is not a solid base on which to erect a theory of value and distribution' (Salvadori 2000: 181; see also Salvadori and Signorino 2007).

4 In his review of the English edition of Antoine-Augustin Cournot's *Researches* Irving Fisher wrote:

> The fault to be found with the reasoning [underlying Cournot's duopoly model] is in his premise that each individual will act on the assumption that his rival's output is constant, and will strive only to so regulate his own output as to secure the largest profits. [...] But, as a matter of fact, no business man assumes either that his rival's output or price will remain constant any more than a chess player assumes that his opponent will not interfere with his effort to capture a knight. On the contrary, his whole thought is to forecast what move the rival will make in response to one of his own.
>
> (Fisher 1898: 126)

On the issue of firms' conjectures within classical duopoly models see Magnan de Bornier (1992) and Giocoli (2003 and 2005).

5 Unlike Sylos Labini (1957), Bain (1956) devoted a long section, 'The probable effects of observed scale economies on the condition of entry', in the final part of Chapter 3, 'Economies of Large Scale as Barriers to Entry', to the analysis of the issue of potential entrants' conjectures about incumbents' likely reaction to actual entry. Bain started from the observation that, in the presence of significant scale economies within a given market, a potential entrant must supply a large percentage of total market capacity in order to

produce at the optimal minimal plant size. This 'percentage effect' of scale economies on entry and the steepness of firm's average cost curve away from the optimal minimal plant size created 'a sort of interdependence between the actions of established sellers and the action of any potential entrants' (Bain 1956: 94). Accordingly, Bain claimed that 'the potential entrant would need to have conjectures about the reactions of established firms to his entry, and in turn about the market situation after his entry... He might make any number of alternate conjectures concerning reactions to his entry, ranging from his acceptance as an equal member of a joint monopoly to aggressive retaliation against him' (Bain 1956: 95). To simplify his analysis Bain assumed product homogeneity and price-elasticity of demand equal to unity and focused on just the three scenarios which he considered the most likely: (i) the pessimistic conjecture (i.e. potential entrants assume that, in the case of actual entry, incumbents will keep their output constant so that the post-entry market price will fall below the pre-entry market price), (ii) the optimistic conjecture (i.e. potential entrants assume that, in the case of actual entry, incumbents will reduce their output enough to allow entrants to gain the market share they wish so that the post-entry market price will not fall below the pre-entry market price) and (iii) an intermediate conjecture. Therefore, given the relative space Bain (1956) and Sylos Labini (1957) devote to the analysis of potential entrants' conjectures, what Modigliani (1958) called the Sylos Postulate should more accurately be rechristened as the Bain postulate.

6 Sylos Labini did not change his mind on this issue with the passage of time. In Sylos Labini (1979: 4) he included among the six main assumptions of his oligopoly pricing model the proposition according to which 'If new firms enter the market, existing firms continue to produce as much as before, not only to discourage the entry of new firms, but also to avoid raising unit costs'.

7 As remarked by Roncaglia (2014: 241), this letter, originally written in Italian, with footnotes containing the annotations by Sylos Labini, was found among Modigliani's papers and translated into English by Antonella Rancan: see Rancan 2014 for a discussion of the historical context of the letter and its theoretical and cultural background.

8 'The production of such hypotheses and solutions has assumed alarming proportions [...] The truth is that there is no stopping on the path of conjectural variations (*Cred'io ch'ei credette ch'io credesse*) [*I believe that he believed that I believed*]. Solutions can be proliferated to infinity and the manufacture of such hypotheses and solutions can become a sort of profession' (Sylos Labini 1962: 19–20). The Italian sentence is a quotation from Dante Alighieri's *The Divine Comedy, Inferno* (Hell), Canto XIII.

9   We shall try to identify such objective elements as may, in real situations, serve as a basis for price determination. Otherwise, we would run the danger of remaining in the fantastic world of reaction curves and conjectural variations – a world where everything might and nothing need happen. And we would risk propounding explanations which may be formally correct but of little or no help in concrete analysis of any particular industry. The only result would be a perpetuation of the serious gap between the theoretical models of oligopoly and modern industrial realities. Without an objective base our explanation, like others before it, would not escape from the vicious circle and would be wide open to R.A. Gordon's sharp rebuke: "Refuge in subjective interpretations of cost and revenue functions is certainly no answer. It leaves theory saying that businessmen do what they do because they do it.

(Sylos Labini 1962: 34)

The quotation is taken from Gordon (1948: 287).

10 According to Sylos Labini a basic feature of concentrated oligopoly, characterised by the production of a homogeneous commodity, is technological discontinuity: incumbent firms within the same market have sharply different plant sizes (on this point see

Roncaglia 1994). This fact implies a number of analytical consequences. In particular, (i) only large-plant firms can exploit scale economies and thus are the most efficient in the sense that, though their average fixed cost is higher, their total average cost is lower than small-plant firms' respective cost curves and (ii) only large-plant firms can fix the price while small-plant firms adapt their supply. According to Sylos Labini, empirical research showed that, in the majority of manufacturing industries, firms' average and marginal cost curves were not U-shaped, as postulated by traditional economic theory. By contrast, marginal cost is constant up to the limit of plant capacity while firms generally produce in regime of decreasing average cost, as suggested by Sraffa (1926), a paper that Sylos Labini quoted as one of the main sources of inspiration for his oligopoly analysis. Formally, for Sylos Labini firms' total cost function $C(x)$ is of the type: $C = k + vx$, where C is total cost, k is the fixed cost, v is the constant marginal and average variable cost and x is the quantity produced: see Sylos Labini 1957: 12 and 38 ff) and Sylos Labini (1962: 10, 29 fn 29 and 35 ff).

11   By "structure" of an industry we mean: (*a*) the absolute size of the market, that is, the volume of sales at a given price; (*b*) the absorption capacity of the market in the narrow sense previously specified (price elasticity of demand); (*c*) the distribution of sales among a number of firms of different types.

(Sylos Labini 1962: 36–37).

12   We distinguish between demand and elasticity of demand with respect to the industry and with respect to individual oligopolistic firms. (If we neglect product differentiation, there is no demand curve for the individual firm as distinct from the demand curve for the industry.) Only the industry demand curve can be said to reflect the tastes and thus the possible reactions of consumers. The individual demand curve reflects a mixture of consumer reactions and of reactions of the firms' (existing and potential) competitors. It is a spurious or, as Kaldor and Sweezy say, an "imagined" demand curve.

(Sylos Labini 1962: 33–34)

Sylos Labini probably referred to Kaldor (1934: 340) and Sweezy (1939: 568).

13 As suggested to me by Nicola Giocoli, Kahn (1937) proposed a similar criticism of Robinsonian demand curves in oligopoly.

14 In modern terminology, Sylos Labini's entry-preventing price is the limit price and Sylos Labini's elimination price is a kind of predatory price that obliges an incumbent small-plant, less efficient, firm to leave the market: see Sylos Labini (1957: 44–45 and 1962: 40).

References

Arena, R. (2007). La théorie de l'oligopole de Sylos Labini: diversité des interprétations et prolongements possibles. *Revue d'économie Industrielle*, **118**: 37–54.

Bain, Joe S. (1942). Market Classifications in Modern Price Theory. *Quarterly Journal of Economics*, **56**(4): 560–574.

Bain, Joe S. (1949). A Note on Pricing in Monopoly and Oligopoly. *American Economic Review*, **39**(2): 448–464.

Bain, Joe S. (1950). Workable Competition in Oligopoly: Theoretical Considerations and Some Empirical Evidence. *American Economic Review*, **40**(2): 35–47.

Bain, Joe S. (1954a). Economies of Scale, Concentration, and the Condition of Entry in Twenty Manufacturing Industries. *American Economic Review*, **44**(1): 15–39.

Bain, Joe S. (1954b). Conditions of Entry and the Emergence of Monopoly. In Edward H. Chamberlin (ed.) (1954). *Monopoly, Competition and their Regulation*. London: Macmillan, 215–241.

Bain, Joe S. (1956). *Barriers to New Competition: Their Character and Consequences in Manufacturing Industries*. Cambridge, MA: Harvard University Press.

Blaug, M. (1997). On the Historiography of Economics. In Mark Blaug, *Not Only An Economist. Recent Essays by Mark Blaug*. Cheltenham, UK and Brookfield, US: Edward Elgar, Chapter 5.

Blaug, M. (1999). Misunderstanding Classical Economics: The Sraffian Interpretation of the Surplus Approach. *History of Political Economy*, **31**(2): 213–236.

Blaug, M. (2002). Is There Really Progress in Economics? In Stephan Boehm, Christian Gehrke, Heinz D. Kurz and Richard Sturn (eds.). *Is There Progress in Economics? Knowledge, Truth and the History of Economic Thought*. Cheltenham, UK and Northampton, MA, USA: Edward Elgar, 21–44.

Bowley, Arthur L. (1924). *The Mathematical Groundwork of Economics*. Oxford: Oxford University Press.

Chamberlin, Edward H. (1929). Duopoly: Value Where Sellers are Few. *Quarterly Journal of Economics*, **44**(1): 63–100.

Chamberlin, Edward H. (1933). *The Theory of Monopolistic Competition. A Re-orientation of the Theory of Value*. Cambridge, MA: Harvard University Press.

Clark, John M. (1940). Toward a Concept of Workable Competition. *American Economic Review*, **30**(2): 241–256.

Fisher, I. (1898). Cournot and Mathematical Economics. *Quarterly Journal of Economics*, **12**(2): 119–138.

Gilbert, Richard J. (1989). The Role of Potential Competition in Industrial Organization. *Journal of Economic Perspectives*, **3**(3): 107–127.

Giocoli, N. (2003). 'Conjecturizing' Cournot: The Conjectural Variations Approach to Duopoly Theory. *History of Political Economy*, **35**(2): 175–204.

Giocoli, N. (2005). The Escape from Conjectural Variations: the Consistency Condition in Duopoly Theory from Bowley to Fellner. *Cambridge Journal of Economics*, **29**(4): 601–618.

Gordon, Robert A. (1948). Short-Period Price Determination in Theory and Practice. *American Economic Review*, **38**(3): 265–288.

Grunberg, Emile and Franco Modigliani (1954). The Predictability of Social Events. *Journal of Political Economy*, **62**(6): 465–478.

Hall, Robert L. and Charles J. Hitch (1939). Price Theory and Business Behaviour. *Oxford Economic Papers*, **2**: 12–45.

Harrod, Roy F. (1933). Review of *The Theory of Monopolistic Competition. By Edward Chamberlin. The Economic Journal*, **43**(172): 661–666.

Harrod, Roy F. (1934). Doctrines of Imperfect Competition. *Quarterly Journal of Economics*, **48**(3): 442–470. Reprinted as Essay 7 of Roy F. Harrod 1952. *Economic Essays*. London: Macmillan, 111–138.

Harrod, Roy F. (1952). Theory of Imperfect Competition Revised. Essay 8 of *Economic Essays*. London: Macmillan, 139–169.

Hartley, James E. (2004). Modigliani's Expectations. *Eastern Economic Journal*, **30**(3): 427–440.

Kahn, R. (1937). The Problem of Duopoly. *The Economic Journal*, **47**(185): 1–20.

Kaldor, N. (1934). Mrs. Robinson's 'Economics of Imperfect Competition'. *Economica*, New Series, **1**(3): 335–341.

Kaldor, N. (1935). Market Imperfection and Excess Capacity. *Economica*, New Series, **2**(5): 33–50.

Kaldor, N. (1938). Professor Chamberlin on Monopolistic and Imperfect Competition. *Quarterly Journal of Economics*, **52**(3): 513–529.

Klaes, M. (2003). Historiography. In Warren J. Samuels, Jeff E. Biddle and John B. Davis (eds). *A Companion to the History of Economic Thought*. Malden, MA and Oxford, UK: Blackwell Publishing Ltd, 491–506.

Magnan de Bornier, J. (1992). The 'Cournot-Bertrand Debate': A Historical Perspective. *History of Political Economy*, **24**(3): 623–656.

Mason, Edward S. (1939). Price and Production Policies of Large-Scale Enterprise. *American Economic Review*, **29**(1): 61–74.

Modigliani, F. ([1956] 2014). A Letter to Sylos Labini. *PSL Quarterly Review*, **67**(270): 283–307.

Modigliani, F. (1958). New Developments on the Oligopoly Front. *Journal of Political Economy*, **66**(3): 215–232.

Osborne, Dale K. (1964). The Role of Entry in Oligopoly Theory. *Journal of Political Economy*, **72**(4): 396–402.

Osborne, Dale K. (1973). On the Rationality of Limit Pricing. *The Journal of Industrial Economics*, **22**(1): 71–80.

Pyatt, G. (1971). Profit Maximisation and the Threat of New Entry. *The Economic Journal*, **81**(322): 242–255.

Rancan, A. (2012). The Origin of the Sylos Postulate: Modigliani's and Sylos Labini's Contributions to Oligopoly Theory. Duke University, Center for the History of Political Economy (CHOPE) Working Paper No. 2012-08; available at SSRN: http://ssrn.com/abstract=2198441, last accessed 28 November 2015. Also published as (2015). *Journal of the History of Economic Thought*, **37**(3): 431–448.

Rancan, A. (2013). Modigliani's and Simon's Early Contributions to Uncertainty (1952–1961). *History of Political Economy*, **45**(1): 1–38.

Rancan, A. (2014). Modigliani's Comments on Sylos Labini's Theory of Unemployment (1956–1958). *PSL Quarterly Review*, **67**(270): 269–282.

Roncaglia, A. (1994). Josef Steindl's Relations to Italian Economics. *Review of Political Economy*, **6**(4): 450–458.

Roncaglia, A. (2006). Paolo Sylos Labini, 1920–2005. *BNL Quarterly Review*, **59**(236): 3–21.

Roncaglia, A. (2014). The Theory of Employment: Two Approaches Compared. *PSL Quarterly Review*, **67**(70): 241–268.

Salvadori, N. (2000). Sraffa on Demand: a Textual Analysis. In Heinz D. Kurz (ed.). *Critical Essays on Piero Sraffa's Legacy in Economics*. Cambridge: Cambridge University Press, 181–197.

Salvadori, N. and R. Signorino (2007). Piero Sraffa: Economic Reality, the Economist and Economic Theory. An interpretation'. *Journal of Economic Methodology*, **14**(2): 187–209.

Sent, Esther-Mirjam. (2002). How (Not) to Influence People: The Contrary Tale of John F. Muth. *History of Political Economy*, **34** (2): 291–319.

Sraffa, P. (1925). Sulle relazioni fra costo e quantità prodotta. *Annali di Economia*, **2**: 277–328. English translation: On the Relations between Cost and Quantity Produced; reprinted in Kurz, Heinz D. and N. Salvadori (eds) (2003). *The Legacy of Piero Sraffa*. Vol. I. Cheltenham, UK and Northampton, MA: Edward Elgar.

Sraffa, P. (1926). The Laws of Returns under Competitive Conditions. *The Economic Journal*, **36**(144): 535–550; reprinted in Kurz, Heinz D. and N. Salvadori (eds) (2003).

The Legacy of Piero Sraffa. Vol. I. Cheltenham, UK and Northampton, MA: Edward Elgar.

Sraffa, P. (1960). *Production of Commodities by Means of Commodities.* Cambridge: Cambridge University Press.

Sweezy, Paul M. (1939). Demand under Conditions of Oligopoly. *Journal of Political Economy*, **47**(4): 568–573.

Sylos Labini, P. (1957). *Oligopolio e Progresso Tecnico.* Second Italian edition (First edition 1956). Milano: Giuffrè.

Sylos Labini, P. (1962). *Oligopoly and Technical Progress.* Cambridge, MA: Harvard University Press.

Sylos Labini, P. (1979). Prices and Income Distribution in Manufacturing Industry. *Journal of Post Keynesian Economics*, **2**(1): 3–25.

Sylos Labini, P. (2005). Franco Modigliani and Oligopoly. *BNL Quarterly Review*, **58**(233–234): 41–48.

Part 6

History of economic analysis

23　What's left of Malthus?

Amitava Krishna Dutt[1]

Introduction

Malthus is regarded as the first major economist to discuss the interaction between economic and population growth in a systematic manner, and his *Essay on the Principle of Population* (Malthus, 1798) is still considered a classic on population, the economy and society and read widely as a Western Great Book. Since Malthus argued that population growth sets limits to economic growth due to resource constraints, the adjectives Malthusian and neo-Malthusian are widely used to characterize those who see population growth and resource constraints as barriers to economic development.

Despite his enormous reputation, however, Malthus's name is often invoked in derision rather than in adulation. Marx's loathing for Malthus, revealed in Chapter 25 of *Capital* which states that the

> *Essay on Population* ... in its first form is nothing but a schoolboyish, superficial plagiarism of Defoe, Sir James Steuart, Townsend, Franklin, Wallace, etc., declaimed in the manner of a sermon, but not containing a single original proposition of Malthus himself
>
> (Marx, 1867, Chapter 25, Note 6)

seems to be a strong reaction to Malthus's idea that inevitable natural forces, rather than forces specific to the exploitative and unjust character of the capitalist system, kept the poor in misery. In more recent times Julian Simon has been a major critic of the ideas of Malthus and the neo-Malthusians who subscribe to the 'limits to growth' approach. Simon and Kahn (1984, p. 45) write that

> Global problems due to physical conditions (as distinguished from those caused by institutional and political conditions) are always possible, but are likely to be less pressing in the future than in the past. Environmental, resource, and population stresses are diminishing, and with the passage of time will have less influence than now upon the quality of human life on our planet.
>
> (Simon and Kahn, 1984, p. 45)

The purpose of this paper is to examine whether there is anything useful left in Malthus's analysis of the relationship between population growth and economic growth. It proceeds to do so by first developing a basic model of Malthus's analytical framework that draws on earlier interpreters and formulators of his system in the next section, and then extending that basic model to examine how it is capable of taking into account factors that Malthus did not take into account, or did not do so adequately or sufficiently. These issues are the nature of technology and technological change in the third section, aggregate demand (something that Malthus actually stressed) in the fourth section, the demographic transition in the fifth section and the environment in the sixth section.

The major motivation of the paper is to examine the analytical structure behind Malthus's analysis of the relation between population growth and economic growth and to evaluate its usefulness by using it to address a variety of issues and to suggest that Malthus's analysis has much to recommend it. A broader motivation is to argue that one should distinguish between two levels of a particular theory – the level of the analytical construct and the level of specific conclusions in the form of broad predictions. The reason for doing so is that even if the theory's conclusions and predictions appear to be at variance with the empirical evidence, the analytical construct can still be valuable for understanding the logic of possible developments, and to analyse why exactly the predictions do not seem to hold.

It should be clarified that the paper does not seek to provide a detailed account of Malthus's contributions by examining his writings or to examine whether or not, and to what extent, Malthus's contributions on population and economic growth are novel, or ascertain in detail whether or not his predictions are valid. Nor does it attempt to develop anything like a complete analysis of population and growth dynamics following Malthus's approach. Its purpose is the more limited one of developing some simple Malthusian models, drawing on some contributions to the literature on specifically Malthusian population and growth models.

A basic Malthusian model

We consider a simple Malthusian model of a closed economy with two classes: workers who work and consume their entire income, and capitalists who save and consume, invest, and organize production.[2] The economy produces one good, the production of which requires only labour as a variable factor of production, and other inputs are ignored for simplicity (or their amounts implicitly taken to be given). Production is given by

$$Y = aL \tag{23.1}$$

where we do not yet make any particular assumption about a, the productivity of labour, and where Y is real output and L the amount of labour employed. Capitalists hire workers at the real wage w and obtain profits given by

$$P = Y - wL \tag{23.2}$$

where P is the real value of profits. Capitalists save a fraction s of their profits, so that

$$S = sP \tag{23.3}$$

where S is total real saving, and consume the rest of it. The entire saving of capitalists is (identically) invested, so that we have

$$I \equiv S, \tag{23.4}$$

where I is real investment in the economy. Investment adds to the wage fund, W, which is the only form of capital in the economy, so that[3]

$$\frac{dW}{dt} = I. \tag{23.5}$$

The wage fund is used by the capitalists to hire workers, so that we have[4]

$$W = wL. \tag{23.6}$$

The rate of population growth depends on the birth rate and the death rate, so that

$$\hat{N} = \beta - \delta \tag{23.7}$$

where the overhat denotes the time-rate of growth of the variable and where N is the total population. We assume that the population is equal to the size of the labour force, the number of capitalists being so small that they can be ignored from the population. The birth rate, ß, increases with the real wage, because more comfortable lives make workers procreate more rapidly while low wages make workers decide to have fewer children, so that

$$\beta = \beta(w) \tag{23.8}$$

where $\beta' > 0$. Malthus (1798) referred to checks on population due to a lower birth rate as preventive checks. The death rate, δ, falls with the real wage because more comfortable lives improve nutrition and living conditions and reduce mortality, so that

$$\delta = \delta(w) \tag{23.9}$$

where $\delta' < 0$. Malthus saw these as positive checks, which operate through illness, malnutrition, and other problems due to low wages and incomes. The relation between the birth and death rates (and hence population growth) and the real wage are shown in Figure 23.1.[5]

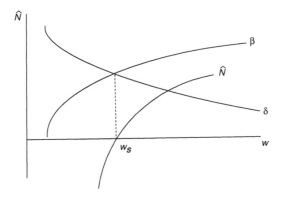

Figure 23.1 Dynamics of population in the basic Malthusian model.

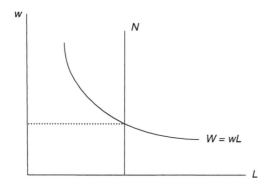

Figure 23.2 Determination of the wage in the basic Malthusian model.

We examine the dynamics of the economy in two runs. In the short run we assume that the population and the wage fund, N and W, are given by past population growth and capital accumulation. In the short run the real wages are flexible, and change to clear the labour market so that in short-run equilibrium the entire labour force or population, N, is employed, implying

$$L = N. \qquad (23.10)$$

The determination of the real wage is shown in Figure 23.2, where the vertical line given by N is the supply curve and the demand curve is given by equation (23.6) for a given wage fund. The equilibrium real wage is shown by the intersection of the two curves, which satisfies equation (23.10), and is determined as

$$w = W/N. \qquad (23.11)$$

In the long run N changes according to equation (23.7) while W changes according to equation (23.5). The dynamics of w, which by using equation (23.10), are given by

$$\hat{w} = \hat{W} - \hat{N}. \tag{23.12}$$

Equation (23.5), using equations (23.1) through (23.4), implies

$$\hat{W} = s[(a/w) - 1]. \tag{23.13}$$

The dynamics of N are given using equations (23.7), (23.8), (23.9) and (23.11), and are given by

$$\hat{N} = \beta \left(\frac{W}{N} \right) - \delta \left(\frac{W}{N} \right). \tag{23.14}$$

Regarding the productivity of labour, for now we assume that

$$a = a(L) \tag{23.15}$$

where $a' < 0$, reflecting diminishing returns to scale if labour is taken to be the only factor of production or diminishing returns to labour for a given level of a fixed factor, such as land, say in the case of agricultural production.[6] Substituting from equations (23.11), (23.12) and (23.15) we get

$$\hat{W} = s \left[\frac{a(N)\,N}{W} - 1 \right]. \tag{23.16}$$

The dynamics of the economy by using equations (23.14) and (23.12), which show the movement of N and W, can be examined using Figure 23.3. The $\hat{N} = 0$ line shows combinations of W and L at which population does not change,

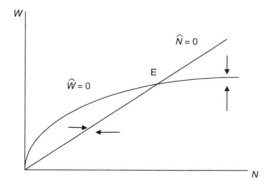

Figure 23.3 Basic Malthusian model with diminishing returns.

according to equation (23.14). Positions on the curve show situations in which the birth rate is equal to the death rate, and the real wage at which this occurs is denoted by w_s, as shown in Figure 23.1. The slope of the curve is given by w_s. At any point above the line, the actual real wage, W/N, exceeds w_s, so population increases, and conversely for points below the line, explaining the direction of the horizontal arrows. The $\hat{W} = 0$ line shows combinations of W and N that keep the wage fund or the stock of capital constant, according to equation (23.16). Positions on the line satisfy the condition $W = a(N)N$, which happens when the wage fund exhausts total output so that profit is zero. At points below the curve positive profits are made, so that the wage fund grows, while at points above it, profits are negative, so that the wage fund shrinks, explaining the direction of the vertical arrows. Given the assumption that at low levels of employment the average product of labour exceeds w_s, and as L tends to infinity a' tends to a zero (or a number less than w_s), the two curves intersect once, at the long-run equilibrium at E, where both N and W reach their constant values, as does output. Clearly, wages are at subsistence and profits are zero. The long-run equilibrium, in fact, is a stationary state.[7] Given the direction of the arrows it can be seen that from any starting position the economy will converge to the unique long-run equilibrium position.

Technology and technological change

Malthus's dismal prognosis regarding economic and population growth has not come true. Much of the world does not live at subsistence, although many undoubtedly do, but for reasons not necessarily connected with Malthus's diagnosis. By assuming diminishing returns, Malthus failed to see the possibility that technology can exhibit constant or even increasing returns and that technological change can counteract the forces of diminishing returns.[8] Although we may conceptually distinguish between these two issues, one relating the average product of labour to increases in labour *given* technology, and the other reflecting how technology changes over time, for our purposes we need not distinguish between them, and simply assume some stable relation between a and L allowing for non-diminishing returns.[9]

If we replace the assumption of diminishing returns by that of increasing returns in the sense that a increases with N, keeping the model otherwise the same, we need only change the shape of the $\hat{W} = 0$ curve in Figure 23.3, drawing it as convex from below as shown in Figure 23.4. If the curve intersects the $\hat{N} = 0$ curve as shown in Figure 23.4, the equilibrium at E, at which the wage will become constant, is saddle-point unstable. If the economy starts below and to the left of the negatively sloped separatrix SS with arrows pointing to E, it will tend towards the destruction of the capitalist economy, but if it starts above the line, it will eventually experience steady growth with increasing population and the wages fund, without ever experiencing a decline in either W or N. However, if the economy is initially in decline, a reduction in the death rate that results in a fall in the subsistence real wage to a position shown by the dashed curve with a lower slope than

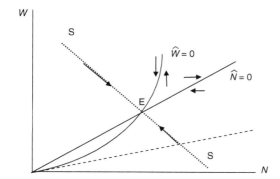

Figure 23.4 Malthusian model with increasing returns.

the initial $\hat{N} = 0$ can reverse the dynamic to result in economic growth. Not so dismal any more, although the population keeps growing rapidly.

The case of $a' = 0$ is instructive and easy to analyse because, in this case, substituting equations (23.11), (23.13) and (23.14) into equation (23.12) we get

$$\hat{w} = s\left[\frac{a}{w} - 1\right] - \beta(w) + \delta(w) \tag{23.17}$$

where a is a constant. At a point in time, since N and W are given, so is w. The movement of w in the long run is given by equation (23.17), which shows that $\hat{w}$ depends on w and the other parameters of the model.

The dynamics can be shown in Figure 23.5. The β and δ curves, showing the birth and death rates, depict equations (23.8) and (23.9), and the $\hat{N}$ curve that shows the vertical difference between the birth rate and death rate at each level of w, depicts equation (23.7).[10] The level of the real wage at which the population becomes stationary, that is, where the birth rate and death rate are equal, is denoted, as in Figure 23.1, by w_s, the subsistence wage at which births just replace deaths. The $\hat{W}$ curve shows how the change in the wage fund depends on the real wage, that is, equation (23.13): a higher real wage squeezes profits and slows down accumulation.[11] The curve intersects the horizontal axis, so that the wage fund becomes stationary, when w is equal to a, so that profit becomes zero and accumulation ceases. The rate of change of the real wage, as shown by equation (23.17), is shown by the vertical difference between the $\hat{W}$ and $\hat{N}$ curves; this could be depicted by a $\hat{w}$ curve, but it is not shown in the figure to avoid clutter. Whenever the $\hat{W}$ curve is above (below) the $\hat{N}$ curve, w increases (decreases) over time; it becomes stationary where the two curves intersect. This level of the real wage is labelled as w_e, the long-run equilibrium real wage. Figure 23.5 assumes that $a > w_s$, that is, the productivity of labour exceeds the subsistence wage.[12] This implies that w_e will lie between w_s and a. Thus, the long-run equilibrium wage

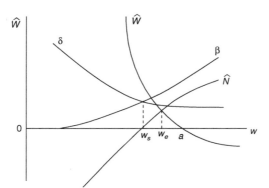

Figure 23.5 Dynamics of the basic Malthusian model with constant returns.

exceeds the subsistence wage, implying that at long-run equilibrium both population growth and capital accumulation will be positive, as will, from equation (23.2)
for a given a, the rate of growth of output and, as we saw, the real wage.

Aggregate demand

Malthus has often been interpreted as an early exponent of the theory of aggregate
demand. The models so far have abstracted from aggregate demand considerations
by assuming that all saving is automatically invested and adds to the stock of
capital or wages fund. We will now use the model with a constant a developed
at the end of the previous section, but relax that assumption and allow aggregate
demand to play a role in determining output and the rate of capital accumulation
by introducing an independent investment function.[13]

We assume that firms make investment plans based on the rate of profit that they
expect to receive and actually receive (making the two equal for simplicity), and
write the investment function as

$$\frac{I}{W} = \gamma_0 + \gamma_1 r, \tag{23.18}$$

where $\gamma_i > 0$ are given investment parameters and where we assume that $\gamma_1 < s$
which, as we shall see, is required for the stability of the model, and where r, the
rate of profit, is given by

$$r = \frac{P}{W} \tag{23.19}$$

that is, profit as a ratio of capital stock or the wages fund.[14] Saving, as before,
is given by equation (23.3). We will assume that in the short run, with W given,

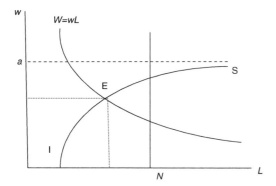

Figure 23.6 Short-run equilibrium in the Malthusian model with aggregate demand.

output adjusts to clear the goods market. Short-run equilibrium therefore implies

$$I = S. \tag{23.20}$$

The adjustment process that clears the goods market is as follows. We assume that the money wage, m, is taken as given throughout.[15] With the price level given by p, the real wage, $w = m/p$, is also given. Producers try to increase production by hiring workers given their wages fund. For the given real wage, they will try to hire as many workers as they can, so that they will want to supply output produced by

$$L = W/w.$$

This curve is shown by the $W = wL$ curve in Figure 23.6. However, for goods market equilibrium, to satisfy equation (23.20) we obtain, using the saving and investment functions,[16]

$$r = \frac{\gamma_0}{s - \gamma_1}.$$

Since $rW = Y - wL = Y - \frac{w}{a}Y$, whatever the level of labour employed, we can solve for the goods-market clearing levels of output and employment as

$$Y = \frac{a\gamma_0 W}{(s - \gamma_1)(a - w)} \quad \text{and} \quad L = \frac{\gamma_0 W}{(s - \gamma_1)(a - w)}.$$

The curve showing the relation between w and L is shown as the IS curve in Figure 23.6. Starting from any given level of the real wage the IS curve shows the level of employment consistent with goods market clearing while the $W = wL$ curve shows the level of employment consistent with full utilization of the wage fund. If, for instance, we start with a real wage lower than the one at point E, firms will want to hire more labour and produce more than the level which clears the goods market; the price level therefore falls and the real wage rises, until we attain the equilibrium level at E. Since the level of employment at this point is lower than the given supply of labour as shown by vertical line, the model allows for the existence of unemployment due to the lack of aggregate demand.[17]

Since unemployment can exist in the economy, we need to distinguish between employment, L, and the population, N. At a point in time the level of population is taken as given. We assume that the birth and death rates depend not on the wage, as before, but on the consumption of each member of the working population, which can be written as the 'adjusted' wage, adjusted by the population,[18]

$$\omega = w\frac{L}{N}.$$ (23.21)

The income of workers is spread over the workers and their families to finance their consumption. If some members of the labour force do not find work and are unable to consume, they die sooner. Thus, we replace equations (23.8) through (23.9) with equations

$$\beta = \beta(\omega)$$ (23.22)

and

$$\delta = \delta(\omega),$$ (23.23)

where the sign of the derivatives are the same as before, and use equation (23.7).

We analyse this model for the case of constant returns to scale, so that the production function is given by equation (23.1) with a constant a. In the short run we have given levels of W and N, and output and employment adjusts to bring saving and investment into equality, to determine the equilibrium level of Y to clear the goods market. Using equations (23.6) and (23.21) we get

$$\omega = \frac{W}{N}.$$ (23.24)

The goods market equilibrium condition (23.20), dividing both sides by W, implies, using equations (23.2), (23.3), (23.6), (23.18) and (23.19), that the market-clearing level of output is given by

$$Y = \left[\frac{\gamma_0}{s - \gamma_1} + 1\right]W.$$ (23.25)

We assume that there is enough labour supply to produce this level of output. Using equation (23.1), the short-run equilibrium level of employment is seen to be given by

$$L = \left[\frac{\gamma_0}{s - \gamma_1} + 1 \right] \frac{W}{a}. \tag{23.26}$$

We also see that an increase in the investment parameters, γ_i, increases Y and L, by increasing aggregate demand, and a rise in s reduces output and employment due the paradox of thrift, as in aggregate demand constrained models. The short-run equilibrium wage for workers is, using equations (23.6) and (23.26), seen to be given as

$$w = \frac{a}{\frac{\gamma_0}{s - \gamma_1} + 1}. \tag{23.27}$$

An increase in labour productivity reduces the level of employment and allows a higher wage out of the given wages fund. An increase in investment demand increases output and employment which implies, given the wages fund, that the wage will be reduced. Since there is an excess supply of labour, employment can be higher even at a lower wage, as determined by the demand for labour.

In the long run W and N change according to equation (23.5), which can be rewritten using (23.3), (23.19) and (23.20) as

$$\hat{W} = s \left(\frac{Y}{W} - 1 \right), \tag{23.28}$$

and (23.7). During the long-run dynamic process the short-run equilibrium conditions are always satisfied. We may analyse the dynamics of this model in terms of the variable ω. Equation (23.24) implies that

$$\hat{\omega} = \hat{W} - \hat{N}, \tag{23.29}$$

which, using equation (23.7), (23.22), (23.23), (23.25) and (23.28), can be written as

$$\hat{\omega} = s \frac{\gamma_0}{s - \gamma_1} - \beta(\omega) + \delta(\omega), \tag{23.30}$$

where the first term of the right hand side is the rate of capital accumulation and the next two terms relate to the rate of population growth.

The dynamics of ω are shown graphically in Figure 23.7, which is similar to Figure 23.2 but with two differences: Figure 23.7 replaces the state variable w, the real wage of workers, by ω, the adjusted real wage, or the per capita consumption of the working classes; and the wage fund accumulation curve is horizontal rather than negatively sloped, since as shown by equations (23.25) and (23.28), the adjusted wage does not affect the rate of accumulation, which is determined only by the saving and investment parameters. The long-run equilibrium level of ω occurs at the intersection of the $\hat{W}$ and $\hat{N}$ curves, at the level ω_e.

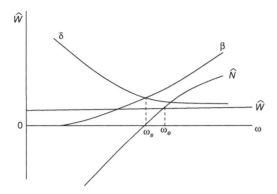

Figure 23.7 Dynamics of the Malthusian model with aggregate demand.

The demographic transition

It has been argued that the greatest failure of Malthus's theory of population growth is its failure to explain fertility transitions from high to low fertility rates, despite increases in per capita income and wages.[19] The subsequently developed theory of demographic transition states that an increase in income first reduces the death rate and increases the birth rate, leading to an increase in the rate of population growth, and then decreases the birth rate, as a variety of socio-economic forces lead families to have fewer babies, which reduces the rate of population growth.[20] Although the case is not analysed by Malthus himself, he clearly recognizes that in some countries population growth can slow down despite there being high wages and incomes, with people postponing marriages and having fewer children after marriage.[21] It is unclear why he does not examine the logical implications of this idea, but a likely explanation is that the demographic transition had not been widely experienced in his time.

Incorporating the demographic transition into the Malthusian framework, for instance by incorporating it into the model with constant returns of the third section, is a simple matter, as shown in Figure 23.8. The figure is exactly the same as in Figure 23.1, in which the birth rate rises with the wage, except that the birth rate in it first rises and then falls with the wage (which makes the β curve inverse U-shaped). This implies that the population growth curve, shown by $\hat{N}$ is first positively sloped and then negatively sloped, eventually flattening out. In this case, it is possible for it to intersect the downward-sloping $\hat{W}$ multiple times. A configuration with three intersections is shown in Figure 23.8. There are three long-run equilibria for the model, where those at E_1 and E_3 are stable and the one at E_2 is unstable. If the wage is initially below w_2, the economy will be pulled back to the low-level equilibrium at E_1 with a high rate of population growth, whereas if it is above w_2 the economy will move to the high wage equilibrium at E_3, with low population growth. The model produces low level equilibrium traps as in early

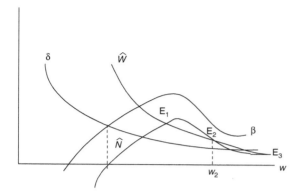

Figure 23.8 Malthusian model with demographic transition.

contributions to development economics and growth theory (see Solow, 1956, p. 90–1).

The model just discussed implies that the economy eventually arrives at a long-run equilibrium with population growth and accumulation rates being positive, but with the wage becoming constant. A further modification, which allows *a* to change over time, can produce a long-run growth path along which the real wage rises over time. Assume that, as in some models of endogenous labour productivity growth (see Dutt, 2013), that labour productivity growth depends positively on the rate of growth of the real wage which, using a simple linear form, yields

$$\hat{a} = \tau_0 + \tau_1 \hat{w} \tag{23.31}$$

where $\tau_i > 0$ are parameters of the technological change function, with $\tau_1 < 1$. Wage increases lead capitalist firms to adopt labour-saving innovations at a faster rate and wage increases lead workers to become more productive at a faster rate due to improved industrial relations. The wage–productivity ratio becomes constant when

$$\hat{a} = \hat{w}. \tag{23.32}$$

For the wage–productivity ratio to become constant, equations (23.31) and (23.32) imply that

$$\hat{a} = \hat{w} = \frac{\tau_0}{1 - \tau_1}. \tag{23.33}$$

If β and δ become constant when the wage goes beyond a certain level, then $\hat{N}$ becomes constant. Let us denote this growth rate by n. Equations (23.17) and (23.33) with constant n imply that

$$\frac{a}{w} = \frac{n + \frac{\tau_0}{1-\tau_1}}{s} + 1. \tag{23.34}$$

Positive growth in the wage is possible, with continuing accumulation at the rate

$$\hat{W} = n + \frac{\tau_0}{1 - \tau_1}, \tag{23.35}$$

which is also seen to be the rate of growth of output. The point of this modification is not to suggest that technological change actually occurs in the smooth manner formalised by equation (23.33) or that the rate of population growth eventually becomes constant, but to show that growth in the wage over long periods of time without attaining a stationary state is possible within the Malthusian framework developed in this paper, with suitable and plausible modifications of assumptions of the basic model.

The environment

In this model we analyse the dynamics of environmental degradation due to production activity, while assuming that the productivity of labour is independent of the scale of output and labour employed. We assume that the environment undergoes a process of natural regeneration and, left to itself, stabilizes at the level $\bar{E}$, its carrying capacity. However, production activity has a negative effect on the environment. We assume that the environmental stock changes according to the equation

$$\dot{E} = \Psi\left(\bar{E} - E\right) - \varepsilon Y, \tag{23.36}$$

where $\bar{E} > 0$ and the function Ψ satisfies the properties $\Psi(0) = 0$, $\Psi' < 0$ for $E < E_m < \bar{E}$, $\Psi'(\bar{E} - E_m) = 0$, and $\Psi' > 0$ for $E > E_m$, the overdot, as before, denotes the time derivative of the variable, and ε is a parameter measuring the per unit environmental damaging effect of production. This equation captures in a simple manner the effect of economic activity on the environment. We also assume that environmental degradation affects production and health conditions. The decline in health and natural resource conditions reduces the productivity of labour, so that we have

$$Y = a(E)L, \tag{23.37}$$

where $a' > 0$, with a' now denoting the effect of an increase in the environmental stock on labour productivity, and a decline in the environment stock increases the death rate, so that we have

$$\delta = \delta\left(w, E\right) \tag{23.38}$$

where the partial derivatives are given by $\delta_w < 0$ as before, and $\delta_E < 0$. The rest of the equations of the model are the same as in the second section. In particular, at any point in time we assume that w adjusts to clear the labour market, so that $L = N$.

The dynamics of the system can be expressed, using equations (23.7), (23.8), (23.13), and (23.36) through (23.38) in terms of three dynamics equations in three variables, W, N and E, that is

$$\hat{W} = s \left[\frac{a(E) N}{W} - 1 \right],$$ (23.39)

$$\hat{N} = \beta \left(\frac{W}{N} \right) - \delta \left(\frac{W}{N}, E \right),$$ (23.40)

and

$$\dot{E} = \Psi \left(\bar{E} - E \right) - \varepsilon a(E) N.$$ (23.41)

Without going into an extensive analysis of the model,[22] we can note that its long-run equilibrium requires stationary values for E, W and N. To show this, let us consider the possibility of another long-run equilibrium in which, as in the second section, we have $\hat{W} = \hat{N}$ without requiring W and N to be stationary. Equations (23.39) and (23.40) imply that this is possible if E attains a stationary value. Let us assume that E does attain a stationary value, and equation (23.41) shows that this is possible for combinations of E and N that satisfy $\dot{E} = 0$. But this requires that if E attains a stationary value, so must N. Thus, equations (23.39) and (23.40) imply that both W and N must attain stationary values. Since E and N are stationary in long-run equilibrium, so is the level of output, Y.

In this model, even though production conditions do not display diminishing returns in the sense that labour productivity falls with output and employment, production results in environmental degradation which has the effect of reducing labour productivity and reducing population growth by worsening health conditions. The result is that output reaches a stationary equilibrium, as in Malthus's model with diminishing returns discussed in the second section, rather than in the models with non-diminishing returns, in the third section, where production and population grow indefinitely at a constant rate.[23] As mentioned earlier, some economists, like Simon, have simply dismissed Malthusian and neo-Malthusian ideas as being unfounded, pointing to improvements in some environmental conditions. However, more recent research on the environment, especially that regarding global climate change, may yet make Malthusian fears – of the growth of production and income, if not population growth – relevant again.

Conclusion

This paper has developed a simple basic Malthusian model of population dynamics and growth that builds on some key assumptions made by Malthus, that is, diminishing returns to labour, the 'law' of population according to which population growth depends positively on the wage, and a saving-investment mechanism in which saving by capitalists is automatically invested in a wage fund. The model has been used to confirm Malthus's pessimistic results on how growth comes to a halt and the system arrives at a stationary state, and that the wage falls to its 'subsistence' level.

The basic model was then modified to take into account some neglected factors to show how Malthus's analytical framework can be modified to incorporate them. Differences due to such issues as non-diminishing returns to labour, aggregate demand, and the demographic transition suggest ways in which Malthus's precise conclusion change without changing his analytical method,[24] thereby emphasizing the need to distinguish the method from specific conclusions and predictions. Not dismissing the method even when the predictions seem to fail can have a valuable role not only in understanding conditions under which the specific results do not hold (for instance, due to non-diminishing returns and demographic transition), but also being aware of reasons why the result can become relevant in the future (for instance, due to global climate change). A lot is left of Malthus.[25]

Notes

1 Prepared for a festschrift in honour of Neri Salvadori, who often reminded me about the importance of the history of economic analysis. I am grateful to conference participants at UNAM, Mexico City and the Federal University of Juiz de Flora, Brazil, for useful comments and suggestions.
2 The model draws from earlier formalizations of Malthus. A fair number of such models are available. In the rest of the paper we will discuss the relation of only a few of those which are directly relevant to the models of this paper.
3 This approach to capital formation follows the formulation of Eltis (1984), although as we will note later, Eltis implicitly does not allow for diminishing returns. Many other formulations of Malthus's approach ignore the dynamics of capital accumulation altogether, concentrating only on population growth and the labour–output relation.
4 The introduction of capital as machinery would require us to modify the analysis to take into account the stocks of both variable capital (for paying labour) and fixed capital.
5 This formulation is similar to a number of formulations of Malthusian population dynamics. Ours is closest to Weir (1987), who distinguishes between workers and capitalists, and between birth and death rates, and Figure 1 is adapted from his diagram.
6 The assumption is implied by Malthus's claim that in a given number of years population increases at a geometric rate while output rises linearly, if we assume that labour is fully employed as we do here.
7 The result is the same as in the standard Ricardian system and in Ricardian models. See, for instance, Pasinetti (1960).
8 Several formulations of the Malthusian system have incorporated technological change and the effects of non-diminishing returns, including Boulding (1955).
9 This assumption rules out technological change when there is no expansion in employment. If we abstract from technological change the three cases reflect diminishing, constant, and increasing returns to scale.
10 The line can be interpreted as being similar to Eltis's (1984) positive relation between the real wage and the rate of growth of the wage fund, although here it is a relation between the rate of growth of population and the real wage, without requiring the wage

fund to grow at the same rate as population, that is, making the real wage constant over time.

11 This curve can be seen as providing a formalization of Eltis's (1984) inverse relation between the wage and the rate of accumulation.

12 If this condition is not satisfied, the two curves will intersect in the negative orthant, and capital stock and population will keep falling. Sooner or later the capitalist mode of production will disappear and people will work only in the subsistence sector.

13 The model draws on Costabile and Rowthorn (1985) but different from it, among other things, in taking time to be continuous, in ignoring land, and in not introducing labour values. Moreover, we assume constant returns to scale with a constant a, whereas they allow for diminishing returns.

14 A similar assumption is made by Eltis (1984) and Costabile and Rowthorn (1985).

15 This is not essential for the analysis. All that we require is that the money wage, if it adjusts to changes in the price level, does so proportionately less than the price level.

16 Variations in r due to variations in Y make the economy converge to this equilibrium given our assumption that $s > \gamma_1$, which also ensures a positive r.

17 If the money wage falls due to the existence of unemployment, the price level will fall proportionately, preventing an increase in employment. Our assumption that the money wage is constant can be due to some norms, but is not the cause of unemployment.

18 This follows Costabile and Rowthorn (1985).

19 See, for instance, Weir (1987, 292).

20 This case was discussed by Boulding (1955) and has become a standard feature of models which examine the dynamics of population growth.

21 Even in the first edition he writes:

> The preventive check appears to operate in some degree through all the ranks of society in England. There are some men, even in the highest rank, who are prevented from marrying by the idea of the expenses that they must retrench, and the fancied pleasures that they must deprive themselves of, on the supposition of having a family. These considerations are certainly trivial, but a preventive foresight of this kind has objects of much greater weight for its contemplation as we go lower.
>
> (Malthus, 1798, 20)

22 See Dutt (forthcoming) for a fuller analysis of this model.

23 It may be argued, as some have done, that increases in output will result in reductions in ε due to improvements in technology and in public policies due to the demand for a cleaner environment. While this can, and does, indeed happen, our results will hold if ε falls, but with a lower bound.

24 We have not provided a characterization of his analytical method with a view to distinguishing between this method and his specific assumptions. Briefly, what we can call his analytical method is the formulation of a system which makes specific assumptions about production conditions, the mechanics of the accumulation and growth process, and the dynamics of population growth using behavioural, technical and institutional assumptions. The specific assumptions relate to the nature of production conditions (whether or not we have diminishing returns, for example), how fertility and mortality are affected by economic and other conditions, and what drives economic growth (aggregate supply or aggregate demand).

25 This provides an illustration of the general idea that it is perilous to forget about contributions in the history of economic thought.

References

Boulding, Kenneth (1955). 'The Malthusian model as a general system', *Social and Economic Studies*, 4, September, 195–205.

Costabile, Liliana and Rowthorn, Bob (1985). 'Malthus's theory of wages and growth', *Economic Journal*, 95 (378), 418–37.

Dutt, Amitava K. (2013). 'Endogenous technological change in classical-Marxian models of growth and distribution', in T. Michl, A. Rezai and L. Taylor, eds., *Social Fairness and Economics. Economic Essays in the Spirit of Duncan Foley*, Abingdon, UK and New York, USA: Routledge, 264–85.

Dutt, Amitava K. (forthcoming). 'A Malthusian model of the environment and economic growth', Department of Political Science, University of Notre Dame, Notre Dame, IN, USA.

Eltis, Walter (1984). *The Classical Theory of Economic Growth*, London: Macmillan.

Malthus, Thomas Robert (1798). *An Essay on the Principle of Population*, London: J. Johnson, St. Paul's Churchyard.

Marx, Karl (1867). *Capital, Volume 1*, English translation, 1885, Moscow: Progress Publishers.

Pasinetti, Luigi (1960). 'A mathematical formulation of the Ricardian system', *Review of Economic Studies*, 27 (2), 267–79.

Simon, Julian and Herman Kahn (eds.) (1984). *The Resourceful Earth: A Response to the Global 2000 Report*, Oxford and New York: Basil Blackwell.

Solow, Robert (1956). 'A contribution to the theory of economic growth', *Quarterly Journal of Economics*, 70 (1), February, 65–94.

Weir, D. R. (1987). 'Malthus's theory of population', in J. Eatwell, M. Milgate and P. Newman, eds., *The New Palgrave*, London: Macmillan.

24 Federico Caffè, a Keynesian on the left

Riccardo Faucci

Introduction

Economist Federico Caffè, born 1914, mysteriously disappeared between 14 and 15 April 1987. This dramatic decision to escape from the world leaving no trace inspired a fine book by E. Rea, *L'ultima lezione*, the last lecture, published in 1992, as well as a movie by F. Rosi with the same title (2001). Independently from this event, a huge mass of reprints of articles by Caffè as well as critical essays on his work have been provided by disciples and estimators. Indeed, it can justifiably be claimed that no other Italian contemporary economist has raised such enduring interest.[1]

Federico Caffè can unhesitatingly be included among the most representative post-1945 Italian economists. As a professor at the University of Rome for almost thirty years, he authored more than 150 academic publications. An outstanding teacher and master, he was the thesis supervisor and advisor who presided over the defense of at least 1200 *tesi di laurea* and trained many excellent scholars, among whom Mario Draghi, Ignazio Visco, Guido M. Rey, Ezio Tarantelli, Marcello De Cecco, and Nicola Acocella (his successor in the Rome chair). But he was not only a renowned teacher. A militant intellectual, his opinions leaned strongly toward the left side of the political spectrum among Italian academic economists, ably defending his ideas in non-professional journals. Countless articles by Caffè appeared in newspapers and magazines.

A perfect balance between scientific and political treatment of economic matters is never easy to reach, as confirmed by our daily experience. Nevertheless, Caffè succeeded in maintaining an appropriate style – or better, two different but not mutually exclusive styles: one featuring a very clear manner of expression and designed for non-professional readers, the other characterised by a rigorous approach and directed to his fellow economists. His main models were undoubtedly Keynes's *Essays in persuasion* as well as Einaudi's *Prediche inutili*.

It should be borne in mind that in the late 1940s, when Caffè began his career, most Italian academic economists were conservative. During twenty years of fascist conformism, many of them had paid lip-service to the regime, which cherished the ambition of imposing its own 'economics', the so-called *corporativismo*.

This was a rehash of old mercantilism with an addition of institutionalism in an ultra-nationalist sauce. Upon the restoration of democracy, *corporativismo* was banned from university courses, after which, however, the easiest solution appeared to be that of merely reviving neoclassical economics. Luigi Einaudi was the most illustrious representative of this latter school, and when, on his return to Italy in December 1944 from exile in Switzerland, he assumed the post of Governor of the Bank of Italy, this decision was highly praised by almost all the political forces.

Another current of economic thought in Italy was Catholic economic doctrine, which was inaugurated by Pope Leo XIII's *Rerum novarum* encyclical of 1891. During Fascism, most Catholic economists aligned themselves with *corporativismo*, interpreting it as consistent with *Rerum novarum*. They were further encouraged in this direction above all after Pius XI's *Quadragesimo anno* of 1931.

In contrast, there were no Marxist economists. Fascism had banned Marx from all university studies, therefore the promising Italian path to the so-called 'revision of Marxism' started by Benedetto Croce during the last decade of the nineteenth century was definitively interrupted.

Within this context, young Federico Caffè – who graduated with Professor G. Masci in 1936 – entered the Bank of Italy as a clerk in 1937, and was awarded a grant for a period of study at LSE in 1947–48. This background enabled him to draw the attention and sympathies of a professional audience without relinquishing his critique of mainstream neoclassical (non-Keynesian) economics, while at the same time always presenting his own position in a polite and to some extent diplomatic manner. As the readers of his works will certainly notice, Caffè often resorted to the rhetorical device of not indicating the names of authors whose ideas he opposed: a device fully in accordance with the well-known motto of Italian (Catholic) wisdom 'you will always indicate the sin, but never the sinner's name'. In Caffè, however, this ploy was not dictated by a calculus of academic opportunism, but rather by the desire to clear the field of any polemical and/or personal excesses.

Caffè's political commitment

Soon after the fall of Fascism, Federico Caffè felt the moral impulse to participate in the economic and political reconstruction of Italy. He therefore resolved to join the *Democrazia del Lavoro*, a small centre-left party which, before the fascist era, had participated in the parliamentary majority led by Giovanni Giolitti. Caffè formed part of the staff of Meuccio Ruini, one of the leaders of the party, who was appointed Minister for reconstruction in 1945.[2]

When the *Democrazia del lavoro* imploded owing to its fragile structure, Caffè joined another party which, although small, had played a much more crucial role in the Resistenza movement: the *Partito d'Azione*, whose leader was Ferruccio Parri, the first premier soon after the Liberazione. But in 1946 even this party collapsed, at which point Caffè joined PSIUP (as the socialist party was named at that time). After 1947 Caffè's political militancy can be considered as definitively concluded.

Many years afterwards, in 1983, he declined the offer by PCI of a senatorial seat as an 'independent on the left'. At that time Caffè's forces were rapidly fading and he did not feel he could take on such a challenging task.

Caffè's academic career was characterised by a steady progression from his private professorship (1949) to the university chair (1954) which he subsequently occupied at the Universities of Messina, Bologna and, from 1959 onwards, Rome. He maintained his relationship with the Bank of Italy, as consultant economist or as director of the Ente Luigi Einaudi, which made research funds available to junior economists. Moreover, during the long period of Guido Carli's office as Governor (1960–75), Caffè contributed to the final versions of the Bank of Italy's annual Concluding Remarks.[3]

In 1979 Caffè felt a moral obligation to defend the behaviour of the Bank of Italy when the *Banco Ambrosiano* scandal was transformed by the political protectors of Michele Sindona into an attack on the governor of the Bank of Italy, Paolo Baffi, and its vice-director, Mario Sarcinelli. Caffè, together with other renowned economists such as S. Steve, P. Sylos Labini and L. Izzo, witnessed in favour of Baffi and Sarcinelli. The trial – one of the most obscure pages of post-war Italian history – led to a general absolution of the Bank of Italy staff.[4]

It was only in the 1970s and 1980s – after concluding his collaboration with the Bank of Italy – that he became active in newspapers such as *Il messaggero* (the most widespread Rome newspaper, politically pro-government, but fairly independent as regards its choice of contributors in the cultural pages), *L'ora* (a Palermo pro-PCI newspaper), and above all *Il manifesto*, the historical voice of the far-left non-parliamentary movement, generally praised for the quality of its reporting.

Moreover, Caffè engaged in an exchange of ideas on political themes with the minority left wing of the CGIL trade union, the so-called 'third component', which represented the internal opposition to the PCI–PSI majority.[5]

Caffè always staunchly defended the coherence of his political choices. He often maintained that he considered himself to be a committed reformist, namely, an intellectual convinced that changing society step by step was the safest way to progress. In this context, he spoke out against the traditional (mainly PCI) parliamentary left, accusing its members of having abandoned any serious project of reform of society in the name of a forced agreement with DC, its traditional adversary. For this reason he bitterly defined himself as a 'lonely marathon runner', or 'lonely reformist', complaining that his voice was becoming more and more isolated even among his fellow economists.[6]

Post-war economic policy and economics

From 1947 onwards Caffè contributed to *Cronache sociali*, a pugnacious periodical of the left wing of DC directed by Giuseppe Dossetti. It also hosted articles by Giorgio La Pira, the jurist and lord mayor of Florence, in whose opinion Keynes was a thinker professing an economic doctrine very close to the teachings of the Gospels. A secularist, yet quite sensitive to the relationship between politics and morals, Caffè deeply admired the earnestness of thought of many Catholic intellectuals engaged in politics.[7]

Caffè always complained that in post-war Italy no serious project had been set up to reconstruct the economy on democratic foundations. In 1945–47 the two parties on the left, PCI and PSIUP (the latter renamed as PSI from 1947 onwards), sat in the cabinet together with DC, which occupied a centre position. Although PSIUP and PCI, taken together, had more votes as well as more seats than DC in the 1946 *Assemblea Costituente*, the two parties on the left were unable to develop a consistent reformist policy. In fact, they were unable to challenge the so-called 'Einaudi line' of economic policy, that presented two different and almost opposite outcomes. In 1946 Luigi Einaudi, as governor of the Bank of Italy, failed to combat inflation that was principally due to banking over-commitment, while in 1947, as Budget minister, he suffocated inflation through a severe budget restraint, with a consequent rise in unemployment.[8]

Moreover, the De Gasperi-Einaudi cabinet relinquished the project of a *cambio della moneta* (currency change), that had been successfully performed by France and Belgium in order to 'uncover' a huge amount of liquidity that was secreted in the hands of the public and derived mainly from the black market. Finally, with the intent of reducing the budget deficit, the government dismantled even the quite modest measures that could have sustained the incomes of the poor, such as the subsidised price of bread. The opposition of the left was altogether inadequate.

According to Caffè, another missed opportunity was that of the *Commissione economica per la Costituente*, a committee established in 1945 by the *Costituente* Minister Pietro Nenni, the socialist leader, and chaired by Professor Giovanni Demaria. Its proceedings, based on reports and hearings, demonstrated that there was a shared awareness that economic reconstruction required some planning of the state's action, to be co-ordinated with a gradual opening to international competition. However, this message was not fully received. On the one side, the attitude of the leading economic minds in Italy was cautious towards genuine international competition, because they were accustomed to the trade regulations and limitations – in other words, protection – as had been the general practice before the war. On the other, the major figures in the world of industry were basically pessimistic with regard to the ability of Italian exports to penetrate foreign markets, and felt that the potential gain from foreign trade could be achieved only by profiting from Germany's temporary inability to compete in the international markets.

Rather than genuine competition, most industrialists who outlined their views to the *Commissione economica* invoked absolute freedom of firing workers as crucial in order to re-launch employment. (The same is frequently repeated today with reference to the much-disputed article 18 of the Worker's Statute.) Consequently, they objected that the elected representatives of the Trade unions in the *consigli di gestione*[9] could worsen the spirit of co-operation between workers and owners of industries. More generally, the masters identified 'reconstruction' with the restoration of power hierarchies within the firms. Internal democracy was considered as a dangerous concession to the 'incompetence' of the Trade union members and therefore rejected. For this reason, these councils were rapidly dismantled.

Finally, there remained the problem of the huge state-owned sector of industry and banking, the legacy of the fascist policy of state intervention in the economy. On this issue, no univocal project emerged from the proceedings of the *Commissione economica*. Incidentally, there was no private capital available to take over the nationalized industry.[10] In a reminiscence written more than twenty years afterwards, Caffè, who acted personally as a technical member of the *Commissione*, complained that structural interventions such as agrarian and educational reforms – *as* requiring some planning – implicitly were not taken into account.[11] In this context, we cannot but underline the change that has come about in the meaning of the phrase 'riforme di struttura' (structural reforms) during these last decades. Originally referring to reforms that *regulate* the market forces, they now imply those measures that *abolish* all impediments to free market.

Only in 1949, two years after the expulsion of the left from the parliamentary majority, did the CGIL Trade Union present the *Piano del lavoro* (labour plan), a fairly ambitious design of development based on an increase in public expenditure through a program of State investment in housing, southern agriculture and electricity. This scheme, apparently Keynesian and illustrated at a public meeting by a respected academic economist, Professor Alberto Breglia, was hastily defined as 'demagogic' by Premier De Gasperi and rapidly discarded. In his reminiscences, Caffè observed that the *Piano del Lavoro* came too late, and the political situation seemed already too severely compromised to allow a true reformist economic policy. Again, the *punctum dolens* (sore point) was that the government had chosen to prefer the mirage of an undisciplined economy over a reasonable policy of planned development.[12]

Caffè believed that a gradual approach in the transition from war to peace was crucial in the short run in order to minimie its social impact on the less protected layers of society. Economic reforms enlarging the domain of free competition would certain be a welcome step, but only once structural reforms in the field of industrial and labour relations had been carried out. The economic and social reforms accomplished by the British Labour cabinet after 1945 were praised by Caffè in a brilliant series of articles. In contrast, he presented the British Conservatives as 'full of money, but poor in ideas'.[13] It should be underlined that Caffè did not assign the merit of the Labour reforms directly to Keynes, but rather to William Beveridge's report *Full employment for a free society* (1944) and to other junior economists.[14]

It is also noteworthy that Caffè praised the Labour government in Britain because – in contrast to what happened in Italy – Labour did not opt in favour of eliminating the instruments of control over prices and quantities introduced during the war. In a retrospective reflection, he deplored the fact that Italy had not followed the British example, which consisted in maintaining all the control measures that were compatible with peacetime. These ideas were to some extent re-launched by Caffè during the various 'oil crises' of the 1970s.[15]

Caffè's 'discourse on method'

The foregoing illustration of the path Caffè followed in politics allows insight into his vision of economics and economic method. Caffè always awarded priority to plain good sense and reasoning based on observation, rejecting all economic *a priori* interpretations of the world – *Weltanschauungen* – that would exclude any possible alternative or different interpretation. For instance, in a 1978 letter to Giorgio Lunghini, Caffè discussed the meaning of the concept of economic equilibrium, which Lunghini, in an article that came out in *Quaderni piacentini* (another extreme-left periodical), had equated to an ideological projection of the existing bourgeois economic order. In opposition to the neoclassical concept of equilibrium, Lunghini put forward the surplus value approach shared by Sraffa and Marx, arguing that such an approach only should be considered as truly scientific. Caffè objected that reducing neoclassical economics *as a whole* to a mere apology of the existing (capitalist) system was a stereotype. For instance, in his view several neoclassical doctrines, such as Fisher's theory of interest, had a general character that was independent of the capitalist system. Furthermore, he felt that dividing economic theories into 'good' and 'bad' was a sterile enterprise.[16]

Si licet parva componere magnis (if we may compare small things with great), I may add that in a private letter written in the same years Caffè criticised a book of mine on classical economics, for the reason that this book appeared to take it virtually for granted that the main historical function of the classical school was to pave the way to Marx's thought. With his typical wit, he observed that *The Wealth of Nations* had already reached countless editions throughout the world 'when Marx was still in his cradle'. Of course, this remark meant that the classical tradition had an enormous intellectual impact *per se*, and could not be considered merely as a preparation to Marxian economics. Caffè's lesson was that all serious historians of economics ought to cultivate an attitude of respect for the true meaning the authors sought to communicate, uncovering their message through a scrupulous weighing of its impact and by avoiding any tendentious or *ad hoc* interpretation.

Can we therefore conclude that according to Caffè *tout comprendre c'est tout pardonner* (understanding everything is forgiving everything)? This was far from being his case. Caffè's profound attitude of philological respect for authors and their ideas by no means led him to neutrality or, worse, to indifference towards the implications of the choices among different issues. His approach to economics was entirely pragmatic. Caffè appears to have shared Joan Robinson's view of economics as a 'toolbox', where the policy-maker could freely choose among a host of analytical instruments that could be considered as comparatively independent of any specific ideology or vision. In Caffè's view, this separation between aims and tools was vital to the policy-maker. Convinced though he was that a choice among alternative routes in no way undermined the importance and strength of the economic interests that come into play in any given context, he realised, on the basis of his knowledge of economic policy, that it is always possible to foresee with sufficient precision the probable effects of a policy decision. Correspondingly, it is always feasible to discuss these effects – and the related alternatives – in a plain and objective manner. In conclusion, economics appears to the policy-maker's eyes as a rich *menu* whose entries can be freely chosen according to logic, coherence and firmness of principles (including moral and political values). Here, he followed Gunnar Myrdal's lesson, but more generally he could not fail to agree with the well-known Marshallian metaphor according to which 'cold heads but warm hearts'[17] must always guide the economist's research.

Caffè's distinction between an approach to 'systems' (which he did not favour) versus an approach to 'tools' (which he preferred) led him, almost by a logical necessity, to a fragmentary vision of the progress of economics. Thus he opted to designate as *Frammenti* a collection of his writings on Italian economics – a title that was dictated not only by his innate modesty, but also by his deep conviction that an empirical approach to economics cannot but lead to a dissection of the various theories. Here one may perceive the lesson of Gustavo Del Vecchio, one of the most influential Italian economists between the two world wars, whose main texts Caffè re-edited.[18] The difference between Del Vecchio and Caffè is, in my opinion, that the former reduced the competition among theories to the adoption of different scientific *languages*, while the latter differentiated them according to their field of *application*.

Caffè's 1966 manual of economic policy contains a critique of Schumpeter's distinction between a theoretical and a practical moment as distinction between knowledge and action (as is well known, in his *History of economic analysis* the Austrian economist concentrates on the former). Caffè objected that according to Schumpeter's dichotomy, economic theory would be useless, while economic policy would be reduced to mere causistry. Neither did the traditional dichotomy between positive and normative economics satisfy Caffè. Instead, he proposed a tri-partition between economic theory, economic policy and applied economics, assigning to economic policy a bridging function that would link the other two, insofar as it represents the 'intermediate phase' between the abstractive-analytical moment and the practical economic action of the state.[19]

Against monetarism

Caffè's outspoken eclecticism is confined to the realm of means, but is excluded from the realm of goals. In his vision, the most important goal concerns the kind of society the economist as intellectual intends to promote. No great economist, from Ferrara to Einaudi to Keynes, could avoid addressing this task.

As far as Caffè is concerned, one finds in his work a conception of economic policy that favourably emphasises the discretional action of the policy-maker, in comparison to the automatic mechanisms preached by modern monetarism.[20]

Caffè's concern regarding the negative effects of a self-functioning market without equity rules, due to an application of monetarism to the functioning of real economic systems, emerges in his comments on the changed role of the IMF.[21] The main responsibility for the situation that arose in the 1980s was to be ascribed to the US policy of high interest rates. The proposal of lowering interest rates in order to support recovery, as suggested by Keynes and Fisher in the 1930s, was put forward again by Caffè in the early 1980s when he denounced the oligopolistic structure of the financial markets as one of the reasons why interest rates did not fall despite declining inflation.[22]

A supporter of international economic co-operation among members acting under equal conditions, Caffè most acutely observed that in the majority of cases two weights and two measures were adopted. Thus Germany was allowed to keep the mark undervalued and to maintain high rates of interest at home, by attracting foreign capital and producing deflation abroad, while the countries that were traditionally debtors, such as those belonging to the third world, were obliged to undertake restrictive policies that were even more deflationist. The surplus countries were treated with kid gloves as they were not obliged to revalue their money. In contrast, the deficit countries were pressed to devalue. In this latter case, relinquishing monetary sovereignty proved to be harmful, insofar as it increased the distance between rich and poor countries. Originally the *stand-by* agreements (which admitted short-term credits for immediate needs) promoted by the IMF had left a margin for domestic policies to restore the balance of payments. From the 1970s onwards, however, the IMF chose a policy of 'arrogance' towards the debtor countries, by making the granting of credit conditional on acceptance of very harsh terms.[23]

Moreover, the dogma of absolute freedom in the movement of international capital hindered any direct control aiming to curb speculative movements, by assigning this task to monetary policy alone, through action on the interest rate, which is by necessity deflationist.[24]

From the analysis Caffè developed on the phenomenon of 'abnormal' capital movements, there emerges his diffidence towards excessively simplistic formulae that assigned the exclusive power of carrying out these policies to supra-national authorities, especially of a technocratic and non-democratic nature. This does not mean that Caffè systematically underrated the results obtained by the international monetary institutions. On the contrary, he suggested amplifying the powers of these institutions, by assigning them the function of 'lenders of last resort' in order to sustain growth. On the other hand, he argued that financial crises should not be considered – as they were by the *laissez-faire* economists – as necessary outcomes of some Darwinian selection, but rather as pathological moments to be overcome through a working international co-operation.[25]

Overall, however, it is indisputable that Caffè always advocated the maintenance of a large list of domestic policy tools, including tariffs, price controls, and public enterprises not subservient to the logic of the private sector.[26]

Caffè maintained that countries like Italy, with serious employment problems, could not *a priori* exclude the adoption of some protection, at least for a limited period of time. In several articles Caffè recalled with favour an essay by Marco Fanno, *Note in margine al mercato comune europeo* (Marginal notes on the European common market) (1958), which expressed reservations concerning the effects of an immediate transition from protection to absolute free trade in a country like Italy, characterized by heavy unemployment. Import-substitution policies,

Caffè argued, could have favourable effects not only in the more backward countries, but in Italy as well.[27]

Interwar Cambridge

Cambridge in the 1930s represented a continuous source of inspiration, not only due to the presence of Keynes, but also on account of Pigou's reformulation of the economics of welfare along lines quite different from Pareto's. A reformer like Caffè could not but follow Pigou. As is well known, Pigou, in contrast to Pareto, advocated income redistribution as an instrument for increasing general welfare. An opponent of Pareto's optimum, Caffè assumed the comparability of personal preferences, and therefore defended the concept of a social welfare function. He championed the legitimacy of study on the effects of redistribution from the rich to the poor classes, a study that could not disregard a prior indication of the economist's value premises.[28]

Secondarily, Cambridge signified the admirable Keynesian construction: a construction that was independent of welfare economics, but aimed to make legitimate an appropriate public intervention.

What aspects of Keynes deserved to be rapidly introduced (and followed) in Italy? Those themes that most attract today's interpreters, such as the theory of expectations, of subjective probability, and so on, were less congenial to Caffè. As a great expert on financial and monetary matters, beyond being a voracious reader, Caffè was acquainted with the contemporary developments of Keynes's interpretations and was very familiar with authors such as Davidson and Minsky.[29] However, his preference for the traditional interpretation should be noted. He followed Hicks in maintaining that Keynes's main theoretical contribution was that of overcoming the so-called classical dichotomy.

Above all, in Caffè's interpretation Keynes was the apostle of full employment and of fiscal measures for economic expansion, according to an interpretation that may seem conventional today, but which substantially influenced post-war policies in the West. Keynes was seen as the heir of the great Bentham–Mill tradition of the State *agenda* and *not agenda*.[30] This tradition has been abandoned by the supporters of absolute *laissez-faire*, like Friedrich von Hayek.[31]

Some interpreters have placed Caffè among the American institutionalists. The story is a little more complicated. Caffè showed no special interest in 'old' institutionalism, whose main representatives were, as is well known, T. Veblen and J. Commons. Rather, he highlighted the presence of significant elements of institutionalism in commenting upon the 'new' welfare economics.[32] He therefore agreed with the critiques raised against the so-called Coase theorem by K. William Kapp.[33]

In the final years of his life, Caffè appeared increasingly pessimistic about the difficulty for a capitalist economy to escape from stagnation. In 1979 he wrote a favourable preface to the Italian edition of James O' Connor's *Fiscal crisis of the state*. In his comment upon O'Connor, Caffè underlined the links between private monopolies and public policy in contemporary capitalism.[34]

An admirer of Cambridge economists, Caffè – *rara avis* among the Italian economists on the left – assigned no special acknowledgment to Piero Sraffa. But rather than taking up a critical stance against Sraffa himself, Caffè criticised the 'Sraffians' who, in Italy, presented a version of *Commodities by means of commodities* in terms of economic policy – mainly based on the assumption of (real) wage as an independent variable that circulated among Italian economists on the left in the 1970s – with which Caffè could not agree. Caffè's position was that the transition from a theoretical model to an interpretation of economic reality required several intermediate steps. Thus, Caffè observed, on the one hand the Sraffians claimed that the essential meaning of Sraffa's contribution is that theoretical rigor involves renouncing any practical application to policy matters. On the other, they calmly proceed 'to implant Sraffa in Keynes's system, thereby extending this discourse to the possible policy implications'. Caffè ironically concluded his comment: 'That such an implant may be fructuous is my sincere hope; but for the moment I see some epistemological confusion in all this'.[35]

Caffè also objected to another legacy of Sraffa's thought, i.e. to the *necessity* of a return to classical political economy against marginalism and all capitalist ideologies. In his 1983 obituary of Sraffa, published in *Manifesto*, Caffè observed that the two articles on costs and returns published by Sraffa in 1925 and 1926 had produced studies, such as Joan Robinson's *Economics of imperfect competition*, that were still carried out along neoclassical lines. Further, Caffè defended marginalism against its identification with 'capitalism': to jettison marginalism as a 'capitalist' ideology was un-historical – even more, it was unjustified from the economic point of view. Again, the 'fragmentary approach' to economics indicated the right way.[36]

Notes

1 See R. Faucci, 'L'economia "per frammenti" di Federico Caffè', *Rivista italiana degli economisti*, 2002, 3, 363–410; and the following books: A. Esposto, M. Tiberi, eds, *Federico Caffè. Realtà e critica del capitalismo italiano*, Meridiana libri, Catanzaro 1995 (a collection of papers on Caffè); G. Amari, N. Rocchi, eds, *Federico Caffè, un economista per gli uomini comuni*, Ediesse, Roma 2007; G. Amari, N. Rocchi, eds, *Federico Caffè, un economista per il nostro tempo*, Ediesse, Roma 2009; G. Amari, ed., *Attualità di Federico Caffè nella crisi odierna*, Ediesse, Roma 2010 (the three last books alternate texts by and on Caffè). Moreover, see three collections of Caffè's articles originally published in various newspapers: F. Caffè, *Scritti quotidiani*, ed. by R. Carlini, preface by P. Ciocca, Manifestolibri, Roma 2007 (a selection of articles on *Il Manifesto*); *Contro gli incappucciati della finanza. Tutti gli scritti: Il Messaggero 1974–1986, L'Ora 1983–1987*, G. Amari, ed., Castelvecchi, Roma 2013; see also an anthology of articles and speeches by Caffè on labour and unemployment: *La dignità del lavoro*, G. Amari, ed., Castelvecchi, Roma 2014. Further, the three-volume collection of *Saggi in onore di FC*, N. Acocella, G. M. Rey, M. Tiberi, eds., Angeli, Milano 1990–1992–1999 should also be kept in mind. Finally, the 'Symposium on Federico Caffè. Public policy and economic thought' with contributions by P. Ramazzotti, R. Schiattarella, L. M. Milone, M. Cangiani and P. Frigato, *History of Economic Ideas*, 2012, n. 1, should not be overlooked. Among Caffè's essays that he himself collected during his lifetime, at least the following volumes should be mentioned: F. Caffè, *Teorie e problemi di politica*

sociale, Laterza, Bari 1970; *Frammenti per lo studio del pensiero economico italiano*, Giuffrè, Milano 1975; *Un'economia in ritardo*, Boringhieri, Torino 1976; *Economia senza profeti. Contributi di bibliografia economica*, Studium, Roma 1977; *L'economia contemporanea*, Studium, Roma 1982; *In difesa del 'welfare state'. Saggi di politica economica*, Rosenberg & Sellier, Torino 1986. A entertaining anthology of Caffè's reflections taken from his works and presented in the form of imaginary interview is G. Amari, ed., *Parla Federico Caffè*, Armando, Roma 2014. For a review of several of these books, see R. Faucci, 'On re-reading Federico Caffè', *Economia politica*, 2010, 1, 211–215.

2 Ruini, a law scholar who was an expert in the field of public works (see his 1913 official report *Le opere pubbliche in Calabria*), had been adamant in rejecting any compromise with the regime during Fascism; he withdrew from politics and published a number of books on economic and intellectual history. See Ruini's profile written by Caffè, in Various Authors, *Protagonisti dell'intervento pubblico*, A. Mortara, ed., Angeli, Milano, 1977, reprinted in F. Caffè, *La dignità del lavoro*, 265–70. Caffè met Meuccio Ruini upon the recommendation of the latter's son, Carlo, Caffè's university friend (later he became professor of agrarian economics). See the letter written in 1984 by Caffè to Carlo Ruini on the occasion of Caffè's last lecture before his retirement. Here Caffè once more expressed his gratitude to his friend for 'having transformed *his* life and changed its meaning'. Letter appended to F. Caffè, *La dignità del lavoro*, 372.

3 Caffè exerted 'moderation' over the most provocative passages in favour of the free market and against the exceedingly suffocating controls (*lacci e lacciuoli*, red tape) introduced by political power over the market. These suggestions were willingly accepted by Carli (see G. Carli, *Cinquant'anni di vita italiana*, Laterza, Roma-Bari 1993, 177–180).

4 See several documents that have been collected by various authors in *In difesa dello Stato, al servizio del Paese*, G. Amari, ed., Ediesse, Roma, 2010.

5 See A. Lettieri, *La dignità del lavoro e il ruolo del sindacato*, in F. Caffè, *La dignità del lavoro*, 23. Antonio Lettieri was one of the leaders of this wing.

6 See the collection of articles of Caffè's edited by N. Acocella and M. Franzini, *La solitudine del riformista*, Bollati Boringhieri, Torino, 1990. The title of the book is drawn from the title of an article by Caffè in *Manifesto* (*Scritti quotidiani*, 81).

7 See several papers of Caffè's published in *Cronache sociali* and reprinted in *La dignità del lavoro*, 191–207.

8 For a defense of the Einaudi line, see G. Carli, *Cinquant'anni di vita italiana*, 15–16. See also A. Gigliobianco, *Via Nazionale. Banca e classe dirigente. Cento anni di storia*, Donzelli, Roma, 2006, 207–208.

9 The *consigli di gestione* – literally, management councils – were introduced in 1946 by the Industry minister, the socialist economist Rodolfo Morandi, in order to allow the workers 'to participate in the general trend of the firm'. In an interview with a CGIL journal, *Sinistra 77* (reprinted in *La dignità del lavoro*, 31–37), Caffè drew a parallel between the timidity of the left in 1947, which only weakly defended the *consigli*, and its timidity in 1977, when the so-called 'historical compromise' between DC and PCI was formulated. On these topics, see also G. Amari, ed., *Parla Federico Caffè*, chapter I; G. Amari, ed., *Attualità di Federico Caffè nella crisi odierna*, 225–231.

10 This was the frank admission made by the President of the *Confindustria* (Confederation of the industry masters), Angelo Costa, in his hearing at the *Commissione economica*. See L. Villari, ed., *Il capitalismo italiano del Novecento*, Laterza, Bari, 1972, 497–498.

11 See F. Caffè, *Un riesame dell'opera svolta dalla Commissione economica per la Costituente* (1969), in *La dignità del lavoro*, 293–302. Caffè was a member of the group of experts on money and foreign trade.

12 See F. Caffè, *Sul 'Piano del lavoro': reminiscenze* (1978), in Caffè, *La dignità del lavoro*, 314–316.

13 F. Caffè, *Annotazioni sulla politica economica britannica in un 'anno d'ansia'*, Tecnica grafica, no indication of place, 1948, 33–34. Several papers collected in this book have been reprinted in F. Caffè, *La dignità del lavoro*, 191–212.

14 See his introduction to F. A. Burchardt, M. Kalecki, G. D. N. Worswick, E. F. Schumacher, T. Balogh, K. Mandelbaum, *L'economia della piena occupazione*, Rosenberg & Sellier, Torino, 1979, reprinted in *La dignità del lavoro*, 336–346.

15 See the interview of July 1977 in *Sinistra 77*, in *La dignità del lavoro*, 31–37.

16 In the later years, Lunghini softened his position: cf. G. Lunghini, 'Né l'apologeta né il becchino', in *Federico Caffè, un economista per il nostro tempo*, 824.

17 *Memorials of Alfred Marshall*, A. C. Pigou, ed., Kelley, New York, 1966, 174.

18 F. Caffè, Introduction to *Antologia di scritti di G. Del Vecchio nel centenario della nascita*, Angeli, Milano, 1983, 15.

19 See Caffè, *Politica economica. Sistematica e tecniche di analisi*, Boringhieri, Torino, 1966, 21.

20 See Caffè, *Politica economica*, vol. 2, *Problemi economici interni*, Boringhieri, Torino, 1972, 213–214; and the entry Moneta in *Enciclopedia del Novecento*, Istituto dell'Enciclopedia italiana, Roma, 1979.

21 The origin and actual functions (or rather, distortions) of the IMF formed the subject of chapter IV of Caffè's *Politica economica*, 2, and also featured in a host of political articles from 1978 to 1984.

22 See F. Caffè, *La problematica degli elevati tassi d'interesse reali*, *Politica ed economia*, XIV, n. 2, Feb. 1983.

23 See F. Caffè, *Alcune trasformazioni recenti del Fondo monetario internazionale*, *La Comunità internazionale*, 1978, 529.

24 See F. Caffè, *Vecchi e nuovi trasferimenti anormali di capitali*, in *Studi in onore di Marco Fanno*, vol. I, Cedam, Padova 1966, 36–41.

25 See F. Caffè, *Appunti sull'economia contemporanea: il ritorno agli studi sulle crisi finanziarie*, *Moneta e credito*, 1979, 452.

26 See F. Caffè, Politica economica – I fondamenti teorici, *Enciclopedia Europea*, Garzanti, Milano, 1979.

27 See F. Caffè, Le dimensioni mondiali della povertà, *Notiziario di geografia economica*, special issue in honour of F. Milone, Roma 1971, 14–15, and several articles collected in *La solitudine del riformista*.

28 See F. Caffè, Benessere (economia del), in *Dizionario di economia politica*, C. Napoleoni, ed., Comunità, Milano 1956, spec. 64–65; Cf. also F. Caffè, Introduction to *Saggi sulla moderna economia del benessere*, Einaudi, Torino, 1956, xiv; see also F. Caffè, Vecchi e nuovi contributi alla sistematica della politica economica, *Cultura e scuola*, n. 1, October 1961.

29 See for instance L'eredità intellettuale keynesiana e gli odierni problemi mondiali, in *In difesa del Welfare state*, 95–111.

30 F. Caffè, La politica economica nel sistema degli economisti classici, chapter two of his manual of *Politica economica. Sistematica e tecniche di analisi*, Boringhieri, Torino, 1966, 26–55. In particular, Caffè insists on the link between theory and policy in David Ricardo, often neglected by interpreters who talk about Ricardo's exceeding propensity for abstract reasoning.

31 Against Hayek, see many hints in Caffè's university courses and in his political articles. Cf. for instance F. Caffè, Che spregiudicato quell'economista, ha scoperto la legge della giungla, *Il Manifesto*, Dec. 7, 1978 (reprinted in *Scritti quotidiani*, 17–18).

32 See among all F. Caffè, ed., *Saggi sulla moderna economia del benessere*, Einaudi, Torino, 1956, where a collection of classics of the post-Pigou literature on welfare is presented.

33 See M. Cangiani, P. Frigato, Federico Caffè and institutional economics, *History of Economic Ideas*, 2012, 1, 131–155; with a rich reference list.

34 See F. Caffè, 'Capitalismo monopolistico', 'Nuovo stato industriale' ed effettiva realtà economica, *Giornale degli economisti e Annali di economia*, 1968, especially 63–69.

35 F. Caffè, Keynes e i suoi contemporanei, in R. Faucci, ed., *John Maynard Keynes nel pensiero e nella politica economica*, Feltrinelli, Milano, 1977, 39.

36 F. Vianello reconstructs this discussion in more conciliatory terms. See his Federico Caffè e l''intelligente pragmatismo', in *Federico Caffè. Realtà e critica del capitalismo storico*, 25–42.

25 What is the labour theory of value and what is it good for?

Duncan K. Foley[1]

Value

In economies where human production is organized through the exchange of products as commodities, the statistical regularities of the exchange process (which may take a wide variety of forms from scattered barter through posted price outlets to highly organized auction markets) establish ratios at which different commodities trade. In well-established commodity systems some form of money typically evolves: the money prices of commodities, that is, the exchange ratios of commodities with money, are the familiar form these exchange ratios take. Under these circumstances it is possible to calculate the value of any collection, or bundle, of commodities by multiplying the quantity of each commodity in the bundle by its price. In mathematical terms, if the vector of commodities representing a bundle is $x = \{x_1, \ldots, x_K\}$ and the vector of money prices of the commodities is $p = \{p_1, \ldots, p_K\}$ the value of the bundle x at price system p is:

$$v[p, x] = p \cdot x = p_1 x_1 + \ldots + p_K x_K \tag{25.1}$$

This is a common ordinary language use of the word 'value', and it is the sense in which I will use it in this paper.

When we discuss production of commodities, as in the case of the labour theory of value, the relevant bundle of commodities represents those newly produced in some period, such as a year or a quarter of a year. In this case the new production generally requires both some existing products as inputs and some labour. Writing the ratios of the inputs used up per unit of new output as the input-output matrix A with a typical element A_{ij} representing the input of product i per unit of output of product j, the inputs used up in producing the bundle x can be conveniently written in matrix notation as $A \cdot x$, and the net output, allowing for the inputs used as $y = x - A \cdot x = (I - A) \cdot x$ where I is the $K \times K$ identity matrix. Then the value added (abstracting from various complications introduced by excise taxes) is

$$p \cdot y = p \cdot (I - A) \cdot x. \tag{25.2}$$

A theory of value such as the labour theory of value is intended to explain value and its changes in this sense. One elementary point is that some changes in money value arise from a uniform proportional change in the money prices of all commodities. If a new price system $p' = \mu p$, the money value of any bundle of commodities will change according to

$$v[p', x] = v[\mu p, x] = \mu p \cdot x = \mu v[p, x]. \tag{25.3}$$

It is natural to regard a proportional change in all money prices as a change in the value of money, rather than a change in the underlying value of the bundle of commodities.

In empirical applications it is common to estimate changes in the value of money using some reference standard or *numéraire, d*:

$$\mu[p, p'] = \frac{p \cdot d}{p' \cdot d}. \tag{25.4}$$

Labour

While the definition of the term 'value' is relatively straightforward because it invokes ordinary day-to-day categories like money price and quantity, the term 'labour' presents more fundamental difficulties. These difficulties arise because human labour transforms subjective experience, such as effort or inconvenience, which is directly accessible only to the labourer, to an objective result, such as a quantity of some usable product, which is inter-subjectively or publicly observable. It is not so difficult to agree on how many bushels of wheat there are in the silo, but it is impossible for anyone but the direct producer to know how much effort it took to get them there.

Adam Smith characteristically treats this transformation of subjective to objective indirectly, referring to labour as the 'ultimate price' human beings pay for usable products. 'The real price of everything, what everything really costs to the man who wants to acquire it, is the toil and trouble of acquiring it' (Smith, 1937, Book I, Chapter 5).

Karl Marx, in the context of his analysis of the wage–labour relation in capitalist economies, noted that what the capitalist purchases in the wage contract is not labour, but the capacity or potential to labour, that is *labour-power*, which can be measured in terms of time. The wage-worker puts a certain amount of his potential labouring time at the disposal of the capitalist in exchange for the money wage. Thus in the case of any particular wage contract there is the question of how much labour effort the capitalist can extract from the worker. It is not hard to imagine experiments that might explore this question in an ordinal sense, with observations that a worker worked harder in one period than in another, or for one employer than another.

It is characteristic of the classical political economy tradition to regard labour effort as comparable in terms of its effects in production across workers and fungible between different tasks (which Marx calls *concrete labours*).

> The difference of natural talents in different men is, in reality, much less than we are aware of; and the very different genius which appears to distinguish men of different professions, when grown up to maturity, is not upon many occasions so much the cause as the effect of the division of labour. The difference between the most dissimilar characters, between a philosopher and a common street porter, for example, seems to arise not so much from nature as from habit, custom, and education. When they came into the world, and for the first six or eight years of their existence, they were, perhaps, very much alike, and neither their parents nor playfellows could perceive any remarkable difference. About that age, or soon after, they come to be employed in very different occupations. The difference of talents comes then to be taken notice of, and widens by degrees, till at last the vanity of the philosopher is willing to acknowledge scarce any resemblance.
>
> (Smith, 1937, Book I, Chapter 2)

Thus one of the substantive claims of the labour theory of value is that there is a relevant sense in which the labour of individual workers can be aggregated in social production despite the subjective quality of labour effort, and the variety of specific tasks, skills, training, and so forth that constitute concrete labour.

> The time spent in two different sorts of work will not always alone determine this proportion. The different degrees of hardship endured, and of ingenuity exercised, must likewise be taken into account. There may be more labour in an hour's hard work than in two hours' easy business; or in an hour's application to a trade which it cost ten years' labour to learn, than in a month's industry at an ordinary and obvious employment. But it is not easy to find any accurate measure either of hardship or ingenuity. In exchanging, indeed, the different productions of different sorts of labour for one another, some allowance is commonly made for both. It is adjusted, however, not by any accurate measure, but by the higgling and bargaining of the market, according to that sort of rough equality which, though not exact, is sufficient for carrying on the business of common life.
>
> (Smith, 1937, Book I, Chapter 5)

Because of the subjective element both Smith and Marx recognize in labour effort, it is impossible to measure labour directly and quantitatively in classical political economy terms. The situation is analogous to the difficulty of third-party enforcement of contracts that specify effort levels (Bowles, 2004, Chapter 8). The results of labour effort in usable output are measurable, but the subjective effort level required to achieve them is not.

Thus while the experience of labour effort is vivid and present to individuals, it is a big leap from this subjective experience to the idea of measuring labour effort in the aggregate over a whole economy. Nonetheless, in Marx's view, the laws of commodity production enforce a relation between social labour time and value added in any commodity-producing economy.

Labour and capital mobility

Smith explains the logic of competitive commodity production in terms of the mobility of labour and capital (which Smith calls 'stock'):

> The whole of the advantages and disadvantages of the different employments of labour and stock must, in the same neighbourhood, be either perfectly equal or continually tending to equality. If in the same neighbourhood, there was any employment evidently either more or less advantageous than the rest, so many people would crowd into it in the one case, and so many would desert it in the other, that its advantages would soon return to the level of other employments. This at least would be the case in a society where things were left to follow their natural course, where there was perfect liberty, and where every man was perfectly free both to choose what occupation he thought proper, and to change it as often as he thought proper. Every man's interest would prompt him to seek the advantageous, and to shun the disadvantageous employment.
>
> (Smith, 1937, Book I, Chapter 10)

There are several aspects of this paragraph worth comment.

First of all, it addresses two fundamental questions: the employment of labour and the employment of capital ('stock'). In both cases the 'whole of the advantages and disadvantages of the different employments' tend to equality in the 'same neighborhood', at least where there is 'perfect liberty'. The mechanism behind this tendency to equality is mobility of labour and capital. But as Smith explains elsewhere, the principles that govern the movement of labour and capital are different. Workers judge the advantages and disadvantages of different employments in terms of the balance between the labour effort, broadly construed, and the money wage (or, more generally to account for 'simple commodity production' where the producer owns the means of production, money income), thereby tending to make the subjective relation between labour expended and the money wage in different employments equal. Employers judge the advantage of different employments of their capital in terms of the profit rate, the ratio of the profit income to the capital invested.

The mobility of labour, then, tends to equalize the relation between the money wage and the subjective disadvantages of labour effort across employments. Marx calls this relation the *rate of exploitation*, or the *rate of surplus value*. The mobility of capital tends to equalize the profit rate across different investments. The subjective disadvantages of labour effort include the time required to acquire necessary skills. The point that the worker subjectively has to compare the effort level of the work with the money income to be had from doing it is crucial. Marx devotes the chapter on Money in the *Grundrisse* (Marx, 1973) to a careful examination of the reasons why commodity-producing labour can be equated only indirectly through the expression of commodity values in money, and cannot be directly equated in the production process itself. This is the reason that Marx's theory of money is an integral and indispensable part of his theory of value. In the case of commodity-producers, whether they are wage-labourers or own their own means of production, the implication is that they move from employment to employment in response to differences in the ratio of labour effort, broadly understood to include training costs, to money income.

Second, we cannot expect any real economy to exhibit the 'perfect liberty' Smith postulates. There are always some obstacles to the completely free mobility of capital and labour, some arising from legislation, and others from other social, cultural, and historical circumstances, such as linguistic differences, racial and gender discrimination, caste, and the like. Marx calls this kind of thought-experiment an *abstraction*. Even though the real level of wages or profits never exactly achieves equality of rates of surplus value or rates of profit, the equalized rate of surplus value and rate of profit positions of the economy are indispensable as an analytical benchmark to understand real situations. For one thing, to a first order approximation, deviations from equality are likely to be symmetrical, with wages in some employments higher and in others lower than justified by differences in labour effort, and therefore offsetting over the whole economy.

But whatever obstacles there may be to labour mobility, they do not include fundamental differences in the talents or capabilities of workers to adapt to the demands of different concrete productive tasks. As Smith explains in the paragraph quoted first above, differences in training and experience can create vast and apparently unbridgeable gaps between the concrete labouring capacities of different workers over their life cycle. But viewed from the point of view of social reproduction, the potential mass of human labour is homogeneous and fungible, in that the distribution of skills and specialization can adapt to requirements of technology and social demand. This perspective suggests the tendency in the abstract conditions of 'perfect liberty' for the balance of advantages and disadvantages of different employments to be *ex ante* equalized. If workers at the beginning of their productive life-cycle are actively pursuing different career paths, that is evidence from Smith's point of view that the paths of training, education, and experience offered by them must be substantially equal in the eyes of those workers. This does not imply that all human beings have the same potential to exert labour effort in any fixed time period. Some may tire more quickly than others, or take longer to perform any task. Employers, to the extent they can detect these differences, will adjust money wages proportionately to the worker's effort relative to the social average. All workers, however, have to choose their sector of employment on the basis of the relation between the money wage and the effort required.

If there are major life-cycle differences in the balance of advantages and disadvantages of different employments in reality, they must be due to limitations on perfect liberty of mobility, not to innate differences in workers' qualitative talents. For example, if some workers have access to finance for training that other workers do not, certain employments that require expensive training will be closed to those who do not have finance. Racial, caste, or gender discrimination would have parallel effects.

Third, the process Smith describes in this paragraph is simultaneously a process of the formation of wages and (through profit rates) of competitive prices and a process of allocation of labour and capital to different sectors of social production. It is differences in rates of surplus value that attract workers from one employment to another (possibly through different educational paths), just as differences in profit rates attract capital from one line of production to another.

Fourth, the equalization of rates of surplus value in different employments implies that labour effort tends to a uniform proportion to money wages, establishing a direct relationship between money and labour effort, broadly construed to include costs of skill acquisition, and other relevant factors such as the health and safety consequences of the work. This proportion entails a parallel proportion between labour effort and aggregate money value added.

Marx's theory of surplus value

Marx uses the term *surplus value* to denote the sum of profits, interest, and rent in a capitalist economy. On the basis of his theory of labour-power, he argues that the ultimate origin of all these components of surplus value is the difference between the money value of commodities productive wage labourers produce and the money value of the wages they receive.

The classical (often called 'Ricardian') theory of rent is the paradigmatic scenario for understanding how surplus value produced by the exploitation of labour at the point of production can be realized in a very different form due to property relations. The owner of a particularly productive natural resource (a waterfall capable of generating useful power, or land naturally situated in favourable circumstances for cultivation, or cheaply mineable mineral deposits) has the legal power to exclude capitalist producers from access to that resource. This gives the resource owner the power to bargain with capitalists seeking to use the resource for a *rent*. The potential capitalist user of the resource values access to it because it will allow the capitalist to produce at lower cost than his competitors, whose costs of production will determine the price of the commodities produced. In these circumstances on average resource owners will be in a position to extract the entire extra profit the capitalist can realize using the resource as rent. If the rent is lower than the extra profit, other similarly situated capitalists will be willing to pay a somewhat higher rent; if the rent is higher than the extra profit, no capitalist will bid for access to the resource. (Again, this argument presupposes a high level of abstraction, since in reality both capitalists and resource owners will have to estimate the advantages of producing with the resource, may make mistakes, may not understand the bargaining situation completely, and so forth.) Once the capitalist rents the resource and begins to produce commodities with it, some part of the surplus value that results winds up in the pocket of the resource owner as rent. From this point of view rents can be seen as allowing the equalization of profit rates between production with superior and inferior resources: capitalists producing on these different resources sell their products as commodities at the same price and face the same prices for labour-power and other inputs to production, so it is the rent that equalizes their costs and rates of profit.

Ordinary commercial language typically denominates rent in terms of the resource (dollars per acre of land, or acre-foot of water, or kilowatt of energy) rather than as a part of the surplus value produced, thus obscuring the origin of the rent in production. This 'irrational' terminology leads 'vulgar' economists to believe that rent originates from the resource itself, not from the property relations and commodity system in which the resource is situated. The inadequacy of this point of view is easy to demonstrate through thought experiments: if production of commodities is small, resources that provide only a small cost advantage may not be utilized at all and as a result their owners cannot appropriate part of the surplus value as rent; if property rights in resources are not secure, productive resources will simply be crowded by producers until average cost using the resource rises to the marginal cost of production using the next-best resource; and so on.

In the manuscripts published as Volume III of *Capital*, Marx systematically discusses each of the various forms in which surplus value is appropriated in capitalist economies, such as interest on financial assets, commercial profit, the employment of unproductive labour, and rents. The first of these discussions, in Part I and Part II, concern the formation of profit and the profit rate itself. While the classical theory of rent is widely understood, and became the foundation of later marginalist and neoclassical price and distribution theory, Marx's theory of profits as a part of surplus value, despite being logically parallel to the classical theory of rent, has been dogged by misunderstanding and controversy.

Marx argues that the exploitation of wage labour over a whole capitalist economy creates an enormous pool of surplus value, which is distributed among capitalists through competition. One basic tendency of competition in the view of the classical political economists is for capital to move to seek the highest profit rate, which, in Smith's language, will tend to equalize the balance of advantages and disadvantages of investment in any line of production from the point of view of capitalists. At the simplest and most abstract level this implies an equalization of rates of profit (subject perhaps to systematic variation depending on risk, seasonality of production, the social acceptability and legality of production, and the like) across different lines of production. If the prospective profit rate (allowing for these long-run systematic difference) in one line of production is higher than the average, capitalists will crowd into that line of production, driving down the price of the output commodity, and lowering the profit rate towards equality with the average. Symmetrically, capital will move out of lines of production with low prospective profit rates.

Thus in Marx's view there is no direct connection between the production of surplus value through the exploitation of wage labour and the appropriation of surplus value as profit. If, however, we maintain the view that the rate of exploitation is tendentially equalized through the mobility of labour, there will tend to be a uniform proportion between the wages of directly productive workers and their actual labour effort. Thus a capitalist who exploits productive workers to the average extent contributes an amount of surplus value to the common pool proportional to the wages he or she pays to them. The same capitalist takes out of the surplus value pool an amount that depends on the prices of the commodities produced, which may be larger or smaller than that capitalist's contribution. In competing to appropriate surplus value from the pool created by the exploitation of wage labour over the whole system of capitalist production, capitalists are exactly in the position of resource owners seeking to maximize rents. One way a capitalist might compete for surplus value in the form of profits would be to lower the actual costs of production by adopting innovative methods of production. This in turn might have a (probably vanishingly small) positive effect on the surplus value pool, but a much bigger effect on the profits of that particular capitalist. Other capitalists might adopt competitive strategies ('business models' in contemporary terminology) that actually reduce the pool of surplus value, but increase their share of the pool. This type of behavior is sometimes called 'rent-seeking' because of its blatant parallel to resource owners' appropriation of rent. But the larger point of Marx's argument is that *all* capitalists are in the same position as resource owners or rent-seekers in their role as appropriators of surplus value.

If the theory of rent proved too subtle and 'non-intuitive' for many economists and most of the public to grasp fully, Marx's theory of surplus value poses even steeper challenges to 'common-sense' perceptions of what is going on in capitalist economies. The rent-appropriating owner of a specialized productive resource is a 'free rider' on the production of surplus value: the landowner as landowner does not contribute one cent to the pool of surplus value by exploiting wage labour, but can bargain for a share of the pool of surplus value by using legally enforced property rights to exclude producers. But because the pool of surplus value in capitalist economies is so large compared to the operations of even the very largest capitalist firms, every single capitalist is effectively a free-rider on pool of surplus value. The direct contribution any capitalist can make to increasing the pool of surplus value by raising the rate of exploitation at one point of production is minuscule compared to the size of the pool itself, which might as well be infinite as far as the capitalist's competitive strategy goes. Thus while the vulgar economist and the public can see that there is *some* connection between the profits of particular firms and the exploitation of that firm's workers, it is very hard to appreciate just how tenuous and indirect that connection is in fact. The main incentive for a particular capitalist to exploit his or her workers more effectively is not to increase the production of surplus value, but to create the strategic conditions under which the capitalist can compete more effectively to appropriate a larger part of the pool of surplus value.

Marx points out that the first-order effect of capitalist innovation to lower costs of production is simply to lower the prices of the resulting products as use-values. This constitutes an immense positive externality of capitalist production from the point of view of social reproduction, since the use-values required for people to live and reproduce become cheaper both in terms of money and in terms of labour effort. But cheapening of commodities has only much smaller second-order effects on the pool of surplus value, which depends on the number of productive labourers and the rate of exploitation or surplus value. Marx puts forward the concept of *relative surplus value*, through which the cheapening of commodities workers consume drives down the money wage relative to labour effort over the whole economy, as the main channel through which the cheapening of commodities might increase the pool of surplus value. But this effect may be (and probably has been in historical experience) diluted by increases in workers' standards of living increasing the amount of use-values they consume (food, clothing, shelter, and so forth) even as these commodities become cheaper.

While Marx appreciated the immense social achievements of capitalist production, he seems to have been appalled at his realization that all those social effects were unintended by-products of an 'irrational', that is, non-transparent and indirect, system of competitive production. Even more striking is the fact that individual capitalists are no more in control of their fates than is bourgeois society as a whole. Despite the fact that the whole edifice is the outcome of the collective enterprise of the capitalists, it depends hardly at all and is basically indifferent to the outcome of any particular enterprise.

It is the mobility of labour, not capitalist competition, that regulates and equalizes the rate of surplus value production, thereby establishing a tendentially uniform relation between labour effort and money in the form of the wage. Individual workers have no more ability to control the overall rate of exploitation than do individual capitalists. Individual workers can respond to a deterioration in the relation between wages and effort in one line of production relative to others by migrating (perhaps with long lag times due to training and other costs) to the more favourable lines of production, and in this way collectively can enforce uniformity of the rate of exploitation. But this movement of labour in and of itself cannot change the average rate of exploitation. Only system-wide factors, such as the labour cost of reproducing the labour power, public policy, trade and labour regulation, and the like, can influence the rate of exploitation and the size of the pool of surplus value.

The 'transformation problem'

Marx attempted to give a quantitative picture of his theory of surplus value in illustrative tables, some of which Engels printed in Chapter IX of Volume III of *Capital*. The attention later scholarship, both sympathetic to and critical of the point of view of the labour theory of value has lavished on these tables and their treatment of the pricing of intermediate inputs to production has tended to obscure the more fundamental question at issue, which is the conservation of surplus value in spite of the deviations between prices of production and embodied labour resulting from the competition of capitals.

If we are reasoning at the level of abstraction (admittedly very high) at which the free mobility of labour equalizes the rate of surplus value production and the free mobility of capital equalizes rates of profit among different lines of commodity production, then the conservation of surplus value in Marx's sense follows directly.

To argue this point verbally, the equalization of the rate of surplus value production means that in every line of production the actual productive social labour expended is proportional to the money wages paid to productive labourers. Thus over the whole sphere of capitalist commodity production the social labour expended is proportional to the money wage bill for productive labour. The aggregate money value added realized from the sale of commodities over the whole system also bears a certain proportion to the aggregate productive money wages. Thus the equalization of the rate of surplus value production implies a proportion between the total productive labour expended in commodity production and the money value added realized. The coefficient representing this proportion will have a magnitude that depends on the units in which we measure productive labour expenditure. Marx consistently uses hours of simple labour time as the unit of labour effort (with skilled labour counting as a multiple of simple labour according to the principles we have reviewed above). But the exact choice of unit for social labour effort is not particularly relevant to the phenomenon of the conservation of surplus value in the process of capitalist competition leading to an equalization of the rate of profit. The important point is that social labour can be consistently compared across lines of production (is *universal* in Marx's sense) and therefore given a quantitative measure in some units. The equalization of the rate of surplus value production in the sense of the quantitative ratio of social labour effort to money wages thus implies a parallel uniform ratio of aggregate money surplus value produced to wages. The competition of capitalists in forcing prices of production above or below proportionality to the living labour time expended can only redistribute surplus value from one line of production to another by altering the location of surplus value realization; it cannot change aggregate surplus value.

To illustrate this point mathematically, suppose the productive labour-power purchased by capitalist employers in sector j is L_j, the wage is w_j, the productive money wage bill is $W_j = w_j L_j$, and the productive labour effort expended is L'_j, given some agreed-on units in which to measure productive labour effort. If the ratio of productive effort expended to the wage is equalized across sectors by the mobility of labour, we have

$$\frac{L'_j}{w_j L_j} = \frac{L'_i}{w_i L_i} = \frac{1}{\mu'} \tag{25.5}$$

for all sectors i, j. The aggregate productive labour effort is then $L' = \sum L'_j = \frac{1}{\mu'} \sum w_j L_j = \frac{1}{\mu'} \sum W_j = \frac{W}{\mu'}$, where $W = w \cdot L = \sum W_j$ is the aggregate productive wage bill. The aggregate ratio of value added to the aggregate productive labour effort is

$$\mu = \frac{p \cdot y}{L'} = \frac{p \cdot y}{wL} \frac{wL}{L'} = \mu'(1 + e) \tag{25.6}$$

where $e = \frac{p \cdot y - W}{W}$ is the aggregate rate of surplus value, the ratio of money surplus value to productive money wages. μ is the *monetary expression of (productive) labour (effort) time (MELT)* in the terminology that became widely used as a consequence of the debate over the 'New Interpretation' of the labour theory of value.

Thus the assumption of the equalization of the rate of surplus value production through the mobility of labour implies that aggregate value added is proportional to aggregate labour effort. As equation (25.6) shows, surplus value under this assumption is transparently proportional to unpaid productive labour time.

The 'New Interpretation' started from the assumption that social labour time could be converted to money through the MELT coefficient, and interpreted surplus value as the labour time equivalent of the difference between money value added and the money wage of productive workers. While the equalization of the rate of surplus value production through the mobility of labour implies the existence of a MELT, the converse is not true. The 'New Interpretation' is a weaker theory than the assertion of the equalization of the rate of surplus value production through the mobility of labour, because it does not rest explicitly on the real process by which competition of labour tendentially equalizes the rate of surplus value production.

The MELT is sometimes estimated for real economies by the ratio of value added to the aggregate labour power in time units, $\frac{p \cdot y}{L}$. Because $L'_j = \mu' w_j L_j$, $L' = \sum \mu' w_j L_j = \mu' \bar{w} L$, where $\bar{w} = \sum w_j \frac{L_j}{L}$ is the average wage of productive labour-power weighted by the productive labour power in each sector. The full labour theory of value thus weights hours of productive labour-power by relative wages in calculating the expenditure of productive labour effort.

The large literature on the 'transformation problem' seeks either to prove or disprove the labour theory of value by considering the equalization of the rate of profit through competition of capitals. Because Marx's tableaux were intended to illustrate the conservation of surplus value in the presence of competition, it is possible to show the consistency of Marx's tableaux with the conservation of surplus in a variety of ways. It is not possible, however, to say much about the labour theory value itself in the context of a discussion of these tableaux, because they presuppose the link between productive labour effort and value added, and a consideration of competition among capitals cannot either support or discredit that connection. It arises not from the mobility of capital that underlies the competition among capitals, but from the mobility of labour that tendentially enforces the equality of the rate of exploitation across productive employments.

The limits of the labour theory of value

The interpretation of the labour theory of value set forth here rests on two key assumptions, which are common to the classical political economists and Marx, but incompatible with later marginalist doctrines. The first assumption is that human labour effort is aggregatable in its productive effects across workers. The second is that the free mobility of labour tends to equalize the subjective ratio of labour effort to money income across employments. The two together imply the proportionality of value-added to productive labour expended in all commodity production, and, more to the point, the conservation of surplus value in capitalist commodity production organized through wage labour.

We might summarize the theory as assuming that labour is *universal* in the sense that social labour effort can be adapted to new technological and social contexts, and *mobile* in the sense that workers seek employments that have the lowest ratio of labour effort to money income. Universality underlies the aggregatability of labour, while mobility implies the proportionality of money value to labour time.

The first assumption is incompatible with the position, widely adopted by post-marginal revolution economics, that there are inherent qualitative differences in productive capacity among individuals. This stance rules out the aggregation of labour effort to a meaningful (though inherently not directly measurable) quantity of productive social effort. For the classical political economists and Marx, however, the comparability of different individuals' labour effort, and therefore the existence of a meaningful aggregate measure of productive labour, apparently raised no philosophical problems. The classical political economists apparently did not question the aggregatability of human labour effort across individuals.

From the point of view of later critiques of the labour theory of value, such as those based on Böhm-Bawerk's argument against the aggregatability of concrete labour efforts (von Böhm-Bawerk, 2007), the important point is that for the classical political economists aggregatability of labour depends on the adaptability or *fungibility* of labour across distinct concrete productive functions. In fact, it does not make sense to aggregate incommensurable concrete labour efforts on the basis of their results in production, since they are not comparable. But it did make sense to the classical political economists and Marx to regard potential social labour effort as fungible between concrete skills because over a long enough time frame, they knew that typical human beings could adapt themselves to new technologies and their skill requirements.

It is true that there is no direct measure of 'universal' or 'abstract' productive labour effort due to the inherently subjective and experiential nature of labour conceived in this way. The economist observing social production 'from outside', as it were, has no direct access to the subjective experience of the workers. But the individual worker does have access to his own subjective experience, and thus can form an opinion of the ratio of labour effort to money income in different employments, and, given mobility of labour, can move to the employment where the ratio of labour effort to money income is lowest. The crucial difference between the classical political economists and Marx, on the one hand, and the post-marginalist tradition is that the classical political economists and Marx go one step further and regard these subjective judgments of individual workers as enforcing the uniformity of the rate of exploitation across productive tasks and sectors. Not only does the individual worker judge the ratio of effort to money income across jobs, but on the whole all workers will make the same judgement, in the view of the classical political economists. Thus Smith, Ricardo, and Marx saw social productive labour time as a definite (though not directly measurable) quantity, which could be allocated across different concrete labour activities in order to accomplish the social division of labour.

The assumption of the free mobility of labour, leading to the equalization of the ratio of subjective labour effort to money wages (income) has the important implication that value can be rigorously regarded as proportional to the expenditure of productive labour effort across the whole system of commodity production, and, as a corollary, that in capitalist commodity production the rate of surplus value constrains the various non-wage incomes and revenue flows, such as employment of unproductive labour and capital, profit, rent, interest, indirect business taxes, and so forth. We can put this point in a number of ways, which all boil down to the same insight. We can say that surplus value is proportional to unpaid productive labour effort, or that competition can reallocate surplus value, but not generate it, or that the capitalist-commodity production system rests on the exploitation of productive labour.

The difficulties that arise from the assumption of free mobility of labour in this story are shared by all the strong abstractions of the classical political economy system. The basic difficulty is that in the real world labour is never completely mobile across employments, which raises the question of whether the labour theory of value has any relevance to real world economic and social relations. One way of thinking through this problem is to consider the assumption of 'perfect liberty' in the free mobility of labour as establishing an abstract benchmark to which reality can be compared. This is the royal road of abstraction, since adherence to the theory compels us to ask why the deviations from equalization of the rate of surplus value we observe are occurring. Are they due to geographic barriers to the mobility of labour, unequal access to credit to support training, gender or racial discrimination? In this way the abstraction pays its way in generating relevant questions for the interpretation of reality. This is the familiar case of a theory with 'auxiliary hypotheses' to account for particular features of a concrete situation. The theory remains useful as long as the auxiliary hypotheses do not become so elaborate and complex as to call into question the correctness the basic insight (as was the case for the epicycles introduced into Ptolemaic astronomy).

We might contrast the relevance of the labour theory of value to situations with particular definable limitations on the mobility of labour with its irrelevance to understanding the division of labour in a non-commodity producing, say, hunter-gatherer, society in which the division of labour and distribution are regulated by tradition and norms rather than by exchange. Human labour may be just as universal and fungible in the hunter-gatherer society, but cannot express its quantitative magnitude in terms of money value because there are no commodities and hence no money.

What the labour theory of value is good for, then, is to provide a framework for understanding the dynamics of accumulation and distribution in capitalist-commodity producing economies.

Productive and unproductive labour

In classical political economy the term *unproductive labour* refers to wage labour that adds no value to products as commodities. One example is the domestic servants rich landowners (who sometimes had made their fortunes in commerce or industry) employed to run large estates. Another example, which became more important with the development of capitalist production, is supervisory and administrative staff employed by capitalists to maximize the appropriation of surplus value through activities such as labour-monitoring, accounting, money-dealing, advertising, and the like. Marx devotes the manuscripts published as Part Four of Volume 3 of *Capital* to the analysis of the origin of the incomes of unproductive labourers in surplus value produced by productive labour.

The implication of the (productive) labour theory of value is that the incomes of unproductive labour depend, like land rent, on the ability of unproductive activities to secure a larger share of the surplus value pool to individual capitalists, not on any contribution unproductive labour makes to the pool of surplus value. The capitalist producer of consumer goods who does not advertise faces a less favourable tradeoff between price and market share than the competitor who does advertise. The employer who fails to monitor employee effort effectively faces a less favourable tradeoff between wage costs and output. From the point of view of social reproduction the unproductive labour contributes nothing to the production of use values or the pool of surplus value. Nonetheless unproductive activities can participate in the appropriation of the pool of surplus value.

There is much more to the phenomenon of unproductive labour than can be addressed in this context. But it is worth mentioning that the interpretation of the labour theory of value put forth here implies that it is possible to define the rate of exploitation of unproductive labour as the gap between the expenditure of labour effort and the money wage paid, just as is the case with productive labour. If the mobility of labour allows workers to shift freely between productive and unproductive employments, the rate of exploitation of unproductive labour will tend to be equalized to the rate of exploitation of productive labour. The subjective situation of productive and unproductive labour is the same: in both cases the capitalist employer extracts more labour effort from labour-power than the worker receives an equivalent for in the money wage. The difference lies in the purposes to which the capitalist directs the labour effort. In the case of productive labour the capitalist organizes the worker's effort to add value to commodities through production; in the case of unproductive labour the worker does not add value to the commodity through production, but may contribute to the capitalist's appropriation of surplus value from the pool created by the exploitation of productive labour.

Conclusion

The labour theory value links the expenditure of productive labour to the money value added to commodities in commodity-producing societies. For the classical political economists and Marx the labour theory of value is a logical implication of the conception of labour effort as a subjective, but socially aggregatable, cost of production, together with the assumption that mobility of labour will lead to the equalization of the ratio of labour effort to money income across employments. The labour theory of value asserts that human labour is universal and fungible, and that in conditions of commodity production, the value added in production is quantitatively proportional to the expenditure of labour effort.

The widespread rejection of the labour theory of value as a foundation for economic analysis seems largely to be the consequence of the rejection of the classical explanation of differences in concrete labor as the result, not the cause, of the division of labour. Post-marginalist labour economics endorses the notion that each worker can balance labour effort against money income (or the commodities that money income can buy), but rejects the aggregatability of social productive labour. The enormous exfoliation of the division of labour that has accompanied the development of capitalist production contributes to the difficulty of seeing the fungibility of human labour in the same light as the classical political economists and Marx. As Smith remarks, it becomes more difficult to think through the process of the differentiation of human skills through training and experience and see the way in which the life-cycle differentiates the 'philosopher' and the 'street porter' (or the surgeon and the receptionist).

The critical analytical issue here is the understanding of the classical theory of rent. In comparing two societies that are otherwise identical but one of which has an endowment of more productive land resources, Marx saw the higher production of the well-endowed society as the result of some social mechanism controlling crowding, whether it was based on private property or social control of the resource. Thus it is not the good land itself that has a 'marginal product' but the social relations that control access to the good land. Even economists who understand the implications of Ricardo's theory of rent often fail to follow its logic to the full labour theory of value and understanding of exploitation of productive labour as the source of surplus value that Marx develops.

Note

1 This paper is a contribution to the festschrift for Neri Salvadori on the occasion of his sixty-fifth birthday. Neri's work in theoretical economics and the history of political economy, which combines mathematical rigor, imagination, historical insight, and impeccable taste, has been a beacon for economists like myself. I would like to thank Jon Cogliano for ongoing conversations on the subject of this paper, which have contributed significantly to clarifying my thinking, and Heinz Kurz, Paul Mattick, Simon Mohun, Jeffrey Stewart and Roberto Veneziani for comments on earlier drafts and explorations of these questions. Any errors remain my responsibility.

References

Bowles, S. (2004). *Microeconomics: Behavior, Institutions, and Evolution*. Princeton University Press, Princeton, NJ.

Marx, K. (1973). *Grundrisse: Foundations of the Critique of Political Economy (Rough Draft)*. Penguin, Harmondsworth.

Smith, A. (1937). *An Inquiry into the Nature and Causes of the Wealth of Nations*. Random House, New York. [1776].

von Böhm-Bawerk, E. (2007). *Karl Marx and the Close of His System*. Ludwig von Mises Institute, Auburn, AL.

26 Self-management and socialism

Bruno Jossa

Introduction

Hobsbawm has written that historians, while drawing a clear-cut distinction between 'Marxists' and 'non-Marxists' and concerning themselves preferably with the former, have actually widened this group through the inclusion of a large selection of authors. In point of fact, he argued, this distinction is necessary if we are to write a reliable history of Marxism (see Hobsbawm, 1979, 61). In our opinion, instead, the most shared opinion is that the line separating what is 'Marxist' from what is not has been progressively blurred. Maxime Rodinson (1969, 9), for instance, has remarked that, despite the efforts of Marx and Marxists to prove previous philosophical systems wrong, it is far from easy to pinpoint what exactly distinguishes the Marxist approach, and some commentators trace this fact to the involvement of an increasing number of intellectuals in academic research on Marxism. Indeed, an attentive Marx commentator such as Rubel has gone so far as to deny the legitimacy of terms such as 'Marxian' or 'Marxist' (see Rubel, 1974, 20–21).

With specific regard to their approach to the next social order, Marxists fall into two broad divisions: those who describe socialism as a command economy founded on planning and those who assume that the correct Marxian view of a socialist economy is one which equates socialism with self-management.[1]

In this paper, we will be arguing that the establishment of a system of cooperative firms reversing the current capital–labour relation is tantamount to a revolution, in that it results in the introduction of a new production mode.[2] Subsequently, we will raise the question: is the idea of a revolution enacted by peaceful and democratic means and in successive steps – until worker-managed firms outnumber capitalistic companies – fully compatible with the letter of Marx and Engels's writings? From our perspective, the prerequisite for such a revolution is a certain amount of support from the public hand, in terms that the State would have to look upon democratic firms as 'merit goods' and make provision for tax and/or other benefits in their favour.

An additional query we deem worth exploring is whether a form of socialism established through State intervention would be compatible with Marx's and Engels's theorisations. Although the best proxy for the system imagined by Marx is doubtless an economy in which labour managed firms operate within a centrally planned system, we wish to argue that a system with self-managed firms would be consistent with Marx's theoretical edifice even though it should fail to adopt central planning.

A system of producer cooperatives as a new production mode

A great many market socialism models have been theorised over the past years; among them, the system with firms run by workers themselves – the one with which we are concerned in this paper – is both the simplest to prefigure and the most widely discussed.[3] The question is: is such a system a new production mode? In the prevailing opinion the only way to evade the control of capital is to do away with it (see, for instance, Mèszàros, 1995, 981).

This opinion misses the point. As capital entails of necessity the existence of the capitalist, the abolition of hired labour will lead to a phaseout of capitalism as a matter of course.

A different line of reasoning leads up to the same conclusion. Whereas capitalists quite obviously strive to maximise profit in the interests of capitalists, the labour-managed firms of the type fleshed out by the theoretical work of Ward (1958) and Vanek (1970) tend to maximise average worker income (or, more precisely, benefits for the workforce or, specifically, for those majority workers who have authority to pass resolutions at meetings). As a result, as soon as economic activity is made to pursue a different goal, the system also (or, more correctly, the mode of production) will change as a matter of course. The well-known Italian philosopher Emanuele Severino (2012, 94) has argued that

> within a logic postulating the existence of goals and means (a logic which has been predominant over the whole span of human history), there can be little doubt (though the conclusion is less dominant than the corresponding starting assumption) that whenever an action – here the capitalistic mode of operation – is made to deflect from its original goal and to start pursuing a different one, this self-same logic determines that the action itself will turn into something different in content, rhythm, intensity, relevance and configuration.

Clues for a better understanding of this point may come from the distinction between two different types of cooperative firms, the LMF and the WMF (see Vanek, 1971a and 1971b). In modern producer cooperative theory (which defines capital consistently with our approach, viz., as the bulk of production means), it is the so-called LMF cooperatives, which segregate labour incomes from capital incomes, that reverse the existing capital–labour relation. Indeed, whereas in capitalistic systems it is the owners of capital that hire workers (either directly or through managers in their service), pay them a fixed income and appropriate the surplus, in LMF-type cooperatives it is the workers running their own firms that *borrow* capital, pay it a fixed income (interest) and appropriate the surplus themselves.

In Marx's approach, the reversal of the capitalistic capital–labour relation triggers a real and proper revolution because it entails a change in actual production relations, not only in legal forms. The moment we accept Marx's claim that the principal contradiction in capitalism is the capital–labour opposition, it quite naturally follows that the reversal of the respective roles of capital and labour triggers a radical change in the existing production mode which unquestionably amounts to a revolution.

A well-known saying by Marx runs that those who control production are also in control of men's lives through the control of tools that enable them to pursue whatsoever aims they may have in mind (see, *inter alia*, Pellicani, 1976, 62 and Bahro, 1977, 23); and this argument goes to reinforce the idea that revolution is to be understood as the handover of production means from capitalists to workers and the concomitant disempowerment of capital.[4]

Marx's approach to producer cooperatives

A number of passages from Marx's works can be quoted in support of our conclusion.

An excerpt from Marx (1864) runs as follows:

> But there was in store a still greater victory of the political economy of labour over the political economy of property. We speak of the cooperative movement, especially of the cooperative factories raised by the unassisted efforts of a few bold 'hands'. The value of these great social experiments cannot be over-rated. By deed, instead of by argument, they have shown that production on a large scale, and in accord with the behest of modern science, may be carried on without the existence of a class of masters employing a class of hands; that to bear fruit, the means of labour need not be monopolised as a means of dominion over, and of extortion against, the labouring man himself; and that, like slave labour, like serf labour, hired labour is but a transitory and inferior form, destined to disappear before associated labour plying its toil with a willing hand, a ready mind, and a joyous heart.
>
> (Marx, 1864, 11)

And in the third volume of *Capital* Marx argues:

> With the development of cooperatives on the workers' part, and joint-stock companies on the part of the bourgeoisie, the last pretext for confusing profit of enterprise with the wages of management was removed, and profit came to appear in practice as what is undeniably was in theory, mere surplus-value, value for which no equivalent was paid.
>
> (Marx, 1894, 513–14)

These passages bear witness to Marx's belief that a system of cooperative firms is not only feasible, but bound to assert itself in history and that it gives rise to a new production mode in which wage labour is swept away and the means of production – what economists term capital – would no longer be used to enslave workers. In such a system, workers would not only cease being exploited; they would be freely and gladly working for firms owned by them.

The system of producer cooperatives envisaged by Marx is a market system where workers become 'their own masters' (Mill, 1871, 739) and where owners of capital are deprived of decision powers concerning production activities. This system is 'in accord with the behest of modern science' and, at the same time, efficient – even more efficient than capitalism – because it entails a new production mode arising spontaneously within the older production mode and improving on it.[5]

This thesis is confirmed by other well-known passages from *Capital*, which clearly reveal how Marx looked upon a system based on producer cooperatives as a new production mode superior to that of capitalism. Immediately before the lines quoted below Marx had described joint-stock companies as a first step toward 'the abolition of capitalist private industry', though 'within the capitalist system itself'.

To understand why Marx emphasised the need to abolish wage labour even in a production system remaining purely mercantile in nature, we have to bear in mind that one main advantage of producer cooperatives (from the perspective of a critic of capitalism) is to realise economic democracy as an essential component of political democracy. As is well known, Marx, Marxists and, generally, critics of society think of political democracy as merely formal, since power remains firmly in the hands of capitalists – or, in other words, since capital is still the economic power holding everything in its sway.

An additional interesting excerpt from *Capital* is reported below:

> Capitalist production has itself brought it about that the work of supervision is readily available quite independent of the ownership of capital. It has therefore become superfluous for this work of supervision to be performed by the capitalist. A musical conductor need in no way be the owner of the instruments in his orchestra, nor does it form part of his function as a conductor that he should have any part in paying the 'wages' of the other musicians. Cooperative factories provide the proof that the capitalist has become just as superfluous as a functionary in production as he himself, from his superior vantage point, finds the large landlord.
>
> (Marx, 1894, 511)[6]

Here, Marx was clearly thinking of a form of market economy in which capitalists would be disempowered.

Solving the capital–labour conflict

All those who hold that parliamentary acts in support of producer cooperatives can phase in a peaceful transition to socialism appear to attach paramount importance to the attainment of a working-class majority in parliament and, hence, to a possible positive solution of the conflict between the interests of the bourgeoisie and those of the working class. In the minds of most Marxists, therefore, the main contradiction of capitalism to be resolved during the transition to socialism is not the plan-market opposition, but the conflict between capital and labour.

The latter contradiction, i.e. the struggle between two opposed classes, occupies centre-stage within the historical process. As is well known, one of Marx's major contributions to the analysis of the society in which we live is the idea that the struggle between opposed classes is the main problem facing any capitalistic economy. As the theme of class struggle first made its appearance in early works dating from years when Marx still had little grounding in political economy, it was not borrowed from any of the writers on whom he drew for his later professional development. The first of these works, the *Critique of Hegel's Philosophy of Law*, was crucial to his later evolution as a theorist (see, *inter alia*, Brewer, 2002, 364) and was written in the autumn of 1843 and issued in the early months of 1844. As is well known, in Marx's approach class struggle is a matter of great consequence because it is assumed to be the main driving force behind history and fits within a dialectical view of social evolution.

The idea that the main contradiction to be addressed upon the abolition of capitalism is the conflict between the class that wields all power and the one that is doomed to passive obedience (rather than the plan–market opposition) has been spelt out in bold letters by more than one Marxist. To think that market – not power – relations are the crux of the issue – Bettelheim wrote – is a gross mistake, because it shifts focus on side issues and diverts attention away from the paramount factor: the existence of a class, the 'bourgeoisie', which is inimical to worker power (see Bettelheim, 1969; see, also, *inter alia*, Marek, 1982, 75).

As Marx himself put it,

> The most essential factor of the labour process is the worker himself, and in the ancient production process this worker was a slave. It does not follow from this that the worker is by nature a *slave* (although Aristotle is not very far removed from holding this opinion) any more than it follows that spindles and cotton are by their nature *capital* because they are at present consumed in the labour process by *wage labourers*.
>
> (Marx, 1863–66, 405)

In Marx's opinion, both Ricardo, who defined capital as that part of the wealth of a country which is employed in production, and other economists who described capital as the bulk of capital goods were the victims of an 'illusion'. And as this illusion caused them to mistake social relations established in the production environment for a natural ownership title to the assets used in production processes, it was 'an absurdity' (though one inherent in the very nature of the capitalistic production process) and 'a very convenient method of demonstrating the eternal character of the capitalist mode of production, or of showing that *capital* is a *permanent natural element* of human production in general' (Marx, 1863–66, 28).

Alienation and the democratic firm

From the claim that 'capital presupposes labour as wage labour' (see Marx, 1894, 811) it follows that the abolition of wage labour in a self-managed system would end both the dominion of dead labour over living labour and the form of alienation generated by the subjection of labour to capital.[7] Indeed, as workers turn into purchasers of production means (instead of being 'bought' by them), the existing capital–labour relation will be reversed, as we have said, and all such alienation as is now caused by the control of capital over labour will be ruled out as a matter of course.[8] Quoting again Marx himself,

> the labourer looks at the social nature of his labour, at its combination with the labour of others for a common purpose, as he would at an alien power; the condition of realising this combination is alien property ... The situation is quite different in factories owned by the labourers themselves, as in Rochdale, for instance.
>
> (Marx, 1894, 179)[9]

In a cooperative firm system, alienation would also be abated thanks to a phase-out of labour division levels (cf. Jossa, 2014, Chapter VIII, Section 4 and Chapter IX, Section 4), and this, too, suggests the reasonable conclusion that a major aim of any revolutionary thrust is the desire of the revolutionaries to reduce, if not altogether end, the conditions inhibiting the free expression of their individuality (see Negt, 1978, 172).

However, while those who endorse Marx's equation of revolution with the abolition of markets and material production predict the ultimate eradication of alienation in all its forms (see Marx, 1844, 296 ff. and, for example, Ollman, 1976, 153), those describing revolution as the reversal of the capitalistic capital–labour relation will argue that alienation would doubtless be abated, but not swept away for good:[10] Without stretching things too far, self-management theorists can safely argue that alienation eliminates 'a form of dehumanization that is particularly acute in the capitalist era' (see Ollman, 1998b, 90).

The conclusion suggested by our line of reasoning is that the prerequisite for cancelling alienation is suppressing material production – a fact that Marx explicitly underscored in the following quote: 'The realm of freedom really begins only where labour determined by necessity and external expediency ends; it lies by its very nature beyond the sphere of material production proper' (Marx, 1894, 958–59);[11] and the reason is that toil turns man from a free being into an animal (see Lukàcs, 1972, 24). Indeed, when work is impelled by the need to earn means of subsistence, what we call freedom turns out to be, not self-realisation, but just the awareness that work is a necessity. Unlike play, it fails to realise basic human needs since it is not a free choice.

The question to be answered at this point is why the lower levels of alienation connoting a labour-managed firm system should afford a new perspective on Marxism. Here, the answer is that the equation of revolution with the establishment of a system of producer cooperatives is far more in tune with Marxian thought than the call for a socio-political order resembling the Soviet model, i.e. a system that proved unable to abate alienation because of the retention of hired labour.

As Ollman puts it (1976, 132), 'without some knowledge of the future millennium, alienation remains a reproach that can never be clarified. An approach to grasping the "logical geography" involved may be made by contrasting the expressions "health" and "disease".' And this is in agreement with our belief that a reasonable amount of knowledge or some reasonable predictions about the coming millennium would shed light on ways to attenuate alienation.

The labour theory of value and alienation in Marx's *Grundrisse*

The view that democratic firm management reduces alienation is supported by a number of passages from the *Grundrisse* which trace alienation to different causes (see Fetscher, 2008).[12]

One of these passages runs as follows (Marx, 1857–58, vol. II, 278):

> And this is labour for Smith, a curse. 'Tranquillity' appears as the adequate stage, as identical with 'freedom' and 'happiness' It seems quite far from Smith's mind that the individual, in his 'normal state of health, strength, activity, skill, facility', also needs a normal portion of work, and of the suspension of tranquillity. Certainly, labour obtains its measure from the outside, through the aim to be attained and the obstacles to be overcome in attaining it. But Smith has no inkling whatever that this overcoming of obstacles is in itself a liberating activity – and that, further, the external aims become stripped of the semblance of merely external natural urgencies, and become posited as aims which the individual himself posits – hence as self-realization, objectification of the subject, hence real freedom, whose action is, precisely, labour.

This means that work is a basic constituent of life. But what kind of work does Marx rate as free?

Another quote from *Grundrisse* (1857–1958, 90–91) may help us forward:

> But in the degree in which large scale industry develops the creation of real wealth becomes less dependent upon labour time and the quantity of labour employed than upon the power of agents set in motion during labour time', 'but depends, rather, upon the general level of development of science and the progress of technology, or on the application of science to production.' At this step of economic development, 'labour no longer appears so much as included in the production process, but rather man relates himself to that process as its overseer and regulator.' While this process of change is under way, 'it is the development of the social individual that appears as the cornerstone of production and wealth' and drives the free growth of individuality, in terms of reducing 'the necessary labour of society to a minimum, to which then

corresponds the artistic, scientific, etc., development of individuals, made possible by the time thus set free and the means produced for all of them.

A major point emphasised by Marx in the *Grundrisse* is that commodities were still priced by reference to the amount of socially required labour time irrespective of the fact that wealth was increasingly generated by science and less so by work. In the opinion of Napoleoni (1985, 76), the resulting incongruity can be explained as follows:

> on the one hand, the fact that capital realises the whole of the exchange value explains why wealth is still determined by reference to the labour time required; on the other hand, upon the introduction of machinery labour time ceases being the assumption for the production of wealth, for this is now mainly governed by science and organisation.

As a result, the point to be clarified is whether science goes to reinforce capital or labour. With respect to capitalistic systems, Marx's answer is that science ultimately adds to misery and exploitation since its benefits are reaped by capital only. And from his perspective, the very fact that productivity gains flowing from scientific progress are never cashed by the majority of the production community, i.e. workers, is an additional factor likely to hasten the advent of a revolutionary crisis.

Turning more specifically to the alienation issue, a close look at the *Grundrisse*, at the excerpts from pages 90–91 quoted above, suggests that the assumptions for relieving man from fatigue are created by progress in machine building first and advancements in automation later. For this reason, Marx held that even at the capitalistic stage of society 'the best-possible proxy for this emancipated mode of production is an orchestra where each player simultaneously looks at himself as part of a whole – as a co-producer of the symphony which, for example, is being performed' (Fetscher, 2008, 113). In other words, according to Fetscher, in Marx's *Grundrisse* work is only described as free provided it is socialised and provided the workers concerned have freely chosen to work in association (see Fetscher, 2008, 112),

Ultimately, Fetscher's conclusion is that any work that is done in a cooperative firm is to be classed as free and that this applies to cooperatives operating in market economies as well.

Dissenting from Fetscher's approach, we do not think that the foregoing excerpts from the *Grundrisse* are to be construed as suggesting that the more mature Marx envisaged the possibility of free work in a market economy. As this conclusion would be at odds with other statements by Marx (including the passage quoted at the beginning of this section),[13] his arguments can at most be accepted as a 'revised' Marxist view.

Concluding, there are reasons for arguing that alienation would only be rooted out at an advanced stage of economic development, when incomes soar to levels at which full employment is a thing achieved, people are no longer obliged to work for their mere subsistence and decisions are jointly made in line with the 'one-man-one-vote' principle. And there is little denying that alienation is not only a descriptive notion, but a call for revolutionary change (in the direction of de-alienation) (see Petrovich, 1991, 11).[14]

The two stages of revolution theorised by Marx

According to Bigo, the need to distinguish between two stages within communism was one of the thorniest issues facing Marx. His aim, he argued, was 'to provide evidence that communism would sweep away alienation in man despite the retention of some forms of value at least at the first stage. On closer analysis, he had actually set himself a very difficult task' (1953, 111) and it will be interesting to examine how he tackled and solved this problem.

Aware that communism could not be achieved within a short timeframe, he postulated a very slow process designed to dismantle inequalities and social constraints while making it absolutely clear that the precondition for its inception was a kind of growth of productive forces that even advanced countries had failed to achieve to his day. The solution worked out by Marx provided for the retention of private property and hired labour throughout the transition period. In the estimation of Bigo (1953, 111), Marx had no option but to maintain – and this is the weak point – that the reason why private property as an institution, wages and salaries as its necessary assumption and the right to freely dispose of the relevant proceeds would no longer cause any alienation was that alienation is a condition specific to capitalistic production.

Bigo has emphasised Marx's firm belief that alienation, far from being caused by the existence of hired labour, the valuation of commodities by reference to abstract value or the existence of money, rests on the fact that prices are determined by the interplay between consumers and competing manufacturers, rather than fixed in lucid decision-making processes. This, he argued, is why a mature Marxian work such as the *Critique of the Gotha Programme* envisages the establishment of a centrally planned system with jointly owned production means, i.e. a social order abolishing the interchange of products between manufacturers.

Quoting Marx (1875, 960):

> Within the collective society based on common ownership of the means of production, the producers do not exchange their products; just as little does the labour employed on the products appear here as the value of these products, as a material quality possessed by them, since now, in contrast to the capitalistic society, individual labour no longer exists in an indirect fashion, but directly as a component part of the total labour.[15]

In Marx's view, in the centrally planned economy that was to rise from the ashes of a capitalistic society, an economy which is 'still stamped with the birthmarks of the older society from whose womb it emerges' (Marx, 1875, 960), each worker would be given a slip stating the amount of work he had performed and this slip would then be used by the worker to purchase commodities in a total cost equalling the value of the hours worked by him. Accordingly, Marx concluded, each worker would ultimately be remunerated with the same amount of labour he/she had contributed to society.

In terms of distribution, therefore, the transitional social order would be governed by the same principle 'as that which regulates the exchange of commodities' (Marx, 1875, 961); a principle which, though not envisaging any class distinctions, would tacitly acknowledge 'the unequal individual endowment and thus productive capacity of the workers as natural privileges' (Marx, 1875, 961) by providing higher remuneration rates for forms of skilled labour (which Marx termed 'complex labour' consisting of multiples of 'simple labour').

The centrally planned system that Marx had in mind at the time he wrote the *Critique of the Gotha Programme* is basically the system which ruinously collapsed in the Soviet Union and Eastern countries. And although it is widely held that we need not concern ourselves with the planned system imagined by Marx, for the purposes of this paper it is interesting to establish where Marx's error in judgment lies.

As was made clear by the socialist calculation debate in the 1930s, Marx's error was to assume that markets could somehow be imitated or used without the concomitant introduction of competition. An additional misjudgement was his belief that the value of complex labour could be determined without allowing markets full play, i.e. without leaving it up to the market to determine the values of individual production activities. Moreover, his claim that alienation would be eradicated in a planned system with markets and money but without competition is barely convincing. In point of fact, the precondition for cancelling alienation is putting an end to scarcity, as mentioned above.

On closer analysis, the heart of the matter is this: if the aim is to induce workers to offer the work output levels that are expected of them there are only two options: introducing competition or the commands of a planning board. A third option simply does not exist.[16] And in either case labour would not be free, but alienated.

Moreover, Marx held that the severest form of fetishism was associated with money (Marx, 1867, 187):

> We have already seen, from the simplest expression of value, x commodity A = y commodity B, that the thing in which the magnitudo of the value of another thing is represented appears to have the equivalent form independently of this relation. We followed the process by which this false semblance became firmly established, a process which was completed when the universal equivalent form became identified with the natural form of a particular commodity, and thus crystallized into the money form.

Be that as it may, since a centrally planned economy does not abolish money, it will retain the severest form of fetishism as a matter of course.

As a result, Bigo's approach is wrong for a number of reasons, including the fact that nowhere in the *Critique of the Gotha Programme* did Marx claim that this centrally planned system was expected to sweep away alienation within a few days of the end of capitalism.[17]

Notes

1 Zolo (1974) has argued that the dirigiste model founded on centralisation was of Engels's rather than Marx's making.
2 A book which describes cooperation as a tendency of human nature and a mode of organising social institutions striving to work out a solution to present crises is Ratner (2009).
3 For Marx's ideas on firms run by workers, see Jossa (2005).
4 Our emphasis on equating the transition from capitalism to a system of producer cooperatives with a real and proper revolution is justified by the awareness that Marxists have always refused to concoct 'recipes for a hypothetical future', i.e. to offer a clear outline of the social order they think will take the place of capitalism. Although Kautsky and many later Marxist theorists were strongly critical of the system that had emerged from the Russian revolution, they did not make it clear how those inimical to the Soviet-type central planning model were to picture to themselves a socialist order (for the Kautsky's silence on this point, see Geary, 1974, pp. 93–94).
5 Numerous authors endorse the notion that this new production mode will arise out of capitalism. Among them, let us mention C. Offe, who stresses the structural incompatibility, within capitalist society, of new sub-systems or structural elements which functionally conflict with the logic of capital valorisation (see Offe, 1972, Chapter 3).
6 In *Antidühring* (1878, p. 642), Engels maintained that following the emergence of joint-stock companies and trusts 'the bourgeoisie demonstrated to be a superfluous class'.
7 In a well-known monograph about alienation theory, Mészàros wrongly equated Marxian alienated labour with wage labour straightaway (see Mészàros 1970, Chapter IV).
8 For an interesting and exhaustive analysis of this point, see Reich and Devine (1981).
9 In an analysis of various degrees of alienation, Sobel (2008) argues that alienation would be extending right into the early stages of the new social order.
10 Interesting historical approaches to the notion of alienation include those by McLellan (1978, 50–52) and Petrovich (1991, 11–16).
11 This particular point of Marxian theory has been addressed, *inter alia*, by Ollman and Hochshild. The former holds that people view one another through the lens of markets in all social relations (Ollman, 1976) and the latter has argued that man under capitalism is alienated even outside of the sphere of material production (see, for example, Hochschild, 1983, 202).
12 As is well known, the most innovative parts of the *Grundrisse* are those concerned with the relations between Marx and Hegel and with alienation (see, *inter alia*, Musto, 2008a, 185).
13 In part, this conclusion is necessitated by the fact that Marx never published the *Grundrisse*, which either raised 'questions that are beyond solution' or developed analyses 'which are not brought to any clear-cut conclusions' (Tronti, 2008, 232).
14 The 'citizenship income' scheme proposed by Sabattini in a recent publication (2009) would be a great stride forward in the direction of abating alienation levels. From our perspective, the ideal solution would be a society founded on democratic firm management and payment of citizen incomes.
15 This recalls Engels's argument that only 'within those social forms in which commodities are not exchanged' could we speak of value (Engels, 1890–1891, 460).

16 Economists think it sign of immaturity or poor intelligence to criticise markets and bureaucracy at the same stroke (see, *inter alia*, Lindbeck, 1972 and Samuelson's introduction to Lindbeck's book, pp. XIII and XIV).

17 In point of fact, Bigo's approach would seem to be validated by the following excerpt from Marx: 'Freedom, in this sphere, can consist only in this, that socialized man, the associated producers, govern the human metabolism with nature in a rational way, bringing it under their collective control instead of being dominated by it as a blind power' (Marx, 1894, 923). Roberts and Stephenson (1970, 196–197) cite this same passage in support of their claim that Marx held centralised planning to cancel alienation (though not the division of labour, as mentioned before) by purging markets of their impersonal and non-manageable mechanisms. But just a few lines before this passage, Marx wrote: 'the realm of freedom really begins only where labour determined by necessity and external expediency ends; it lies, by its very nature, beyond the sphere of material production proper'. As a result, it is possible to argue that both Bigo and Roberts and Stephenson have failed to realise that in Marx's approach it is only labour that is freely undertaken for the sake of the pleasure it offers, and not also work done for earning one's daily bread, that is classified as non-alienated.

Bibliography

Bahro, R. (1977). *Eine Dokumentation*. Frankfurt: Europäische Verlagsanstalt.

Bettelheim, C. (1969). Sulla transizione tra capitalismo e socialismo. In *Monthly Review*, Italian edition, March–April, pp. 6–9.

Bigo, P. (1953). *Marxismo e umanismo*, Italian Translation. Milan: Bompiani, 1963.

Bottomore, T. (ed.) (1991). *A Dictionary of Marxist Thought*, 2nd edition. Oxford: Blackwell, pp. 23–30.

Brewer, A. (2002). The Marxist Tradition in the History of Economics. In Weintraub, 2002.

Engels, F. (1878). *Anti-Dühring*. In Marx and Engels, *Collected Works*, vol. 25.

Engels, F. (1890–1891). In the Case of Brentano versus Marx. Regarding Alleged Falsification of Quotation. In Marx and Engels, *Collected Works*, vol. 27.

Fetscher, I. (2008). Emancipated Individuals in an Emancipated Society; Marx's Sketch of Post-Capitalist Society in the 'Grundrisse'. In Musto, 2008b.

Geary, R.J. (1974). Difesa e deformazione del marxismo in Kautsky. In Istituto Giangiacomo Feltrinelli, 1974.

Hobsbawm, E.J. (1979). La cultura europea e il marxismo fra Otto e Novecento. In Hobsbawm *et al.*, 1978–1982, vol. II.

Hobsbawn, E.J., Haupt, G., Marek, F., Ragionieri, E., Strada, V. and Vivanti, C. (eds) (1978–1982). *Storia del marxismo*, 5 vol. Turin: Einaudi.

Hochschild, A. R. (1983). *The Managed Heart: Commercialization of Human Feeling*. Berkeley: University of California Press.

Istituto Giangiacomo Feltrinelli (1974). *Storia del marxismo contemporaneo*. Milan: Feltrinelli.

Jossa, B. (2005). Marx, Marxism and the Cooperative Movement. *Cambridge Journal of Economics,* vol. 1, January, pp. 3–18.

Jossa, B. (2014). *A System of Cooperative firms as a New Production Mode*. London: Routledge.

Lindbeck, A. (1972). *The Political Economy of the New Left: an Outsider's View*. New York: Joanna Cotler Books.

Lukàcs, G. (1972). *L'uomo e La rivoluzione*, Italian Translation. Rome: Editori Riuniti, 1973.

Marek, F. (1982). Teorie della rivoluzione e fasi della transizione. In Hobsbawn *et al.*, 1978–1982.

Marx, K. (1844). *Economic and Philosophic Manuscripts of 1844*. In Marx and Engels, *Collected Works*, vol. 3.

Marx, K. (1857–1858). Economic Manuscripts of 1857–58. In Marx and Engels, *Collected Works*, vols. 28 and 29.

Marx, K. (1863–1866). *Il capitale: libro I, capitolo VI inedito*, Italian translation. Florence: La Nuova Italia, 1969.

Marx, K. (1864). Inaugural Address of the Working Men's International Association. In Marx and Engels, *Collected Works*, vol. 20.

Marx, K. (1867). *Capital*, vol. I. Harmondsword: Penguin Books, 1986.

Marx, K. (1875). *Critica al programma di Gotha*. In Marx and Engels, 1966.

Marx, K. (1894). *Capital*, vol. III. Harmondsworth: Penguin Books, 1981.

Marx, K. and Engels, F. (1966). *Opere scelte*, ed. by L. Gruppi. Rome: Editori Riuniti.

Marx, K. and Engels, F. *Collected Works*. London: Lawrence & Wishart.

McLellan, D. (1978). La concezione materialistica della storia. In Hobsbawm *et al.*, 1978–1982.

Mèszàros, I. (1970). *La teoria dell'alienazione in Marx*, Italian translation. Rome: Editori Riuniti, 1976.

Mèszàros, I. (1995). *Beyond Capital*. London: Merlin Press.

Mill, J. S. (1871). *Principi di economia politica*, 3rd edition, Italian translation. Turin: UTET, 1953.

Musto, M. (2008a). Dissemination and Reception of the *Grundrisse* in the World. In Musto, 2008b.

Musto, M. (ed.) (2008b). *Karl Marx's Grundrisse*. London: Routledge.

Napoleoni, C. (1985). *Discorso sull'economia politica*. Turin: Boringhieri.

Negt, O. (1978). L'ultimo Engels. In Hobsbawm *et al.*, 1978–1982.

Offe, C. (1972). *Lo Stato nel capitalismo maturo*, Italian translation. Milan: Etas Libri, 1977.

Ollman, B. (1976). *Alienation; Marx's Conception of Man in Capitalistic Society*, 2nd edition. Cambridge: Cambridge University Press.

Ollman, B. (ed.) (1998a). *Market Socialism: the Debate among Socialists*. London: Routledge.

Ollman, B. (1998b). Market Mystification in Capitalist and Market Socialist Societies. In Ollman, 1998a.

Pellicani, L. (1976). Socialismo ed economia di mercato. *Mondoperaio*, June, pp. 7–14.

Petrovich, G. (1991). Alienation. In Bottomore, 1991.

Ratner, C., (2009). Cooperativism: A Social, Economic and Political Alternative to Capitalism. *Capitalism, Nature, Socialism*, vol. 20, n. 2, pp. 44–73.

Reich, M. and Devine, J. (1981). The Microeconomics of Conflict and Hierarchy in Capitalist Production. *Review of Radical Political Economics*, vol. 12, January, pp. 27–45.

Roberts, P.C. and Stephenson, M.A. (1970). A Note on Marxian Alienation. Reprinted in Wood, 1988.

Rodinson, M. (1969). Sociologia marxista e ideologia marxista. In Spinella, 1969.

Rubel, M. (1974). *Marx critique du marxisme. Essais*. Paris: Payot.

Sabattini, G. (2009). *Welfare State; nascita, evoluzione e crisi. Le prospettive di riforma*. Milan: F. Angeli.

Severino, E. (2012). *Capitalismo senza futuro*. Milan: Rizzoli.

Sobel, R. (2008). Travail et justice dans la société communiste chez Marx. Un commentaire à propos de quelques ambiguïtés naturalistes de 'l'etage du bas' de La 'phase superieure' du communisme. *Économies et Sociétés*, vol. 40, n. 5, pp. 20–34.

Spinella, M. (ed.) (1969). *Marx Vivo*. Milan: Mondadori.

Tronti, M. (2008). Dissemination and Reception of the *Grundrisse* in the World: Italy. In Musto, 2008b.

Vanek, J. (1970). *The General Theory of Labour-Managed Market Economies*. Ithaca: Cornell University Press.

Vanek, J. (1971a). Some Fundamental Considerations on Financing and the Form of Ownership under Labor Management. Reprinted in Vanek, 1977.

Vanek, J. (1971b). The Basic Theory of Financing of Participatory Firms. Reprinted in Vanek, 1977.

Vanek, J. (1977). *The Labor Managed Economy: Essays by J. Vanek*. Ithaca: Cornell University Press.

Walras, L. (1860). *L'économie politique et La justice; examen critique et réfutation des doctrines économiques de M. P.J. Proudhon*. Paris: Guillaumin.

Ward, B. (1958). The Firm in Illyria: Market Syndicalism. *American Economic Review*, vol. 48, n. 4.

Weintraub, E.R. (2002). *The Future of the History of Economics*. Durban and London: Duke University Press.

Wood, J.C. (ed.) (1988). *Karl Marx's Economics: Critical Assessments*. New South Wales: Croom Helm.

Zolo, D. (1974). *La teoria comunista dell'estinzione dello Stato*. Bari: De Donato.

27 Institutions, economies, technologies

Two Italian founders (1821–1921)

Alberto Quadrio Curzio[1]

Introduction

I would like to express my gratitude to Heinz Kurz for having been invited to contribute to the volume in honour of a man and an economist who deserves much appreciation, Neri Salvadori.

Choosing the subject, however, has not been easy. I was tempted by various alternatives: a theoretical contribution on structural dynamics with scarce resources along my long-standing line of research; an analysis of Salvadori's most important theoretical contributions; a consideration of some Italians that I have defined as 'institutional economists' who in the nineteenth and twentieth centuries contributed significantly to building an industrialized nation thanks to their broad vision and innovative implementations. I chose the last option, because the first would have been a review of my previous, well-known, works while the second would have required an effort that I cannot undertake at the moment. Moreover, the third solution is related to one of my long-standing interests in the historical roots of economic development. The analysis here proposed has two topical aspects. The first regards Italian industrial development, which 150 years after national unification, has not yet spread to the whole country. I have already devoted considerable attention to industrial and technologically-applied economics in my works.[2] The second is to place, within an international setting, such as this book in honour of Neri Salvadori, the role of two eclectic personalities who marked Italian institutional and economic history during the Italian *Risorgimento* and the period which immediately followed the unification of Italy.

While my contribution is not theoretical, in my opinion, it remains also coherent with Neri Salvadori's research for two reasons. First because he has always pursued an independent and original approach, when considering the importance of production and technologies without complying to the mainstream school of thought. Second, because he has devoted interesting works[3] to the relationships between social and economic institutions and growth processes. Both approaches are adopted herewith for presenting two Italians who were concretely engaged in the building of a new State and a new Economy between 1821 and 1921. They are Carlo Cattaneo (1801–1869) and Giuseppe Colombo (1836–1921). In 1821, Cattaneo was 20 years old and already very active as an original thinker; in 1921

Colombo died. It is during this century that Italy was shaped and our two personalities advanced and further expanded the ideas of Illuminists, such as Pietro Verri
(1728–1798) and Cesare Beccaria (1738–1794).[4]

Two Italian innovators in ideas and facts

Carlo Cattaneo and Giuseppe Colombo were prominent contributors to Italy's economic growth and industrialization, set within an institutional context oriented
toward the nation's conscious involvement in Europe.

They were outstanding 'architects' of Italy's economic development. Their
views were rationally systematic, rooted in the value given to innovation and
action oriented. Yet, they were neither theorists nor entrepreneurs. In my previous works, I mentioned Cattaneo and Colombo for their link to Lombardy's
Enlightenment, as men of 'rational pragmatism',[5] which in my view is the most
appropriate and concise description. In other works, with specific reference to
Colombo and personalities akin to him, I defined them as 'economic-engineers'
or 'technology-entrepreneurs'.[6] These are all valid characterizations but none are
fully inclusive of their specific economic analysis approach. Perhaps, their contributions could be connected, in general terms, to structural institutional-economic
dynamics; meaning a change in an economy caused by the interactions among
institutions, production processes, technology and market mechanisms considered
in the long run.[7]

Institutional reforms and structural dynamics

Carlo Cattaneo was, and is, one of the most important figures of the Italian
Risorgimento,[8] a period in which national political unification was coupled by
institutional and economic modernization. This process of modernization was
marked by structural dynamics with science and technology playing a crucial role
in thrusting Italy towards more developed European countries. My interest in Cattaneo is long-standing.[9] Many of his works deserve patient attention as they are
conceptually complex. In fact, Cattaneo was in Einaudi's words 'encyclopedic
(. . .) [and had a] universal mind'.[10]

Although I make reference to many of my previous works on Cattaneo, his contributions are here examined only to highlight his relevance on those issues we
aim to discuss. That is *Risorgimento* and civilizing process, or in Italian, *Incivilimento*; economic expansion founded on learning, science and technology; industry
and entrepreneurship; transport, communications and global markets. It should be
noted that the above list comprises most of the components of structural dynamics.

'Risorgimento per Incivilimento'

As a man of the *Risorgimento*, Cattaneo believed that the modernization of
Italy could be realized by absorbing 'Italian culture and material needs within a
European and even an international context'.[11] He was the ingenious successor
of the eighteenth century luminaries such as Cesare Beccaria, Pietro Verri,

Melchiorre Gioja, Gianrinaldo Carli and Gian Domenico Romagnosi. These personalities, as did Cattaneo, regarded economic policies as 'governmental instruments' suitable to guide in freedom. Furthermore, Cattaneo also believed that Europe was the appropriate arena for disseminating ideas and that Italy should belong to a common geo-economic (and in some respects geo-political) area.[12] He went even further than his eighteenth century predecessors in believing that economic growth was determined by scientific and technological advances applied to the various productive sectors and to transports. In conclusion, he can be considered a true man of the *Risorgimento* with a federalist conception of the state that was not implemented during the Italian unification process.

Civilizing process or *Incivilimento* was the core of Cattaneo's thoughts and actions. This concept, introduced by his mentor, G.D. Romagnosi (1761–1835),[13] was adopted by Cattaneo without supplying a precise definition in his article 'Ricerche economiche sulle interdizioni imposte dalla legge civile agli israeliti' (English translation: 'Economic research on interdictions imposed by civil law on Israelis').[14] According to Cattaneo, 'civilizing' is the historical process arising from human needs and the desire to command increasingly better living conditions. Progress is gradual and the ensuing results, in terms of economic development, are favoured by scientific and technological innovations and by the evolution of the existing institutions.[15]

Let us now focus on the main aspects that in Cattaneo's view should characterize economic development. My impression is that, in his view, institutions and civil society, in their various complementary components, have a relevant role, in the way Europe does when considered as an area for circulating ideas and goods. This latter view is fully developed in his considerations on European federalism.[16]

Economic development, learning, science and technology

Cattaneo's designs for economic development were specifically aimed at Lombardy but they can and must be placed in a more general framework. Accordingly, he should not be seen as supporting 'localism', since the Lombard paradigm envelopes a rich structural system covering education and science, productive sectors and entrepreneurship, transport and the international markets. However, at the same time, the reference to Lombardy is important because, if this region is one of the most developed in Europe today, it is also due to the influence of Cattaneo's paradigm.

He emphasized the crucial role of learning not only for a general education but also for preparing highly qualified professionals such as engineers, technical experts and specialized workers. In fact, his aim was 'to promote the study of sciences and perfect industrial and agricultural development by coordinating the arms of the inventors and the minds of the scholars'.[17] This is a crucial aspect of Cattaneo's paradigm of development because, in his view, the 'intellect' combined with other factors of production increases an economic system's productivity and thus generates income: 'Before every work, before any capital, when all things lie still in nature's womb, it is the intellect that shapes, and for the first time, imprints the character of wealth'.[18]

Cattaneo promoted this structural system of learning, science and technology in many ways among which through the journal he created in 1838, *Il Politecnico. Repertorio mensile di studi applicati alla prosperitá e coltura sociale* (English translation: 'The Politecnico. Monthly review of studies applied to social prosperity and culture'). The *Journal* remained under his direction until 1845, and again, when the second series was launched in 1860, until 1862.

The Politecnico is one of the best expressions of Cattaneo's paradigm because it aimed 'to provide fellow citizens with a sporadic collection of immediate knowledge of that part of truth from the arduous regions of Science that can easily be led to fertilize the field of practice and increase support and comfort to common prosperity and civil co-habitation'.[19]

The *Journal* published the results obtained from the 'intellects of the nation', as well as the scientific research, the discoveries and the initiatives for improving production and living conditions. It also called for a European-wide educational and technical training system. At the beginning of 1842, he affirmed that education and technical training 'should not be commanded by short-sighted local or national considerations ... but should conform to the broader European views for Europe to fully appreciate Italy and not compare it to a waned nation'.[20]

Productive sectors, institutions and entrepreneurship

Cattaneo emphasized the nexus between productive activities and institutions for economic development and hence for the 'civilizing process' (*Incivilimento*). In particular, institutions should promote and safeguard private property and individual initiative. This approach is not conceptual and does not correspond to *laissez faire* as it is intended today.

Cattaneo explained that, besides the favourable geological and geographical aspects of Lombardy's land, specific institutions would make it possible to appraise the land and thus the transition from land with zero value to land with a positive value. The value of cultivated land and its exploitation would further increase income and the nation's overall wealth.[21]

It is very important to consider Cattaneo's suggestion on how to speed up the agricultural progress, from the last of a number of letters that he, as requested by the Milanese government, addressed to Robert Campbell. The letters were the reply to some questions posed by the English government on the causes of the advanced system of agricultural production in northern Italy.[22] In a list that sums up the principles introduced to implement efficient agricultural production, Cattaneo stressed the relevance of the following institutional aspects: 'the promotion of full and free property rights;[23] the right to water followed by canalization and appropriate work on the land, on the basis of technical expert opinions without specific laws or parliamentary intervention';[24] a property registry; the definition of the contractual terms and standards between landowners and tenants on the basis of a code elaborated by engineers that establish rules for continuous land improvements (the principle of long-standing rent and of 'delivery and refund for improvements to the advantage of tenants'[25]); and finally, the construction of infrastructure. Cattaneo also remarked, with reference to other European countries (for example, Ireland)[26] and Italian territories (like Sardinia),[27] that a delay in economic development is mainly caused by the persistence of feudal institutions and oppressive jurisdictions.

The relevance of private property and individual initiative in economic development emerges also in the writings devoted to Lombardy's industrial development. Cattaneo considered the industrial sector as the most dynamic productive sector in a modern economy, and capable of increasing a country's productive capacity in the long run.[28] In his view, an entrepreneur has to organize and coordinate human resources, find commodities and expand the market.[29] Cattaneo also remarked that an entrepreneur should employ the capital at his disposal in production activities, even better if they are diversified, and should not indulge in 'momentary ambition' which is characteristic of speculation.[30] I consider Cattaneo a social-liberal with a strong predisposition for a real economic system.

Transport and international trade

Other issues in Cattaneo's structural dynamics paradigm are transport and communications system, access to markets and international trade.

As for the analyses and proposals of transport systems, Cattaneo adopted a broad view that took into account economic, social and demographic factors, as well as all types of distances.[31]

In contrast to engineers, who studied transportation infrastructure from a technical viewpoint, Cattaneo looked at infrastructure mainly as a choice, both economic and social, in which technological aspects must also be considered. In particular, he focused on the economic factor. In considering the costs deriving from constructing and maintaining roads, to keep expenditures low, he suggested the use of local materials while bearing in mind the environmental surroundings of where the road would be constructed. Technical innovations were obviously taken into account as well. Moreover, he emphasized the indirect advantages and returns from developing transport infrastructure: it was a propelling factor of a country's wealth. He also underscored the relevance of building roads that would connect Italy to other European countries as well as the need for a European zone.

Cattaneo showed a similar avant-garde approach in his analyses and proposals concerning international trade and markets.[32] He believed that free trade allows countries to distribute their nationally produced goods to other countries and receive goods that are not produced at home, thereby increasing a country's available wealth. Thus, creating an industry limited to a narrow national market or to adopt protectionist measures was inefficient: those

> who impose protectionist tariffs on foreign industry hold a double-edged sword, and it is hard to tell who will be harmed the most. The fence, that

halts foreign industry, holds back national industry as well; and in the end, when the whole area is caged-in, the prisoner with the smallest cage will be the worst off and live the most listless life.[33]

According to Cattaneo, free trade has two further positive effects. First, it creates anonymous foreign offshore companies: foreign capital is a factor that promotes productive activities.[34] Nonetheless, Cattaneo believed that national companies must reflect intelligence, uphold legality in business practices, and have foresight. Second, free trade develops a positive correlation between international economic integration, and the dissemination of ideas, scientific discoveries and the promotion of a better understanding of different cultures. In his view, these conditions favoured economic development for a host of nations.[35]

Two developments of the Risorgimento

As often happens when studying personalities of stature from the past, one builds paradigms that have been developed by selecting those elements which strengthen personal convictions.

Accordingly, my social liberalism paradigm – based on institutions, society and economy[36] – not only influenced my previous analyses of Cattaneo's contributions, but also deepened my convictions.

Among which is the conviction that Cattaneo continued in the tradition of Lombard Illuminists, who had among their most eminent protagonists Pietro Verri and Cesare Beccaria,[37] and had innovative ideas concerning economics and its links to institution, society, science and technology.

In our view, two streams stemmed from Cattaneo's contributions: one followed by Luigi Einaudi (1874–1961): the science of government and of political economy; the other followed by Giuseppe Colombo: the science of government and of the connection between economics and technology. Other scholars could be mentioned for further developing Cattaneo's ideas on federalism. Unfortunately, neither Einaudi's nor Colombo's streams have been fully implemented in Italy's economic development since its birth 150 years ago. Federalism, for instance, was introduced late in 2001, but it was awkwardly set in place, without solving, or perhaps even aggravating, the North/South chasm.

Of the many guidelines provided by Cattaneo, only technological progress will be considered below.

A polyvalent engineer: from science to industry

Giuseppe Colombo resumed Cattaneo's connection between technological and economic progress and strengthened it to engineering and firms. In my view, he was one of the most significant Italian 'economic-engineers' or 'technological-entrepreneurs' that ever lived between the end of the nineteenth and the beginning of the twentieth centuries.

On the basis of my previous works,[38] I will here consider three aspects of his contributions: Colombo as a scientist and technologist, as an engineer and entrepreneur, and as an institutionalist-engineer.

The training and education of the engineers

After his degree in Mathematics obtained at the University of Pavia, at the young age of twenty, Colombo devoted most, but not all, of his life to studying and teaching at two institutions that played a crucial role in Lombardy's industrialization: the Società di Incoraggiamento di Arti e Mestieri, where he taught for 26 years, from 1857 to 1883; the Politecnico di Milano, where he taught for 56 years, from 1865 to 1921, and was Rector for 24 years, from 1897 to 1921, succeeding Francesco Brioschi (1827–1897).

At the Società, where Cattaneo had also taught and had strongly influenced, Colombo was a teacher of great relevance. While there, he came into contact with the most important entrepreneurs of Milan and Lombardy and acquired their esteem.[39]

At the Politecnico, on the fiftieth anniversary of its foundation, he affirmed that his mission was to bring 'to the nation the guiding light of applied science to industry'.[40]

Colombo's teaching activity was of broad spectrum. He dealt with all branches of engineering, perhaps with a predilection for industrial mechanics and the construction of machinery; he also taught these subjects as Full Professor at the Politecnico. His book *Manuale dell'Ingegnere* (1877), edited by Hoeply, is the exemplification of his extraordinary competence and polyvalence in engineering. The handbook, with its many editions translated in many foreign languages, has become an essential instrument in the study and work of any engineer, and it is often called 'the Colombo'.

At the inaugural address held at the Politecnico of Turin in 1997, Edoardo Vesentini, a Former President of the Accademia Nazionale dei Lincei (National Lincei Academy), defined 'the Colombo' as:

> a 'Summa Ingegneristica' of all the knowledge and practice that a scholar of the Politecnico should learn – or should have learned – and would need throughout his professional life: a sort of bridge between academic knowledge and the technology that an engineer finds in his work. (...). Whoever has leafed through Colombo's handbook will find a subdivision of the various subjects studied and taught in the Engineering courses and (in part) a Degree in Architecture: Math, Mechanics, Electro-techniques [...], a teaching that was addressed, as much as possible, to a wide public, made up not only of engineering and architecture students, but also students pursuing other degrees (Mathematics, Physics, ...).[41]

Moreover, convinced that the applied activity of an engineer was a necessary part of an education in engineering and that students had to become familiar with executing industrial projects, Colombo organized visits to industrial plants in Italy and foreign countries, and, as we can see below, encouraged students to undertake planning and projects.

The industrial culture

To carry out his mission and bring to 'the country the guiding light of applied science to industry', Colombo also became active in publishing. In particular, he wrote for *Il Politecnico, Annuario scientifico ed industriale, Industriale, Nuova Antologia* and *La Perseveranza*.[42]

He became the editor of *Il Politecnico* in 1866 and contributed, with Brioschi, to renovating and shifting the focus of the *Journal* and providing more room for engineering issues as opposed to the liberal arts.[43] This change, that also led to the merger of *Il Politecnico* and *Giornale dell'Ingegnere*, did not stop Colombo from dropping his economic engineering approach. Evidence of his continued interest in economics can be seen in his articles in *La Perseveranza*. Published in October–December 1861, one of his most famous articles analyses the Italian Industry Exhibition organized in Florence that same year. In this article, Colombo developed the main precepts of his necessary features for industrial development, precepts he would adhere to throughout his life.[44] On the same matter, his contributions to *Nuova Antologia* were equally important, for example *Le industrie meccaniche italiane all'Esposizione di Torino* (1898) and *I progressi dell'elettrotecnica in Italia* (1900).[45]

His many scientific and technical contributions will not be discussed here, but it is worthy of mention that many of his works appeared in the proceedings of the Istituto Lombardo – Accademia di Scienze e Lettere (Lombard Institute – Academy of Sciences and Liberal Arts) and of the Accademia Nazionale dei Lincei, two institutions to which he dedicated much effort.[46]

An innovative entrepreneur

Colombo was a Schumpeterian entrepreneur for many years.[47]

In 1872, with Eugenio Cantoni and Colin MacKenzie, he founded the Cantoni–Colombo–MacKenzie company for the planning and procurement (also by importing from foreign countries) of industrial machinery (steam fuelled machines for the paper and food industries ... only to mention a few). The firm likewise promoted and disseminated information of new machineries and technologies for entrepreneurs through the journal *L'Industriale*.[48]

Colombo also backed the business start-ups of two Lombard businessmen who would become leaders of entrepreneurship. One was the Cotonificio Cantoni, founded by Eugenio Cantoni in 1872.[49] The firm gave an important contribution to Lombardy's industrialization, also thanks to the support of the Cantoni–Colombo–Mackenzie company mentioned above.

The second was the firm established by Giovan Battista Pirelli in 1872. Colombo, who contributed as stakeholder at the beginning,[50] became a member of the board of directors and then a statutory auditor.[51] Giovan Battista Pirelli, who had had Colombo as a professor at the Politecnico of Milan from where he graduated in Engineering in 1870, was strongly influenced by him. As a matter of fact, it was Colombo who had encouraged him to study rubber production and financially supported his travels abroad for study and training.

Finally, Colombo contributed to the founding of Società Edison, and became the *dominus* of the company for the first 40 years. From 1877, when his interest in electricity began, to 1921, Edison was one of the main concerns of his professional activity.

Colombo, on the basis of his scientific and technical analyses, became convinced that progress in electro-techniques would make lighting possible for considerable distances as well as for extended areas. When he examined Thomas Edison's system at the International Paris Exhibition in 1881, he became determined to introduce and apply it to Italy.[52] Thereafter, in the autumn of 1881, he created a Committee for the application of an electricity-grid in Italy. He invited an Edison collaborator to Milan for economic and technical expertise then he negotiated with the Edison Continental companies for an exclusive license of Edison's patent for Italy. He obtained it in July 1881.[53] Later, he went to the US and met Edison, and brought another of Edison's collaborators to Italy.[54]

A brief overview of Edison's first developments in Italy is here proposed for two reasons. Colombo's professional life and the Edison in Italy are linked for 44 years. He was the managing director of the company from 1844 to 1891 and then its President from 1896 until his death in 1921, and he dedicated the five years in between to political activity (see the next section). Also, the Edison was the most important innovative entrepreneurial initiative undertaken by Colombo.

Starting as a single electricity company, it has become, through shareholdings in other electricity companies, the front line of many local electricity companies. This development has, on the one hand, reduced Edison's overall administrative costs and, on the other hand, favoured the spread of electricity services to small territories.

Moreover, Edison has become a sort of 'mixed' industrial and financial company. This also explains the close contacts, first, with the Banca Commerciale Italiana and, then, with the Credito Italiano.[55] Since the creation of the Committee promoting the Edison electricity system in Italy, Colombo involved many bankers from the Milanese financial circles: Enrico Rava, director of the Milan branch of the Banca Generale and later its general director; Giuseppe Crespi, managing director of the Credito Lombardo; Pacifico Cavalieri, a banker from Ferrara; representatives of the Banca di Milano, Banca di Credito Italiano, Banca Generale and Banca Villa. Thus, the relations between the Edison and the banks were constant and fruitful. On this, one should mention that Colombo was President of the Credito Italiano from 1909 to 1921.

An institutional economist-engineer

His roles as a local administrator in Milan and a politician at the national level, where he became Minister and, then, President of Parliament (Chamber of Deputies), complete our examination of Colombo's contributions to the development of Italy.

Considering his political contributions is relevant in order to emphasize aspects of his dual role as an institutional-engineer and an economist-engineer.

As an engineer, Colombo saw the benefits of science and technology for industrial development. Similarly, in his public role, he conceived laws and a fiscal system to foster economic development. He was a city councilman in Milan from 1881–1889. In 1885, as member of the Committee for the new Regulatory Plan, he advanced technical solutions to deal with problems arising from the rapid urban growth and the creation of new urban areas, sewer systems and aqueducts.[56] His proposals were characterized by accuracy, typical of the engineer, and creativity, typical of an architect dedicated to civil and economic aspects of development.

In 1886, he was elected to the Chamber of Deputies, on the liberal moderates party ticket (also defined neo-conservative by some). Colombo represented the interests of Lombard entrepreneurs that were different from the agrarian interests upheld by the conservatives. In Parliament, he distinguished himself for his criticism of inadequate technical teaching in schools and for denouncing the fiscal policies of the Leftist governments.[57]

In February 1891, he became Minister of Finance in Antonio Di Rudinì's government. He resigned in May 1892, refusing to introduce new taxes to finance military expenditure.[58] He then opposed Francesco Crispi because he disagreed with the fiscal policy proposals and colonial expansionism.

On 15 November 1899 he was elected President of the Italian Parliament and had to deal with 'extreme' filibustering against the special laws proposed by Luigi Pelloux. He was re-elected on 2 April 1900 and dissolved the Assembly because of the flare-up from the filibustering. He was elected once again on 3 June 1900, but not from his electoral constituency. When, on 11 November 1900, he was nominated Senator, he became a member of the Senate Finance Committee, and continued to work on fiscal matters.[59]

A founder

Vilfredo Pareto defined Colombo as 'a man of talent and true value', while Francesco Nitti considered him the only 'really modern' member of a Right-wing party.[60] In truth, his political predisposition is not particularly relevant if we consider that his ability to actively promote technological innovation and industrial and economic growth are the main aspects that make him an emblematic figure of a new conception of Italian development.

My aim with this contribution is to reveal a personality who is not well known today, as is the case of Quintino Sella (1827–1884), especially among economists. He was, as I have described him on other occasions, an engineer, a scientist, a statesman, a technologist and an economist.[61]

Concluding remarks

In Italy, there have been and there are streams of thought and practices that can be considered coherent with the approach of the two 'architects' of economic development here considered. However, it is not possible to consider them here because increasing specialization makes it difficult to pin down polyvalent figures such as Cattaneo and Columbo. Nonetheless, there are some men who in some respect have the same stature of Cattaneo and/or Colombo in the sense that they made remarkable political contributions acting in their sectorial professionalism. The link between the vision *á la* Cattaneo and those more concentrated in a specific field is Luigi Einaudi (1874–1961) whose latitudinous intellect is an exemplary expression of the continuity of Italian political thought. Other personages worthy of mention are Bonaldo Stringher (1854–1930), Alberto Beneduce (1877–1944), Raffaele Mattioli (1895–1973), Donato Menichella (1896–1984), Pasquale Saraceno (1903–1991), Enrico Mattei (1906–1962), Enrico Cuccia (1907–2000) and Giudo Carli (1914–1993). There are of course other renowned men who are alive today and who could be added to the list.

The choice of names might seem risky, and perhaps it is. These distinguished men were born either in the second half of the nineteenth century or the first decade of the twentieth century. They all lived influenced by the civil ethics of the *Risorgimento* that, for some of them, concretely translated into Republican Reconstruction. They all had a structural concept of political economy in which economic (in particular industrial growth with a focus on technological innovation) and finance were complementary and not alternatives. They were all conscious that overcoming the existing territorial dualism was the last step toward national unification. I have written of some of these personalities,[62] I hope to write of others since in all of them I can identify a vision of complementarity between institutions, society and economic growth and in none a reductive bipolar economy of State and market. When using my paradigm, all those mentioned seem to belong to rational pragmatism and social liberalism which represent, in my view, the distinctive element of Italian national unification and its openness toward Europe.

Notes

1 I would like to thank Ilaria Pasotti for her useful suggestions and for the English translation with the assistance of Micaela Tavasani. The usual caveats apply.
2 For example: Quadrio Curzio and Fortis (eds), 2000a,b, 2005, 2006, 2008, and 2014.
3 Salvadori and Opocher (eds.), 2009; Salvadori, Commendatore and Tamberi (eds.), 2009; Salvadori (ed.), 2010.
4 Quadrio Curzio and Scazzieri, 2008.
5 Quadrio Curzio, 2007.
6 Quadrio Curzio, 1995.
7 Quadrio Curzio and Scazzieri, 1990.
8 There is no equivalent English word that fully captures the definition that is a period leading to unification of Italy in 1861.
9 See: Quadrio Curzio, 2007b; Quadrio Curzio, 2013a.
10 Einaudi, 1939, 10.
11 Bertolino, 1956, 358.
12 Quadrio Curzio, 1996.
13 Romagnosi was the author of: *Dell'indole e dei fattori dell'incivilimento, con esempio del suo risorgimento in Italia* (1832).
14 'Now Eastern Europe is that area where the capacity for growth and the desired growth rate of the population is much greater, because space is extremely abbundant and

the civilizing process is recent and superficial' ('Ora la parte orientale dell'Europa è quella in cui la capacità di popolarsi e l'aumento sperabile della popolazione è di gran lunga maggiore; perché lo spazio è vastissimo e l'incivilimento è ancora recente e superficiale'), Cattaneo, 1836, 178–342.

15 Cattaneo, 1836, 180.

16 Cattaneo, 1850–1855.

17 Original text: 'promuovere ad un tempo lo studio delle scienze e il perfezionamento dell'Industria e dell'Agricoltura coordinando ad un medesimo intento le braccia delli artefici e le menti delli studiosi', Cattaneo, 1846, 51.

18 Original text: 'Prima d'ogni lavoro, prima d'ogni capitale, quando le cose giacciono ancora non curate e ignote in seno alla natura, è l'intelligenza che comincia l'opera, e imprime in esse per la prima volta il carattere di ricchezza', Cattaneo, 1861, 344.

19 Original text: 'appianare ai nostri concittadini con una raccolta periodica la più pronta cognizione di quella parte di vero che dalle ardue regioni della Scienza può facilmente condursi a fecondare il campo della Pratica e crescere sussidio e conforto alla prosperità comune e alla convivenza civile', Cattaneo, 1839a, 7.

20 Original text: 'non devono essere sollecitati da anguste preoccupazioni municipali o nazionali, ma devono adeguarsi alle idee generali d'Europa perchè l'Europa intenda l'Italia e non la consideri al pari di un paese decaduto', Cattaneo, 1842, 944.

21 Einaudi wrote: 'nobody, better than Cattaneo, [has studied] more in depth the specific problem of appraising cultivated land' (Original text: 'nessuno, meglio di Cattaneo, (. . .), [ha scrutato] più a fondo un problema particolare: la edificazione della terra coltivata'), Einaudi, 1939, 10.

22 Cattaneo, 1847, 201–202.

23 Original text: 'il promovimento della piena e libera proprietà', Cattaneo, 1847, 201.

24 Original text: 'esercitata *a giudizio d'esperti*, senza leggi speciali, senza intervento parlamentario', Cattaneo, 1847, 201.

25 Original text: 'consegna e [il] *rimborso del miglioramento*, a vantaggio dei fittuari', Cattaneo, 1847, 201.

26 Cattaneo (1847), 133–204.

27 Cattaneo, 1841, 660–716.

28 Cattaneo, 1839b, 252–253.

29 See Cattaneo, 1839b, 252.

30 Original text: 'ardimenti istantanei', Cattaneo, 1839c, 118–122.

31 Bertolino, 1956, 362–363.

32 Cattaneo, 1843, 1219–1278.

33 Original text: 'chi oppone all'industria straniera una dogana protettiva, impugna un'arme a due tagli, e non può dirsi se nuocerà più ad altri o a sé. Il recinto, che arresta i passi dell'industria straniera, arresta anche quelli della nazionale; e infine del conto quando tutto lo spazio è ripartito in recinti, sta peggio e vive più languida vita quel prigioniero che ha il recinto più angusto', Cattaneo, 1843, 1271.

34 Cattaneo, 1839d, 163–165.

35 Cattaneo, 1843, 1219–1278.

36 See Quadrio Curzio, 2002.

37 Quadrio Curzio and Scazzieri, 1992; Quadrio Curzio, 2007b.

38 Quadrio Curzio, 2007d.

39 See Lacaita (ed.), 1985, 14.

40 See Lacaita (ed.), 1985, 467.

41 Original text: '. . . una "Summa Ingegneristica" di quasi tutto ciò che l'allievo del Politecnico aveva appreso – o avrebbe dovuto apprendere – e di gran parte di quello di cui avrebbe avuto bisogno nell'intero arco della sua vita professionale: una specie di tramite fra la preparazione universitaria di base e la tecnologia che l'ingegnere avrebbe trovato nel suo lavoro. (. . .). Chi avesse sfogliato il manuale del Colombo, vi avrebbe

trovato una ripartizione fra le varie discipline coltivate nei corsi di laurea in ingegneria e (almeno in parte) di architettura: Matematica, Meccanica, Elettrotecnica [...] espressione di una didattica che si rivolgeva, nei limiti del possibile, ad un uditorio allargato, costituito non solo dagli allievi di ingegneria e di architettura, ma anche dagli studenti di altri corsi di laurea (matematica, fisica, ...)', quoted in Quadrio Curzio, 2007d, 162.

42 See Lacaita (ed.), (1985).
43 See Lacaita (ed.), (1985).
44 See Lacaita (ed.), 1985.
45 On this see also Scherillo, 1921.
46 See Quadrio Curzio, 2007d, 164–165.
47 See Lacaita (ed.), 1985, 39.
48 See Lacaita (ed.), 1985, 42; Cambria, 1982, 217.
49 See Cambria, 1982, 217
50 See Lacaita (ed.), 1985, 42.
51 See Cambria, 1982, 216.
52 See Lacaita (ed.), 1985, 48 and following.
53 See Cambria, 1982, 217.
54 See Lacaita (ed.), 1985, 50.
55 See Lacaita (ed.), 1985, 80.
56 See Cambria, 1982, 219.
57 See Lacaita (ed.), 1985.
58 See Lacaita (ed.), 1985.
59 See Lacaita (ed.), 1985.
60 See Lacaita (ed.), 1985, 7.
61 After obtaining a degree in Hydraulic Engineering at the University of Turin in 1847, he studied in France, German and England, where he became interested in manufacturing. He returned to Turin in 1852 where he first became a teacher at the Regio Istituto Tecnico and then professor at the University. His interests were in science and its applications but he also gave an important contributions to mathematics, mineralogy, crystallography, and in the policy of science and technique. He contributed, both directly and indirectly, to the foundation of the Politecnical Universities of Turin and Milan, and he reorganized the Science Faculty of the University of Rome. Also, he played a crucial role in the re-founding the Lincei National Academy between 1870 and 1873. As a statesman, he played a fundamental role as Finance Minister (March–December 1862; September 1864–December 1865; December 1869–July 1873) by contributing to balancing the national budget (even though it was achieved after the end of his term in office), which was essential for the nation's stability (Quadrio Curzio, 2013b).
62 Quadrio Curzio, 1992; Quadrio Curzio and Rotondi, 2007, 2012.

Bibliography

Bertolino, A. (1956). 'Introduzione' in C. Cattaneo (1956), *Scritti economici*, republished in Barucci, P. (ed.) (1979). *Scritti e lezioni di storia del pensiero economico*. Milan: Giuffrè, 357–366.

Cambria, R. (1982). 'Giuseppe Colombo', in *Dizionario biografico degli italiani*. *Vol. XXVII*. Rome: Istituto dell'Enciclopedia Italiana.

Cattaneo, C. (1836). 'Ricerche economiche sulle interdizioni imposte dalla legge civile agli israeliti', in Cattaneo, C. [1956, 178–342].

Cattaneo, C. (1839a). 'Prefazione al primo volume del "Politecnico"', in Cattaneo, C. [1989, 7–11].

Cattaneo, C. (1839b). 'Della beneficenza pubblica', in Cattaneo, C. [1956, 223–255].

Cattaneo, C. (1839c). 'La scienza dei conti', in Cattaneo, C. [1989, 118–122].

Cattaneo, C. (1839d). 'Andamento di alcune compagnie anonime straniere', in Cattaneo, C. [1956, 163–165].

Cattaneo, C. (1841). 'Di varie opere sulla Sardegna', in Cattaneo, C. [1989, 660–716].

Cattaneo, C. (1842). 'Prefazione al volume quinto del 'Politecnico'', in Cattaneo C. [1989, 991–994].

Cattaneo, C. (1843). 'Sistema nazionale d'Economia Politica', in Cattaneo, C. [1989, 1219–1278].

Cattaneo, C. (1846). 'Le scuole industriali della Cassa d'Incoraggiamento d'Arti e Mestieri', in Cattaneo, C. [2002, 47–51].

Cattaneo, C. (1847), 'D'alcune istituzioni agrarie dell'Alta Italia applicabili a sollievo dell'Irlanda. Lettere a Roberto Campbell', in Cattaneo, C. [1939, 133–204].

Cattaneo, C. (1850–1855). *Archivio triennale delle cose d'Italia dall'avvenimento di Pio IX all'abbandono di Venezia.* Capolago: Tip. Elvetica Chieri.

Cattaneo, C. (1861). 'Del pensiero come principio d'economia pubblica', in Cattaneo C. [1956, 337–372].

Cattaneo, C. (1939). *Saggi di economia rurale* (L. Einaudi, ed.). Turin: Einaudi.

Cattaneo, C. (1956). *Scritti economici* (A. Bertolino, ed.). Florence: Le Monnier.

Cattaneo, C. (1989). *Il Politecnico: 1839–1844* (L. Ambrosoli, ed.). Turin: Bollati Boringhieri.

Cattaneo, C. (2002). *Scritti sulla Lombardia.* Milan: Mondadori.

Einaudi, L. (1939). 'Introduzione', in Cattaneo C. (1939). *Saggi di economia* rurale. Turin: Einaudi.

Lacaita, C.G. (ed.) (1985). *Giuseppe Colombo. Industria e politica nella storia d'Italia. Scritti scelti: 1862–1916.* Milan: Cariplo-Laterza.

Quadrio Curzio, A. (1992). *Pasquale Saraceno: 1903–1991* (commemoration held on March 12, 1992, at the Istituto Lombardo di Scienze e Lettere), in *Rendiconti*, vol. 126, Istituto Lombardo Accademia di Scienze e Lettere, 1994, 281–290, republished in Quadrio Curzio, A. [2007a, 266–280].

Quadrio Curzio, A., (1995). 'Gli ingegneri-economisti e i tecnologi-imprenditori nello sviluppo lombardo', in *Milano e La Lombardia nella civiltà nazionale*, Lezioni dell'Istituto Lombardo di Scienze e lettere 1994/95. Milan: Istituto Lombardo, 169–183.

Quadrio Curzio, A. (1996). 'Introduzione', in Quadrio Curzio, A. (ed.) (1996). *Alle Origini del Pensiero Economico in Italia. Economia e istituzioni: il paradigma lombardo tra i secoli XVIII e XIX.* Bologna: Il Mulino, 7–14.

Quadrio Curzio, A. (2002). *Sussidiarietà e sviluppo. Paradigmi per l'Europa e l'Italia,* Milan: Vita e Pensiero.

Quadrio Curzio, A. (2007a). *Economisti ed economia.* Bologna: Il Mulino.

Quadrio Curzio, A. (2007b). 'Cesare Beccaria e Pietro Verri: l'economia civile per il governo della "cosa pubblica"', in Quadrio Curzio, A. [2007a, 43–56].

Quadrio Curzio, A. (2007c). 'Carlo Cattaneo: l'economia e la tecnologia per le riforme e l'Europa', in Quadrio Curzio, A. [2007a, 101–116].

Quadrio Curzio, A. (2007d). 'L'identità e le eredità degli ingegneri innovatori imprenditori', in Quadrio Curzio, A. [2007a, 153–180].

Quadrio Curzio, A. (2013a). 'Sviluppo economico per l'"incivilimento" italiano in Europa: Istituzioni ed economia', in Lacaita, G. C. and Masoni, F. (eds.) (2013). *Carlo Cattaneo: Federalismo e sviluppo.* Florence: Le Monnier, pp. 133–140.

Quadrio Curzio, A. (2013b). 'Quintino Sella: uno scienziato statista italiano ed europeo', in *Quintino Sella. Scienziato e Statista per l'Unità di Italia,* (Roma, 5–6 dicembre 2011), Atti dei Convegni Lincei, n. 269, Accademia Nazionale dei Lincei, Rome: Scienze e Lettere Editore Commerciale, 9–16.

Quadrio Curzio, A. and Scazzieri, R. (1990). 'Introduzione', in Quadrio Curzio, A., Scazzieri, R. (eds.) (1990). *Dinamica economica strutturale.* Bologna: Il Mulino, pp. 11–51.

Quadrio Curzio, A. and Scazzieri, R. (1992). 'Dall'economia politica al governo dell'economia: riflessioni sul contributo di Cesare Beccaria e Pietro Verri sulla teoria e pratica della moneta', in Acocella, N., Rey, G.M. and Tiberi, M. (eds.). *Saggi di politica economica in onore di Federico Caffè,* vol. II, Milan: Franco Angeli reprinted in Quadrio Curzio, A. (2007), *Economisti ed economia.* Bologna: Il Mulino, 57–99.

Quadrio Curzio, A. and Fortis, M. (eds.) (2000a). *Il Made in Italy oltre il 2000.* Bologna: Il Mulino.

Quadrio Curzio, A. and Fortis, M. (eds.) (2000b). *Complexity and Industrial Clusters.* Heidelberg: Physica-Verlag.

Quadrio Curzio A. and Fortis M. (eds.) (2005). *Research and Technological Innovation.* Heidelberg: Physica-Verlag.

Quadrio Curzio, A. and Fortis, M. (eds.) (2006). *Industria e Distretti. Un Paradigma di perdurante competitività italiana.* Bologna: Il Mulino.

Quadrio Curzio, A. and Rotondi, C. (2007a). 'Luigi Einaudi: liberalismo, federalismo, Europa', in Quadrio Curzio, A. (2007). *Economisti ed economia.* Bologna: Il Mulino, 189–226.

Quadrio Curzio, A. and Fortis, M. (eds.) (2008). *The EU and the Economies of the Eastern European Enlargement.* Heidelberg: Physica-Verlag.

Quadrio Curzio, A. and Scazzieri, R. (2008). 'Historical stylizations and monetary theory', in Scazzieri R., Sen, A. and Zamagni, S. (eds.) (2008), *Markets, Money and Capital. Hicksian Economics for the Twenty-First Century.* Cambridge: Cambridge University Press, 85–203.

Quadrio Curzio, A. and Rotondi, C. (2012). 'Ezio Vanoni (1903–1956)', in Pinchera, M. and Sinigaglia, E. (eds.). *Protagonisti dell'intervento pubblico in Italia, Volume II.* Milano: Nino Arango Editore, 1117–1143.

Quadrio Curzio, A. and Fortis, M. (eds.) (2014). *L'economia reale nel Mezzogiorno.* Bologna: Il Mulino.

Salvadori, N. (ed.) (2010). *Institutional and Social Dynamics of Growth and Distribution.* Cheltenham: Edward Elgar.

Salvadori, N. and Opocher, A. (eds.) (2009). *Long-run Growth, Social Institutions and Living Standards.* Cheltenham: Edward Elgar.

Salvadori, N., Commendatore, P. and Tamberi, M. (eds.) (2009). *Geography, Structural Change and Economic Development.* Cheltenham: Edward Elgar.

Scherillo, M. (1921). 'Discorso in occasione della Commemorazione di Giuseppe Colombo tenuta nell'adunanza del 27 gennaio 1921', in Reale Istituto Lombardo, *Rendiconti,* Milano: Hoepli, 1921, serie II, vol. LIV, 7–89.

Publications by Neri Salvadori

Books (author)

1 (with Heinz Kurz) *Theory of Production. A Long-Period Analysis*, Cambridge: Cambridge University Press, 1995; reprint, 1997; paperback, 1997.
2 (with Heinz Kurz) *Understanding 'Classical' Economics. Studies in Long-Period Theory*, London and New York: Routledge, 1998.
3 (with Heinz Kurz) *Classical Economics and Modern Theory: Studies in Long-period Analysis*, London and New York: Routledge, 2003.
4 (with Heinz Kurz) Теория производства, traduzione russa del volume, *Theory of Production. A Long-Period Analysis*, Mosca: Finansi i statistica, 2004.
5 (with Heinz Kurz) *Interpreting Classical Economics: Studies in Long-period Analysis*, London and New York: Routledge, 2007.
6 (with Simone D'Alessandro and Domenico Fanelli) *Elementi di Economia Industriale*, Turin: Giappichelli, 2012.
7 (with Heinz Kurz) *Revisiting Classical Economics: Studies in Long-period Analysis*, London and New York: Routledge, 2014.

Books (editor)

1 *Esperimenti Intellettuali ed Economia Politica. Saggi sullo Schema Teorico di P. Sraffa*, Milan: Franco Angeli Editore, 1981.
2 (with Ian Steedman) *Joint Production of Commodities*, Aldershot, UK: Edward Elgar, 1990.
3 (with Carlo Panico) *Post Keynesian Theory of Growth and Distribution*, Aldershot, UK: Edward Elgar, 1993.
4 (with Heinz Kurz) *Elgar Companion to Classical Economics*, Aldershot, UK: Edward Elgar, 1998.
5 *The Theory of Economic Growth: A 'Classical' Perspective*, Cheltenham, UK: Edward Elgar, 2003.
6 *Old and New Growth Theories: An Assessment*, Cheltenham, UK: Edward Elgar, 2003.
7 (with Heinz Kurz) *The Legacy of Piero Sraffa*, Cheltenham, UK: Edward Elgar, 2003.
8 (with Richard Arena) *Money Credit and the Role of the State: Essays in honour of Augusto Graziani*, Aldershot, UK: Ashgate, 2004.

9   (with Renato Balducci) *Innovation, Unemployment and Policy in the Theories of Growth and Distribution*, Cheltenham, UK: Edward Elgar, 2005.
10   (with Carlo Panico) *Classical, Neoclassical and Keynesian Views on Growth and Distribution*, Cheltenham, UK: Edward Elgar, 2006.
11   *Economic Growth and Distribution. On the Nature and Causes of the Wealth of Nations*, Cheltenham, UK: Edward Elgar, 2006.
12   (with Heinz Kurz and Luigi Lodovico Pasinetti) *Piero Sraffa: The Man and the Scholar*, London and New York: Routledge, 2008.
13   (with Pasquale Commendatore and Massimo Tamberi) *Geography, Structural Change and Economic Development*, Cheltenham, UK: Edward Elgar, 2009.
14   (with Arrigo Opocher) *Long-run Growth, Social Institutions and Living Standards*, Cheltenham, UK: Edward Elgar, 2009.
15   *Institutional and Social Dynamics of Growth and Distribution*, Cheltenham, UK: Edward Elgar, 2010.
16   (with John Vint, Stanley Metcalfe, Heinz D. Kurz and Paul A. Samuelson), *Economic Theory and Economic Thought. Essays in honour of Ian Steedman*, London, UK: Routledge, 2010.
17   (with Christian Gehrke) *Keynes, Sraffa and the Criticism of Neoclassical Theory. Essays in honour of Heinz Kurz*, London and New York: Routledge, 2011.
18   (with Christian Gehrke, Ian Steedman and Richard Sturn) *Classical Political Economy and Modern Theory. Essays in Honour of Heinz Kurz*, London and New York: Routledge, 2012.
19   (with Heinz Kurz) *Elgar Companion to David Ricardo*, Cheltenham, UK: Edward Elgar, 2015.

Articles in journals

1   "Sulle macchine utilizzate congiuntamente: note ad un dibattito", *Studi Economici*, XXXII, pp. 151–167, 1977.
2   "Determinatezza del saggio di profitto nella teoria post-keynesiana. Un commento [a L. L. Pasinetti]", *Giornale degli Economisti e Annali di Economia*, 37(7/8), pp. 479–481, 1978.
3   "The Technology Frontier in Capital Theory. A Comment [to K. Sato]", *Economic Notes*, pp. 117–124, 1979.
4   "Mutamento dei metodi di produzione e produzione congiunta. Un commento al § 96 di Produzione di Merci a mezzo di Merci", *Studi Economici*, 34(7), pp. 79–94, 1979.
5   "Sulle macchine utilizzate congiuntamente: una replica [a P. Varri]", *Studi Economici*, XXXIV, pp. 75–85, 1979.
6   (with Massimo Marrelli) "The rate of Profit in an Expanding Economy: Some Existence, Uniqueness, and Stability Conditions", *Australian Economic Papers*, 18(33), pp. 283–293, 1979.
7   "On a Generalized von Neumann Model", *Metroeconomica*, 32(1), pp. 51–62, 1980.
8   "Falling Rate of Profit with a Constant Real Wage. An Example", *Cambridge Journal of Economics*, 5(1), pp. 59–66, 1981; reprinted in King J. E. (a cura di) *Marxian Economics*, Aldershot, UK: Edward Elgar, 1990.

9   (with Elido Fazi) "The Existence of a Two-Class Economy in the Kaldor Model of Growth and Distribution", *Kiklos*, 34(4), pp. 82–592, 1981.

10 "Existence of Cost-Minimizing Systems within the Sraffa Framework", *Zeitschrift für Nationalökonomie*, 42(3), pp. 291–298, 1982; reprinted in Steedman I. (Ed.), *Sraffian Economics*, Aldershot, UK: Edward Elgar, 1988.

11 (with Massimo Marrelli) "Tax Incidence and Growth Models", *Public Finance*, 38(3), pp. 409–418, 1983.

12 "A New Variety of Rent", *Metroeconomica*, 35(1–2), pp. 73–85, 1983.

13 "Falling Rate of Profit with a Constant Real Wage: A Reply to Fujimoto", *Kagawa University Economic Review*, 57(1), pp. 208–211, 1984.

14 (with Liliana Basile) "Kalecki's Pricing Theory", *Jounal of Post-Keynesian Economics*, 7(2), pp. 249–262, 1984–85; reprinted in Blaug M. (Ed.), *Michal Kalecki (1899–1970)*, Aldershot, UK: Edward Elgar, 1992, and in Sawyer M. C. (Ed.), *The Legacy of Michal Kalecki*, Aldershot, UK: Edward Elgar, 1999.

15 "Switching in Methods of Production and Joint Production", *The Manchester School*, 53(2), pp. 156–178, 1985; reprinted in Steedman I. (a cura di) *Sraffian Economics*, Aldershot, UK: Edward Elgar, 1988.

16 (with Elido Fazi) "The Existence of a Two-Class Economy in a General Cambridge Model of Growth and Distribution", *Cambridge Journal of Economics*, 9(2), pp. 155–164, 1985.

17 (with Ian Steedman) "Cost Functions and Produced Means of Production: Duality and Capital Theory", *Contributions to Political Economy*, 4(1), pp. 79–90, 1985.

18 "Was Sraffa Making No Assumptions on Returns?", *Metroeconomica*, 37(2), pp. 175–186, 1985; reprinted in Blaug M. (Ed.) *Piero Sraffa (1898–1983)*, Aldershot, UK: Edward Elgar, 1992.

19 (with Liliana Basile) "Kalecki's Pricing Theory: A Reply [a F. Lee]", *Jounal of Post-Keynesian Economics*, 9(1), pp. 159–160, 1986.

20 "Il capitale fisso come 'specie' del 'genere' produzione congiunta", *Economia Politica*, 3(1), pp. 21–38, 1986.

21 (with Heinz Kurz) "A comment [on A. L. Levine]", *Journal of Post-Keynesian Economics*, 9(1), pp. 163–165, 1986.

22 "Land and Choice of Techniques within the Sraffa Framework", *Australian Economic Papers*, 25(46), pp. 94–105, 1986.

23 (with Heinz Kurz) "Burmeister on Sraffa and the Labour Theory of Value: a Comment", *Journal of Political Economy*, 95(4), pp. 870–881, 1987.

24 "Il Capitale fisso come 'specie' del 'genere' produzione congiunta. Ulteriori precisazioni ed una risposta [a S. Baldone e P. Varri]", *Economia Politica*, 4, pp. 265–275, 1987.

25 "Fixed Capital within a von Neumann-Morishima Model of Growth and Distribution", *International Economic Review*, 29(2), pp. 341–351, 1988.

26 (with Ian Steedman) "Joint Production Analysis in a Sraffian Framework", *Bulletin of Economic Research*, 40(3), pp. 165–196, 1988.

27 (with Ian Steedman) "A Note About The Interest Rate and The Revenue Function", *Eastern Economic Journal*, 14(2), pp. 153–156, 1988.

28 "Fixed Capital within the Sraffa Framework", *Zeitschrift für Nationalökonomie*, 48(1), pp. 1–17, 1988.

29 (with Ian Steedman) "No Reswitching? No Switching!", *Cambridge Journal of Economics*, 12(4), pp. 481–486, 1988.

30 "The Existence of a Two-Class Economy in a General Cambridge Model of Growth and Distribution. An Addendum", *Cambridge Journal of Economics*, 12(2), pp. 273–279, 1988.

31 (with Ian Steedman) "Four Questions concerning Joint Production", *Political Economy*, 4(2), pp. 223–229, 1988.

32 (with Liliana Basile) "Kalecki's Pricing Theory Revisited: a Comment", *Journal of Post-Keynesian Economics*, 13(2), pp. 293–297, 1990.

33 (with Heinz Kurz) "Morishima on Ricardo: A review article", *Cambridge Journal of Economics*, 16(2), pp. 227–247, 1992.

34 (with Heinz Kurz) "Von Neumann's Growth Model and the 'Classical' Tradition", *The Europian Journal of the History of Economic Thought*, 1(1), pp. 129–160, 1993.

35 (with Heinz Kurz) "The Non-Substitution Theorem: Making Good a Lacuna", *Zeitschrift für Nationalökonomie*, 59(1), pp. 97–103, 1994.

36 (with L. Basile) "On the Existence of a Solution to Kalecki's Pricing Equations", *Jounal of Post-Keynesian Economics*, 16(3), pp. 435–438, 1994.

37 (with C. Panico) "Sraffa, Marshall and the Problem of Returns", *The European Journal of the History of Economic Thought*, 1(2), pp. 323–343, 1994.

38 (with Heinz Kurz) "Choice of Techniques in a Model with Fixed Capital", *European Journal of Political Economy*, 10(3), pp. 545–569, 1994.

39 (with Ch. Bidard) "Duality between Prices and Techniques", *European Journal of Political Economy*, 11(2), pp. 379–389, 1995.

40 (with Ch. Bidard) "Solutions to Linear Equations depending on a Parameter", *Rivista di Matematica per le Scienze Economiche e Sociali*, 19(1), pp. 103–112, 1996.

41 (with Heinz Kurz) "Exhaustible Resources in a Dynamic Input–Output Model with 'Classical' Features", *Economic Systems Research*, 9(3), pp. 235–252, 1997.

42 (with Heinz Kurz) "Morishima on Ricardo: A Rejoinder", *Cambridge Journal of Economics*, 22(2), pp. 227–239, 1998.

43 "Sraffa sulla 'domanda': Un'analisi testuale", *Il Pensiero Economico Italiano*, 6(1), pp. 243–262, 1998.

44 "A Linear Multisector Model of 'Endogenous' Growth and the Problem of Capital", *Metroeconomica*, 49(3), pp. 319–335, 1998.

45 (with Heinz Kurz) "Reverse Capital Deepening and the Numeraire: A Note", *Review of Political Economy*, 10(4), pp. 415–426, 1998.

46 (with Heinz Kurz) "¿Pertencen á traditión clásica os modelos de crecemento 'endoxeno'?", *Revista Galega de Economía*, 8(1), pp. 89–118, 1999.

47 (with Heinz Kurz) "The Dynamic Leontief Model and the Theory of Endogenous Growth", *Economic Systems Research*, 12(2), pp. 255–265, 2000.

48 (with Heinz Kurz) "'Classical' Roots of Input–Output Analysis: A Short Account of its Long Prehistory", *Economic Systems Research*, 12(2), pp. 153–179, 2000.

49 (with Heinz Kurz) "Economic Dynamics in a Simple Model with Exhaustible Resources and a Given Real Wage Rate", *Structural Change and Economic Dynamics*, 11(1–2), pp. 167–179, 2000.

50 (with Heinz Kurz) "On a recent 'Review Essay' in JHET", *Journal of the History of Economic Thought*, 22(4), pp. 487–489, 2000.

51 (with Heinz Kurz) "Production Theory: An Introduction", *Indian Economic Journal*, 47(4), pp. 15–29, 2001.

52 (with Heinz Kurz) "Sraffa and von Neumann", *Review of Political Economy*, 13(2), pp. 161–180, 2001.

53   (with Heinz Kurz) "Classical Economics and the Problem of Exhaustible Resources", *Metroeconomica*, 52(3), pp. 282–296, 2001.

54   (with Heinz Kurz) "Mark Blaug on the Sraffian Interpretation of the Surplus Approach", *History of Political Economy*, 34(1), pp. 225–236, 2002.

55   (with Heinz Kurz) "One Theory or Two? Walras's Critique of Ricardo", *History of Political Economy*, 34(2), pp. 365–398, 2002.

56   (with Heinz Kurz) "The Aggregate Neoclassical Theory of Distribution and the Concept of a Given Value of Capital: A Reply [to Paola Potestio]", *Structural Change and Economic Dynamics*, 12(4), pp. 479–485, 2001.

57   (with Heinz Kurz) "Fund–flow versus Flow–flow in Production Theory. Reflections on Georgescu-Roegen's Contribution", *Journal of Economic Behavior and Organization*, 51(4), pp. 487–505, 2003.

58   (with Christian Gehrke and Heinz Kurz) "Ricardo on Agricultural Improvements: A Note", *Scottish Journal of Political Economy*, 50(3), pp. 291–296, 2003.

59   (with Heinz Kurz) "Von Neumann, the Classical Economists and Arrow-Debreu: Some Notes", *Acta Oeconomica*, 54(1), pp. 39–62, 2004.

60   (with Heinz Kurz) "'Man from the Moon': On Sraffa's Objectivism", *Economies et Societes, "Histoire de la pensee economique"*, No. 35, 8–9/2004, pp. 1545–1557, 2004.

61   "Il contributo di Piero Sraffa alla scienza economica", *Il Filangieri*, Anno I, No. 3, pp. 423–441, 2005.

62   (with Heinz Kurz) "Representing the Production and Circulation of Commodities in Material Terms: On Sraffa's Objectivism", *Review of Political Economy*, 17(3), pp. 413–441, 2005.

63   (with Heinz Kurz) "Removing an 'Insuperable Obstacle' in the Way of an Objectivist Analysis: Sraffa's Attempts at Fixed Capital", *The European Journal of the History of Economic Thought*, 12(3), pp. 493–523, 2005.

64   (with Giuseppe Freni and Fausto Gozzi) "Existence of Optimal Strategies in Linear Multisector Models", *Economic Theory*, 29(1), pp. 25–48, 2006.

65   (with Heinz Kurz) "Input–Output Analysis from a Wider Perspective: A Comparison of the Early Works of Leontief and Sraffa", *Economic Systems Research*, 18(4), pp. 373–390, 2006.

66   (with Rodolfo Signorino) "Piero Sraffa: Economic Reality, the Economist and Economic Theory: An Interpretation", *Journal of Economic Methodology*, 14(2), pp. 187–209, 2007.

67   (with Simone D'Alessandro) "Pasinetti versus Rebelo: Two Different Models or Just One?", *Journal of Economic Behavior & Organization*, 65(3), pp. 547–554, 2008.

68   (with Heinz Kurz) "Sraffa y la Teoría del Valor de Trabajo", *Circus. Revista Argentina de Economía*, 2, pp. 25–58, 2009.

69   (with Amitava Krishna Dutt, Harvey Gram, Alan Kirman, Heinz D. Kurz, Bertram Schefold, Ian Steedman, Stephen J. Turnovsky), "Paul Anthony Samuelson (1915–2009)", *Metroeconomica*, 61(3), pp. 427–441, 2010.

70   (with De Francesco), "Oligopoli simmetrici ed oligopoli asimmetrici", *Studi Economici*, 100, pp. 65–89, 2010.

71   (with Heinz Kurz), "In Favor of Rigor and Relevance: A Reply to Mark Blaug," *History of Political Economy*, 43(3), pp. 607–616, 2011.

72   (with Massimo De Francesco), "Bertrand–Edgeworth Competition in an Almost Symmetric Oligopoly", *Journal of Microeconomics*, 1(1), pp. 99–105, 2011; reprinted in *Studies in Microeconomics*, 1(2), pp. 213–219, 2013.

73   (with Rodolfo Signorino), "The Classical Notion of Competition Revisited," *History of Political Economy*, 45(1), pp. 149–175, 2013.
74   (with Rodolfo Signorino), "Adam Smith on Monopoly Theory. Making Good a Lacuna", *Scottish Journal of Political Economy*, 61(2), pp. 178–195, 2014.
75   (with Rodolfo Signorino), "Defense versus Opulence? An Appraisal of the Malthus–Ricardo 1815 Controversy on the Corn Laws", *History of Political Economy*, 47(1), pp. 151–184, 2015.
76   (with Rodolfo Signorino), "From Stationary State to Endogenous Growth: International Trade in the Mathematical Formulation of the Ricardian System", *Cambridge Journal of Economics*, first published online April 1, 2015, doi:10.1093/cje/bev018.

Special issues of journals (editor)

1   *Omaggio a Piero Sraffa (1898–1983). Storia Teoria Documenti*, special issue of *Il Pensiero Economico Italiano*, 6(1), 2002.
2   *Old and New Growth Theories – Historical and Methodological Issues*, special issue of *History of Economic Ideas*, 10(20), 1998.
3   *Theories of Economic Growth – Recent Developments*, special issue of *Metroeconomica*, 54(2–3), 2003.
4   *Contributions to the History of Economic Growth*, special issue of *The European Journal of the History of Economic Thought*, 10(1), 2003.
5   *Piero Sraffa 1898–1983*, special issue of *Review of Political Economy*, 17(3), 2005.
6   *Growth and Distribution – Recent Developments*, special issue of *Metroeconomica*, 58(1), 2007.
7   *Institutional and Social Dynamics of Growth and Distribution*, special issue of *Metroeconomica*, 61(1), 2010.
8   *Scritti in Memoria di Liliana Basile*, special issue of *Studi Economici*, 100, 2010.

Chapters in books

1   "Blaug e la critica della teoria neoclassica della distribuzione" in M. Blaug (Ed.), *La Rivoluzione di Cambridge*, Naples: Liguori, 1977.
2   "Le Choix des techniques chez Sraffa: le cos de la production jointe" in Ch. Bidard (Ed.), *La Production Jointe, Nouvaux Débates*, Paris: Economica, 1984.
3   "Les ressouces naturelles rares dans la théorie de Sraffa" and (with Antonio D'Agata) "Sur quelques paradoxes en théorie de la rente, in Ch. Bidard (Ed.), *La Rente, Actualité de l'Approche Classique*, Paris: Economica, 1987.
4   "Sul prezzo di una merce non base che entra nella propria riproduzione. Una soluzione dinamica ad un problema lasciato insoluto dall'analisi statica", in Alberto Quadrio Curzio and Roberto Scazzieri (Eds), *Dinamica Economica e Strutturale*, Bologna: Il Mulino, 1990.
5   "Su un sistema di disequazioni alle differenze", *Atti del Tredicesimo Convegno A.M.A.S.E.S.* (Verona Settembre 1989), Bologna: Pitagora Editrice, 1991.

6   "Post-Keynesian Theory of Distribution in the Long Run", in E. Nell and W. Semmlar (Eds), *Nicholas Kaldor and Mainstream Economics: Confrontation or Convergence?*, New York: Macmillan, 1991.

7   (with Heinz Kurz) "The 'Standard Commodity' and Ricardo's Search for an 'Invariable Measure of Value'", in M. Baranzini and G. C. Harcourt (Eds), *The Dynamics of the Wealth of Nations. Growth, Distribution and Structural Change*, London: Macmillan, 1993.

8   (with Heinz Kurz) "Competition and Long-Period Positions in Classical and Neo-Classical Economics", in Perrotta C. and Gioia V. (Eds), *Where Is Economics Going? Historical Viewpoints*, Lecce: Congedo Editore, 1994.

9   "'Demand' in Production of Commodities by Means of Commodities", in Harcourt, G., Roncaglia, A. and Rowley, R. (Eds), *Income and Employment in Theory and Practice*, London: Macmillan, and New York: Macmillan and St. Martin's Press, 1995.

10   "'Productivity Curves' in The Accumulation of Capital", in Marcuzzo, C., Pasinetti, L. L., and Roncaglia, A. (Eds), *The Economics of Joan Robinson*, London and New York: Routledge, 1996.

11   (with Heinz Kurz) "In the Beginning all the World was Australia . . .", in Arestis Ph., Palma G. and Sawyer M. (Eds), *Capital Controversy, Post-Keynesian Economics and the History of Economic Thought. Essays in Honour of Geoff Harcourt*, London and New York: Routledge, 1996.

12   (with Heinz Kurz) "On Critics and Protective Belts", in Salanti, A. and Screpanti, E. (Eds.), *Pluralism in Econonomics: New Perspective in History and Methodology*, Aldershot, UK: Edward Elgar, 1997.

13   (with Heinz Kurz) "The 'New' Growth Theory: Old Wine in New Goatskins", in Coricelli F., Di Matteo M. and Hahn F. H. (Eds), *New Theories in Growth and Development*, London: Macmillan, and New York: St. Martin's Press, 1998. Spanish translation in Bricall J.M. and de Juan O. (Eds), *Economia Politica del crescimento, fluctuaciones y crisis*, Barcellona: Editorial Ariel, S.A.

14   (with Heinz Kurz) "Piero Sraffa and Mainstreem Theory", in Holt R., Pressman S. (Eds), *Economics and its Discontents: Twentieth Century Dissenting Economists*, Aldershot, UK: Edward Elgar, 1998.

15   "Transferable Machines with Uniform Efficiency Paths", in Mongiovi G. and Petri F. (Eds), *Value, Distribution and Capital*, London and New York: Routledge, 1999.

16   (with Heinz Kurz) "Theories of 'Endogeneous' Growth in Historical Perspective", in Murat R. Sertel (Ed.), *Contemporary Economic Issues. Proceedings of the Eleventh World Congress of the International Economic Association, Tunis. Volume 4 Economic Behaviour and Design*, London: Macmillan, and New York: St. Martin's Press, 1999.

17   (with Heinz Kurz) "Reswitching. Simplifying a Famous Example", in Martin M. G. Fase, Walter Kanning and Donal A. Walker (Eds), *Economics, Welfare Policy and the History of Economic Thought. Essays in Honour of Arnold Heertje*, Cheltenham, UK: Edward Elgar, 1999.

18   "Modelli di crescita 'endogena' nell'analisi 'classica'", in Enzo Sciacca (Ed.), *Una Facoltà nel Mediterraneo. Studi in occasione dei trent'anni della Facoltà di Scienze Politiche di Catania*, Milan: Giuffré, 2000.

19   (with Heinz Kurz) "Walras and Ricardo", in Pierre Dockès, Ludovic Frobert, Gérard Klotz, Jean-Pierre Potier and André Tiran (Eds), *Les traditions economiques françaises*, Paris: CNRS Editions, 2000.

20 "Sraffa on Demand: A Textual Analysis", "Comment on Mainwaring and Steedman", (with Heinz Kurz) "Comment on Samuelson", (with Heinz Kurz) "Piero Sraffa's Contributions to Economics: A Brief Survey", in Kurz H. (Ed.), *Critical Essays on Piero Sraffa's Legacy in Economics*, Cambridge: Cambridge University Press, 2000. "Comment on Samuelson" has been reprinted in Janice Murray (Ed.), *The Collected Scientific Papers of Paul A. Samuelson, Volume 6*, Cambridge, MA: The MIT Press, 2011, pp. 444–455.

21 (with Heinz Kurz) "Sraffa and the Mathematicians: Frank Ramsey and Alister Watson", in T. Cozzi and R. Marchionatti (Eds), *Piero Sraffa's Political Economy. A Centenary Estimate*, London and New York: Routledge, 2000.

22 (with Heinz Kurz) "Sraffa e von Neumann", M. Pivetti (Ed.), *Piero Sraffa: Contributi per una biografia intellettuale*, Roma: Carocci Editore, 2000, Spanish translation in M. Pivetti (Ed.), *Piero Sraffa: Contributiones para una biografia intrlectual*, Mexico: UNAM, 2008.

23 (with Heinz Kurz) "On the Long-period Method. A Comment on Ravagnani", S. Böhm, Ch. Gehrke, H. D. Kurz and R. Sturn (Eds), *Is there Progress in Economics? Knowledge, Truth and the History of Economic Thought*, Cheltenham, UK: Edward Elgar, 2002.

24 (with Heinz Kurz) "'Classical' vs. 'Neoclassical' Theories of Value and Distribution and the Long-period Method", F. H. Hahn and F. Petri (Eds), *General Equilibrium: Problems and Prospects*, London: Routledge, 2003.

25 (with Giuseppe Freni and Fausto Gozzi) "Endogeneous Growth in a Multi-sector Economy" and (with Heinz Kurz) "Theories of Economic Growth Old and New", in Neri Salvadori (Ed.), *The Theory of Economic Growth: A 'Classical' Perspective.* Cheltenham, UK: Edward Elgar, 2003.

26 (with Heinz Kurz) "Endogenous Growth in a Stylised 'Classical' Model", in Pere Mir (Ed.), *Produccion, productividad y crecimiento*, Lleida, Spain: Edicions de la Universitat de Lleida, 2003.

27 "Wealth in Post-Keynesian Theory of Growth and Distribution", in G. Argyrous, M. Forstater and G. Mongiovi (Eds), *Growth, Distribution and Effective Demand: Essays in Honor of Edward J. Nell*, New York: M. E. Sharpe, 2003.

28 "Is Ricardian Extensive Rent a Nash Equilibrium?", in Richard Arena and Neri Salvadori (Eds), *Money Credit and the Role of the State: Essays in honour of Augusto Graziani*, Aldershot, UK: Ashgate, 2004.

29 (with Heinz Kurz) "On the Collaboration between Sraffa and Besicovitch: The Cases of Fixed Capital and Non-Basics in Joint Production", in *Atti dei Convegni Lincei, Convegno internazionale Piero Sraffa (Roma, 11–12 febbraio 2003)*, Roma: Accademia Nazionale dei Lincei, 2004.

30 (with Heinz Kurz) "La costruzione delle curve di offerta di lungo periodo: Note alla critica di Sraffa alle analisi di equilibrio parziale", in Antonio D'Agata, Emilio Giardina and Enzo Sciacca (Eds), *Economia e Società. Studi in memoria di Giovanni Montemagno*, Milano: Giuffrè, 2006.

31 (with Heinz Kurz) "Endogeneous Growth in a Stylised 'Classical' Model", George Stathakis and Gianni Vaggi (Eds), *Economic Development and Social Change*, London: Routledge, 2006.

32 "On a Proof by Sraffa's" and (with Heinz Kurz) "On the Collaboration between Sraffa and Besicovitch: The 'Proof of Gradient'", in Guglielmo Chiodi and Leonardo Ditta (Eds), *Sraffa or an Alternative Economics*, New York: Palgrave Macmillan, 2008, pp. 253–259 and pp. 260–274.

33 (with Heinz Kurz) "New Growth Theory and Development Economics", Amitava Krishna Dutt and Jaime Ros (Eds), *International Handbook of Development Economics*, Cheltenham, UK: Edward Elgar, 2008.

34 (with Heinz Kurz) "Ricardo on Exhaustible Resources, and the Hotelling Rule", Aiko Ikeo and Heinz D. Kurz (Eds), *A History of Economic Theory. Essays in honour of Takashi Negishi*, London, UK: Routledge, 2009.

35 (with Heinz Kurz) "Spurious 'Margins' Versus the Genuine Article", in Adriano Birolo, Duncan K. Foley, Heinz D. Kurz, Bertram Schefold and Ian Steedman (Eds), *Production, Distribution and Trade: Alternative Perspective. Essays in honour of Sergio Parrinello*, London, UK: Routledge, 2010, pp. 101–118.

36 (with Heinz Kurz) "Trade Equilibrium Amongst Growing Economies: Some Extensions" and (with Heinz Kurz) "Sraffa and the Labour Theory of Value: A Few Observations", in John Vint, Stanley Metcalfe, Heinz D. Kurz, Neri Salvadori and Paul A. Samuelson (Eds), *Economic Theory and Economic Thought. Essays in honour of Ian Steedman*, London, UK: Routledge, 2010, pp. 106–114 and pp. 189–215.

37 (with Heinz Kurz) "The Post-Keynesian Theories of Growth and Distribution: A Survey", in M. Setterfield (Ed.), *Handbook of Alternative Theories of Economic Growth*, Cheltenham, UK: Edward Elgar, 2010, pp. 95–107.

38 (with Heinz Kurz) "Exhaustible Resources: Rents, Profits, Royalties and Prices", in Volker Caspari (Ed.), *The Evolution of Economic Theory. Essays in Honour of Bertram Schefold*, London, UK: Routledge, 2011, pp. 39–52.

39 "Besicovitch, Sraffa, and the Existence of the Standard Commodity", in Neri Salvadori and Christian Gehrke (Eds), *Keynes, Sraffa and the Criticism of Neoclassical Theory. Essays in Honour of Heinz Kurz*, London and New York: Routledge, 2011, pp. 113–131.

40 (with Heinz Kurz) "On the 'vexata questio of value': Ricardo, Marx and Sraffa", in Lance Taylor, Armon Rezai and Thomas Michl (Eds), *Social Fairness and Economics. Economic Essays in the Spirit of Duncan Foley*, Abingdon, UK: Routledge, 2013, pp. 213–227.

41 (with Giuseppe Freni) "The Construction of the Long-run Market Supply Curves: Some Notes on Sraffa's Critique of Partial Equilibrium Analysis", in Enrico Sergio Levrero, Antonella Palumbo and Antonella Stirati (Eds), *Sraffa and the Reconstruction of Economic Theory: Volume Three. Sraffa's Legacy: Interpretations and Historical Perspectives*, Basingstoke, UK: and New York (USA): Palgrave Macmillan, 2013, pp. 189–216.

42 (with Heinz Kurz) "The 'Classical' Approach to Exhaustible Resources: Parrinello and the Others", in Heinz Kurz and Neri Salvadori (Eds), *Revisiting Classical Economics: Studies in Long-period Analysis*, London and New York: Routledge, 2014.

43 (with Heinz Kurz) "On the Beginning of Sraffa's Path to *Production of Commodities by means of Commodities*: A Comment on De Vivo", in Heinz Kurz and Neri Salvaadori (Eds), *Revisiting Classical Economics: Studies in Long-period Analysis*, London and New York: Routledge, 2014.

44 (with Heinz Kurz) "Piero Sraffa's Early Work on Joint Production: Probing into the Intricacies of Multiple-Product Systems", in Fabrice Tricou and Daniella Leeman (Eds), *Èconomie mathématique et Histoire: Hommage à Christian Bidard*, Paris: Presses universitaires de Paris Ouest, 2014.

45 (with Heinz Kurz) "A Single Commodity Produced by Labour and Land", in Mauro Baranzini, Claudia Rotondi and Roberto Scazzieri (Eds), *Resources, Production and Structural Dynamics*, Cambridge, UK: Cambridge University Press, 2015.

Entries in scientific dictionaries

1 "Non-Substitution Theorems" and "Basics and Non-Basics", in J. Eatwell, M. Milgate and P. Newman (Eds), *The New Palgrave*, London, Macmillan Press Ltd, 1987.
2 (with Heinz Kurz) "Free Disposal and the 'Rule of Free Goods'", (with Heinz Kurz) "Given Quantities", (with Heinz Kurz) "Growth", (with Heinz Kurz) "Machines", (with Heinz Kurz) "Neumann, John von", (with Heinz Kurz) "Ricardo, David", (with Heinz Kurz) "Wage Differentials", (with Heinz Kurz) "Wicksell Effects", in Kurz H. D. and Salvadori N. (Eds), *Elgar Companion to Classical Economics*, Aldershot, UK: Edward Elgar, 1998.
3 (with Heinz Kurz) "Capital Theory Debates", (with Heinz Kurz) "Invariable Measure of Value", in O'Hara Ph. (Ed.) *Encyclopedia of Political Economy*, London and New York: Routledge, 1999.
4 (with Heinz Kurz) "Cambridge Controversy", (with Heinz Kurz) "Classical Economics", (with Heinz Kurz) "Growth", (with Heinz Kurz) "Neo-Ricardian Economics", (with Heinz Kurz) "Ricardo", (with Heinz Kurz) "Sraffa Piero", (with Heinz Kurz) "Sraffian Economics", (with Heinz Kurz) "Theory of Production", in Jonathan Michie (Ed.), *Reader's Guide to the Social Sciences*, London: Fitzroy Dearborn Publishers, 2001.
5 "Non-substitution Theorems" and (with Heinz Kurz) "Neo-Ricardian Economics", in Steven N. Durlauf and Lawrence E. Blume (Eds), *The New Palgrave Dictionary of Economics, Second Edition*, London: Palgrave Macmillan, 2008.
6 (with Heinz Kurz) "Endogenous Growth", (with Heinz Kurz) "Exhaustible Resources and Mines", (with Heinz Kurz) "Invariable Measure of Value", (with Heinz Kurz) "*Principles of Political Economy and Taxation*", (with Heinz Kurz) "Samuelson, Paul Anthony, on Ricardo", (with Heinz Kurz) "Sraffa, Piero, on Ricardo", (with Heinz Kurz) "Walras, Marie-Esprit-Léon, on Ricardo", in H. D. Kurz and N. Salvadori (Eds), *Elgar Companion to David Ricardo*, Aldershot, UK: Edward Elgar, 2015.

Reviews

1 "Review of 'Caravale G (a cura di), *La crisi nelle teorie economiche*, Milan: F. Angeli, 1983", *Studi Economici*, XXXIX, 1(22), pp. 152–153, 1984.
2 "Review of 'Laise D. and Tucci M., *Capitale, moneta e tempo*, Padua: Cedam, 1984", *Studi Economici*, XL, 3(27), pp. 177–180, 1985.
3 "Review of 'Pellizzari F., *La teoria economica delle risorse naturali*, Milan: F. Angeli, 1985", *Studi Economici*, XLI, 2(29), pp. 203–204, 1986.
4 (with Marco Lippi) "Review of *Aggregation: Aggregate Production Functions and Related Topics, Collected papers by Franklin M. Fisher*, edited by John Monz, Cambridge, Massachusetts: The MIT Press", *Journal of Economic Behavior and Organization*, 24(2), pp. 241–245, 1994.

5   "Review of *On Political Economists and Modern Political Economy, selected essays of G. C. Harcourt*, edited by Claudio Sardoni. London and New York: Routledge, 1992", *European Journal of History of Economic Thought*, 1(3), pp. 623–625, 1994.

6   (with Heinz Kurz) "Review of *Piero Sraffa (1898–1983)*, edited by Mark Blaug, *Pioneers in Economics 44, an Elgar Reference Collection*, Aldershot, UK, 1992: Edward Elgar Publishing Limited, 178 plus x pages", *Contibutions to Political Economy*, 12(1), pp. 115–117, 1993.

7   (with Giuseppe Freni) "Review of *Property and Prices. Toward a Unified Theory of Value*, by André Burgstaller, Cambridge: Cambridge University Press, 1994", *Economics and Philosophy*, 12(2), pp. 240–243, 1996.

8   (with Rodolfo Signorino) "Review of *Piero Sraffa. His life, Thought and Cultural Heritage*, by Alessandro Roncaglia, Routledge Studies in the History of Economics, London and New York: Routledge, 2000, pp. 129, ISBN 0-415-23480-8", *Economic Systems Research*, 14(1), pp. 99–102, 2002.

9   "Review of *The Collected Interwar Papers and Correspondence of Roy Harrod*, edited by Daniele Besomi. Cheltenham, UK: Edward Elgar Publishing Limited. Volume I, Correspondence, 1919–35; Volume II, Correspondence, 1936-39; Volume III, Essays and Press Items", *Studi Economici*, LIX, 82, pp. 145–147, 2004/1.

10   (with Rodolfo Signorino) "Review of '*Mark Blaug: Rebel with Many Causes*', edited by Marcel Boumans and Matthias Klaes, Cheltenham, UK and Northampton, MA, USA: Edward Elgar, 2013, pp. ix + 302. ISBN 978 1 78195 566 6", *Journal of History of Economic Thought*, 37(4), pp. 615–623. 2015.

Author Index

Subject Index

For Product Safety Concerns and Information please contact our EU
representative GPSR@taylorandfrancis.com
Taylor & Francis Verlag GmbH, Kaufingerstraße 24, 80331 München, Germany

www.ingramcontent.com/pod-product-compliance
Ingram Content Group UK Ltd.
Pitfield, Milton Keynes, MK11 3LW, UK
UKHW021023180425
457613UK00020B/1038